Novell®
Certified Linux® Engineer 9 (CLE 9)
Study Guide

ROBB H. TRAC

Novell PRESS™
Novell®

Published by Pearson Education, Inc.
800 East 96th Street, Indianapolis, Indiana 46240 USA

Novell® Certified Linux Engineer 9 (CLE 9) Study Guide

International Standard Book Number: 0-672-32787-2

Library of Congress Catalog Card Number: 2004195537

Printed in the United States of America

First Printing: September 2005

08 07 06 05 4 3 2 1

Special and Bulk Sales

Pearson offers excellent discounts on this book when ordered in quantity for bulk purchases or special sales. For more information, please contact

U.S. Corporate and Government Sales
1-800-382-3419
corpsales@pearsontechgroup.com

For sales outside of the U.S., please contact

International Sales
international@pearsoned.com

Acquisitions Editor
Jenny Watson

Development Editor
Emmett Dulaney

Managing Editor
Charlotte Clapp

Senior Project Editor
Matthew Purcell

Copy Editor
Barbara Hacha

Indexer
Heather McNeill

Proofreader
Suzanne Thomas

Technical Editor
David Coughanour

Publishing Coordinator
Vanessa Evans

Book Designer
Gary Adair

Page Layout
Brad Chinn

Novell Press is the exclusive publisher of trade computer technology books that have been authorized by Novell, Inc. Novell Press books are written and reviewed by the world's leading authorities on Novell and related technologies, and are edited, produced, and distributed by the Que/Sams Publishing group of Pearson Education, the worldwide leader in integrated education and computer technology publishing. For more information on Novell Press and Novell Press books, please go to www.novellpress.com.

Associate Publisher
Mark Taber

Program Manager, Novell, Inc.
Darrin Vandenbos

Marketing Manager
Doug Ingersoll

Contents at a Glance

Table of Contents

About the Author

With 10 years of teaching experience, Robb H. Tracy is an expert in the Information Technology training industry.

Robb has a Master of Science degree in Instructional Technology from Utah State University. There he learned the principles of teaching and learning from some of the finest minds in the field.

Since leaving the university, Robb has designed and implemented technical training curricula for major industry hardware and software vendors since 1994. Robb spent some time working for Novell, Inc. in the 1990s, developing courseware for all CNE training programs since NetWare 4.11. Robb has also served on the CompTIA Network+ Certification Advisory committee.

In 2002, Robb co-founded Nebo Technical Institute, Inc., a leading provider of technical training development services. When not rushing to finish yet another project, Robb can be found relaxing in a boat on a high-mountain lake with a fishing pole in hand.

Dedication

This book is dedicated to all the individuals who have made a difference in my life. To my Dad, for instilling in me a love of teaching and all things mechanical. To my Mom, for teaching me the value of hard work and devotion.

To my mentor Dennis Simmons, for teaching me to strive for excellence in all I do. Finally, to my wife and best friend, for supporting and loving me through the process of writing this book. (Now that it's complete, I promise I'll get the landscaping done!)

Acknowledgments

The title page of this book lists Robb H. Tracy as its author. However, this attribution is deceiving. By no means was this a one-man job. Behind every book is a team of people who rarely get the credit they deserve. They are the unsung heroes who make sure the job gets done.

First, I would like to acknowledge the efforts of my beautiful wife, Kimberly. She's kept the bills paid, got the kids to school on time, and kept me sane as I endeavored to hit my deadlines. Without her support, this title would never have happened. Next, I would like to acknowledge the patience shown by Jessica, Joshua, Brittany, and Natasha while Dad tapped away at the keyboard most nights and weekends. It's time to spend some time at the lake, kids!

I would also like to acknowledge the efforts of the production team behind this book. These folks were the glue that kept everything together. Thanks to Jenny Watson for giving me the opportunity to write this book. I appreciate your confidence in me! Thanks to Emmett Dulaney as well for managing the development process. I've been in his shoes before, and you don't get a lot of sleep. Thanks, Emmett!

Thanks also go out to Barbara Hacha for her copyediting efforts. You have to have eyes like a hawk to do her job. Thanks for catching my typos! Speaking of editors, thanks also to Matt Purcell, the project editor behind this book. His positive attitude was contagious!

Finally, a huge thank you to Dave Coughanour at Novell. Dave reviewed each and every word and exercise step in this book for technical accuracy. His efforts kept me honest and were absolutely invaluable, dramatically increasing the overall quality of this title. Dave spent many late nights testing the lab exercises in this book, ensuring you have a successful experience. Thanks, Dave!

We Want to Hear from You!

As the reader of this book, *you* are our most important critic and commentator. We value your opinion and want to know what we're doing right, what we could do better, what topics you'd like to see us cover, and any other words of wisdom you're willing to pass our way.

You can email or write me directly to let me know what you did or didn't like about this book—as well as what we can do to make our books better.

Please note that I cannot help you with technical problems related to the topic of this book and that due to the high volume of mail I receive I may not be able to reply to every message.

When you write, please be sure to include this book's title and author as well as your name and email address or phone number. I will carefully review your comments and share them with the author and editors who worked on the book.

Email: feedback@novellpress.com

Mail: Mark Taber
Associate Publisher
Novell Press/Pearson Education
800 East 96th Street
Indianapolis, IN 46240 USA

Reader Services

For more information about this book or others from Novell Press, visit our website at www.novellpress.com. Type the ISBN or the title of a book in the Search field to find the page you're looking for.

Introduction

Congratulations on your choice to become a Certified Linux Engineer (CLE)! By purchasing this book, you are on your way to earning one of the hottest certifications around.

Introduction

Welcome to the world of Linux! As you will see in later chapters of this book, Novell has yet again revolutionized the Information Technology industry by providing one of the finest Linux distributions available: SUSE LINUX Enterprise Server 9 (SLES 9).

By providing an inexpensive, yet highly stable and scalable network operating system, Novell has raised a standard that other vendors will be hard pressed to match. In accordance, Novell Training Services has rolled out a certification program for SLES 9: The Certified Linux Engineer 9 (CLE 9).

Because of the complexity of the CLE 9 certification, Novell wants to make sure candidates really know their stuff with SLES 9. To do this, Novell has implemented a practical test for the certification. To pass, you must be able to walk the walk, not just talk the talk.

By gaining your CLE 9 certification, you tell the world that you can actually manage an SLES 9 deployment, not just answer a bunch of questions about the product in a multiple-choice exam. This gives you a strong competitive edge in a tight job market.

However, this hands-on approach to testing means the CLE 9 exam is much more difficult than most other certification exams you may have taken. The CLE 9 practical exam has a higher failure rate than most written IT certification exams. To pass, you must thoroughly prepare yourself.

That's where this book comes in! By reading this book and completing the lab exercises, you will be much better prepared than the average CLE 9 candidate.

In Chapter 1, "Introduction to the Certified Linux Engineer (CLE) Certification," I introduce you to the SLES 9 product and the CLE 9 certification program. I also provide you with some important exam tips and strategies that will increase your chances of passing.

In Chapter 2, "Introduction to SUSE Linux Enterprise Server 9," you are introduced to the SLES 9 operating system. You learn how to install a SLES 9 server and review how to manage the system configuration.

In Chapter 3, "Configuring DNS on SLES 9," you learn how to install and configure a BIND DNS server on your SLES 9 system.

In Chapter 4, "Configuring DHCP on SLES 9," you learn how to configure the DHCP service on your SLES 9 system.

In Chapter 5, "Configuring CUPS on SLES 9," you learn how to use CUPS to provide print services for your users.

In Chapter 6, "Configuring File and Print Services for Windows Clients on SLES 9," you learn how Linux can cross over into the Windows world by providing domain authentication and file storage services for Windows workstations.

In Chapter 7, "Implementing Email Services on SLES 9," you learn how to turn the simple Postfix daemon on your SLES 9 server into a full-fledged email solution with SMTP authentication and POP3/IMAP support.

In Chapter 8, "Using SLES 9 to Manage Network Traffic," you learn how to deploy and use a wide range of network monitoring utilities on your SLES 9 system. These include ntop, Nagios, ethereal, tcpdump, and an SNMP agent.

In Chapter 9, "Securing the SLES 9 Server," you are introduced into the wild world of network security. You learn steps you can take to secure your SLES server and learn how to use cryptography to secure services running on your server . This chapter also discusses network-related security issues as well as how to detect intruders who are trying to break into your system.

In Chapter 10, "Implementing Packet Filter Firewalls with SLES 9," you learn how to secure your network from intruders using a variety of firewall technologies that can be implemented right on your SLES 9 server.

In Chapter 11, "Implementing Virtual Private Networks with SLES 9," you learn how to implement WAN and remote access functionality over the Internet using VPNs.

Finally, in Chapter 12, "Putting It All Together: Adding OpenSLP and Tomcat to Your Server," you learn how you can implement an automated system for locating services in the network with the Service Location Protocol (SLP). You also learn how to deploy a web application server with Tomcat.

As you progress through this book, my goal is to provide you with a quality learning experience. I hope you find this book well written and easy to understand. I also hope you find it to be adequate preparation for your CLE 9 exam. However, no text is perfect. If you have suggestions for improvement, features you would like to see added, or corrections you believe need to be made, please feel free to email me at support@nebo-tech.com.

Best of luck to you in your CLE 9 certification pursuits!

CHAPTER 1

Introduction to the Certified Linux Engineer (CLE) Certification

Congratulations on your choice to become a Certified Linux Engineer (CLE)! By purchasing this book, you are on your way to earning one of the hottest certifications around.

By gaining your CLE 9 certification, you can prove to your employer and your co-workers (and to yourself, for that matter) that you truly know your stuff with Linux. That's because Novell's practical testing strategies ensure that anyone certified as a CLE 9 really can do the job. No paper certifications allowed here! We'll go into more depth on CLE 9 in just a moment. Before doing so, let's take a look at what will be covered in this chapter:

- Introduction to the CLE 9
- Introduction to the CLE 9 Test Environment
- Using this Study Guide
- Strategies and tips for the CLE 9 Practicum

Let's start by introducing the latest version of the CLE: CLE 9!

Introduction to the CLE 9

For years, Novell certifications have represented the pinnacle of Information Technology industry skills assessment. Novell pioneered the certification industry with the Certified Novell Engineer (CNE) and Certified Novell Administrator (CNA) programs.

Novell continues this venerable tradition with the Certified Linux Engineer 9 program. Before discussing the CLE 9 certification, you need to understand that there are two versions of the CLE. Let's take a look at the differences between them.

CLE Versus CLE 9

If you've been around in the Novell world, you know that Novell launched the original CLE certification early in 2004. However, the CLE 9 certification we're going to focus on in this book is completely and utterly different from the original CLE.

The original CLE certification focused on implementing Novell Nterprise Linux Services (NNLS) on the Linux platform. NNLS was a suite of products containing traditional Novell services ported to run on Linux. It was really cool. You could run services such as eDirectory, iFolder, NetMail, DirXML, and iPrint on the Linux platform.

In terms of certification, the original CLE was a Linux-based equivalent of the CNE certification. Novell's CNE, over the years, has become heavily focused on implementing and managing Novell's powerful network services. In fact, the original CLE didn't include very many Linux-specific objectives. Novell expected you to enter the program with a fair degree of Linux knowledge already under your belt.

NOTE

The original CLE assumed you had your LPIC-1 certification (or equivalent knowledge) coming into the program.

The CLE 9 certification, on the other hand, is different. You might be wondering why the original CLE was given such an overhaul. There are several reasons:

- Between the time that the original CLE was released and the CLE 9 certification was developed, Novell purchased SUSE LINUX. Novell wanted to create a certification program surrounding its new network operating system (SUSE LINUX Enterprise Server) in the same way that it created the CNE certification around NetWare.
- NNLS, as a product, was assimilated into the latest Novell product release: Open Enterprise Server (OES). OES is built around Novell's world-class network services. When implementing OES, you have the option of selecting which operating system you want to deploy them on: Linux or NetWare. As a result, development on NNLS as a standalone product has all but stopped. Simply put, it's difficult to maintain a certification program centered around a product that isn't available any more.

- Using the term *Certified Linux Engineer* didn't accurately portray the knowledge domain of the original CLE. You could get the impression that a CLE must be an absolute guru with Linux. Although the original CLE did have to know a substantial amount about Linux, it wasn't the focus of the certification.

For these reasons, Novell has completely revamped the CLE. As you may have guessed from the first item in the preceding list, the CLE 9 no longer covers NNLS. In harmony with the second item, the CLE 9 is now truly what it sounds like: It's an advanced-level Linux certification (based on Novell's SUSE LINUX Enterprise Server 9 distribution). Anyone who attains this certification can truly be regarded as a Linux expert.

Paths to the CLE

Because of the new nature of the certification, the path to the CLE has changed as well. With the original CLE, anyone who had the suggested prerequisites could enter the program. This isn't the case with the CLE 9. If you want to be certified as a CLE 9, you must first obtain your Certified Linux Professional (CLP) certification from Novell.

Basically, the new CLE works in a manner similar to the CNE certification. Before you can become a CNE, you have to obtain your CNA certification. The CNA is an entry-level NetWare certification. The CNE is a much more advanced certification. The CLE works in much the same way. You first obtain your CLP, and then you advance to the CLE. This path is depicted in Figure 1.1:

FIGURE 1.1
The path to your CLE.

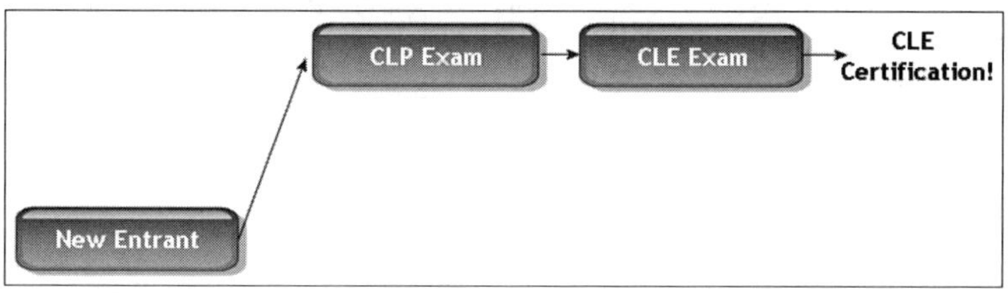

In this study guide, I'm going to assume that you already have your CLP (or have an equivalent level of knowledge). Accordingly, I will address only the CLE objectives not covered by the CLP certification.

The path depicted in Figure 1.1 is intended for those interested in certification. However, there are always those who participate in these programs who are interested in gaining the knowledge provided by the certification, but aren't interested in actually getting certified.

Novell has accounted for folks in this category, as well. There's a secondary path for individuals who already have their Red Hat Certified Engineer (RHCE) or their Linux Professional Institute Certification Level 1 (LPIC-1) certifications. This path is depicted in Figure 1.2.

FIGURE 1.2
An alternative path to CLE knowledge.

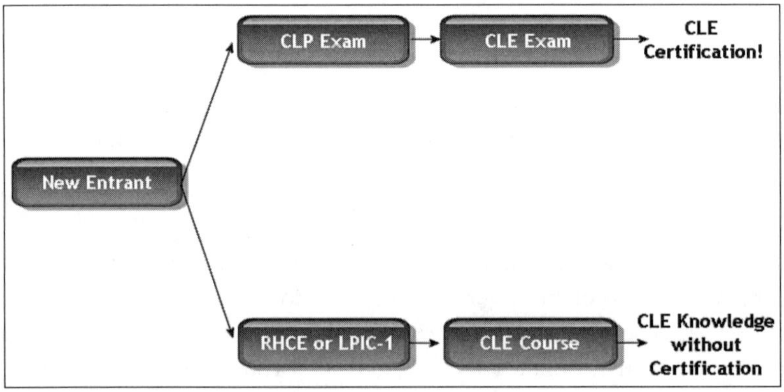

To accommodate this audience, Novell has provided *Course 3019: Migrating to SUSE LINUX*. The goal of this course is to teach someone who has experience with a different Linux distribution how to accomplish familiar tasks on SUSE Enterprise Linux Server 9 (SLES 9).

I recognize that some readers may be in this second category. To accommodate this audience, I've included content in Chapter 2 of this study guide that will help bring you up to speed on the SLES 9 distribution.

In addition to a solid background in Linux, you should also have a firm understanding of computer networking before attempting to complete this study guide. The CLE 9 certification assumes that you already have your Network+ certification from CompTIA or have equivalent experience.

If you can answer the question, "What's the default subnet mask for a Class B IP address?" without hesitation, you are probably prepared to begin study for the CLE 9. If not, you should probably study basic network concepts before beginning this study guide.

Now that you know who the CLE is for and the paths you can take to reach it, let's review the CLE 9 certification objectives.

CLE 9 Objectives

With the CLE 9, be aware that you will be expected to both *know* the concepts and *do* the tasks specified in each objective.

With many other IT certifications in the marketplace today, it's possible to pass the associated exam even if you lack proficiency with some of the objectives, as long as you have a good understanding of the remaining objectives. Basically, the cut score is low enough that you can get away with missing a number of questions.

With the CLE 9, however, you must have a strong working knowledge of *all* the objectives. To be blunt, the CLE 9 Practicum is an unforgiving pass/fail exam. You might be surprised to know that more candidates fail Novell practical exams than pass them.

NOTE

Novell has implemented practical exams for a number of certification programs, including the Certified Linux Professional (CLP).

This is because of the way Novell structured the CLE 9 exam. It incorporates multiple objectives into a given testing scenario. If you lack proficiency with one of the objectives, you could potentially fail the entire scenario, thus failing the exam.

Now that I've scared you to death, let's talk about what you need to know for the exam. The material needed to obtain your CLE 9 certification is defined in two Novell courses:

- Course 3057: SUSE Linux Network Services
- Course 3058: SUSE Linux Security

This study guide will address the objectives from both courses. Talk about a two-for-one deal! Here's what this study guide covers:

- Configuring a DNS server
- Configuring a DHCP server
- Implementing Samba to provide file and print services
- Implementing network printing using CUPS
- Configuring email services
- Implementing a proxy server with SQUID
- Monitoring traffic on your network
- Implementing OpenSLP

- Implementing a web application server with Tomcat
- Implementing general security practices
- Implementing host security
- Implementing network security
- Securing services with cryptography
- Relating general firewall concepts
- Implementing a packet filter
- Implementing an application level gateway
- Implementing a VPN
- Detecting intruders
- Responding to security breaches

As you can see, these are some advanced Linux topics. We're going to have a lot of fun as we traverse them in this book!

With these objectives under our belt, let's talk about the CLE 9 exam itself.

Introduction to the CLE 9 Test Environment

As mentioned earlier, for the CLE 9 Novell has implemented a practical exam called the *Practicum* to ensure that you really have the skills required.

NOTE

The mere mention of the phrase *Practicum* has been known to send network administrators shrieking in fear!

Instead of a written exam, the CLE 9 tests you in a hands-on, live environment that certifies that you are sufficiently skilled in advanced Linux topics. Let's review the difference between practical exams and traditional exams.

Practical Testing Versus Traditional Testing

With a multiple-choice test, some network administrators have discovered over the years that, many times, you can pass without studying extensively. After all, you have a 1 in 4 chance of getting the right answer without any knowledge at all. With a little bit of networking background, many candidates can discern the correct response without really understanding the concepts behind the question. Your score won't be anything to write home about—but hey, you passed!

Traditional certification exams in the IT industry usually provide the student with a series of multiple-choice, fill-in-the-blank, and matching questions, as shown in Figure 1.3.

FIGURE 1.3
The traditional testing method.

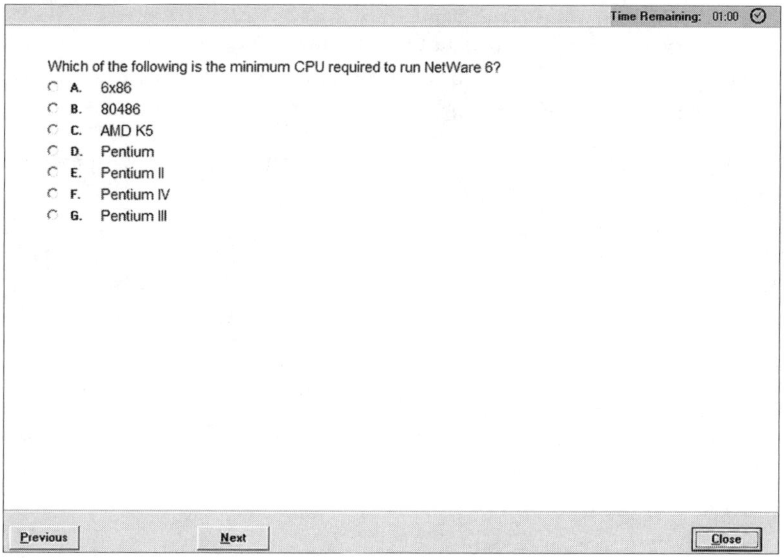

The strength of these exams is that they are very effective at evaluating your mastery of theoretical concepts. They are also relatively easy to create and deliver. That's why they are used so extensively.

Their main weakness is that they don't test your ability to actually perform the tasks specified in the objectives. In other words, they tend to evaluate what you *know* instead of what you can *do*. You may have heard the term "paper certified" before. This term refers to network administrators who have passed the multiple-choice exam for their certification, but who can't actually perform on the job. You can't just magically summon the "vast powers of certification."

This won't happen with the CLE 9 Practicum. Novell has been a pioneer in the field of practical testing since its Certified Directory Engineer (CDE) certification was introduced in 1999. Novell practical exams present you with a scenario and then require you, without guidance, to determine the proper resolution and implement that resolution on a running server. Your server is then evaluated to see whether you did it correctly. If you did, you pass. If you missed something or did it incorrectly, you fail.

The strength of this strategy is that it truly verifies whether you have mastered the skills specified in the objectives. You've got to be able to "walk the walk and talk the talk" or you will fail miserably.

In spite of the pain associated with practical exams, they can actually be very beneficial to you. Students who pass a practical test are much more likely to be able to perform on the job than those who pass only traditional exams.

To a job applicant, this is of great value. It gives you bargaining power with an employer, allowing you to truly certify your skill set.

Unfortunately, other "certified" IT job applicants have burned many employers over the years. Because their skills were verified only at the conceptual level, their ability to actually do the job was sometimes less than what was necessary. (In many cases, it was a lot less.)

Practical certification testing helps employers filter out less-qualified job applicants. When you apply for a job, employers can have a high degree of confidence in your abilities if you have successfully completed a practical exam. In fact, because of the flood of paper-certified applicants, many employers relate that the only certifications that mean anything to them now are those that are based on practical testing.

Accordingly, be aware that the pass rate on practical exams tends to be much lower than on traditional exams. To pass the CLE 9 practical exam, you will probably have to spend twice as much time preparing as you would for a traditional certification exam.

Interestingly, Novell reports that even though the pass rate on their practical exams is lower than traditional exams, most candidates feel the tests are quite fair—even those who fail. This is because most people dislike being tested on "stuff" that doesn't matter. They respect an exam that reveals where they really stand in relation to relevant skills—whether they pass or fail!

Let's talk about what you will experience when you take your CLE 9 practical exam.

How the CLE 9 Practicum Works

To complete the Practicum, you must schedule a test with a Novell education partner center. This can be done by visiting http://practicum.novell.com/partner_search.php.

When you arrive at the testing center, you will be assigned a workstation. The practical exam will be delivered to you through this computer. The CLE 9 Practicum is composed of the components shown in Figure 1.4.

FIGURE 1.4
The CLE Practicum.

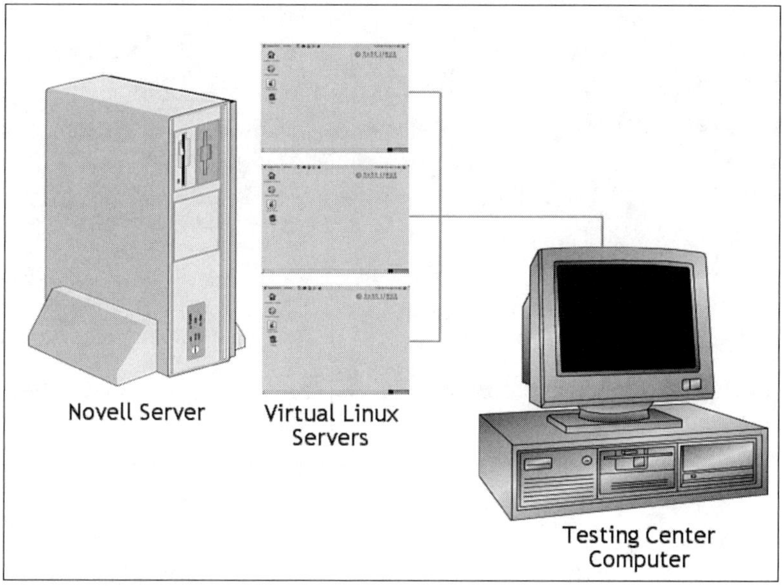

The role of each of these components is described in the sections that follow.

THE TESTING CENTER COMPUTER

The first component in the CLE Practicum is the testing center workstation where you will be seated. From this system, you will use a web browser to access virtual servers running on the Novell server. A sample CLE exam interface is shown in Figure 1.5.

THE NOVELL SERVER

The second component in the Practicum is the Novell server. This server is maintained at Novell's Provo campus and runs VMWare, a product that allows multiple operating systems to be run simultaneously on a single computer. Using this product, the Novell server provides you with access to multiple virtual SLES 9 servers.

NOTE

More information about VMWare can be found at http://www.vmware.com.

FIGURE 1.5
The CLE Practicum interface.

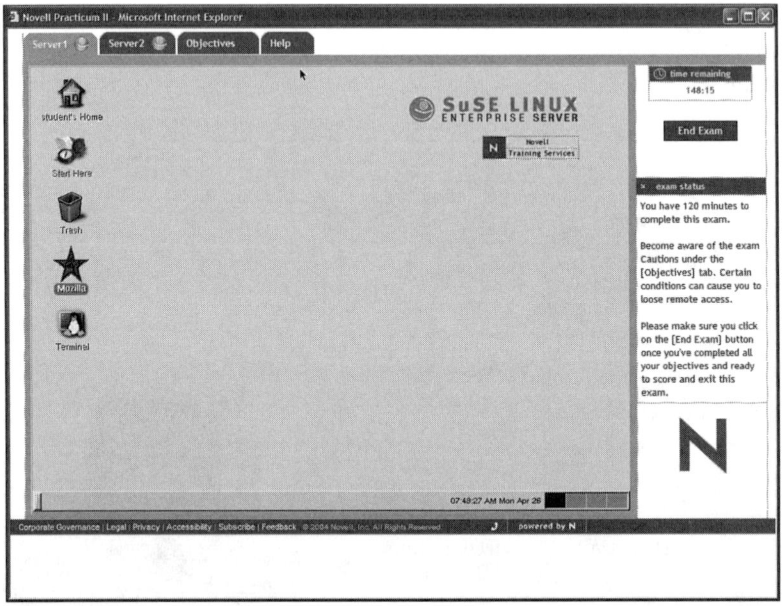

VIRTUAL SERVERS

The final Practicum component is a group of virtual server sessions running on the Novell server. Each session is a separate SLES 9 virtual server. These virtual servers have been preconfigured according to a specific scenario designed by the testing team at Novell.

Depending on what scenario you are required to complete, you will probably find that these servers have been deliberately configured incorrectly. To pass the exam, you must correct any errors and implement the requirements of the scenario on these virtual servers.

Now that you've been acquainted with the CLE 9 certification and with the practical testing environment, let's talk about how you can use this book to get yourself ready.

Using This Study Guide

As we've discussed, to pass the CLE 9 exam you must have both the theoretical knowledge and the technical skills reflected in the objectives. This study guide is designed to provide you with both of these elements.

First, each chapter will present you with a thorough review of the conceptual matter associated with one or more CLE 9 objective.

Then, each chapter in this book (with the exception of this one) will provide you with one or more hands-on exercises to help you gain the SLES 9 skills required to pass the CLE 9 exam. As you progress through this guide, you will build a complete SLES 9 implementation, piece by piece, from the ground up.

It is absolutely critical that you complete these exercises. The CLE 9 practical exam requires that you be able to complete these tasks in a live environment without any books or any help. Everything you do has to come from your brain!

To complete the lab exercises in this book, you will need the following equipment:

- A lab PC—This computer must meet the following specifications:
  - CPU—Pentium III 800MHz or later
  - Memory—256MB minimum
  - Hard disk—6GB or more
  - Peripherals—A CUPS-compatible printer, a monitor, a mouse, and a keyboard.

- A copy of SLES 9—An evaluation copy of SLES 9 is available from Novell at http://www.novell.com. In Chapter 2, "Introduction to SUSE Linux Enterprise Server 9," you will be provided with specific instructions for downloading and burning a copy.

If you've got this equipment, you're ready to go. Before we dig in, there's one more thing we need to discuss—how to prepare for your practical exam.

Strategies and Tips for the CLE Practicum

Taking a practical exam can be unnerving. If you've ever taught a networking class or presented a technical demonstration, you know that what worked perfectly back in your office will, with certainty, blow up in front of a live audience.

The same Murphy's Law corollary applies to your practical exam. How do you deal with it? You prepare as if the fate of the entire world depends on it! I'm going to finish this chapter with several tips and strategies you should keep in mind as you go through this book and prepare for your practical exam. They will save you a lot of trouble:

- When you begin your exam, you will be presented with detailed instructions describing how to complete the exam. Don't skip reading these. Follow all instructions to the letter!
- Remember that you are accessing the virtual servers using a TCP/IP connection. You should never change the IP address, subnet mask, router address, or DNS server address of your virtual servers. Doing so will totally disrupt your ability to access them.
- You will be automatically logged in to the virtual server as a nonroot user. If you need root-level access, open a terminal session and use the `su` or the `sux` command. Under no circumstances should you log out. You won't be able to log back in.
- Remember that the virtual Linux server has several key processes running on it that provide you with remote access from your testing center. Don't kill a running process unless you are absolutely sure you know what it is. If you accidentally kill a process that provides remote access, your session will be closed.
- You should never exit the X Window System. If you need access to a shell prompt, open a terminal session.
- If you need to restart your server, use the **`reboot`** command. You should never use the `halt` or `logout` command.
- On occasion, your mouse cursor may disappear when you are using a web browser within the virtual server desktop. It may or may not come back. (Sometimes wiggling the mouse quickly will cause it to reappear.) If you can't get your cursor back, you must exit the browser by pressing Ctrl+Q and then restart it.
- It can take some time to load some utilities on your server for the first time. Be patient. After the utilities are loaded into memory on your virtual server, it should run at a reasonable speed thereafter.
- Remember that you are completing the exam on a virtual server being accessed through a remote-access web connection. It's going to run much slower than a real server. Exercise patience and don't get "click happy."
- Read the scenario. Remember that Novell uses a number of CLE scenarios. Each one is slightly different from the others. When you sign on at the testing center, you will be randomly assigned one of these scenarios to complete. When you receive your scenario, keep the following points in mind:
- Analyze the scenario thoroughly. Because of the time constraints imposed on the Practicum, your first impulse will be to get working right away on your virtual server. Avoid this impulse at all costs. It is imperative that you read through your scenario line by line. The time spent will be time well invested.

- Identify the problem or error condition in the scenario.
- Look for any special or unusual conditions identified in the scenario.
- Identify what criteria must be met for the scenario to be considered resolved. (It is critical that you list each item!)
- Determine what tests you can run to verify that each criteria has been successfully met.
- Don't assume that your server has been configured properly as you read the scenario. Depending on your scenario, you may have to isolate and resolve various misconfigured parameters.
- After you have read through and analyzed your scenario, read it again! Chances are you will find one or more items that you missed. Add these to your scenario analysis.
- Plan your strategy. After you have thoroughly read and analyzed your scenario, you will again be tempted to immediately dive in and start working on your virtual server. Avoid this impulse at all costs! Before working on your server, it is imperative that you use your scenario analysis to create a plan of action. Using scratch paper or whiteboard (provided by the testing center), identify each tasks you must complete to resolve the condition in the scenario. List them in the order that they must be completed.
- Implement your plan. After you have thoroughly analyzed your scenario and have planned your strategy, you can give in to your impulse and actually start working on your virtual servers. If you've organized yourself properly, you should be able to complete the scenario quickly and methodically. As you do, it is important that you keep your eyes open for hidden issues that may not have been overtly described in the scenario. Be prepared to reevaluate your plan at any time.
- Test the resolution. As a part of your overall plan, you should have identified how you will test your resolution to ensure that you have completed each criterion in the scenario. (It's interesting to note that many practical exam-takers fail to complete this simple task.) When you have completed each task in your plan, implement your evaluation plan and verify that the scenario has been truly completed. There's a better-than-average chance that you will find one or more problems remain unresolved. Identify each of these and develop a plan for how you will work them out.

If you study the material in this book, practice with the lab exercises, follow the exam instructions, plan your strategy, and test your implementation, you will greatly increase your chances of passing the CLE Practicum.

Before we move on, let's review what you learned in this chapter.

Summary

In this chapter, you were introduced to the CLE 9 certification from Novell. You learned about its purpose, its audience, and about how it is delivered.

You then learned about the nature of the CLE 9 practical testing environment. You learned about the various components that compose the practical exam.

Finally, you were presented with some test-taking tips and strategies for increasing your chances of passing the CLE 9 practical exam.

The next chapter will present you with a brief introduction to SLES 9. After that, the remaining chapters will dig right into the CLE 9 objectives.

CHAPTER 2

Introduction to the SUSE Linux Enterprise Server 9

This chapter covers the following prerequisite requirements for Novell's Certified Linux Engineer (CLE) 9 certification:

1. Describe the SUSE Linux Enterprise Server (SLES) 9 Linux Distribution.
2. Install SLES 9.
3. Use YaST.
4. Manage the SLES 9 system configuration.

Before you dig into the main topics of this book, you should know that Novell has specified a number of prerequisite skills and tasks that you need to understand to have a successful experience when preparing for the CLE exam. Recall from Chapter 1, "Introduction to the Certified Linux Engineer (CLE) Certification," that you should already have your Certified Linux Professional (CLP) certification from Novell (if you're planning to become CLE certified) or have some other Linux certification, such as the RHCE or the LPIC-1 (if you're not planning to pursue CLE certification).

If you have your CLP, you're in good shape. However, if you have a different Linux certification, you will need a brief introduction to SLES 9 because the SLES 9 distribution is slightly different from many other common Linux distributions.

Even though all Linux distributions are based on a common kernel, the operating systems built around the kernel by the various Linux vendors vary quite a bit; it's a fact of life we have to deal with in the Linux world.

In this chapter, we'll go through these differences to bring you up to speed with SLES 9. Of course, if you have your CLP certification, you will probably already be familiar with the content of this chapter. Even if this is the case, I recommend that you work your way through this chapter anyway. I say this for two reasons:

- It never hurts to review.
- In this chapter's labs, you will install and configure a basic SLES 9 system that will be used in the labs in later chapters.

Let's begin by introducing you to the SLES 9 Linux distribution.

An Introduction to SUSE Linux Enterprise Server 9

TEST OBJECTIVE COVERED:

1. Describe the SUSE Linux Enterprise Server (SLES) 9 Linux Distribution.

SUSE Linux has been around for quite some time. Like most Linux distributions, it was initially developed and released in the early 1990s.

The SUSE organization itself was established in Germany. Back then, the name of the company was S.u.S.E., which was an acronym for *Software und System Entwicklung* (German for *Software and System Development*). Later on, the name was changed to just SuSE.

There is an ongoing debate in the industry about how to pronounce the name *SUSE*. If you ask most native English-speakers, they will say it is pronounced *soo-see, soo-zuh,* or *soo-suh*. If you speak with someone at Novell, more than likely they will pronounce it in this manner.

However, I've had occasion over the last couple of years to converse with SUSE employees in Germany and their pronunciation is a little different. They generally say *zuu-zah*. Either way, understand that we're talking about the very same Linux distribution.

The first version of S.u.S.E. Linux (version 1.0) was released in 1994. The German SuSE organization maintained a series of releases over the years up to version 8.0, which was released in 2002. Then, in mid-2004, Novell acquired SuSE. When the purchase was complete, Novell changed the name of the company to *SUSE* (which I might add, is very difficult to type when you're used to *SuSE*).

Since Novell's acquisition, the SUSE Linux distribution has been released in three variations:

- Novell Linux Desktop (NLD) 9—This version of SUSE Linux is designed as a replacement for Microsoft Windows on the user's desktop. It comes with a series of productivity applications, such as OpenOffice.org (which provides Microsoft Office functionality), Evolution (a powerful email client), and the Mozilla Firefox web browser. Its intent is to make the switch to Linux from Windows as painless as possible.
- SUSE Linux Professional 9—As NLD is intended for Windows users, SUSE Linux Professional is a Linux desktop operating system intended for more experienced Linux users and enthusiasts.
- SUSE Linux Enterprise Server 9 (SLES 9)—Both NLD and SUSE Linux Professional are designed as desktop operating systems. SUSE Linux Enterprise Server 9, on the other hand, is designed to function as a high-end server system. Instead of running end-user applications, this operating system is optimized to provide network services, such as Samba, CUPS, MySQL, and Apache. It also provides the underlying operating system for Novell's new Open Enterprise Server (OES) product offering.

The CLE 9 certification requires you to know only SLES 9. Therefore, in this course, we are going to be concerned only with this operating system.

Before we can go much further, you will need a server system to work with. Let's start by learning how to install a base SLES 9 server.

Installing SLES 9

TEST OBJECTIVE COVERED:

2. Install SLES 9.

Installing SLES 9 is a snap. SLES uses an installation and configuration utility called *YaST*, which stands for Yet another Setup Tool. YaST is an integral part of SLES 9 and we'll spend more time later in this chapter discussing in detail how to use it to configure your system. For now, understand that YaST makes SLES 9 one of the easiest Linux distributions to install.

Before you actually start the installation, you need to verify that your server hardware meets the minimum requirements for SLES 9.

SLES 9 System Requirements

To install SLES 9, your server must meet the following system requirements:

- Memory: 256MB (512MB recommended)
- Hard Disk Space: 4GB (minimum)

NOTE

In this course, your system will need a hard disk that is at least 6GB in size.

- Network Interface: 1 Ethernet interface *or* a modem
- Supported CPUs:
  - x86
  - AMD64
  - Intel EM64T
  - Itanium
  - IBM Power, zSeries, and S/390
- Miscellaneous Hardware
- X-compatible display adapter and monitor
- Keyboard
- Mouse (recommended)

In this course, we're going to stick with the x86 version of SLES. This is also the version you will use in the CLE 9 practicum.

Be aware that the preceding requirements are minimum requirements. If you implement SLES in a high-load environment, you will probably need to upgrade your hardware. The best operating system in the world can't compensate for lousy hardware.

After you've got your system ready, the next thing you need to do is get a copy of SLES 9.

Obtaining SLES 9

Like most Linux distributions, SLES 9 is available as a free download. To get an evaluation copy, open a browser window and navigate to http://www.novell.com/products/linuxenterpriseserver/eval.html. From this link, you can select the appropriate distribution for your processor architecture. More than likely, you will use the x86-AMD64-EM65T distribution shown in Figure 2.1.

FIGURE 2.1
Getting ready to download SLES 9.

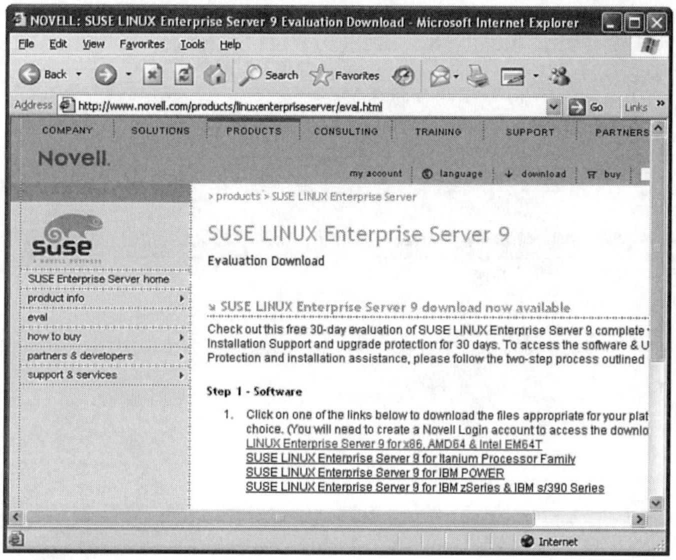

After selecting the appropriate link, you'll be prompted to log in as shown in Figure 2.2.

FIGURE 2.2
Logging in to Novell's website.

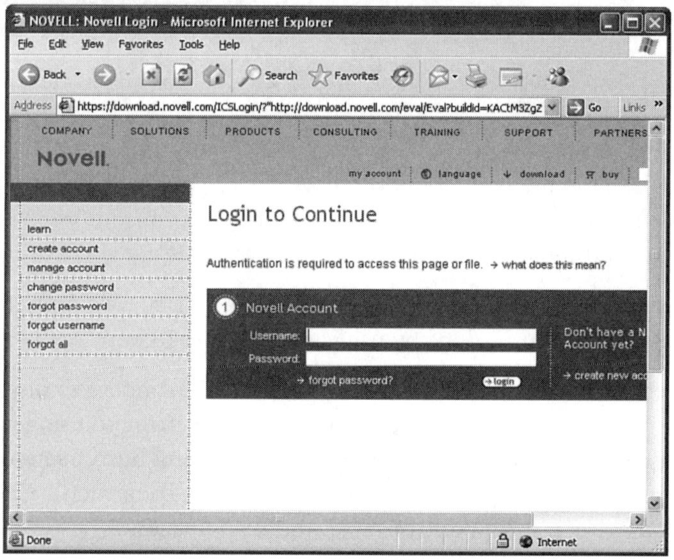

If you already have a Novell account, you can use your existing username and password. If you don't have an account, select Create a New Account and follow the prompts. The account is free and you can specify whether you want to be added to Novell's mailing list.

After logging in, you will see links to the six ISO images used to create the SLES 9 installation CDs, as shown in Figure 2.3.

FIGURE 2.3
SLES 9 ISO images ready for download.

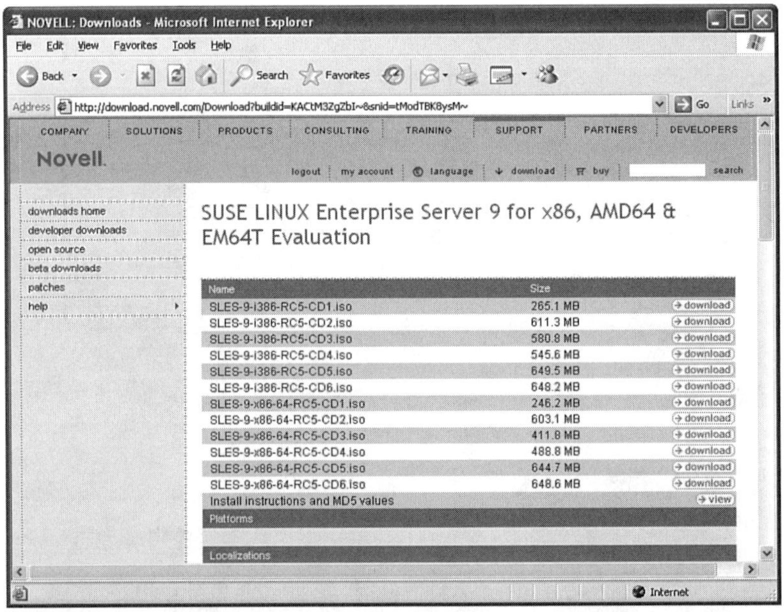

Notice that these images are very large. Don't even think about trying to download these using a dial-up connection to the Internet unless you have a very patient ISP who won't drop your connection and you, yourself, can wait a week or so for the downloads to complete. Even with a 1Mbps broadband Internet connection, these downloads are going to take a while.

After you get the images downloaded, you will need to create a set of CDs from which you can install a SLES 9 server. This is done by using a CD burner to burn the ISO images to disc.

This is a point of confusion for many. When I say "burn the ISO image to disc," I'm not referring to putting the image file itself on the CD. Instead, I'm referring to using your CD burning software to extract all the individual files from the image file and burn them to disc. Most CD burning software packages are capable of doing this; however, some aren't. Check your package's documentation to see if it supports burning from ISO images.

Installing SLES 9

After the CDs are burned, you're ready to install SLES 9.

NOTE

The lab exercises in this chapter assume you have a clean machine on which to install SLES 9. You can install SLES 9 on a system that already has an operating system installed as long as about 4GB or so of *unpartitioned* space is available on one of your drives. GRUB should detect the existence of the other bootable partitions on the drive and add a corresponding menu item, allowing you to choose the OS on startup. If it doesn't, you will need to manually configure GRUB so you can access each OS on the system.

The SLES installation process is pretty straightforward, thanks to YaST. In this chapter, we will first review the steps for installing SLES in a generic manner with explanations as to what the various options do. Then you will be presented with a lab exercise that you can use to perform the actual installation on your own hardware. You should read through the conceptual portion first before attempting the lab exercise.

NOTE

You can use VMWare to install SLES 9 as a virtual machine. VMWare is a really cool product that allows you to run multiple guest operating systems on your host system operating system. You don't have to worry about disk partitions or boot loaders. You can download an evaluation copy from http:/www.vmware.com. However, if you choose to use VMWare, an issue exists with the SLES 9 installation routine that makes the graphical screens unreadable.

To get around this issue, you can press F2 in the first installation screen and select Text Mode. It's not pretty, but it gets the job done.

Fortunately, there's a second option that I like a lot better. You can enter **VNC=1** into the Boot Options field. This will allow you to view the installation process from within a browser window. For more information on this option, visit http://www.novell.com/coolsolutions/qna/1805.html.

To install SLES 9, complete the following:

1. Insert Disc 1 into your server's CD drive and boot from it. After a few seconds, the screen shown in Figure 2.4 is displayed.
2. Before starting, configure installation parameters necessary for your environment. Some of the more important options you should consider include the following:
   - F2—Allows you to configure a text-based or graphical installation as well as the screen resolution if you're using a graphical install.

- F3—Allows you to specify your installation source.
- F6—Allows you to update the drivers used for systems that use unusual or specialized hardware.

3. Select **Installation**. It will take a few minutes for the installation to initialize.
4. In the License Agreement screen, select **I Agree**. The screen in Figure 2.5 is displayed.

FIGURE 2.4
SLES 9 initial installation screen.

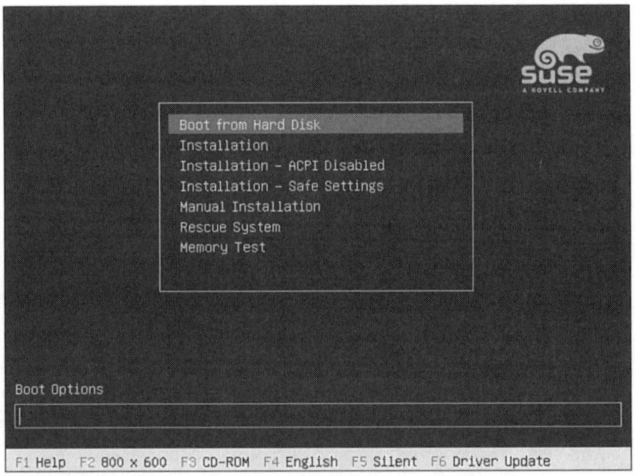

TIP

Notice that a progress indicator is displayed on the left side of the screen.

5. Select your **Language**, and then select **Accept**. The Installation Settings screen, shown in Figure 2.6, is displayed.

FIGURE 2.5
Configuring the system language.

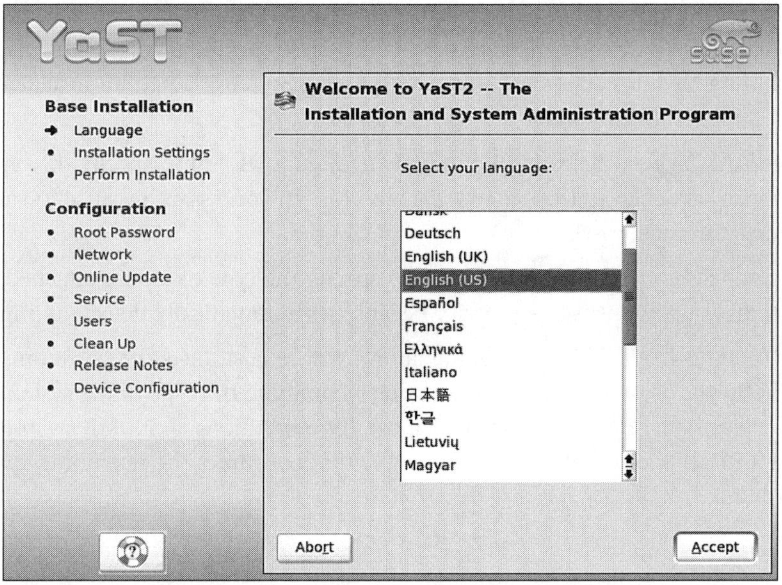

FIGURE 2.6
Configuring Installation Settings.

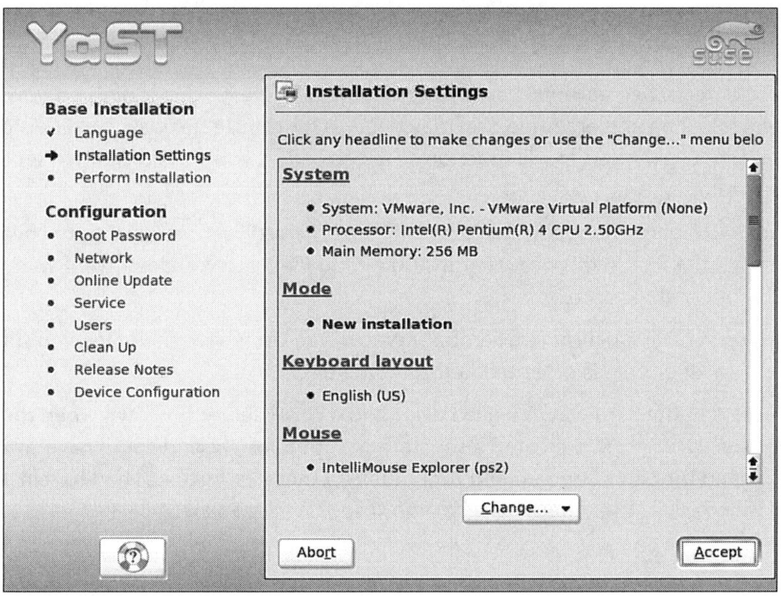

6. Customize your installation settings. You have the following options:
   - System—Selecting System causes YaST to run a full hardware detection probe of your system.
   - Mode—Selecting Mode allows you to configure a specific type of installation, including New Installation, Update an Existing System, Repair an Installed System, and Boot Installed System.
   - Keyboard Layout—Selecting Keyboard Layout allows you to specify the type of keyboard attached to the system. Usually this isn't necessary because it's automatically detected in most cases.
   - Mouse—Selecting Mouse allows you to specify the type of mouse attached to the system. Usually this isn't necessary because it's automatically detected in most cases.
   - Partitioning—Selecting Partitioning allows you to customize the partitioning scheme used by your system. It also allows you to configure the type of file system used for your partitions. By default, YaST proposes two partitions: a 500MB swap partition and a Reiser root partition (mounted at /) that consumes the remaining space on the hard disk.

NOTE

In this book, we will exclusively use the Reiser file system. SLES 9 works fine with ext3 or ext2 file systems, which are commonly implemented in Linux systems. However, Reiser has some advantages over these other two. Reiser is a journaling file system just like ext3 (in fact, it was the very first journaling file system). Reiser provides faster file access and system recovery than ext3, and that is why we're using it here.

Generic partitioning schemes work well for some servers. However, depending on how your particular server will be implemented, you may need to customize the way the disk is partitioned. For example, if the server will function as a web server, you should create a separate partition for web data.

It's a good idea to create a separate partition for `/var`. The services we're going to cover in this course create a lot of files in this directory, including log files, and you don't want your root partition running out of disk space.

As well, if the server will function as a Samba server where users save their files, you should create a separate partition that is mounted at the /home directory.

I learned this lesson the hard way. A while back, I had a Linux server go down when the root partition got corrupted. If I had created a separate partition for `/home`, I could have simply reinstalled the OS and probably been up and running in 15 minutes. Instead, I had to reinstall from scratch and then restore users' data from backup. It took a LONG time.

If you do customize the partitioning scheme, be sure you use a swap partition that is at least 500MB in size. Also be sure that the partition that contains the root directory is at least 3.5GB in size.

- Software—Selecting Software will give you the option of customizing the packages that will be installed on the system during installation. You can select from four predefined options: Minimum System, Minimum Graphical System, Full Installation, or Default System. You can also select Detailed Selection to manually specify the packages you want installed.
- Booting—Selecting this option allows you to configure your boot loader type and the various parameters it will use.
- Time Zone—This option allows you to specify the time zone where the server resides.
- Language—This option allows you to specify the server language.
- Default Runlevel—Using this option, you can specify whether your system boots to a text-based shell (runlevel 3) or into a graphical environment (runlevel 5).

7. When you have finished configuring your installation, select **Accept**.
8. When prompted to start the installation, select **Install**.
9. When prompted, insert the remaining SLES 9 installation CDs. As the installation proceeds, YaST displays a progress indicator, shown in Figure 2.7.
10. Wait while the base installation is completed. You will be prompted to configure your new system. The first task is to set the root password. The screen shown in Figure 2.8 is displayed.
11. In the Password fields, enter a password for your root user account; then select **Next**.

    Novell recommends that you use a mixture of upper- and lowercase characters and numbers in the password. If you don't, you will be presented with a security warning.

    After selecting Next, the Network Configuration dialog box is displayed; as shown in Figure 2.9.
12. In the Network Configuration dialog box, you can configure the following settings:
    - Network Interfaces—Use this option to configure the NIC in your server. If you have a single NIC in your system, it should be automatically detected and configured to use DHCP.

      However, in a multiple-NIC system, the first NIC is detected and automatically configured to use DHCP; usually, the NIC is installed in the lowest-numbered PCI slot. But NICs in subsequent PCI slots are usually detected but left unconfigured. If you select **Network Interfaces**, the screen in Figure 2.10 is displayed.

FIGURE 2.7
YaST installation progress indicator.

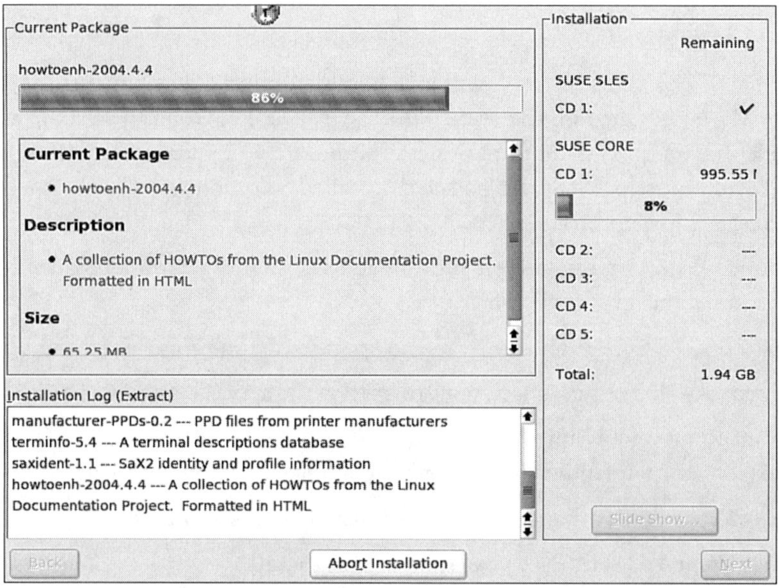

FIGURE 2.8
Setting the root password.

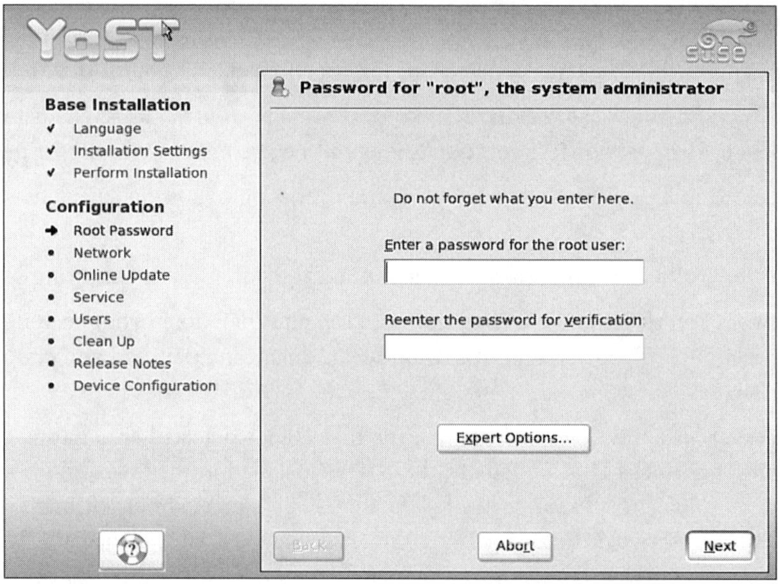

FIGURE 2.9
Configuring network settings.

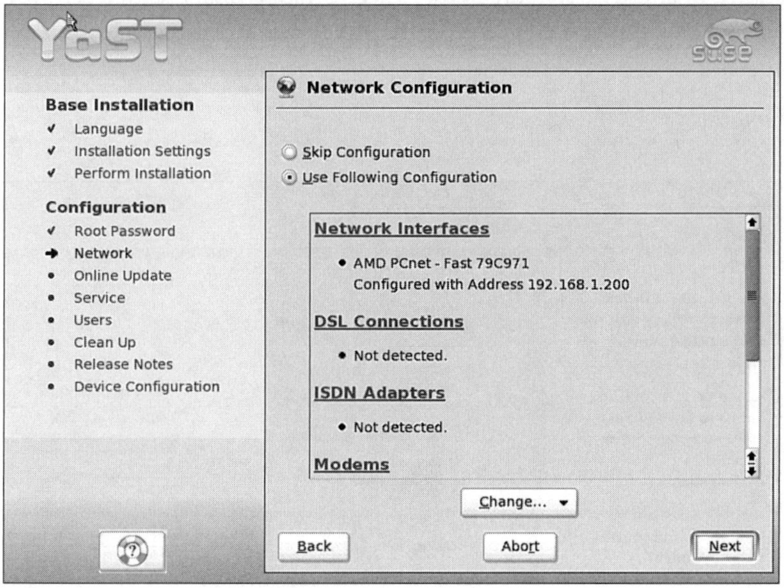

FIGURE 2.10
Configuring NICs.

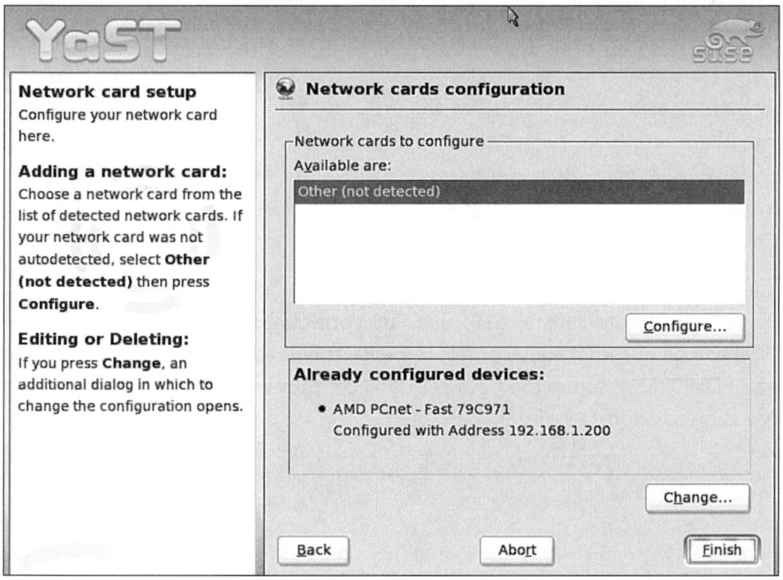

To configure your additional NICs, you will need to select them from the Available Are field and select **Configure**.

To modify an already-configured NIC, select **Change** underneath the Already Configured Devices field and select **Edit**. The screen in Figure 2.11 is displayed.

FIGURE 2.11
Configuring protocols.

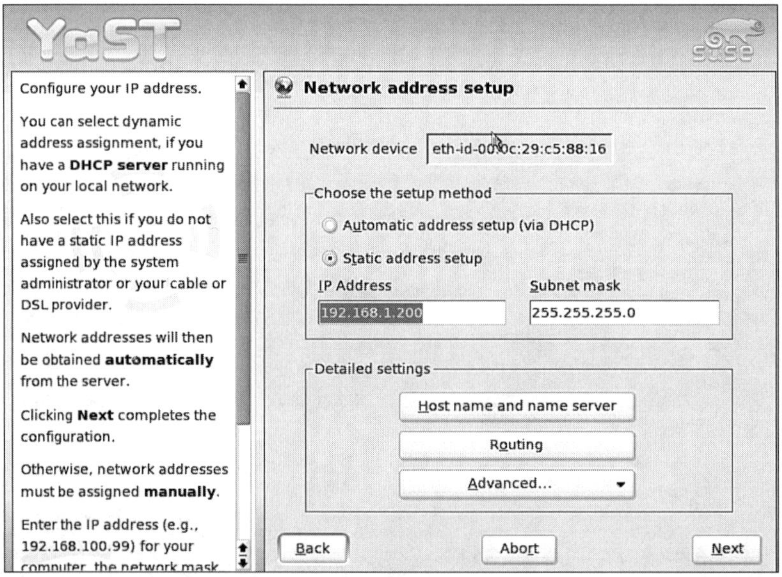

In this screen, you can specify that the NIC use DHCP or that it use a static IP address. You can also configure the system's hostname, DNS server address, and default gateway router address. If you are using a wireless NIC in your server, you can also use this screen to configure wireless settings, such as your SSID and your WEP key.

TIP

If you are using VNC to remotely install SLES and you configured VNC to use a static IP address, the detected NIC will be automatically configured with the IP address you specified instead of configured to use DHCP. That's how the figures in this chapter were created, and that's why you see a statically assigned address in Figures 2.9–2.11.

When you have your NIC configured select **Next, Finish**.

Other choices available include the following:

- DSL Connections—Use this option to configure any DSL interfaces installed in your server system.
- ISDN Adapters—Use this option if you have an ISDN adapter installed in the system that needs to be configured.
- Modems—Use this option to configure a modem installed in or connected to the system.
- Proxy—Use this option to configure your server to use a proxy server and to provide it with a proxy username and password.
- VNC Remote Administration—VNC stands for Virtual Network Computing. VNC allows you to use either a VNC client (using port 5901) or a Java-enabled web browser (using port 5801) to remotely access the server's desktop. A sample VNC session where a SLES 9 server is being installed is shown in Figure 2.12.

FIGURE 2.12
Using VNC in a web browser.

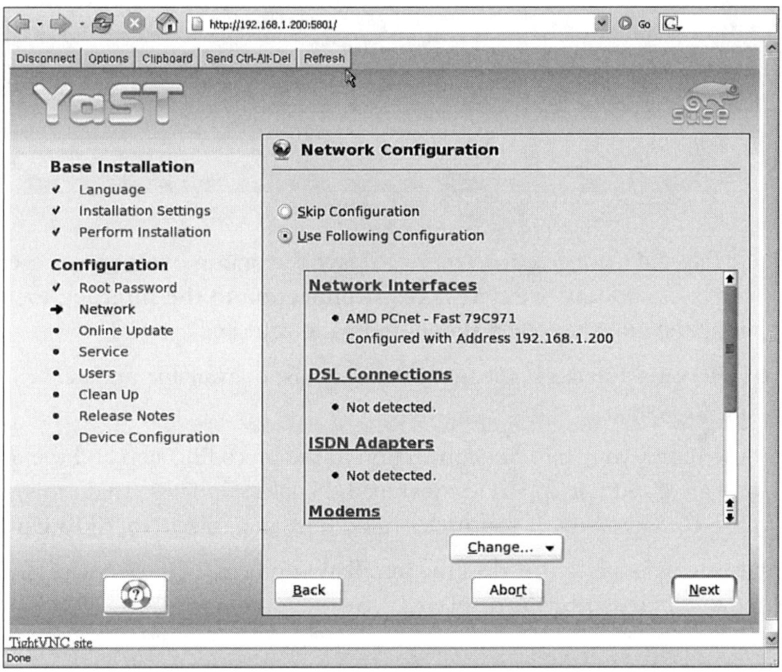

Selecting this option allows you to enable this service on your server.

13. Select **Next**.
14. Wait while your configuration settings are saved. When complete, the screen shown in Figure 2.13 is displayed.

FIGURE 2.13
Configuring your Internet connection test.

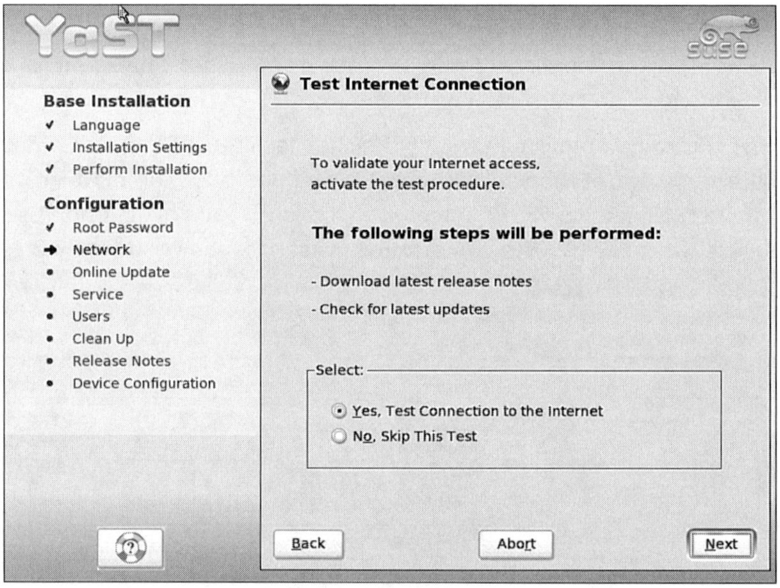

15. In the Test Internet Connection screen, you have the option of testing your connection to the Internet. To do this, select **Yes, Test Connection to the Internet**; then select **Next**. During the test, the screen shown in Figure 2.14 is displayed:

    If the test succeeds, the latest release notes and a list of available updates will be downloaded to your system.
16. If you chose to test your Internet connection in the preceding step and the test was successful, you are given the option to download the latest updates. To do this, select **Yes, Run Online Update Now**. If you prefer to do this later, select **No, Skip Update**.
17. After updating, you are returned to the installation process. The Service Configuration screen shown in Figure 2.15 is displayed.

FIGURE 2.14
Testing your Internet connection.

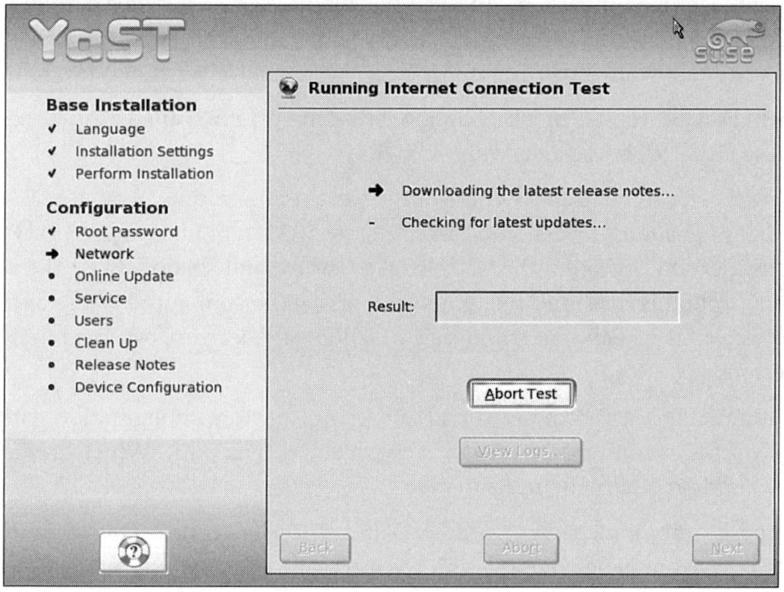

FIGURE 2.15
Configuring services.

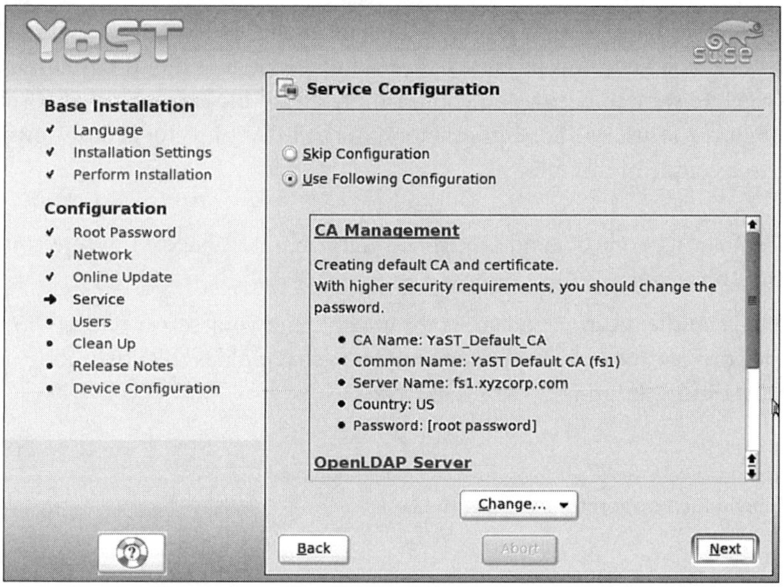

In this screen, you can configure the following options:

- CA Management—Selecting this option allows you to specify how security certificates are handled on your system. You can specify that this server be a certificate authority (CA) and generate its own certificate. If you already have a CA in your network, you can configure your server to import a certificate you've generated from the CA.
- OpenLDAP Server—Using this option, you can customize the LDAP directory service that is installed, by default, with SLES 9.

  This service can be used to store your server's user accounts. As you will see later in the installation process, you can configure PAM in SLES 9 to use LDAP for authentication instead of the traditional password and shadow files. The advantage of this option is that multiple Linux systems can be configured to use a single set of user accounts (much like NIS does), which greatly decreases your administrative overhead.

  In addition to user accounts, the LDAP server can store configuration settings for many services running on your server (which NIS can't do). Why is this a big deal? Let's consider a hypothetical situation:

  Suppose your Linux server provides DNS services for your network. Your DNS zone data is saved in `named.hosts`, which is a text file. What would happen if your server had a catastrophic hardware failure? Suppose the hard disk where `named.hosts` was stored died. What are your options? Basically, you must reinstall the OS and then restore `named.hosts` (hopefully) from your backups. That could take some time, during which your network is without DNS services.

  On the other hand, suppose your DNS zone data is stored in an LDAP directory that is replicated among several servers instead of a local text file. If the same catastrophic disk failure were to occur, you could simply install BIND on a different server and configure it to use the zone information in the LDAP directory. Your down time is cut to a couple of minutes.

18. After configuring your CA and OpenLDAP service, select **Next**. The screen in Figure 2.16 is displayed:
19. In the User Authentication screen, you can configure your server to use NIS, LDAP (default), or your local `/etc/passwd` and `/etc/shadow` files to authenticate users. Select the *method* you want to use; then select **Next**.

TIP

If you're not sure which option to use, go with LDAP.

The next screen displayed depends on the authentication method you chose. Because LDAP is so powerful, we're going to assume you chose this option. The screen in Figure 2.17 is displayed:

FIGURE 2.16
Configuring User Authentication.

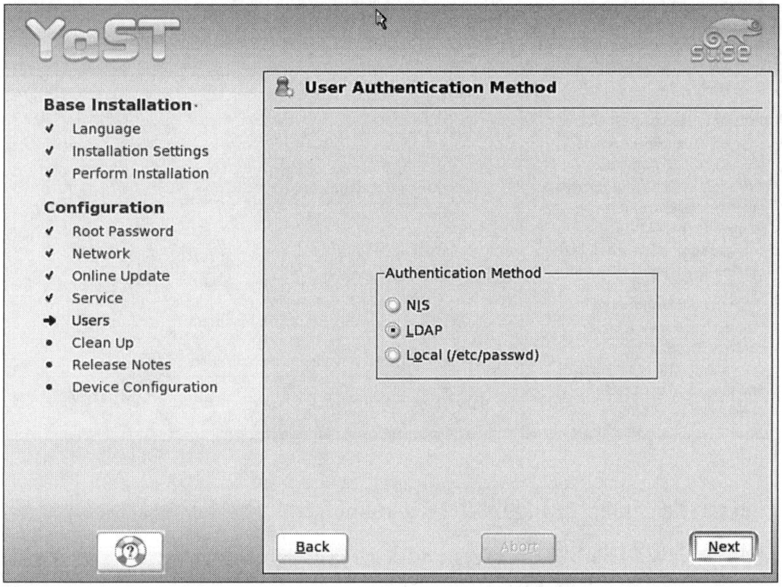

20. In this dialog box, you can configure the following options:

- LDAP Base DN—Remember that LDAP organizes information into a hierarchical tree (much like Novell's eDirectory). Each level in the tree is either a container or a leaf. Containers can hold other containers or a leaf entry. A leaf is an entry that represents a single network resource, such as a user account. In this field, you are basically identifying where in this hierarchy the LDAP client is going to look for information.
- Addresses of LDAP Servers—Earlier I mentioned that information hosted by the LDAP server can be shared with other LDAP servers. In this field, you can specify the addresses, separated by a space, of the LDAP servers in your network. If one is down or otherwise unreachable, your LDAP client can access other servers hosting the same information, making your life as a system administrator MUCH easier.

  If you're not sure how to configure these parameters, go with the default values.

FIGURE 2.17
Configuring the LDAP client.

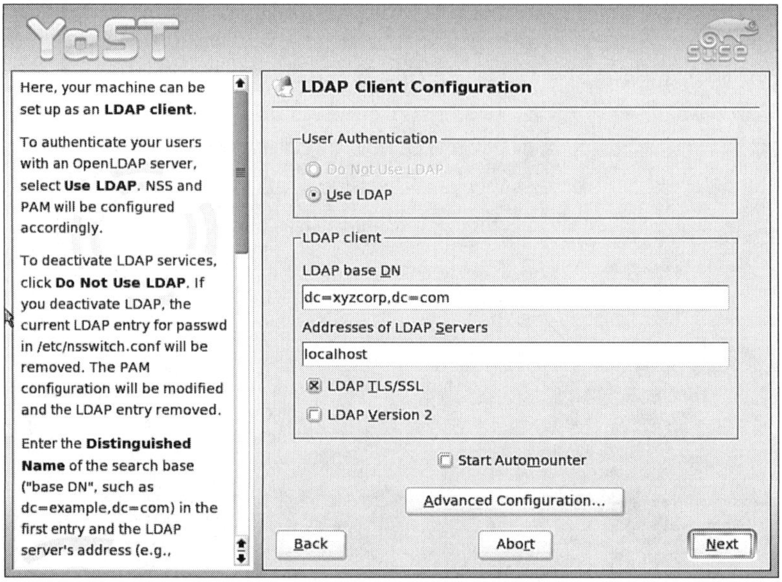

21. Select **Next**. The screen in Figure 2.18 is displayed:
22. In the Add a New LDAP User screen, add users for your system. If you want to add multiple users, select **User Management**.
23. When you're done adding users, select **Next**.
24. Wait while the system is configured. When configuration is complete, the Release Notes screen is displayed, as shown in Figure 2.19.
25. Read the Release Notes; then select **Next**.
26. Wait while your system hardware is probed. When the probe is complete, a screen similar to Figure 2.20 is displayed.
27. Configure your hardware by selecting the appropriate heading (as needed); then select **Next**.
28. Wait while the configuration changes are applied. When they are complete, the screen shown in Figure 2.21 is displayed:
29. In the Installation Completed screen, select **Finish**.

You are now ready to install your own SLES 9 server system. Lab Exercise 2-1 will walk you through the process.

FIGURE 2.18
Adding users.

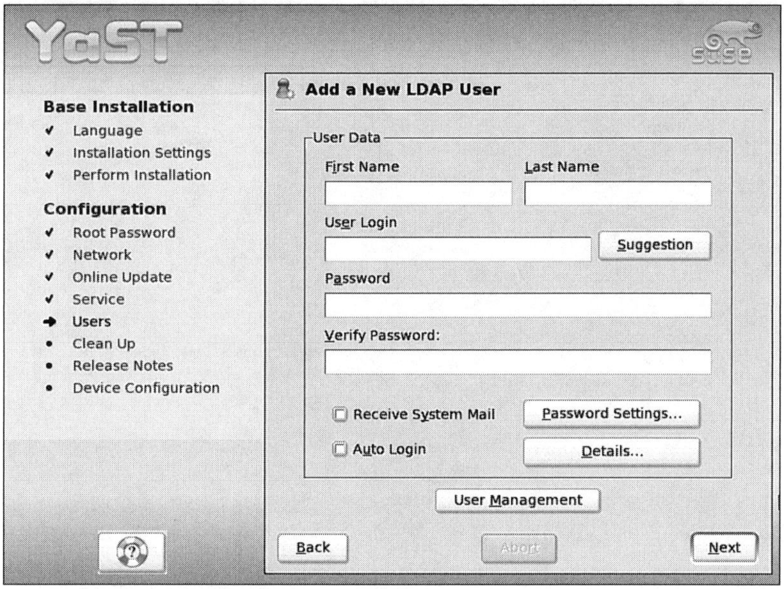

FIGURE 2.19
SLES 9 Release Notes.

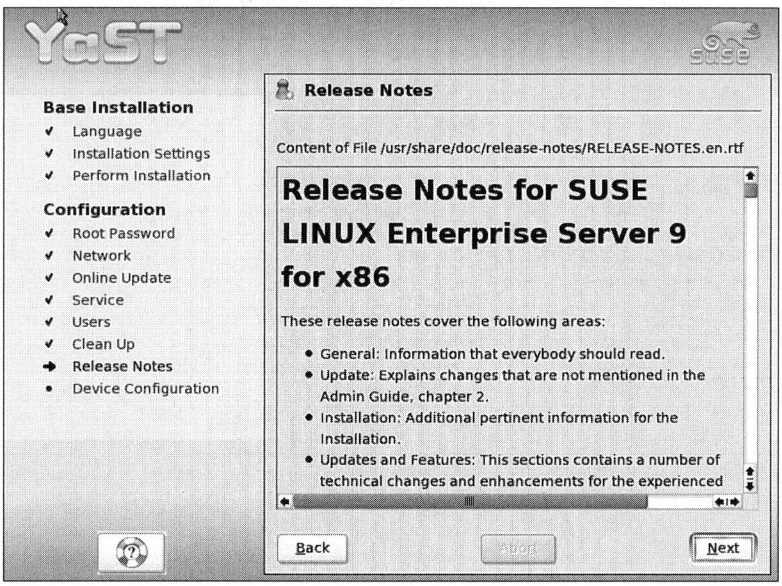

FIGURE 2.20
Detected hardware.

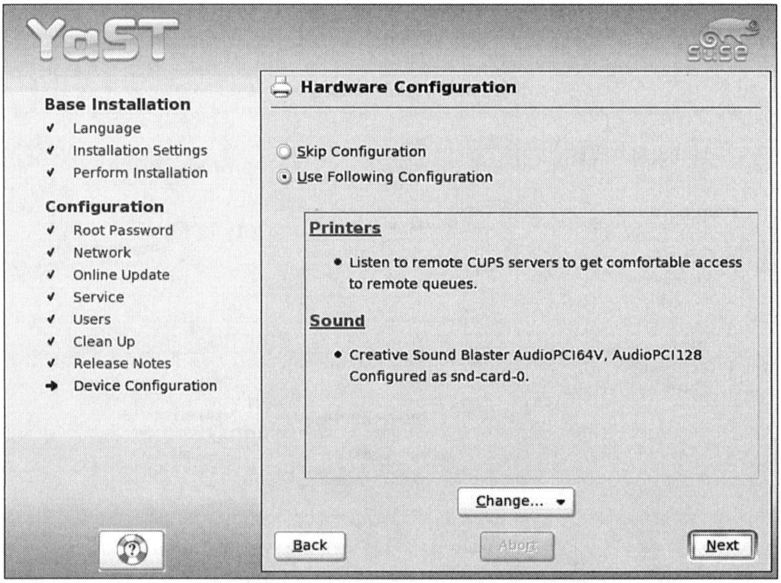

FIGURE 2.21
SLES 9 Installation complete!

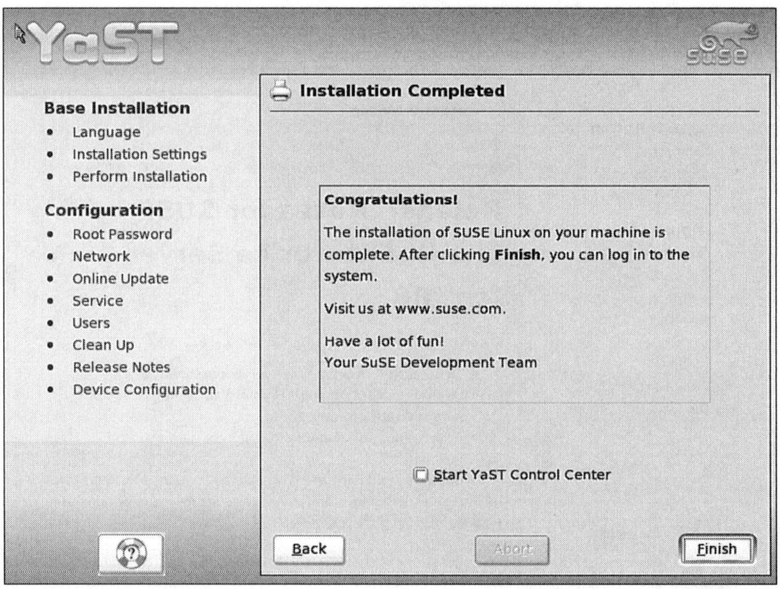

Lab Exercise 2.1: Installing a SLES 9 Server

In this lab exercise, you will install and configure a SLES 9 server system that you will use throughout the rest of this course.

NOTE

It's important that you follow the steps presented here exactly. If you don't, lab exercises later in this course may not work properly without a lot of reconfiguration.

In addition, you really should use a lab system to complete this exercise. The steps are written with the assumption that you can use the entire hard disk for SLES partitions. If you're installing on a system that already has an OS installed, you need to ensure there is sufficient space to install SLES. Then you will need to configure GRUB so that you can boot to SLES or to the existing OS.

If the system you're going to install on has important data, be sure you make a backup before you start this exercise!

If you want to save yourself a lot of trouble in this regard, I highly recommend VMWare. With VMWare, you don't have to worry about managing partitions, nor do you need to worry about losing critical data. You can download an evaluation copy that will run for 30 days from http://www.vmware.com.

To complete this exercise, you will need the following items:

- A lab PC system that meets the requirements presented earlier in this chapter.
- A copy of SLES 9 (which you will need to download from http://www.novell.com).

To install SLES on your system, complete the following:

1. Access the CMOS Setup program in your server system and configure it to boot from its CD or DVD drive first.
2. Insert *SUSE LINUX Enterprise Server 9 CD 1* in your server's CD or DVD drive and boot the system from it.
3. In the initial installation screen, select **Installation**.

NOTE

If you're using VMWare to install your SLES 9 system, be sure to either configure the system to install in text mode or enable VNC.

4. Wait while the Linux kernel is loaded.

NOTE

If you're using VNC, you'll need to open a web browser on a different computer system (or the host system if you're using VMWare) and access http://*your_SLES_server_IP_address*:5801.

5. In the SLES 9 License Agreement screen, select **I Agree**.
6. In the Language screen, select *your language*; then select **Accept**.
7. If an Installation Mode screen appears, select **New Installation, OK**.

NOTE

You will see this screen only if you already have an existing SLES installation.

8. Configure your server's disk partitions by completing the following:
   a. Scroll down to and select **Partitioning**.
   b. Select Create Custom Partition Setup; then select **Next**.
   c. Select Custom Partitioning For Experts; then select **Next**.

      If your system already has an operating system on it, remove any existing partitions. Be sure to back up anything you want to save first!
   d. Create a swap partition by selecting **Create**.
   e. Mark **Primary Partition** and select **OK**.
   f. In the File System drop-down list, select **Swap**.
   g. In the End field, enter **+500M**; then select **OK**.
   h. Create an extended partition by selecting **Create**.
   i. Mark **Extended Partition** and select **OK**.
   j. In the Create an Extended Partition window, select **OK**.
   k. Create a partition for the root directory by selecting **Create**.
   l. Make sure the File System drop-down list is set to **Reiser**, and then enter **+1GB** in the End field.

m. Make sure the Mount Point drop-down list is set to / and then select **OK**.

n. Repeat this process to create a 1GB partition mounted at `/home`, a 1GB partition mounted at `/var`, and a 2.5 (or larger) partition mounted at `/usr`.

NOTE

These partitions are sized for a typical lab system. If you were implementing a SLES server for a production environment, you would need to use a much larger hard disk drive.

o. Select **Next**.

9. In addition to the default packages, configure the following packages to be included in the installation by doing the following:

   a. Select **Software**.

   b. Select **Detailed Selection**.

   c. Mark **C/C++ Compiler and Tools**.

   d. Mark **File Server (NFS, Samba)**.

   e. Mark **DHCP and DNS Server**.

   f. Mark **Mail and News Services**.

   g. Mark **Simple Webserver**.

   h. In the Filter drop-down list, select **Search**.

   i. In the Search field, enter **`ntop`**.

   j. Mark the **ntop** package.

   k. In the Search field, enter **`nagios`**.

   l. Mark each **nagios** package.

   m. In the Search field, enter **`squid`**.

   n. Mark the **squid** package.

   o. Select **Accept**.

   p. When prompted to implement dependent packages, select **Continue**.

10. Scroll down to and select **Time Zone**.

11. Select your time zone; then select **Accept**.

12. Confirm the proposal and start the installation by selecting **Accept**.
13. When prompted to start the installation, select **Yes**, **Install**.
14. When prompted, insert your *SUSE LINUX Enterprise Server 9 CD 2* and then select **OK**.
15. Wait while your system is installed.
16. Insert CDs 3 and 4 as prompted.

NOTE

The YaST will reboot the system after it's done with CD 4. If you're using VNC to install, you will need to wait for a message to appear on the server indicating that the system is ready for a VNC connection. Then select **Reconnect** in your VNC applet in the browser window.

17. In the Password for root screen, enter a password of **`tuX123`**; then select **Next**.
18. Configure your network connection by completing the following:
    a. Select **Network Interfaces**.

NOTE

Your network interface should have been automatically detected and configured. If not, select **Configure** under the Network Cards to Configure field to configure your network interface.

    b. Under Already Configured Devices, select **Change**.
    c. Select your interface card and then select **Edit**.
    d. Mark **Static Address Setup**.
    e. In the IP Address field, enter an *IP address* appropriate for your network.

NOTE

If your server will reside on a network at your place of employment, be sure to get permission from your organization's network administrator to put this server up. Also, consult with the administrator to secure a static IP address assignment. They tend to get a bit testy if you arbitrarily grab one and start using it without their knowledge.

f. In the Subnet Mask field, enter the appropriate subnet mask for your network segment.

g. Select **Host Name** and **Name Server**.

h. In the Host Name field, enter **`fs1`**.

i. In the Domain Name field, enter **`cle9.com`**.

j. In the Name Server fields, enter the *IP address* you assigned to your server.

TIP

You do this because in the next chapter, you will configure the BIND service on your SLES server.

k. Select **OK**.

l. Select **Routing**.

m. In the Default Gateway field, enter the *IP address* of the default gateway router for your network segment.

n. Select **OK**.

o. Select **Next**.

p. Select **Finish**.

q. In the Network Configuration screen, select **Next**.

19. In the Test Internet Connection screen, mark **No**, **Skip This Test**; then select **Next**.

20. In the Service Configuration screen, select **Next**.

21. In the User Authentication Method screen, ensure that LDAP is marked and then select **Next**.

22. In the LDAP Client Configuration screen, ensure that the LDAP Base DN is set to **`dc=cle9, dc=com`** and that the IP address of the LDAP server is set to **localhost**; then select **Next**.

23. In the Add a New LDAP User screen, enter the following to create a new user:

    - First Name: **`Tux`**
    - Last Name: **`Penguin`**

- User Login: **tux**
- Password: **SuSE789**

24. Select **Next**.
25. In the Release Notes screen, read the release notes and then select **Next**.
26. In the Hardware Configuration screen, verify that your display adapter and monitor have been properly detected and configured and then select **Next**.

TIP

If you're installing in VMWare using VNC, no monitor or display adapter will be detected. You will have to first install VMWare Tools from a shell prompt and then manually configure your display after the installation is complete.

27. When prompted that the installation is complete, select Finish. The system will reboot and the login screen will be displayed.

Congratulations! You now have a fully functional SLES 9 server! Next, you need to learn how to configure your server using YaST.

Now that you have your system up and running, we need to review some of the key differences between SLES 9 and other Linux distributions.

SLES 9 Differences

One of the first differences you will notice is the directory where CDs and floppy disks are mounted. If you're familiar with Red Hat (and many other Linux distributions), you know that, by default, you mount these devices using subdirectories within the `/mnt` directory, as shown in Figure 2.22:

FIGURE 2.22
Mount points on a Red Hat Linux system.

Although the `/mnt` directory exists on a SLES 9 system, it's not used for mounting removable media. As you can see in Figure 2.23, the mount points for the floppy and CD drives don't exist in this directory.

FIGURE 2.23
The `/mnt` directory on a SLES 9 system.

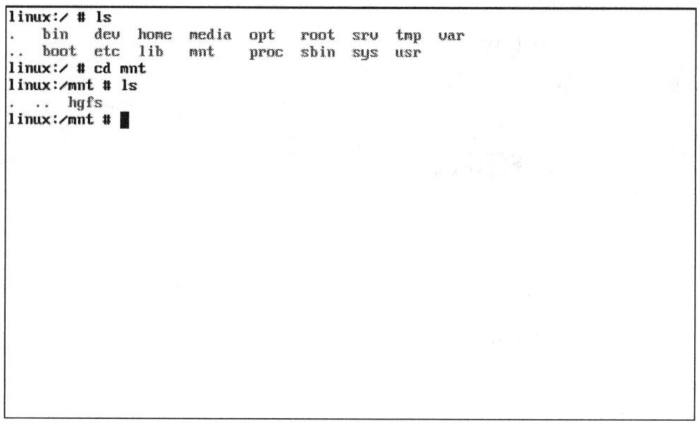

On a SLES 9 system, these devices are mounted in the `/media` directory. These mount points are shown in Figure 2.24:

FIGURE 2.24
Mount points on a SLES 9 system.

```
linux:/media # ls
.  ..  cdrecorder  floppy
linux:/media #
```

Could you create directories in `/mnt` on a SLES 9 system that serve as mount points for removable media drives? Absolutely. But be aware that your system is going to default to the directories in `/media` to mount these devices. As you can see in Figure 2.25, the fstab file on a SLES 9 system is configured by default to use `/media`.

FIGURE 2.25
Default mount points defined in `fstab`.

```
linux:/mnt # cat /etc/fstab
/dev/hda2            /                    reiserfs   acl,user_xattr        1 1
/dev/hda1            swap                 swap       pri=42                0 0
devpts               /dev/pts             devpts     mode=0620,gid=5       0 0
proc                 /proc                proc       defaults              0 0
usbfs                /proc/bus/usb        usbfs      noauto                0 0
sysfs                /sys                 sysfs      noauto                0 0
/dev/cdrecorder      /media/cdrecorder    subfs      fs=cdfss,ro,procuid,nosuid,
nodev,exec,iocharset=utf8 0 0
/dev/fd0             /media/floppy        subfs      fs=floppyfss,procuid,nodev,
nosuid,sync 0 0
linux:/mnt #
```

If you insist on using `/mnt` to mount removable media drives, you should edit your fstab file to reflect this preference. However, if you give it a chance, pretty soon you will find yourself just as comfortable using `/media` as you have been with `/mnt`.

Another key aspect of SUSE Linux that you need to understand is that the first SUSE distribution back in 1994 was derived from the Slackware Linux distribution. Because of this, SLES 9 implements system init scripts in a slightly different manner.

If you're familiar with Red Hat Linux, you know that it uses System V-type init scripts. Within the `/etc/rc.d` directory are subdirectories named `rc0.d` through `rc6.d`; as shown in Figure 2.26:

FIGURE 2.26
System V script directories.

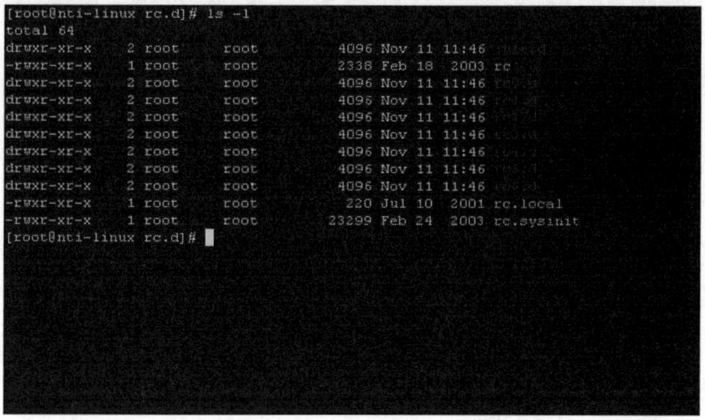

Each of these subdirectories is associated with a particular kernel runlevel (0, 1, 2, 3, 4, 5, and 6). Within each subdirectory are symbolic links that point to the init scripts for services associated with a given runlevel. The init scripts themselves are located in the `/etc/rc.d/init.d` directory, as shown in Figure 2.27.

SLES 9, on the other hand, uses BSD-style init scripts; these reside in the `/etc/init.d` directory, as shown in Figure 2.28.

When the runlevel on a SLES 9 system needs to be changed, the init process uses the inittab configuration file, located in `/etc`. Using this file, init runs the `/etc/init.d/rc` script; sending it the runlevel to switch the system to.

Depending on what runlevel the system is currently in and what runlevel the system is being switched to, the `rc` script uses the symbolic links within the `rc0.d` through `rc6.d` subdirectories within `/etc/init.d` to stop and then start services associated with the runlevel.

These are some of the key differences you will notice. With this in mind, let's turn to a more detailed discussion of another difference; that is, the tool used to manage the configuration of your SLES 9 server: Yet another Setup Tool (YaST).

FIGURE 2.27
Init scripts on Red Hat Linux.

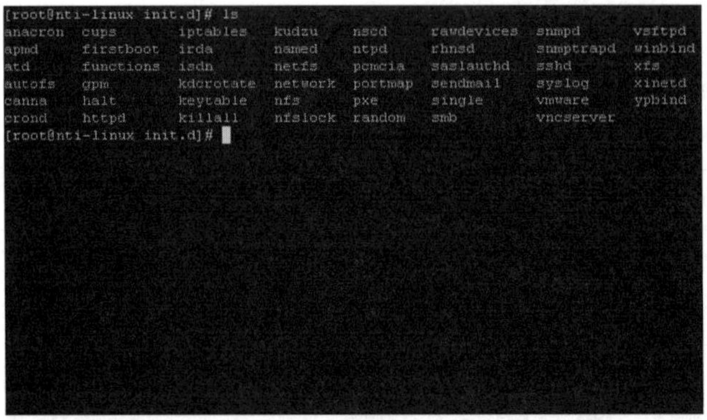

FIGURE 2.28
SLES 9 initialization scripts.

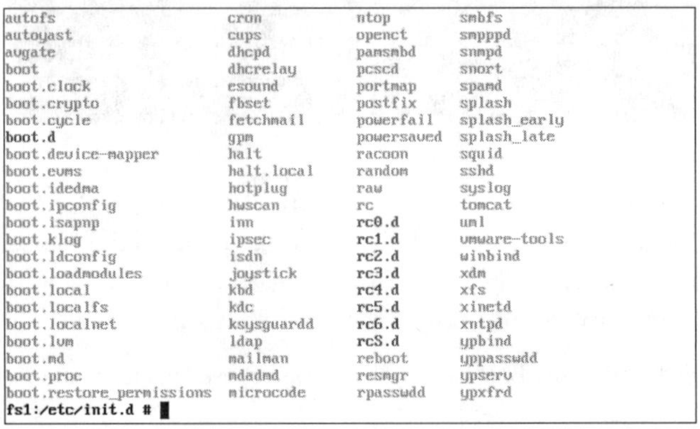

Working with YaST on SLES 9

TEST OBJECTIVE COVERED:

3. Use YaST.

By now you've had a chance to use YaST to install SLES 9 on your server. With your system up and running, you can use YaST to configure your system as well.

If you're coming to SUSE Enterprise Linux Server 9 from another Linux distribution, such as Red Hat, you may have some reservations about switching to YaST. I understand your trepidation. I balked at using this tool the first time I was exposed to it. However, after using YaST for a while, it's awfully hard to go back! Simply put, YaST makes administering your Linux system easier and faster.

Permit me to share an example. Several years ago, I had the chance to set up a SLES 8 server for a client. This was my first real exposure to SLES, and I knew very little about YaST.

To make a long story short, my client wanted to use the SLES server as a NAT router between network segments. To accommodate this request, I installed two network boards in the system and then sat down to write an init script to enable NAT routing between them. I had developed a base script years before, based on the IPMASQ HOWTO, that I'd implemented on various Red Hat and Caldera Linux systems; so I decided to use it here as well.

After about 8 hours of tweaking and testing, I finally had the script working correctly. I was pretty proud of myself. Then, about a year later, I was experimenting with a SLES server installed on one of my lab systems and discovered that I could use YaST to enable NAT routing between two network interfaces. The difference? About 7 hours and 59 minutes. Literally, what took 8 hours of manual scripting I was able to do with a couple of mouse clicks with YaST.

Now, many experienced Linux enthusiasts will insist that, to be a truly effective administrator, you need to know what's going behind the GUI interface. They argue that we've got an entire generation of network administrators who've been trained on Windows who can't handle any operating system that requires them to use a command or shell prompt. As a result, they shy away from utilities like YaST.

I'm actually in complete agreement with these folks. You really do need to understand what's happening behind the snazzy graphical interface. However, after you have this understanding, why not use a utility such as YaST if it makes your job faster?

In addition to making your job faster, YaST reduces errors on the part of the administrator. How many times have you edited a configuration file using a text editor and inadvertently made a typo? All of us have, and you know the effect. You spend hours (with bloodshot eyes) trying to figure out why the particular service isn't working the way it should, during which time you mutter inane things such as "I've done this a million times, why won't it work?"

YaST all but eliminates this problem. As long as you enter the proper parameters in the utility, your configuration files are written correctly without human-introduced errors. Again, this makes your life as a system administrator much easier.

The first thing you need to understand about YaST is that it's a modular utility. Each module is used to configure a specific component of the SLES 9 system. If you enter **yast -l** at a shell prompt, you can view the different modules YaST can use to configure your system, as shown in Figure 2.29.

FIGURE 2.29
YaST modules.

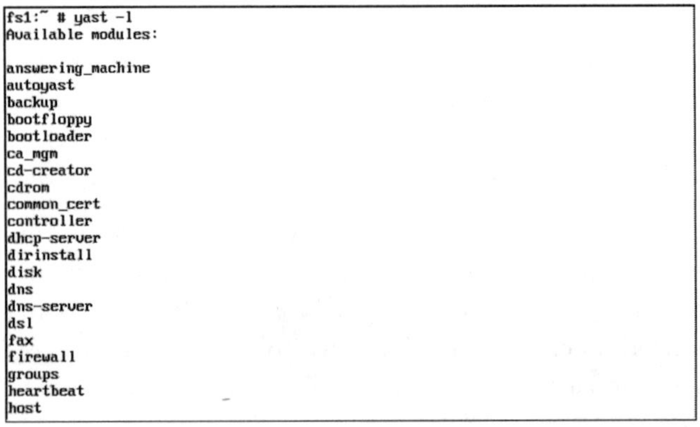

It's important to remember that to run YaST, you must have root privileges . Fortunately, when you first start YaST, you are given the opportunity to su to root if you aren't currently logged in as root. This is shown in Figure 2.30.

FIGURE 2.30
Changing to root in YaST.

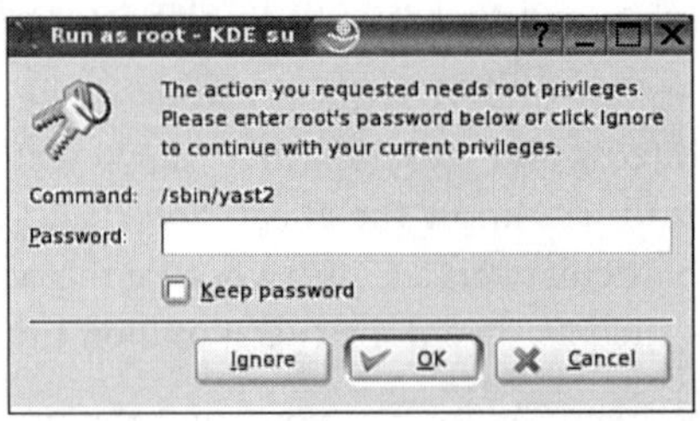

There are actually two versions of YaST. In this chapter, we will focus on the graphical version. You can start this version by selecting YaST from the System menu, as shown in Figure 2.31.

FIGURE 2.31
Accessing YaST from the System menu.

You can also access the graphical version of YaST from the shell prompt by running **`yast2`**. If you choose this option, you can use the **`sux`** command before running yast2 to first get root privileges.

This begs the question, then, of what to do if you need to access YaST on your server from a remote location. For example, suppose you're sleeping blissfully at home when you get an emergency 3:00 a.m. phone call from work. It sure would be nice to be able to access YaST on the office server from a system at your house. Otherwise, you're going to have to drive to work in your pajamas.

Never fear, because you can access YaST remotely in two ways. First, you can use a local Linux system to run YaST on your remote SLES 9 system. To do this, complete the following:

1. On your local system, open a terminal session.
2. At the shell prompt, enter **`ssh -X root@`***`your_server's_IP_address`*.
3. Authenticate with root's password.
4. Run yast2.

TIP

You can also do this using a local Windows workstation if you install an X client, such as WinaXe, and an ssh utility, such as PuTTY.

There is a second option: YaST also comes in a text-only version. This can be run from a shell prompt, including a remote ssh session, by entering **`yast`**. The text version of YaST is shown in Figure 2.32.

FIGURE 2.32
The text-only version of YaST.

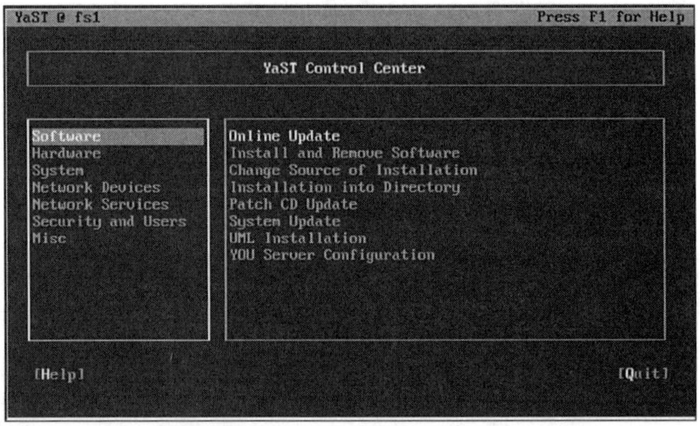

This is also useful for systems where X Window isn't running. Many Linux administrators don't like the overhead X adds to their servers, so they keep their system at runlevel 3. If you're in this camp, you can also use the text version of YaST.

Let's take a look at how YaST is laid out. In Figure 2.33, the main YaST screen is displayed.

The left frame displays several categories. When you select one of these categories, you are presented with icons that represent the various YaST modules that have been assigned to the category. To use a particular module, just click it.

NOTE

When using YaST, you only need to single-click a category or a module to access it. Don't worry if you forget and use double-clicks. YaST will ignore the extra click.

When you use one of these modules to configure your system, the configuration files in `/etc` and in `/etc/sysconfig` are modified. These files are shown in Figure 2.34.

Many services have configuration files in both locations. For example, the xntpd daemon has a configuration file in `/etc` named `ntp.conf`. A portion of this file is shown in Figure 2.35.

FIGURE 2.33
The graphical YaST interface.

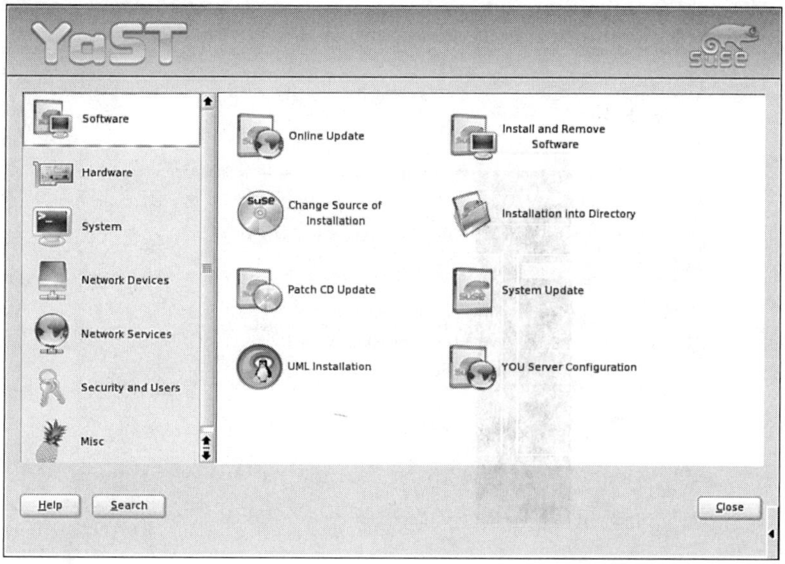

FIGURE 2.34
Configuration files in `/etc/sysconfig`.

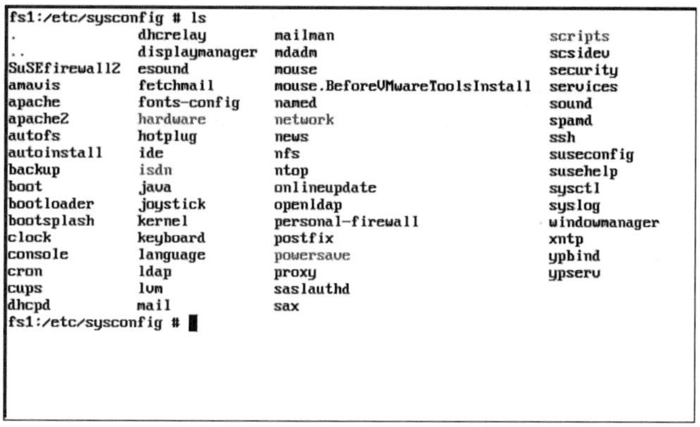

FIGURE 2.35
The `ntp.conf` file in `/etc`.

```
fs1:/etc # cat ntp.conf
################################################################################
## /etc/ntp.conf
##
## Sample NTP configuration file.
## See package 'xntp-doc' for documentation, Mini-HOWTO and FAQ.
## Copyright (c) 1998 S.u.S.E. GmbH Fuerth, Germany.
##
## Author: Michael Andres,  <ma@suse.de>
##
################################################################################

##
## Radio and modem clocks by convention have addresses in the
## form 127.127.t.u, where t is the clock type and u is a unit
## number in the range 0-3.
##
## Most of these clocks require support in the form of a
## serial port or special bus peripheral. The particular
## device is normally specified by adding a soft link
## /dev/device-u to the particular hardware device involved,
## where u correspond to the unit number above.
##
## Generic DCF77 clock on serial port (Conrad DCF77)
```

In this file, you specify which servers the xntpd daemon will use as a time provider. Anytime you modify a daemon's configuration file, you need to stop and then restart that service for the changes to be applied.

The xntpd daemon also has a configuration file in `/etc/sysconfig` named `xntp`. This file is shown in Figure 2.36.

FIGURE 2.36
The `xntp` file in `/etc/sysconfig`.

```
fs1:/etc/sysconfig # cat ./xntp
## Path:           Network/NTP
## Description:    Network Time Protocol (NTP) server settings
## Type:           string
## Default:        AUTO-2
## ServiceRestart: xntpd
#
# Usually it's a good idea to get the current time and date
# from some other ntp server, before the local xntpd is started.
# - Set XNTPD_INITIAL_NTPDATE="AUTO" to query ALL servers listed
#   in the configuration file (/etc/ntp.conf).
# - Set XNTPD_INITIAL_NTPDATE="AUTO-{NUMBER}" to query the first {NUMBER}
#   servers listed in the configuration file. E.g. "AUTO-2".
# Otherwise provide a space-separated list of ntp servers to query, or
# set XNTPD_INITIAL_NTPDATE="" to do no initial query at all.
#
XNTPD_INITIAL_NTPDATE="AUTO-2"

## Type:           string
## Default:        "-u ntp"
#
# Additional arguments when starting ntpd. The most
# important ones would be
# -u user[:group]   to make xntpd run as a user (group) other than root.
```

This file contains various parameters that control how the service is started. For example, you can configure which user account the daemon will run as. If your `ntp.conf` file contains multiple time providers, you can configure which one is queried first.

In essence, your SLES 9 system configuration is controlled by the files in `/etc/sysconfig`. Anytime a file in `/etc/sysconfig` is modified, you need to run a special SLES utility called SuSEconfig.

SuSEconfig applies the settings in the various configuration files. It also modifies other system files based on the changes made to the files in the `/etc/sysconfig` directory. This utility is composed of many different modules. These modules reside in `/sbin/conf.d`, as shown in Figure 2.37.

FIGURE 2.37
SuSEconfig modules in `/sbin/conf.d`.

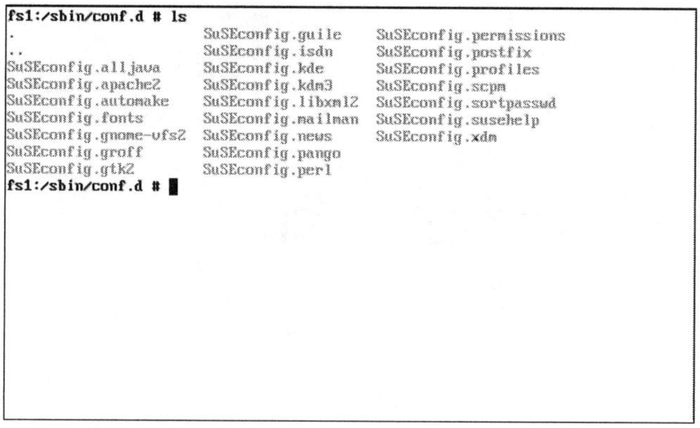

The good news is that if you use YaST to manage your system configuration, it automatically stops and restarts any affected services and it automatically runs SuSEconfig to apply any changes to files in `/etc/sysconfig`. This is shown in Figure 2.38.

TIP

You can also modify the files in `/etc/sysconfig` manually. To do this, you must first change to runlevel 1 by entering `init 1`. You can then edit the appropriate files with a text editor. When you're done, run SuSEconfig to apply the changes. Then return to your original runlevel.

Now that you know how YaST works, you need to learn how to configure your SLES 9 server using YaST.

FIGURE 2.38
YaST applying changes using SuSEconfig.

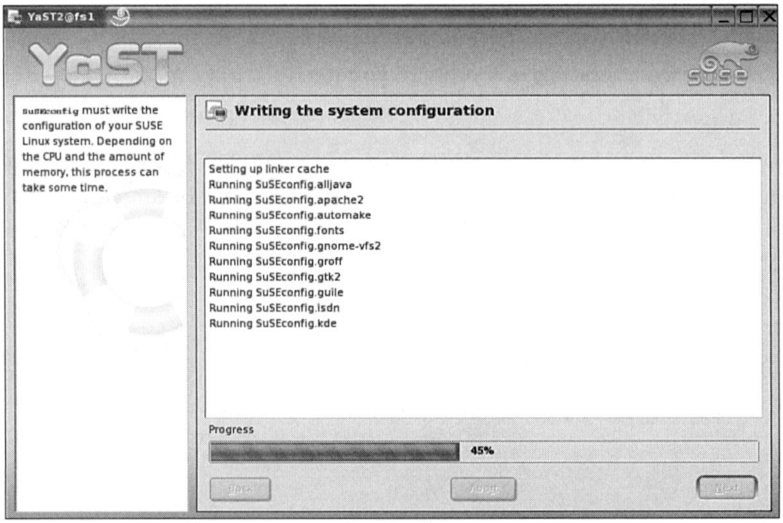

Managing SLES 9 with YaST

TEST OBJECTIVE COVERED:

4. Manage the SLES 9 system configuration.

Before we end this chapter and start digging into the meat of the CLE, we need to review how to complete some basic administration tasks on SLES 9 using YaST. Specifically, we're going to talk about the following:

- Managing network settings
- Managing server hardware
- Managing user accounts
- Managing services

Let's first talk about how you manage network settings.

Managing Network Settings Using YaST

If you're experienced with another Linux distribution, you probably already know how to manage IP parameters using ifconfig. So why spend time talking about how to do it with YaST? It's all about time.

Remember the example I presented earlier in this section about configuring NAT? The principle applies to managing IP address parameters on SLES 9 as well. Let's look at an example. Suppose that you configured your SLES server to use a dynamically assigned IP address when you installed it. This configuration has worked fine in your environment until recently.

Now, however, you need to implement an http service on your SLES 9 server and it really needs to have a static IP address assigned. If you were to do this manually, you would have to do the following:

1. In a text editor, open the appropriate configuration file for your interface, located in `/etc/sysconfig/network`, as shown in Figure 2.39.

FIGURE 2.39
Manually configuring network parameters.

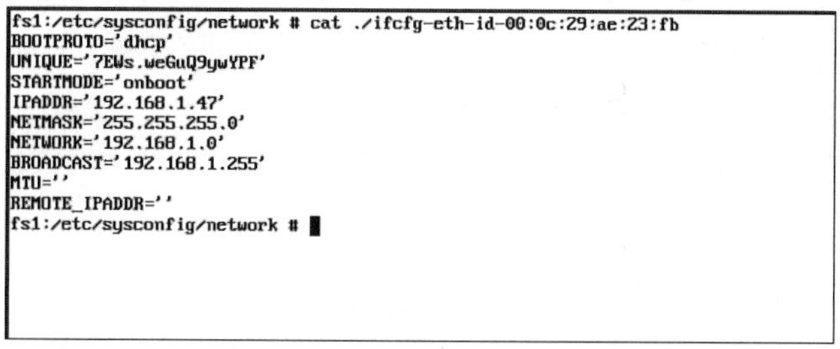

2. Edit the file to use a static IP address.
3. Open `/etc/resolv.conf` in a text editor, as shown in Figure 2.40.
4. Edit the file to use a static DNS server address.
5. Open `/etc/sysconfig/network/routes` in a text editor, as shown in Figure 2.41.
6. Enter the default route in the file.
7. Run SuSEconfig to apply the changes.

FIGURE 2.40
Manually setting the DNS server address.

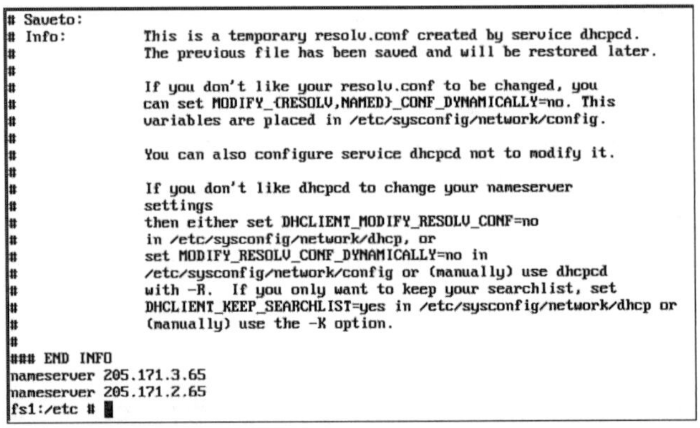

```
# Saveto:
# Info:          This is a temporary resolv.conf created by service dhcpcd.
#                The previous file has been saved and will be restored later.
#
#                If you don't like your resolv.conf to be changed, you
#                can set MODIFY_{RESOLV,NAMED}_CONF_DYNAMICALLY=no. This
#                variables are placed in /etc/sysconfig/network/config.
#
#                You can also configure service dhcpcd not to modify it.
#
#                If you don't like dhcpcd to change your nameserver
#                settings
#                then either set DHCLIENT_MODIFY_RESOLV_CONF=no
#                in /etc/sysconfig/network/dhcp, or
#                set MODIFY_RESOLV_CONF_DYNAMICALLY=no in
#                /etc/sysconfig/network/config or (manually) use dhcpcd
#                with -R.  If you only want to keep your searchlist, set
#                DHCLIENT_KEEP_SEARCHLIST=yes in /etc/sysconfig/network/dhcp or
#                (manually) use the -K option.
#
### END INFO
nameserver 205.171.3.65
nameserver 205.171.2.65
fs1:/etc #
```

FIGURE 2.41
Manually configuring the default router address.

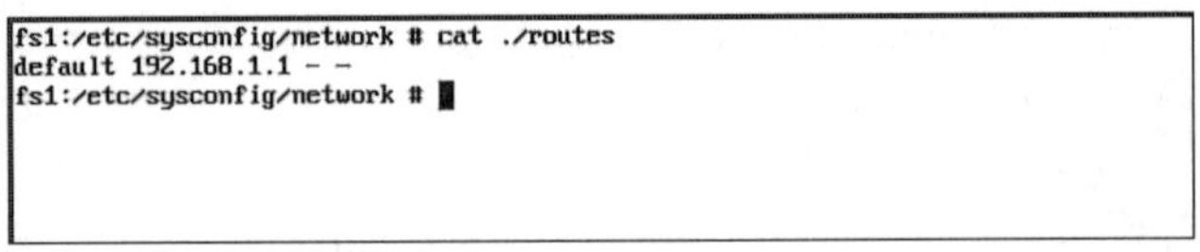

```
fs1:/etc/sysconfig/network # cat ./routes
default 192.168.1.1 - -
fs1:/etc/sysconfig/network #
```

TIP

You can also perform these tasks using command line tools, such as ifconfig, ip, and routes. However, remember that these changes aren't persistent. You need to save the changes to the appropriate configuration files to have them take effect the next time the system is booted.

That's a lot of work. In addition, if you have large fingers like mine, you may also introduce errors into the configuration by making typos.

Conversely, you can complete the same task in a single interface using YaST. To manage network parameters in YaST, complete the following:

1. From your graphical desktop, select **N, System, YaST**.
2. Supply your root user's *password*.
3. In the left frame, select **Network Devices**.
4. In the right frame, select **Network Card**. The screen in Figure 2.42 is displayed.

FIGURE 2.42
Selecting a network interface to configure in YaST.

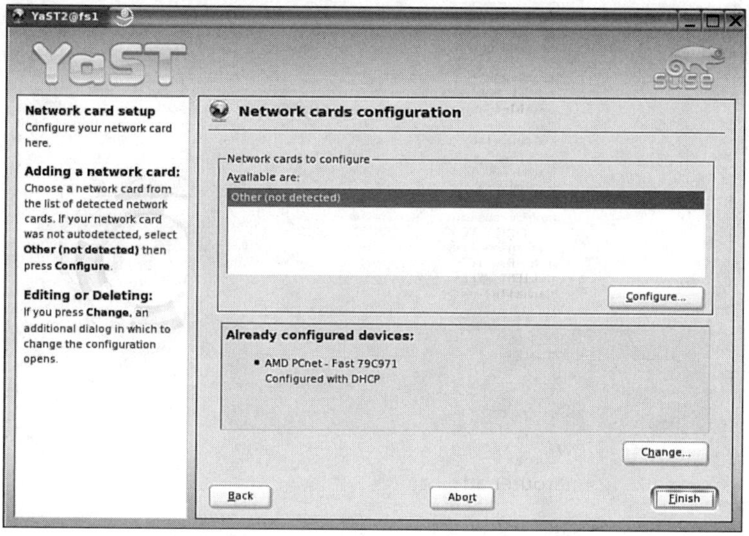

5. Under Already Configured Devices, select **Change**. If, for some reason, your network interface isn't configured, do the following:

   a. Under Network Cards to Configure, select **Configure**. The screen in Figure 2.43 is displayed.

   b. Configure the network configuration and the kernel parameters; then select **Next**.

TIP

If you don't know what kernel module to use, select **Select from List**.

   c. Skip to step 7.

6. Select the *network interface* you want to modify, and then select **Edit**. The screen in Figure 2.44 is displayed.

7. If you want to use dynamic addressing, mark **Automatic Address Setup**. If you want to manually specify an address, mark **Static** and then do the following:

   a. In the IP Address field, enter an appropriate *IP address* for your network segment.

   b. In the subnet mask field, enter the appropriate **subnet mask** for your network segment.

FIGURE 2.43
Configuring a new network interface in YaST.

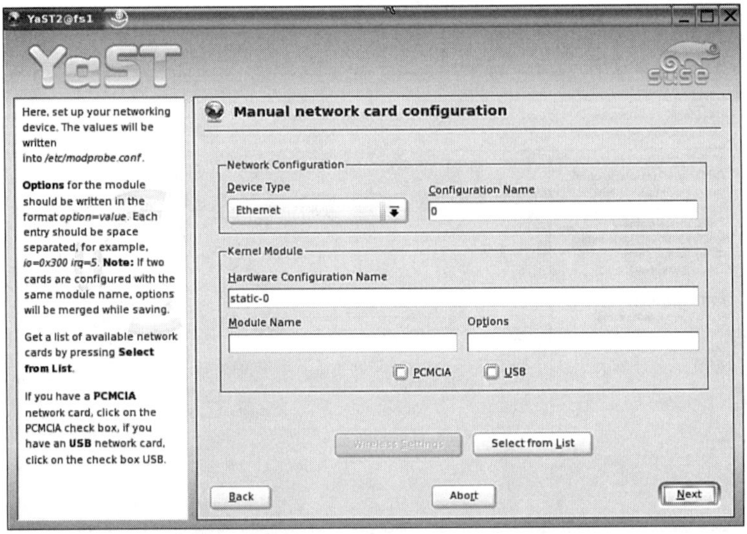

FIGURE 2.44
Configuring IP parameters.

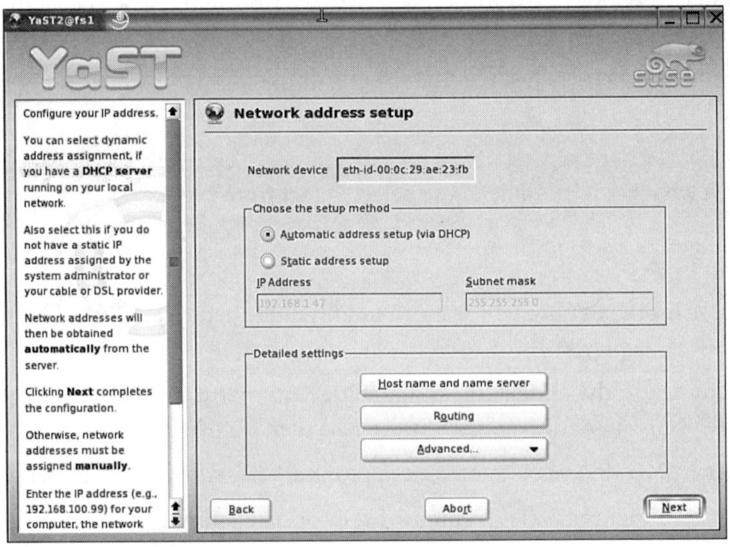

c. Select Hostname and Name Server.

d. If prompted that the `resolv.conf` file has been modified by dhcpcd, select **Modify**. The screen in Figure 2.45 is displayed.

FIGURE 2.45
Configuring IP name resolution parameters.

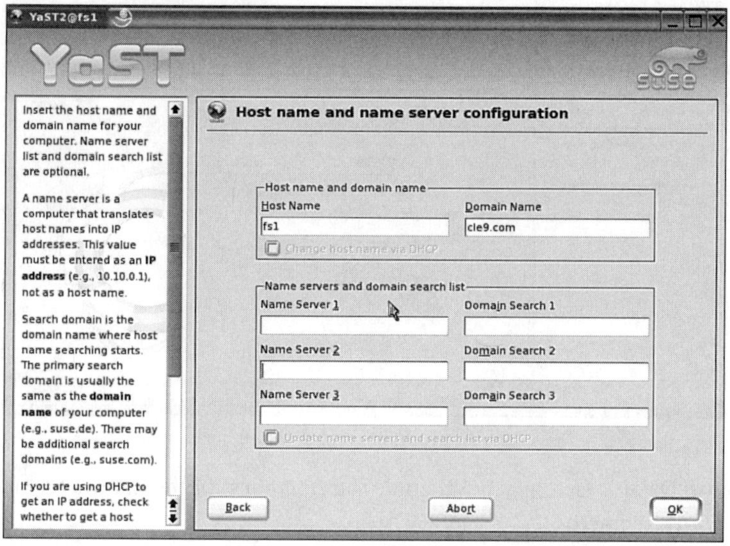

e. Enter the appropriate *hostname*, *domain name*, name *server addresses*, and *search domains* in the respective fields.

TIP

Remember that the search domain is used to create a fully qualified domain name (FQDN). If you submit only a hostname, the domain specified in the search domain is appended to the hostname for the DNS server to resolve.

f. Select **Next**.

g. Select **Routing**. The screen in Figure 2.46 is displayed.

FIGURE 2.46
Configuring the default gateway router.

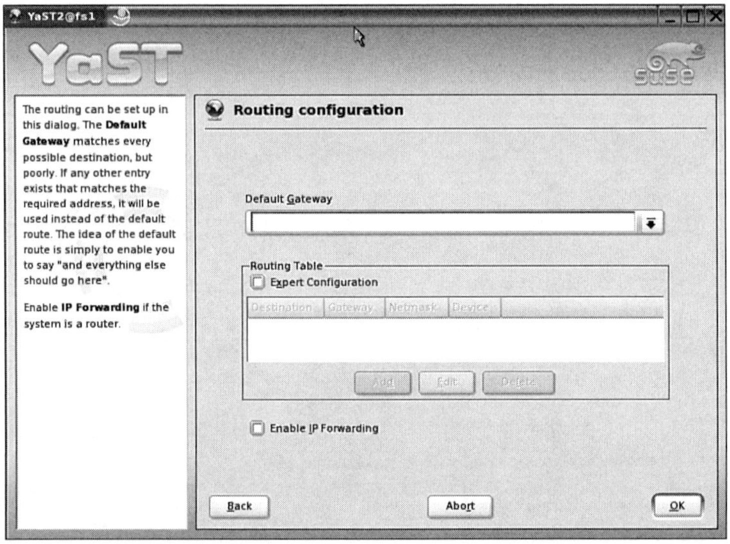

h. In the Default Gateway field, enter the *IP address* of the gateway router for your network segment.

i. If you want to specify additional static routes, mark **Expert Configuration**; then select **Add** to add additional static routes.

j. Select **OK**.

8. Select **Next, Finish**.

After selecting Finish, the information you entered is written to the various configuration files and SuSEconfig is automatically run to apply the changes.

Again, I agree that it's important to know what files YaST is affecting when you use it to configure your system. However, after you do, why continue to do things the hard way? Go YaST!

Let's now review how to use YaST to configure your system hardware.

Managing Server Hardware with YaST

In addition to configuring network interfaces, you can also use YaST to configure your server hardware. As with network interfaces, you could manually configure hardware devices in your SLES 9 server.

As with other Linux distributions, you can use `modprobe` to load modules and `rmmod` to remove modules. You can also use `lsmod` to list currently loaded modules. On a SLES 9 system, the module files are stored in a subdirectory within `/lib/modules`, based on the kernel version.

Configuration parameters for many devices, such as hot-pluggable devices, are stored in `/etc/sysconfig/hardware` on your SLES 9 server. An example of a file used to configure a network interface is shown in Figure 2.47.

FIGURE 2.47
Configuration file for a network interface.

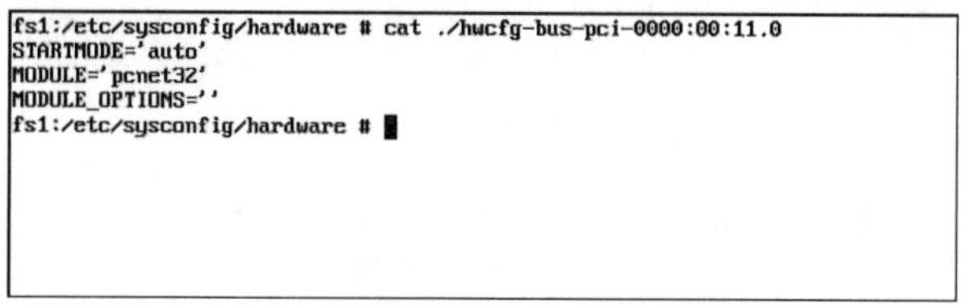

In this example, the STARTMODE parameter specifies that the device is started automatically when the system is booted. The MODULE parameter specifies which kernel module is to be loaded for the device. The MODULE_OPTIONS parameter allows you to pass module-specific options to the kernel module.

As with network interfaces, it's important that you understand the manual way of managing server hardware. However, after you have this understanding, using YaST to manage hardware streamlines the process. To do this, complete the following steps:

1. Start YaST.
2. In the left frame, select **Hardware**. When you do, the screen in Figure 2.48 is displayed.
3. In this screen, select the *hardware item* you want to manage from the right frame. For example, if you needed to manage your hard disk controller, you could select the Disk Controller icon. When you do, the screen in Figure 2.49 is displayed.

FIGURE 2.48
Configuring hardware in YaST.

FIGURE 2.49
Configuring the hard disk controller in YaST.

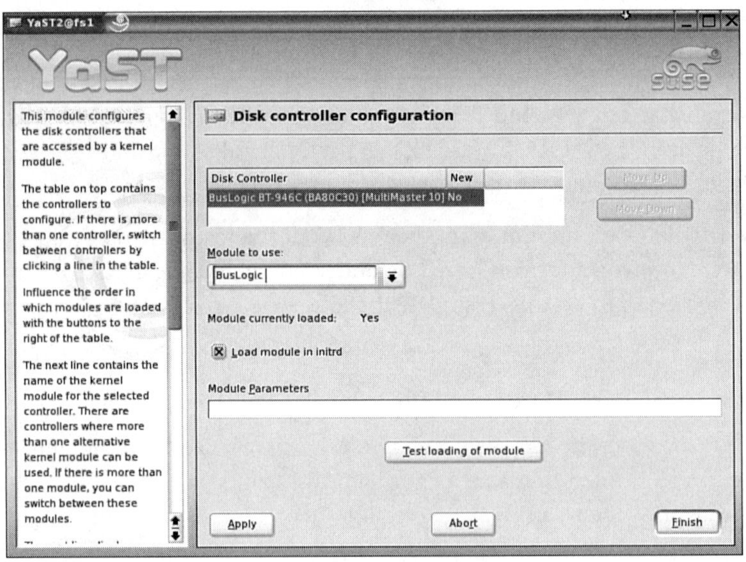

Notice that in this interface, you can configure the module to be used for the device. You can also configure how the module for the devices is loaded. Because the disk controller must be loaded to access the disk partition mounted at /, it's been configured to be loaded in initrd.

4. Configure *parameters* specific to your hardware and select **Finish**. When you do, your changes are written out to the appropriate configuration files; then SuSEconfig is run automatically to apply your changes.

If you're used to manually managing your Linux hardware modules, I think you'll find that YaST makes the process much easier and faster.

In addition to managing hardware, you can use YaST to configure users and groups on your SLES 9 server.

Configuring Users and Groups in YaST

SLES 9 uses the elements of users, groups, ownership, and permissions just like any other Linux distribution. In addition, the command-line utilities you're familiar with also work. For users, you can use `useradd` to create new accounts. You can use `passwd` to set user passwords, `usermod` to modify an existing account, and `userdel` to delete an account.

When you use `useradd`, the default values specified in `/etc/login.defs` and `/etc/default/useradd` are applied unless you use `useradd` switches that will override these values. Portions of these two files are shown in Figures 2.50 and 2.51.

FIGURE 2.50
The `/etc/login.defs` file.

```
fs1:/etc # cat ./login.defs |more
#
# /etc/login.defs - Configuration control definitions for pwdutils package.
#
# Comment lines (lines beginning with "#") and blank lines are ignored.
# Please read the manual page for more information (login.defs.5).
#

#
# Should login be allowed if we can't cd to the home directory?
# Default is yes.
#
DEFAULT_HOME            yes

#
# The default PATH settings (used by login):
#
ENV_PATH                /usr/local/bin:/usr/bin:/bin

#
# The default PATH settings for root (used by login):
#
ENV_ROOTPATH            /sbin:/bin:/usr/sbin:/usr/bin
--More--
```

FIGURE 2.51
The `/etc/default/useradd` file.

```
fs1:/etc/default # cat ./useradd
GROUP=100
HOME=/home
INACTIVE=-1
EXPIRE=
SHELL=/bin/bash
SKEL=/etc/skel
GROUPS=dialout,uucp,video,audio
fs1:/etc/default #
```

Likewise, you can use the **`groupadd`** utility to add groups, the **`groupmod`** utility to modify an existing group, and the **`groupdel`** utility to delete a group.

Now let's look at a faster way to manage SLES 9 users and groups: YaST. To manage users in YaST, you need to do the following:

1. In YaST, select **Security and Users**, **Create and Edit Users**.
2. If you've configured your system to use LDAP to store user account information, you will be prompted to authenticate to the LDAP directory. Enter your root *password* and the screen in Figure 2.52 is displayed next.

FIGURE 2.52
Managing users in YaST.

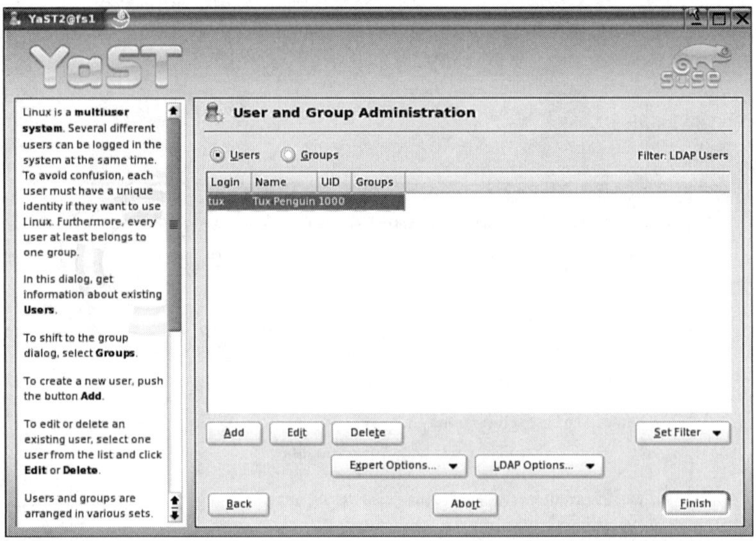

TIP

Many experienced Linux system administrators get confused when they see this screen for the first time because only user accounts used for authentication are displayed. The system user accounts appear to be missing.

Don't worry, they're still there. YaST assumes that if you're managing user accounts, you don't want to see system accounts; likewise, if you're working with system accounts, you don't want to see authentication user accounts. If you want to see system user accounts select **Set Filter, System Users**.

3. To add a user account, do the following:

   a. Select **Add** to display the screen shown in Figure 2.53.

FIGURE 2.53
Adding a user in YaST.

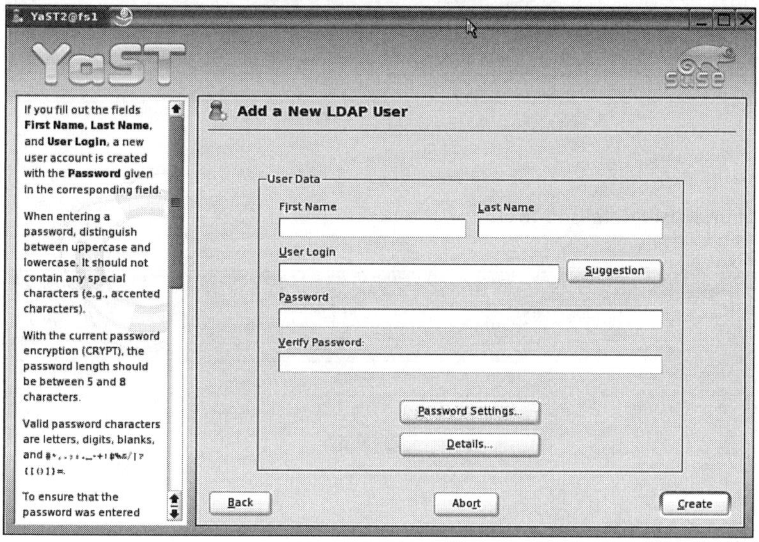

   b. Provide the requested parameters for the new account, including the *first and last name*, *user login*, and *password*.

   c. Select **Details**. The screen in Figure 2.54 is displayed.

   d. Configure details of the user account, including *user ID*, *home directory*, *login shell*, and *group memberships*.

   e. Select **Next** to display the screen shown in Figure 2.55.

FIGURE 2.54
Configuring user details in YaST.

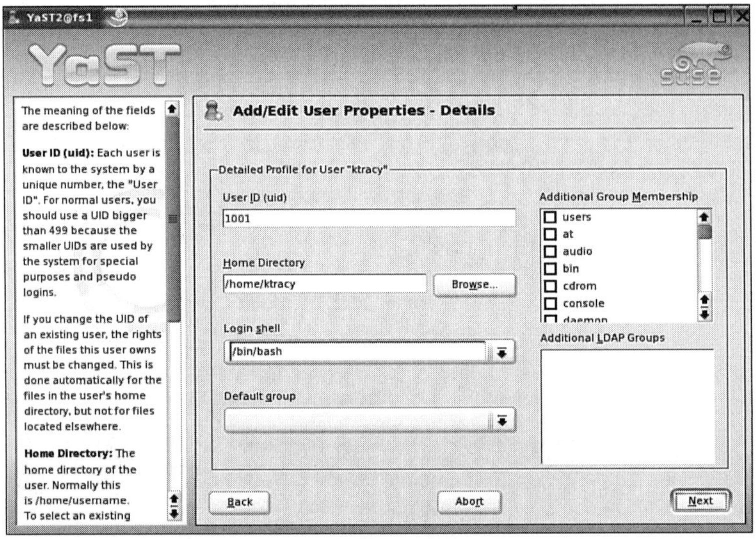

FIGURE 2.55
Configuring optional user details in YaST.

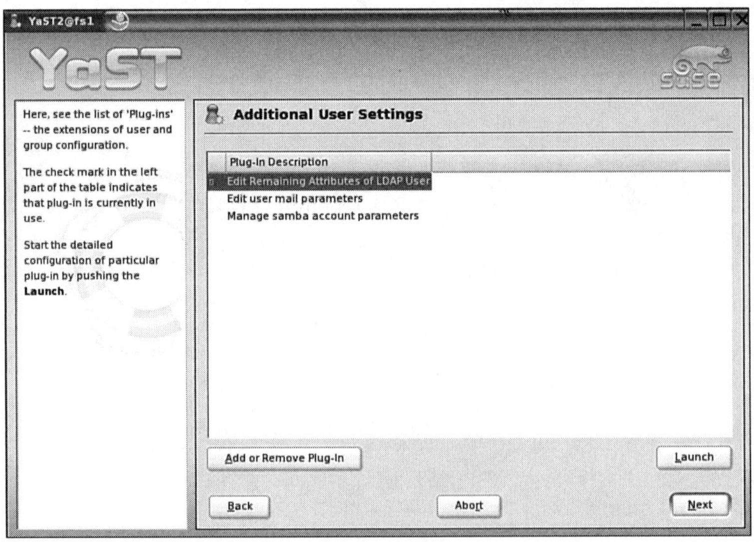

f. In this screen, you can configure optional LDAP, mail, and Samba parameters for the user account. When you're finished, select **Next**.

g. Select **Create**.

4. To edit an existing account, do the following:

   a. Select the *account* you want to modify.

   b. Select **Edit**.

   c. Modify parameters of the account as needed, and then select **Next**.

5. When you are finished, select **Finish**.

As you can see, using YaST to manage user accounts makes the process slick and easy. Before going any further, there's an important point you need to understand. If you've configured your SLES 9 server to store user accounts in an LDAP directory, you need to alter the way you use the `useradd` command.

Let's look at an example. Suppose I need to add a new user named dcoughanour to the system. Being an old-timer, I decide to use the `useradd` utility to do this, as shown in Figure 2.56.

FIGURE 2.56
Creating a user with `useradd`.

```
fs1:/etc # useradd dcoughanour
fs1:/etc # █
```

Notice that I didn't supply any extra command switches, so the defaults determined during installation were used. Now, if I open up YaST's Create and Edit Users module, notice that the user dcoughanour is conspicuously missing, as you can see in Figure 2.57.

What happened to the new user account? The problem is that, by default, `useradd` creates the new account in the `/etc/passwd` and `/etc/shadow` files instead of in the LDAP directory. In YaST, if I select **Set Filter, Local Users**, the account I just created is displayed, as shown in Figure 2.58.

FIGURE 2.57
The new user is missing in YaST.

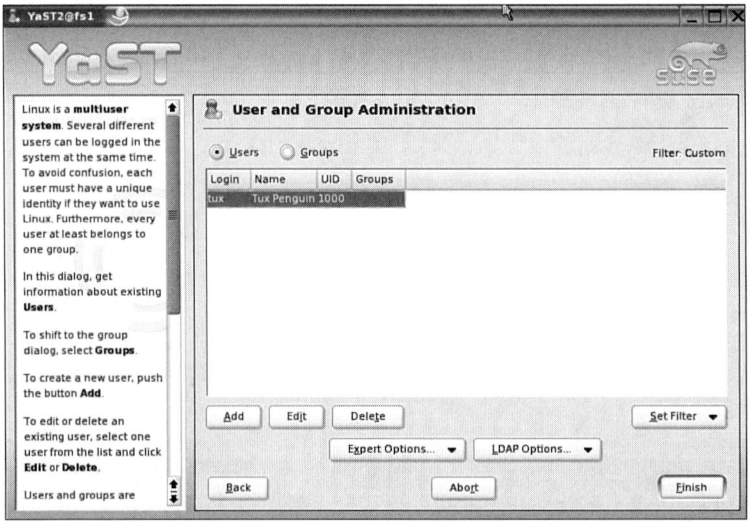

FIGURE 2.58
The new user is found in YaST.

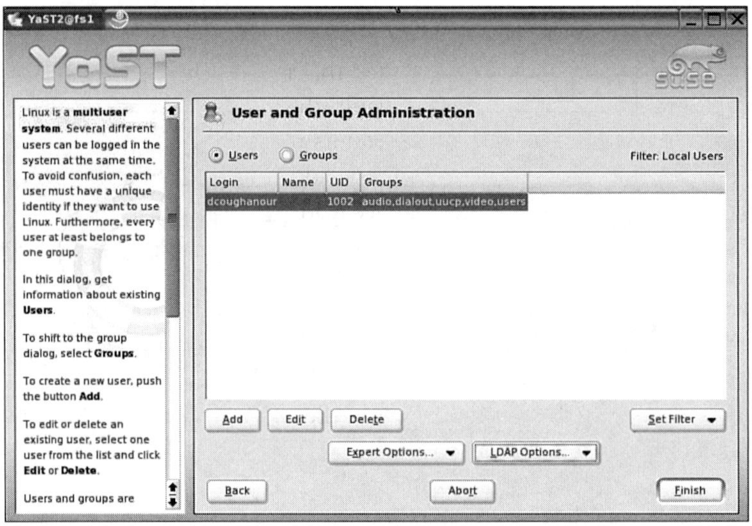

To use **useradd** to add users to the LDAP directory, you must use two switches:

- `--service ldap`—This specifies that useradd should place the new user in the LDAP directory instead of in the **/etc/passwd** file.
- `--binddn (or -D)`—This switch allows you to specify which user account to use to bind to the LDAP service.

For example, to add dcoughanour to the LDAP directory using **useradd**, I would enter the following command:

```
useradd --service ldap --binddn  cn=administrator,dc=cle9,dc=com dcoughanour
```

Remember that administrator is the user account you set up during installation that has permission to manage the LDAP directory on your server. After entering the command, you are prompted to supply administrator's password (which, on the server you installed in the preceding lab exercise, is the same as your root user's password: **tuX123**). This is shown in Figure 2.59.

FIGURE 2.59
Adding a new user to LDAP using `useradd`.

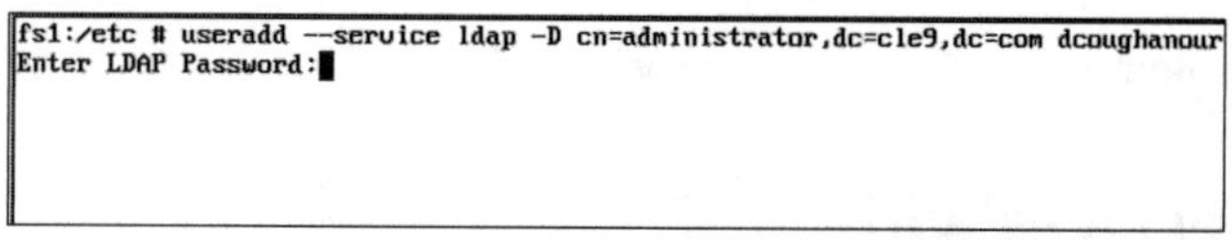

After supplying the password, you are prompted that the user has been added and into what LDAP context the user account resides. By default, the user is placed in the ou=people container. This is where all of your LDAP user accounts reside. You will probably also be prompted with errors indicating that the user couldn't be added to several groups. Remember our **/etc/default/useradd** file? The useradd utility reads this file for user defaults even if we're adding the account to the LDAP service. The problem is that the default groups specified in this file are *local* groups. They don't exist in the LDAP directory.

To fix this, you have two options. First, you could add these groups to your LDAP directory. Alternatively, you could edit your default file and remove these directories.

The good news is that, even if **useradd** can't find the default directories, the user account is still created, as shown in Figure 2.60.

FIGURE 2.60
New user added to LDAP directory.

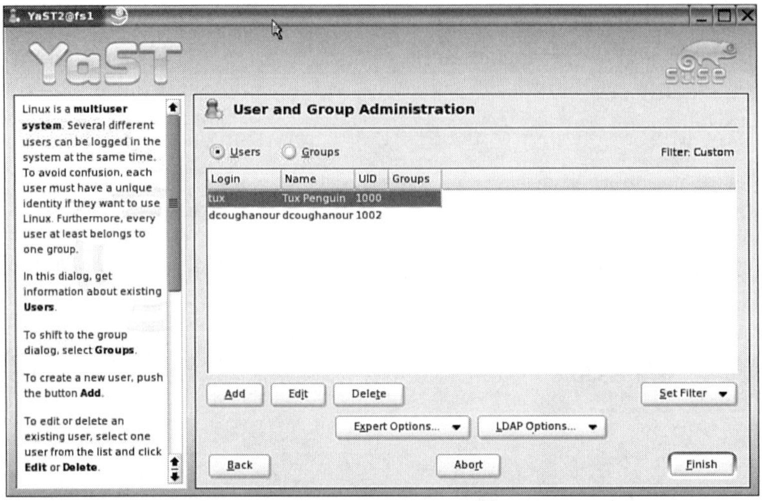

Next, it's time to look at managing system services with YaST.

Managing Services with YaST

If you've managed daemons on other Linux distributions, you know that you must

- Install the service on your system.
- Edit the service's configuration file.
- Start the service.
- Configure the runlevels where the service will be automatically run.

To install the service, you use the `rpm` utility. Then you use a text editor, such as vi, to modify the `.conf` file for the service. When you're done, you run the service using the init scripts in `/etc`. Then you use `chkconfig` to set the runlevels where the service is enabled.

Again, YaST streamlines this process for you. Let's look at how this is done.

To install a service on your system, complete the following:

1. Start YaST.
2. Select **Software, Install and Remove Software**. When you do, the screen in Figure 2.61 is displayed. In this screen, you can use the Filter drop-down list to see packages by Selection or Package Group. Alternatively, you can use a Search option to look for a specific package.

FIGURE 2.61
Adding New Services with YaST.

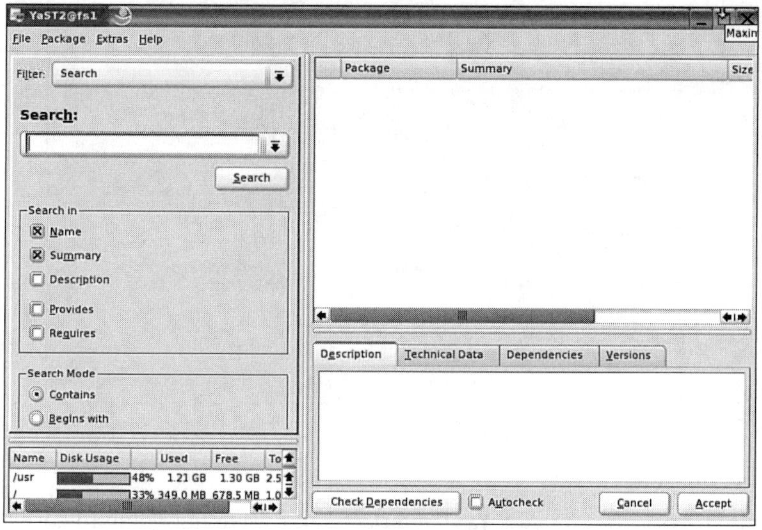

3. Mark the *packages* you want to install and then select **Accept**.

The next task is to configure the service. Again, you can do this with YaST. Many daemons provide YaST modules that are plugged in when the service is installed.

NOTE

Not all daemons have a YaST module. If you don't see the appropriate item in YaST, you'll have to configure the service the old-fashioned way.

To use these modules to perform configuration tasks, you need to do the following:

1. In YaST, locate the *module* used to configure the appropriate service. Most network-related modules are in the Network Service group, shown in Figure 2.62.

FIGURE 2.62
Network Service modules in YaST.

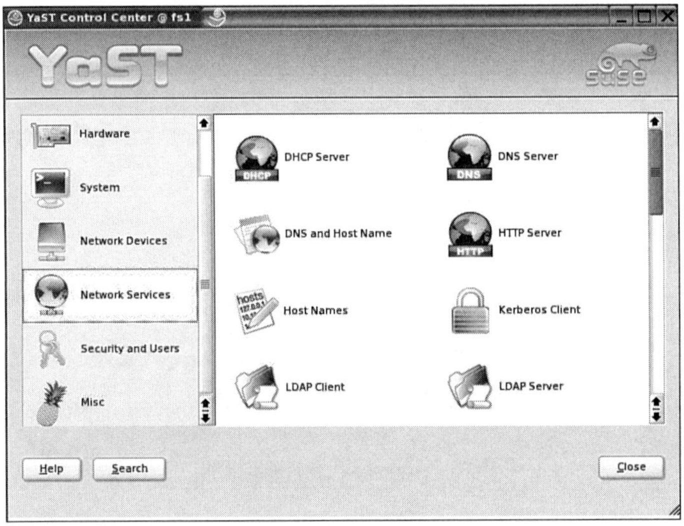

2. Select the **module**.
3. Each module provides its own YaST interface (and we're not going to cover all of them here). Follow the prompts to configure the service.
4. Select Finish.

With the service installed and configured, the next tasks are to start the service and to set the runlevels. Unlike the preceding task, you can use YaST to perform these tasks on all services on your SLES 9 server. To do this, complete the following:

1. Start YaST.
2. Select System, Runlevel Editor.
3. Select **Expert Mode** to display the screen shown in Figure 2.63.

FIGURE 2.63
Configuring Services in YaST.

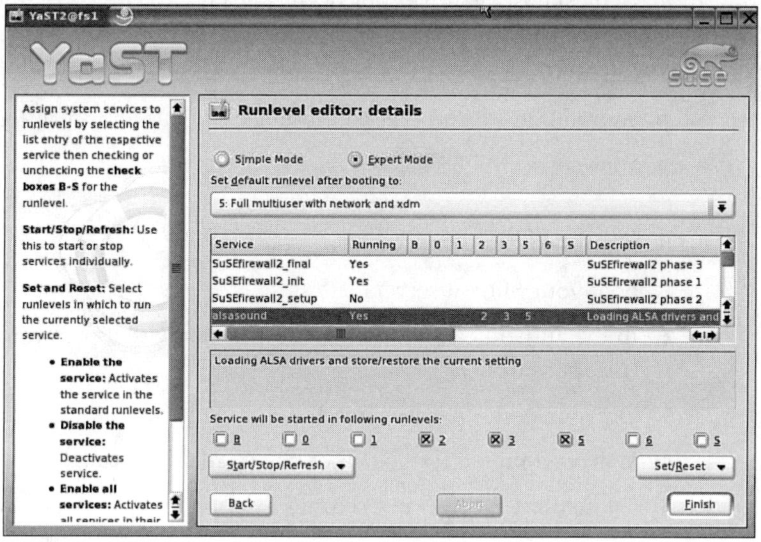

4. Under Services, scroll down to and select the *service* you want to modify.
5. To start the service, select **Start/Stop/Refresh, Start Now**.
6. Mark the *runlevels* in which the service should be automatically started, and then select **Finish**.

YaST is pretty cool, huh? As I said earlier, the key advantages of YaST is that it makes your administration work easier, faster, and less mistake-ridden. Let's now spend some time practicing with YaST.

Lab Exercise 2.2: Working with YaST

In this lab exercise, you will practice using YaST to complete some typical Linux administration tasks. To complete this exercise, you will need the following items:

- Your lab PC system that you installed SLES 9 on in Lab Exercise 2.1.
- Your copy of SLES 9.

Complete the following:

1. Boot your SLES 9 server.
2. In the authentication screen, log in as **`tux`** with a password of **`SuSE789`** (case sensitive).
3. On your desktop, select **YaST**.
4. When prompted for your root password, enter **`tuX123`**.
5. Configure your network settings by completing the following:

TIP

Your network card should have already been configured during installation. We left one parameter out then that we are going to edit in this exercise.

   a. Select **Network Devices**, **Network Card**.
   b. Under Already Configured Devices, select **Change**.
   c. In the Overview screen, mark your *network interface* and then select **Edit**.

TIP

Your system should be configured with a static address from Lab Exercise 2.1.

   d. Select **Host Name** and **Name Server**.
   e. Ensure that your hostname is set to **fs1** and that your domain is set to **cle9.com**.
   f. Ensure that the correct *DNS server address* has been entered.
   g. In the Domain Search 1 field next to your DNS server address, enter **`cle9.com`**.

h. Select **OK**.

i. Select **Next**, **Finish**.

j. Test the configuration by opening a terminal session and entering **`ping fs1`**.

k. The `ping` utility should report that it is pinging `fs1.cle9.com`. Press **Ctrl+C** to stop the pinging.

6. Use YaST to add a user to your system by completing the following:

   a. In the left frame of YaST, select **Security and Users**.

   b. Select **Create and Edit Users**.

   c. When prompted for your LDAP password, enter **`tuX123`**.

   d. Select **Set Filter**, **LDAP Users**.

   e. Select **Add**.

   f. Enter the following information:

      - Name: **`Jason Corry`**
      - User Login: **`jcorry`**
      - Password: **`Anne1`**

   g. Select **Details**.

   h. In the Additional Group Membership field, mark the users group.

   i. Select **Next**.

   j. Select **Next**.

   k. Select **Create**.

   l. Select **Finish**.

7. Install a new package on your server using YaST by completing the following:

   a. Select **Software**, **Install and Remove Software**.

   b. In the Search field, enter **`howto`**.

   c. Mark the **howto** package.

   d. In the search field, enter **`ethereal`**.

   e. Mark the **ethereal** package.

TIP

Be sure you do this because we will be using ethereal in later lab exercises.

f. Select **Accept**.

g. When prompted, insert the appropriate CDs.

h. Wait while the packages are installed.

8. Use YaST to configure services on your SLES server by completing the following:

    a. Select **System**, **Runlevel Editor**.

    b. Select **Expert Mode**.

    c. Under Service, scroll down to and select **apache2**.

    d. Select **Start/Stop/Refresh**, **Start Now**.

    e. When prompted that the service is running, select **OK**.

    f. Configure the apache2 service to automatically start at runlevels 3 and 5 by marking **3** and **5**.

    g. Select **Finish**.

    h. When prompted that the changes will be saved, select **Yes**.

Congratulations! You now know how to use one of the finest system configuration utilities known to the Linux world: YaST!

That's it for this chapter. Before we go to Chapter 3, "Configuring DNS on SLES 9," let's review what you've learned.

Summary

This chapter is designed mostly for readers who have a non-Novell Linux certification, such as RHCE or LPIC-1, but who don't have their CLP certification. The objective of this chapter was to bring the reader up to speed on Novell's SLES 9 distribution.

To do this, we first introduced the history of SUSE and the various distributions currently available. Then we went through the SLES 9 installation process. In Lab Exercise 2.1 we practiced installing a base system that we will use throughout the rest of this study guide.

After installing, we reviewed some of the more obvious differences between SLES 9 and other popular Linux distributions, such as the `/media` directory for mounts and the location of init scripts.

Finally, we spent some time getting used to YaST. We talked about the relationship between YaST and SuSEconfig. Then we practiced using YaST to perform common system administration tasks, such as managing network settings, managing server hardware, managing user accounts, and managing services.

With that, you're ready to dive into Chapter 3, where we will start building our SLES 9 deployment by implementing DNS and DHCP.

CHAPTER 3

Configuring DNS on SLES 9

This chapter covers the following requirements for Novell's Certified Linux Engineer (CLE) 9 certification:

1. Configure a DNS server using BIND.

On a modern IP-based network, users take for granted the fact that they can access local network and Internet resources using easy-to-remember domain names instead of IP addresses. I doubt that a single work day goes by that the typical employee doesn't access some website with a URL that uses a domain name, such as `http://www.novell.com`. As a Linux system administrator, it's your job to know how to provide users with this functionality.

In this chapter, we're going to do just that. We're going to discuss how to implement domain name service (DNS) on your SLES 9 server.

Let's begin!

The Need for DNS

TEST OBJECTIVE COVERED:

1. Configure a DNS server using BIND.

Let's visit an imaginary world; a world without DNS. In this world, users can't use the domain names that we are so used to in our modern lexicon.

Your coworker comes to you and says, “Hey, I found a great website for searching the Internet. Just go to 66.102.7.99.” Later, you're watching television and you see an advertisement for an online auction website. The slogan for it goes, “I found just what I needed on 66.135.192.124.” It's not very catchy, is it?

Fortunately, in the real world, this isn't a problem. We have DNS. As you probably know, DNS is a network service that allows you to map easy-to-remember host and domain names to IP addresses. Before going any farther, let's review a little bit of the history behind DNS.

Life Before DNS

Believe it or not, DNS hasn't always been with us. In the early days of IP-based computer networks, we had two choices:

- Don't use any kind of name resolution.
- Use the *hosts* file for name resolution.

As you can guess, the first option wasn't terribly popular. If you're a tech-head (and you probably are if you're pursing the CLE 9 certification), you probably could handle using IP addresses instead of hostnames. It wouldn't be easy, but as soon as you memorized a list of frequently used IP address, you could probably get by.

However, this option would be a support nightmare for your typical network users. Could you imagine how many help-desk calls you would get? For whatever reason, humans have a tough time memorizing long numbers. Our brains tend to just jumble up the numbers.

NOTE

Some psychological researchers have actually studied this phenomenon. If you want to have a little fun, get a friend and try this experiment.

Have your friend say a number and then ask you to recite the number he or she just said. Then have your friend say two new numbers and have you repeat them back. Continue adding more numbers (be sure to use new numbers each time) until you can no longer accurately repeat back the numbers. The average person can only recall between 5–9 numbers before they can't do it any more.

Imagine what would happen if you sent out the memo in Figure 3.1 to your users.

I can tell from personal experience that your phone will be ringing off the hook. It's just hard for the typical user to comprehend IP addresses.

FIGURE 3.1
The World without name resolution.

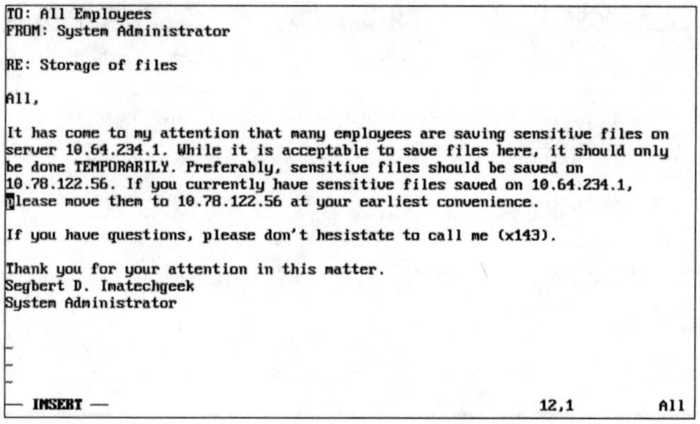

```
TO: All Employees
FROM: System Administrator

RE: Storage of files

All,

It has come to my attention that many employees are saving sensitive files on
server 10.64.234.1. While it is acceptable to save files here, it should only
be done TEMPORARILY. Preferably, sensitive files should be saved on
10.78.122.56. If you currently have sensitive files saved on 10.64.234.1,
please move them to 10.78.122.56 at your earliest convenience.

If you have questions, please don't hesitate to call me (x143).

Thank you for your attention in this matter.
Segbert D. Imatechgeek
System Administrator

~
~
~
-- INSERT --                                      12,1          All
```

Because of this, most system administrators used the second option. Instead of requiring users to memorize IP addresses, they instead used the hosts file to provide a simple form of name resolution.

Most operating systems are designed to use some type of hosts file to map hostnames to IP addresses. A sample hosts file from a Linux system is shown in Figure 3.2:

FIGURE 3.2
A sample Linux hosts file.

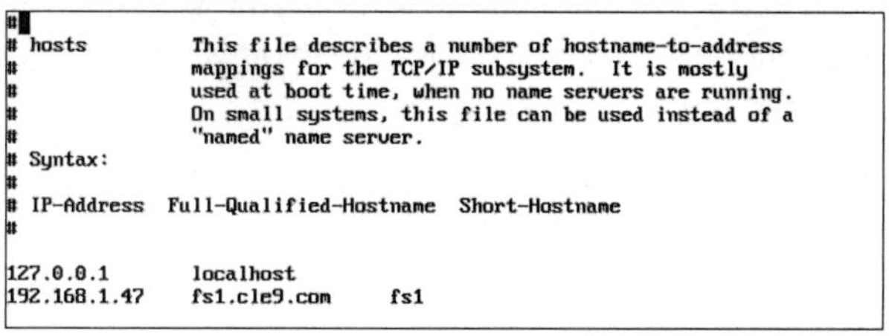

```
#
# hosts         This file describes a number of hostname-to-address
#               mappings for the TCP/IP subsystem.  It is mostly
#               used at boot time, when no name servers are running.
#               On small systems, this file can be used instead of a
#               "named" name server.
#
# Syntax:
#
# IP-Address  Full-Qualified-Hostname  Short-Hostname
#

127.0.0.1       localhost
192.168.1.47    fs1.cle9.com      fs1
```

On a Linux system, this file resides in `/etc`. Even the latest Windows operating system still has a hosts file available should it be needed. On a Windows XP system, this file resides in the `\windows\system32\drivers\etc` directory. A sample hosts file from a Windows system is shown in Figure 3.3:

FIGURE 3.3
A sample Windows hosts file.

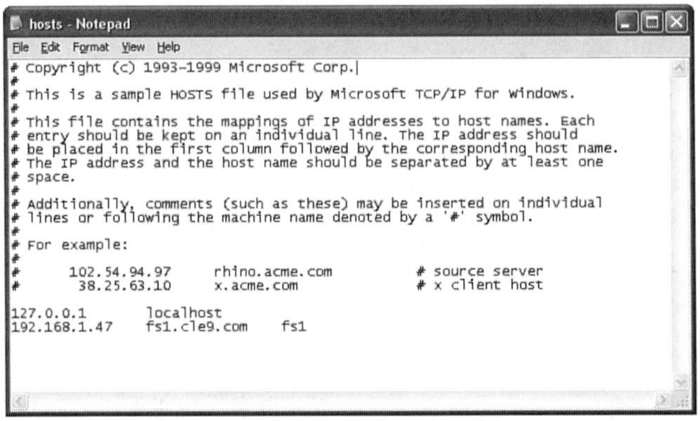
```
# Copyright (c) 1993-1999 Microsoft Corp.
#
# This is a sample HOSTS file used by Microsoft TCP/IP for Windows.
#
# This file contains the mappings of IP addresses to host names. Each
# entry should be kept on an individual line. The IP address should
# be placed in the first column followed by the corresponding host name.
# The IP address and the host name should be separated by at least one
# space.
#
# Additionally, comments (such as these) may be inserted on individual
# lines or following the machine name denoted by a '#' symbol.
#
# For example:
#
#      102.54.94.97     rhino.acme.com          # source server
#       38.25.63.10     x.acme.com              # x client host

127.0.0.1       localhost
192.168.1.47    fs1.cle9.com    fs1
```

TIP

NetWare servers can also use a hosts file. It resides on the SYS volume in the ETC directory.

Notice in Figures 3.2 and 3.3 that each mapping resides on a single line. The syntax is as follows:

```
IP_address     Host_Name          Alias
```

The IP_address parameter is the IP address of the host you want the hostname mapped to. The `Host_Name` parameter is the alphanumeric hostname you want mapped to the IP address. The Alias parameter is an optional, secondary hostname you want mapped to the same IP address. It's usually shorter than the hostname.

For example, in the preceding figures, the IP address 192.168.1.47 is mapped to the hostname of fs1.cle9.com. Notice that you're not limited to a hostname only for this parameter. You can also use a fully qualified domain name (FQDN).

TIP

The FQDN is composed of two elements: the hostname of the system concatenated with the DNS domain (which we'll discuss later in this chapter). In this example, fs1 is the hostname and cle9.com is the domain name.

This can be a point of confusion. Frequently in the industry you will hear the FQDN referred to as simply the "domain name." Just remember that they are probably talking about the FQDN. The domain name itself probably has many different hosts within it. FQDN refers to one specific host within a domain.

The Alias parameter is usually a shorter, easy-to-remember name that you want additionally mapped to the specified IP address. In Figures 3.2 and 3.3, we've also mapped the alias of fs1 to 192.168.1.47 in addition to the FQDN. With this hosts file, we can use either fs1.cle9.com or fs1 to access the host configured with the IP address 192.168.1.47.

Sounds pretty easy, huh? Can you still use hosts files to provide name resolution services on your network? Absolutely. This can be configured on your Linux host using the `/etc/host.conf` file. The order directive in this file specifies whether you are going to use hosts files and, if so, where to look first.

Do system administrators still use hosts files to provide name resolution services? Very rarely. Although editing the hosts file to define mappings is relatively uncomplicated, using hosts files has two major shortcomings.

First, maintaining hosts files on a small network is somewhat feasible. However, if a network gets very large at all, it becomes an impossible task. Suppose, for example, that you are responsible for managing an IP-based network that has 800 hosts on it. If you were to add a server to the network, you would have to manually update 800 hosts files with the new server's IP address and hostname. Unless you're the type of person who lives for tedium, this really isn't feasible, especially if your network is a growing, dynamic network. However, in the "old days," this was the only real name resolution option available and system administrators did the best they could.

The second problem with hosts files relates to Internet access. If an organization allowed very few users to access the Internet from their desktops, this wasn't an issue. You could maintain your users' hosts files (very tediously) with mappings of IP address to hostnames for systems on your network.

However, imagine the problem you would face if you wanted to implement hosts files to allow users to access hosts on the Internet. Basically, each user with Internet access would need a hosts file that contained mappings for all Internet hosts (or at least the ones you want them to be able to access). Yikes! This task sounds almost impossible.

To make this possible, the registration of Internet host names was centrally managed by the InterNIC (Network Information Center) at Stanford. This organization kept a master hosts file. Early system administrators would have to download new versions of this file regularly. They would then have to add mappings to the file for hosts on their own network. When they were done, they would copy the file around to all of the systems on their network.

Essentially, with hosts files, the smallest change required a great deal of manual effort to implement and distribute. That's where DNS comes into play.

How DNS Works

DNS makes name resolution on your IP network a much easier administrative task. The main weakness with hosts files was that name resolution was decentralized. Each computer system had its own hosts file. Any change in the network required each hosts file on every system to be changed.

DNS rectifies all that. Where the hosts file was a decentralized name resolution system, DNS is a centralized name resolution system.

Recall that when we installed and configured our SLES 9 server in the previous chapter, we configured the system with the IP address of a DNS server, as shown in Figure 3.4:

FIGURE 3.4
Configuring the IP address of the DNS resolver.

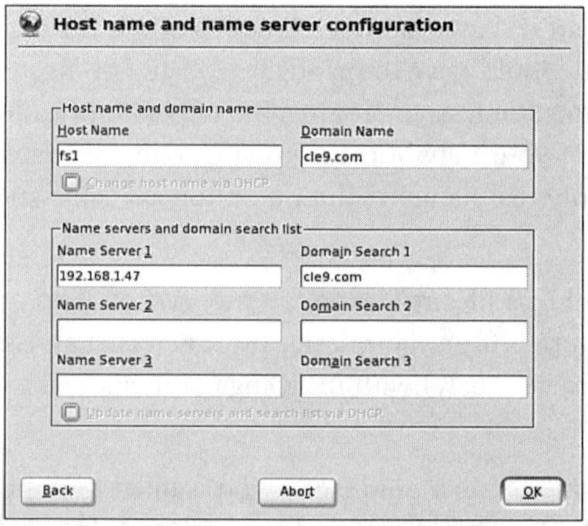

Instead of relying on the hosts file, the system will instead send requests for resolving host-names into IP addresses (and vice versa) to the DNS server.

NOTE

Even though your system is configured to use a DNS server for name resolution, you can still manually enter a hostname-IP address mapping in the hosts file. If your `/etc/host.conf` file is configured to do so, the system can use the hosts file to resolve that particular hostname.

This strategy provides distinct advantages over hosts files. Key among these is that name resolution services are centralized in the network. Recall the example we looked at earlier. You have 800 computer systems in your network and you've just added a new server. You need to update your name resolution system with the new hostname and IP address of the server.

We related that when using hosts files, you would have to make 800 manual updates; every hosts file would have to be edited or copied. With DNS, however, you would have to make a single update to the DNS server. As soon as you add the mapping, the hostname can immediately be resolved for any host on the network. That's a lot of time saved on your part.

Let's review how DNS works.

THE DNS NAMESPACE

One of the key differences between DNS and hosts files is that DNS employs a hierarchy of *domains* and *zones*. This hierarchy is called the *DNS namespace*.

By way of comparison, refer back to Figure 3.2. The hosts file is flat. What does the term "flat" mean? It means there is no structure to the file that would allow records to be nested within units of organization. All records in a hosts file reside at the same level.

For example, you could enter the following list of hostnames and IP addresses in a single hosts file:

```
192.168.1.47    fs1.cle9.com        fs1
130.57.4.27    www.novell.com        novell
192.168.1.1    gateway.cle9.com    gateway
195.135.220.3    www.suse.com        suse
```

Notice that the mappings aren't arranged in any particular fashion. They don't appear in any particular order nor are similar records grouped together. For a small hosts file, this isn't a problem. However, imagine how messy a hosts file could become if there were hundreds or even thousands of different records in the hosts file.

DNS, on the other hand, organizes hosts into a highly structured domain structure. Think of this structure as an inverted tree, as depicted in Figure 3.5.

To understand how DNS domains organize hostnames, let's analyze a sample domain name: www.novell.com.

At the top of the DNS hierarchy is the root domain. It's denoted by a simple period, as shown in Figure 3.5. This will be the right-most domain in any DNS domain name.

FIGURE 3.5
The DNS domain hierarchy.

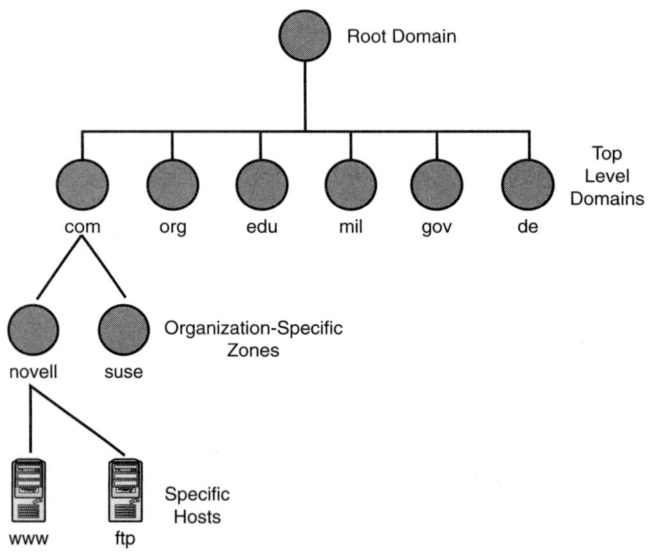

Notice the period at the end of www.novell.com. This period represents the root domain. Now, as you visit websites, you probably don't include the trailing period in the URL. Most people don't. However, you should always remember that a properly written FQDN name ends with a trailing period denoting the root domain.

As an experiment, try opening a web browser and navigating to your favorite websites using a trailing period after the domain name. You'll find that it works! In Figure 3.6, you see Novell's website opened using just this type of URL:

FIGURE 3.6
Using a trailing period in a URL.

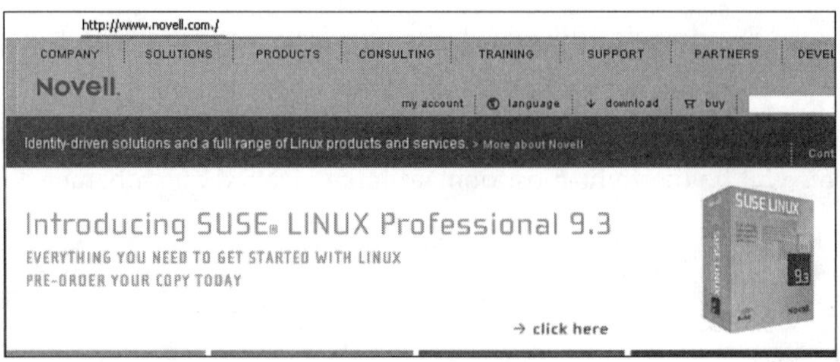

The root domain contains a number of top-level domains (TLDs). If you've visited websites on the Internet, you're probably already familiar with these top-level domain names, which include

- com—Contains commercial organizations.
- edu—Contains educational organizations.
- org—Contains nonprofit organizations.
- gov—Contains United States government organizations.

This list isn't all-inclusive. In recent years, new top-level domains have been added, including tv, biz, and info. In addition, top-level domains exist for specific countries. For example, the top-level domain for Australia is au. The top-level domain for Spain is es.

In our www.novell.com. example, the next domain after the root domain is com.

Within the top-level domains reside thousands of subdomains or *zones*. Zones are specific to an organization.

TIP

Occasionally you'll hear your fellow system administrators arguing over whether a zone is a domain. Some DNS purists get rankled if you refer to a zone as a subdomain. However, in common usage, the two terms are interchangeable.

Zones themselves can contain either subzones or specific hosts. In our example, the zone comes immediately to the left of the top-level domain; in this case, novell.

In Figure 3.5, you'll notice that the novell zone contains two specific records; one for www and one for ftp. These records contain mappings, just like in a hosts file, that map a hostname to an IP address. In our example, www specifies a specific host within the novell zone.

With this in mind, let's look at how the name resolution process works with DNS.

RESOLVING HOSTNAMES WITH DNS

Recall that with a hosts file, the system needing to resolve a hostname parses the locally stored file until it finds a match and reads the appropriate IP address. The process is quite a bit more complex when using DNS to resolve hostnames. However, it's this complexity that makes DNS a much more manageable system than using hosts files.

The DNS name resolution system uses DNS servers. Instead of reading a local file, a computer system that needs to resolve a hostname into an IP address sends a resolution request to the DNS server it's been configured to use; as shown in Figure 3.4.

What happens after that gets a little more complex. The process is depicted in Figure 3.7:

FIGURE 3.7
The Name resolution process.

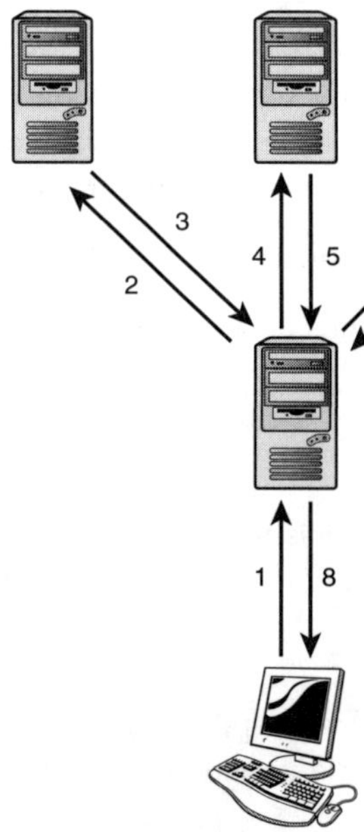

Here's how it works:

1. The system needing to resolve a hostname to an IP address sends a request to the DNS server it's been configured to use on IP port 53. If the DNS server is *authoritative* for the zone where the hostname being requested resides, it responds with the IP address. If not, the process continues to step 2.

NOTE

The DNS server is said to be authoritative if it has a record for the FQDN being requested in its local database.

2. The DNS server sends a request to a root-level DNS server. There are 13 root-level DNS servers on the Internet. When you install your own DNS server, it's automatically configured with the IP addresses of these servers, as shown in Figure 3.8. These root-level servers are configured with records that resolve to authoritative DNS servers for each top-level domain.

FIGURE 3.8
Root-level DNS servers.

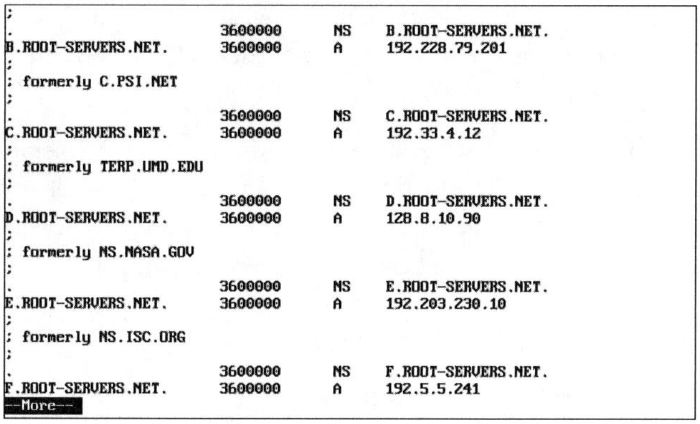
```
;
.                       3600000    NS    B.ROOT-SERVERS.NET.
B.ROOT-SERVERS.NET.     3600000    A     192.228.79.201
;
; formerly C.PSI.NET
;
.                       3600000    NS    C.ROOT-SERVERS.NET.
C.ROOT-SERVERS.NET.     3600000    A     192.33.4.12
;
; formerly TERP.UMD.EDU
;
.                       3600000    NS    D.ROOT-SERVERS.NET.
D.ROOT-SERVERS.NET.     3600000    A     128.8.10.90
;
; formerly NS.NASA.GOV
;
.                       3600000    NS    E.ROOT-SERVERS.NET.
E.ROOT-SERVERS.NET.     3600000    A     192.203.230.10
;
; formerly NS.ISC.ORG
;
.                       3600000    NS    F.ROOT-SERVERS.NET.
F.ROOT-SERVERS.NET.     3600000    A     192.5.5.241
--More--
```

TIP

On your SLES 9 server, the IP addresses of the root-level DNS servers are contained in the `/var/lib/named/root.hint` file.

3. The root-level DNS server contacted responds to your DNS server with the IP address of a DNS server that's authoritative for the top-level domain of the FQDN in question.
4. Your DNS server sends a resolution query for the FQDN to the top-level domain authoritative DNS server.
5. The top-level domain DNS server responds to your DNS server with the IP address of the DNS server that's authoritative for the DNS zone of the FQDN that you need to resolve.
6. Your DNS server sends a resolution request to the DNS server that's authoritative for the zone where the FQDN resides.
7. The authoritative DNS server for the FQDN responds to your DNS server with the respective IP address.
8. Your DNS server responds to the system that originated the request with the IP address.

At this point, something very important happens. When your DNS server resolves a hostname for which it is not authoritative, it saves that address in its *name cache*. In the future, if it receives a request to resolve the same hostname again, it will pull the IP address out of its cache and respond to the requesting system directly instead of going through the entire resolution process again. This saves both time and network traffic, especially on a heavily utilized DNS server.

With this in mind, you need to know a couple of things about the DNS server's name cache. First, the cache resides in the server's memory; it's not saved in a file. This is significant because, many times, system administrators want to manipulate their DNS server's cache, such as manually editing it to add hosts or to copy it to another DNS server. Simply put, you can't do it.

This brings to bear the second point: The name cache on a given DNS server isn't persistent. Because it resides in memory only, it's lost if you stop the DNS service or if you reboot the server system that's running the service. Many administrators want to save the cache to a file and then reload it when the service comes back up. The idea is a good one; rather than wait for the name cache to be rebuilt, they want to force the service to use an existing cache, saving time and reducing network traffic. Unfortunately, it can't be done.

Before we go any further, we need to discuss the two roles that a DNS server can take: master or slave.

MASTER AND SLAVE DNS SERVERS

One of the problems with current DNS implementations is fault tolerance. If you have your DNS database hosted on a particular server and it goes down, name resolution for your network is gone.

To provide a degree of redundancy, BIND allows you to configure *master* and *slave* DNS servers. A master server is a DNS server that hosts zone files. Any changes made to the zone are made to the zone files on the master server.

A slave DNS server, on the other hand, is configured to get its zone data from a master DNS server. Every so often, the slave server contacts the master server and downloads zone data. This transfer is called a *zone transfer*.

By configuring your DNS implementation with master and slave servers, you provide a degree of fault tolerance. That's because a slave DNS server can resolve hostnames just like a master DNS server. Your workstation doesn't know the difference between the two.

In fact, you'll notice that most organizations and ISPs provide two or more DNS server addresses for client workstations. One is usually a master server, the others slave servers. If your master server were to go down, workstations can still use the slave server for name resolution.

In addition to knowing about master and slave servers, you also need to understand that two types of zones can be hosted by a DNS server. Let's look at those next.

FORWARD- AND REVERSE-LOOKUP ZONES

DNS servers can perform two types of lookups performing name-resolution tasks. The first type is called a *forward lookup*. A forward lookup is the type of lookup we've been focusing on in the beginning pages of this chapter. When performing a forward lookup, the client system sends a request to the DNS server asking it to resolve a hostname into an IP address.

However, this process also works in reverse. These are called *reverse lookups*. During a reverse lookup, the client system sends a request to the DNS server that asks it to resolve an IP address into a hostname.

At first glance, you may conclude that the DNS server can use the same zone data to perform both types of lookup. After all, it's just a matter of direction, right?

Well, it doesn't work that way. If you want a DNS server to provide forward and reverse lookups, you have to create two zones: a forward zone and a reverse zone. Both zones contain the same data; it's just formatted in a slightly different fashion. We'll look at the difference later in this chapter.

Now that you know how DNS works conceptually, you need to learn how to implement it on your SLES 9 server.

Installing DNS on SLES 9

TEST OBJECTIVE COVERED:

1. Configure a DNS server using BIND.

To implement a DNS service on your SLES 9 server, you can choose from several packages. However, the most widely implemented DNS package is Berkeley Internet Name Domain (BIND) package. For your CLE 9 certification, this is the package you need to know how to deploy.

Let's briefly discuss the BIND package itself.

About BIND

BIND was originally developed in the early 1980s at the University of California at Berkeley. Its initial development was funded by a grant from the United States Department of Defense.

Subsequent versions, up to version 4.9, were sponsored by DEC. Versions since have been maintained by the Internet Systems Consortium (ISC). The latest versions of BIND can be downloaded from http://www.isc.org. However, you don't need to do that because the BIND 9 package is included on your SUSE Linux Enterprise Server 9 CD 3; as shown in Figure 3.9:

FIGURE 3.9
BIND package on SLES 9 CD 3.

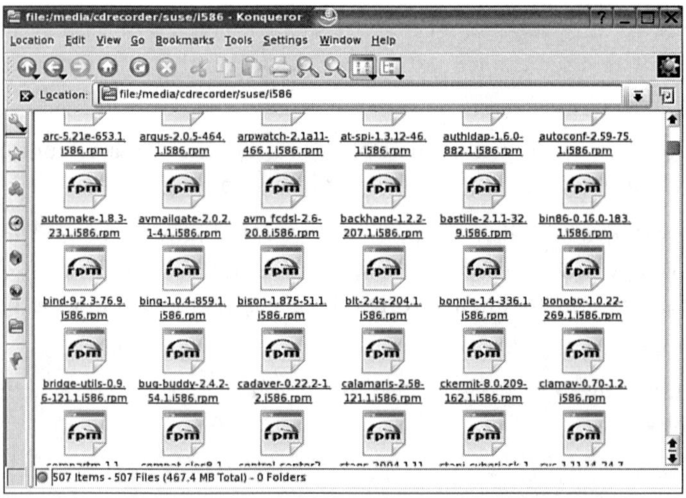

Let's now review how to install the BIND package on your SLES 9 server.

Installing BIND

You install BIND on a SLES 9 server the same as you would any other software package. You can use either YaST or the `rpm` command-line utility. Let's look at how to do this with YaST. Complete the following:

1. From your SLES 9 desktop, select **YaST**.
2. When prompted, provide your *root password*.

3. In the left frame, select **Software**.
4. In the right frame, select **Install and Remove Software**. The screen in Figure 3.10 appears:

FIGURE 3.10
YaST software management screen.

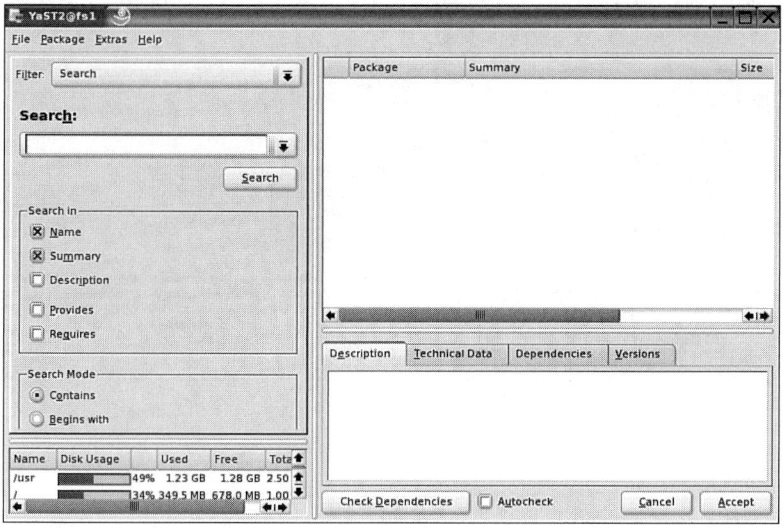

5. In the Search field, enter **`bind`**; then select **Search**.
6. In the right frame, mark the bind and the bind-utils packages; as shown in Figure 3.11.
7. Select **Accept**.
8. When prompted, insert the appropriate CDs.
9. Wait while the packages are installed and SuSEconfig is run; as shown in Figure 3.12.
10. Close YaST by selecting **Close**.

If you want to use the `rpm` utility to install the package from a shell prompt, do the following:

1. Insert your SLES 9 CD 3 into your server's CD-ROM drive.
2. Open a terminal session and enter **`rpm -i /media/cdrecorder/suse/i586/bind-9.2.3-76.9.i586.rpm`**.

FIGURE 3.11
Installing BIND packages.

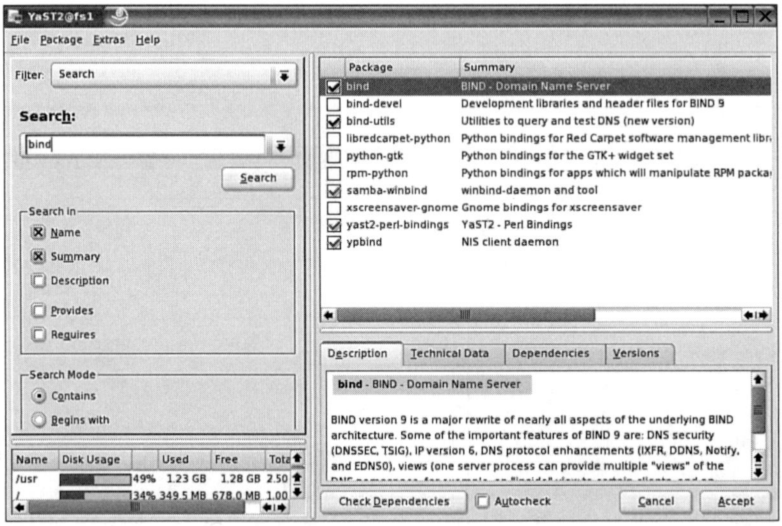

FIGURE 3.12
Running SuSEconfig after installing BIND.

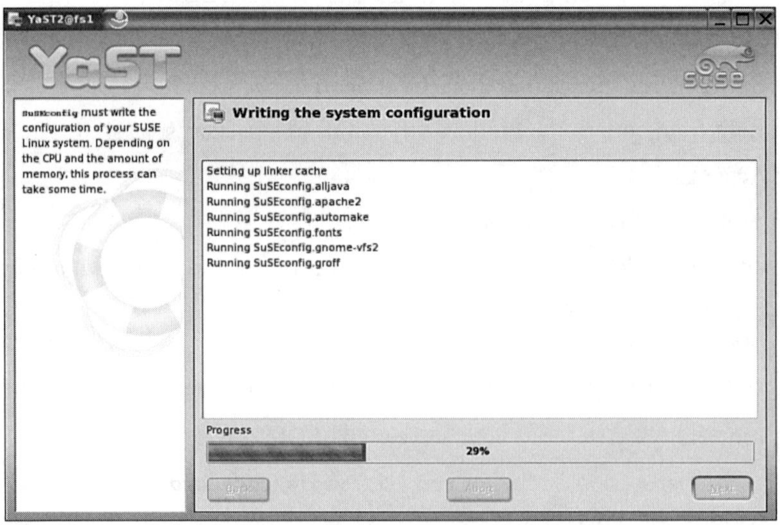

TIP

If you want a prettier display while the package is being installed, enter **`rpm -ihv /media/cdrecorder/suse/i586/bind-9.2.3-76.9.i586.rpm`**. You can also install the rpm by browsing to it in Konqueror. Right-click the file; then select **Actions, Install with YaST**.

If you followed the steps in the lab exercises in the previous chapter, your SLES 9 system should already have the BIND package installed.

To verify that it's there, open YaST and select **Software, Install and Remove Software**. In the search field, enter **`bind`**, and then select **Search**. You should see the bind and bind-utils packages marked with blue check marks, as shown in Figure 3.13:

FIGURE 3.13
BIND is already installed.

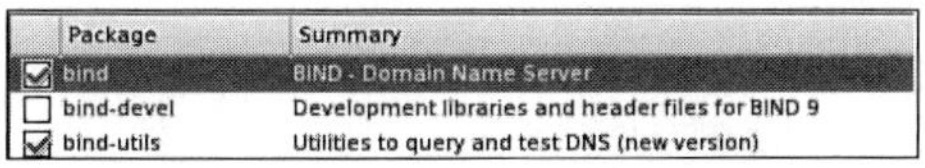

If, for some reason, the BIND packages aren't installed on your SLES 9 system, follow the preceding steps to install them.

After the BIND packages are installed, the service is started and stopped using the `named` (pronounced "*name dee*") init script in `/etc/init.d`, as shown in Figure 3.14:

FIGURE 3.14
The BIND startup script.

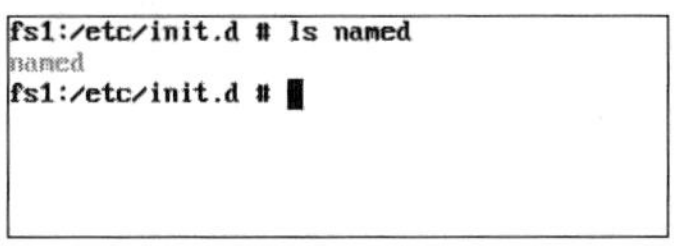

The actual binary that provides this service is the `named` executable located in `/usr/sbin` shown in Figure 3.15.

Like other daemons, you use the `/etc/init.d/named` script to start, stop, or restart `named`. This is done by simply calling the script and supplying the appropriate parameter. Some examples of commands you can use include the following:

- `/etc/init.d/named start`—Starts the named daemon.
- `/etc/init.d/named stop`—Stops the named daemon.
- `/etc/init.d/named restart`—Restarts the named daemon.

If you don't want to use the full path, you can also enter **`rcnamed`** from the shell prompt along with the `start`, `stop`, or `restart` parameters to manage the named daemon.

FIGURE 3.15
BIND binary.

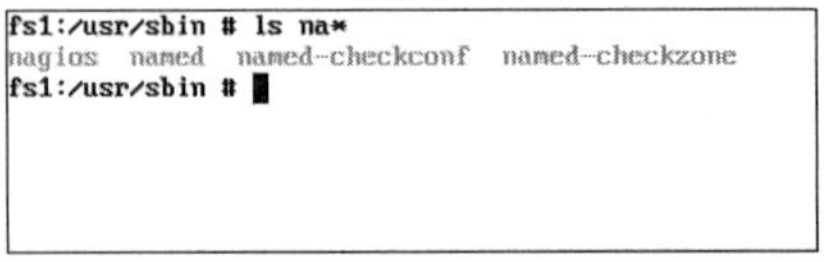

TIP

If you just enter *`rcscript`* at the shell prompt without any parameters, a list of available parameters will be displayed.

After BIND is installed on your system, you're ready to configure and start the service on your server. However, before doing so, you need to have a solid understanding of the BIND configuration files.

BIND Configuration Files

In this chapter, we're going to use YaST to set up the named service on your SLES 9 server. However, as discussed in Chapter 2, "Introduction to SUSE LINUX Enterprise Server 9," I believe that it's critical that you thoroughly understand what's happening "under the hood" of YaST's graphical interface.

With that in mind, let's look at the files that are used to configure the named service running on your server.

CONFIGURING named USING named.conf

The first file you need to be familiar with is `named.conf`. This file resides in `/etc`, as shown in Figure 3.16:

FIGURE 3.16
The `named.conf` file in `/etc`.

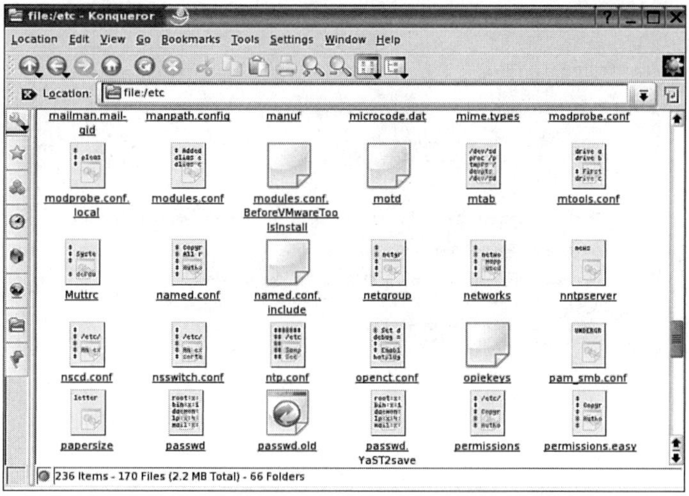

The **`named.conf`** file is the main configuration file for the named service. **`named.conf`** is composed of *directives* along with *blocks* of information associated with those directives.

TIP

A *block* is composed of lines of data enclosed in brackets. After the last bracket is a semicolon.

The directives within the **`named.conf`** file include the following:

- options—This directive defines general configuration options for the named service.
- logging—This directive configures logging channels for the named service. These channels could include sending logging information to the syslog service or to a specific file.
- zone—These directives define zones serviced by named.

The **`named.conf`** file has many configuration parameters. At this point, we're going to focus on two of them. We'll look at several of the others later on in the chapter.

The first parameter you need to be aware of is the **`directory`** parameter within the options directive, shown in Figure 3.17:

FIGURE 3.17
Setting the working directory for named.

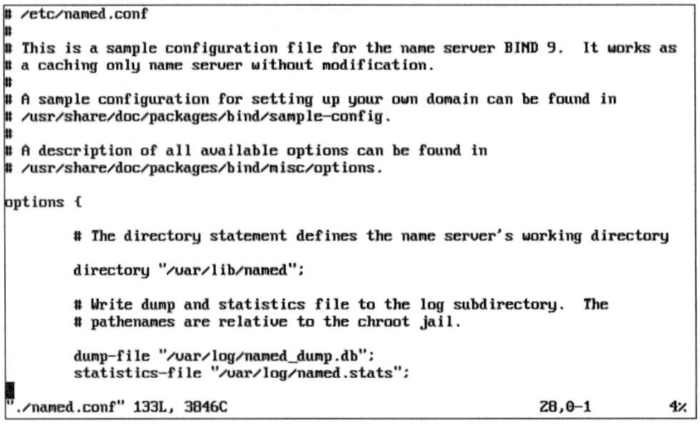

This option specifies the directory where the zone database files used by the named service will reside. By default, these reside in `/var/lib/named`, as shown in Figure 3.18:

FIGURE 3.18
Files for named in `/var/lib/named`.

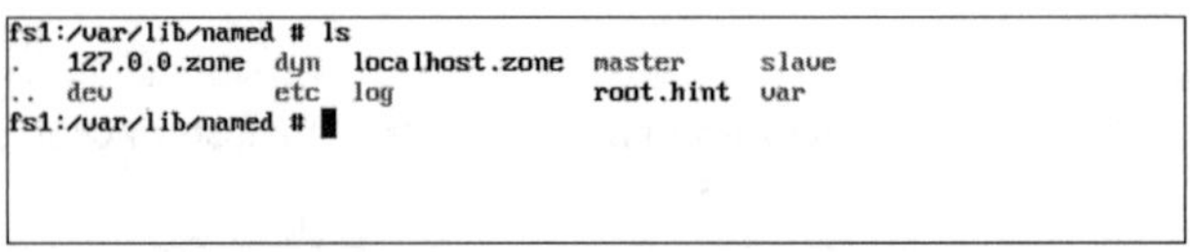

Anytime a filename is specified in any directive that follows the directory parameter in the `named.conf` file, it is assumed to reside in the specified directory.

The second set of parameters you need to be familiar with are the zone directives. These are found farther down in the file after the options directive, as shown in Figure 3.19.

The zone directives in `named.conf` define the zones that will be serviced by named. Notice in Figure 3.19 that a zone directive is composed of several parts:

- Zone Name—The zone name comes right after the zone directive. The zone name is enclosed in quotes. In Figure 3.19, three zones have been defined: ., *localhost*, and *0.0.127-in-addr.arpa*:

FIGURE 3.19
Zone directives in `/etc/named.conf`.

```
# The following zone definitions don't need any modification.  The first one
# is the definition of the root name servers.  The second one defines
# localhost while the third defines the reverse lookup for localhost.

zone "." in {
        type hint;
        file "root.hint";
};

zone "localhost" in {
        type master;
        file "localhost.zone";
};

zone "0.0.127.in-addr.arpa" in {
        type master;
        file "127.0.0.zone";
};

# Include the meta include file generated by createNamedConfInclude.  This
# includes all files as configured in NAMED_CONF_INCLUDE_FILES from
# /etc/sysconfig/named

                                                  127,0-1       94%
```

- Name Space—The name space declaration comes after the zone name. In Figure 3.19, each of the three zones has been configured to use the Internet name space, denoted by *in*.

TIP

The Internet name space is used almost exclusively. It's very unlikely that you will encounter any other name spaces when implementing a DNS server.

- Type—The type declaration identifies whether the server will be a *master* DNS server or a *slave* DNS server.
- File—The file declaration identifies the file where the zone data is stored. The file name is enclosed in quotes. The file is assumed to be in the directory specified in the options directive.

In Figure 3.19, you can see that three zones are defined by default in `named.conf`. The first zone is called `.` and is configured as a hint file. The records in this zone point to the root-level name servers on the Internet. This zone is used by named when it receives a request to resolve a hostname residing in a zone for which it isn't authoritative. The IP address for these root-level name servers is contained in the `root.hint` file, shown in Figure 3.20:

FIGURE 3.20
Root-level DNS server IP addresses in `root.hint`.

```
.                        3600000  IN  NS    A.ROOT-SERVERS.NET.
A.ROOT-SERVERS.NET.      3600000      A     198.41.0.4
;
; formerly NS1.ISI.EDU
;
.                        3600000      NS    B.ROOT-SERVERS.NET.
B.ROOT-SERVERS.NET.      3600000      A     192.228.79.201
;
; formerly C.PSI.NET
;
.                        3600000      NS    C.ROOT-SERVERS.NET.
C.ROOT-SERVERS.NET.      3600000      A     192.33.4.12
;
; formerly TERP.UMD.EDU
;
.                        3600000      NS    D.ROOT-SERVERS.NET.
D.ROOT-SERVERS.NET.      3600000      A     128.8.10.90
;
; formerly NS.NASA.GOV
;
.                        3600000      NS    E.ROOT-SERVERS.NET.
E.ROOT-SERVERS.NET.      3600000      A     192.203.230.10
;
"./root.hint" 80L, 2517C                          40,1          29%
```

The root.hint file is automatically copied to `/var/lib/named` when the BIND package is installed.

The next default zone defined in `named.conf` is localhost. This zone contains only a single record that simply maps localhost to the IP address 127.0.0.1.

The last default zone is called 0.0.127.in-addr.arpa. That name may sound a little confusing, but it actually isn't. This zone is a *reverse* zone. It maps the IP address 127.0.0.1 to the localhost hostname. We'll look at reverse-lookup zones a little later.

As you may have noticed, these three default zones don't define any real DNS zones. Can the named service installed on the server do any meaningful work in this configuration? Your first impression might be that it can't. What can it resolve if it has records only for the localhost hostname? However, it can actually function very nicely. In this default configuration, the named service operates as a *caching-only* name server.

Recall, as discussed earlier in this chapter, that a DNS server will query root-level name servers when it's asked to resolve a hostname that it isn't authoritative for. The DNS server will use the information supplied by the root-level DNS server to locate an authoritative DNS server for the requested hostname.

When the hostname is finally resolved, the DNS server stores that information in its cache. The next time it receives a request to resolve the same hostname, it simply pulls the information out of its cache.

This type of configuration is appropriate for situations where you don't have your own domain and you want to provide users with the capability to browse the web.

However, it's more likely that you will need to provide resolution services for a domain using the name daemon. To do this, you will need to create your own zone files and configure named to use them.

Let's talk about how to do that next.

CREATING ZONE FILES

Suppose you are the system administrator for an organization named CLE9 (what a coincidence!). You've secured the cle9.com domain name for your organization. Previously, you configured your SLES 9 server to be a caching-only name server. However, now you need to configure named to provide authoritative resolution services for the cle9.com zone. What do you need to do?

First, you need to edit your `/etc/named.conf` file and add a new zone directive. This is shown in Figure 3.21:

FIGURE 3.21
Adding a New Zone to `named.conf`.

```
# The following zone definitions don't need any modification.  The first one
# is the definition of the root name servers.  The second one defines
# localhost while the third defines the reverse lookup for localhost.

zone "." in {
        type hint;
        file "root.hint";
};

zone "localhost" in {
        type master;
        file "localhost.zone";
};

zone "0.0.127.in-addr.arpa" in {
        type master;
        file "127.0.0.zone";
};

zone "cle9.com" in {
        file "master/cle9.com";
        type master;
};
-- INSERT --                                           105,1         87%
```

In this example, we've added the cle9.com zone. The DNS server will be a master, authoritative server for the zone. The next thing we need to do is to create a file for the zone. Notice that we've specified the file to be `master/cle9.com`. Because we've specified that our directory is `/var/lib/named`, the zone file will, therefore, be `/var/lib/named/master/cle9.com`.

After saving the file, the next thing we need to do is open the zone file and add the appropriate information. This is where things get a little more complicated. I'm going to show you a basic zone file I've created for the cle9.com zone. This is shown in Figure 3.22:

FIGURE 3.22
The cle9.com zone.

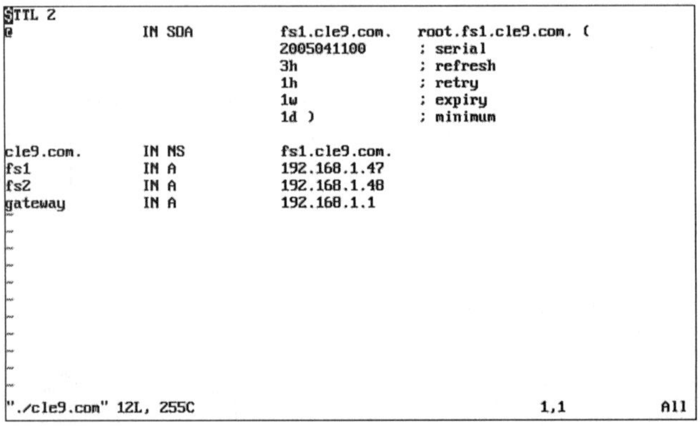

```
$TTL 2
@               IN SOA          fs1.cle9.com.   root.fs1.cle9.com. (
                                2005041100      ; serial
                                3h              ; refresh
                                1h              ; retry
                                1w              ; expiry
                                1d )            ; minimum

cle9.com.       IN NS           fs1.cle9.com.
fs1             IN A            192.168.1.47
fs2             IN A            192.168.1.48
gateway         IN A            192.168.1.1
~
~
~
~
~
~
~
~
~
"./cle9.com" 12L, 255C                                  1,1          All
```

In this zone, there are three hosts: fs1, fs2, and gateway. Let's explore each element of the zone file in a little more depth:

- $TTL—This stands for Time To Live. This value specifies the default time to live for each record. If a record has an explicit time to live value, it takes precedence over the TTL value specified here. If no unit is specified, the value is assumed to reference seconds. Figure 3.22 shows 2 seconds, which is probably too small a value. You can also specify units in days by placing a D after the value; for example, 2D.
- IN—Specifies that the file uses the Internet namespace.
- SOA—SOA stands for Start Of Authority. The SOA is actually a record, just like the records you see in Figure 3.22 for fs1 and fs2. However, the SOA record has a special purpose. It must be placed immediately after the $TTL parameter. The role of the SOA record is to identify the following:
  - Which DNS server is the authoritative server for the zone? In Figure 3.22, fs1.cle9.com. is identified as the authoritative DNS server for the cle9.com zone.

NOTE

Remember to use trailing periods wherever you use a FQDN in the zone file!

- The email address of the system administrator who maintains the zone. In this example, this is root@fs1.cle9.com.
- The zone's serial number. This number is used by slave DNS servers for this zone to determine whether they should update their databases. You can use any initial value you want in this field. However, the general practice is to use the date the zone file was created concatenated with a zero. In Figure 3.22, the zone file was created on April 8, 2005. If you use YaST to update your zone, this number will be automatically incremented (that's why we start with a zero at the end). If you update the zone file with a text editor, you should manually increment the last digit of the serial number. This tells slave DNS servers that the zone file has changed and that they need to update their database from the master server.
- The periodic interval, specified by the refresh parameter at which slave DNS server should update their databases from the master server. Notice in Figure 3.22, the refresh interval is set to 3 hours.
- How many attempts slave servers should make before giving up when updating their database from the master server. This is specified by the retry parameter.
- How long before zone data on slave servers expire. This is specified by the expiry parameter. If zone data expires, slave servers will not be allowed to respond to name resolution requests until it downloads updated zone data from the master server.
- How long failed name resolution requests should be stored in the cache of slave servers. This is specified by the *minimum* parameter.

- Hostname records—After the SOA record come a series of records for network hosts. The general syntax is:

```
host_name          name_space       record_type     IP address or host_name.
```

  Let's review each of these parameters:

  - Hostname—This the hostname assigned to the particular system.
  - Name space—This specifies the name space used for the record. More than likely, you will always used the Internet (IN) namespace.
  - Record type—This parameter specifies what type of DNS record this is.

- IP address or hostname—This parameter specifies the IP address or hostname you are mapping a the hostname to. Remember, if you use a hostname, you have two options. First, you can just specify the hostname being mapped to. If you do this, it will be assumed to be in the zone specified in the SOA. Second, you can use a FQDN. If you do, you must use a trailing period.

When creating DNS records, you can create several types. These include the following:

- NS—An NS record is used to specify the hostname of the DNS server that hosts the specified zone. Instead of mapping to an IP address, an NS record maps to the hostname of the DNS server. The DNS server referenced by the NS record must, itself, be represented by an A record in the zone.
- A—An A record maps a hostname to an IP address. The host is usually just the hostname, as shown in Figure 3.22. In this case, the host is assumed to be in the zone specified in the SOA record. However, you can also specify a FQDN (with a trailing period).
- CNAME—A CNAME record is an alias. Instead of mapping to an IP address, it maps a hostname to another hostname in the zone. For example, in Figure 3.22, you could create a CNAME record that maps the hostname of MyServer to fs1. If you do this, you must create an A record for the hostname being mapped to. In preceding example, you would have to have an A record for fs1.
- MX—An MX record represents a mail server. Like a CNAME record, an MX record maps a hostname to another hostname instead of an IP address. For example, suppose fs2 in Figure 3.22 is running a mail service. You could create an MX record in your zone for the hostname mail that points to fs2. Like a CNAME record, you must have an A record in the DNS zone that maps the second hostname to an IP address.

At this point, we need to discuss an interesting fact about the way named handles records in a zone file. The question frequently arises as to how to handle hosts with multiple IP addresses. This situation arises for two reasons.

First, to provide a degree of fault tolerance and to balance the network load between the NICs, many network administrators will install multiple NICs in their servers. In this situation, a server may have two or more IP addresses.

Second, many network administrators will provide a given service on multiple hosts. For example, to accommodate network load, an organization may divide its HTTP service among several servers in a server farm. For example, if you use dig or nslookup to resolve www.yahoo.com, you will see that there are multiple A records for this single hostname, as shown in Figure 3.23:

FIGURE 3.23
Multiple address for www.yahoo.com.

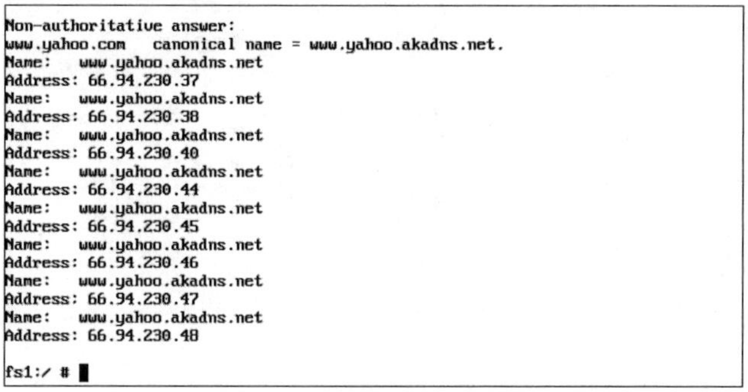

```
Non-authoritative answer:
www.yahoo.com	canonical name = www.yahoo.akadns.net.
Name:	www.yahoo.akadns.net
Address: 66.94.230.37
Name:	www.yahoo.akadns.net
Address: 66.94.230.38
Name:	www.yahoo.akadns.net
Address: 66.94.230.40
Name:	www.yahoo.akadns.net
Address: 66.94.230.44
Name:	www.yahoo.akadns.net
Address: 66.94.230.45
Name:	www.yahoo.akadns.net
Address: 66.94.230.46
Name:	www.yahoo.akadns.net
Address: 66.94.230.47
Name:	www.yahoo.akadns.net
Address: 66.94.230.48

fs1:/ #
```

If you are in either situation, you need to configure your zone file so that named will resolve multiple IP addresses to a single hostname. Additionally, you probably want to make sure that named doesn't give out the same address for the multiaddress hostname over and over. One of your major goals behind implementing a multi-NIC server or a multiserver service is to balance the load. This goal would be undermined if your DNS server resolves only one of the addresses assigned to the hostname.

So what do you do? The good news is that named is designed with this scenario in mind. If you have a hostname that has multiple IP addresses, all you have to do is create multiple A records for the same hostname in your zone; each resolving to a different IP address. The named daemon will then automatically rotate which address is resolved to the hostname, thereby distributing the network load on your server or service for you. Pretty powerful stuff!

At this point, we need to switch gears. Everything we've been talking about in this topic has been based on forward-lookup zones. Before continuing, we need to also review how to create reverse zones.

CONFIGURING REVERSE-LOOKUP ZONES

As discussed earlier in this chapter, a reverse-lookup zone operates in the opposite manner of a standard forward-lookup zone. Instead of resolving hostnames into IP addresses, a reverse zone resolves IP addresses into hostnames.

Before your named daemon can perform this type of lookup, you need to configure a companion reverse zone for your forward zone. An example of a reverse zone for the cle9.com zone is shown in Figure 3.24:

FIGURE 3.24
The reverse-lookup zone for cle9.com.

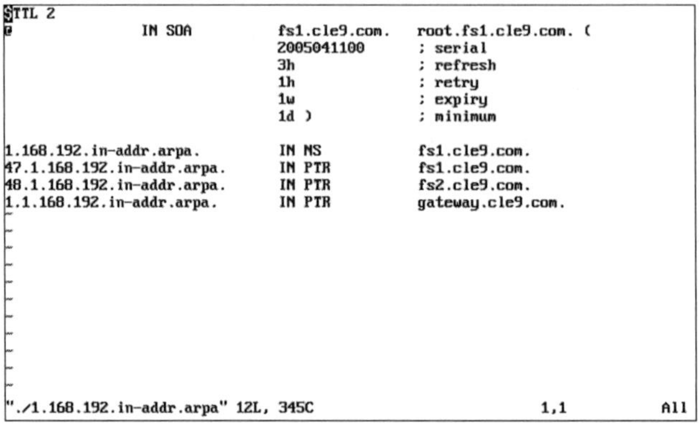

```
$TTL 2
@               IN SOA          fs1.cle9.com.    root.fs1.cle9.com. (
                                2005041100       ; serial
                                3h               ; refresh
                                1h               ; retry
                                1w               ; expiry
                                1d )             ; minimum

1.168.192.in-addr.arpa.         IN NS            fs1.cle9.com.
47.1.168.192.in-addr.arpa.      IN PTR           fs1.cle9.com.
48.1.168.192.in-addr.arpa.      IN PTR           fs2.cle9.com.
1.1.168.192.in-addr.arpa.       IN PTR           gateway.cle9.com.
~
~
~
~
~
~
~
~
~
"./1.168.192.in-addr.arpa" 12L, 345C                       1,1          All
```

You'll notice that the **$TTL** parameter and the SOA record are pretty much the same as the forward-lookup zone. However, similarities end there.

Locate the NS record in Figure 3.24. Notice the odd zone name used. Instead of cle9.com, the zone's name is **1.168.192.in-addr.arpa.**. Reverse zone names are constructed in the following way:

`reversed_network_address.in-addr.arpa.`

For example, in Figure 3.24, the network address for the hosts in the zone is 192.168.1.0. Therefore, the zone name is **1.168.192.in-addr.arpa.**.

Accordingly, the hosts in the zone are referenced in the following way:

host_portion_address.reversed_network_address.in-addr.arpa.

For example, the reverse hostname for fs1.cle9.com is **47.1.168.192.in-addr.arpa.**.

TIP

Just like a forward-lookup zone, FQDNs in a reverse name must have a trailing period.

With the reverse zone running, you can send reverse resolution requests, as shown in Figure 3.25:

FIGURE 3.25
Performing a reverse-lookup.

```
fs1:/etc # host 192.168.1.47
47.1.168.192.in-addr.arpa domain name pointer fs1.cle9.com.
fs1:/etc #
```

In this example, the DNS server has resolved the IP address of 192.168.1.47 to fs1.cle9.com.

Now that you know about forward and reverse zone as well as the files that compose them, you are ready to configure BIND on your server. Let's do that next.

Configuring BIND on SLES 9

To configure BIND on SLES 9, you basically have two options: You can manually create and edit the necessary files or you can use YaST. For your CLE 9 certification, you need to know how to do this with YaST. Let's dig right in and do it. To configure BIND on SLES 9, complete the following:

1. From the desktop of your SLES 9 server, start YaST.
2. Select **Network Services, DNS Server**, as shown in Figure 3.26:

FIGURE 3.26
Configuring DNS in YaST.

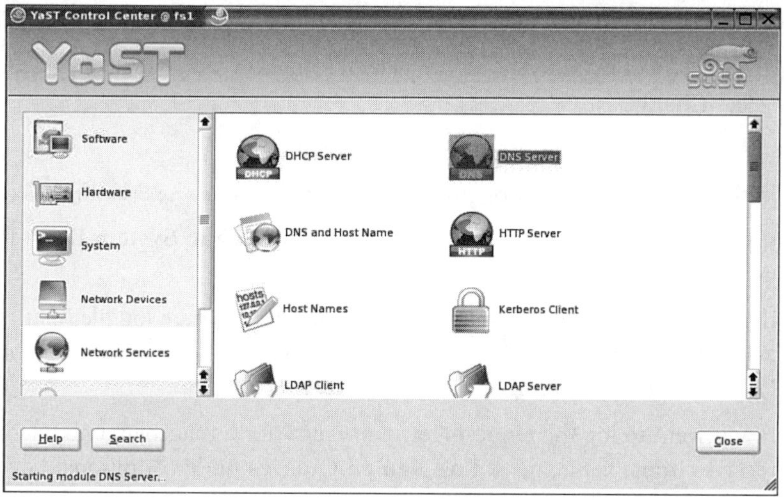

3. Configure the named files directory by completing the following:

    a. In the left frame, select **Basic Options**. The screen in Figure 3.27 is displayed:

FIGURE 3.27
Configuring named Basic Options.

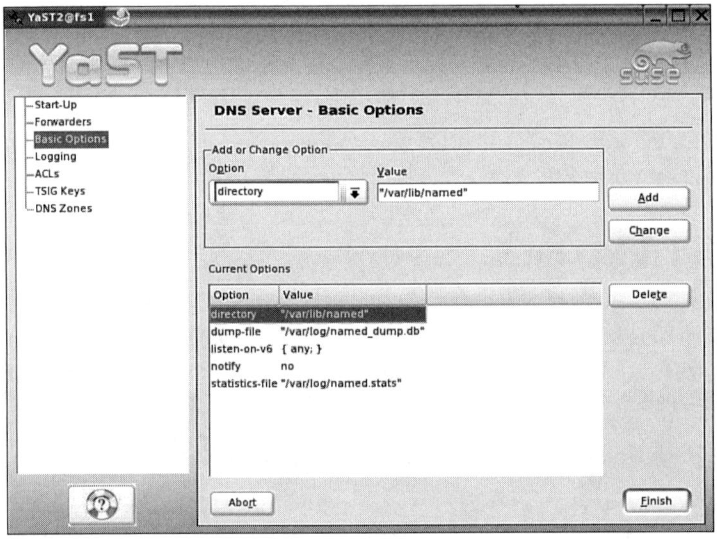

    b. In the Option drop-down list, select **Directory**.

    c. In the Value field, enter the directory where the named files reside, enclosed in quotes.

    d. Select **Change**.

4. To configure named logging, complete the following:

    a. In the left frame, select **Logging**. The screen in Figure 3.28 is displayed.

    b. If you want named to use the system log, mark **Log to System Log**. (This is the default behavior.)

    c. If you want named to write log information to a separate log file, mark **Log to File**; then enter a *filename*, *maximum log size* (in MB), and a *maximum number of log versions* to be saved.

    d. If you want to log the requests for name resolution that the named daemon receives from clients, mark **Log Named Queries** under Additional Logging.

FIGURE 3.28
Configuring named Logging options.

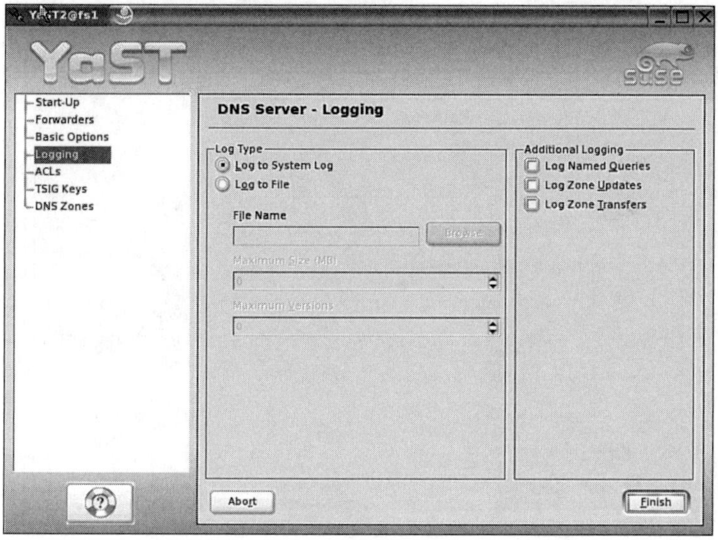

TIP

I strongly recommend that you use this option for testing and troubleshooting only. If you leave this option turned on for a heavily utilized server, your log file will get really big really fast.

   e. If you want to log modifications made to the zone, mark **Log Zone Updates**.

   f. If you want to log zone transfers, mark **Log Zone Transfers**.

5. Configure your zones by completing the following:

   a. In the left frame, select **DNS Zones**. The screen shown in Figure 3.29 is displayed.

   b. To create a new zone, enter the *name* of the zone in the Zone Name field.

TIP

If you're creating a reverse zone, enter the reverse zone name in this field.

   c. Select **Add**.

   d. Under Configured DNS Zones, select the *zone* you just created, and then select **Edit Zone**.

   e. Select the **NS Records** tab. The screen in Figure 3.30 appears.

FIGURE 3.29
Configuring DNS Zones in YaST.

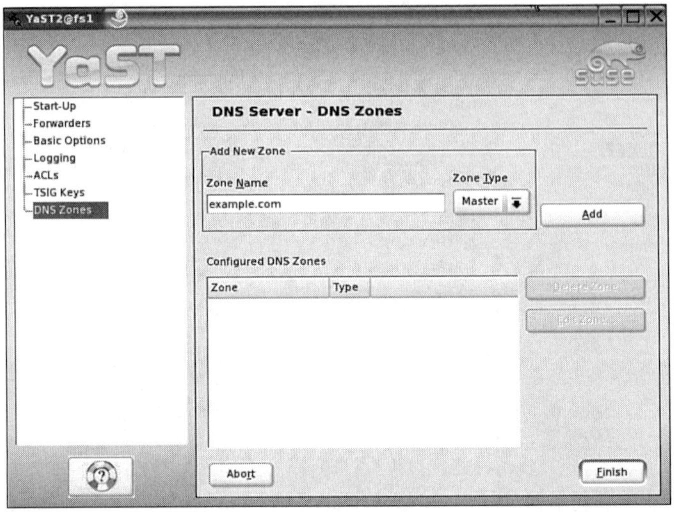

FIGURE 3.30
Configuring NS Records in YaST.

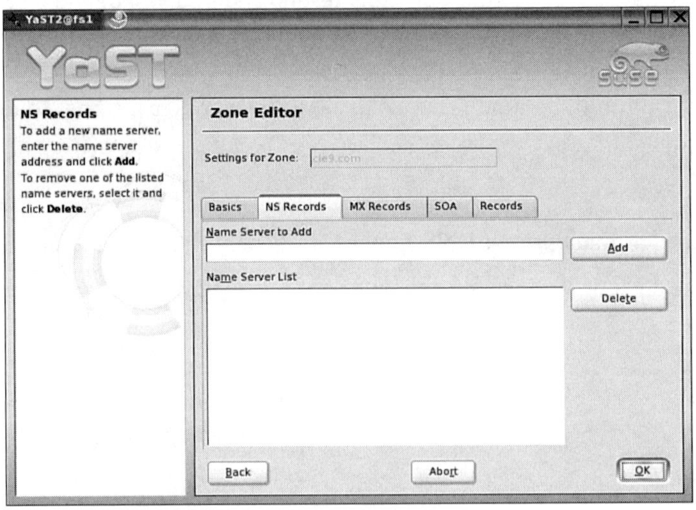

f. In the Name Server to Add field, enter the **FQDN** of the server that is running named.

TIP

If you forget to add a trailing period. YaST will add it for you.

g. Select **Add**.

h. Select the **SOA** tab. The screen shown in Figure 3.31 is displayed:

FIGURE 3.31
Configuring the SOA Record in YaST.

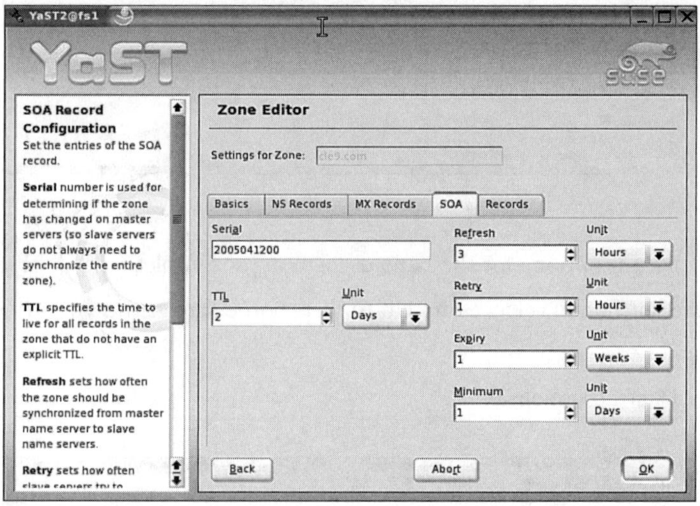

i. Configure your SOA ***directives*** as desired.

j. Select the **Records** tab. The screen in Figure 3.32 is displayed.

k. In the Record field, enter the *hostname* or the *FQDN* for a host you want to add to the zone.

l. In the Type drop-down list, select the *type of record* you are adding.

m. In the value field, enter the *IP address* (for A records) or *FQDN* (for CNAME records) assigned to the host.

n. Select **Add**.

o. Repeat these steps for all the hosts you want to add to the zone.

p. When you're done, select **OK**.

FIGURE 3.32
Configuring Zone Records in YaST.

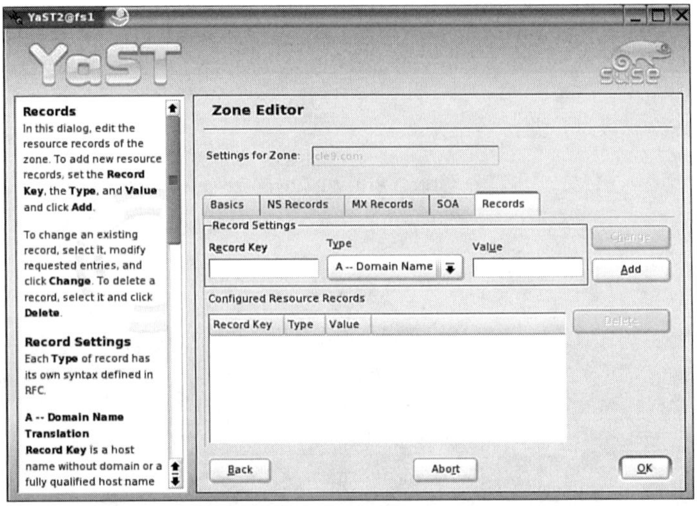

6. Configure startup options for the named daemon by completing the following:
   a. In the left frame, select **Start-Up** to display the screen shown in Figure 3.33:

FIGURE 3.33
Configuring named Startup Options in YaST.

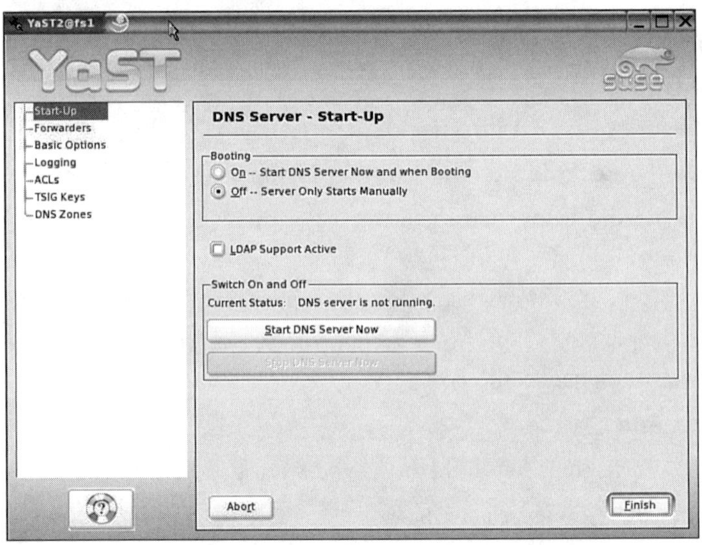

   b. To start named, select **Start DNS Server Now**.
   c. If you want named to automatically start on boot, mark **On** under Booting.

7. Apply the changes by selecting **Finish**.

That's all there is to it. You're probably ready to get your own DNS server up and running; let's do that in Lab Exercise 3.1.

Lab Exercise 3.1: Configuring DNS

In this lab exercise, you will use YaST to configure the DNS service on your SLES 9 server. To complete this exercise, you will need your lab PC system that you installed SLES 9 on in Lab Exercise 2.1.

TIP

If you've already accessed the YaST DNS Server module prior to this exercise, some of the functionality may be slightly different. The first time the module is run, it operates in wizard mode. After the first time, you must manually select the component you want to configure in the left frame. This exercise is written under the assumption that the module is operating in wizard mode.

Complete the following:

1. Boot your SLES 9 server.
2. Authenticate as **`tux`** with a password of **`SuSE789`**.
3. Start YaST.
4. When prompted, supply the root password of **`tuX123`**.
5. Select Network Services, DNS Server.
6. In the Forwarder Settings screen, select **Next**.
7. In the DNS Zones screen, complete the following:
    a. In the Zone Name field, enter **`cle9.com`**.
    b. Select **Add**.
    c. Under Configured DNS Zones, ensure the **cle9.com** zone is selected; then select **Edit Zone**.
    d. Select the **NS Records** tab.
    e. In the Name Server to Add field, enter **`fs1.cle9.com.`**.
    f. Select **Add**.
    g. Select the **SOA** tab.
    h. Change the TTL directive to **3 days**.
    i. Select the **Records** tab.
    j. In the Record Key field, enter **`fs1`**.
    k. Ensure that the Type drop-down list is set to **A**.

l. In the Value field, enter the *IP address* of your SLES 9 server.

m. Select **Add**.

n. Select **OK**.

8. Create a reverse-lookup zone by completing the following:

   a. In the DNS Zones screen, enter the appropriate *name* for a reverse zone for your network segment. For example, if your network address is 192.168.1.0, you would enter **`1.168.192.in-addr.arpa.`**.

   b. Select **Add**.

   c. Under Configured DNS Zones, select your *reverse zone*.

   d. Select **Edit Zone**.

   e. Select the **NS Records** tab.

   f. In the Name Server to add field, enter **`fs1.cle9.com.`**.

   g. Select **Add**.

   h. Select the **SOA** tab.

   i. Change the TTL directive to **3 days**.

   j. Select the **Records** tab.

   k. In the Record Key field, enter the appropriate *reverse FQDN* for your SLES 9 server. For example, if the IP address of your server were 192.168.1.47, you would enter **`47.1.168.192.in-addr.arpa.`**.

   l. Ensure that the Type drop-down list is set to **PTR**.

   m. In the Value field, enter **`fs1.cle9.com.`**.

   n. Select **Add**.

   o. Select **OK**.

   p. In the DNS Zones screen, select **Next**.

9. In the Finish Wizard screen, mark **On** under Start-Up Behavior.

10. Select **Finish**.

11. Open a terminal session.

12. At the shell prompt, enter su – and provide a password of tuX123.

13. At the shell prompt, enter **`tail /var/log/messages`**.

14. Verify that your forward and reverse zones were loaded properly by named.
15. Verify that your system is configured with the correct DNS server address by completing the following:
    a. At the shell prompt, enter **`cat /etc/resolv.conf`**.
    b. There should be a line that reads nameserver *your_server's_IP_address* and a line that reads search cle9.com. If this isn't the case, use YaST to make the necessary changes. (See Lab Exercise 2.2 for specific steps.)
16. Test your zones by completing the following:
    a. At the shell prompt, enter **`dig fs1.cle9.com`**. This should resolve to your DNS server's IP address.
    b. At the shell prompt, enter **`host`** ***`your_server's_IP_address`***. Your named daemon should return fs1.cle9.com as the hostname associated with IP address.

Congratulations! You now have a functional DNS server running on SLES 9.

With named running, you're ready to explore some advanced DNS features. Let's do that next.

Advanced DNS Configuration

TEST OBJECTIVE COVERED:

1. Configure a DNS server using BIND.

The DNS server you configured in Lab Exercise 3.1 is well suited for many networks. However, you should be aware of some advanced features and security issues. Although there are many subjects we could address, in this topic we'll focus on the following:

- Configuring forwarding
- Securing the DNS server
- Configuring LDAP support

Let's start with configuring DNS forwarding.

Configuring Forwarding

Recall that at the beginning of this chapter, we discussed how the DNS name resolution process works. We said that your DNS server, if asked to resolve a hostname for which it isn't authoritative, will first contact a root-level name server. The root-level name server will provide the IP address of a TLD name server. Your DNS server will then send the request to the TLD name server, which will respond with the IP address of the DNS server that is authoritative for the zone where the host resides (see Figure 3.7).

This process works reasonably well. However, two problems are associated with it:

- It creates a fair amount of network traffic.
- It can be somewhat slow.

If you want to see just how slow, give it a try on your SLES 9 server. Open a shell prompt and enter **dig** `www.novell.com` (or any other hostname for which your server isn't authoritative). You'll notice that it takes up to 3 seconds for you to get a response. If you enter the command a second time, dig provides a response instantly. That's because your named daemon cached the information the first time it made the query.

Forwarding is a feature of DNS that speeds things up. When you configure forwarding, your DNS server will directly contact another specified DNS server when it needs to resolve a name for which it isn't authoritative. The assumption is that the second DNS server has tons of names already in its cache. This saves the laborious process of finding the root server, then the TLD server, and then the authoritative server.

Forwarding is generally implemented in two situations:

- Your organization has implemented a DNS server hierarchy.
- Your network is connected to the Internet using an ISP who supplies a DNS server for customers to use.

I've never actually worked for an organization that uses a DNS server hierarchy; however, I've heard of some that do. Those that I know of are academic institutions that have many networks, usually each owned by a particular department. Each department has its own DNS server.

Rather than having all these separate DNS servers walking the DNS domain tree to resolve outside hostnames, they are configured to resolve up a chain of internal DNS servers. As a result, only one or two DNS servers go outside on the Internet. These servers cache huge numbers of names, which really speeds up the resolution process. This situation is depicted in Figure 3.34 below:

FIGURE 3.34
A sample DNS hierarchy for a college.

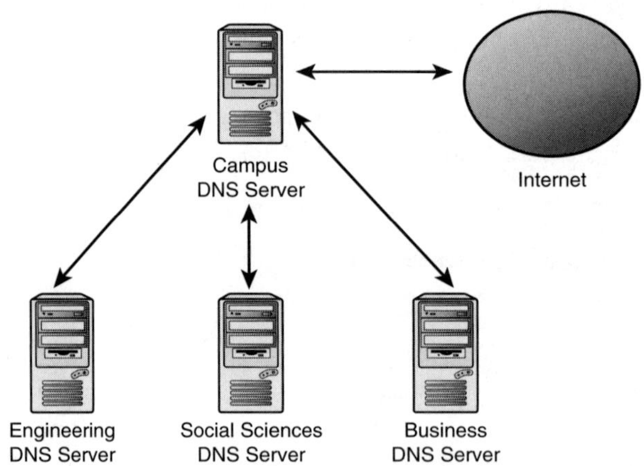

The situation I've seen more frequently is the second scenario presented. Many organizations go through an ISP to connect their network to the Internet. Most ISPs provide one or more DNS servers for their customers to use. You can use forwarding to point your DNS server to your ISP's DNS server. The assumption is that your ISP's DNS server gets used a lot and, therefore, has a lot of names in its cache. Again, this configuration saves your DNS server from having to walk the DNS tree to resolve names it's not authoritative for.

Forwarding is relatively easy to implement. To do this, complete the following:

1. Open `/etc/named.conf` file in a text editor.
2. Locate the Options directive and find the **`forwarders`** parameter, as shown in Figure 3.35:

FIGURE 3.35
Enabling DNS forwarding.

```
# Write dump and statistics file to the log subdirectory.  The
# pathenames are relative to the chroot jail.

dump-file "/var/log/named_dump.db";
statistics-file "/var/log/named.stats";

# The forwarders record contains a list of servers to which queries
# should be forwarded.  Enable this line and modify the IP address to
# your provider's name server.  Up to three servers may be listed.

#forwarders { 192.0.2.1; 192.0.2.2; };

# Enable the next entry to prefer usage of the name server declared in
# the forwarders section.

#forward first;

# The listen-on record contains a list of local network interfaces to
# listen on.  Optionally the port can be specified.  Default is to
# listen on all interfaces found on your system.  The default port is
# 53.
--More--
```

3. Uncomment the `forwarders` line.
4. Within the curly brackets, enter the IP addresses of the servers you want your DNS server to forward requests to (separated by semicolons).
5. Uncomment the `forward first` line.

With these option enabled, the server will first query the DNS servers listed in the `forwarders` line. If, for some reason, it can't get an answer, it will proceed with the traditional DNS name resolution process.

Now that you understand forwarding, let's look at some steps you can take to increase the security of your DNS server.

Securing the DNS Server

In the past, a number of attacks on servers have been perpetrated through the BIND service. Fortunately for us, many of these attacks have been mitigated because vulnerabilities were fixed in BIND version 9.*x*. In spite of these fixes, you still need to do a number of things to secure your DNS service as well as the server it runs on. These include the following:

- Running named in a chroot Jail
- Restricting Zone Transfers
- Using ACLs

Let's first look at putting your named daemon in jail!

RUNNING NAMED IN A CHROOT JAIL

One of the main problems in earlier BIND releases was that the named daemon ran as root by default. The service needed access to a variety of files in the file system as well as access to the system log; to make this possible, named ran as root.

Although this accomplished the goal, it also opened up a big security hole. Because named ran as root, it had full and unfettered access to the entire system. If a hacker were to discover a way to exploit the named daemon (and it did actually happen) then he or she could gain access to the system with root-level access. Yikes!

To fix this problem, you need to configure named to run as a different user. Better still, you need to create a chroot jail and run named within it.

NOTE

I'm assuming here that you already know about chroot jails from your CLP courseware. If you need more information, see the SLES 9 documentation available from http://www.novell.com.

By doing this, you deny named root access and you deny it access to anything outside its own directory structure in the file system.

So, how do you go about doing this? In the old days we had to do this manually. It was a fairly complicated process, not for the faint of heart.

TIP

A great HOWTO is available from http://www.tldp.org that goes through the process step by step. It's called chroot-BIND HOWTO.

Fortunately for us, we don't have to worry about it. Why not? The version of BIND 9 that you installed in Lab Exercise 2.1 automatically installs named into a chroot jail! To verify this, open `/etc/sysconfig/named` in a text editor, as shown in Figure 3.36.

FIGURE 3.36
Running named in a chroot jail.

```
## Path: Network/DNS/Name Server
## Description: Names server settings

## Type: yesno
## Default: yes
## ServiceRestart: named
#
# Shall the DNS server 'named' run in the chroot jail /var/lib/named/?
#
# Each time you start 'named' with the init script, /etc/named.conf,
# /etc/named.conf.include, /etc/rndc.key, and all files listed in
# NAMED_CONF_INCLUDE_FILES will be copied relative to /var/lib/named/.
#
# The pid file will be in /var/lib/named/var/run/named/named.pid.
#
NAMED_RUN_CHROOTED="yes"

## Type: string
## Default: ""
## ServiceReload: named
#
# If you enter the names of any include files here, all conf files will
# be copied relativ to /var/lib/named/, when 'named' is started in the
"./named" 61L, 1800C                                        1,1          Top
```

Notice that, by default, the `NAMED_RUN_CHROOTED` parameter is set to `yes`. The chroot jail is located in `/var/lib/named`. Notice also that each time the service is stated, the various named configuration files are copied from their locations elsewhere in the file system into the jail, eliminating the need for named to access other directories and files in the file system.

Because named now runs in a chroot jail by default, it no longer runs as root. Have a look at Figure 3.37.

Notice that named runs using the named user account. Hats off to the BIND 9 developers! They have really made our lives as system administrators a lot easier.

Now that we've discussed running named in a chroot jail, let's look at our next security topic: restricting user access to your DNS server.

RESTRICTING USER ACCESS TO THE DNS SERVER

By default, the DNS service running on your server is wide open for anyone to use. Depending on your situation, this may or may not be an issue for you.

If your DNS server resides on your local area network behind your organization's firewall, restricting user access may not be an issue. Because of where it's located, the only users who will be able to access it are authorized users.

FIGURE 3.37
Running named using the named User Account.

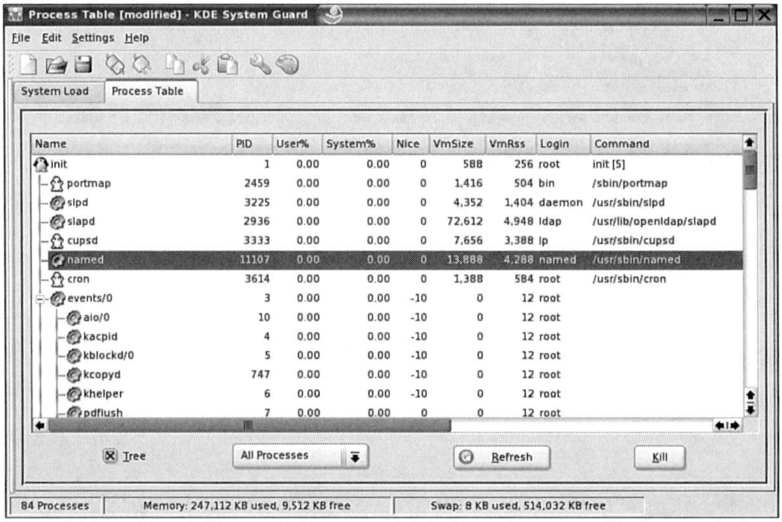

However, if your DNS server resides in your organization's demilitarized zone (DMZ), which is a very common situation, you may want to configure restrictions that define who can use the service. Otherwise, it's wide open for anyone on the Internet (who know its IP address) to use.

To restrict user access, you use the *allow-query* directive. Inserting this directive in your `named.conf` file allows you to specify a list of IP addresses that are allowed to submit queries for name resolution to the DNS service. The allow-query directive is followed by a list of IP addresses, separated by semicolons.

NOTE

Unfortunately, BIND doesn't offer a way to control access with user authentication. The only option you have is to create restrictions based on the IP address of the system sending the query.

You may be saying at this point, "Whoa! I don't want to have to list each and every IP address that's allowed to use the DNS server!" You're right—that could represent a monumental task, especially if your network is a big one. Fortunately, the allow-query directive allows you to use network addresses as well as IP addresses. This allows the DNS server to respond to queries from all hosts on the specified network. This is shown in Figure 3.38:

FIGURE 3.38
Restricting user access.

```
# should be forwarded.  Enable this line and modify the IP address to
# your provider's name server.  Up to three servers may be listed.

#forwarders { 192.0.2.1; 192.0.2.2; };

# Enable the next entry to prefer usage of the name server declared in
# the forwarders section.

#forward first;

allow-query {192.168.1.0/24; };


# The listen-on record contains a list of local network interfaces to
# listen on.  Optionally the port can be specified.  Default is to
# listen on all interfaces found on your system.  The default port is
# 53.

#listen-on port 53 { 127.0.0.1; };

# The listen-on-v6 record enables or disables listening on IPv6
# interfaces.  Allowed values are 'any' and 'none' or a list of
# addresses.
-- INSERT --                                          40,40         23%
```

In Figure 3.38, the allow-query directive has been inserted within the options statement of the `named.conf` file. By placing this directive here, the restriction will apply to all zones hosted by the local DNS server. In this example, the DNS server has been configured to respond only to queries that come from systems whose IP address is 192.168.1.*x*.

NOTE

The /24 parameter after the network address specifies the subnet mask associated with the address. The parameter *24* indicates how many bits are in the subnet mask. Remember that each octet of an IP address or subnet mask is composed of 8 bits (hence the term "octet"). Each bit can have a value of 0 or 1.

In this case, 24 bits indicates that the first three octets of the subnet mask each have all their bits set to the value of 1. The last octet has all of its bits set to 0. The decimal equivalent of the binary number 11111111 is 255. Therefore, the /24 parameter indicates that the subnet mask for this address is 255.255.255.0.

If a host with an IP address outside the specified range sends a query for name resolution to the DNS server, it will deny the request.

TIP

You can also use any as a parameter with the allow-query directive instead of IP addresses. However, that's the named daemon's default behavior; I haven't seen it used this way very often.

There may be situations in which your DNS server is hosting multiple zones and you want to restrict access on a per-zone basis. Can you do it with the allow-query directive? You bet!

In addition to the options statement, you can also place allow-query directives within each zone declaration. By doing so, you can customize the hosts that can query each zone.

For example, suppose your DNS server has two zones: cle9.com and somedomain.com. You want to restrict the cle9.com zone to users on the network segment that has the IP address of 192.168.1.0. Likewise, you want to restrict somedomain.com to users on a different network segment: 192.168.2.0. To do this, you would add the allow-query directive to each zone, as shown:

```
zone "cle9.com" in {
    file "master/cle9.com";
    type master;
    allow-query (192.168.1.0/24;);
};

zone "somedomain.com" in {
    file "master/somedomain.com";
    type master;
    allow-query (192.168.2.0;);
};
```

Now that you know how to lock down user access to your DNS server, the next thing you need to know is how to restrict zone transfers.

RESTRICTING ZONE TRANSFERS

Recall our earlier discussion of master and slave DNS servers. We said that slave DNS servers are implemented to provide a degree of fault tolerance to your name resolution system. They do this by periodically transferring zone information from your master DNS server. This process is called a *zone transfer*.

After a zone transfer has occurred, the slave DNS server can resolve hostnames just like a master DNS server. However, any modifications or updates that need to be made to the zone must be made to the master server and then replicated out to the slave server. Any changes you make to a slave DNS server will be lost when the next zone transfer occurs.

The problem with zone transfers is that, by default, your master server is wide open. Anyone who knows your server's IP address can initiate a zone transfer. Although there may be some who don't care, the rest of us care a great deal. It adds significant overhead to your DNS server and it also provides the other party with a list of hostnames and IP addresses on your network that you probably don't want them to have.

The good news is that you can lock down zone transfers. This is done with the *allow-transfer* directive in your `named.conf` file. This directive allows you to specify which slave servers are allowed to initiate a zone transfer with your server. The allow-transfer directive is followed by a list of IP addresses of servers, separated by a semicolon, that are allowed to transfer zone data from your server.

If you want to establish a blanket rule for all zones hosted by the DNS server, you can insert an allow-transfer directive within the options statement in your `named.conf` file, just like the allow-query directive. An example is shown in Figure 3.39:

FIGURE 3.39
Restricting zone transfers.

```
        # interfaces.  Allowed values are 'any' and 'none' or a list of
        # addresses.

        listen-on-v6 { any; };

        # The next three statements may be needed if a firewall stands between
        # the local server and the internet.

        #query-source address * port 53;
        #transfer-source * port 53;
        #notify-source * port 53;

        # The allow-query record contains a list of networks or IP addresses
        # to accept and deny queries from. The default is to allow queries
        # from all hosts.

        #allow-query { 127.0.0.1; };

        allow-transfer {192.168.1.48; };

        # If notify is set to yes (default), notify messages are sent to other
        # name servers when the the zone data is changed.  Instead of setting
        # a global 'notify' statement in the 'options' section, a separate
-- INSERT --                                                66,41          39%
```

In Figure 3.39, the named daemon has been configured to allow zone transfers only with the DNS server that has an IP address of 192.168.1.48. Because it's listed within the options statement, zone transfers for all zones hosted by named on this server are limited to this single slave DNS server.

Suppose you don't use a slave DNS server and you don't want anyone to be able to initiate a zone transfer? You can do this as well with the allow-transfer directive. Simply add the following somewhere within the options statement of your server's named.conf file:

```
allow-transfer {"none"; };
```

You may encounter situations in which you need to configure zone transfer restrictions on a per-zone basis. Many times, you many want one zone on your DNS server to synchronize with one slave DNS server and other zone on your DNS server to synchronize with a different slave server.

This can also be done with the allow-transfer directive. Instead of putting the directive in the options statement of **named.conf**, you put it within the zone declaration itself in the file.

For example, suppose your DNS server hosts two zones; cle9.com and somedomain.com. You want zone transfers for cle9.com to be restricted to a slave server with an IP address of 192.168.1.48. You also want zone transfers for somedomain.com to be restricted to a slave server with an IP address of 192.168.1.49. To do this, you would configure each zone declaration within your **named.conf** file with its allow-transfer directive, as shown:

```
zone "cle9.com" in {
    file "master/cle9.com";
    type master;
    allow-transfer (192.168.1.48;);
};

zone "somedomain.com" in {
    file "master/somedomain.com";
    type master;
    allow-transfer (192.168.1.49;);
};
```

If you're managing a large DNS implementation with many zones and complex access rules for user queries and zone transfers, you may want to consider using Access Control Lists (ACLs) for your DNS server to simplify this process. Let's look at those next.

USING ACLS

With DNS you can define ACLs that you can use to configure your restrictions.

NOTE

Don't confuse DNS ACLs with the ACLs used in your Linux server's file system. They are two different things.

With a DNS ACL, you define an access control list in your **named.conf** file. Then you can reference these ACLs when you use the allow-query and allow-transfer directives. The general syntax in the named.conf file is the following:

```
acl acl_name {list_of_addresses; };
```

The `acl` statement is parallel with the options and zone statements. Be sure you don't place it within the options statement. The **acl_name** parameter is any name you want to give the ACL. You will use this name in other directives, such as allow-query, to reference back to the ACL. The list of addresses parameter is a list of IP addresses or network addresses you want to include in the ACL.

For example, suppose you want to configure your DNS server so that queries are restricted to two network segments: 192.168.1.0 and 192.168.2.0. You could create an ACL in your `named.conf` file as shown:

```
acl allowedhosts {192.168.1.0; 192.168.2.0; };
```

Then you could insert an allow-query directive within the options statement that references the ACL, as shown:

```
allow-query {allowedhosts;};
```

Using ACLs can save you a lot of typing and prevent a lot of typos. You can also use YaST to define ACLs in your named.conf file by doing the following:

1. Start YaST.
2. Select **Network Services, DNS Server**.
3. In the left frame, select **ACLs**. When you do, the screen in Figure 3.40 is displayed:

FIGURE 3.40
Defining ACLs in YaST.

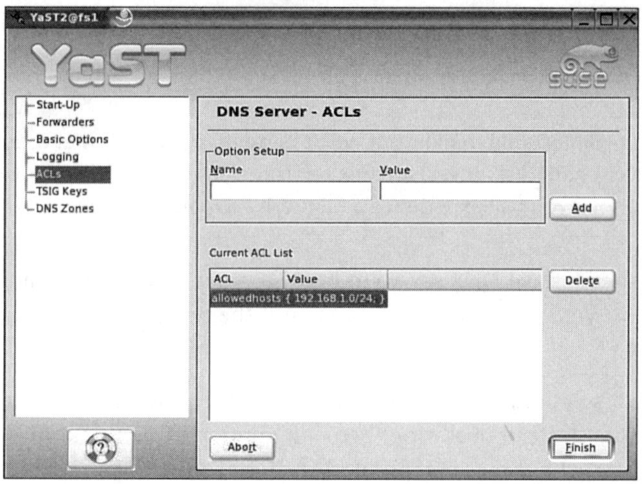

4. In the Name field, enter a *name* for your ACL.
5. In the Value field, enter the IP address(es) you want included in the ACL. If you use more than one, be sure to separate them with a semicolon. Don't worry about entering brackets; YaST puts them in automatically for you.
6. Select **Add, Finish**.

Recall earlier that I mentioned that you could use **any** and **none** in your allow-query and allow-transfer directives? These are predefined ACLs that are automatically implemented when you installed BIND.

Now that you've learned how to lock down your DNS server, we need to cover one last topic in this course—configuring your DNS server to store information in the LDAP directory.

Configuring LDAP Support

Recall that in Chapter 1 when we were discussing LDAP, I mentioned that one of the advantages of LDAP was that, in addition to user accounts, you could store your DNS configuration in the directory.

Why would you want to? Admittedly, this is a new concept for most Linux system administrators. I've not seen many production systems configured to work this way. It may take a while to catch on. However, after you understand the benefits of using LDAP for DNS, you may have a hard time going back.

The main problem with the traditional DNS configuration is that important information is stored locally in text files. If something were to happen to your server, your name resolution system is gone.

NOTE

Don't let yourself get comfortable thinking, "It won't happen to me...." Remember that computer components (especially hard disk drives) are mechanical/electrical devices that wear out over time. It's not a matter of *if* you will experience a failure, it's a matter of *when*.

Even if you configured a slave DNS server to back up your zone data, a natural catastrophe could still take down your name resolution system if the servers were located in the same geographic location.

Storing your name resolution information in LDAP, on the other hand, makes your DNS system less server-centric. Instead of storing the configuration in local text files, the data is stored in the LDAP directory, which can be replicated and used among many servers.

In the event of a hardware failure or a natural disaster, any other server in the network can instantly take the role of the DNS server. There's no backups to restore, no files to copy.

TIP

If you've ever worked with Novell's DNS implementation on NetWare 5 and later, you already know how useful this can be. NetWare stores its DNS configuration in eDirectory, which is an LDAP-compliant, distributed, and replicated directory service. If the NetWare server hosting DNS goes down, any other NetWare server in the directory tree can immediately take over by simply loading `NAMED.NLM` and pointing it to the configuration information in the eDirectory tree.

To integrate your DNS server into the LDAP directory, complete the following:

1. Start YaST and su to root.
2. Select **Network Services**, **DNS Server**.
3. In the left frame, select **Start-Up**. The screen in Figure 3.41 is displayed:

FIGURE 3.41
Configuring LDAP Support.

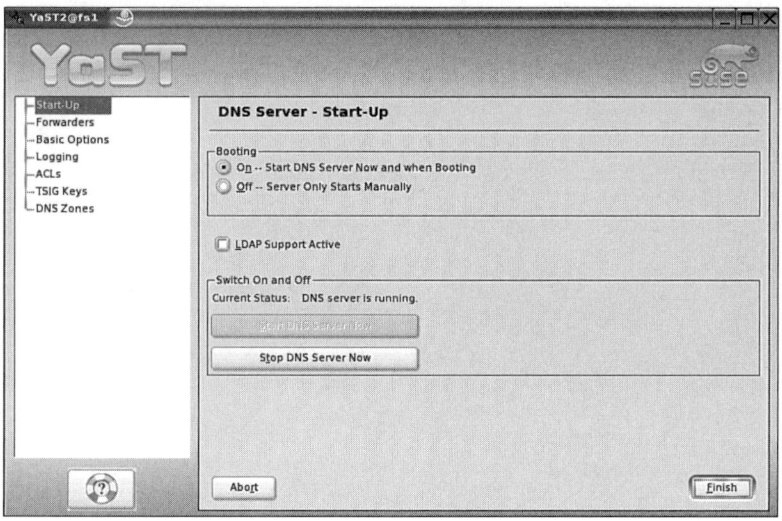

4. Mark **LDAP Support Active**; then select **Finish**.
5. When prompted, enter the password for your Administrator LDAP user account.
6. Wait while the changes are applied.

Your DNS zone information is then saved in the LDAP directory, as shown in Figure 3.42:

FIGURE 3.42
DNS Zones in LDAP.

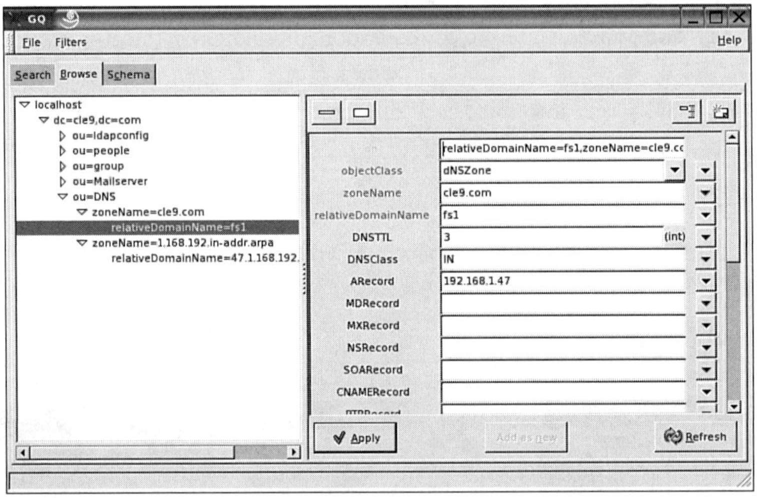

Let's practice performing these tasks on your DNS server in Lab Exercise 3.2.

Lab Exercise 3.2: Advanced DNS Configuration

In this lab exercise, you will use YaST to configure forwarding, DNS security, and LDAP support. To complete this exercise, you will need your lab PC system that you installed SLES 9 on in Lab Exercise 2.1 and configured in Lab Exercise 3.1.

Complete the following:

1. Boot your SLES 9 server.
2. Authenticate as **tux** with a password of **SuSE789**.
3. Start YaST.
4. When prompted, supply a root password of **tuX123**.
5. Select **Network Services**, **DNS Server**.
6. Configuring DNS forwarding by completing the following:
   a. In the left frame, select **Forwarders**.
   b. Mark **Set Forwarders Manually**.
   c. In the IP Address field, enter the *IP address* of your ISP's DNS server.
   d. Select **Add**.
7. Configure an ACL by completing the following:
   a. In the left frame, select **ACLs**.
   b. In the Name field, enter **allowedhosts**.
   c. In the Value field, enter your *network address* and *subnet mask*. For example, if your network address is 192.168.1.0 and your subnet mask is 255.255.255.0, you would enter **192.168.1.0/24**.
   d. Select **Add**.
8. Restrict DNS queries to hosts on your network segment by completing the following:
   a. In the left frame, select **Basic Options**.
   b. In the Option drop-down list, select **allow-query**.
   c. In the Value field, enter **{allowedhosts; }**.
   d. Select **Add**.

9. Select **Finish**.

10. Verify the changes by completing the following:

    a. Open a terminal session.

    c. Switch to your root user.

    b. At the shell prompt, enter **`cat /etc/named.conf |more`**.

    c. Verify that your changes were made.

11. Configure LDAP support by completing the following:

    a. In YaST, select **DNS Server**.

    b. In the left frame, select **Start-Up**.

    c. Mark LDAP Support Active.

    d. When prompted that perl-ldap needs to be installed, select **Continue**.

    e. When prompted, insert your *SLES 9 CD 3*; then select **Continue**.

    f. Wait while the package is installed. (Leave your CD in the drive; we'll need it in just a minute.)

    g. In the DNS Server Start-Up screen, select **Finish**.

    h. When prompted for the LDAP Server password, enter **`tuX123`**.

12. To view the contents of the LDAP directory on your server, you have to install the gq client. To do this, complete the following:

    a. In YaST, select Software, Install and Remove Software.

    b. In the Search field, enter **`gq`**; then select **Search**.

    c. Mark the **gq** package; then select **Accept**.

    d. Wait while the package is installed.

13. Verify that your DNS zone information was imported into your LDAP directory by doing the following:

    a. Select **N**, **System**, **GQ LDAP Client**.

    b. Select **File, Preferences**.

    c. Select **Servers**.

    d. Select **localhost, Edit**.

e. Select **Details**.

f. In the Bind DN field, enter **`cn=Administrator,dc=cle9,dc=com`**.

g. Select **OK, OK**.

h. Select the **Browse** tab.

i. Expand **localhost**.

j. When prompted for a password, enter **`tuX123`**.

k. Expand **dc=cle9,dc=com**.

l. Expand **ou=DNS**.

m. Browse your zone records to verify that they were imported properly.

14. Close GQ and YaST.

Congratulations! You now have a locked-down DNS server that's integrated with your LDAP directory.

That's it for this chapter. Before we go to Chapter 4, "Configuring DHCP on SLES 9," let's review what you've learned.

Summary

In this chapter, we first reviewed the way DNS works. We talked about the DNS namespace and the process a DNS server goes through to resolve hostnames. We then reviewed the difference between forward- and reverse-lookup zones. Then we discussed implementing master and slave DNS servers to increase fault tolerance.

We finally implemented BIND on our SLES 9 server and reviewed the various files that are used to configure the named services, including `named.conf`, `root.hint`, and zone files.

We then shifted gears and looked at some more advanced DNS configuration issues. First we looked at using forwarding to speed up the response time of your DNS server.

Next, we looked at a variety of DNS security issues. We reviewed how to run named in a chroot jail as a nonroot user. We also talked about restricting access to the DNS server using DNS ACLs.

Finally, you learned how to integrate your DNS server configuration into an LDAP directory service.

We're ready now to move on to Chapter 4, where you will learn how to implement a DCHP server on SLES 9. However, we're not through with DNS yet. In Chapter 4, you will learn how to tie your DNS service and your DHCP service together so that your DNS database is automatically updated whenever your DHCP server assigns an IP address.

CHAPTER 4

Configuring DHCP on SLES 9

This chapter covers the following requirement for Novell's Certified Linux Engineer (CLE) 9 certification:

1. Use DHCP to manage networks.

In the previous chapter, we discussed how users expect to be able to fire up a browser and wander the Web. To provide this functionality, you learned how to implement BIND on your SLES 9 server.

Even more basic than name resolution, users also expect to be able to come into the office at the beginning of the workday, turn on their workstations, and have everything just "work."

When it comes to configuring network settings, they don't want to touch anything—and you probably don't want them to. You need to automate the process by implementing the Dynamic Host Configuration Protocol (DHCP) in your network.

In this chapter, we're going to cover how to do that by implementing the dhcpd daemon on your SLES 9 server. Let's begin by talking about how DHCP works.

Managing DHCP Networks

TEST OBJECTIVE COVERED:

1. Use DHCP to manage networks.

We pretty much take for granted that the majority of computer networks in the world today run on the TCP/IP protocol. However, it wasn't long ago that this wasn't necessarily the case. Until the mid-1990s, there was a fairly even split between networks that ran using the Internetwork Packet Exchange (IPX) protocol, the Network Basic Input/Output System (NetBIOS) protocol, and the Internet Protocol (IP). Basically, if you had a Novell NetWare network, you ran IPX. If you had a Microsoft Windows network, you ran NetBIOS. If you were running Unix, you were running IP.

Although they aren't used extensively anymore, IPX and NetBIOS had some unique characteristics that made them very user friendly. Key among these was that they provided automatic address configuration functionality. As long as the protocol was installed, all you had to do was plug a network host into the wall jack and turn it on. The protocol stack would automatically configure its own network settings and everything just "worked."

Today, IPX and NetBIOS networks aren't implemented very often. IP has become the network protocol of choice for most organizations. IP runs reasonably fast and its advanced routing capabilities make it ideal for worldwide networks such as the Internet.

However, IP doesn't have automatic address configuration capabilities built into the protocol itself. By default, the IP protocol must be manually configured on each host in the network. This is called *static configuration*. Let's look at how it works.

Statically Configuring IP Addresses

How do you statically configure IP addresses? Basically, you do it the hard way. You, as the network administrator, walk around to each and every network host on the network and manually configure (at a minimum) the following:

- IP address
- Subnet mask
- Default gateway router address
- DNS server address

On a small, static network, this is generally a doable task. Annoying, perhaps, but doable. If you can get the initial configuration done, everything should function properly thereafter with little additional work on your part.

However, on a large network (more than about 20 systems), using a static configuration strategy can become completely unmanageable. You would probably spend most of your time just running around configuring IP addresses. Aside from initially assigning addresses, several other problems occur with the manual addressing strategy.

First, a very small change to your network requires a huge amount of work. For example, suppose you support an IP network with 300 hosts and your DNS server just underwent a major hardware meltdown. To keep things running, you've moved the DNS service over to another server in your network.

So far so good. However, for the other hosts on the network to use the new DNS server, you will have to walk around to each and every system and manually change its DNS server address. As you can probably guess, this process can be labor intensive and time consuming, which costs your organization money it probably doesn't want to spend.

Second, static IP addressing is very inefficient in terms of address allocation. For some administrators this is a serious issue; for others, it isn't. If your organization uses a private addressing scheme in conjunction with a NAT router, you probably don't care whether your addressing strategy is efficient. You've got addresses to burn.

NOTE

In RFC 1918, the Internet Assigned Numbers Authority (IANA) specifies three blocks of IP addresses that anyone can use for private addressing. These are 10.0.0.0 to 10.255.255.255 (Class A), 172.16.0.0 to 172.31.255.255 (Class B), and 192.168.0.0 to 192.168.255.255 (Class C).

Networks using these address ranges are usually implemented in conjunction with a Network Address Translation (NAT) router that connects the private network to a public network that uses registered IP addresses. This allows an entire network segment to consume only a single registered IP address, which is assigned to the public interface of the NAT router.

However, not all organizations use private addressing. Many larger organizations use a block of registered IP addresses that are assigned to all hosts on the network, including servers, workstations, and printers. In this situation, efficient use of addresses is very important to you. Organizations that use all registered IP addresses usually find themselves in a constant battle to keep usage of addresses to a minimum. There's never enough addresses to go around.

The heart of the problem is that, when statically assigning addresses, you have to permanently allocate one address for each and every host in your network. That host consumes that address 24 hours a day, 7 days a week, regardless of whether the host is actually in use.

For example, suppose your company runs two shifts: days and nights. In this scenario, only about one-half of your employees are actually on site at any given time. Likewise, only about one-half of your computer systems will be powered on at a time. The half that are powered off are consuming costly registered addresses even though they aren't in use.

How do you get around these problems? You use a dynamic address assignment strategy.

Dynamically Assigning Addresses

With a dynamic address assignment strategy, you configure a server in your network to automatically assign IP addresses to hosts when they connect to the network. Over the years, three approaches have been implemented:

- RARP
- BOOTP
- DHCP

Let's look at each of these.

RARP

Back in the early days of IP networks, the Reverse Address Resolution Protocol (RARP) was used to assign IP addresses to network hosts. RARP worked in the opposite manner as the Address Resolution Protocol (ARP).

To understand how RARP can be used to assign IP addresses, you need to understand that IP addresses are associated with the Network layer of the OSI model. If you move down the OSI model to the Data Link layer, you can't use IP addresses to identify network hosts; you have to use Media Access Control (MAC) addresses.

A MAC address is a 48-bit hexadecimal address that is burned into the read-only memory (ROM) chip on every network board in the world. Theoretically, every network board manufactured has a globally unique MAC address. No two NICs should have the same MAC address.

If you want to see the MAC address assigned to your network board, you can issue the `ifconfig` command at a shell prompt, as shown in Figure 4.1.

TIP

You can also view this information with the `ip address show` command.

FIGURE 4.1
Viewing a host's MAC address.

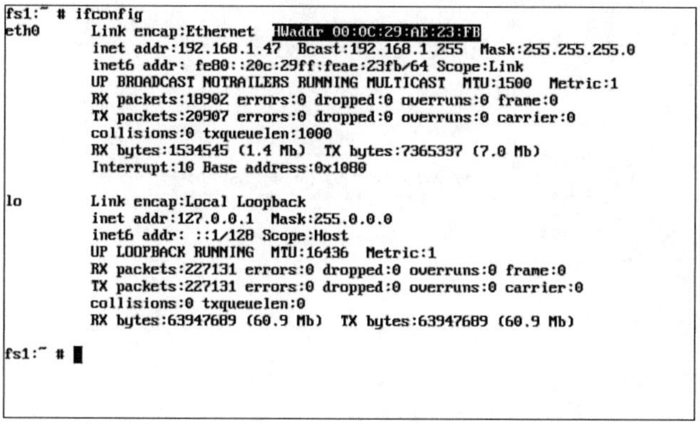

In Figure 4.1, the NIC in the system has a MAC address of 00:0C:29:AE:23:FB. When you initiate any communication between two IP hosts, the sending system must first resolve the destination system's IP address into a MAC address. This is done using the ARP protocol, which is automatically installed whenever you install the IP protocol on a network host.

The sending host sends out an ARP broadcast asking for the hardware address of the host with the specified IP address, as shown in Figure 4.2:

FIGURE 4.2
The ARP process.

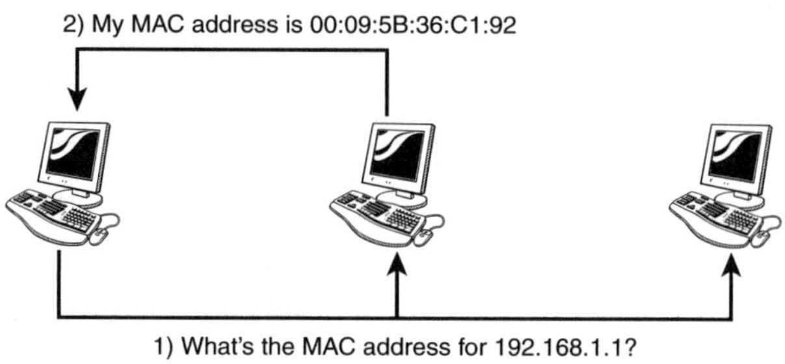

The host configured with the requested IP address responds to the ARP; all other hosts ignore the request. The responding host replies to the sending station with its MAC address, as shown in Figure 4.2.

After this is done, the sending host stores the IP address-to-MAC address mapping in its ARP table. You can view the ARP table on a host by issuing the **`arp -a`** command from a shell prompt, as shown in Figure 4.3:

FIGURE 4.3
The ARP table.

```
fs1:~ # arp -a
? (192.168.1.1) at 00:09:5B:36:C1:92 [ether] on eth0
? (192.168.1.46) at 00:0A:E9:0E:A1:92 [ether] on eth0
fs1:~ #
```

If the sending host needs to contact the destination host again in the future, it checks its ARP table first and pulls the MAC address from there instead of sending another ARP request.

The RARP process works in the opposite manner. Instead of requesting the MAC address of another host, with RARP a host sends out a request that essentially says, "What's the IP address for my MAC address?" This is shown in Figure 4.4:

FIGURE 4.4
The RARP process.

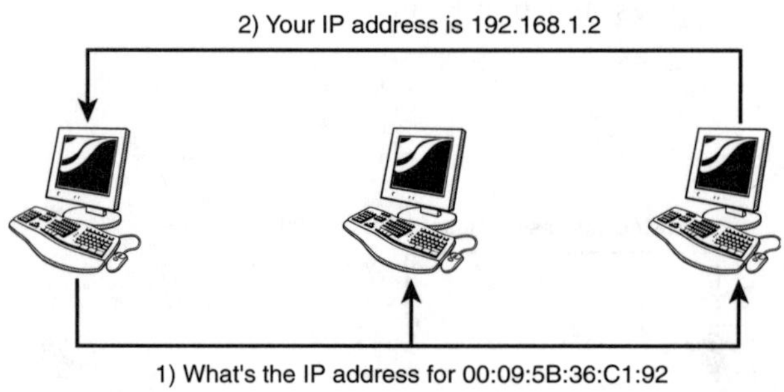

The RARP server responds with an IP address. The system administrator must configure the RARP server beforehand with a table that maps MAC addresses to IP addresses.

This process for assigning IP addresses worked, but it had some limitations:

- It still required a considerable amount of manual configuration to set up. The network administrator had to go around to each host and record its MAC address. Then he or she had to create the mapping table on the RARP server to link the IP address with associated MAC addresses.

- Because the system administrator had to establish a one-to-one mapping between IP and MAC addresses, RARP didn't conserve IP addresses.
- RARP could assign only an IP address to a host. It couldn't assign the subnet mask, gateway router address, or DNS server address.

To address these limitations, another protocol was developed and implemented called BOOTP. Let's review BOOTP next.

BOOTP

The BOOTP protocol is defined in RFC 951. The BOOTP protocol is much more complex than RARP. It was originally designed for workstations without hard or floppy disk drives, but can be used by regular systems as well. The BOOTP process is divided into two phases:

- Phase 1—In phase 1, the host system needing an IP address sends out a broadcast on the network. The BOOTP server responds with an IP address and other associated parameters, such as the subnet mask, DNS server address, and gateway router address.
- Phase 2—In phase 2, the BOOTP server transfers operating system startup files to the requesting system using the Trivial File Transfer Protocol (TFTP). The host uses these files to boot the operating system.

As you can see, BOOTP is much more powerful than RARP. It enables you to fully configure the IP stack on the requesting workstation. However, it still had a key limitation. Like RARP, a BOOTP server used a one-to-one mapping of MAC addresses to IP addresses.

Therefore, as with RARP, the system administrator still had to gather all the MAC addresses on the network and build a table of mappings from them. Accordingly, BOOTP didn't conserve IP addresses very well because of the one-to-one mapping of IP addresses to MAC addresses. Even though a given machine may not be powered on, it still had an IP address allocated to it, and no one else could use it.

As you can probably guess, RARP and BOOTP aren't widely implemented anymore. Instead, we use a much more powerful protocol: DHCP.

DHCP

DHCP is defined in RFC 2131 and is based on the BOOTP protocol. With the DHCP service running on a server in your network, hosts configured to use DHCP broadcast a request for IP configuration parameters when they boot. The DHCP server responds to the broadcast and the two negotiate an IP address assignment (we'll talk more about this process later in the chapter).

NOTE

DHCP still supports many BOOTP functions, which allows it to provide IP addresses to BOOTP clients as well as DHCP clients.

DHCP is widely implemented because it's very powerful. Like RARP and BOOTP, DHCP eliminates the need for you to walk around to every system and manually configure IP address parameters. It's all taken care of automatically when the host boots.

Like BOOTP, it also configures more than just the IP address. With DHCP, you can configure network hosts with IP addresses, the subnet mask, the DNS server IP address, and the address of the gateway router.

Also like BOOTP, DHCP makes it easy to deploy changes in your network. Previously, I presented a scenario where the address of the DNS server in your network had changed. With DHCP, this change is very easy to deploy. You modify the appropriate option in the DHCP server's configuration and the new address will be automatically deployed the next time systems renew their DHCP leases.

DHCP also addresses the shortcomings associated with RARP and BOOTP. First, DHCP doesn't have to use a one-to-one mapping of IP addresses to MAC addresses the way RARP and BOOTP do. DCHP offers three modes of allocating IP addresses:

- Manual Allocation—This mode operates in the same manner as RARP and BOOTP. In the DHCP server's configuration, you manually map a given MAC address to a specific IP address. This ensures that a particular host will always have the same IP address. This is useful for network hosts, such as servers.

NOTE

Personally, I don't use manual allocation very often. If I have a network host (such as a server) that must always have the same IP address, I usually assign it statically and create an exclusion for that address in the DHCP server's configuration. There are pros and cons to both approaches.

- Automatic Allocation—This mode is similar to the manual allocation mode, except the administrator doesn't have to manually create the MAC-to-IP address mappings. With automatic allocation, the DHCP server assigns a particular host an IP address from a defined range of addresses. The DHCP server records the MAC address to which the IP address was assigned. From then on, the host with that MAC address will always be assigned that same IP address.

NOTE

Sometimes you will see automatic allocation referred to as *permanent allocation.* In my experience, automatic allocation mode is rarely implemented.

- Dynamic Allocation—In dynamic allocation mode, you configure your DHCP server with a range of IP addresses that it can assign to network hosts. When it receives a request from a network host, the DHCP server takes the next available address from the range and assigns it to the host for a fixed period of time, called the *lease*. When the lease expires or when the host system is shut down, the IP address is released and can be assigned to another network host.

Using the dynamic allocation mode, DHCP helps you conserve IP addresses. Only the systems that are powered on and in use consume addresses. This rectifies the shortcoming associated with static configuration, RARP, and BOOTP, where each host on the network is allocated an IP address regardless of whether it is in use.

For example, earlier we discussed a scenario where a company runs two shifts of employees. With static addressing, RARP, or BOOTP, every system in the network must be allocated an IP address. If the company had 500 systems, you would need 500 addresses.

With DHCP, however, you assign addresses only to systems that are powered on. In this scenario, only 250 or so addresses would be needed at any given time. This is a real benefit to organizations that use registered IP addresses.

NOTE

Since 1998, you have to pay for every IP address that is registered to your organization.

Because of these benefits, DHCP is very widely implemented, and you need know how to properly implement and maintain a DHCP server. In this chapter, you'll learn how to do this on your SLES 9 server.

Before doing so, however, it's critical that you understand what happens "under the hood" of DHCP. Let's take a look at the DHCP in more detail.

How DHCP Works

The first thing you need to understand about DHCP is that it is a client/server protocol. For DHCP to work, you must have the following:

- A DHCP service running on one of your network servers.
- A DHCP client service running on the network hosts that will request IP addresses from the DHCP server.

To obtain an IP address, the DHCP client and the DHCP server communicate with each other using the process shown in Figure 4.5:

FIGURE 4.5
The DHCP process.

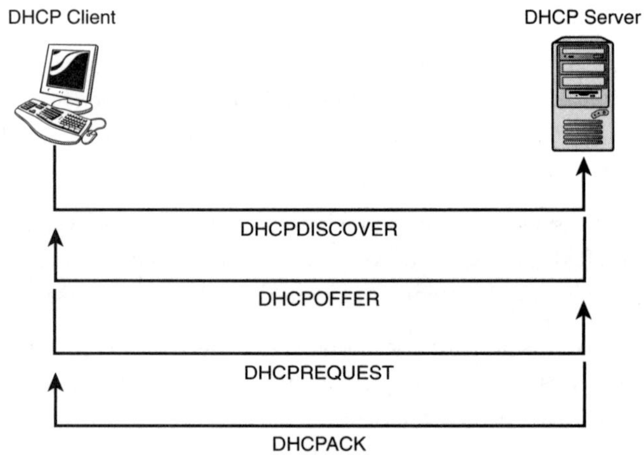

When a network host that is configured as a DHCP client is booted, it sends out a DHCPDISCOVER broadcast, as shown in Figure 4.5. The DHCP server receives the broadcast and selects an IP address from its range of available addresses that it can assign to the DHCP client.

NOTE

For the DHCP service to work on your server, you must have broadcasting enabled on your NIC. Use `ifconfig` to verify that this is so.

The server creates a proposal and sends the information in a DHCPOFFER message back to the requesting host, as shown in Figure 4.5. If more than one DHCP server is on the network segment, the DHCP client will receive a DHCPOFFER message from each server.

The DHCP client will then select the offer it wants to accept. If multiple DHCPOFFER messages were sent, the client usually opts for the first one it received.

After it has selected an offer, the DHCP client sends a DHCPREQUEST broadcast, as shown in Figure 4.5. This broadcast accomplishes two things:

- It informs the selected DHCP server that it has accepted the addressing information it has offered.
- It informs the other DHCP servers that sent a DHCPOFFER message that their offer has been rejected and they can retract their offers.

NOTE

Remember that the DHCPREQUEST message is a broadcast. That's why it can communicate with all the DHCP servers at once.

The DHCP server whose offer was accepted then responds to the DHCP client with a DHCPACK message, as shown in Figure 4.5. The DHCPACK message contains an IP address, the appropriate subnet mask, the gateway router's IP address, the DNS server's address, and a *lease*. The DHCP lease is a set period of time during which the DHCP client may use the IP address it has sent.

DHCP leases provide you with a valuable tool in managing your network's IP addresses. To understand DHCP leases, you need to understand that there are two ways in which an assigned IP address can be returned to the pool of addresses available for assignment:

- If the DHCP client host is powered off.
- If the DHCP lease expires.

The RARP and BOOTP protocols didn't use the concept of a lease. Because these older protocols used a one-to-one mapping of IP to MAC addresses, there wasn't a need to limit the amount of time a client host could use the given IP address.

With DHCP, however, you can configure how long the DHCP client can keep the IP address the DHCP server has assigned. If the lease time expires, the DHCP server puts the associated IP address back into its pool of available addresses.

At this point, you may be asking, "What happens if the workstation is left running for a period of time longer than the lease time?" You don't need to worry. Your workstations won't suddenly lose their IP addresses. Instead, the DHCP client will make several attempts to renew the lease.

The first attempt is made when the lease is halfway consumed. The DHCP client will send a DHCPREQUEST to the DHCP server it originally obtained its IP address from. In the DHCPREQUEST message, the DHCP client will specify the IP address it wants to renew, as shown in Figure 4.6:

FIGURE 4.6
The DHCP lease renewal process.

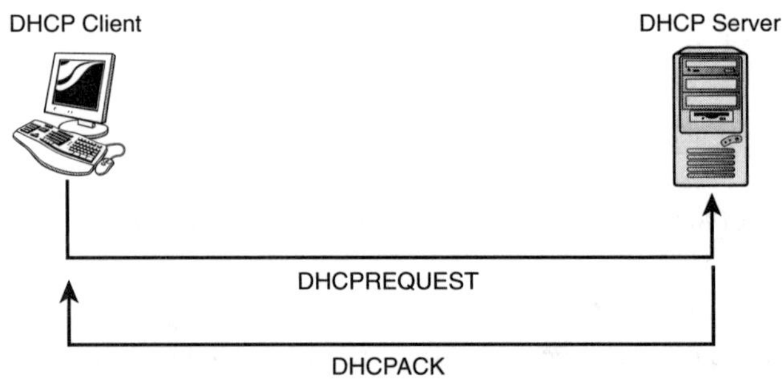

The DHCP server will then respond back with a DHCPACK message, confirming that the lease has been renewed.

If, for some reason, the DHCP client can't establish contact with the DHCP server, the DHCP client will wait until the lease is 87.5% consumed; then it will send another DHCPREQUEST message to renew the lease.

Later in this chapter, we'll look at how you can configure the length of your DHCP leases. How long you choose to make them depends on your network and your organization's priorities. Longer leases create less network traffic, but they also don't use addresses as efficiently. Conversely, short leases use addresses more efficiently, but they also create more network traffic because the leases have to be renewed more often.

With DHCP theory behind us, let's now take a look at how you install the DHCP service on your server.

Installing the DHCP Daemon

TEST OBJECTIVE COVERED:

1. Use DHCP to manage networks.

As with DNS, there are many different DHCP packages you can install on your SLES 9 server. For your CLE 9 certification, you need to know how to install and configure the DHCP daemon provided by the Internet Systems Consortium (ISC). This is the same organization that currently maintains the BIND package we worked with in the previous chapter. For more information, visit http://www.isc.org.

To install the DHCP service on your SLES 9 server, complete the following:

1. From your SLES 9 desktop, select **YaST**.
2. When prompted, provide your *root password*.
3. In the left frame, select **Software**.
4. In the right frame, select **Install and Remove Software**. The screen shown in Figure 4.7 appears:

FIGURE 4.7
YaST software management screen.

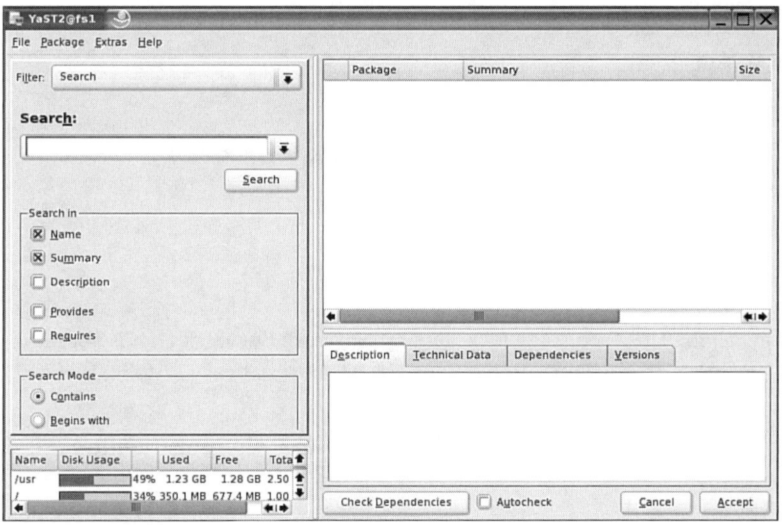

5. In the Search field, enter **dhcp**, and then select **Search**.
6. Mark the **dhcp**, **dhcp-server**, **dhcp-tools**, and **yast2-dhcp-server** modules, as shown in Figure 4.8:

FIGURE 4.8
Installing DHCP packages.

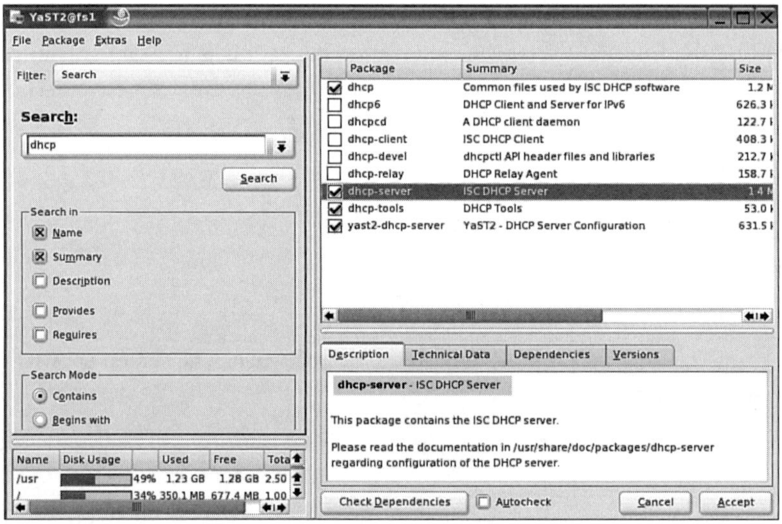

7. Select **Accept**.
8. When prompted, insert the appropriate CDs.
9. Wait while the packages are installed and SuSEconfig is run.
10. Close YaST by selecting **Close**.

TIP

You can also install the DHCP package by accessing **Network Services, DHCP Server** in YaST. If the package isn't installed, the DHCP Server module will automatically install it for you.

If you followed the steps in the lab exercises in Chapter 2, "Introduction to SUSE LINUX Enterprise Server 9," your SLES 9 system should already have the DHCP server package installed.

To verify that it's there, open YaST and select **Software, Install and Remove Software**. In the search field, enter **dhcp**, and then select **Search**. You should see the dhcp, dhcp-server, dhcp-tools, and yast2-dhcp-server packages marked with blue check marks, as shown in Figure 4.9:

FIGURE 4.9
The DHCP server is already installed.

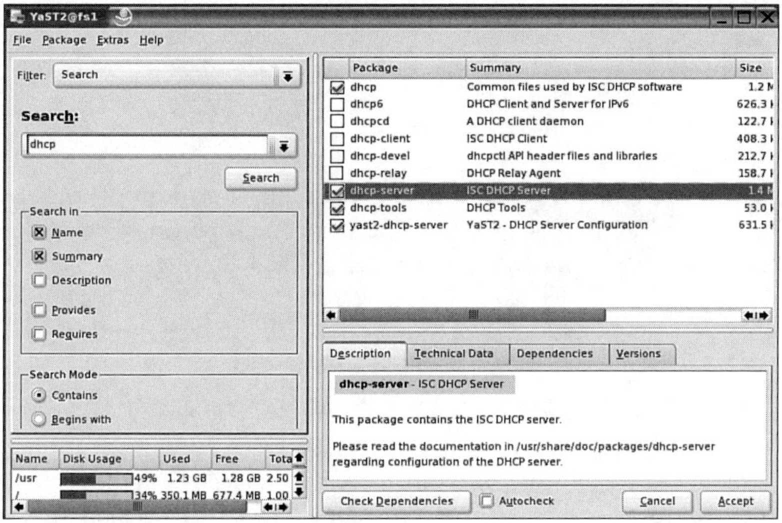

If, for some reason, the DHCP packages aren't installed on your SLES 9 system, follow the steps previously presented to install them.

After the packages are installed, the service is started and stopped using the **dhcpd** init script in `/etc/init.d`, as shown in Figure 4.10:

FIGURE 4.10
The DHCP startup script.

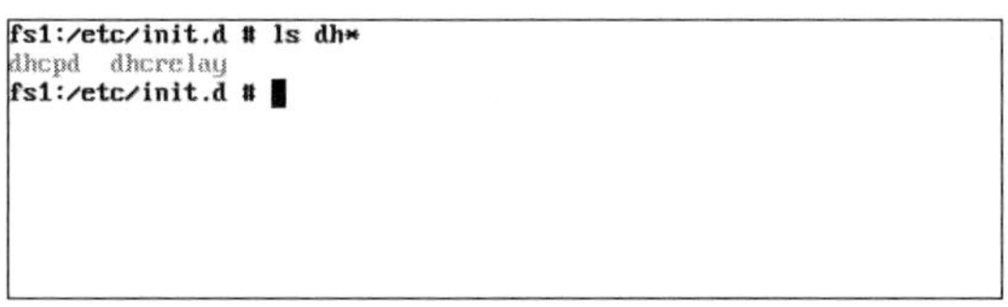

The actual binary that provides this service is the **dhcpd** executable located in `/usr/sbin`, as shown in Figure 4.11:

FIGURE 4.11
The DHCP binary.

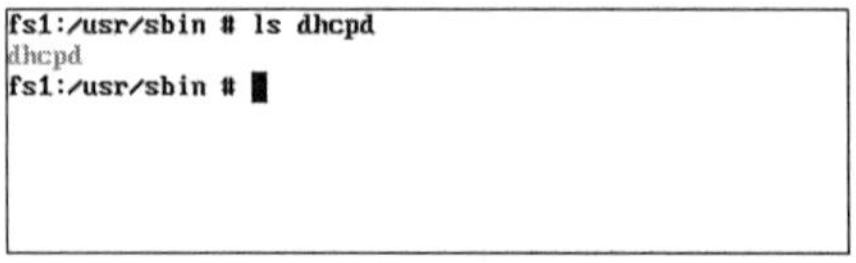

Like other daemons, you use the `/etc/init.d/dhcpd` script to start, stop, or restart the DHCP service on your server. This is done by calling the script and supplying the appropriate parameter. Some examples of commands you can use include the following:

- `/etc/init.d/dhcpd start`—Starts the dhcpd daemon.
- `/etc/init.d/dhcpd stop`—Stops the dhcpd daemon.
- `/etc/init.d/dhc restart`—Restarts the dhcpd daemon.

If you don't want to use the full path, you can also enter **rcdhcpd** from the shell prompt along with the `start`, `stop`, or `restart` parameters to manage the DHCP daemon. As with the named script we discussed in the previous chapter, you can enter **rcdhcpd** to see a list of available options.

After the DHCP service is installed on your system, you're ready to configure and start the service on your server. However, before doing so, you need to have a solid understanding of the DHCP daemon's configuration files. Let's look at those next.

Configuring the DHCP Daemon

TEST OBJECTIVE COVERED:

1. Use DHCP to manage networks.

I'm probably sounding like a broken record, but again, we're going to focus this chapter on the text files that are used to configure dhcpd. Only when you are thoroughly familiar with them will we look at how to use YaST to speed up the configuration process.

Let's do just that; let's take a look at the dhcpd configuration files. The first one we need to look at is `/etc/dhcpd.conf`.

Configuring the `/etc/dhcpd.conf` File

The `/etc/dhcpd.conf` file is the primary configuration file for the dhcpd daemon on your server. A sample `dhcpd.conf` file is shown in Figure 4.12:

FIGURE 4.12
The `/etc/dhcpd.conf` file.

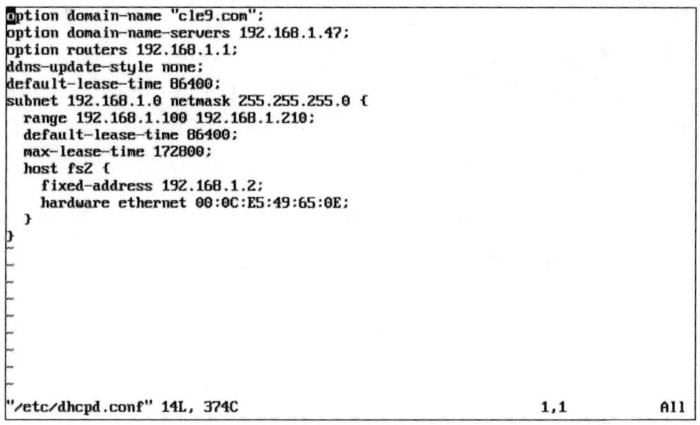

```
option domain-name "cle9.com";
option domain-name-servers 192.168.1.47;
option routers 192.168.1.1;
ddns-update-style none;
default-lease-time 86400;
subnet 192.168.1.0 netmask 255.255.255.0 {
  range 192.168.1.100 192.168.1.210;
  default-lease-time 86400;
  max-lease-time 172800;
  host fs2 {
    fixed-address 192.168.1.2;
    hardware ethernet 00:0C:E5:49:65:0E;
  }
}
~
~
~
~
~
~
~
~
~
"/etc/dhcpd.conf" 14L, 374C                         1,1           All
```

The key element in this file is the *subnet* declaration. This is used to define the IP addresses that can be distributed by the dhcpd daemon, which is probably your foremost concern when configuring the DHCP service.

CONFIGURING A SUBNET

The syntax of the subnet declaration is as follows:

```
subnet network_address netmask subnet_mask {
    range start_address end_address;
    default-lease-time lease_duration;
    max-lease-time maximum_lease_duration;
}
```

The ***`network_address`*** and ***`subnet_mask`*** parameters are used to specify the network address and the subnet mask of the network segment where dhcpd will be assigning addresses. In Figure 4.12, the dhcpd daemon is configured to operate on a network segment with an address of 192.168.1.0 and with a subnet mask of 255.255.255.0.

The **range** parameter identifies which IP addresses dhcpd will assign to network hosts. The ***start_address*** parameter identifies the first address in the range it can assign. The ***end_address*** parameter identifies the last address in the range that it can assign. In Figure 4.12, the dhcpd daemon has been configured to assign addresses within the range of 192.168.1.100 to 192.168.1.210.

The last parameters configure the lease time for assigned IP addresses. The **default-lease-time** parameter within the subnet block sets the default lease time, in seconds, for this address range. DHCP client systems must renew their leases within this time frame. In Figure 4.12, the default lease time has been set to 24 hours (86400 seconds).

You've probably noticed in Figure 4.12 that there are two **default-lease-time** parameters. One is within the subnet declaration; the other is placed earlier in the file. The one within the subnet declaration is specific to the address range. It overrides the **default-lease-time** parameter that is listed earlier in the file, which is applied only if a **default-lease-time** isn't specified within a particular subnet declaration.

The **default-lease-time** parameter is used if the DHCP client doesn't request a specified lease-expiration time. If, for some reason, the DHCP client has been configured to request a specific amount of time in its address lease, the **max-lease-time** parameter is used instead of the **default-lease-time**.

This parameter specifies the absolute maximum lease length you're willing to assign. If the lease being requested is less than this **max-lease-time** parameter, it will be granted as requested. If it is longer, the value in the **max-lease-time** parameter will be issued instead. In Figure 4.12, the maximum lease time has been set to 48 hours (172800 seconds).

In Figure 4.12, notice that there is a **host** declaration within the subnet declaration. This declaration is used to assign a specific IP address to a DHCP client with a specific MAC address. The syntax of the host declaration is as follows:

```
host hostname {
    fixed-address IP_address
    hardware hw_type MAC_address
}
```

The ***hostname*** value specifies the hostname of the system to be assigned a fixed IP address. In Figure 4.12, the hostname of the system is fs2. The **fixed-address** parameter specifies the IP address that is to be always assigned to the particular host. In Figure 4.12, the address to be assigned to fs2 is 192.168.1.2.

The **hardware** parameter has two values. The ***hw_type*** value specifies the type of network board in the client system that is to always be assigned the same address. The possible values are token-ring and ethernet. The ***MAC_address*** value is the hardware address of the client system to whom the same IP address is always to be assigned. In Figure 4.12, fs2 uses an ethernet card with a MAC address of 00:0C:E5:49:65:0E.

TIP

You must include the colons in the MAC address.

In addition to configuring the subnet, you can also configure optional parameters that can be delivered to DHCP clients in the `/etc/dhcpd.conf` file. Let's look at those next.

CONFIGURING DHCP OPTIONS

One of the key benefits of DHCP is its capability to deliver additional parameters to DHCP clients beyond an IP address.

NOTE

BOOTP was provided with "vendor information extensions" in RFC2132 that could function in a manner similar to DHCP options.

These options enable you to configure DHCP clients with a variety of parameters. Some of the more useful options are shown in Table 4.1:

TABLE 4.1
Useful DHCP Options

OPTION	NAME	DESCRIPTION
1	Subnet Mask	The client's subnet mask
3	Router	The IP address of the gateway router
6	Domain Server	The IP address of the DNS server
12	Host Name	The hostname for the client
15	Domain Name	The DNS domain for the client
28	Broadcast Address	The broadcast address for the client
40	NIS Domain	The NIS domain for the client
41	NIS Servers	The IP address of the NIS server
42	NTP Servers	The IP address of the NTP time server
58	Renewal Time	The lease time for the DHCP lease
64	NIS-Domain-Name	The NIS+ domain name for the client
65	NIS-Server-Address	The NIS+ server's IP address
79	Service Scope	The SLP service agent scope

If you want a full list of DHCP options, see RFC2132. In Figure 4.12, three options have been defined. Because these appear outside of the subnet declaration, these options would apply to all DHCP clients if more than one subnet was defined in this file.

The syntax for defining options is as follows:

```
option option_name option_value
```

The first option defined in the `dhcpd.conf` file in Figure 4.12 sets the domain name for the client to cle9.com. The next option delivers the IP address of the network's DNS server; in this case 192.168.1.47. The last option delivers the IP address of the network segment's gateway router, which is 192.168.1.1.

NOTE

We'll cover the `ddns-update-style` statement later in the chapter.

With the `dhcpd.conf` file configured in this manner, we've got a basic DHCP service ready to go. However, before moving on, we need to go a little deeper and review one other dhcpd configuration file: `/etc/sysconfig/dhcpd`.

Configuring the `/etc/sysconfig/dhcpd` File

As with the named daemon, covered in the previous chapter, the configuration file for dhcpd in `/etc/sysconfig` provides you with advanced configuration features for the service itself. A portion of a sample `/etc/sysconfig/dhpcd` file is shown in Figure 4.13:

FIGURE 4.13
The `/etc/sysconfig/dhcpd` file.

```
## Path:        Network/DHCP/DHCP server
## Description: DHCP server settings
## Type:        string
## Default:     ""
## ServiceRestart: dhcpd
#
# Interface(s) for the DHCP server to listen on
# (separated by spaces)
#
# Examples: DHCPD_INTERFACE="eth0"
#           DHCPD_INTERFACE="eth0 eth1 eth2 tr0 wlan0"
#
DHCPD_INTERFACE="eth-id-00:0c:29:ae:23:fb"

## Type:        yesno
## Default:     yes
## ServiceRestart: dhcpd
#
# Shall the DHCP server dhcpd run in a chroot jail (/var/lib/dhcp)?
#
# Each time you start dhcpd with the init script, /etc/dhcpd.conf will
# be copied to /var/lib/dhcp/etc/.
#
"/etc/sysconfig/dhcpd" 80L, 2209C                    1,1          Top
```

You need to be aware of three key parameters. First is the `DHCPD_INTERFACE` parameter. This is a very useful parameter if your server has more than one interface. By default, the dhcpd daemon will bind to all interfaces in the server. This may or may not be a desired behavior.

For example, suppose you've configured your Linux server as a NAT router, connecting a private network to a public network, which is a very common implementation. In addition, you want your Linux server to provide DHCP services.

In this situation, you need to make sure the dhcpd daemon doesn't respond to DHCP requests on the public network interface. Otherwise, it will be handing out IP addresses for the private network on the public network. This would not be a good thing. Your help desk would be swamped with calls from frustrated users trying to figure out why they can't get to their servers.

NOTE

I've seen this very type of situation. Several years ago, a co-worker set up a server running DHCP configured for his private lab network.

This server was also running as his NAT router to the regular corporate network. Pretty soon we had a widespread network outage because his Linux system would respond to `DHCPDISCOVER` messages faster than the corporate DHCP server. As a result, everyone was getting his 10.0.0.x IP addresses for their workstations and no one could read email, browse the Web, and so on.

In this situation, you can use the `DHCPD_INTERFACE` parameter to configure which network interface in the server the dhcpd daemon is to listen on for `DHCPDISCOVER` messages.

In the `/etc/sysconfig/dhcpd` file, you can also configure dhcpd to run in a chroot jail, just as with the named daemon we looked at in the previous chapter. This is done with the `DHCPD_RUN_CHROOTED` parameter, shown in Figure 4.14.

Running dhcpd chrooted is a highly advisable practice. If the dhcpd daemon were to be compromised by a hacker, his or her file system access would be limited to the file structure of the chroot jail. By default, this is `/var/lib/dhcp`.

As with named, the dhcpd daemon, when running the chroot jail, will copy all the files it needs to the `/var/lib/dhcp` on startup. These files include the following:

- `/etc/dhcpd.conf`
- `/etc/host.conf`
- `/etc/hosts`
- `/etc/resolv.conf`
- `/etc/localtime`

FIGURE 4.14
Running dhcpd chrooted.

```
# be copied to /var/lib/dhcp/etc/.
#
# Some files that are important for hostname to IP address resolution
# (/etc/{hosts,host.conf,resolv.conf,localtime}, /lib/libnss_dns.so.2,
# /lib/libresolv.so.2) will also be copied to the chroot jail by the
# init script when you start it (about 100kB altogether).
#
# The pid file will be in /var/lib/dhcp/var/run/dhcpd.pid.
#
DHCPD_RUN_CHROOTED="yes"

## Type:          string
## Default:       ""
## ServiceRestart: dhcpd
#
# Since version 3, dhcpd.conf can contain include statements.
# If you enter the names of any include files here, _all_ conf
# files will be copied to $chroot/etc/, when dhcpd is started in the
# chroot jail. (/etc/dhcpd.conf is always copied.)
#
# For your convenience, you can also specify entire directories, like
# "/etc/dhcpd.conf.d".
#
                                                    22,1          36%
```

When you install dhcpd on SLES 9, it is installed into a chroot jail by default. In accordance, dhcpd daemon runs as the dhcpd user instead of root. This is configured using the last critical parameter in the `/etc/sysconfig/dhcpd` file we'll mention here: `DHCPD_RUN_AS`, shown in Figure 4.15:

FIGURE 4.15
Running dhcpd as a nonroot user.

```
# "/etc/dhcpd.conf.d".
#
# Example: "/etc/dhcpd.conf.shared /etc/dhcpd.conf.bootp-clients"
#
DHCPD_CONF_INCLUDE_FILES=""

## Type:          string
## Default:       "dhcpd"
## ServiceRestart: dhcpd
#
# Leave empty or enter "root" to let dhcpd run as root.
# Enter "dhcpd" to run dhcpd as user 'dhcpd'.
#
DHCPD_RUN_AS="dhcpd"

## Type:          string
## Default:       ""
## ServiceRestart: dhcpd
#
# Other arguments that you want dhcpd to be started with
# (e.g. "-p 1234" for a non-standard port to listen on)
#
DHCPD_OTHER_ARGS=""
                                                    43,1          73%
```

Be sure you don't leave this parameter without a value. The default behavior, if left blank, is to run the daemon as root; which you probably don't want to do.

Now that you understand the files that are used to configure dhcpd on your server, you can learn how to use YaST to expedite the process.

Configuring dhcpd with YaST

Just as with other network services, using YaST to configure the dhcpd daemon on your server makes the process fast and very easy.

NOTE

The first time you start the dhcpd configuration module in YaST, it runs in wizard mode. Subsequently, it starts in advanced mode, which we will discuss here.

To use YaST to configure dhcpd, complete the following:

1. Start YaST.
2. When prompted, supply your root user's password.
3. Select **Network Services**, **DHCP Server**. The screen in Figure 4.16 is displayed:

FIGURE 4.16
Configuring DHCP server startup options.

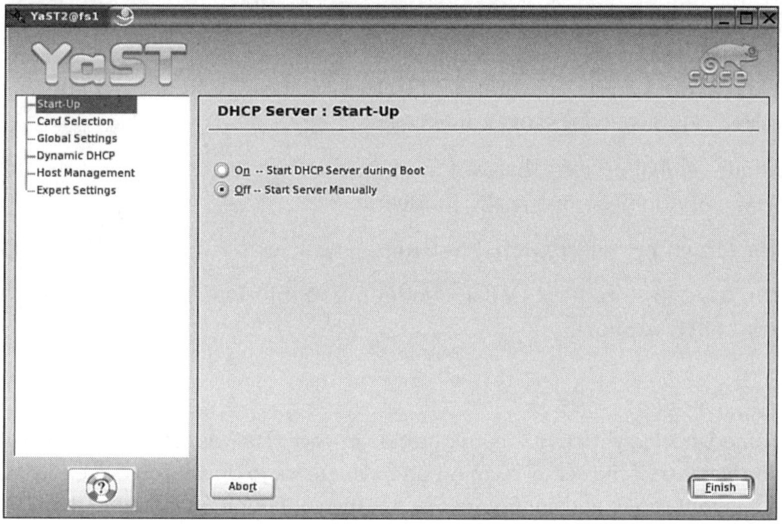

4. To configure your DHCP service to start automatically, mark **On**; otherwise, mark **Off**.
5. To configure the interface the dhcpd daemon should listen on, complete the following:
   a. In the left frame, select **Card Selection**. The screen in Figure 4.17 is displayed:

FIGURE 4.17
Configuring interfaces used by dhcpd.

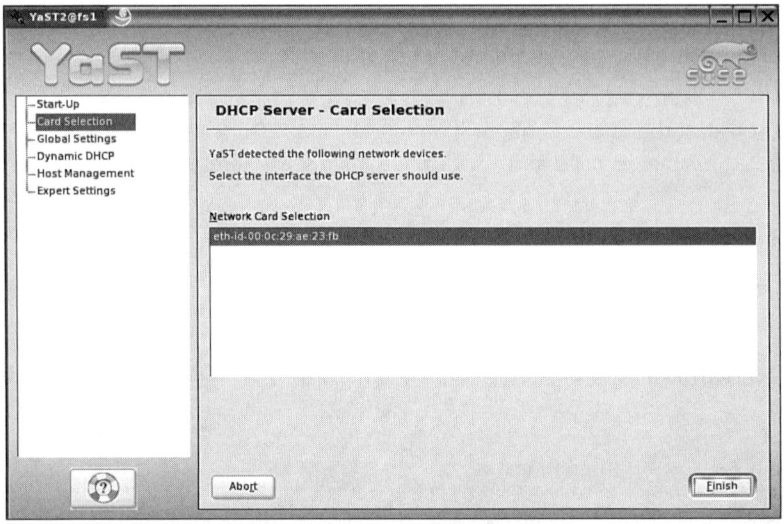

b. In the Network Card Selection field, select the *network interface(s)* you want dhcpd to listen on for `DHCPDISCOVER` messages.

6. To configure global options that will apply to all dhcp leases (unless overridden by subnet-specific options), complete the following:

a. In the left frame, select **Global Settings**. The screen in Figure 4.18 is displayed.

b. If you want to store your DHCP configuration information in your LDAP directory, mark **LDAP support**.

NOTE

Just as with named, storing your DHCP configuration in your LDAP directory provides you with a degree of fault tolerance. If the server running dhcpd were to go down, you can easily start the daemon on a different server and configure it to use the configuration stored in the LDAP directory (assuming your LDAP directory service is replicated on multiple servers).

c. In the various fields provided, configure the DHCP options you want assigned to DHCP clients.

FIGURE 4.18
Configuring global DHCP options.

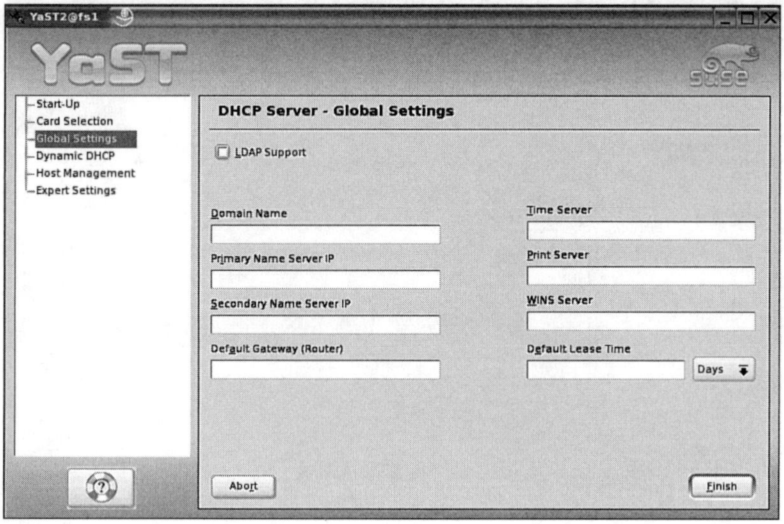

TIP

These DHCP options are optional. You can configure all, some, or none of them.

7. To configure a DHCP subnet, complete the following:
   a. In the left screen, select **Dynamic DHCP**. The screen in Figure 4.19 is displayed.
   b. In the First IP Address field, enter the *first IP address* in the range you want dynamically assigned to DHCP clients.
   c. In the Last IP Address field, enter the last *IP address* in the range you want dynamically assigned to DHCP clients.
   d. In the Lease Time fields, enter the *default lease time* and the *max lease time*.
8. (Optional) If you want to create a one-to-one mapping of a specific IP address to a specific computer system, complete the following:
   a. In the left frame, select **Host Management**. The screen in Figure 4.20 is displayed.

FIGURE 4.19
Configuring a DHCP subnet.

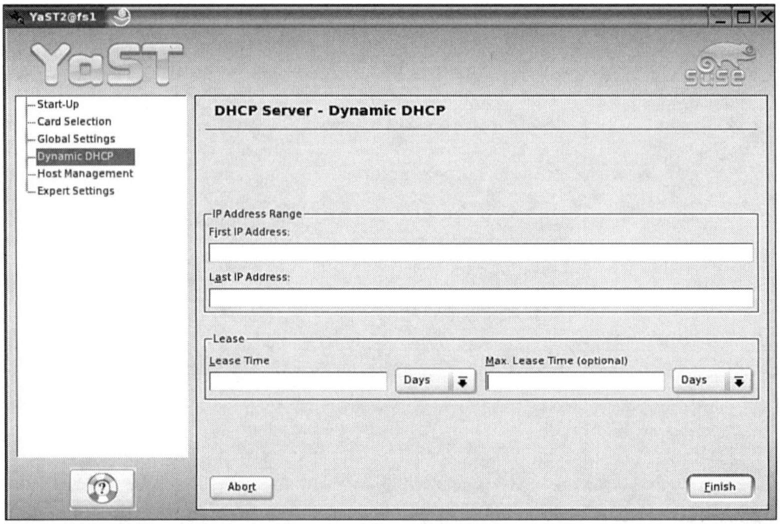

FIGURE 4.20
Configuring a one-to-one mapping.

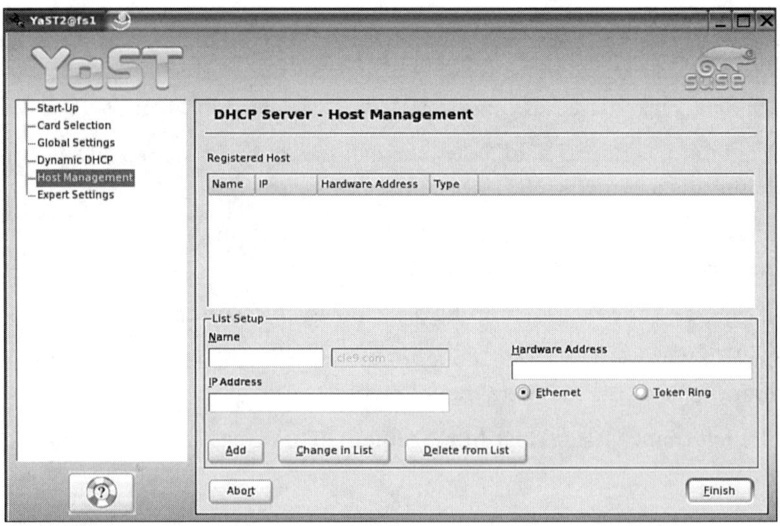

   b. In the Name field, enter the *hostname* of the system you are creating the mapping for.

   c. In the IP Address field, enter the *IP address* you want assigned to the specific host.

   d. Under Hardware Address, mark **Ethernet** or **Token Ring**.

   e. In the Hardware Address field, enter the MAC address of the system you are creating the mapping for. Be sure to enter the MAC address using colons.

   f. Select **Add**.

9. Apply your changes by selecting **Finish**.

Enough talk! Let's get DHCP running on your SLES 9 server in Lab Exercise 4.1.

Lab Exercise 4.1: Configuring DHCP on SLES 9

In this lab exercise, you will configure the DHCP daemon on your SLES 9 server that you installed in Chapter 2.

NOTE

You really should complete this exercise on an isolated lab segment. If you set up a DHCP server on a production segment, you're probably going to have a lot of people very upset with you.

To complete this exercise, you will need the following systems:

1. Your SLES 9 server with named running.
2. A second workstation with an operating system already installed to function as a DHCP client. As an option, you can download a copy of Novell Linux Desktop from http://www.novell.com and use it as the DHCP client.

To configure the dhcpd daemon on your system, complete the following:

1. Boot your SLES 9 server and authenticate as **tux** with a password of **SuSE789**.
2. From your desktop, start YaST.
3. When prompted, enter a root password of **tuX123**; then select **OK.**
4. Select Network Services, DHCP Server.
5. In the Card Selection screen, mark the *interface* you want the DHCP daemon to listen on.
6. Select **Next**.
7. In the Global Settings screen, complete the following:
    a. Mark LDAP Support.
    b. In the Domain Name field, enter **cle9.com**.
    c. In the Primary Name Server IP field, enter the *IP address* of your SLES 9 server.
    d. In the Default Gateway (Router) field, enter the *IP address* of the gateway router for your network segment.

   e. In the Default Lease Time field, specify **1 day**.
   f. Select **Next**.
8. Configure your DHCP subnet by completing the following:
   a. In the First IP Address field, enter the *first IP address* in the range you want to assign to DHCP clients.
   b. In the Last IP Address field, enter *last IP address* in the range you want to assign to DHCP clients.

NOTE

Again, make sure it's OK for you to use these IP addresses. It is best if you set this system up on an isolated lab segment where you won't interfere with any other systems!

   c. In the Lease Time field, specify **1 day**.
   d. In the Max Lease Time field, specify **2 days**.
   e. Select **Next**.
9. Select **Finish**.

TIP

We're not going to configure the DHCP daemon to automatically start in this exercise.

10. When prompted for the password to the LDAP server, enter **`tuX123`**.
11. Open a terminal session.
12. At the shell prompt, enter **`su -`**.
13. When prompted, enter a password of **`tuX123`**.
14. At the shell prompt, enter **`rcdhcpd start`**.
15. Test your configuration by completing the following:
    a. Make sure your workstation system is connected to the same network segment as your SLES 9 server.
    b. Configure your workstation operating system to obtain its IP address using DHCP.
    c. Open a terminal session on your workstation.

TIP

I'm assuming you're using a Linux system as your workstation in this step. If you're using Windows, use the `IPCONFIG /ALL` command to check the IP parameters.

d. At the shell prompt change to root by entering **`su -`** and supplying a password of **`tuX123`**.

e. At the shell prompt, enter **`ifconfig`**.

f. Verify that the system was able to obtain an IP address from your DHCP server.

g. At the shell prompt, enter **`route`**.

h. Verify that an entry for the default route appears in the list of routes. A sample is shown in Figure 4.21:

FIGURE 4.21
Default route delivered via DHCP.

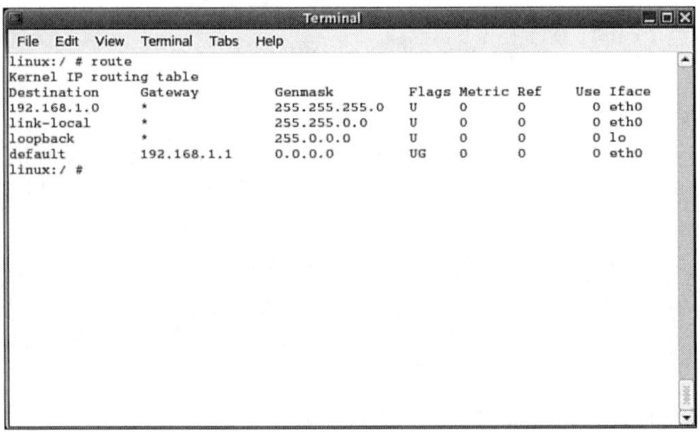

i. At the shell prompt enter **`cat /etc/resolv.conf`**.

j. Verify that this file is being created by dhcpd, as shown in Figure 4.22:

FIGURE 4.22
Name resolution parameters delivered by DHCP.

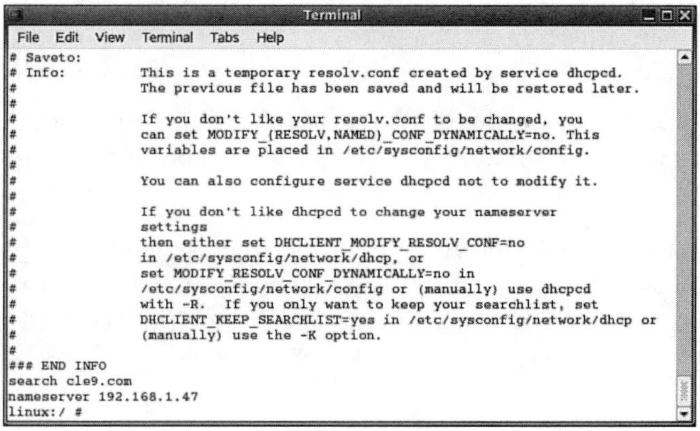

Congratulations! You now have a working DHCP server. Now you need to learn how to work with DHCP relay agents.

Configuring the DHCP Relay Agent

TEST OBJECTIVE COVERED:

1. Use DHCP to manage networks.

The DHCP server we've configured thus far in this chapter would work great on a single-segment network. If this server were intended for deployment in a small organization, we'd be in business.

However, as you probably know, the networks in medium and large organization will, more than likely, be composed of many network segments connected by routers. If this server were to be implemented in this type of environment, we would have a problem. Let's look at the cause of this problem.

The Problem with DHCP in a Routed Network

Do you recall what type of communication is used by DHCP clients to discover the DHCP server? Yes, it uses *broadcasts*. This represents a problem for us. That's because most routers, by default, will not forward broadcast messages between network segments.

NOTE

Occasionally, you will run into systems where routers have been configured to forward broadcasts. This is a very bad idea. Not only does it create a lot of unnecessary network traffic, it also opens up your network to exploitation by Denial of Service (DoS) attacks.

Some DoS attacks, such as the Smurf attack, require an unwitting intermediary (patsy) network that is configured to forward broadcasts to do its dirty work.

Consider the network shown in Figure 4.23:

FIGURE 4.23
DHCP in a network with more than one segment.

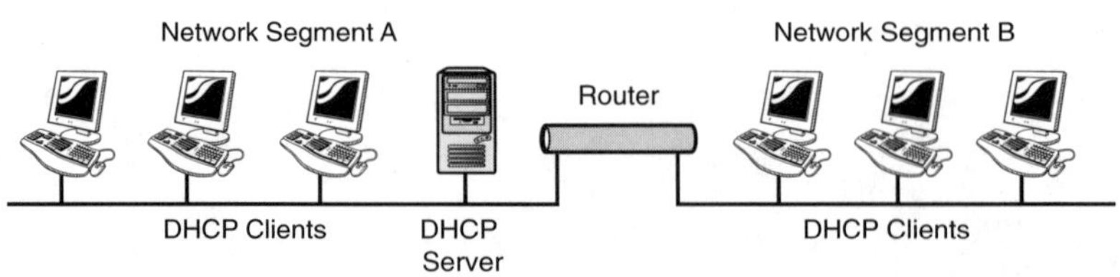

In this configuration, the DHCP clients on Network Segment A will be able to contact the DHCP server because it resides on the same side of the router as they do.

However, because broadcasts (hopefully) can't cross the router, the DHCP clients on Network Segment B will not be able to reach the DHCP server and, therefore, won't be able to obtain IP address leases from it. How do you make DHCP work in this kind of network? Let's find out.

Making DHCP Work in a Routed Network

To make DHCP work in a network composed of many network segments, you have three options. The first option is to configure your routers to forward broadcasts. However, as we've discussed, this is not a good idea in most situations. In fact, many routers don't even provide you with the option.

The second option is to implement a separate DHCP server on each and every network segment. This is a viable option and many organizations do this. The problem with it is that it can really increase your administrative overhead. Instead of managing one DHCP server for your organization, you have to manage a whole bunch of them.

Another option is to implement a DHCP relay agent. This is a slick way to do things. Instead of setting up a DHCP server on each network segment, you set up a single DHCP server that services your entire organization. Because each network segment has a different network address, you next need to create a separate `subnet` declaration for each segment in your `/etc/dhcpd.conf` file. Each declaration contains the appropriate parameters for the particular segment, such as address range, subnet mask, and gateway router address.

Then—and this is the cool part—you configure one server on each segment to run a DHCP relay agent. This is provided by the dhcrelay daemon. The relay agent listens on the local network segment for DHCPDISCOVER broadcasts from DHCP clients. When it receives one, it forwards the DHCPDISCOVER message, using a unicast transmission that can traverse routers, to the DHCP server on a different network segment.

The DHCP server sends a DHCPOFFER back, but not to the DHCP client. Instead, it sends it back to the system running the relay agent. The relay agent then forwards the message on to the DHCPCLIENT. The rest of the DHCP negotiation continues using the same process. Essentially, the DHCP relay agent acts as an intermediary between the DHCP server and the DHCP client. This is shown in Figure 4.24.

TIP

Don't run a DHCP relay agent and a DHCP server on the same segment. You need only one service per segment that responds to DHCP broadcast messages.

FIGURE 4.24
Configuring DHCP relay agents.

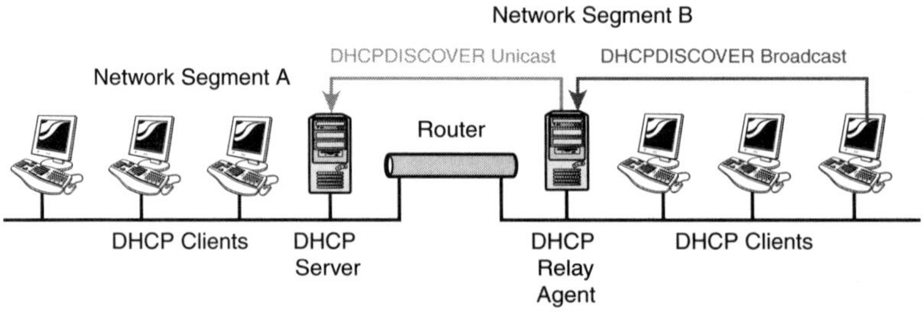

Using DHCP relay agents can be a great benefit for you as a network administrator. Instead of managing multiple DHCP servers, you can configure your network with just one, making your life a little easier.

Let's look at how you go about configuring the DHCP relay agent.

Configuring the dhcrelay Daemon

The dhcrelay daemon is fairly easy to configure. The first thing you need to do is to verify that the package is installed on the system by following these steps:

1. Run YaST and select **Software**, **Install and Remove Software**.
2. In the Search field, enter **dhcp**; then select **Search**.
3. Verify that the dhcp-relay package is installed, as shown in Figure 4.25.
4. If the package isn't installed, mark the **dhcp-relay** package and then select **Accept**.
5. Follow the prompts to complete the installation.

With the package installed, you're ready to configure the service. Unlike other services you may be familiar with, dhcrelay doesn't have a `.conf` file in `/etc`. Instead, all configuration is done using the dhcrelay file in `/etc/sysconfig`. This file is shown in Figure 4.26.

FIGURE 4.25
Installing the DHCP relay agent package.

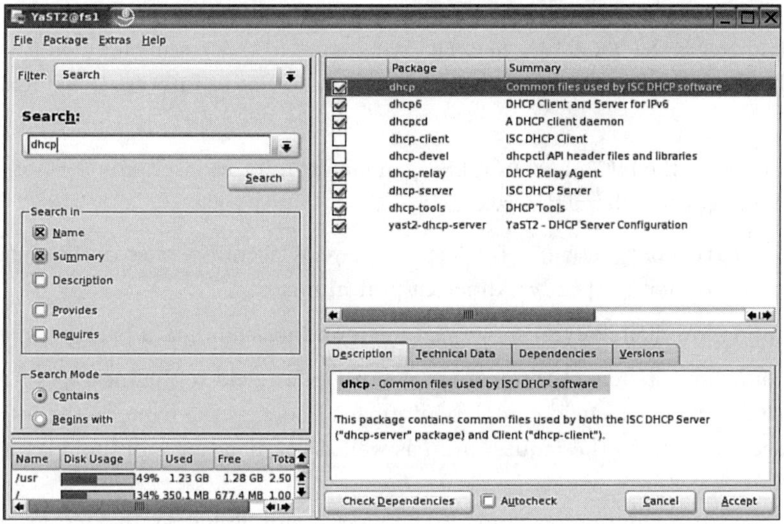

FIGURE 4.26
The `/etc/sysconfig/dhcrelay` file.

```
#
# Interface(s) for DHCP relay agent to listen on:
# (separated by spaces, e.g. "eth1")
#
DHCRELAY_INTERFACES=""

## Type:          string
## Default:       ""
## ServiceRestart: dhcrelay
#
# DHCP servers to be used by DHCP relay agent
# (separated by spaces, e.g. "192.168.0.11 191.168.0.12")
#
DHCRELAY_SERVERS=""

## Type:          string
## Default:       ""
## ServiceRestart: dhcrelay
#
# Additional options
# Example: "-c 8"
#
DHCRELAY_OPTIONS=""
                                              28,1          Bot
```

There are only three options you need to be concerned with. The first is the `DHCRELAY_INTERFACES` parameter. Use this parameter to specify which network interfaces the daemon should listen on. If you leave the parameter blank, it will listen on all configured interfaces.

TIP

The relay agent will respond to both DHCP and BOOTP client messages.

The next parameter is the `DHCRELAY_SERVERS` parameter. In this parameter, you specify the IP address of the DHCP server(s) you want the dhcrelay daemon to forward DHCP client messages to.

The last parameter is the `DHCRELAY_OPTIONS` parameter. You can insert any (or none) of the following options for the dhcrelay service:

- `-p alternate_port_number`—By default, the relay agent operates on IP port 67. You can use this option to specify a different port number.
- `-d`—Configures dhcrelay to run in the foreground instead of as a background service.
- `-a`—Configures dhcrelay to append an Agent Option field to the messages it forwards to the DHCP server. This field contains information such as the name of the interface the relay agent is sending the request from as well as the IP address of the relay agent.

Of these options, the `-a` option is definitely the most useful. By using this option, the DHCP server can determine which network segment the forwarded DHCP request is coming from. If you have configured your `/etc/dhcpd.conf` file with multiple subnet declarations, you should always configure the relay agent with the `-a` option. This will allow the DHCP server to determine which subnet to use to assign an IP address.

After you've edited the `/etc/sysconfig/dhcrelay` file, you can start the dhcrelay service. This is done by opening a terminal session, changing to root, and then entering **`rcdhcrelay start`** at the shell prompt.

Because this service is absolutely critical to the proper functioning of your network, you should configure dhcrelay to automatically start at runlevels 3 and 5. This can be done using the `chkconfig` command or by selecting **System, Runlevel Editor** in YaST, as shown in Figure 4.27.

FIGURE 4.27
Configuring dhcrelay to automatically start.

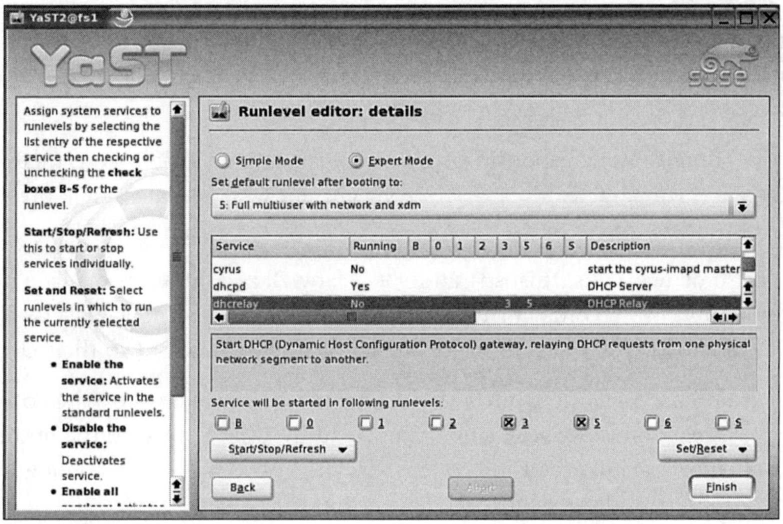

Now that you know how to configure DHCP relay agents, you need to take a look at one more DHCP-related topic: Dynamic DNS.

Implementing Dynamic DNS

TEST OBJECTIVE COVERED:

1. Use DHCP to manage networks.

If you're not familiar with Dynamic DNS, you're probably wondering why we're covering a DNS topic in this DHCP chapter. Dynamic DNS is way for us to connect our DHCP server to our DNS zone. In the next section, you'll learn how it works.

How DDNS Works

One of the problems with DNS is that DNS zones are static in nature. The DNS server simply knows that there are bunch of records in the zones it serves that map hostnames to IP addresses and vice versa. The DNS server doesn't know whether the particular host represented by the hostname in the zone is up or down. It doesn't know if that host even still exists.

In addition, if you were to add hosts to the network or change the IP addresses assigned to existing hosts, the DNS server has no idea what you've done. It assumes that whatever data it currently has in its zone is correct and up to date.

This situation is exacerbated when DHCP comes into the picture. Network hosts are assigned and reassigned IP addresses every day. There's a very good chance that a particular network host may have several different IP address throughout the course of the week.

As the network administrator responsible for your organization's DNS server, there is no possible way you could manually keep your DNS zone current with the latest IP address assignments from your DNS server.

Admittedly, for some networks, this isn't an issue. Many DNS administrators care only about keeping "important" DNS records current. These include devices such as servers, routers, and printers. They don't worry about putting DNS records for workstations in their DNS zones.

However, be aware that many network services (including some web sites) are configured to perform *reverse lookups* on hosts accessing them. Basically, it looks at who the host says it is and runs a DNS query against the DNS zone where the host claims to be coming from to see if the host name and IP address match up. This is done to prevent spoofing.

In this situation, your DNS zone must contain records for workstations as well as servers, routers, and printers. If you're using DHCP, which just about everyone does, this can be an insurmountable problem.

Fortunately, there is a way to deal with it. The named and dhcpd daemons from ISC both support Dynamic DNS (DDNS). With DDNS, your dhcpd daemon can be configured to automatically create records in your DNS zone every time it hands out an IP address. Likewise, when a lease is released or expires, the dhcpd services removes those records from the zone. This is shown in Figure 4.28:

FIGURE 4.28
Updating DNS zones with DDNS.

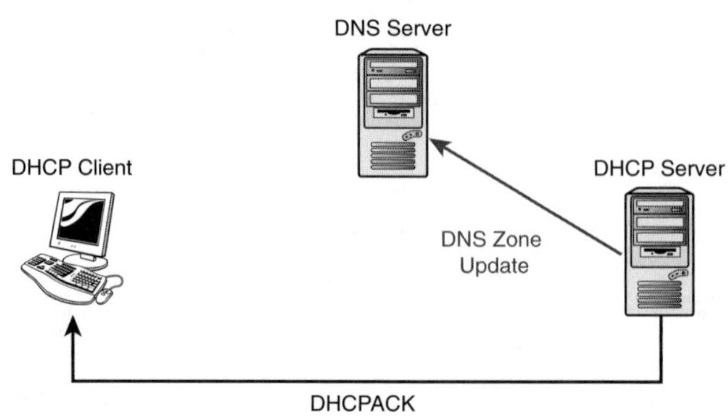

When you implement DDNS, your DNS zone contains accurate DNS records for all the DHCP-configured hosts in your network. Let's look at how DDNS is configured on your SLES 9 server.

Configuring DDNS on SLES 9

A key component of DDNS on SLES 9 are transaction signatures (TSIGs). TSIGs are used to secure the zone update between the DHCP server and the DNS server. In the "old days" of DDNS, the update was sent clear text without authentication. The only real restriction you could create was based on the IP address. This worked, but IP addresses can be spoofed.

To increase DDNS security in today's world, we generate a TSIG key on the DNS server. This key is saved in a local file that is copied to the DHCP server where it is used to secure transmissions between the two servers. The same key must exist on both.

NOTE

Zone transfers between master and slave DNS servers can also be secured with TSIG keys. The TSIG key is generated by the master server and then copied by the administrator to the slave server.

In fact, you can't configure DDNS in ISC's current release of named and dhcpd without configuring TSIGs. To generate TSIGs and configure DDNS, complete the following:

1. Start YaST.
2. Select **Network Services**, **DNS Server**.
3. Configure a TSIG key by completing the following:
   a. In the left frame, select **TSIG Keys**. The screen in Figure 4.29 is displayed.
   b. In the Key ID field, enter an *identifier* for your TSIG key.
   c. In the File Name field, enter a *filename* for the key, including the full path to the file.
   d. Select **Generate**.
   e. When prompted to generate the key, select **Yes**.
4. Configure your DNS zones to support dynamic updates by completing the following:
   a. In the left frame, select **DNS Zones**.
   b. Under Configured DNS Zones, select your *zone*.
   c. Select **Edit Zone**. The screen in Figure 4.30 is displayed.

FIGURE 4.29
Generating the TSIG Key.

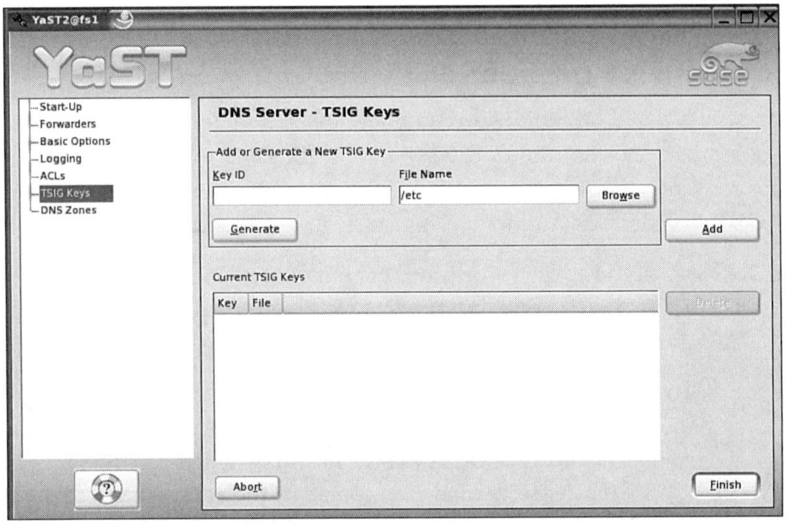

FIGURE 4.30
Configuring your zone to support DDNS.

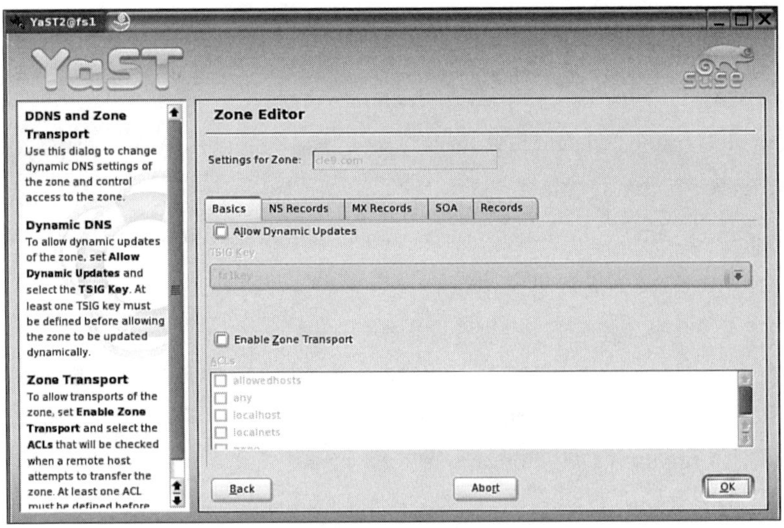

d. Mark Allow Dynamic Updates.

e. In the TSIG Key drop-down list, select the *TSIG key* you just created.

f. Select **OK**.

g. Repeat this process on your *reverse zone*.

TIP

You must have both forward and reverse zones running on your DNS server for DDNS to work. After enabling dynamic updates, the zone files will be moved from `/var/lib/named/master` to `/var/lib/named/dyn`.

h. Select **Finish**.

5. Copy the TSIG key you just created to your DHCP server.

6. Configure your DHCP server to send zone updates to your DNS server by completing the following:

   a. In YaST, select Network Services, DHCP Server.

   b. In the left frame, select **Expert Settings**.

   c. When prompted to continue, select **Yes**. The screen in Figure 4.31 is displayed:

FIGURE 4.31
Configuring the DHCP server.

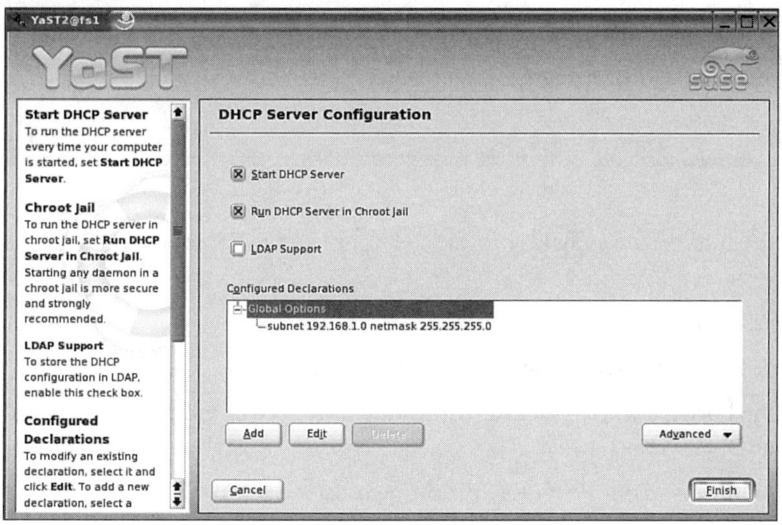

TIP

After DDNS is configured, the DHCP Server YaST module will display only the Expert Settings screen.

d. If not already done, mark **Start DHCP Server**.

e. Under Global Options, select the *subnet* you want to enable DDNS on.

f. Select **Edit**.

g. Select **Dynamic DNS**. The screen in Figure 4.32 is displayed.

FIGURE 4.32
Configuring the TSIG Key on the DHCP server.

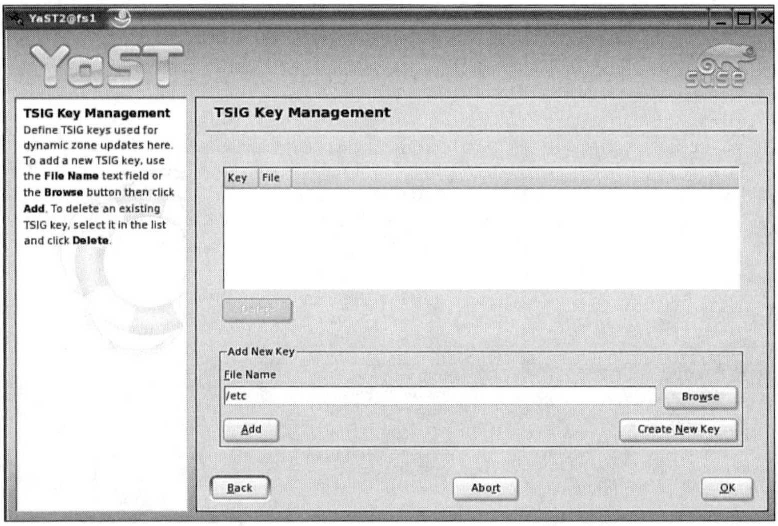

h. In the Add New Key field, browse to and select the *TSIG key* you copied from your DNS server.

i. Select **Add, OK**. The screen in Figure 4.33 is displayed.

j. Mark **Enable Dynamic DNS for This Subnet**.

k. In the Forward Zone TSIG Key drop-down list, select the *TSIG key* copied from your DNS server.

l. In the Reverse Zone TSIG Key drop-down list, select the *TSIG key* copied from your DNS server.

FIGURE 4.33
Enabling DDNS on the DHCP server.

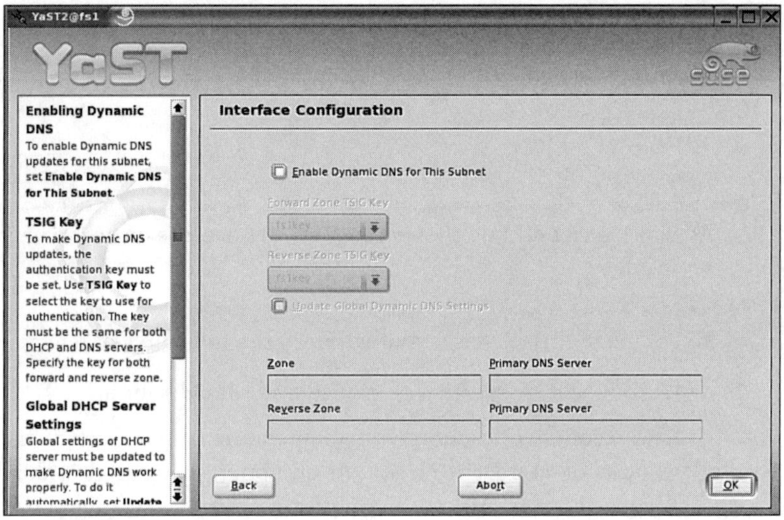

m. Mark **Update Global Dynamic DNS Settings**.

n. In the Zone field, enter the *name* of your forward zone.

o. In the Primary DNS Server field, enter the *IP address* of your DNS server.

p. In the Reverse Zone field, enter the *name* of your reverse zone.

q. In the Primary DNS Server field, enter the *IP address* of your DNS server.

r. Select **OK**.

s. Select **OK**, **Finish**.

Your DNS and DHCP servers are now tied together. When DHCP clients get an address from the DHCP server, their hostname and IP address will be added as an A record in your DNS zone and as a PTR record in your reverse DNS zone.

Let's give it a try on your SLES 9 server in Exercise 4.2.

Lab Exercise 4.2: Configuring DDNS on SLES 9

In this lab exercise, you will configure the DHCP daemon on your SLES 9 server to send dynamic updates to the DNS server you configured in Chapter 3.

NOTE

As with Exercise 4.1, you should complete this exercise on an isolated lab segment.

To complete this exercise, you will need the following systems:

1. Your SLES 9 server with named and dhcpd running.
2. A second workstation with an operating system already installed to function as a DHCP client. As an option, you can download a copy of Novell Linux Desktop from http://www.novell.com and use it as the DHCP client.

To configure DDNS on your system, complete the following:

1. Boot your SLES 9 server and authenticate as **tux** with a password of **SuSE789**.
2. Start YaST.
3. When prompted for the root password, enter **tuX123**.
4. Select **Network Services**, **DNS Server**.
5. Deselect LDAP Support Active.

NOTE

Because named must authenticate to the LDAP directory when making changes to the zone, dynamic updates won't work with this configuration. To make things simple, we're going to disable LDAP support for the DNS and the DHCP servers.

6. Select **Finish**.
7. Select **DHCP Server**.
8. In the left frame, select **Global Settings**.

9. Deselect **LDAP Support**.
10. Select **Finish**.
11. Select **DNS Server**.
12. Configure a TSIG key by completing the following:
    a. In the left frame, select **TSIG Keys**.
    b. In the Key ID field, enter **`fs1key`**.
    c. In the File Name field, enter **`/etc/mykey`**.
    d. Select **Generate**.
    e. When prompted to generate the key, select **Yes**.
13. Configure the cle9.com zone to support dynamic updates by completing the following:
    a. In the left frame, select **DNS Zones**.
    b. Under Configured DNS Zones, select **cle9.com**.
    c. Select **Edit Zone**.
    d. Mark **Allow Dynamic Updates**.
    e. In the TSIG Key drop-down list, select **fs1key**.
    f. Select **OK**.
    g. Select your reverse zone.
    h. Select **Edit Zone**.
    i. Mark **Allow Dynamic Updates**.
    j. In the TSIG Key drop-down list, select **fs1key**.
    k. Select **OK**.
    l. Select **Finish**.

TIP

Because your DNS and DHCP services are running on the same server, you don't need to copy the key between machines.

14. Configure your DHCP server to send zone updates to your DNS server by completing the following:
    a. In YaST, select **Network Services**, **DHCP Server**.
    b. In the left frame, select **Expert Settings**.

c. When prompted to continue, select **Yes**.

d. If not already done, mark **Start DHCP Server**.

e. Under Global Options, select the subnet you created in Exercise 4.1.

f. Select **Edit**.

g. Select **Dynamic DNS**.

h. In the Add New Key field, browse to and select `/etc/mykey`.

i. Select **Add**, **OK**.

j. Mark **Enable Dynamic DNS for This Subnet**.

k. In the Forward Zone TSIG Key drop-down list, select **fslkey**.

l. In the Reverse Zone TSIG Key drop-down list, select **fslkey**.

m. Mark **Update Global Dynamic DNS Settings**.

n. In the Zone field, enter **`cle9.com`**.

o. In the Primary DNS Server field, enter the *IP address* of your DNS server.

p. In the Reverse Zone field, enter the name of your reverse zone.

TIP

Be sure you spell the name of the reverse zone correctly. If you don't, DDNS won't work. This is the number one mistake I made when configuring DDNS.

q. In the Primary DNS Server field, enter the *IP address* of your DNS server.

r. Select **OK**.

s. Select **OK**, **Finish**.

TIP

At this point, you may need to manually restart the DHCP daemon. YaST should do this for you; however, on several occasions, I've had to manually restart the DHCP daemon to get DDNS to work.

15. Boot the workstation system you used in Lab Exercise 4.1, allowing it to obtain an IP address from your DHCP server.

16. Check to see whether a lease was assigned by completing the following:

a. Open a terminal session.

b. At the shell prompt, enter **`su -`**.

c. When prompted, enter a password of **`tuX123`**.

d. At the shell prompt, enter **`cat /var/lib/dhcp/db/dhcpd.leases`**.

e. Verify that a lease was assigned to your workstation and that A, PTR, and TXT records for the DHCP client were added to your cle9.com zone, as shown in Figure 4.34.

FIGURE 4.34
Leases in the `dhcpd.leases` file.

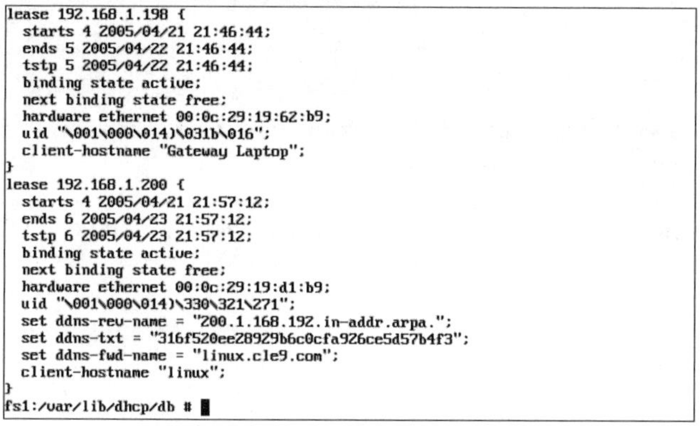

```
lease 192.168.1.198 {
  starts 4 2005/04/21 21:46:44;
  ends 5 2005/04/22 21:46:44;
  tstp 5 2005/04/22 21:46:44;
  binding state active;
  next binding state free;
  hardware ethernet 00:0c:29:19:62:b9;
  uid "\001\000\014)\031b\016";
  client-hostname "Gateway Laptop";
}
lease 192.168.1.200 {
  starts 4 2005/04/21 21:57:12;
  ends 6 2005/04/23 21:57:12;
  tstp 6 2005/04/23 21:57:12;
  binding state active;
  next binding state free;
  hardware ethernet 00:0c:29:19:d1:b9;
  uid "\001\000\014)\330\321\271";
  set ddns-rev-name = "200.1.168.192.in-addr.arpa.";
  set ddns-txt = "316f520ee28929b6c0cfa926ce5d57b4f3";
  set ddns-fwd-name = "linux.cle9.com";
  client-hostname "linux";
}
fs1:/var/lib/dhcp/db #
```

17. Use YaST to check for a new record in your zone.

TIP

It may take up to 5 minutes before the record update is complete.

a. Select **DNS Server**.

b. Select **DNS Zones**.

c. Select the **cle9.com zone**; then select **Edit Zone**.

d. Select the **Records** tab.

e. Verify that the record for your workstation has been added, as shown in Figure 4.35.

FIGURE 4.35
DDNS records in the DNS zone.

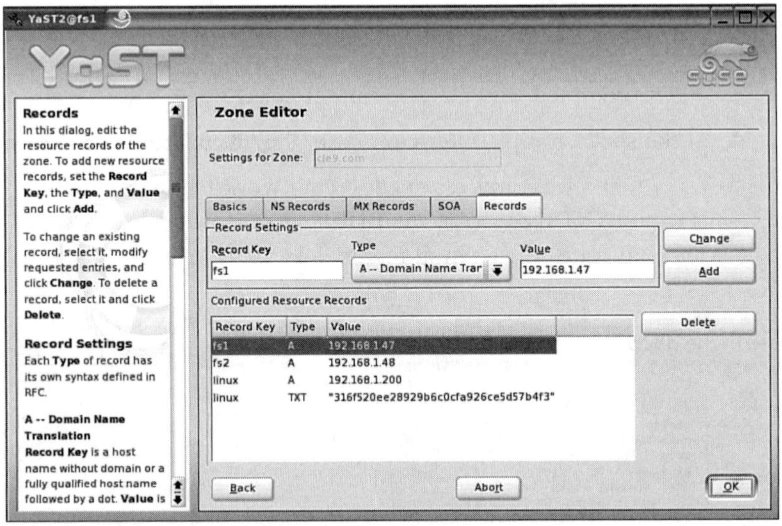

Congratulations! Your DHCP server is now integrated with your DNS server, providing instant updates whenever it hands out an IP address.

That's it for this chapter. Before you go to Chapter 5, "Configuring CUPS on SLES 9," let's review what you've learned.

Summary

In this chapter, you learned how to implement DHCP on your SLES 9 server. We first reviewed the difficulty associated with manually managing IP address assignments in your network. We also reviewed the three methods used to dynamically assign IP addresses: RARP, BOOTP, and DHCP.

We then investigated DHCP in depth. We first reviewed the DHCP transaction process: DHCPDISCOVER, DHCPOFFER, DHCPREQUEST, and DHCPACK. Then we discussed how leases are implemented in DHCP to manage the amount of time IP addresses are assigned to hosts.

With DHCP theory out of the way, we spend the rest of the chapter discussing how to implement DHCP on SLES 9. We first reviewed how to install the DHCP packages on your server.

Then we discussed how to configure the dhcpd daemon on your server using the `/etc/dhcpd.conf` file. We also discussed how to configure DHCP options in the **`dhcpd.conf`** file to pass additional IP configuration parameters to DHCP clients.

After discussing `/etc/dhcpd.conf`, we also discussed how to configure the behavior of the dhcpd daemon itself using the `/etc/sysconfig/dhcpd` file.

After reviewing the text files used to configure dhcpd, we shifted gears and learned how to expedite the DCHP configuration process with YaST. You finished this part of the chapter by completing Lab Exercise 4.1, where you implemented DHCP on your SLES 9 server.

The next topic we addressed was the problem with DHCP broadcasts. We discussed how you can use DHCP relay agents to extend DHCP services to other segments in a routed network with many subnets. The dhcrelay daemon is used on SLES 9 to provide this service.

Finally, we ended the chapter learning about Dynamic DNS. With DDNS, you link your DHCP and your DNS servers together. Whenever your DHCP server assigns an IP address to a DHCP client, it automatically updates your DNS zone with the appropriate DNS records for the host.

In Chapter 5, you're going to learn how to provide users with a powerful Linux printing solution: CUPS!

CHAPTER 5

Configuring CUPS on SLES 9

This chapter covers the following requirement for Novell's Certified Linux Engineer (CLE) 9 certification:

1. Configure network print server using CUPS.

In Chapters 3 and 4, you learned how to set up core network infrastructure services (DNS and DHCP) on your SLES 9 server. With these services running, your users can come to work, turn on their systems, and have everything "work."

With everything running, your users now need to be able to use the network to enhance their productivity. After all, organizations don't implement networks just for the fun of it. They are expensive to install and even more expensive to maintain. Why do they do it if it's so expensive? Because they increase productivity, thereby saving more money than they cost.

One of the most fundamental services provided by a network that increases user productivity is printing. Today, users take for granted that they can send a print job from their workstation to a printer in the copy room. As with the services discussed in earlier chapters, users expect this process to just "work."

In this chapter, we're going to cover how to do that by implementing the cupsd daemon on your SLES 9 server. Let's begin by talking about how printing with CUPS works.

How CUPS Works

TEST OBJECTIVE COVERED:

1. Configure network print server using CUPS.

There's no question that Linux is a high-power server operating system. Review any of the *objective* tests available on a variety of Internet websites and you will see that, on comparable hardware, Linux runs circles around other network operating systems. Basically, Linux is faster, cheaper, and more reliable.

Unfortunately, there's one network service that, historically speaking, Linux hasn't done very well: network printing. In the past, network printing under Linux was accomplished using the line printer daemon (lpd). Print jobs were submitted to the network print server from the command line. For you and I, this doesn't present much of a problem. We're comfortable with Linux shells and it doesn't bother us to compose print jobs with lp or lpr.

However, for the average user in any given organization today, this presents a huge obstacle. Most users have grown up with a graphical user interface on their PCs. They expect to be able to click **File, Print** in any productivity application, such as a spreadsheet or word processor, and have the operating system magically send the print job to the network printer. With lp and lpr, that wasn't possible.

To be viable in the workplace, Linux has to provide network printing services. How do we do that? We use CUPS!

Welcome to the World of CUPS

Fortunately, a new printing daemon was introduced in the late 1990s—the Common Unix Printing System (CUPS). CUPS makes Linux a viable option as a print server. CUPS is built around the Internet Printing Protocol (IPP). IPP is a newer protocol that was introduced in 1999. IPP is an IP-based protocol that functions at the Application layer of the OSI model and uses IP port 631.

NOTE

The IPP protocol is defined in a series of RFCs. For a high-level overview, see RFC 2568.

What's the big deal about IPP? Two words: Internet printing! IPP allows users to send print jobs to remote printers or print servers over any IP network, including your local LAN or even the Internet. To do this, IPP is tightly integrated with the Hypertext Transfer Protocol (HTTP) version 1.1. HTTP is a solid protocol that has been widely implemented.

In addition, HTTP can be easily extended. IPP itself is an extension to the HTTP protocol. Many of the existing functions and methods associated with HTTP are leveraged by IPP.

For example, you probably know that you can use the HTTP POST method to send data from a form in a web page on the client system to a web server. IPP leverages this functionality. IPP uses the HTTP POST function to send print jobs from the client system to the IPP printer or print server. Using HTTP methods, IPP provides users with the capability to submit, kill, pause, restart, or query print jobs.

To understand the full import of IPP, imagine the following scenario. You are a salesperson visiting clients in a remote city. After arriving in your hotel room one evening, you receive a phone call from your home office. Your supervisor desperately needs a printout of your sales presentation for a meeting early the next morning.

Using the wireless Internet connection provided by the hotel, you open a web browser and select an IPP-compatible printer at your home office. You then print your sales presentation over the Internet to the printer. This is shown in Figure 5.1:

FIGURE 5.1
Using IPP to print over the Internet.

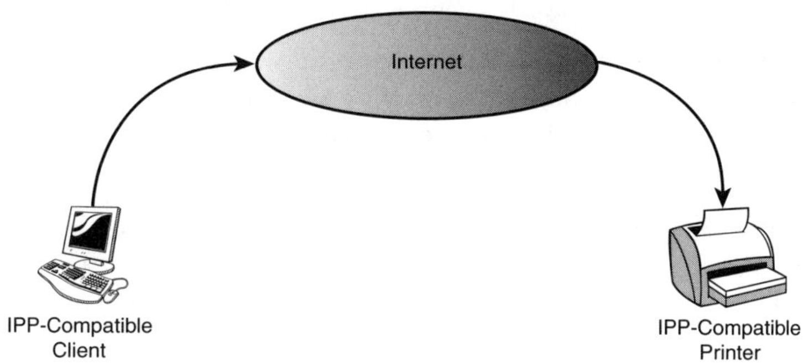

As you can see, IPP is a powerful printing protocol. It lets us do things we could only dream of just 10 years ago. When you implement CUPS on your Linux system, you gain all the benefits of IPP, providing users with a powerful network printing solution. Before you implement it, however, it's imperative that you have a solid understand of how CUPS works. Let's look at that next.

The CUPS Architecture

CUPS was designed from the ground up to make network printing as easy as possible. The CUPS daemon, cupsd, on the print server automatically announces the availability of its print queues on the local network. CUPS client systems listen to these announcements, allowing the user to select the printer he or she wants with little networking knowledge.

To provide this functionality, the CUPS system is composed of several component parts. These include the following:

- The CUPS scheduler
- CUPS filters
- CUPS backends
- PPD files
- CUPS classes
- CUPS administration web front-end

Let's look at the role played by each of these components.

THE CUPS SCHEDULER

The first CUPS component you need to be familiar with is the CUPS scheduler. Recall earlier that we said the IPP protocol is an extension to the HTTP protocol. As such, IPP (and therefore, CUPS) needs some kind of HTTP web server to function. The CUPS scheduler is just that. It's a web server that is used specifically to handle IPP requests from CUPS clients.

If you have experience working with other web servers, you may be wondering whether you can implement CUPS if another web server, such as Apache, is already running on the Linux system. The good news is that yes, you can. Remember that a typical HTTP server runs on two ports: 80 and 443.

NOTE

That's not to say you can't configure your web server to run on ports other than 80 and 443. However, most web browsers assume that any http:// URL is pointing to port 80 on the server and that any https:// URL is pointing to port 443.

If you were to configure your web server to use ports other than these, users would have to append the custom port numbers to the URL in order to access your website. For this reason, just about everyone sticks with 80 and 443 for their HTTP servers.

IPP, however, doesn't run on ports 80 or 443. Instead, it uses port 631. POST requests sent from IPP clients to the CUPS scheduler are sent using this port, allowing it to comfortably coexist with traditional web servers.

Later in this chapter, you'll look at the CUPS configuration file. When you do, you'll see that it looks a lot like the Apache web server's configuration file. In fact, many of the features and functionality associated with Apache are also available with the CUPS HTTP server.

In addition to processing print jobs, the CUPS scheduler functions as a typical web server, providing CUPS documentation as well an administration tool (discussed later) in a browser interface.

The next component you need to be familiar with is the CUPS filters.

THE CUPS FILTERS

To understand CUPS filters, you must first understand that modern printers use a variety of *printer description languages* (PDLs). In a Linux system, most applications, by default, generate print jobs using Adobe's PostScript PDL. Standardizing on PostScript makes life much easier for programmers. Instead of having to devise output specific for each make and model of printer on the market, they format print jobs in PostScript, relying on the PostScript interpreters in the printer itself to rasterize the print job onto paper.

NOTE

The printer rasterization process operates in a manner similar to the way a television or CRT computer monitor works. A TV set draws a frame on the screen by aiming its CRT guns at the top-left corner of the screen and moving it from left to right, drawing each frame one line at time.

A print job has to be rasterized as well. In the case of a laser printer, a print job is processed by the printer one page at a time. Each page is divided into tiny strips that are transferred one at a time to the drum by the laser, just like the CRT guns in a TV set.

This strategy works well if you have a PostScript-compatible printer. However, not all printers have PostScript support built in. To include PostScript support, the printer manufacturer must pay hefty licensing fees to Adobe, which can dramatically increase the price of the unit. To get around this, many printer manufacturers, such Hewlett-Packard, use the Printer Control Language (PCL) PDL. Other manufacturers, such as Epson, use the ESC/P PDL.

NOTE

Unless you work for an organization that deals with high-end printing, the printers you will support as a CLE most likely won't be PostScript-compatible. They are just too expensive.

What do you do if you don't have a PostScript-compatible printer? You use CUPS filters, which convert a print job from PostScript into the appropriate format using the PDL of the printer to which it is being sent. These filters are located in `/usr/lib/cups/filters`, as shown in Figure 5.2.

FIGURE 5.2
CUPS filters.

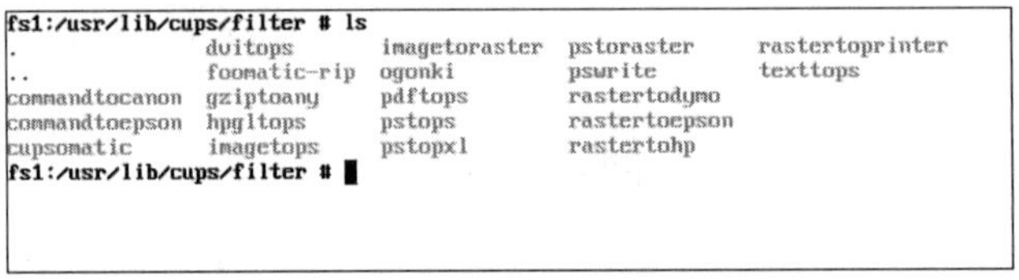

The next component you need to know about is the CUPS backends. Let's look at these next.

CUPS BACKENDS

CUPS backends are a critical component in the CUPS printing system. Backends are responsible for providing the interface between the scheduler and the actual printer hardware. The CUPS backends are located in `/usr/lib/cups/backends`, as shown in Figure 5.3.

FIGURE 5.3
CUPS backends.

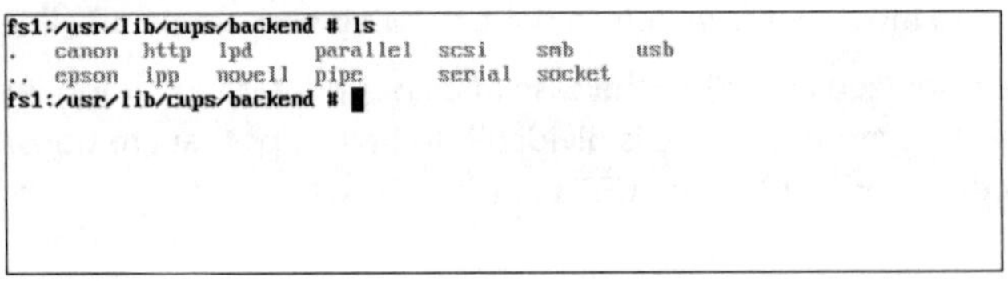

As you can see in Figure 5.3, CUPS provides backends for a variety of different printer interfaces, including the following:

- Parallel
- Serial
- USB
- IPP

- lpd
- Novell
- Samba

NOTE

The smb backend is actually installed with the Samba package. If you don't have Samba installed, you won't have the smb backend. Other backends may be installed if you install other packages on the system. For example, if you install Blackberry support on the server, you will also have a Blackberry backend installed for CUPS to use.

When the cupsd daemon starts, it queries each backend installed on the system. The backends respond to the daemon, reporting whether a printer is connected to the interface. If a printer is connected, they report specific parameters for the printer, such as the make, model, and other connection information.

The next CUPS component we will explore is the PPD files.

PPD FILES

The acronym PPD stands for PostScript Printer Description. These files are used by CUPS to determine the capabilities of a given printer. Every printer configured on your system has a PPD associated with it. These PPD files are stored in `/etc/cups/ppd`.

Now we need to look at CUPS classes.

CUPS CLASSES

Classes are a really cool component of the CUPS printing system. A CUPS class is a logical group of printers that you define. When a class has been defined, print jobs are sent to the class instead of a particular printer. The CUPS daemon then determines which printer in the class is available and sends the job to it.

This can be exceptionally useful in large organizations with many printers. For example, to increase manageability, many organizations will install all the printers for a particular floor or area in a copy room. If the printing load is large, there may be four or five printers in the copy room for users to choose from.

In this situation, you, as the network administrator, would need to configure each user workstation for each of the printers in the copy room. From the users' perspective, this presents a quandary: Which printer should they print their document to?

The Grocery Line Corollary to Murphy's Law invariably will come into play in this situation. Have you ever noticed that no matter what checkout line you choose at the grocery store, the one you choose is always the slowest one? Likewise, no matter which printer in the copy room your users choose to print to, it will invariably be the one on which a 500-page document is already printing.

CUPS classes fix this for you. In the preceding example, you could configure all the printers in the copy room into a class. Then your users can print to the class, allowing the CUPS daemon to automatically determine the next available printer and forward the document to it.

In addition, CUPS provides you with the capability to configure *implicit classes*. Implicit classes are groups of print servers. When a print job is sent to the implicit class, the next available print server is identified and the document is sent to it for processing by the printer it services.

Implicit classes provide your printing system with a degree of fault tolerance. For example, suppose you have an implicit class composed of three print servers. If one of them were to have a major hardware meltdown and become unavailable, the other two print servers automatically assume the load. All of this is completely transparent to your users. They have no idea that anything has happened. Printing just keeps working, and everyone knows that users just like things to "work."

The last CUPS component we will explore here is the web-based administration utility. Let's do that next.

THE CUPS WEB-BASED ADMINISTRATION FRONT-END

To configure the CUPS service on your Linux system, you have two options: command-line tools or a web-based graphical interface. I've done it both ways and the web-based interface is by far the fastest and easiest way to go.

The web-based administrative interface is provided by the CUPS Scheduler. Remember that the CUPS Scheduler is actually an HTTP server. As such, it can be used to serve up web pages and web-based applications such as the CUPS administration utility. The important point to remember is that it runs on port 631, not port 80 as with a typical web server.

To access the CUPS web-based administration utility, open a browser window and navigate to http://*your_server_IP*:631. When you do, the screen in Figure 5.4 is displayed.

This utility can be used to set up a printer, create classes, and manage print jobs.

With these various components in mind, let's briefly review how they work together to provide a printing solution for your network.

FIGURE 5.4
The CUPS web-based administration utility.

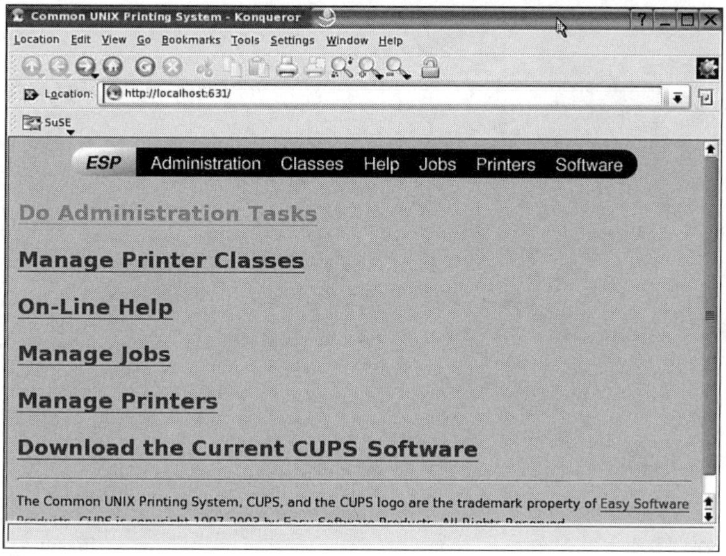

The CUPS Printing Process

When a print job is submitted to a CUPS server, the process depicted in Figure 5.5 occurs.

1. An application on the client system generates a print job and sends it to the CUPS scheduler (cupsd) on the server.
2. The scheduler saves the job in the print queue spooling directory. As it does so, the print job is split into two parts:
   - Queue and filter information from the print job are saved in `/var/spool/cups`. It is saved in a file that is named with c concatenated with a print job number assigned by cupsd; for example, **c00015**.
   - The document itself to be printed is saved in `/var/spool/cups`. It's saved in a file named with a d concatenated with the print job number assigned by cupsd, such as d00015-001.
3. The print job is sent to the filter for conversion to the appropriate PDL.

FIGURE 5.5
The CUPS printing process.

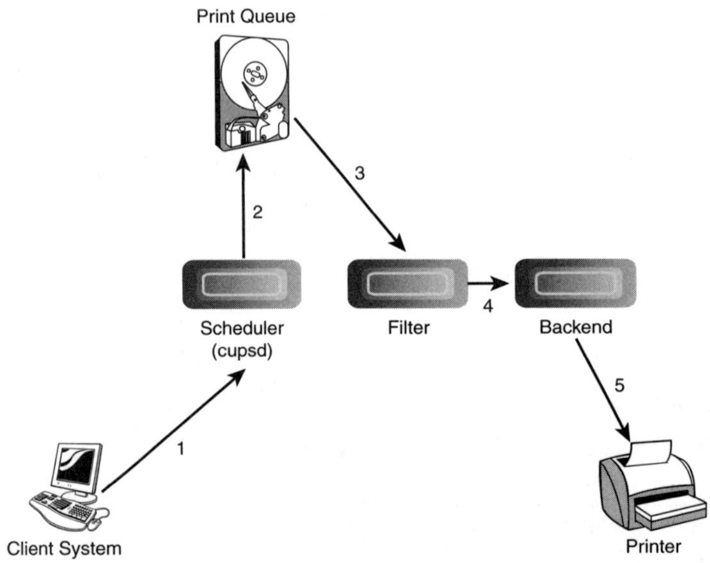

NOTE

Depending on the type of printer used, it's possible that more than one filter will be needed. If this is the case, a *filter chain* will be established; passing the job from filter to filter until it is in the correct format for the particular printer being used.

4. The converted print job is sent from the filter to the backend.
5. The backend sends the job to the printer.

When the backend is finished sending the job to the printer, it notifies the cupsd daemon, which then deletes the print job from the print queue.

Now that you know how the CUPS printing system works, you need to learn how to implement and configure it on a SLES 9 system.

Installing CUPS on SLES 9

TEST OBJECTIVE COVERED:

1. Configure network print server using CUPS.

With the DNS and DHCP services we explored in previous chapters, you could choose from a variety of packages to install the particular daemon on your SLES 9 system. This isn't the case with CUPS. There's only one version of CUPS, provided by Easy Software. This is the package you need to know about to pass your CLE 9 certification exam. For more information about CUPS, visit `http://www.cups.org`.

To install the CUPS service on your SLES 9 server, complete the following:

1. From your SLES 9 desktop, select **YaST**.
2. When prompted, provide your root password.
3. In the left frame, select **Software**.
4. In the right frame, select **Install and Remove Software**. The screen in Figure 5.6 appears.

FIGURE 5.6
YaST software management screen.

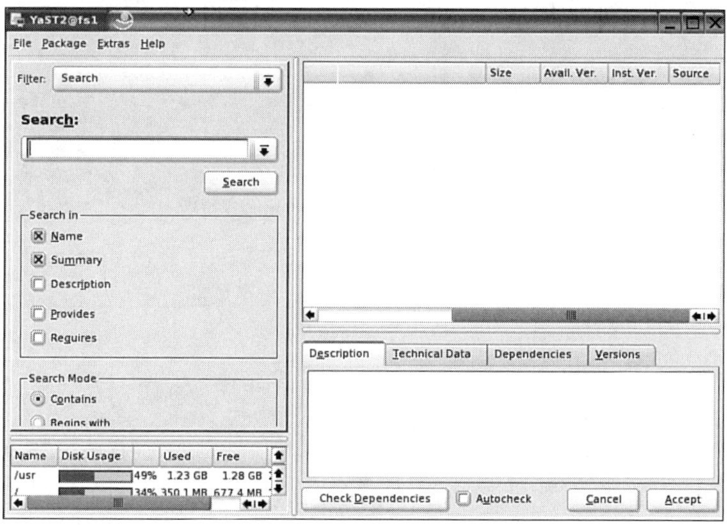

5. In the Search field, enter **cups**; then select **Search**.
6. Mark the following packages (as shown in Figure 5.7):
    - **cups**
    - **cups-client** (optional)
    - **cups-drivers**
    - **cups-drivers-stp** (optional)
    - **cups-libs**
    - **cups-SUSE-ppds-dat**
    - **xpp**

FIGURE 5.7
Installing CUPS packages.

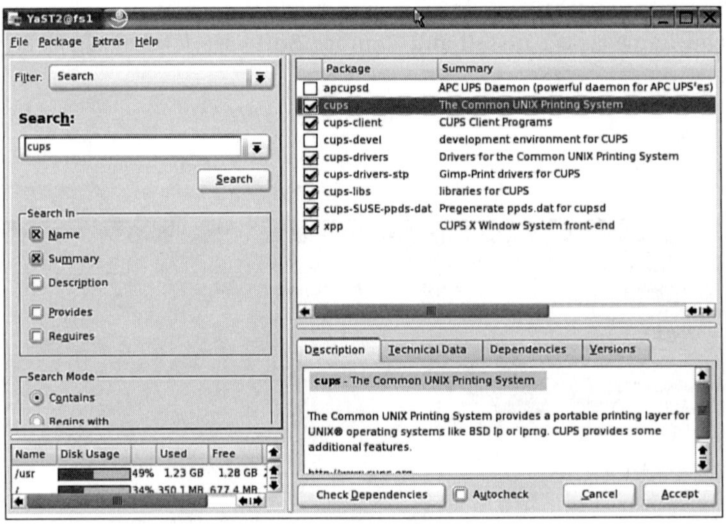

7. Select **Accept**.
8. When prompted, insert the appropriate CDs.

TIP

Be aware that CUPS has a lot of dependencies. It may take some time to complete the installation.

9. Wait while the packages are installed and SuSEconfig is run.
10. Close YaST by selecting **Close**.

If you followed the steps in the lab exercises in Chapter 2, your SLES 9 system should already have the CUPS server and client packages installed.

To verify that it's there, open YaST and select **Software, Install and Remove Software**. In the search field, enter **cups** and then select **Search**. You should see various CUPS packages marked with blue check marks, as shown in Figure 5.8.

FIGURE 5.8
CUPS packages that are already installed.

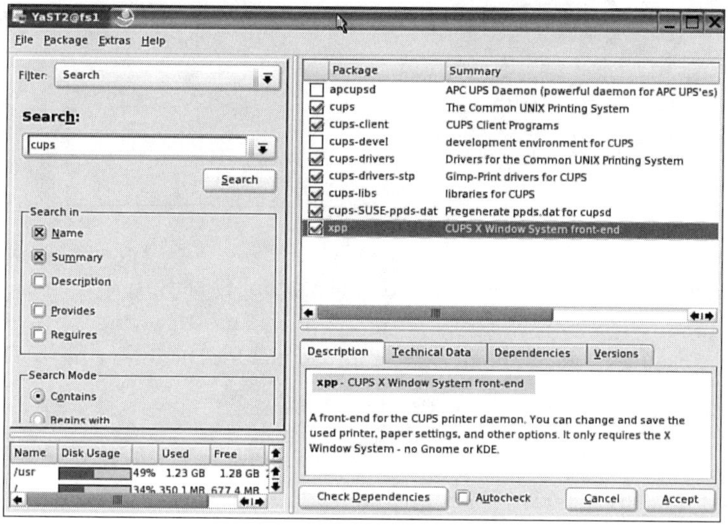

If, for some reason, the CUPS packages aren't installed on your SLES 9 system, follow the previous steps to install them.

After the packages are installed, the service is started and stopped using the `cups` init script in `/etc/init.d`, as shown in Figure 5.9.

The actual binary that provides this service is the `cupsd` executable located in `/usr/sbin`, as shown in Figure 5.10.

FIGURE 5.9
CUPS startup script.

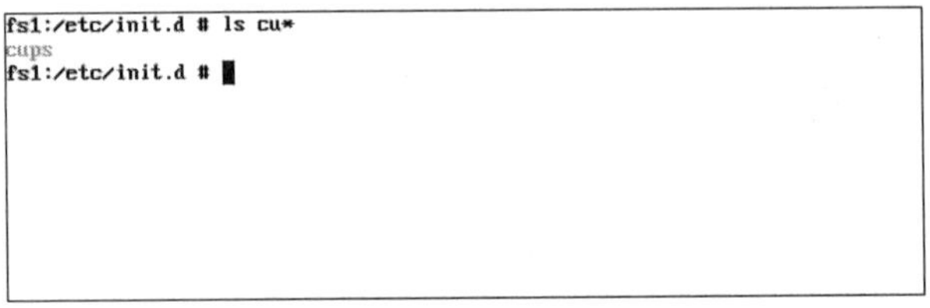

FIGURE 5.10
CUPS binary.

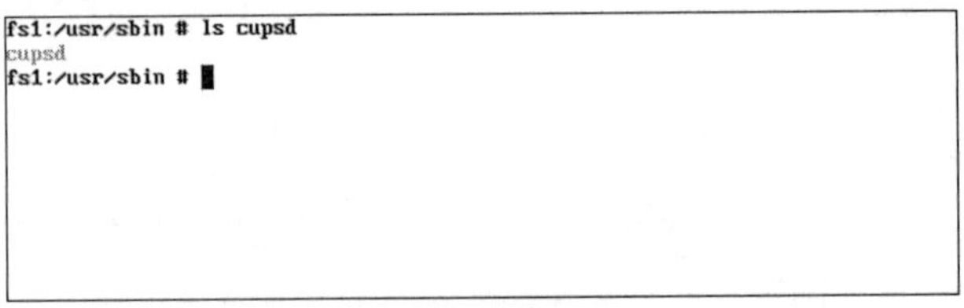

Like other daemons, you use the `/etc/init.d/cups` script to start, stop, or restart the cupsd daemon on your server. This is done by calling the script and supplying the appropriate parameter. Some examples of commands you can use include the following:

- `/etc/init.d/cups start`—Starts the dhcpd daemon.
- `/etc/init.d/cups stop`—Stops the dhcpd daemon.
- `/etc/init.d/cups restart`—Restarts the dhcpd daemon.

If you don't want to use the full path, you can also enter **`rccups`** from the shell prompt along with the **`start`**, **`stop`**, or **`restart`** parameters to manage the cupsd daemon.

After the DHCP service is installed on your system, you're ready to configure and start the CUPS service on your server. However, before doing so, you need to have a solid understanding of the cupsd daemon's configuration files. Let's look at those next.

Working with CUPS on SLES 9

TEST OBJECTIVE COVERED:

1. Configure network print server using CUPS.

From the preceding pages in this chapter, you may have reached the conclusion that CUPS is a complex system, and you would be correct. CUPS has a higher degree of complexity than DNS or DHCP, which we covered in earlier chapters. Fortunately, in spite of its complexity, CUPS is relatively easy to implement and administer. In this part of this chapter, you'll learn how this is done. Let's begin by learning about the files that are used to configure CUPS.

CUPS Configuration Files

As with any other Linux service, CUPS is configured using several text files in the `/etc` directory. CUPS configuration files are stored in the `cups` directory within `/etc`. As I've said many times already in this book, you really should have a solid understanding of these files before you start configuring and deploying the service.

To do this, we're going to spend a considerable amount of time reviewing these files. After you're comfortable with them, you'll then learn how to use a GUI interface to make some of your administrative work easier and faster.

NOTE

Of the files we're going to look at here, `cupsd.conf` is the *only* one you should ever attempt to edit manually. Easy Software, the author of CUPS, recommends that all other files should be configured using the GUI interface.

However, we're going to have to break with tradition when we reach that point. Unlike DNS and DHCP, YaST doesn't include a module for configuring CUPS. Instead, we will use the CUPS web-based administration interface to perform our configuration work.

Let's begin. The first file we need to look at is `cupsd.conf`.

cupsd.conf

The `/etc/cups/cupsd.conf` file is the main configuration file you will use to configure the cupsd service. Recall that we said cupsd is really a type of HTTP server. As such, the `cupsd.conf` file is similar to the conf files used to configure other web servers, such as Apache. A sample `cupsd.conf` file is shown in Figure 5.11.

FIGURE 5.11
The cupsd.conf file.

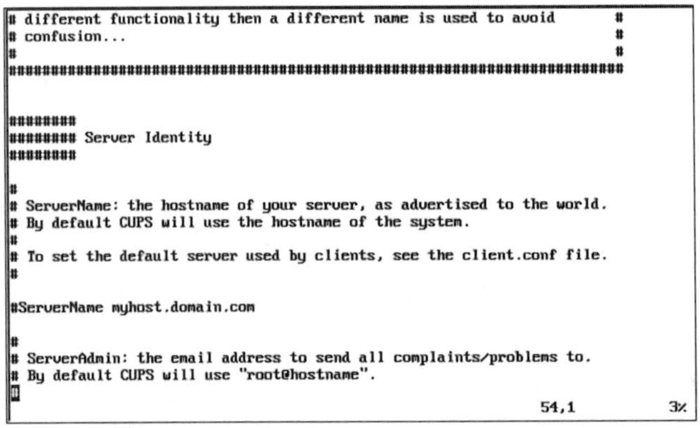

The **cupsd.conf** file is a very long file. Only a very small portion of it is shown in Figure 5.11. The **cupsd.conf** file is composed of many server directives that control the way cupsd operates.

Before we go any further, understand that there are more directives in this file than we can possible cover here (at least, not without putting you to sleep). Some of the directives are more useful than others. In this part of the chapter, I'm going to present a relative handful of directives that I find most useful. If you want to learn more about all of the directives contained in the cupsd.conf file, either visit http://www.cups.org or, on your CUPS server, open http://localhost:631/sam.html. Both of these locations will provide you with an exhaustive list of the many directives in this file.

TIP

When you're taking your CLE practical exam, don't forget that you are allowed to use the various documentation sources available on your server. Being able to look at a man page or the on-line CUPS documentation could be a real lifesaver!

If you look at the **cupsd.conf** file, you'll notice that it is divided into several logical groupings of directives. This makes it relatively easy to locate a particular directive you need to modify. The groupings include the following:

- Server Identity
- Server Options

- Fax Support
- Encryption Support
- Filter Options
- Network Options
- Security Options

Some of the more useful `cupsd.conf` directives within these groups that you need to be familiar with include the following:

- Server Identity
  - `ServerName`—This directive specifies the server name that is announced to CUPS clients. If not explicitly specified here, cupsd will default to the server's hostname.
  - `ServerAdmin`—This directive specifies the email address users can use to contact the CUPS administrator.

- Server Options
  - `DataDir`—This directive specifies the directory where CUPS data files are stored. By default, this is `/usr/share/cups`.
  - `DocumentRoot`—Just as with any other HTTP server, you need to specify where documents cupsd servers to clients are located. This directive specifies the directory where these files reside. By default, this is `/usr/share/doc/packages/cups`.
  - `LogLevel`—This directive specifies the level of detail stored in log files. You must use one of the following options as a value for this directive:
    - none—Log nothing.
    - error—Log only errors.
    - warn—Log errors and warnings.
    - info—Log errors, warnings, and all print requests. (Default)
    - debug—Log just about all messages from cupsd.
    - debug2—Log all messages from cupsd.

  - `PreserveJobHistory` and `PreserveJobFiles`—These directives can be used to keep jobs in the print queue after they have been processed. Although not advisable for day-to-day operations, this can be a useful troubleshooting tool. The default value is `no`.

- `MaxCopies`—This directive can be used to set a limit on the number of copies a user can request for a particular print job. The default value is 100.
- `MaxJobsPerUser`—This directive can be used to limit the number of print jobs a user can have active. By default, there's no limit.
- `ServerRoot`—This directive specifies the location of the configuration files used by cupsd. By default, this is `/etc/cups`.

- Encryption Support
  - `ServerCertificate`—This directive specifies the SSL certificate to be used by cupsd. By default, this is `/etc/cups/ssl/server.crt`.
  - `ServerKey`—This directive specifies the key file to be used by cupsd. By default, this is `/etc/cups/ssl/server.key`.

- Filter Support
  - `User`—This directive specifies the user that cupsd runs as. By default, this is the lp user.
  - `Group`—This directive specifies the group that cupsd runs as. By default, this is the lp group.

- Network Options
  - `Port`—This directive specifies the IP port that cupsd runs on. By default, it uses the IPP port of 631.
  - `MaxClients`—This directive sets a limit on the number of concurrent client connections. By default this is set to 100.

- Browsing Options
  - `Browsing`—This directive specifies whether or not cupsd will announce its printers via broadcasts on the local network segment. The default value is on.
  - `BrowseProtocols`—This directive specifies the protocol that cupsd should use to announce printers. You can use cups, slp, or all (which uses both cups and slp) as values for this directive. The default value is cups.
  - `BrowseAddress`—This directive specifies the broadcast address cupsd should use to announce its printers. This directive is disabled by default. Until you enable it, cupsd won't announce its printers. You should use the broadcast address of your subnet as the value for this parameter. For example, if your network address is 192.168.1.0, you would use 192.168.1.255.

TIP

This is the number one problem I've observed folks encounter when using CUPS. CUPS administrators just assume that printer announcement is enabled by default. If you find that your clients can't see the printers on your CUPS server, this directive should be the first thing you check.

- `BrowseInterval`—This directive specifies the interval, in seconds, between printer announcements. The default value is 30 seconds.
- `ImplicitClasses`—This directive enables implicit classes on your network. By default this directive is set to on. When enabled, you can create an implicit class by configuring all the printers you want in the implicit class with the same name (such as HPLJ5). All printers with the same name are automatically put into an implicit class of the same name. If a client system then sends a print job to the printer name, it is automatically forwarded to the first available print queue on the associated CUPS server.
- `HideImplicitMembers`—If ImplicitClasses is enabled, then this directive, if enabled, will configure cupsd to show all print queues in the class as a single queue. This directive is enabled by default.

As I alluded earlier, there's no graphical utility available for editing cupsd.conf. To make changes, you have use your trusty old vi or kate text editor.

After you've got cupsd.conf edited the way you want, you need to understand the role of the `classes.conf` file. Let's look at this file next.

classes.conf

The `/etc/cups/classes.conf` file is used to define printer classes in your network. This file doesn't contain any parameters for implicit classes, however. Only regular printer classes can be defined in `classes.conf`. A portion of a sample `classes.conf` file is shown in Figure 5.12.

The directives within `classes.conf` include the following:

- *<Class name>*—The Class directive defines a class and must begin any class definition.
- Info—The Info directive allows you to specify descriptive information about the class you are defining.
- Location—The Location directive allows you to specify the physical location of the printer, such as "2nd Floor Copy Room."
- State—The State directive allows you to set the initial state of the class. The possible values are Idle and Stopped.

FIGURE 5.12
The `classes.conf` file.

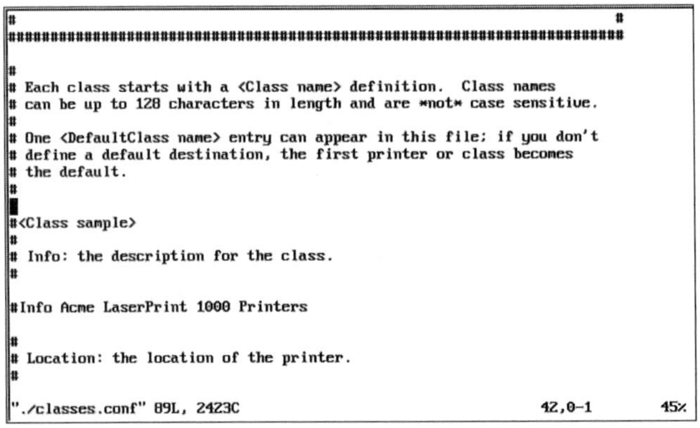

```
#                                                                   #
#####################################################################

#
# Each class starts with a <Class name> definition.  Class names
# can be up to 128 characters in length and are *not* case sensitive.
#
# One <DefaultClass name> entry can appear in this file; if you don't
# define a default destination, the first printer or class becomes
# the default.
#

#<Class sample>
#
# Info: the description for the class.
#

#Info Acme LaserPrint 1000 Printers

#
# Location: the location of the printer.
#
"./classes.conf" 89L, 2423C                          42,0-1        45%
```

- Accepting—This directive specifies whether the class can accept new jobs. The possible values are Yes and No.
- Printer—The Printer directive includes a specific print queue in the class.
- *</Class>*—This directive is used to end the class definition.

You should never manually edit this file. Instead, you should use the CUPS web-based front end to configure this file.

TIP

Alternatively, you can also use the `lpadmin` utility from a shell prompt. To see how to use this utility to configure `classes.conf`, see the lpadmin man page.

The next CUPS configuration file you need to be familiar with is the **`printers.conf`** file.

`printers.conf`

The `/etc/cups/printers.conf` file is used to configure the printers serviced by cupsd. A portion of a sample `printers.conf` file is shown in Figure 5.13.

The directives used in the `printers.conf` file include the following:

- <Printer *name*>—The Printer directive begins a printer definition. The *name* parameter specifies the name of the printer being defined.
- Info—The Info directive enables you to specify descriptive information about the printer you are defining.

FIGURE 5.13
The `printers.conf` file.

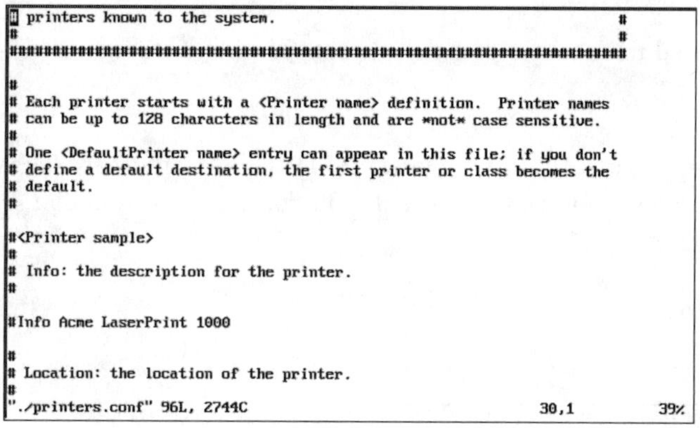

```
# printers known to the system.                                          #
#                                                                        #
##########################################################################

#
# Each printer starts with a <Printer name> definition.  Printer names
# can be up to 128 characters in length and are *not* case sensitive.
#
# One <DefaultPrinter name> entry can appear in this file; if you don't
# define a default destination, the first printer or class becomes the
# default.
#

#<Printer sample>
#
# Info: the description for the printer.
#

#Info Acme LaserPrint 1000

#
# Location: the location of the printer.
#
"./printers.conf" 96L, 2744C                                 30,1          39%
```

- Location—The Location directive enables you to describe the physical location of the printer.
- DeviceURI—The DeviceURI directive enables you to specify a URI for the printer. CUPS URIs can take the following forms:
  - IPP printer—`ipp://host/path`
  - Parallel printer—`parallel://dev/lp0`
  - USB printer—`usb://dev/usb/lpx`
  - Shared Samba printer—`smb://`*`host/printer`*

TIP

URI stands for Uniform Resource Identifier. It's a super-ordinate class of Internet name-space identifiers. A URI includes the protocol used to access a resource, the name of the host where the resource resides, and the specific name of the resource. A URL is a type of URI. A typical URL includes the protocol (http), the name of the host (www.novell.com), and the specific resource (such as index.html).

- State—The State directive enables you to set the initial state of the printer. The possible values are Idle and Stopped.
- Accepting—This directive specifies whether the printer can accept new jobs. The possible values are Yes and No.
- </Printer>—This directive ends the printer definition.

As with `classes.conf`, we're discouraged from manually editing the `/etc/cups/printers.conf` file. Instead we're encouraged to use either lpadmin or the CUPS web-based administration utility.

The next file you need to be aware of is the `mime.types` file. Let's look at this file next.

`mime.types`

Like the `mime.types` file associated with other HTTP services, the `/etc/cups/mime.types` file is used to associate a given file with a particular file format. A portion of a sample `mime.types` file is shown in Figure 5.14.

FIGURE 5.14
The `mime.types` file.

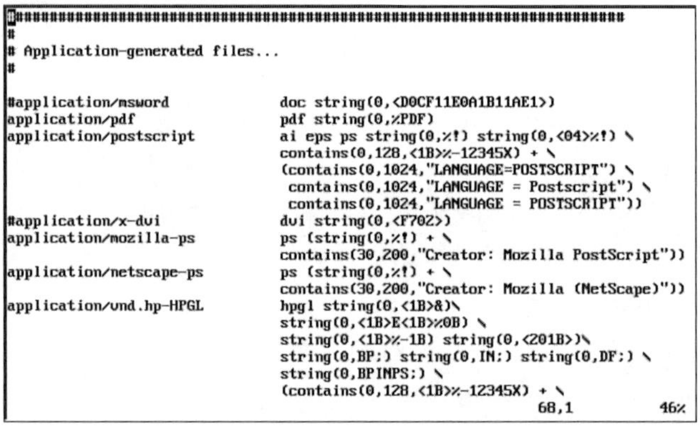

```
############################################################################
#
# Application-generated files...
#

#application/msword             doc string(0,<D0CF11E0A1B11AE1>)
application/pdf                 pdf string(0,%PDF)
application/postscript          ai eps ps string(0,%!) string(0,<04>%!) \
                                contains(0,128,<1B>%-12345X) + \
                                (contains(0,1024,"LANGUAGE=POSTSCRIPT") \
                                 contains(0,1024,"LANGUAGE = Postscript") \
                                 contains(0,1024,"LANGUAGE = POSTSCRIPT"))
#application/x-dvi              dvi string(0,<F702>)
application/mozilla-ps          ps (string(0,%!) + \
                                contains(30,200,"Creator: Mozilla PostScript"))
application/netscape-ps         ps (string(0,%!) + \
                                contains(30,200,"Creator: Mozilla (NetScape)"))
application/vnd.hp-HPGL         hpgl string(0,<1B>&)\
                                string(0,<1B>E<1B>%0B) \
                                string(0,<1B>%-1B) string(0,<201B>)\
                                string(0,BP;) string(0,IN;) string(0,DF;) \
                                string(0,BPINPS;) \
                                (contains(0,128,<1B>%-12345X) + \
                                                          68,1          46%
```

You probably will not need to make any changes to this file. The `mime.types` file works hand-in-hand with the `mime.convs` file. Let's look at it next.

`mime.convs`

The `/etc/cups/mime.convs` file works with the `mime.types` file to define specific filters to be used with each file type. A portion of a sample `mime.convs` file is shown in Figure 5.15.

As with the `mime.types` file, you probably won't ever need to edit the `mime.convs` file.

Those are the files that are used to configure the cupsd daemon running on your server. You're probably getting tired of learning CUPS theory, so let's shift gears and start implementing it!

FIGURE 5.15
The `mime.convs` file.

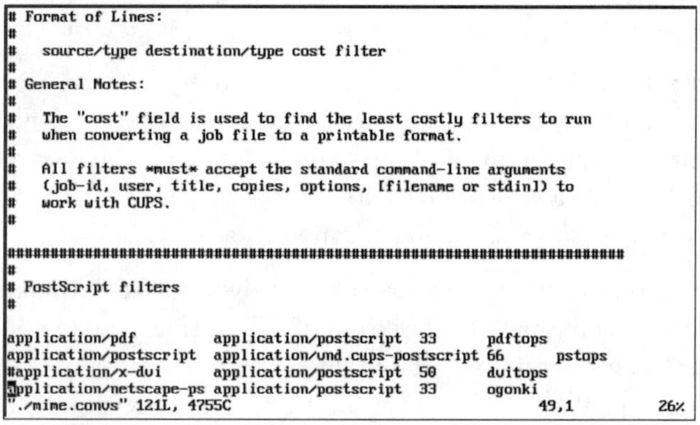

```
# Format of Lines:
#
#   source/type destination/type cost filter
#
# General Notes:
#
#   The "cost" field is used to find the least costly filters to run
#   when converting a job file to a printable format.
#
#   All filters *must* accept the standard command-line arguments
#   (job-id, user, title, copies, options, [filename or stdin]) to
#   work with CUPS.
#

########################################################################
#
# PostScript filters
#

application/pdf         application/postscript  33      pdftops
application/postscript  application/vnd.cups-postscript 66      pstops
#application/x-dvi      application/postscript  50      dvitops
application/netscape-ps application/postscript  33      ogonki
"./mime.convs" 121L, 4755C                              49,1          26%
```

Configuring CUPS on SLES 9

Let's get CUPS running on SLES 9. To do so, you need to complete the follow tasks:

- Configure a CUPS administrator.
- Configure and start cupsd.
- Configure a CUPS printer.
- Configure Linux CUPS clients.
- Create classes.

Let's begin by setting up a user account to serve as the CUPS administrator.

CONFIGURING A CUPS ADMINISTRATOR

To understand why you need to configure a CUPS administrative user account, you first need to understand that, by default on SLES 9, CUPS is not configured to use the same user accounts that your Linux system uses. Instead, CUPS is configured to use Digest authentication. This is controlled within the `/etc/cups/cupsd.conf` file using the `AuthType` directive. The `AuthType` directive has three possible values:

- None—This value configures CUPS to provide anonymous user access. No username or password is required to use the system.
- Basic—This value configures CUPS to use your Linux system's `/etc/passwd` file to authenticate users.

- Digest—This value configures CUPS to use Digest authentication to authenticate users. This is the default value when you install CUPS on SLES 9. In this configuration, user accounts are stored in a separate file called `passwd.md5`, which is located in `/etc/cups`.

At first glance, you may be thinking that Basic authentication might be the better choice. Unfortunately, it has some weaknesses. With Basic authentication, usernames and passwords are transmitted clear-text when authenticating to the printing system. For most network administrators, this keeps us awake at night. It's just too easy for someone on the network with a sniffer to capture sensitive user authentication data.

Digest authentication, on the other hand, doesn't actually send the username and password to authenticate. Instead, it sends an MD5 checksum of the username and password. This makes it much more secure than Basic authentication. Even if someone were to capture the checksum, it's very unlikely that they would be able to decipher it back into the original username and password.

With that background in mind, you can now see why we need to configure a CUPS administrative user. Our root user account doesn't exist in the `passwd.md5` file. To add an administrative user to the Digest authentication system, we use the `lppasswd` command from a shell prompt. To create an administrative user in the `passwd.md5` file named root who is a member of the CUPS administration group named sys, you use the following command:

```
lppasswd -g sys -a root
```

Until you do this, you won't be able to use the CUPS web-based administration utility. For security purposes, the folks at SUSE recommend that, if you use root, you don't use the same password as your Linux system root user.

Now that we've got an administrative user set up, your next task is to configure your `cupsd.conf` file.

CONFIGURING THE `cupsd.conf` FILE AND STARTING CUPSD

The way you configure `cupsd.conf` will largely depend on the particular situation you are implementing the system in. The good news is that, for a basic implementation, you don't need to do a whole lot.

However, as mentioned earlier, you must enable the `BrowseAddress` directive or CUPS won't announce its printers. This directive isn't enabled by default. I'd like to have a nickel for each time I've been asked "Why can't my Linux clients see my CUPS printer?" Every single time, it's because the administrator hasn't uncommented the `BrowseAddress` directive. This directive can use the following possible values:

- `@LOCAL`—This value will cause CUPS to send its printer announcement broadcasts to all local interfaces in the system. This is the value that is most typically used.
- `@IF(interface_name)`—If you have multiple interfaces in the server, you can use this value to cause CUPS to send its broadcasts to a specific network interface.
- `Broadcast_Address:631`—You can also specify a specific broadcast address to send printer announcements to. For example, you could use 255.255.255.255 or 192.168.1.255. If you use this option, be sure to remember to add the :631 port number to the end of the broadcast address.

NOTE

The `cupsd.conf` file points out that if you use a networkwide broadcast address of 255.255.255.255:631, the printer announcements will be sent to all network interfaces in the system, including dial-up connections. Using the @LOCAL value will cause the broadcasts to be sent only to nondialup network interfaces.

A sample `cupsd.conf` file with the `BrowseAddress` directive enabled is shown in Figure 5.16.

FIGURE 5.16
Enabling printer announcements in `cupsd.conf`.

```
# Class A, B, C, or D netmask (i.e. no CIDR support).
#
# Note: Using the "global" broadcast address (255.255.255.255) will
# activate a Linux demand-dial link with the default configuration.
# If you have a LAN as well as the dial-up link, use the LAN's
# broadcast address.
#
# The @LOCAL address broadcasts to all non point-to-point interfaces.
# For example, if you have a LAN and a dial-up link, @LOCAL would
# send printer updates to the LAN but not to the dial-up link.
# Similarly, the @IF(name) address sends to the named network
# interface, e.g. @IF(eth0) under Linux.  Interfaces are refreshed
# automatically (no more than once every 60 seconds), so they can
# be used on dynamically-configured interfaces, e.g. PPP, 802.11, etc.
#

#BrowseAddress x.y.z.255
#BrowseAddress x.y.255.255
#BrowseAddress x.255.255.255
#BrowseAddress 255.255.255.255
BrowseAddress @LOCAL
#BrowseAddress @IF(name)

-- INSERT --                                        512,1         61%
```

After you have your `cupsd.conf` file configured, you can start your cupsd daemon. This is done using the `/etc/init.d/cups` init script. It can also be done using the `rccups` command, which was discussed earlier in the chapter.

With your `cupsd.conf` file configured and the cupsd daemon running, your next task is to configure a CUPS printer and queue on the server.

CONFIGURING A CUPS PRINTER

Remember that CUPS printers are defined in the `/etc/cups/printers.conf` file. Although you could manually edit it, the folks at both Easy Software and SUSE strongly recommend that you use the CUPS web-based administration utility instead. Frankly, I agree. Configuring a CUPS printer is a snap when you use this utility. To configure a CUPS printer, complete the following on your CUPS server:

1. From your server, start a web browser.
2. Navigate to `http://localhost:631`. The screen shown in Figure 5.17 is displayed.

FIGURE 5.17
Accessing the CUPS web-based administration utility.

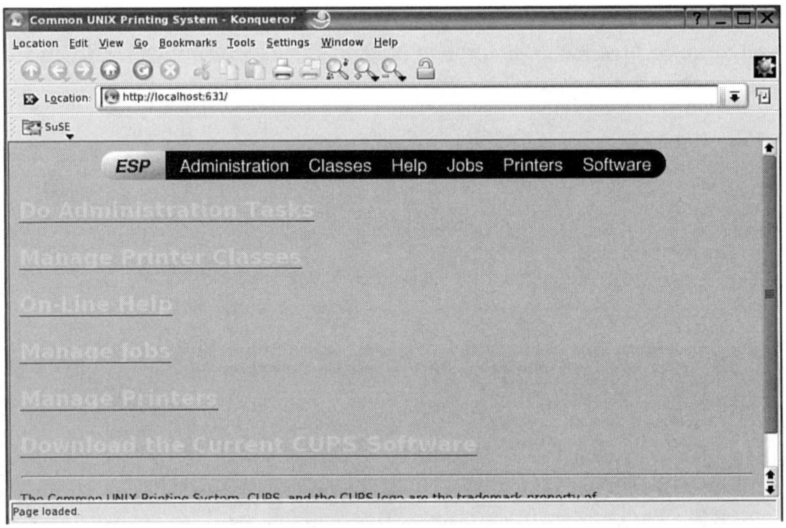

3. Select **Administration**.
4. When prompted, authenticate as the *user* you configured earlier using lppasswd. The screen shown in Figure 5.18 is displayed.
5. Under Printers, select **Add Printer**. The screen shown in Figure 5.19 is displayed.
6. In the Name field, enter a name for the printer.
7. In the Location field, enter a descriptive location for the printer.
8. In the Description field, enter a description of the printer.
9. Select **Continue**. The screen shown in Figure 5.20 is displayed.

FIGURE 5.18
CUPS System Administration page.

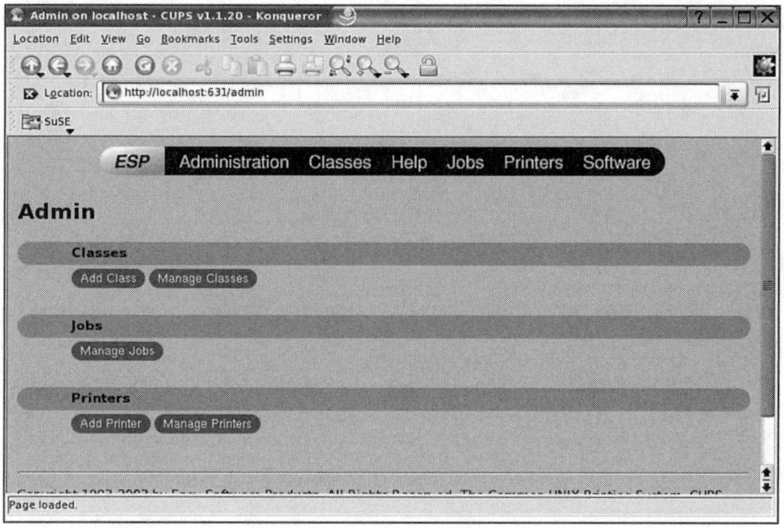

FIGURE 5.19
Configuring a CUPS printer.

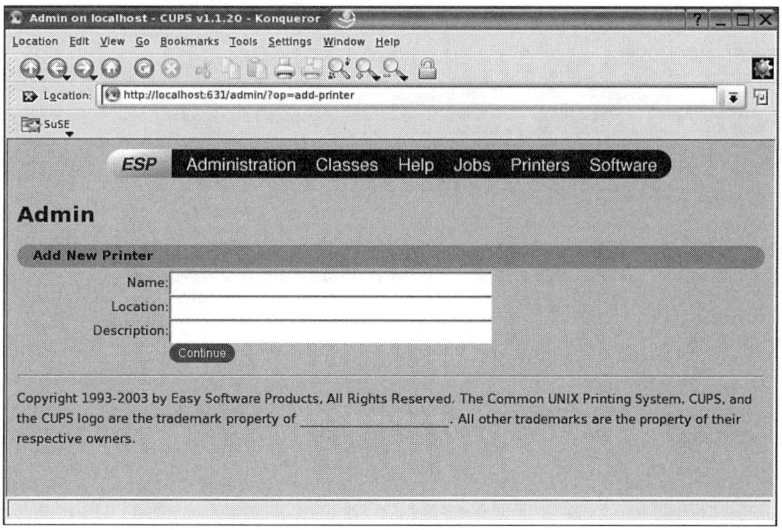

FIGURE 5.20
Configuring the printer device.

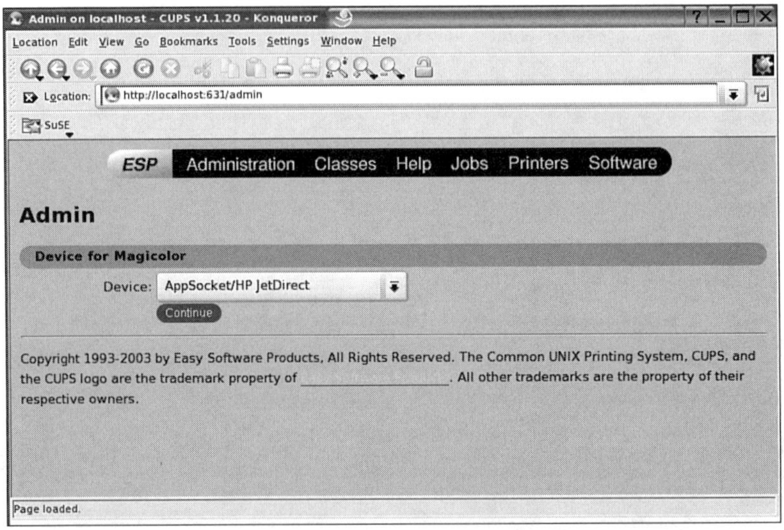

10. In the Device drop-down list, select the *interface* where the printer is connected.
11. Select **Continue**. The screen shown in Figure 5.21 is displayed.

FIGURE 5.21
Configuring the printer driver.

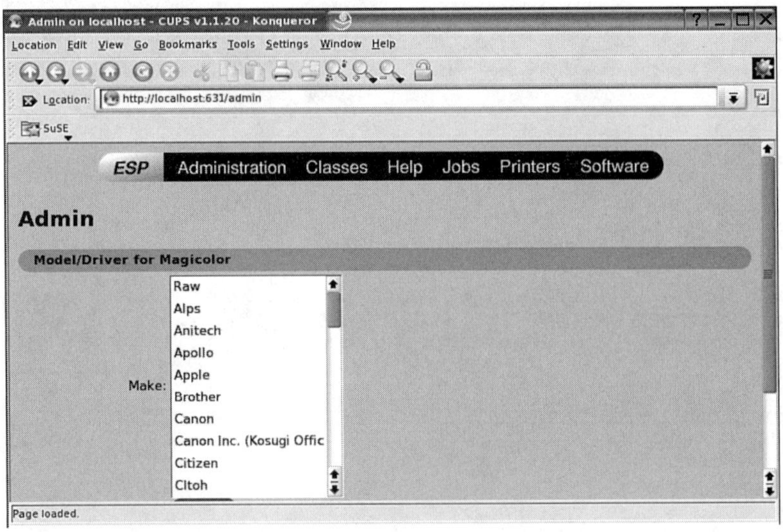

12. In the Model/Driver screen, select the *printer manufacturer*.
13. Select **Continue**.
14. In the Model field, select your *printer model*.
15. Select **Continue**. A page is displayed indicating that the printer has been added.
16. To see the current status of your printer, select the link for your printer. The screen shown in Figure 5.22 is displayed.

FIGURE 5.22
CUPS printer status.

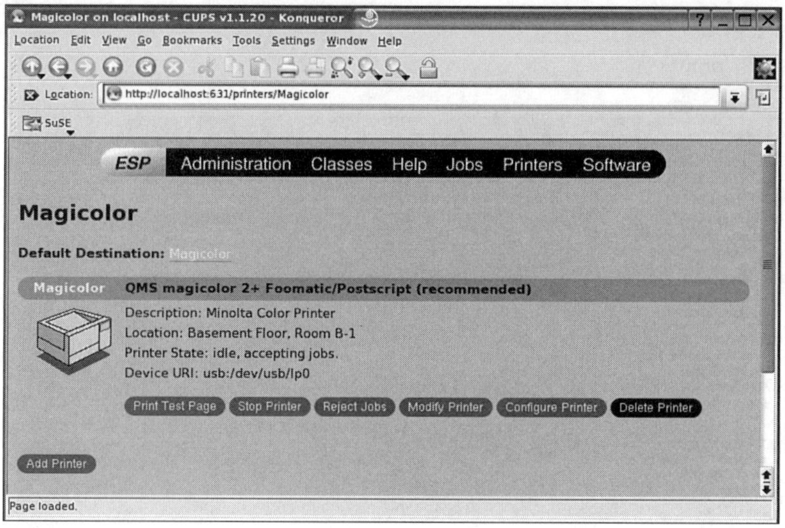

From the Printer Status page, you can control your CUPS printer. You can send a test page, stop the printer, kill print jobs, modify the printer properties, or delete the printer.

With your printer up and running, your next task is to configure CUPS clients to use the printer you just set up.

CONFIGURING CUPS CLIENTS

This is where CUPS really shines. The cupsd daemon on your server sends out a broadcast every 30 seconds (by default) announcing the printers it has available. For your client systems to use it, you need to configure them to listen for CUPS printers on the network.

How this is done varies from distribution to distribution. For your CLE 9 certification, you only need to know how to do this on a SUSE client system, so that's what we're going to cover here.

On a Novell Linux Desktop 9 system, you configure a CUPS printer by doing the following:

1. Start YaST by selecting **System**, **Administrator Settings**.
2. Authenticate as your root user.
3. Select **Hardware, Printer**. If you specified that the system listen for CUPS servers when you installed the OS, the screen in Figure 5.23 will be displayed. This is the default option for NLD, so it's very likely that this is the case. If so, your job is done! If not, continue on to step 4.

FIGURE 5.23
Listening for CUPS printers.

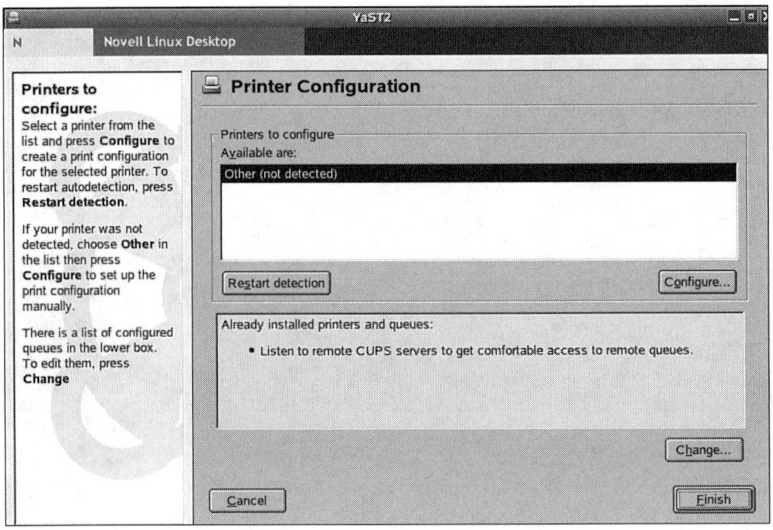

4. If your system isn't already configured to listen for CUPS broadcasts, do the following:
   a. Under Already Installed Printers and Queues, select **Change**.
   b. Select **Add**.
   c. Mark **Print via CUPS Network Server**, as shown in Figure 5.24.

FIGURE 5.24
Configuring NLD 9 to listen for CUPS servers.

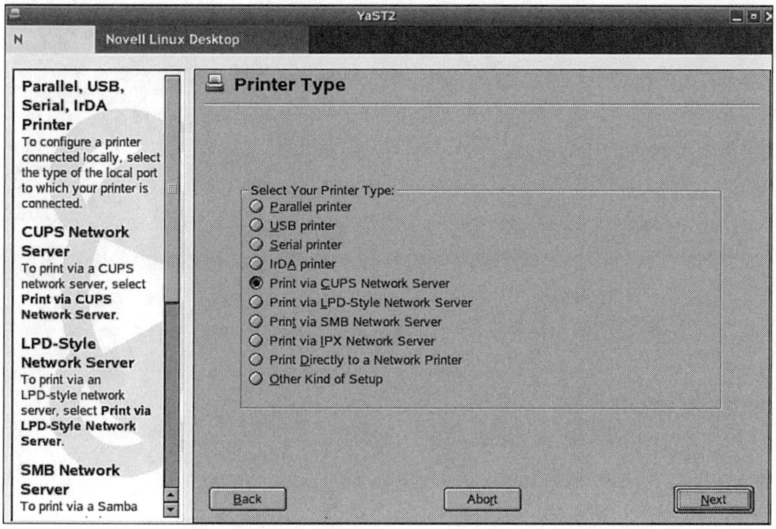

d. Select **Next**.

e. In the Connection Type screen, mark **CUPS Using Broadcasting**, as shown in Figure 5.25.

f. Select **Next**.

g. In the Listening to Remote CUPS Servers screen, ensure **Listen to IPP Broadcast Packets** is marked; then select **OK**.

h. Select **Finish**.

5. Test the configuration by completing the following:

   a. On the NLD 9 system, open an application from which you can generate a print job.

      OpenOffice.org works really well for this.

   b. Select **File, Print**. Your CUPS printer should be displayed as an available printer; as shown in Figure 5.26.

From this demonstration, you should now begin to grasp the power and value of CUPS. All the configuration work is done at the server, not at the client. This is unique among the various printing services available with other network operating systems. If you make a change to an existing printer, delete a printer, or add a printer, your modifications are almost immediately made available to your users. You don't have to walk around from system to system to reconfigure them. That makes life nice for you and me.

FIGURE 5.25
Configuring NLD 9 to listen for CUPS broadcasts.

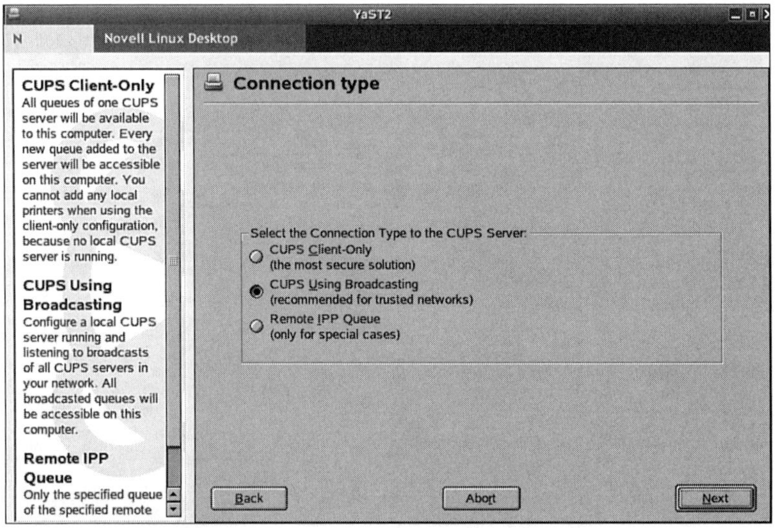

Before we move on to Lab Exercise 5.1 where you will set up your own CUPS system, we need to cover one more topic for your CLE 9 exam: configuring printer classes.

FIGURE 5.26
Printing to a CUPS printer.

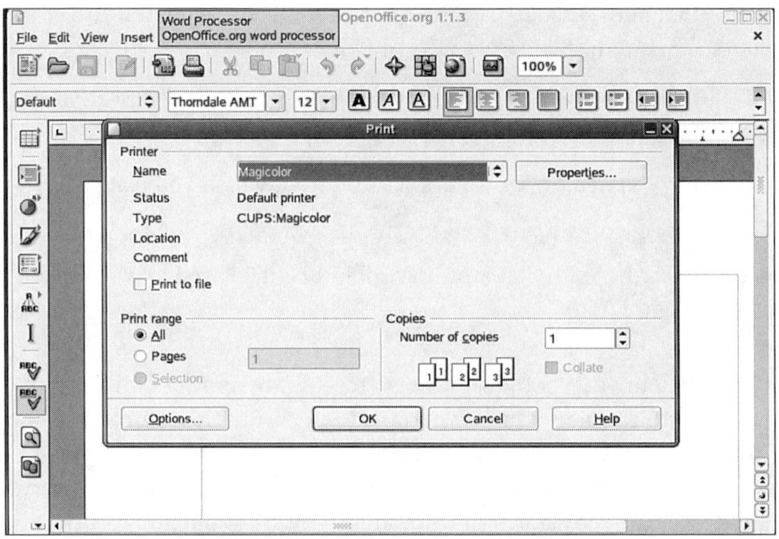

CONFIGURING CUPS PRINTER CLASSES

CUPS classes are defined in the `/etc/cups/classes.conf` file. As with the `printers.conf` file, the folks at Easy Software and SUSE strongly recommend that you don't manually edit this file. Instead, you should use the CUPS web-based administration utility. To define a printer class, complete the following on your CUPS server:

1. From your server, start a web browser.
2. Navigate to `http://localhost:631`.
3. Select **Administration**.
4. When prompted, authenticate as the administrative user you configured earlier using lppasswd.
5. Under Classes, select **Add Class**. The screen in Figure 5.27 is displayed.

FIGURE 5.27
Creating a Printer class.

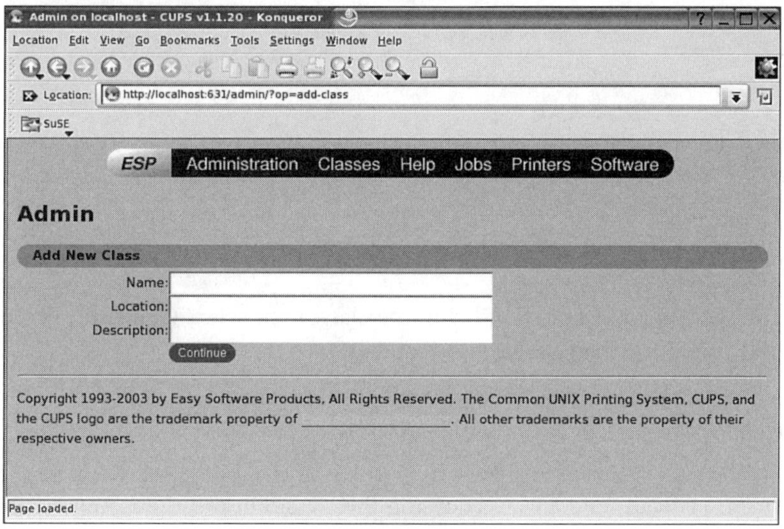

6. In the Name field, enter a name for the class.
7. In the Location field, enter a description location for the printer serviced by the class.
8. In the Description field, enter a description of the class.
9. Select **Continue**. The screen shown in Figure 5.28 is displayed.

FIGURE 5.28
Adding members to a class.

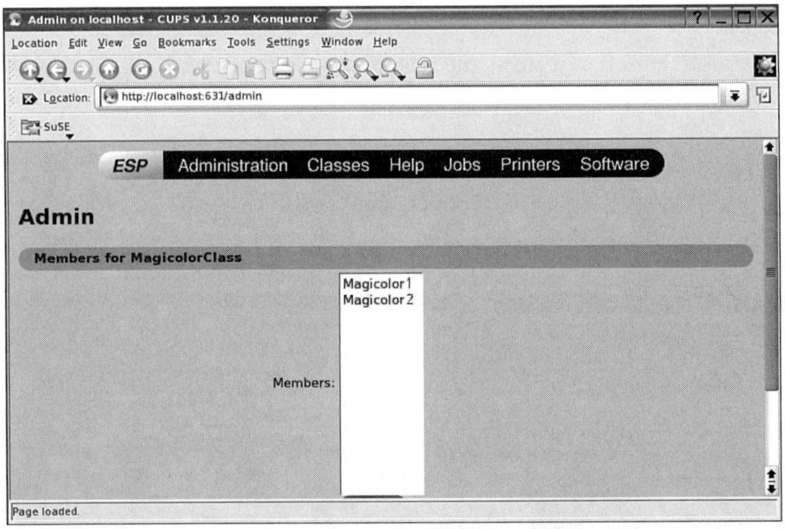

10. Mark the *printers* you want included in the class; then select **Continue**. A screen is displayed indicating the class has been added.
11. To view the class, select the link displayed. The screen shown in Figure 5.29 is displayed.

From this screen, you can send a test page, stop the class, kill print jobs, modify the class's properties, or delete the class.

With that, you're now ready to configure your own CUPS implementation. Let's do that in Lab Exercise 5.1.

FIGURE 5.29
Managing a printer class.

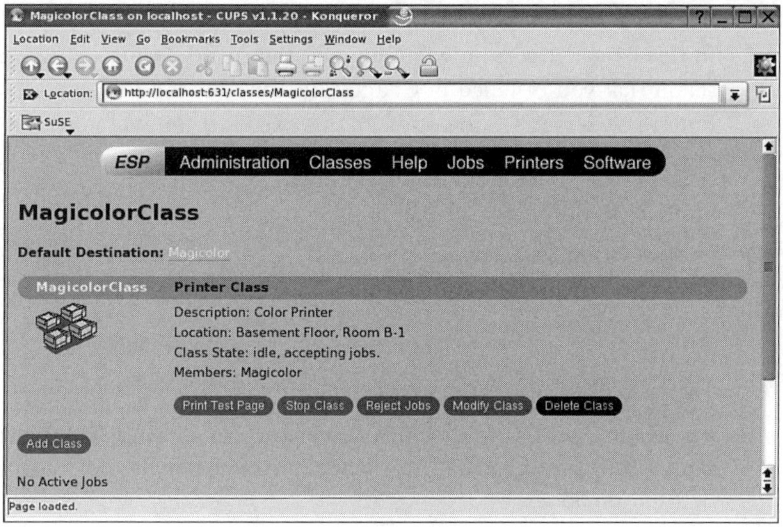

Lab Exercise 5.1: Configuring CUPS on SLES 9

In this lab exercise, you will configure the cupsd daemon on the SLES 9 server that you installed in Chapter 2, "Introduction to SUSE LINUX Enterprise Server 9." To complete this exercise, you will need the following components:

- Your SLES 9 server with named running.
- (Optional) A Novell Linux Desktop 9 workstation to test the configuration with. You can download a copy of Novell Linux Desktop from http://www.novell.com.

TIP

If you don't want to use a second system, you can use your SLES 9 system as both a CUPS server and a CUPS client at the same time. It's not as cool, but it gets the job done.

- A printer for sending CUPS print jobs to.

To configure the cupsd daemon on your system, complete the following:

1. Connect your printer to your SLES 9 server.
2. Boot your SLES 9 server.
3. Open a terminal session.
4. Change to root by entering **`su -`** and a password of **`tuX123`**.
5. Edit your `cupsd.conf` file to enable broadcasting by completing the following:
    a. At the shell prompt, enter **`vi /etc/cups/cupsd.conf`**.
    b. Scroll down to the `BrowseAddress @LOCAL` directive.
    c. Press **Ins**.
    d. Delete the `#` from the beginning of the `BrowseAddress @LOCAL` line.
    e. Press **Esc**.
    f. Enter **`:exit`**.
    g. At the shell prompt, enter **`rccups restart`**.

6. Create a CUPS administrative user cupsboss by completing the following:
   a. At the shell prompt, enter **lppasswd -g sys -a cupsboss**.
   b. When prompted for a password, enter **Penguin1**.
   c. When prompted to reenter the password, enter **Penguin1**.
7. Create a CUPS printer by completing the following:
   a. On your SLES 9 server, select the **Web Browser** icon in the bottom menu bar.
   b. In the Location field, enter **http://localhost:631**.
   c. Select Administration.
   d. When prompted to authenticate, enter **cupsboss** in the Username field.
   e. Enter **Penguin1** in the Password field; then select **OK**.
   f. Under Printers, select **Add Printer**.
   g. In the Name field, enter a *name* for your printer.
   h. In the Location field, enter a *location description* for your printer.
   i. In the Description field, enter a *description* of your printer.
   j. Select **Continue**.
   k. In the Device drop-down list, select the *interface* to which your printer is connected.
   l. Select **Continue**.
   m. In the Make field, select your printer's *manufacturer*.
   n. Select **Continue**.
   o. In the Model field, select your printer's *model*.
   p. Select **Continue**. You should be prompted that the printer has been successfully added.
   q. Select the *link* for your printer.
8. Configure your CUPS client by completing the following:

NOTE

If you're using your SLES 9 system as the CUPS client, switch back to YaST and begin with step 8d.

a. Boot your NLD 9 workstation.

b. Start YaST by selecting **System, Administrator Settings**.

c. Authenticate as your root user.

d. Select **Hardware, Printer**.

e. Check to see whether the system has already been configured to listen for CUPS servers. If so, skip ahead to step 9. If not, complete the remaining steps in step 8.

f. Under Already Installed Printers and Queues, select **Change**.

g. Select **Add**.

h. Mark Print via CUPS Network Server.

i. Select **Next**.

j. In the Connection Type screen, mark **CUPS Using Broadcasting**.

k. Select **Next**.

l. In the Listening to Remote CUPS Servers screen, ensure **Listen to IPP Broadcast Packets** is marked; then select **OK**.

m. Select **Finish**.

n. Select **Close**.

9. Test the configuration by completing the following:

   a. On your NLD 9 system, select **Programs, Office, Word Processor**.

NOTE

If you're using your SLES 9 server, select **N, Utilities, Editor**.

   b. Enter some text in the document.

   c. Select **File, Print**. Your CUPS printer should be displayed as an available printer.

   d. Select **OK** to send the print job.

   e. Verify that the job prints correctly on your printer.

Congratulations! Your CUPS server is ready to serve Linux print clients.

That's it for this chapter. Before we go to Chapter 6, "Configuring File and Print Services for Windows Clients on SLES 9," let's review what you've learned.

Summary

In this chapter, you learned how to implement CUPS on your SLES 9 system. We first discussed the IPP protocol. Then you learned how CUPS is built around IPP.

After that, you learned about the various components that make up the CUPS server, including

- CUPS scheduler
- CUPS filters
- CUPS backends
- PPD files
- CUPS classes
- CUPS web-based administration utility

With these components in mind, we discussed the CUPS printing process, tracing a print job from the CUPS client through the CUPS server to the printer.

We then discussed how to install the CUPS package on a SLES 9 server. Then we spend a great deal of time reviewing the various files that are used to configure the CUPS daemon cupsd. These include

- `cupsd.conf`
- `classes.conf`
- `printers.conf`
- `mime.types`
- `mime.convs`

Finally, we configured CUPS on a SLES 9 system. To do this, we configured the following:

- A CUPS administrative user
- The `cupsd.conf` file
- A CUPS printer
- A CUPS class

You ended this chapter by configuring CUPS on your SLES 9 system in Lab Exercise 5.1.

With this CUPS background behind you, you're ready to move on to Chapter 6, where you will learn how to implement Samba on your SLES 9 server. You may have noticed in this chapter that we didn't say much about printing from a Windows workstation to a CUPS printer. In Chapter 6, you'll learn how this can be done!

CHAPTER 6

Configuring File and Print Services for Windows Clients on SLES 9

This chapter covers the following requirement for Novell's Certified Linux Engineer (CLE) 9 certification:

1. Configure a Primary Domain Controller on SLES 9.

In this chapter, you will learn how to implement Samba on your SLES 9 system. Samba is one of the most powerful of all Linux services. In my opinion, Samba is one of the key reasons Linux has made significant inroads into modern corporate networks. As a CLE 9, there's a pretty good chance that you will be responsible for managing a Samba deployment in your Linux network.

Let's begin this chapter by learning how Samba works.

An Overview of Samba

TEST OBJECTIVE COVERED:

1. Configure a Primary Domain Controller on SLES 9.

Linux (especially SLES 9) makes for one heck of a network server. Linux is powerful, fast, inexpensive, and reliable. As you've seen in the preceding chapters, Linux can do just about everything more expensive network operating systems can do, usually a lot better!

Because of this, Linux is really gaining traction in the corporate network as a server. Anyone who's had to deal with the high price of user licensing with other operating systems knows what a financial black hole they can be. Linux, on the other hand, costs the same, regardless of whether you have one user or a thousand.

As you may have noted in the preceding paragraph, I said that Linux has made great progress against other network operating systems. Unfortunately, Linux hasn't done as well on the desktop. There are two key reasons for this:

- Historically, there has been a lack of desktop productivity applications available for Linux. This situation, fortunately, has been getting better lately. The adoption of the OpenOffice.org suite has helped make Linux a viable option for the desktop. However, the breadth of applications available for the Windows desktop still isn't available for Linux desktops yet.
- The average user finds Linux somewhat intimidating. For you and I, this isn't a problem. We like using Linux as our desktop operating system. We know how to use it to increase our productivity. We know how to run programs, install services, and mount file systems. Unfortunately, the average user in most organizations learned how to use a computer with some version of Windows installed. They don't want to learn a new OS.

For these reasons, Linux has established itself primarily in the server room. It may be a few more years before we see dramatic acceptance on the desktop.

NOTE

On that note, I think the Linux community has really stepped up to the plate on this issue. Productivity applications, such as OpenOffice.org, as well as specific distributions such as the Novell Linux Desktop, are a step in the right direction.

Until then, we're still going to have to deal with Windows on the desktop. That presents us with a quandary. How do we provide services typically associated with Windows servers using Linux as our network operating system?

To answer that question, first we have to look at what desktop services are typically provided by Windows servers. Much as the folks who design network operating systems would like to disavow it, there are three key services desktop users consume:

- User authentication
- File storage
- Shared printing

NOTE

In the course of my career, I've had the opportunity to be a member of several network operating system core teams. In our core team meetings, the product managers in charge usually expressed a lack of interest in file and print services. They just aren't very flashy. They wanted to create network operating systems with the latest and greatest network services.

The problem I observed, however, is that file and print services are the *core* of any network operating system. If you don't provide them (and provide them well), no one cares what other cool services the OS offers.

In my experience, 99 percent of the usage a typical Windows server experiences from Windows clients involves the storage of user files and processing print jobs for network servers.

Replicating this functionality with a Linux server presents a problem. How do we access the file system on a Linux server? Traditionally we have done this with NFS, right? Do Windows client operating systems natively support NFS? Sort of. To mount a remote NFS export with a Windows client, you have to install the Microsoft Client for NFS service. Unfortunately, this service doesn't appear to be included with all Windows XP versions. It wasn't the easiest service to configure in the first place. It also didn't provide the browseability users are accustomed to when using My Network Places on their Windows desktop systems.

How about printing? In the old days, we used the lpd daemon to provide network printing on a Linux system. Today, we use CUPS. Can you use a Windows desktop system to print to either of these Linux printing systems? With Microsoft's Print Services for Unix, you could use Window's `lpr` command to send print jobs to a Linux printer. However, again it didn't provide the same degree of friendliness users were accustomed to when printing to printers managed by a Windows server. With CUPS, the news is even worse. Windows desktop operating systems don't support CUPS printers at all.

As you can see, we have a tall order to fill when replacing a Windows server with Linux. It all comes down to the fact that the Linux server must provide authentication, file and print services, as well as the Windows server everyone is used to. Installing Microsoft's Unix-related services on the Windows desktop just doesn't cut it. Instead, we need a service on our Linux servers that replicates the file and print functionality of a Windows server. Fortunately, we have just that: Samba! Let's talk about what Samba is and how it works.

Welcome to the World of Samba

Samba is a really cool, really powerful service you can install on your SLES 9 server. When you do, your Linux server can, basically, emulate a Windows NT server on your network.

Using only the native Microsoft Client for Microsoft Networks client and the File and Printer Sharing for Microsoft Networks service, shown in Figure 6.1, users can browse to shared directories and connect to CUPS printers on your Linux server:

FIGURE 6.1
Required workstation components for Samba.

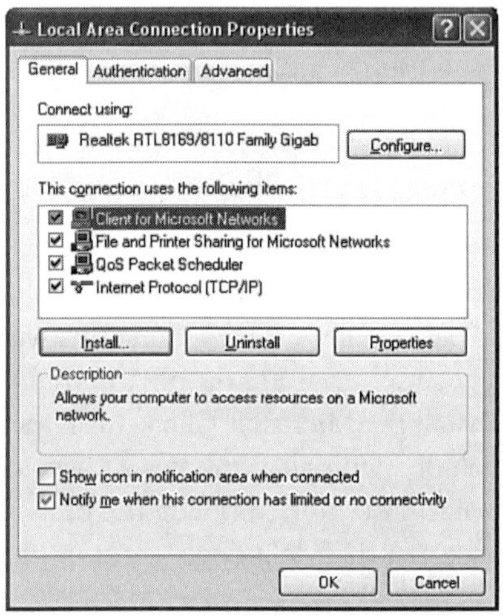

NOTE

In various industry marketing pieces, you'll hear references made to "clientless" or "native" Windows connections. This is a serious misnomer. What they are referring to are connections made using the Microsoft Client for Microsoft Networks. If you want to have a little fun during a marketing demo, ask the presenter to demonstrate their "clientless" system after removing the Microsoft client.

In addition, Samba can turn your Linux server into a Windows Primary Domain Controller (PDC), allowing hosting a domain and providing authentication services for your Windows desktop systems. Again, all this functionality is supported by the client configuration shown in Figure 6.1. There's nothing special to install or configure on the Windows workstations.

In addition to providing PDC, file, and print services, Samba can also do the following:

- Allow the Linux server to participate in a Microsoft Active Directory tree.
- Use another Windows Domain Controller to authenticate users.
- Provide a Windows Internet Name Service (WINS) server.

To this point, I've emphasized the usefulness of Samba in connecting Windows desktops to a Linux server. However, the usefulness of Samba goes even further. A Samba client package is available for Linux systems as well. This client package allows Linux desktops to connect to a Samba service running on a Linux server or to any other Windows server.

This has some significant advantages for folks running a heterogeneous networking environment. In the past, organizations running both Windows and Linux had to, for the most part, run two separate networks. The Windows systems didn't interact or share data with the Linux network and vice versa.

The Windows network used Microsoft Domains to authenticate users and the Microsoft Client for Microsoft Networks to provide file and print access. The Linux systems, on the other hand, typically used NIS+ to authenticate users, lpd or CUPS to provide printing, and NFS to share files. As we discussed previously, getting these two different networking systems to play together was an ugly process.

Now, with Samba, everything can come together nicely. By implementing Samba, both Windows and Linux systems can interact. Using Samba to replace NIS+ and NFS on the Linux servers and desktops does this. This allows Linux desktops to communicate with both Linux and Windows servers. Likewise, Windows desktops can communicate with both Linux and Windows servers. This scenario is depicted in Figure 6.2.

FIGURE 6.2
All One Happy Family with Samba.

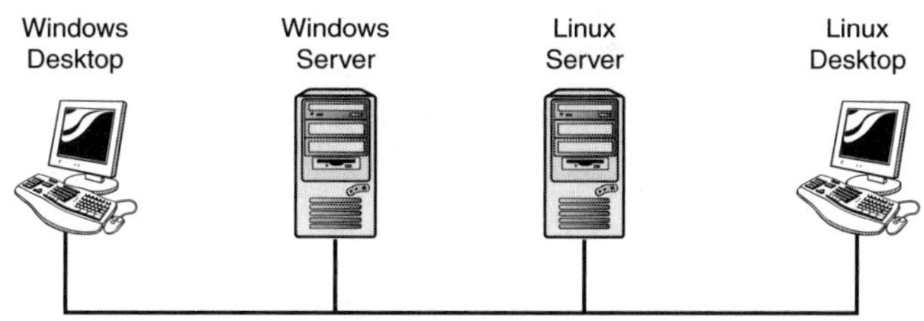

Sounds like a mighty friendly world! How does Samba do all this? The key is the protocol that is uses. Samba is based on the Server Message Block (SMB) protocol. Let's first discuss SMB fundamentals to prepare you to implement Samba in your network.

The Server Message Block Protocol

The earliest version of the SMB protocol was developed by IBM in the mid-1980s. In the early 1990s, Andrew Tridgell developed an SMB implementation that would run on Unix. Mr.

Tridgell is still leading the development of Samba today. The SMB protocol was later adopted and widely deployed by Microsoft, beginning with Windows 95 and Windows NT. It has since become the backbone of Microsoft's networking system.

NOTE

Microsoft uses the name Common Internet File System (CIFS) to describe its SMB implementation. CIFS interoperates very nicely with Samba.

The SMB protocol makes server files and printers available to SMB clients through a process called *sharing*. Shared resources on a server are referenced using the Universal Naming Convention (UNC). The syntax for referring to a particular share using UNC is as follows:

```
\\server_name\share_name
```

For example, if I had a Linux system named server1 with Samba installed and running, I could share the `/tmp` directory in my server's file system for users to store temporary files. Using the Samba configuration file (which we'll discuss later) I could create a share for `/tmp` and give it a name; let's say **`tempfiles`**. To refer to the share, I would use a UNC of **`\\server1\tempfiles`**.

TIP

This directory was selected for sharing by way of example. Remember that `/tmp` gets periodically cleaned out by the system. I've actually seen Linux administrators share `/tmp` for users without telling them this. Users get mighty upset when they find their files gone!

It's also possible, with some applications, to use URLs when referencing an SMB share. This is done using the format of:

```
smb://server_name/share_name
```

Using the preceding example, we would use a URL of `smb://server1/tempfiles`.

The SMB protocol operates at the Application and Presentation layers of the OSI model. At its core, SMB is a file and print access protocol. Its job is to provide SMB clients with access to the file system of a SMB server. Likewise, it's designed to provide SMB clients with access to shared printers on the SMB server. The protocol is designed to use the internal security system of the operating system to determine what the SMB client can and cannot do in the file system. In the case of Linux, the file system ACLs are used to control access.

SMB can be implemented with a variety of middle-layer protocols, including IPX. However, the most common implementation is to use SMB with NetBIOS on IP. Because of this, you need to have a basic understanding of NetBIOS to effectively manage a Samba implementation. We'll talk about that next.

ABOUT NETBIOS

NetBIOS (Network Basic Input/Output System) is a networking protocol that operates at the Session layer of the OSI model. Like the SMB protocol, the NetBIOS protocol was original developed by IBM in the mid-1980s. Microsoft subsequently adopted NetBIOS as the basic networking protocol for its Windows operating systems.

Because NetBIOS operates at the Session layer of the OSI model, it has no inherent internetworking capabilities. Basically, it's designed to work on a single network segment. It doesn't know how to move between routers.

To make NetBIOS work in a routed network, you have to piggyback it on top of another Network-layer protocol. Various implementations have been developed over the years that run NetBIOS on top of a variety of Internetwork protocols, including IPX/SPX. However, the most popular method is to piggyback NetBIOS on top of TCP/IP or UDP/IP. This relationship between SMB, NetBIOS, and IP is shown in Figure 6.3.

FIGURE 6.3
SMB and the OSI model.

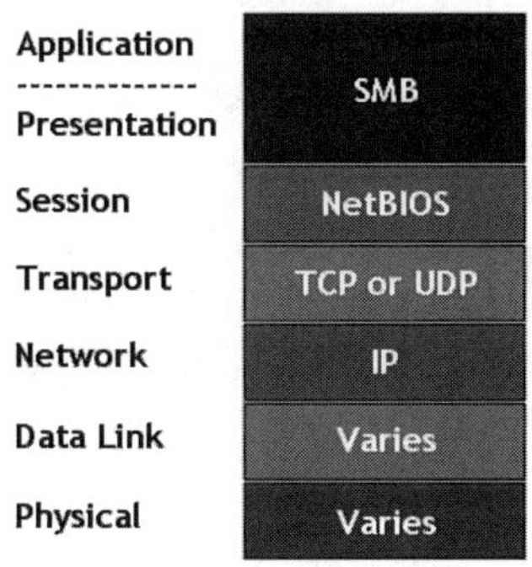

In the context of this chapter, we're going to limit our discussion to this type of implementation.

TIP

NetBIOS running on top of TCP/IP is frequently referred to as NBT or sometimes as NetBT.

As you know, most Network-layer protocols, such as IPX or IP, use a numerical host address to uniquely identify hosts on the network. NetBIOS doesn't do this. Instead, it uses a 16-byte, 15-character alphanumeric name to uniquely identify hosts on the network.

TIP

The NetBIOS name and the hostname of a given system are two different things. You could have a system with a hostname of Server1 and a NetBIOS name of XYZCORP-S1. As you might guess, this could get really messy. The folks at SUSE recommend that you use the same name for both the NetBIOS and the hostnames. The good news is that Samba, by default, does this for you.

This works fine at the Session layer. However, as two hosts establish communications, we have to move down the OSI model. As we do, the NetBIOS name no longer suffices. When we reach the Network layer, we have to know the IP addresses.

To accommodate this, we need to be able to resolve NetBIOS names to IP addresses. This sounds familiar, doesn't it? In Chapter 3, "Configuring DNS on SLES 9," we talked about resolving DNS names to IP addresses. We need to be able to do the same thing with NetBIOS names when we're using Samba. This is done using a WINS (Windows Internet Naming Service) server. Similar to a DNS server, a WINS server resolves NetBIOS names into IP addresses. However, unlike a DNS server, a WINS server is considerably more dynamic.

When a NetBIOS host is booted, it does one of two things. If a WINS server is up and running, the NetBIOS host will register itself with the server. If the name is not in use, the WINS server will put the host's name and IP address into its database. All other NetBIOS hosts can then query the WINS server to get the IP address associated with the particular NetBIOS host name.

If a WINS server is not detected on the network, then, on boot, the NetBIOS host simply broadcasts the name it has been configured with. If another NetBIOS host is already using that name, it will generate an error and respond back indicating that a conflict exists. Otherwise, the host simply takes the name.

In this WINS-less scenario, however, we still need to resolve NetBIOS names into IP addresses. How do we do it without a WINS server? NetBIOS uses a mechanism similar to that used by ARP, which we discussed briefly in Chapter 3.

In this situation, the NetBIOS host sends out a broadcast whenever it needs to contact another host. The host with the requested NetBIOS name responds back with its IP address. Obviously, this type of configuration can cause a great deal of network traffic. Broadcasts are the bane of a network administrator's existence. Using a WINS server can dramatically reduce this traffic to a manageable level.

The Samba package on Linux includes a NetBIOS name resolver that provides WINS functionality. This is provided by the nmbd daemon. You can configure your Samba deployment to use this name resolution service, or you can configure it to use an existing WINS server in your network.

You need to remember one other aspect of NetBIOS names as well. Recall that we said the SMB protocol is based on a client/server networking model. This model is supported by the NetBIOS protocol.

Remember that a NetBIOS name can be a maximum of 15 characters long, each character consuming one byte. However, a NetBIOS name is 16 bytes in length. The very last byte of a NetBIOS name is used to identify the type of service the host is providing. It's called the NetBIOS Suffix.

A workstation will have a value of `00` (hexadecimal) in this byte. A server will have a hex value of `20`, and a domain controller will have a hex value of `1C` in this byte.

NOTE

For more information on the values that are used in the NetBIOS Suffix, look at Knowledgebase Article 163409 at http://support.microsoft.com.

Why is all this important? Why do you need to know about NetBIOS in the modern world of TCP/IP? When you attempt to open a SMB connection, the NetBIOS protocol is used to establish a connection at the Session layer of the OSI model between the sending and the receiving host. If you don't understand NetBIOS, you're going to have a difficult time troubleshooting SMB issues.

With this NetBIOS background in mind, we'll look at how SMB communications work.

HOW SMB PROTOCOL COMMUNICATIONS WORK

After a NetBIOS session has been established at the Session layer, SMB clients and SMB servers communicate with each other at the Application and Presentation layers of the OSI model using Server Message Blocks (hence the name of the protocol). These SMBs contain specific, structured commands that establish communication and provide access to shared resources.

To give you an idea of how the SMB protocol works, let's step through a sample session. In this scenario, a user on an SMB client workstation wants to create a file on an SMB server, edit the file, and then save it. The transactions involved are shown in Figure 6.4.

SMBs work on a command/response model. Either node can issue an SMB command, and either node can send an SMB response. To create the file in this scenario, the following SMBs are sent:

1. The SMB client sends an SMBNegProt SMB command to the SMB server. This SMB tells the server which dialect of SMB it's using. The server then sends a SMBNegProt response back to the client, agreeing on a dialect along with a series of networking parameters for the client to use.

FIGURE 6.4
Opening and saving a file using SMB.

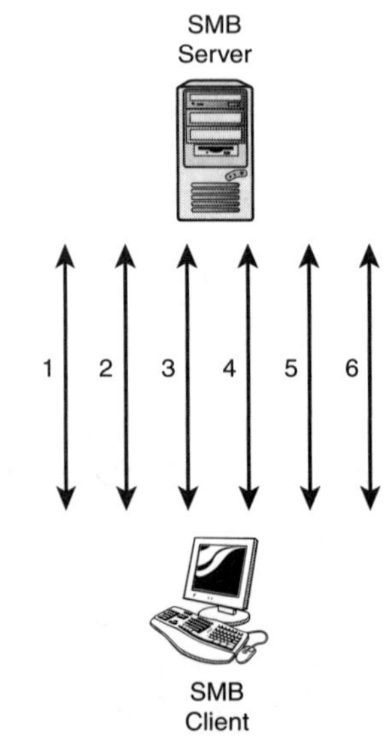

NOTE

Because the SMB protocol has been around a while, many software vendors have produced their own versions of SMB. These different versions are called *dialects*. There are SMB dialects from Microsoft, IBM, and others. The good news is that Samba can handle all these dialects. Part of the SMBNegProt transaction involves the client and the server agreeing upon a particular dialect to use for the session.

2. The client then sends an SMBSesssetup SMB to the server. This command contains the username and password of the user. If the server accepts the credentials, it responds with a SMBSesssetup response indicating that the authentication has been granted.
3. The client sends the server a SMBtcon command, in which the client tells the server which shared resource it wants to use. The server responds to the client with an SMBtcon response, indicating that the client has been granted permission to use the resource.
4. The client sends an SMBmknew command to the server, instructing the server to create a new file. The server sends an SMBmknew response when the file has been created.
5. The client sends an SMBopen command to the server, instructing it to open the file that was just created.

6. The client sends an SMBread command to the server. The server responds by sending the requested file to the client. At this point, the user can edit the file with the appropriate application on the client workstation.

When the editing is complete, the user saves the file and exits the application. Accordingly, the client system sends a SMBwriteclose command to the server. The server system saves the file to disk and closes it. Then it responds to the client, indicating whether the process was successful.

NOTE

Sometimes you'll see SMB commands with an X appended to the end. The X indicates that multiple commands are being sent in the same SMB. For example, if you see an SMBmknewX command, it indicates that the server should make a new file and then execute the next SMB embedded within the SMBmknew command (such as SMBopen).

In addition to the commands previously listed, a plethora of other SMB commands are used to manipulate files and directories on the server as well as to submit print jobs. For example, the SMBcopy command copies files, the SMBmove command moves files, and the SMBsplopen command opens a spool for printing.

With all this SMB theory in mind, we'll now talk about how you implement and configure Samba on your Linux system to create the happy, friendly, heterogeneous world we talked about at the beginning of this chapter. We'll start with installing the Samba package on your server.

Installing Samba on SLES 9

TEST OBJECTIVE COVERED:

1. Configure a Primary Domain Controller on SLES 9.

As with CUPS, only one Samba package is available for Linux systems. Samba is maintained by a team of developers. You can learn more about them and the Samba product itself by visiting http://www.samba.org.

The current version of Samba is 3.0. This is the version you need to be familiar with to pass your CLE 9 certification exam.

To install the Samba service on your SLES 9 server, complete the following:

1. From your SLES 9 desktop, select **YaST**.
2. When prompted, provide your root password.
3. In the left frame, select **Software**.
4. In the right frame, select **Install and Remove Software**.
5. In the Search field, enter **samba**; then select **Search**.
6. Mark the following packages (as shown in Figure 6.5):
   - **kdebase3-samba**
   - **libsmbclient**
   - **samba**
   - **samba-client (optional)**
   - **samba-doc**
   - **samba-pdb**
   - **samba-winbind**
   - **yast2-samba-client (optional)**
   - **yast2-samba-server**

FIGURE 6.5
Installing Samba packages.

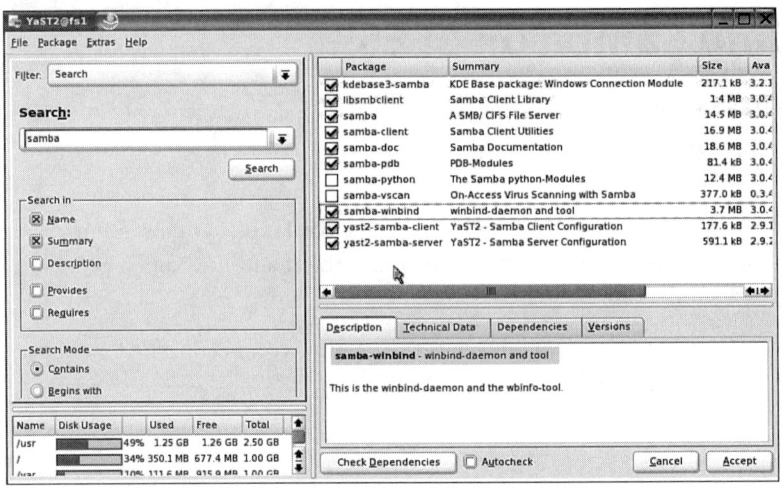

TIP

The samba-client and yast2-samba-client packages are needed only if you want your SLES 9 server to function as *both* a Samba server and as a Samba client. If you want it to be only a Samba server, you can omit these packages.

7. Select **Accept**.
8. When prompted, insert the appropriate CDs.
9. Wait while the packages are installed and SuSEconfig is run.
10. Close YaST by selecting **Close**.

As with the other products we've covered so far in this book, your SLES 9 system should already have the Samba server and client packages installed if you followed the steps in the lab exercises in Chapter 2, "Introduction to the SUSE Linux Enterprise Server 9."

To verify that it's there, open YaST and select **Software, Install and Remove Software**. In the search field, enter **cups**, and then select **Search**. You should see various CUPS packages marked with blue check marks, as shown in Figure 6.6.

FIGURE 6.6
Samba packages already installed.

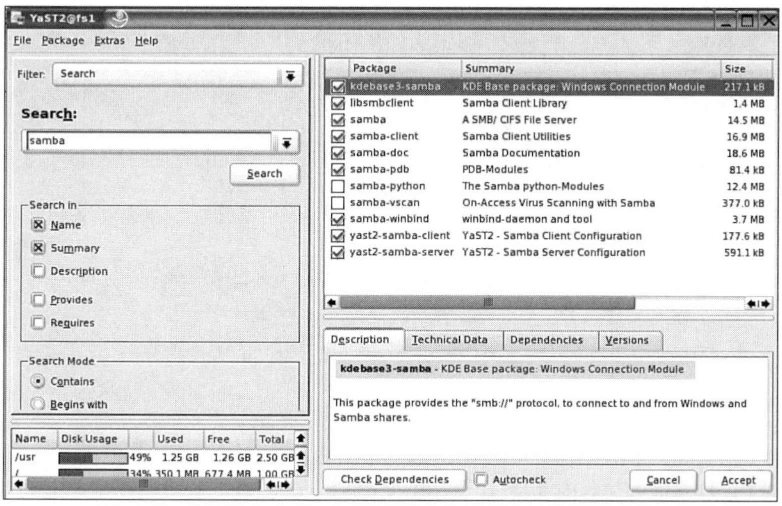

If, for some reason, the Samba packages aren't installed on your SLES 9 system, follow the preceding steps to install them.

After installation, the following daemons are used on your SLES 9 system to provide the Samba service:

- smbd—The smbd daemon is your SMB server. It is used to share SMB resources with SMB clients.
- nmbd—The nmbd daemon is a Linux implementation of a Windows WINS server. It provides NetBIOS to IP address resolution services for your SMB server and SMB clients.
- winbindd—The winbindd daemon connects your Linux Samba implementation to a traditional Microsoft Windows network. With this daemon, you can configure Samba users to authenticate through a domain controller running on a separate Windows server instead of on the local Linux server.

After the daemons are installed, the Samba service is started and stopped using the smb, nmb, and winbind init scripts in `/etc/init.d`, as shown in Figure 6.7.

FIGURE 6.7
Samba startup script.

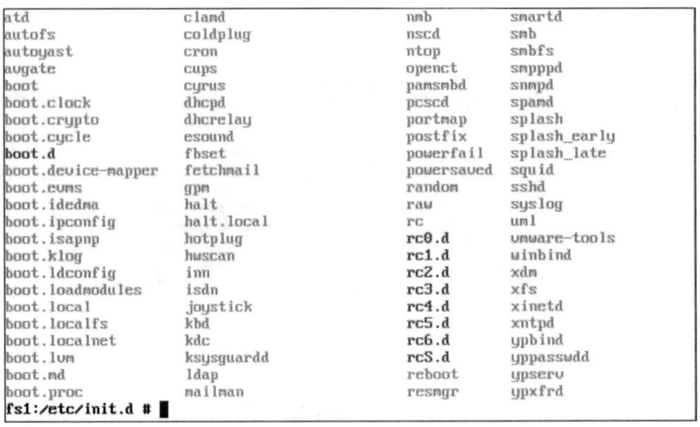

NOTE

In `/etc/init.d`, you will also see an init script called smbfs. This is a file system driver and, as such, is part of the Linux kernel itself. It's not part of the Samba package.

After the Samba package is installed on your system, you're ready to configure and start the service on your server. Let's talk about how to do that next.

Configuring Samba on SLES 9

TEST OBJECTIVE COVERED:

1. Configure a Primary Domain Controller on SLES 9.

Samba is very powerful product. As such, it's quite extensive—probably more so than any of the products we've covered thus far in this book. You're going to need a considerable amount of background knowledge to be an effective Samba administrator—knowledge you will also need to pass your CLE 9 exam.

To make you a Samba expert, we're going to cover the following topics:

- Windows networking overview
- Working with the Samba configuration files
- Samba-enabling Linux users
- Configuring a PDC on Samba
- Configuring a PDC using YaST

We'll begin by reviewing some basic Windows networking concepts.

Windows Networking Overview

As we've discussed, Microsoft adopted SMB in the 1990s as its primary networking system. Because of this, Windows networking and SMB have become tightly intertwined. By extension, Samba and Windows networking concepts have also become tightly intertwined. Many Windows functions are woven into the Samba package on your Linux system.

Much as we may dislike doing so, we have to become Windows-networking savvy in order to be an effective Samba administrator. If you're coming into your CLE certification from a Windows background, you're in great shape. However, if you're like me, you cut your networking teeth on non-Windows operating systems such as NetWare, Unix, or Linux. For us, Windows networking concepts are somewhat foreign.

Before going any further in this chapter, we're going to spend some time reviewing some Windows networking basics. Otherwise, you're going to be scratching your head when we hit particular sections of the `smb.conf` file. Specifically, we're going to cover the following:

- Workgroups
- Domains
- Domain Controllers
- Trusts

NOTE

Note that we're not trying to make you a Microsoft Certified Systems Engineer (MCSE) in this chapter. We're going to cover these Windows concepts at a very basic level. If you're already experienced with Windows, please stifle your yawns and snickers.

Let's begin by discussing Windows workgroups.

WINDOWS WORKGROUPS

A Windows *workgroup* is nothing more than a logical organization of hosts that have been grouped together on a network. A workgroup is usually confined to the network hosts on a single network segment. A Windows system can be configured to participate in a workgroup using the System applet, as shown in Figure 6.8.

FIGURE 6.8
Setting the Windows Workgroup.

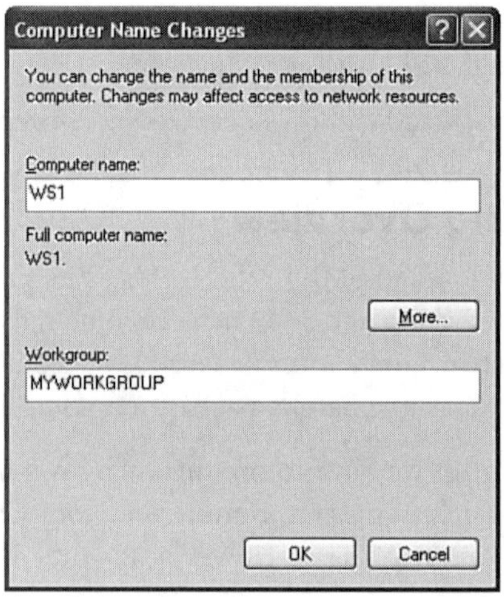

All you have to do to create a workgroup is to enter the same name in the Workgroup field on all the workstations that will be members. After it is configured, users can browse shared resources provided by hosts that are members of the workgroup, as shown in Figure 6.9.

This browsing functionality makes Windows networking much easier for users. Instead of having to know the UNC path to the shared resource they want to access, they can browse through the workgroup to the particular host and select the resource.

To make browsing possible, one computer system in the workgroup is elected to be the *master browser*. The master browser keeps a list of all hosts and shared resources in the workgroup.

FIGURE 6.9
Browsing systems within a workgroup.

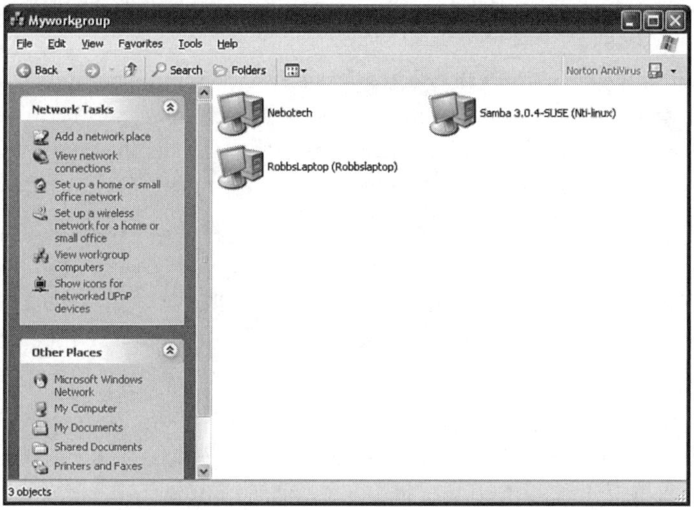

TIP

The master browser is sometimes referred to as the *local master browser*. Browsing works with Windows domains as well as workgroups. We'll discuss domains later in the chapter.

When systems in the workgroup are booted, they go through an election process to decide which system will be the master browser. Using factors such as system load and the length of time a host has been up, one system is elected to be the master browser for the workgroup.

Why do Windows workgroups use a master browser? Without one, each individual desktop system in the workgroup would have to go out and query each host in the workgroup to identify the resources each has to share whenever the user opened My Network Places to browse the workgroup. This would take a considerable amount of time and would generate a lot of unnecessary network traffic, especially in a large workgroup with a lot of systems.

To speed things up, the master browser alone does all the probing to discover shared resources in the workgroup. Then, when a user browses the workgroup, his or her desktop system contacts the master browser to get a list of shared resources. This process is much faster and generates considerably less network traffic. As network administrators, we like that!

Windows workgroups don't require a Windows server, although they aren't prevented from participating in a workgroup. Windows 9*x*, ME, NT (Server and Professional), 2000 (Server and Professional), XP (Home and Professional), and Server 2003 systems can all share resources in a workgroup.

Any of these systems can also function as a master browser in a workgroup. In addition, a Linux Samba server or client can participate in a Windows workgroup. In fact, the other Windows systems in the workgroup don't know the difference. As far as they are concerned, your Linux Samba system is just another Windows host.

As neat as workgroups may sound, they actually aren't widely implemented. Workgroups have a major shortcoming that limits their usefulness; that is, each computer system has to maintain its own separate set of user accounts. This means that if users in the workgroup want to access resources on another system in the workgroup, they must have a user account configured on the remote system.

If users need to use resources located on multiple systems, they must authenticate separately to each host. Now, if the user passwords are the same on all hosts, this works process works relatively well. The local username and password will be used by the remote system for authentication.

However, if different passwords are used on each system, workgroups can turn into a real nightmare for users and, by extension, the network administrator. As you can probably guess, keeping user accounts synchronized in a large network can quickly become an impossible task.

In addition, because of the way NetBIOS uses broadcasts, it's very difficult to implement a workgroup on a routed network. For these reasons, workgroups usually aren't implemented in large organizations. Instead, most large Windows networks are configured to use *domains*.

WINDOWS DOMAINS

A Windows *domain* is a logical grouping of computer systems on a network, much like a workgroup.

NOTE

Windows domains are not the same thing as DNS domains. Occasionally, this is a point of confusion for new network administrators.

Unlike a workgroup, however, a domain uses one central database of user accounts that all systems that are members of the domain use for authentication. Instead of configuring duplicate user accounts on each host, a single server is configured with the user account database (the domain).

Domains remedy the weaknesses associated with workgroups. First, domains can span routers, allowing them to support very large corporate networks. In addition, domains create a single point of administration. All account-management tasks are done using a single database.

Domains also eliminate the need for multiple user logins. Because access to all resources in the domain is controlled by the domain database, users need to authenticate only once to the domain. After they are authenticated, they can access whatever domain resources they need, based on the permissions they have been granted.

TIP

The Windows XP Home operating system can operate only in a workgroup. To use domains for authentication if you want to use Windows XP, you must use Windows XP Professional.

The system that hosts the domain database is called the *domain controller*.

DOMAIN CONTROLLERS

In a Windows network, the domain controller is a Windows server (Windows NT, 2000 Server, or Server 2003) that runs a service called the Security Account Manager (SAM).

NOTE

Desktop Windows systems, such as Windows 9*x*, Windows 2000 Professional, and Windows XP, can't function as domain controllers. If you don't have a Windows server in the network, you can't use domains. A Windows workgroup is your only option.

Each domain must have one or more domain controllers. On a Windows network, one server is configured as a Primary Domain Controller (PDC). The PDC is the "boss" of the domain. It's the authoritative source of domain data. Each domain can have only one PDC.

However, for fault-tolerance purposes, we need to have more than one domain controller. Imagine what would happen in the typical workplace if the one and only domain controller in the network were to go down. No one would be able to log in, no work would get done, and the network administrator would be checking the Help Wanted section of the classified ads.

For redundancy purposes, a Windows network can be configured with a Backup Domain Controller (BDC). A BDC has a copy of the domain database from the PDC. If the PDC goes down, the BDC jumps in and takes over, ensuring that the network keeps working. A Windows network can have multiple BDCs.

You should remember that a BDC is nonauthoritative in a Windows network. By way of comparison, it's a lot like a slave DNS server. Just as a slave DNS server gets its zone data from a master DNS server, a BDC synchronizes its domain database from the PDC.

Likewise, just as you don't update the zone database on a slave DNS server, you don't update the domain database on a BDC. Instead, you make all changes to the PDC domain database. At periodic intervals, the PDC then synchronizes the domain with all BDCs in the domain.

A desktop system that is a member of a domain can use either a PDC or a BDC to authenticate to the domain, much like a slave DNS server can still resolve name resolution queries as well as a master DNS server can. A hypothetical domain is shown in Figure 6.10.

FIGURE 6.10
A typical Windows domain.

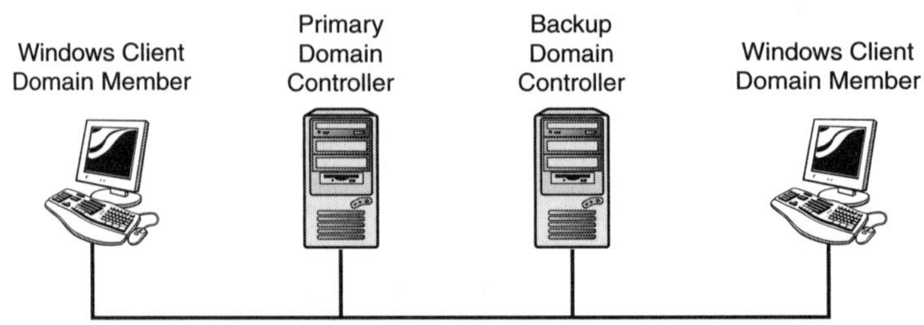

NOTE

It's also possible for a Windows server to exist in a domain without being a PDC or a BDC. In this case, its simply called a *member server*.

Can a Linux Samba client participate in a Windows domain? Absolutely. With the winbindd daemon, a remote Windows domain controller can even handle authentication. Can a Linux Samba server participate in a Windows domain? You bet; however, there are some limitations. A Linux Samba server can function as a PDC in a Windows NT network. It can also function as a BDC if the PDC is another Samba server. If the PDC is a Windows server, it can't function as a BDC.

NOTE

From what I understand, however, this is scheduled to be fixed in a later release.

A Linux Samba server can also function as a member server in a Windows NT domain.

If, however, you are using Windows 2000 Server or Server 2003, your options are a little more limited. Windows 2000 Server and later use Active Directory to store user accounts; Samba support for Active Directory is very limited. Your Linux Samba server can function only as a member server in a Windows 2000 or 2003 domain. It can't be a PDC.

TIP

This is true if your Windows server is running in *native mode*. If you configure your Windows server to run in *mixed mode*, your Linux Samba server can participate in the domain as either a member server or as a PDC.

Now that you understand workgroups and domains, you next need to understand the concept of *trusts*.

WINDOWS TRUST RELATIONSHIPS

Windows trust relationships are a little tricky and most administrators don't like using them. However, they are a necessary part of running a Windows network, so we learn to live with them.

You can establish trust relationships between two Windows domains to allow users in one domain to access resources in the other domain; including shared folders or printers. In and of itself, this relationship is relatively straightforward and easy to configure.

The problems start when you have multiple domains configured with a spider web of trusts. We then have to deal with what are called *transitive trusts*. We're not going to delve into this topic here. Whole books have been written about how to deal with transitive trusts. For now, just understand what trust relationships do and that Samba supports them.

Now that you understand workgroups, domains, domain controllers, and trusts, you're ready to work with the Samba configuration files on your Linux system.

Working with Samba Configuration Files

As with DNS and DHCP, a fantastic YaST module for Samba makes configuration and administration a breeze. However, as I've said before, I think it's absolutely critical that you understand the actual text files that are used to configure Samba. When you do, feel free to make your work fast and easy using YaST.

The files you need to be familiar with reside in the `/etc/samba` directory. They include the following:

- `lmhosts`
- `smbfstab`
- `smbpasswd`
- `smbusers`
- `smb.conf`

Let's start with `lmhosts`.

lmhosts

The `/etc/samba/lmhosts` file as a function very similar to that of the `/etc/hosts` file on your Linux system. Recall that your hosts file is used to provide a simple mapping of hostnames to IP addresses. By and large, we don't use the hosts file that much any more. Instead, we try to use a DNS server to accomplish this task wherever possible.

The `lmhosts` file, shown in Figure 6.11, provides a static mapping of NetBIOS names to IP addresses.

FIGURE 6.11
The /etc/samba/lmhosts file.

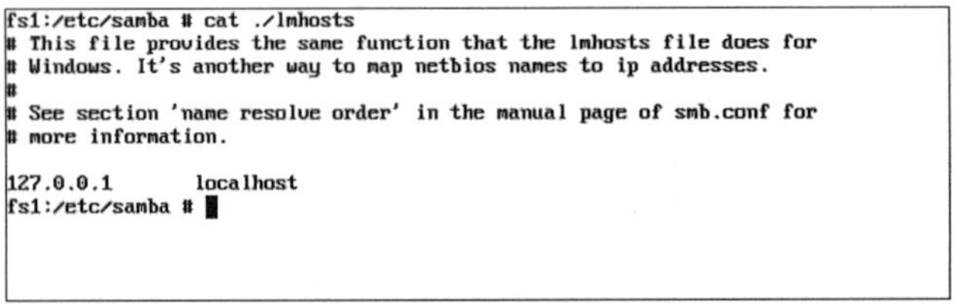

```
fs1:/etc/samba # cat ./lmhosts
# This file provides the same function that the lmhosts file does for
# Windows. It's another way to map netbios names to ip addresses.
#
# See section 'name resolve order' in the manual page of smb.conf for
# more information.

127.0.0.1        localhost
fs1:/etc/samba #
```

In the absence of a WINS server, `lmhosts` can be used to provide simple NetBIOS name resolution. Like `/etc/hosts`, we don't usually use `lmhosts` that much. All the weaknesses associated with the `/etc/hosts` file are applicable to the `/etc/samba/lmhosts` file. Using the nmbd daemon on your Linux server provides a much more robust NetBIOS name-resolution system.

smbfstab

The `/etc/samba/smbfstab` file is used when configuring the Samba client on your system. It's not required when configuring your system as a Samba server only. The `smbfstab` file is used to automatically mount a shared directory on a remote system when the system is booted. A sample `smbfstab` file is shown in Figure 6.12.

To do this, you specify the *share*, the local *directory* where it's to be mounted, the remote *file system type* (cifs or smbfs), and various *options*, such as the username and password needed to authenticate to the remote server.

The next file we need to look at is the `smbpasswd` file.

smbpasswd

The `/etc/samba/smbpasswd` file is a critical file that you must be aware of when managing a Samba deployment. Do you recall, in the previous chapter, that the CUPS service on your Linux server can be configured to use Digest authentication? If you choose to do so, CUPS can no longer use the `/etc/passwd` file to authenticate users. Instead, a new file is created using MD5 encryption to store user accounts.

FIGURE 6.12
The `/etc/samba/smbfstab` file.

```
fs1:/etc/samba # cat ./smbfstab
# This file allows you to mount SMB/ CIFS shares during system boot while
# hiding passwords to other people than root.  Use /etc/fstab for public
# available services.  You have to specify at least a service name and a mount
# point.  Current default vfstype is smbfs.
#
# Possible vfstypes are smbfs and cifs.
#
# The options are explained in the manual page of smbmount and mount.cifs.
#
# service        moint-point     vfstype options

;//fjall/test    /data/test      cifs    username=tridge,password=foobar
fs1:/etc/samba #
```

Samba works in much the same way. The smbd daemon, by default, uses `/etc/samba/smbpasswd` file to store Samba user accounts. This drove me nearly crazy the first time I set up a Samba server back in the late 1990s. I could get publicly shared directories to work without any trouble. But I couldn't authenticate to my users' home directories to save my life.

After reading a bunch of web pages, I finally discovered why. I hadn't Samba-enabled my users. As soon as I did, everything worked beautifully. We'll talk more about how to add users to `smbpasswd` later in this chapter.

TIP

Samba version 3 can actually use other options to store user account information, including an LDAP directory service.

The next file you need to be familiar with is `smbusers`.

smbusers

The `/etc/samba/smbusers` file is used by the Samba server to map usernames from client systems to user accounts on the local server. A sample `smbusers` file is shown in Figure 6.13.

For example, you may have a user who authenticates to her local Windows workstation as KimberlyT. However, her user account on the Samba server is KTracy.

The problem here is that, by default, when the client attempts to access a resource on the server, it sends the credentials that were used to authenticate to the desktop system. If they aren't the same, the user will have to manually supply the correct Samba username and password. To fix this, you could

- Live with it, requiring the user to authenticate twice.
- Manually synchronize the accounts.
- Map the client username to a server user account in the `smbusers` file.

FIGURE 6.13
The /etc/samba/smbusers file.

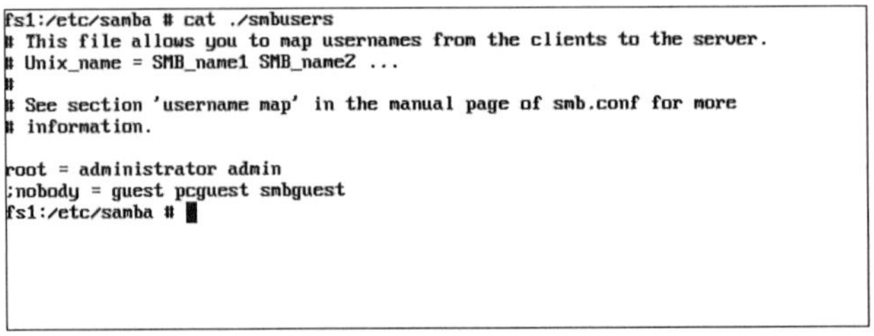

In the `smbusers` file, you use the following syntax:

```
Samba_server_username = client_username
```

With the exception of `smbpasswd`, you probably won't have to do much with the preceding configuration files when setting up a Samba system. The file that you will spend most of your time with is the `smb.conf` file. We'll look at this file next.

smb.conf

The `/etc/samba/smb.conf` file is the heart of your Samba configuration. Most of your configuration work will be done in this file. It is divided into two parts: *global options* and *shared resources*. The [global] section is used to define options that apply serverwide. The shared resources section is used to define resources on the server that can be accessed by SMB clients. A portion of a default `smb.conf` file is shown in Figure 6.14.

FIGURE 6.14
The /etc/samba/smb.conf file.

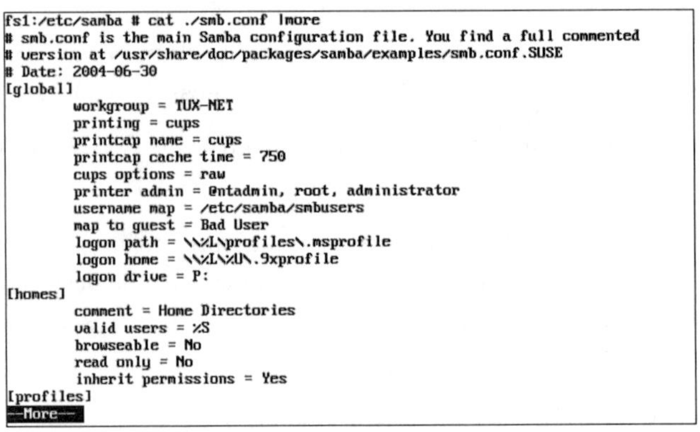

Let's look at the parameters in the [global] section first.

THE [GLOBAL] SECTION OF `smb.conf`

There are actually a ton of parameters that you can use in the [global] section of **smb.conf**, most of which you will never use. If you want to see list of all possible parameters, see the man page for **smb.conf**. For the purposes of the CLE certification, you need to be familiar with only a handful of parameters. These include the following:

- `workgroup`—This parameter defines the name of the workgroup *or* domain the Samba server will participate in.
- `netbios name`—This parameter is used to manually set the NetBIOS name of the Samba server. If you don't include this parameter in **smb.conf**, the NetBIOS name will default to the server's hostname.
- `server string`—This parameter is used to provide a description of the Samba server that will be displayed in My Network Places for Windows clients. This text string can contain any value you want. If you don't include this parameter in **smb.conf**, smbd will default to Samba ***samba_version_number***, as shown in Figure 6.15.

FIGURE 6.15
The server string parameter default value.

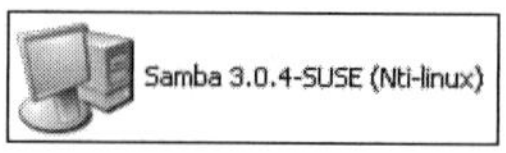

- `os level`—This parameter is used to configure how well your Samba server will do when electing a master browser. If you don't include this parameter, the Samba server is assigned an `os level` value of `20` and will win out over any other Windows systems in the workgroup or domain except for a PDC or a BDC. If you want to ensure that the Samba server wins over *any* other system in a browser election, include this parameter and set it to `65`.
- `encrypt passwords`—This parameter is used to configure smbd to use encrypted passwords. This should always be set to **on** because every version of Windows since Windows 98 requires encrypted passwords.
- `domain logons`—This parameter is used to configure Samba as a domain controller. When set to **yes**, the Samba server runs the netlogon service, which allows users to authenticate to the domain.

- `domain master`—This parameter is set to yes when configuring a PDC; it is set to no when configure the server to be a BDC.
- `preferred master`—This parameter configures the Samba server to be the preferred master browser for the workgroup or domain. If set to `yes`, an election will be forced when the service is started. If `domain master` is set to `yes`, the Samba server will win the election.
- `passdb backend`—This parameter is used to identify where Samba user accounts are stored.
- `wins server`—If a WINS server is already running on your network, include this parameter in your `smb.conf` file and set its value to the IP address of the WINS server.
- `wins support`—If your network doesn't already have a WINS server, use this parameter to run nmbd as a WINS server by setting its value to `yes`. The default value for this parameter is `no`.
- load printers—This is a really useful parameter. If you include this parameter in your `smb.conf` file, all printers defined in `/etc/printcap` will be automatically shared for SMB clients to use.

NOTE

Remember that back in Chapter 5 we said that Windows desktop systems don't support CUPS printers? Well here's our answer! By using Samba, we can share our CUPS printers with Windows SMB clients. Samba rocks!

- `security`—This is a critical parameter that is frequently overlooked by new Samba administrators. This parameter determines how smbd will authenticate users. There are five possible values:
  - `user`—Authentication is handled on a per-user basis. This value is usually used for workgroups on the network. When the security parameter is set to user, an SMB client must first authenticate with a valid username and password to the Samba server before it is allowed to access shared resources on the server. This is the default behavior if the security parameter isn't included in `smb.conf`.
  - `share`—Authentication is handled on a per-share basis. This value is usually used when using workgroups on the network. When the security parameter is set to share, each share in the system is assigned its own individual password. Client systems can access the share by providing the share's password. Usernames are not checked.
  - `domain`—This value is usually used for a domain on the network. When set to `domain`, all authentication processes are handled by a remote PDC or a BDC.

  - `server`—This value is usually used for a workgroup. When set to server, all authentication requests are forwarded to a different SMB server. This could be a different Samba server or it could be a Windows system.
  - `ads`—This value is used when the Samba server is a member of an Active Directory realm. When set to **`ads`**, all authentication processes will be handled by an AD domain controller.

- `printing`—This parameter defines the type of printing system on the server that will be managed by Samba. The possible values are **CUPS**, **LPRNG**, **PLP**, **SYSV**, **AIX**, **HPUX**, **QNX**, **SOFTQ**, and **BSD**. For the most part, you will probably use **CUPS** for this parameter.
- `username map`—This parameter allows you to specify the file that is used to map SMB client user names to local system user names. The default file to use for this purpose is /etc/samba/smbusers.

The next section you need to know about is [homes]. Let's look at it next.

THE [HOMES] SECTION OF `smb.conf`

If you refer back to Figure 6.15, you will see a section in **`smb.conf`** called [homes]. This section of the file is designed to automatically share the home directories of users on your server. When a user authenticates to the Samba server, the user's home directory is shared, as shown in Figure 6.16.

FIGURE 6.16
A shared home directory.

In addition to these shared home directories, you can also use **`smb.conf`** to define your own shared directories. We'll look at how to do that next.

CREATING A SHARED DIRECTORY

You can share any directory in your Linux file system. To do this, you add a section to your `smb.conf` file using the following syntax:

```
[share_name]
    comment = share_description
    path = path to shared directory
    other_smb_options
```

The *share_name* parameter specifies the name of the share. You can then use the following parameters to configure the share:

- `comment`—This parameter is used to provide a description of the share.
- `path`—This parameter specifies the full path to the shared directory. Be sure you configure the directory with the appropriate permissions.

NOTE

The path parameter is required. Those that are listed next are optional.

- `browseable`—This parameter specifies whether the share can be browsed in My Network Places. If you don't include this parameter, the default value of `yes` is assumed.
- `read only`—If set to `yes` (the default value), users are not allowed to create or edit files in the shared directory.
- `writeable`—This is basically the same parameter as `read only`, just in reverse. If set to `yes`, users are allowed to create or edit files in the shared directory (assuming the file system permissions will allow it).
- `public`—This parameter, when set to `yes`, allows users to connect to the shared directory without supplying a password. Because of this, the user will be connected using the nobody system account. This is used only with share-level security. The default value for this parameter is `no`.
- `valid users`—This parameter specifies the users who are allowed to access the share. You can separate multiple users with a comma. You can also specify a group by entering *@group_name*. If you don't include this parameter in `smb.conf`, anyone is allowed to access the share.
- `guest ok`—When set to yes, this parameter specifies that users don't need to supply a password to access the shared resource. The default value is `no`.
- `printable`—When set to `yes`, the parameter allows client systems to create spool files for printing in the shared directory. The default value is `no`.

As with the [global] section of **smb.conf**, there are about a bazillion other parameters that you can use when configuring a share—many more than we can cover here. Again, most of them are parameters that you will probably never use. Those previously listed are Linux file system. To do this, you add a section to your **smb.conf** file using the the ones you will probably use on a day-to-day basis.

After you have your **smb.conf** file configured, the next task you need to complete is to Samba-enable your users.

Samba-Enabling User Accounts

As was mentioned earlier, smbd doesn't use the **/etc/passwd** file to store user accounts. Instead, it uses the **/etc/samba/smbpasswd** file. By default, **smbpasswd** doesn't have anything in it, as shown in Figure 6.17.

FIGURE 6.17
An empty smbpasswd file.

```
fs1:/etc/samba # cat ./smbpasswd
# This file is the authentication source for Samba if 'passdb backend' is set
# to 'smbpasswd' and 'encrypt passwords' is 'Yes' in the [global] section of
# /etc/samba/smb.conf
#
# See section 'passdb backend' and 'encrypt passwords' in the manual page of
# smb.conf for more information.
fs1:/etc/samba #
```

TIP

In addition to the smbpasswd file, the Samba server can also use an LDAP directory or a MySQL database as a user store. You don't need to know how to do this for the CLE, so we're not going to cover it here. However, if you want to play with this, you can do so in the Identity tab of YaST. Select **Advanced Settings, User Authentication Sources, Add.** In the dialog box presented, you can select the database you want to use for Samba user accounts.

How do you populate the **smbpasswd** file? You use the **smbpasswd** utility. To do this, complete the following:

1. Open a terminal session.
2. At the shell prompt, switch to root.

TIP

If you run `smbpasswd` as any user other than root, it will perform operations only for the currently logged in user account. If you want to manage accounts other than your own, you must have root privileges.

3. At the shell prompt, enter **`smbpasswd -a`** ***`username`***. An example is shown in Figure 6.18.

FIGURE 6.18
Samba-enabling a user account.

```
fs1:/etc/samba # smbpasswd -a dcoughanour
New SMB password:
```

4. When prompted, enter a password for the SMB user account.

TIP

There's some debate as to whether you should use the same password for the SMB user account as for the system account. I like using the same password so I don't have to maintain two separate sets of passwords. However, those who are a little more security paranoid than I am insist that different passwords be used. I'll let you decide for yourself.

5. When prompted, reenter the password. You will be prompted that the user account as been added, as shown in Figure 6.19.

FIGURE 6.19
A Samba-enabled account.

```
fs1:/etc/samba # smbpasswd -a dcoughanour
New SMB password:
Retype new SMB password:
Added user dcoughanour.
fs1:/etc/samba #
```

This user account is now in the `/etc/samba/smbpasswd` file; as shown in Figure 6.20.

FIGURE 6.20
The Samba user account in smbpasswd.

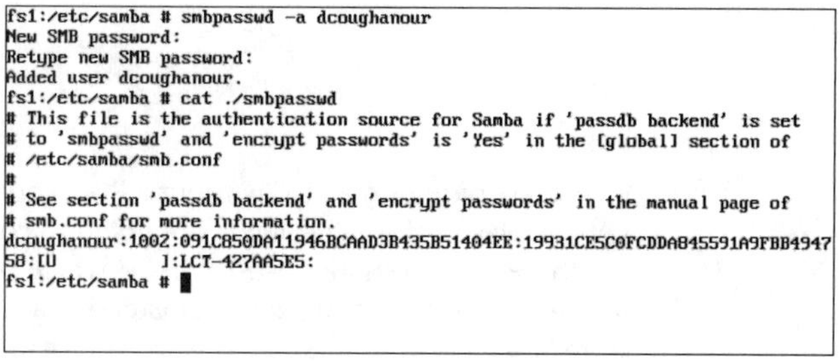

At this point, the user will be able to authenticate to the Samba server. Now that you understand how Windows network works, how to configure the Samba configuration files, and how to Samba-enable user accounts, you're ready to deploy your Samba server as a PDC.

Configure a PDC Using Samba on SLES 9

Configuring Samba to function as an SMB server in a workgroup is relatively easy. However, for your CLE 9 certification, you have to know how to deploy a Samba server as a PDC. To do this, you need to do the following:

- Configure [global] `smb.conf` options.
- Create a [netlogon] share.
- Create a [profile] share.

CONFIGURE [GLOBAL] OPTIONS IN SMB.CONF FOR A PDC

To set up your Samba server as a PDC, you need to add the parameters with the associated values shown in Table 6.1 to your `smb.conf` file:

TABLE 6.1
Required PDC `smb.conf` Parameters

PARAMETER	VALUE
`workgroup`	Use the *name of your domain* for the value.
`os level`	32 (or higher)
`domain logons`	yes
`domain master`	yes (for a PDC) or no (for a BDC)

TABLE 6.1
Required PDC `smb.conf` Parameters (continued)

PARAMETER	VALUE
`preferred master`	`yes`
`security`	`user`
`encrypt passwords`	`yes`
`passdb backend`	If you're configuring a PDC without a BDC, you can use `smbpasswd` for the value. If you are going to configure a BDC for this PDC, you should use `ldapsam`, which configures Samba to use an LDAP directory service instead of a local text file to store SMB user accounts. See the `smb.conf` man page to learn how to do this.

When your [global] settings complete, you next need to add a share named [netlogon] to your `smb.conf` file.

CONFIGURING THE [NETLOGON] SHARE

All PDCs or BDCs on a Windows network provide a share called [netlogon]. It's used to store logon scripts and group policies. The folks on the Samba team recommended that you, likewise, create a [netlogon] share on your Samba server. However, implementing this share is optional. In fact, when you use YaST to create a PDC 9 (as we'll do later in this chapter) you'll see that the [netlogon] share isn't created. At any rate, the syntax for the [netlogon] share is as follows:

```
[netlogon]
comment = Network Logon Service
path = /var/lib/samba/netlogon
browseable = No
guest ok = Yes
```

After your [netlogon] share has been defined, the next thing you need to do is configure another share; this one is named [profiles].

CONFIGURING THE [PROFILES] SHARE

The [profiles] share stores user profiles. To do this, the user must have read/write permissions to the directory where his or her profile is stored. The easiest way to do this is to use the user's home directory. That way you don't have to worry about permissions (although you certainly can use a different directory and manually set it up, if you want to).

A sample [profiles] share is shown next:

```
[profiles]
comment = Network Profiles Service
path = %H
read only = no
store dos attributes = yes
create mask = 0600
directory mask = 0700
browseable = yes
guest ok = no
printable = no
```

Notice that the path parameter uses a variable: `%H`. This variable represents the home directory of the logged-in user. You can use a variety of variables in the **`smb.conf`** file. A brief list is shown in Table 6.2:

TABLE 6.2
Variables That Can Be Used in `smb.conf`

VARIABLE	VALUE
%H	The user's home directory.
%U	The user's username.
%h	The hostname of the Linux system.
%m	The NetBIOS name of the SMB client system the user has authenticated from.
%L	The NetBIOS name of the Samba server.
%I	The IP address of the user's client system.

After you have your [global] options configured and your [netlogon] and [profiles] shares created, restart your Samba server with **`rcsmb restart`** and you've got a PDC!

Now you'll learn how to do it the easy way with YaST!

Configuring a PDC with YaST

Now that you know all about the configuration files used to set up Samba, you'll learn how to do it with YaST. Specifically, you'll look at configuring Samba as a PDC. To do this, you need to complete the following:

1. Start YaST.
2. When prompted, provide your root password.
3. Select **Network Services, Samba Server**. The screen in Figure 6.21 is displayed.

FIGURE 6.21
Setting the domain name.

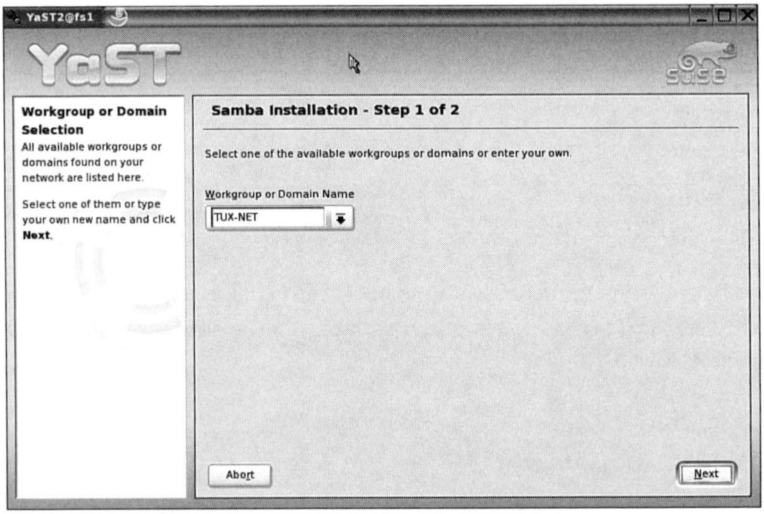

TIP

Like the DNS and the DHCP YaST modules, the first time you run the Samba module, it runs in wizard mode. You won't see some of these screens the next time you start the module.

4. In the Workgroup or Domain Name field, enter the *name of the domain* your Samba server will serve as a PDC for.
5. Select **Next**. The screen in Figure 6.22 is displayed.
6. In the Type Selection for SAMBA Server field, mark **Primary Domain Controller (PDC)**.
7. Select **Next**. The screen in Figure 6.23 is displayed.
8. In the Startup tab, mark **On**.
9. Select the **Shares** tab. You will see that a variety of shares have already been defined by default. These are shown in Figure 6.24.
10. You can configure new shares by completing the following:
    a. Select **Add**.
    b. In the Share Name field, enter the *name* of the new share.
    c. In the Share Description field, enter a *description* of the share.
    d. Under Share Type, mark the type of share you are configuring.

e. If you marked **directory**, enter the path to the shared directory in the Share Path field.

f. Select **OK**.

FIGURE 6.22
Configuring the server role.

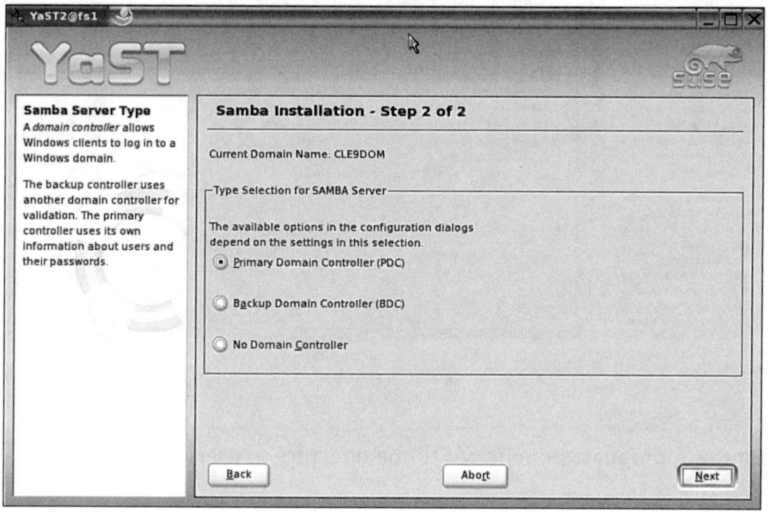

FIGURE 6.23
Configuring Samba startup options.

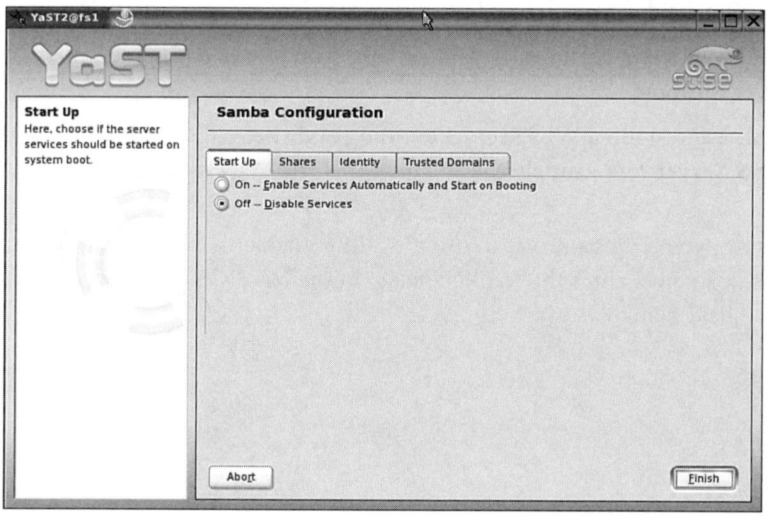

FIGURE 6.24
Configuring Samba shares.

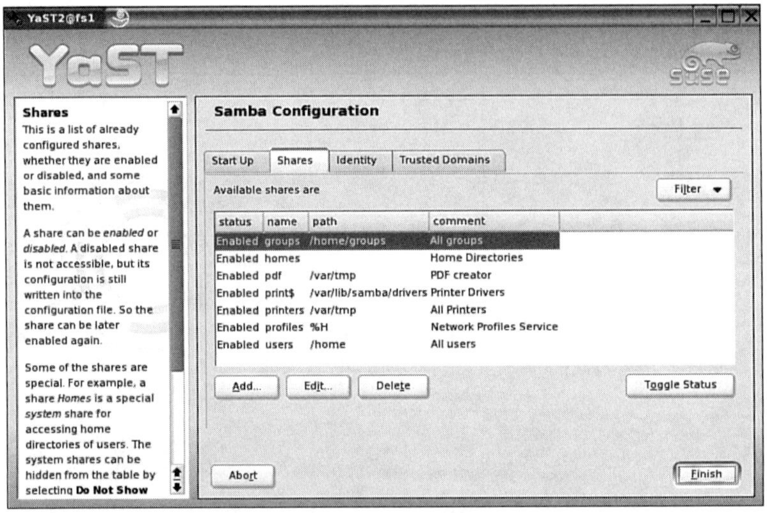

TIP

Be sure to grant the appropriate permissions to the directory so users can access it.

11. Select the **Identity** tab. The screen in Figure 6.25 is displayed.
12. In the Base Settings field, verify that your *domain* and *server role* have been configured properly.
13. In the WINS field, complete the following:
    a. If you want your Samba server to also function as a WINS server, mark **WINS Server Support**.
    b. If you want to use a WINS server running elsewhere in the network, mark **Remote WINS Server**; then supply the IP address of the WINS server.
14. If you want your Samba server to use a NetBIOS name that is different from the Linux system's hostname, enter the *NetBIOS name* in the NetBIOS Host Name field. Otherwise, leave the field blank.

FIGURE 6.25
Configuring the Samba server identity.

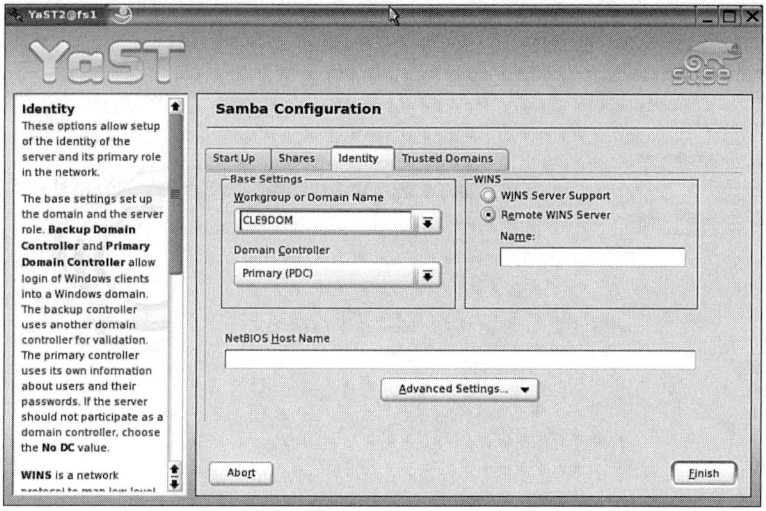

TIP

Leaving this field blank will cause Samba to use the system hostname as its NetBIOS name.

15. If you want to include additional parameters in your `smb.conf` file that haven't been addressed in the wizard, do the following:
    a. Select **Advanced Settings, Expert Global Settings**. The screen in Figure 6.26 is displayed.
    b. To add a parameter not listed, select **Add**.
    c. In the Selected Option drop-down list, select the *parameter* you want to add to the `smb.conf` file, as shown in Figure 6.27.
    d. Select **OK**.
    e. Configure the parameter and then select **OK**.

TIP

You can also use the **Edit** button to change an existing parameter.

    f. When you're finished configuring advanced settings, select **OK**.

FIGURE 6.26
Configuring advanced Samba server parameters.

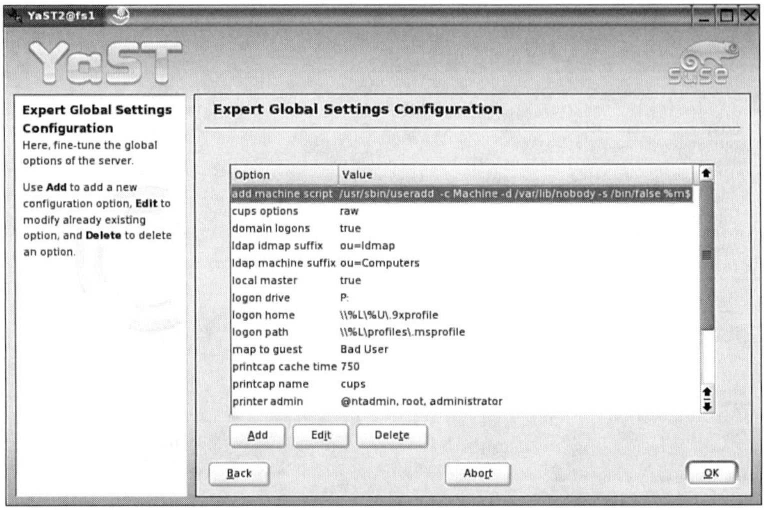

FIGURE 6.27
Adding a parameter to the smb.conf file.

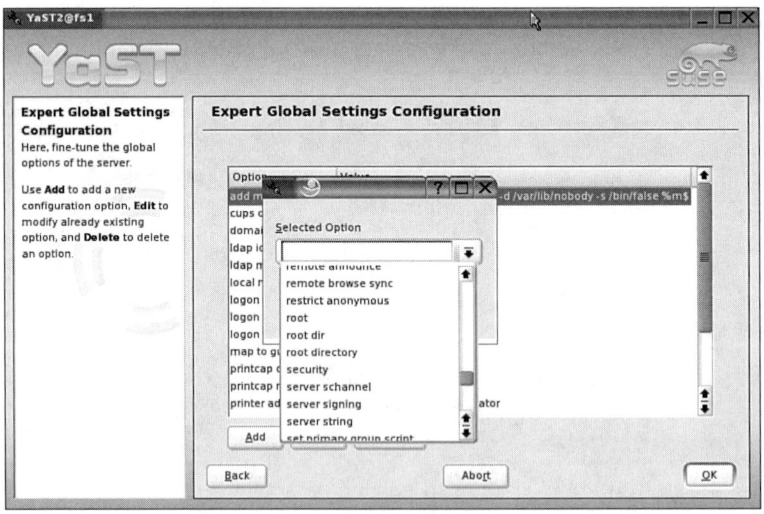

16. If you need to configure a trust relationship with another domain, complete the following:

   a. Select the **Trusted Domains** tab. The screen in Figure 6.28 is displayed.

FIGURE 6.28
Configuring trusts.

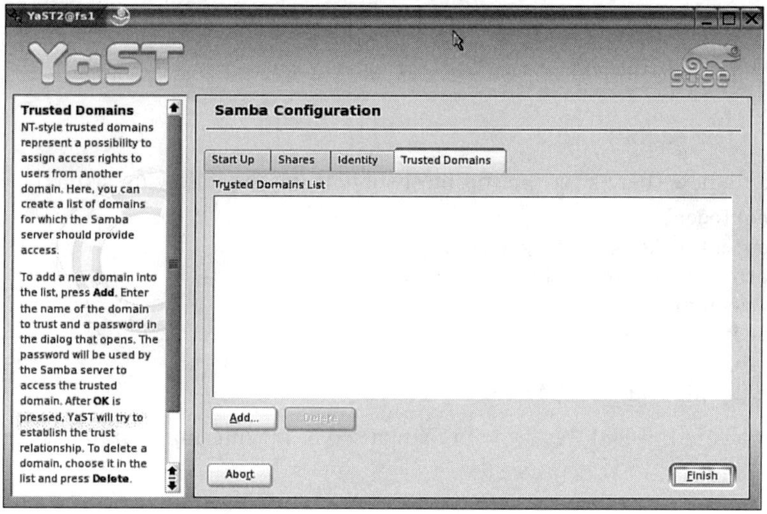

   b. Select **Add**.

   c. In the Domain field, enter the *name* of the trusted domain.

   d. In the Password field, enter the password required to authenticate to the trusted domain. You would have configured this password when you set up the domain and configured the trust relationship.

   e. Select **OK**.

17. Select **Finish**.

18. When prompted, provide your *root password*.

19. Select **OK**.

20. Samba-enable your users by completing the following:

   a. Open a terminal session.

   b. At the shell prompt, change to root.

   c. At the shell prompt, enter **`smbpasswd -a`** ***`username`***.

   d. When prompted, provide an *SMB password* for the user.

   e. Repeat this process for each user you want to be able to access your Samba server.

21. Add the [netlogon] share by completing the following:

TIP

You have to have root permissions to do this!

   a. Run a text editor (such as vi).

   b. Insert a new share after the [profiles] share using the following syntax:

```
[netlogon]
comment = Network Logon Service
path = /var/lib/samba/netlogon
browseable = No
guest ok = Yes
```

   c. Save the file and exit the editor.

22. When you are finished, restart your Samba server by entering **`rcsmb restart`** at the shell prompt.

TIP

This is another one of those "gotcha"—mistakes that many Samba administrators (including myself) frequently make. After editing the `smb.conf` file or adding users with `smbpasswd`, you must restart Samba.

That's all there is to it. Now you can practice in Lab Exercise 6.1.

Lab Exercise 6.1: Configuring a PDC

In this lab exercise, you will configure the Samba service on your server as a PDC for the CLE9DOM domain. You will also create a shared directory where all users can share files. To complete this exercise, you will need the following systems:

1. Your SLES 9 server with DNS, DHCP, and CUPS running.
2. (Optional) A Windows XP workstation to join the domain with.

To configure a PDC on your server, complete the following:

1. Boot your SLES 9 server and authenticate as **`tux`** with a password of **`SuSE789`**.
2. Prepare a directory for shared files by completing the following:
    a. Open a terminal session.
    b. At the shell prompt, enter **`su -`**.
    c. Supply a password of **`tuX123`**.
    d. At the shell prompt, enter **`mkdir /resources`**.
    e. Grant all users read/write access to `/resources` by entering **`chmod 666 /resources`**.
3. Start YaST.
4. When prompted for the root password, enter **`tuX123`**.
5. Select Network Services, Samba Server.
6. In the Workgroup or Domain Name field, enter **`CLE9DOM`**.
7. Select **Next**.
8. In the Type Selection for SAMBA Server field, mark **Primary Domain Controller (PDC)**.
9. Select **Next**.
10. In the Startup tab, mark On—Enable Services Automatically and Start on Booting.
11. Select the **Shares** tab.
12. Create a share for the `/resources` directory by completing the following:

a. Select **Add**.
b. In the Share Name field, enter **`ShareRes`**.
c. In the Share Description field, enter **`Shared resources for all users`**.
d. Under Share Type, mark **Directory**.
e. In the Share Path field, enter **`/resources`**.
f. Select **OK**.
g. Under Available Shares, select the **ShareRes** share; then select **Edit**.
h. Select **Add**.
i. In the Selected Option drop-down list, select **browseable**.
j. Select **OK**.
k. Mark **browseable**; then select **OK**.
l. Select **OK**.

13. Create a [netlogon] share by completing the following:

a. Select **Add**.
b. In the Share Name field, enter **`netlogon`**.
c. In the Share Description field, enter **`Network Logon Service`**.
d. Under Share Type, mark **Directory**.
e. In the Share Path field, enter **`/var/lib/samba/netlogon`**.
f. Select **OK**.
g. In the warning screen, select **Continue**.
h. Under Available Shares, select the **netlogon** share; then select **Edit**.
i. Select the **writable** option; then select **Delete**.
j. Select **Add**.
k. In the Selected Option drop-down list, select **browseable**.
l. Select **OK, OK**.
m. Select **Add**.
n. In the Selected Option drop-down list, select **guest ok**.
o. Select **OK**.
p. Mark **guest ok**; then select **OK**.
q. Select **OK**.

14. Select the **Identity** tab.
15. In the Base Settings field, verify that the domain has been set to **CLE9DOM** and that the server is configured to be a **PDC**.
16. In the WINS field, mark **WINS Server Support**.
17. Select **Finish**.
18. When prompted, enter **`tuX123`** as your root password; then select **OK**.
19. Samba-enable your users by completing the following:
    a. Switch to your terminal session.
    b. At the shell prompt, enter **`smbpasswd -a jcorry`**.
    c. When prompted, provide an SMB password of **`Anne1`**.
    d. Repeat this process to make root an SMB user.

TIP

You have to add root to the `smbpasswd` file; otherwise, you won't be able to add users and systems to the domain!

20. Restart your Samba server by entering **`rcsmb restart`** at the shell prompt.
21. Check your configuration by entering **`testparm`** at the shell prompt.
22. (Optional) Test your system by joining the domain from a Windows workstation. Complete the following:

NOTE

These steps are written for Windows 2000/XP Professional. If you're using Windows 9x or ME, see the documentation at http://www.samba.org for instructions.

    a. Configure your WINS server address by selecting Start, Control Panel, Network and Internet Connections, Network Connections.
    b. Right-click the appropriate *LAN connection*; then select **Properties**.
    c. Select **Internet Protocol**; then select **Properties**.
    d. Make sure your IP addressing information is correct; then select **Advanced**.
    e. Select **WINS**.

f. Select **Add**.

g. Enter the *IP address* of your Samba server.

h. Under NetBIOS Setting, mark **Enable NetBIOS over TCP/IP**; then select **OK**.

i. Select **Start**, **Right-click My Computer**.

j. Select **Properties**.

k. Select **Computer Name**.

l. Select **Change**.

m. Under Member of, mark **Domain**.

n. In the Domain field, enter **`CLE9DOM`**; then select **OK**.

o. When prompted for a user with permission to join the domain, enter **`root`** with a password of **`tuX123`**; then select **OK**.

p. Wait while the system is added to the domain.

q. When prompted that the system has been added to the domain, select **OK**.

r. When prompted to restart the system, select **OK**.

s. In the System Properties dialog box, select **OK**.

t. When prompted to reboot, select **Yes**.

u. When the system comes back up, press **Ctrl+Alt+Del**; then select **Options**.

v. In the Log On To Field, select **CLE9DOM** from the drop-down list.

w. Authenticate as **`jcorry`** with a password of **`Anne1`**.

TIP

Don't try to join the domain when you are initially installing Windows XP. If you do, you will get an error message indicating that a trust relationship doesn't exist between the workstation and the domain controller. Instead, install into a simple workgroup. Then join the domain after installation using the preceding steps.

23. From the Windows XP system, select **Start**, **My Computer**. You will see a drive mapped to jcorry's home directory, as shown in Figure 6.29.

FIGURE 6.29
Mapped Samba home directory share.

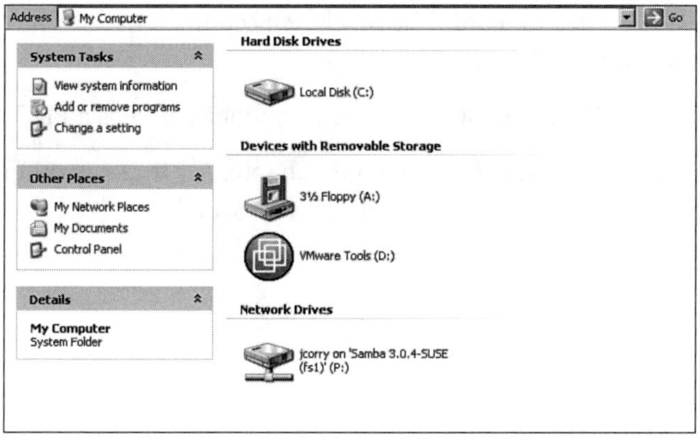

You can also browse your Samba server in My Network Places to see the shared resources it has been configured with, as shown in Figure 6.30.

FIGURE 6.30
Browsing shared resources on the Samba server.

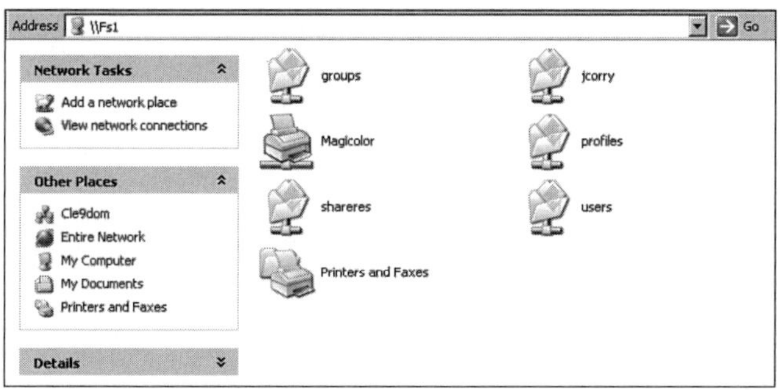

Notice in Figure 6.30 that the CUPS printer you configured in Chapter 5 has been automatically shared and is ready to service Windows clients. You've got to love Samba!

The next time you boot your SLES 9 server, you'll also see that a new user account has been added to the system using your workstation's system name. When configured as a PDC, Samba uses an add machine script (which simply calls good old useradd) that creates this user account. This script is specified in smb.conf. The machine account is used to access the domain when you're authenticating.

Congratulations! Your Samba server has been configured as a PDC.

That's it for this chapter. Before we go to Chapter 7, "Implementing Email Services on SLES 9," let's review what you've learned.

Summary

In this chapter, you learned how to implement Samba on your SLES 9 system. We first discussed how Samba makes your Linux system function like a Windows server on the network. Samba does this by implementing the Server Message Block (SMB) protocol, which is the backbone protocol of Windows servers.

You also saw how the SMB protocol uses the NetBIOS and TCP/IP or UDP/IP protocol at lower layers in the OSI model to provide printer and file sharing.

With the basics of SMB behind you, we then explored the various packages that are used to provide the Samba service on your SLES 9 server. Then we reviewed the process for installing them.

Before going any further, we reviewed several key Windows networking concepts that are key components of Samba, including

- Workgroups
- Domains
- Domain controllers
- Trusts

With Windows networking under our belt, we then discussed the various files used to configure and run the Samba service, including

- `lmhosts`
- `smbfstab`
- `smbpasswd`
- `smbusers`
- `smb.conf`

We then spent a great deal of time reviewing the way **`smb.conf`** is constructed. You also learned how to create a new share in **`smb.conf`**.

After that, you learned about how to Samba-enable users so they can access shared resources on the server from SMB client systems. In the remaining pages of the chapter, you learned how to configure your Samba server as a Primary Domain Controller (PDC).

In the next chapter, you're going to learn how to implement an email on your SLES 9 system. Stay tuned!

CHAPTER 7

Implementing Email Services on SLES 9

This chapter covers the following requirement for Novell's Certified Linux Engineer (CLE) 9 certification:

1. Use SLES 9 as a mail server.

In modern organizations, email has become the backbone of communication. If you have any doubt about this statement, just visit any office where the mail server has gone down. All productive work grinds to a halt.

Because email has become such an integral component of most networks, you need to know how to deploy and manage a mail server. Accordingly, the CLE 9 certification expects you to be able to do this on SLES 9 using Postfix.

Let's begin this chapter by introducing you to Postfix.

An Introduction to Postfix

TEST OBJECTIVE COVERED:

1. Use SLES 9 as a mail server.

Let's take a trip back in time (at least back to the early 1990s). If you needed to communicate with someone in your organization, you had three options:

- You could walk down to the person's office and communicate face to face.
- You could call the person on the telephone.
- You could write the person a memo.

Although it may seem foreign in today's work environment, back then we usually went for the last option. Why? Because it provided a paper trail. Whenever you sent someone a memo, you always made two copies: one for the recipient and one for yourself. Here's how the process went:

1. You typed up your memo using a word processor and printed two copies.
2. You put one copy of your memo in your filing cabinet.
3. You put the other copy of your memo in the mail slot of the recipient.
4. You waited a day or so for the recipient to get around to checking his or her mail slot.
5. You waited another day or so for the recipient to compose a response to your memo and put it in your mail slot.

Frankly, this was a very inefficient process that wasted a lot of paper. The inefficiencies were further magnified if you ever had to distribute an organization-wide memo.

For example, suppose you needed to notify everyone of a company picnic. You (or your administrative assistant) would have to compose a memo and then make a copy for every person in the company. What a waste of time and paper.

Thankfully, email has made the memo obsolete. I can't remember the last time I received a paper memo. The only thing I get in my mail slot now is junk mail. All other communications have been taken over by email.

You could argue, as I hinted earlier, that we've become a little too dependent on email. I find it humorous that co-workers, sitting in adjacent cubicles, will carry on conversations over email when they could simple pop their heads up and talk face-to-face over the cubicle wall.

At any rate, email is here to stay. In this chapter, you will learn how to deploy a mail server on SLES 9 using Postfix. Postfix is a very powerful and very extensive mail service that runs on Linux.

Postfix is extensive enough that entire books have been written about it. We don't have the time or the space here to address email in that kind of depth. Instead, we will focus on implementing POP3 and IMAP with Postfix to create an email solution.

NOTE

If you already have some experience with other Linux operating systems, you might be scratching your head about using Postfix. Postfix is a replacement for the Sendmail daemon you may already be familiar with.

I think you'll find, as we go through this chapter, that Postfix is somewhat easier than Sendmail to work with. As you deploy Postfix, you'll probably find it to be much more scalable than Sendmail, as well.

Let's begin by reviewing the email process.

How Email Works

To understand how Postfix works and how to deploy it, you need to understand how the email process itself works. The first thing you need to understand is the fact that the process is modular.

Different components play different roles as messages are sent from the sender to the recipient. These components and the overall message delivery process are shown in Figure 7.1.

FIGURE 7.1
The email process.

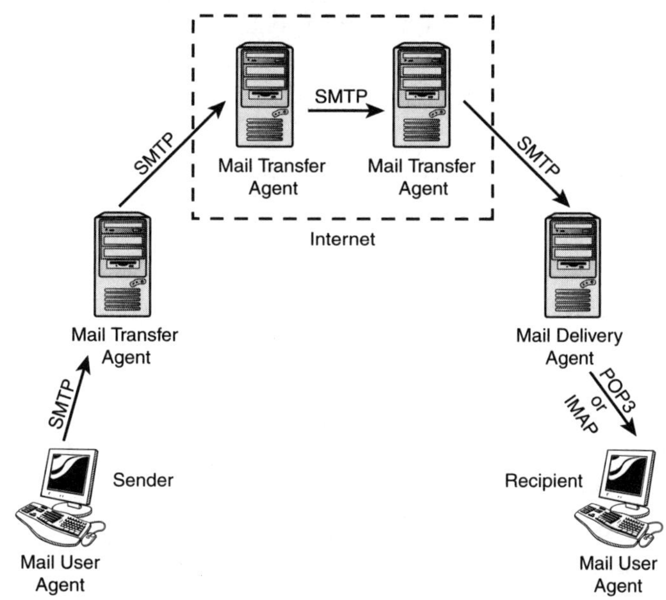

Let's review how it works. The following steps occur as the message is originated at the sender and transferred to the recipient:

1. A user at the sending workstation uses email client software to compose an email message. This client software is called the Mail User Agent (MUA). If you've ever used Outlook Express on a Windows system or Evolution on a Linux system, you've used a MUA. The MUA has no idea how to get the message to the intended recipient. Instead, it's configured to send outgoing messages to a mail server.
2. When the user selects **Send** in the MUA, it uses the Simple Mail Transfer Protocol (SMTP) to transfer the message to the mail server that it has been configured to use. SMTP is a very simple, IP-based email protocol, running on port 25, that functions at the upper layers of the OSI model. The sole purpose of SMTP is to transfer mail messages between email agents.

TIP

An enhanced version of SMTP, called the Extended Simple Mail Transfer Protocol (ESMTP), is also used to send binary files, such as graphics, audio, and video, as email messages.

3. Using SMTP, the email message is transferred from the MUA on the sender's workstation to the Mail Transfer Agent (MTA) on the mail server the MUA has been configured to use. The MTA is the "brains" of the email system. After receiving the mail message from the MUA, the MTA transfers the mail message to the next MTA between it and the destination system.

NOTE

If the message is intended for another user in your same domain, the message is held by the local MTA for delivery to the recipient's MUA. It doesn't get shuffled from one MTA to another, as depicted in Figure 7.1.

For example, if you were to send a message to your co-worker Chris (who works in an adjacent cubicle), it wouldn't be sent through a series of MTAs on the Internet to finally reach him. Instead, it would go directly to the MDA (which we'll discuss shortly) to await delivery to his MUA.

4. The email message is transferred from MTA to MTA on the Internet until it finally arrives at the MTA used by the message's recipient. The MTAs use the SMTP protocol to accomplish the transfers.
5. The destination MTA transfers the email message to the Message Delivery Agent (MDA) for the system where the recipient resides. The MDA's job is to hang on to the message until the MUA of the recipient requests it. The MDA is sometimes called the Message Store for this reason.

6. The recipient uses the MUA on his or her workstation to connect to the MDA and pull down email messages. To do this, the MUA can use either the Post Office Protocol (POP) version 3 or the Internet Message Access Protocol (IMAP). Both protocols are supported by most MDAs and MUAs. Which one you choose to implement is based on what the MUA needs to be able to do. Keep the following points in mind:
   - POP3 is the simpler of the two protocols. POP3 resides at the upper layers of the OSI model and operates using port 110. POP3 is basically designed to pull messages down from the MDA, deleting the messages from the MDA in the process. It doesn't do much more than that.

NOTE

Some implementations of POP3 allow you to keep a copy of your messages on the server.

   - IMAP is a more powerful mail protocol. IMAP also functions at the upper layers of the OSI model; using port 143. Instead of downloading the entire message, IMAP allows you to pull down the message headers only, allowing the user to decide which messages to completely download. IMAP allows you to keep a copy of downloaded messages on the MDA server, which can be very useful if you're using a web-based MUA in conjunction with a typical MUA client. IMAP also enables you to create custom folders on the MDA for sorting your messages.
7. The recipient uses the MUA on his or her workstation to read the message from the sender.

At a high level, that's how email works. In the next section, you'll learn how Postfix fits into this model.

How Postfix Works

Postfix functions as an MTA in the model displayed in Figure 7.1. Its job is threefold:

- It accepts messages from MUAs.
- It stores accepted messages in a queue in the server's file system.
- It forwards messages from the queue on to their next destination.

Postfix uses the SMTP protocol to accomplish these tasks, as discussed earlier. It's important to note, however, that Postfix does *not* include any POP3 or IMAP support. Accordingly, Postfix has limited functionality as an MDA. It can function as an MDA only for mail messages intended for user accounts on the local machine.

Most likely, however, you will want users to be able to use their own MUA client software to attach to your mail server and download their messages. To allow remote MUAs to pull messages down, you have to implement a POP3/IMAP service in conjunction with Postfix. We'll discuss how to do that later in the chapter.

To accomplish its three jobs, Postfix uses a series of modular daemons. If you've ever worked with Novell's NetMail email server on NetWare or Linux, you will be acquainted with the modular nature of Postfix.

Instead of rolling all the services and functions Postfix is to perform into a single daemon, it uses the master daemon along with multiple worker daemons, which are started only when needed. When the tasks assigned to the worker daemons are complete, the master daemon automatically shuts them down.

The master daemon and the worker daemons function together as a unit to process email messages through the Postfix MTA. Figure 7.2 shows the flow of these messages as they are processed.

FIGURE 7.2
Message flow through the Postfix MTA.

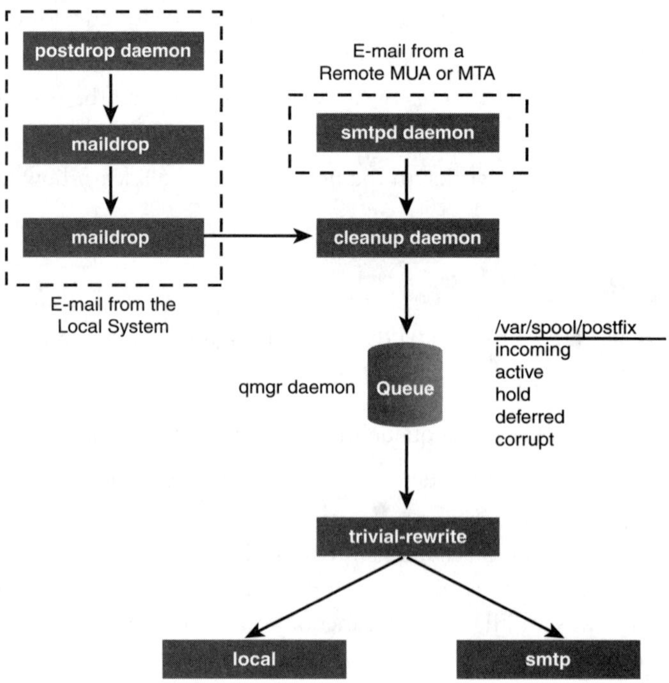

The following happens to each message as it is processed:

1. If an email message is sent to the Postfix MTA by a remote MTA or remote MUA, it is accepted into the system by the smtpd worker daemon. The smtpd daemon forwards the message to the cleanup daemon.
2. If an email message is sent to the Postfix MTA by a user using a shell prompt on the local system, the following occurs:
   a. It is accepted into the system by the postdrop daemon, which is also a Postfix worker daemon.
   b. The postdrop daemon places the email message in the maildrop directory in `/var/spool/postfix`, as shown in Figure 7.3.

FIGURE 7.3
Postfix queues.

```
fs1:/var/spool/postfix # ls
.  active  corrupt  deferred  hold      maildrop  private  saved
.. bounce  defer    flush     incoming  pid       public   trace
fs1:/var/spool/postfix #
```

   c. The pickup daemon transfers the message from the maildrop directory and forwards it to the cleanup daemon.
3. The email message, regardless of whether it originated remotely or on the local system, is then processed by the cleanup daemon.
4. The cleanup daemon places the email message in the incoming queue, which is also located in `/var/spool/postfix` (see Figure 7.3).
5. The cleanup daemon notifies the Queue Manager daemon (qmgr) that a message has been added to the incoming queue.
6. The qmgr daemon moves the email message to one of five message queues, all of which are located in `/var/spool/postfix`:
   - incoming—This queue contains incoming messages that have been processed by the cleanup daemon.
   - active—This queue contains messages that arrived intact, were processed correctly, and are ready to be forwarded on to the next MTA or MDA.
   - hold—This queue contains messages whose delivery, for some reason, has been put on hold.

- deferred—This queue contains messages that could not be delivered on the first try. The qmgr daemon will wait a while; then it will make several more delivery attempts.
- corrupt—This queue contains messages that were damaged somewhere in transit and are no longer readable.

7. The qmgr daemon then invokes the trivial-rewrite daemon, which identifies the next MTA or MDA to which the message should be sent.
8. The qmgr daemon then passes the message to the appropriate delivery agent. If the message is intended for a local user account, the local agent is used. If the message is intended for another MTA or an MDA, the smtp agent is used.
9. The selected agent transfers the email message to the appropriate system.

I'll bet you didn't know that so much work went into delivering an email message! Now that you know how Postfix works, you need learn how to configure it on your system.

Configuring Postfix on SLES 9

TEST OBJECTIVE COVERED:

1. Use SLES 9 as a mail server.

Configuring Postfix is an interesting adventure. Like most of the other services we've covered in this book, the service is configured using a text file in the `/etc` directory. As we've done in other chapters, we'll first look at the Postfix configuration file; then we'll talk about how to configure Postfix graphically with YaST.

As we do, you'll see why I say Postfix configuration is an adventure. Postfix is installed automatically when SLES 9 is installed. The default configuration that is created during installation works nicely right out of the box. From that standpoint, Postfix is relatively easy to implement.

However, as soon as you try to customize Postfix beyond the defaults, you'll see that, of all the services we cover in this book, Postfix is one of the more difficult to configure. As I mentioned earlier, entire volumes have been written on the topic. We have space here to cover only a basic configuration (which is good, because that's what you need to know for the CLE 9 exam).

NOTE

As challenging as Postfix may be to configure, Sendmail is much more difficult!

The Postfix service is started and stopped using the **postfix** init script in **/etc/init.d**, as shown in Figure 7.4.

FIGURE 7.4
Postfix startup script.

```
atd                  clamd                nmb          smartd
autofs               coldplug             nscd         smb
autoyast             cron                 ntop         smbfs
avgate               cups                 openct       smpppd
boot                 cyrus                pamsmbd      snmpd
boot.clock           dhcpd                pcscd        spamd
boot.crypto          dhcrelay             portmap      splash
boot.cycle           esound               postfix      splash_early
boot.d               fbset                powerfail    splash_late
boot.device-mapper   fetchmail            powersaved   squid
boot.evms            gpm                  random       sshd
boot.idedma          halt                 raw          syslog
boot.ipconfig        halt.local           rc           uml
boot.isapnp          hotplug              rc0.d        vmware-tools
boot.klog            hwscan               rc1.d        winbind
boot.ldconfig        inn                  rc2.d        xdm
boot.loadmodules     isdn                 rc3.d        xfs
boot.local           joystick             rc4.d        xinetd
boot.localfs         kbd                  rc5.d        xntpd
boot.localnet        kdc                  rc6.d        ypbind
boot.lvm             ksysguardd           rcS.d        yppasswdd
boot.md              ldap                 reboot       ypserv
boot.proc            mailman              resmgr       ypxfrd
fs1:/etc/init.d #
```

The actual Postfix daemons themselves reside in the **/usr/lib/postfix** directory on your SLES 9 system, as shown in Figure 7.5.

FIGURE 7.5
Postfix daemons.

```
fs1:/usr/lib/postfix # ls
.       cleanup  lmtp    nqmgr   pipe      qmqpd  smtpd   trivial-rewrite
..      error    local   oqmgr   proxymap  showq  spawn   verify
bounce  flush    master  pickup  qmgr      smtp   tlsmgr  virtual
fs1:/usr/lib/postfix #
```

In this part of the chapter we'll get a basic Postfix deployment running. Then, to make our mail server available to remote email clients, we'll learn how to add IMAP and POP3 support to Postfix.

To accomplish this task we're going to cover the following topics:

- Creating MX records on the DNS server
- Configuring Postfix
- Configuring SMTP authentication
- Configuring IMAP and POP3 support

You'll begin by learning how to add records to your DNS server to support email.

Configuring MX Records

A properly functioning DNS server is a key component of your Postfix configuration. Think about it: If a user needs to send an email message to support@somedomain.com, your Postfix MTA needs to be able to resolve the IP address for somedomain.com. If the MTA doesn't have access to a properly configured DNS server, this isn't going to happen.

In addition, MTAs outside your domain need to be able to resolve the IP address of your mail server; otherwise, they won't be able to get mail from outside to the MTA for your domain. To do this, you need to configure a Mail Exchange (MX) record. An MX record identifies the MTA that's responsible for handling mail messages for a given domain.

For example, suppose someone out on the Internet were to send an email message to jcorry@cle9.com. Assuming we've registered the cle9.com domain for our organization, the MTA to whom the user's MUA sent the message needs to forward the message to our MTA. However, notice that the email address includes only the domain name: cle9.com. The MTA doesn't know which server within the cle9.com is the MTA for the domain.

To provide this information, you configure your DNS server with an MX record. To do this on your SLES 9 server, you would complete the following:

1. Start YaST.
2. When prompted, supply your root password.
3. Select **Network Services**, **DNS Server**.
4. Select **DNS Zones**.
5. Select the domain the MTA will service; then select **Edit zone**.
6. Select the **Records** tab. The screen in Figure 7.6 is displayed.
7. Create an A record for your MTA by completing the following:
    a. In the Record Key field, enter a *DNS name* for your MTA. For example, `mail.cle9.com.`.

TIP

Don't forget the trailing period!

    b. Make sure the Type drop-down list is set to **A – Domain Name Translation**.
    c. In the Value field, enter the *IP address* of the server where the MTA is running.
    d. Select **Add**.

FIGURE 7.6
Adding mail server records.

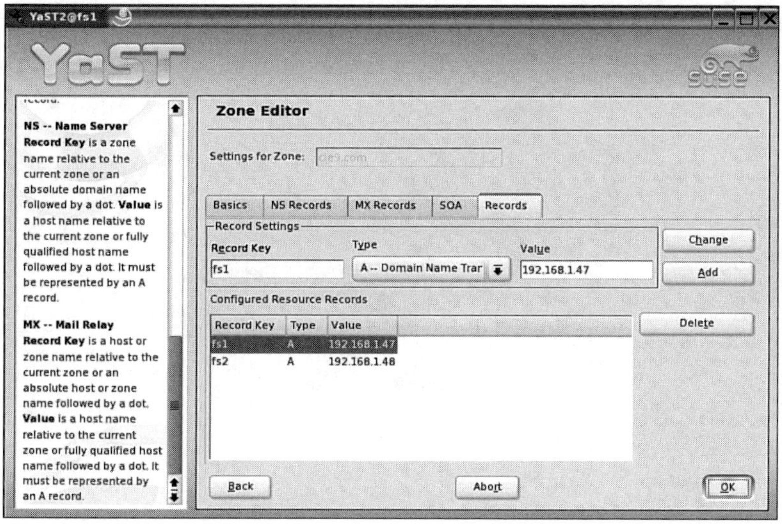

8. Create an MX record for your domain by completing the following:

   a. In the Record Key field, enter the *domain name* that will be serviced by your MTA server. For example, **`cle9.com.`**

   b. In the Type drop-down list, select **MX—Mail Relay**.

   c. In the Value field, enter the *DNS name* of the MTA (which you just created). For example, **`mail.cle9.com.`**.

   d. Select **Add**. Your Configured Resource Records field should appear similar to that shown in Figure 7.7.

9. Select the **MX Records** tab. You should see something similar to Figure 7.8.

NOTE

Notice the Priority field in Figure 7.8. If you have more than one mail server for the zone, you can add them in this screen and set their priority level.

10. Select **OK**.

11. In the DNS Server—DNS Zones screen, select **Finish**.

FIGURE 7.7
An A record for `mail.cle9.com`.

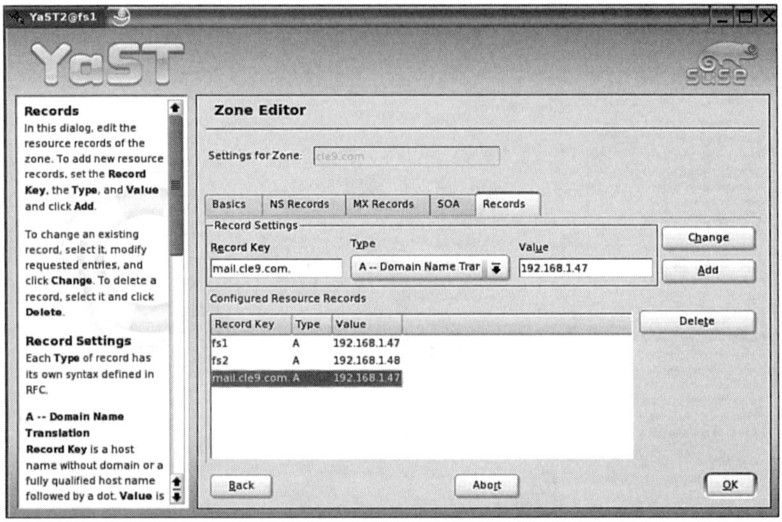

FIGURE 7.8
An MX record for the cle9.com zone.

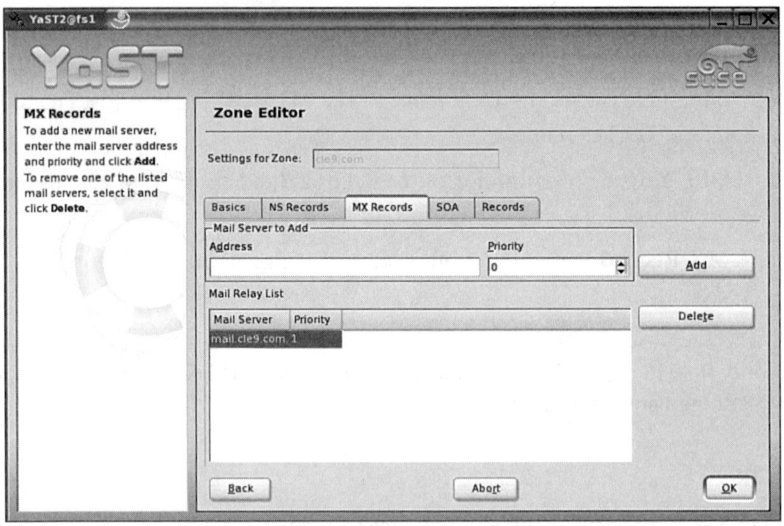

TIP

If you have DDNS running, the preceding procedure won't work. You'll find that the changes aren't written out to the zone file.

Alternatively, you can also use a text editor, such as vi, to manually edit your zone file. You can use the cle9.com zone file shown in Figure 7.9 as an example.

FIGURE 7.9
A zone file configured with an MX record.

```
fs1:/var/lib/named/dyn # cat cle9.com
$ORIGIN .
$TTL 43200
cle9.com                IN SOA  fs1.cle9.com. root.fs1.cle9.com. (
                                2005042106 ; serial
                                10800      ; refresh (3 hours)
                                3600       ; retry (1 hour)
                                302400     ; expire (3 days 12 hours)
                                43200      ; minimum (12 hours)
                                )
                        NS      fs1.cle9.com.
mail.cle9.com.          A       192.168.1.47
cle9.com.               MX      1       mail.cle9.com.
$ORIGIN cle9.com.
fs1                     A       192.168.1.47
fs2                     A       192.168.1.48

fs1:/var/lib/named/dyn #
```

With your DNS server ready to service your MTA, you next need to configure the Postfix service itself.

Configuring Postfix

During installation, Postfix is automatically configured to function as an MTA. This makes life nice for us. We don't have to do a whole lot to get it working. The configuration files used to configure Postfix are located in `/etc/postfix`, as shown in Figure 7.10.

Your jaw probably dropped when you first saw the incredible number of files in this directory. The good news is that for the basic configuration we're going to be working with in this chapter, you don't need to do much of anything with most of them.

TIP

I wasn't kidding when I said advanced configuration of Postfix is somewhat complicated!

FIGURE 7.10
Postfix configuration files.

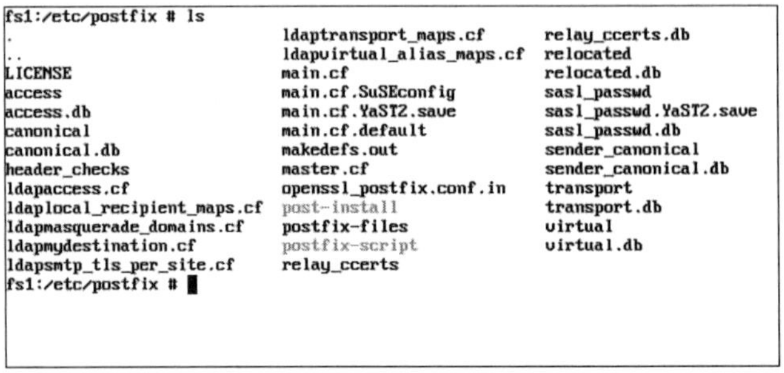

In fact, we really need to be concerned only with `main.cf`, which is used to configure the overall Postfix service's behavior. The `main.cf` file uses the typical format of

`parameter = value`

To modify the parameters within `main.cf`, you have three options: You can use a traditional text editor, such as kate or vi. A sample `main.cf` file open in vi is shown in Figure 7.11.

FIGURE 7.11
Editing `main.cf` in vi.

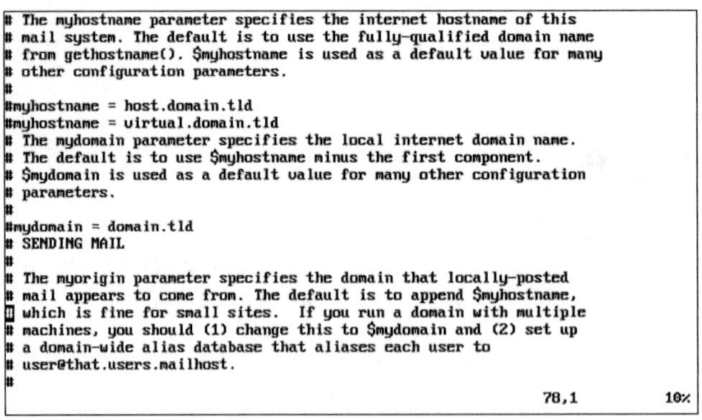

You can use the `postconf` command to change parameters within the file. This is done using the following syntax:

`postconf -e parameter=value`

The `-e` switch tells postconf to edit the parameter specified.

Finally, you can also use YaST, as shown in Figure 7.12.

FIGURE 7.12
Editing `main.cf` with YaST.

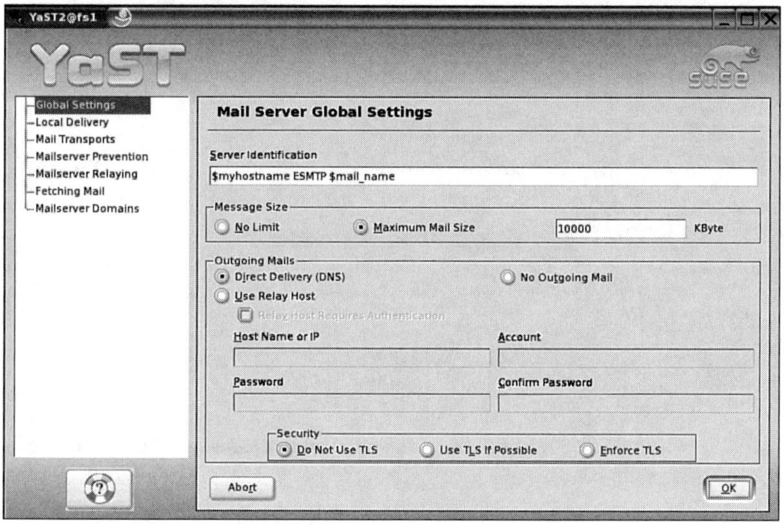

Having configured Postfix all three ways, I much prefer YaST. This is primarily because `main.cf` can be configured using more than 300 possible parameters. If you don't work with Postfix every day, it's easy to forget what combination of parameters you need to accomplish a certain task. It's nice to let YaST remember them for you.

The problem with YaST, however, is that it allows you to configure only a small subset of the many `main.cf` parameters. In fact, a couple of the basic parameters that are required for Postfix to run properly can't even be modified with YaST. Therefore, you have to know `main.cf`!

With that in mind, let's look at some of the `main.cf` parameters you will most likely need to work with. These include the following:

- `queue_directory`—This parameter specifies the directory in the local server's file system that Postfix will use as its mail queue. By default, this is **/var/spool/postfix**.
- `mail_owner`—This parameter is used to specify the user account the postfix daemons will run as. By default, this is the postfix system user. On a SLES 9 system, the postfix user is a member of two groups: mail and postfix, as shown in Figure 7.13.

FIGURE 7.13
The postfix user account.

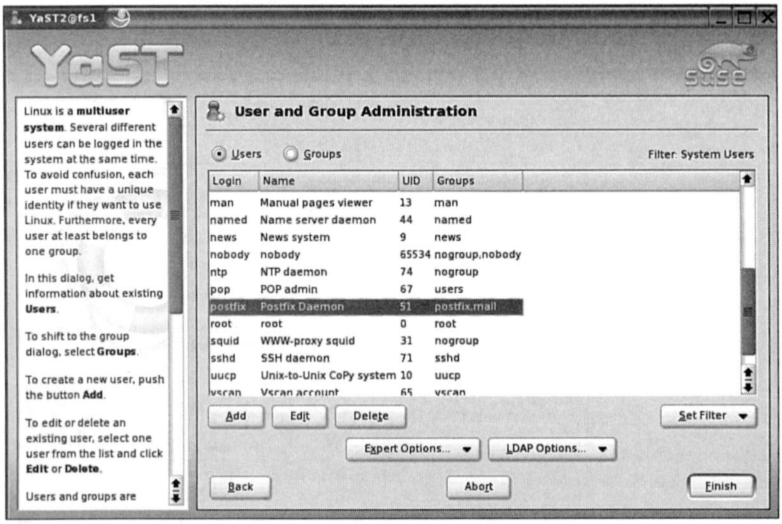

- `myhostname`—This parameter is used to specify the hostname of the server where the Postfix MTA is running. If you enter a hostname only in this parameter, you'll need to set the value of mydomain to your domain. If you set myhostname to the FQDN of your system, the **`mydomain`** parameter is not needed. The system will automatically parse out your domain name from the value in the **`myhostname`** parameter.

NOTE

Make sure this parameter is configured correctly! If it isn't, Postscript won't function properly.

- `mydomain`—This parameter is used to specify the domain of the host running Postfix. If you use a FQDN in the **`myhostname`** parameter, you don't need to use this parameter.

TIP

Postfix uses the `$myhostname` and the `$mydomain` variables to store the values of the `myhostname` and `mydomain` parameters in `main.cf`.

- `myorigin`—This parameter is used to append domain information to email recipient messages where the sender doesn't include a domain name in the To address. When enabled, this parameter is really useful for interoffice email. For example, I could set `myorigin` equal to **`cle9.com`**. Then, if I wanted to send an email to my co-worker Chris in the next cubicle, I could simply send the message to **`chris`** instead of **`chris@cle9.com`**.

- `inet_interfaces`—This parameter is used to specify which network interfaces can be used to receive mail messages. By default, Postfix listens for mail on all active network interfaces.
- `proxy_interfaces`—This parameter is used to specify the IP address of the network's proxy server.
- `mydestination`—This parameter is a critical one. It is used to define the domains that the Postfix MTA will service.
- `home_mailbox`—This parameter is used to define where users' mailbox files will be stored. By default, they are stored in `/var/spool/mail/`*`user_name`*. This is configured by setting this value to **`Mailbox`**. You can also store the users' mailbox files within their home directories. To configure this behavior, set this parameter to the relative path to the mailbox directory in your users' home directories. For example, if you want mail delivered to `/home/`*`user_name`*`/Mail`, you would enter **`Mail/`**.

Be sure to include the / after `Mail`!

NOTE

If you want to deliver mail to the Cyrus IMAP server, which we'll discuss later, you need to include this parameter in `main.cf`, but it should be set to a null value.

In addition to `main.cf`, the `/etc/sysconfig/postfix` file is used to configure Postfix on a SLES 9 system. A sample Postfix file is shown in Figure 7.14.

This file is edited when you use YaST to configure Postfix. Many of the virus and spam protection parameters used with Postfix are configured with this file. We'll discuss these later in this chapter.

With your `main.cf` file configured, next you need to configure SMTP authentication to your Postfix MTA.

Configuring SMTP Authentication

If you refer back to Figure 7.1, you will notice that the SMTP protocol is used to submit mail messages from MUAs on client workstations to your Postfix MTA. SMTP is a relatively simply protocol. One of the problems with it is that it doesn't verify the credentials of the user.

FIGURE 7.14
The `/etc/sysconfig/postfix` file.

```
fs1:/etc/sysconfig # cat ./postfix |more
## Path:        Network/Mail/Postfix
## Description: Basic configuration of the postfix MTA
## Type:        string
## Default:     ""
## Config:      postfix
#
# Should we use a mailrelay?
# NOTE: ALL mail that is not considered to be my destination
# (POSTFIX_LOCALDOMAINS), will be sent to this host.
# If this host is not your MX, then you have to use [square brackets]
# around the hostname, e.g. [relay.example.com]
# You may also specify an alternate port number, e.g.
# relay.example.com:26 or [relay.example.com]:26 to prevent MX lookups.
#
POSTFIX_RELAYHOST=""

## Type:        string
## Default:     ""
## Config:      postfix
#
# Comma separated list of domains that must have their subdomain
--More--
```

This presents you, as the mail administrator, with a fairly serious security problem. Without any authentication system, you MTA will accept mail messages from anyone and forward them on. Sure, you could use parameters (which we haven't discussed) in `main.cf` to restrict SMTP access to a particular subnet or domain. The problem is, you can fake a lot of information in the header of email messages, making them appear to be coming from a particular subnet or domain.

Without an authentication mechanism, your mail server is said to be an *open relay server*. In other words, it simply relays messages sent to it via SMTP to the various recipients without checking to see whether the messages are authorized.

Several years ago, I had a friend at work who set up a UnixWare server (this was back when Novell still owned Unix). It ran a version of Sendmail that, using its default configuration, didn't require any kind of SMTP authentication. Several of my co-workers and I discovered this and had a great deal of fun with it. Using spoofed return addresses, we sent all kinds of bogus email messages to unsuspecting co-workers. It was just like being in junior high school all over again.

Our antics with Sendmail were all done in fun. However, this kind of MTA can be used maliciously, causing a great deal of trouble. Open relay servers are a favorite device of spammers.

Because they will send messages without checking where they are coming from, an open relay server in your network can (without your knowledge) be used by a spammer to send unsolicited email with spoofed return addresses. If you were to try to trace down where these spam messages came from, guess where they would appear to originate from? Yep, your server, as shown in Figure 7.15.

FIGURE 7.15
The dangers of a relay server.

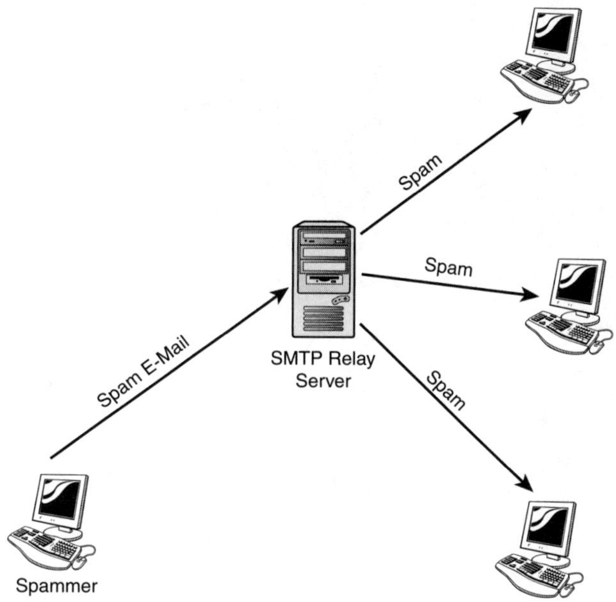

To keep this from happening, you should configure your MTA with a means of authenticating users before sending their messages. Doing this creates a much more secure mail system than simply restricting access based on domain or subnet.

This is done use the Simple Authentication and Security Layer (SASL) version 2 service. This service integrates with our Postfix MTA and is used to authenticate users to the mail system before allowing them to send SMTP messages through, as shown in Figure 7.16.

Several SASL are packages available. However, the most popular one is the Cyrus SASL package. This is what we will use to configure SMTP authentication in this chapter.

To use this package, you need to make sure the appropriate packages are installed on your server. The main package you need is the cyrus-sasl package, shown in Figure 7.17.

FIGURE 7.16
Preventing unauthorized relay with SASL authentication.

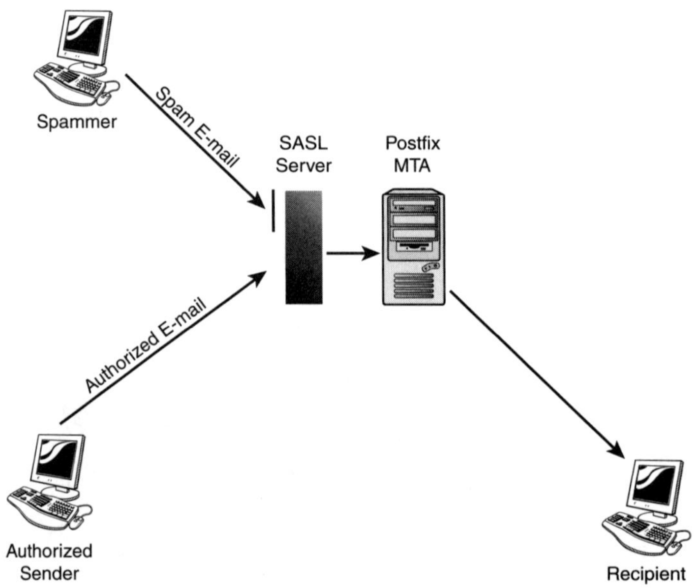

FIGURE 7.17
Installing the Cyrus SASL packages.

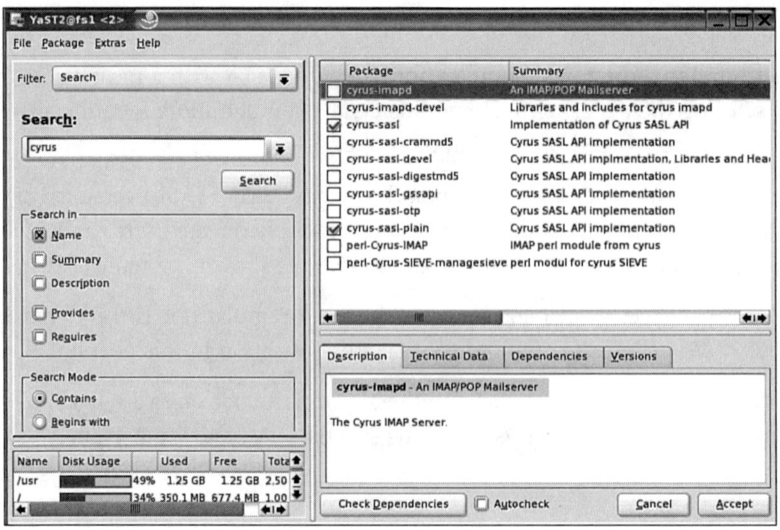

NOTE

The Cyrus SASL server is maintained by Carnegie Mellon University. For more information, visit http://asg.web.cmu.edu/cyrus.

Notice in Figure 7.17 that there are also a series of additional cyrus-sasl packages, including cyrus-sasl-plain, cyrus-sasl-digestmd5, and so on. The Cyrus SASL server allows you to customize how you want to manage your SASL authentication process. For example, if you want to use basic authentication, you would use cyrus-sasl-plain. If want to use Digest authentication, you would use the cyrus-sasl-digestmd5.

The SASL service is provided by the saslauthd daemon. Two files are used to configure this daemon:

- `/etc/sysconfig/saslauthd`
- `/usr/lib/sasl2/smtpd.conf`

Let's look at the saslauthd file first. A sample file is shown in Figure 7.18.

FIGURE 7.18
Configuring saslauthd daemon in `/etc/sysconfig/saslauthd`.

```
fs1:/etc/sysconfig # cat ./saslauthd
## Path:           System/Security/SASL
## Type:           list(getpwent,kerberos5,pam,rimap,shadow,ldap)
## Default:        pam
## ServiceRestart: saslauthd
#
# Authentication mechanism to use by saslauthd.
# See man 8 saslauthd for available mechanisms.
#
SASLAUTHD_AUTHMECH=pam
fs1:/etc/sysconfig #
```

The only parameter you can configure in this file is `SASLAUTHD_AUTHMECH`. You use this parameter to specify the type of authentication mechanism you want to use. You have the following options:

- `pam`—This authentication method specifies that the saslauthd daemon use PAM on the local server to authenticate users. This parameter allows you to use the PAM modules your system has been configured with. This is the default (and most flexible) value, as shown in Figure 7.18.
- `getpwent`—This authentication method bypasses PAM and directly accesses your `/etc/passwd` file. Obviously, if you use shadow passwords, this option won't do much for you.

- `kerberos4` or `kerberos5`—These authentication methods allow saslauthd to authenticate to your local Kerberos realm, if you are using Kerberos on your Linux server.
- `shadow`—This authentication method allows saslauthd to use your `/etc/shadow` file to authenticate SMTP users.
- `ldap`—This authentication method configures saslauthd to use an LDAP directory service to authenticate users.

You also configure saslauthd using the `/usr/lib/sasl2/smtpd.conf` file, shown in Figure 7.19.

FIGURE 7.19
Configuring saslauthd daemon in `/usr/lib/sasl2/smtpd.conf`.

```
fs1:/usr/lib/sasl2 # cat ./smtpd.conf
pwcheck_method: saslauthd
mech_list: plain login
fs1:/usr/lib/sasl2 #
```

There are two different parameters you can configure:

- `pwcheck_method`—Setting this parameter to **`saslauthd`** configures the saslauthd daemon to authenticate SMTP users.
- `mech_list`—This parameter specifies the authentication mechanisms that will be used to log in SMTP users. You can use the following mechanisms:
- `plain`—The plain authentication mechanism sends usernames and passwords as clear text. If you choose this mechanism, you should also configure your system to use TLS to encrypt data as it is sent between the client and the server.
- `login`—The login authentication mechanism is used to support older MUA client software that used an SMTP authentication scheme called LOGIN.
- `digest-md5`—This authentication mechanism uses Digest authentication to authenticate SMTP users. To use this parameter here, you must configure the `SASLAUTHD_AUTHMECH` parameter of `/etc/sysconfig/saslauthd` to use Digest authentication.
- `kerberos`—This authentication mechanism is used when you have implemented a Kerberos realm on your Linux server.

To configure your Postfix implementation to use Cyrus SASL to authenticate SMTP users, complete the following:

1. Verify that the appropriate cyrus-sasl packages have been installed on your server.
2. Edit your `/etc/sysconfig/saslauthd` file and configure the `SASLAUTHD_AUTHMECH` parameter.

TIP

The default value of `pam` will work best for most deployments.

3. Edit your `/usr/lib/sasl2/smtpd.conf` file and set the value of `pwcheck_method` to saslauthd.
4. Set the value of `mech_list` to the authentication method you configured in `/etc/sysconfig/saslauthd`.

TIP

I recommend starting with the default values of `plain` and `login`. These are the easiest to work with. Later in the chapter, we'll look at how to use TLS to encrypt the data.

5. Open `main.cf` in a text editor and make the following changes:
   a. Configure Postfix to use SASL SMTP authentication by setting the value of `smtpd_sasl_auth_enable` to **`yes`**.
   b. Disable anonymous SMTP authentication by setting the value of `smtpd_sasl_security_options` to **`noanonymous`**.
   c. Enable Postfix to relay email messages only for authenticated SMTP users by setting the value of `smtpd_recipient_restrictions` to **`permit_sasl_authenticated, permit_mynetworks, reject_unauth_destination`**.
6. Start the saslauthd daemon and configure it to automatically start at runlevels 3 and 5.
7. Restart the Postfix service.

At this point, your Postfix server is configured to authenticate SMTP users using the Cyrus SASL server. Spammers be gone!

The last thing you need to do to get a basic Postfix mail server running is configure POP3/IMAP support.

Configuring IMAP and POP3 Support

As we've mentioned several times in this chapter, Postfix has no IMAP or POP3 support built in. If you want to deliver mail to local mail accounts, this isn't a problem. Postfix can do that.

However, usually most organizations need a somewhat more robust solution. You probably don't want users having to ssh into your mail server to read their mail. Most likely, you will want users to use an email client on their local workstation to send and receive email.

The sending part isn't a problem. Postfix can use SMTP, as we've just discussed, to receive and send mail from MUAs. However, if we want users to be able to pull down their email from the Postfix MTA, then we have to implement a POP3 and/or IMAP server along with the Cyrus SASL Server and Postfix, as shown in Figure 7.20.

FIGURE 7.20
Adding POP3/IMAP support to Postfix.

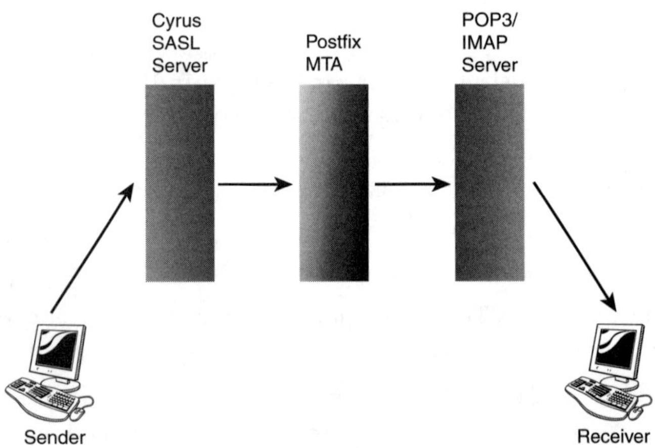

There are a variety of POP3/IMAP server packages available that will do this. Some of them rely on Postfix to deposit received email messages in the mail spool directory. When a MUA attaches via the POP3 or IMAP protocol, the POP3/IMAP server pulls their messages from the mail spool directory and sends them down to the mail client.

This type of POP3/IMAP server usually must be installed on the same server as the Postfix daemon. It works really well in smaller environments. The WU-IMAP package is an example of this type of server.

Some deployments, on the other hand, will require that the POP3/IMAP server be installed on a separate Linux server in the network. For this type of implementation, you will need to use a package such as the Cyrus IMAP Server. This server uses the Local Mail Transport Protocol (LMTP) to transfer mail messages from the Postfix MTA.

NOTE

The LMTP protocol is based on the SMTP protocol. Unlike SMTP, LMTP is designed for transferring mail messages only on the local network instead of over the Internet.

Because it uses LMTP, the Cyrus IMAP server doesn't require the messages to be stored in a local queue. The Cyrus IMAP server works best in large environments with lots of users and servers (where scalability is a key factor).

For this book, we're going to look at both types of POP3/IMAP servers. Let's start with the Cyrus IMAP server.

IMPLEMENTING THE CYRUS IMAP SERVER

The Cyrus IMAP server is implemented by installing the cyrus-imapd, perl-Cyrus-IMAP, and perl-Cyrus-SIEVE-managesieve packages, as shown in Figure 7.21.

FIGURE 7.21
Installing the Cyrus IMAP server.

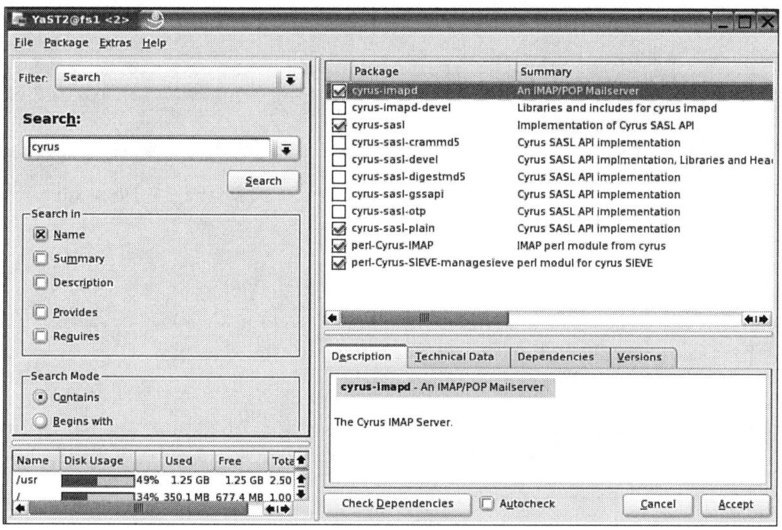

Configuring a basic Cyrus IMAP implementation is fairly straightforward. To do this, complete the following:

1. Open `/etc/cyrus.conf` in a text editor, as shown in Figure 7.22.

FIGURE 7.22
Editing the `/etc/cyrus.conf` file.

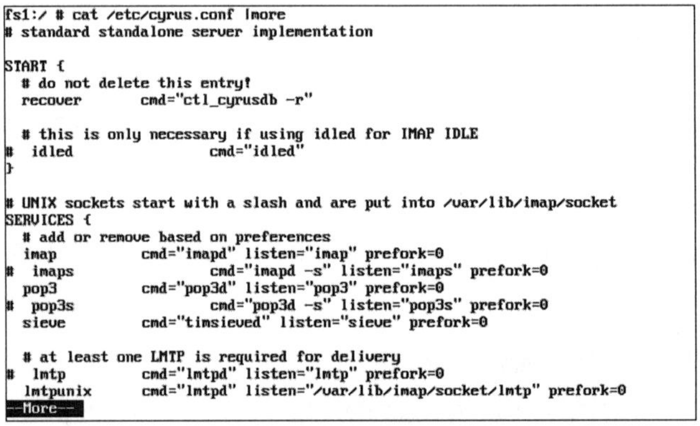

```
fs1:/ # cat /etc/cyrus.conf |more
# standard standalone server implementation

START {
  # do not delete this entry!
  recover       cmd="ctl_cyrusdb -r"

  # this is only necessary if using idled for IMAP IDLE
#  idled                 cmd="idled"
}

# UNIX sockets start with a slash and are put into /var/lib/imap/socket
SERVICES {
  # add or remove based on preferences
  imap          cmd="imapd" listen="imap" prefork=0
#  imaps                 cmd="imapd -s" listen="imaps" prefork=0
  pop3          cmd="pop3d" listen="pop3" prefork=0
#  pop3s                 cmd="pop3d -s" listen="pop3s" prefork=0
  sieve         cmd="timsieved" listen="sieve" prefork=0

  # at least one LMTP is required for delivery
#  lmtp         cmd="lmtpd" listen="lmtp" prefork=0
  lmtpunix      cmd="lmtpd" listen="/var/lib/imap/socket/lmtp" prefork=0
--More--
```

2. Uncomment the following lines by removing the # sign:
   - `imaps`
   - `pop3s`
3. Make sure a line exists that reads

   `lmtpunix          cmd="lmtpd" listen="/var/lib/imap/socket/lmtp" prefork=0`
4. Save the changes and close the file.
5. Restart the Cyrus IMAP server by entering **`rccyrus restart`** at the shell prompt.
6. Open `/etc/postfix/master.cf` in a text editor.

NOTE

The `master.cf` file is the configuration file for the Postfix master daemon.

7. Verify that an entry exists for the lmtp protocol using the syntax shown in Figure 7.23.

FIGURE 7.23
Editing the `/etc/postfix/master.cf` file.

```
cleanup   unix  n     -     n     -      0    cleanup
qmgr      fifo  n     -     n     300    1    qmgr
#qmgr     fifo  n     -     n     300    1    oqmgr
#tlsmgr   fifo  -     -     n     300    1    tlsmgr
rewrite   unix  -     -     n     -      -    trivial-rewrite
bounce    unix  -     -     n     -      0    bounce
defer     unix  -     -     n     -      0    bounce
trace     unix  -     -     n     -      0    bounce
verify    unix  -     -     n     -      1    verify
flush     unix  n     -     n     1000?  0    flush
proxymap  unix  -     -     n     -      -    proxymap
smtp      unix  -     -     n     -      -    smtp
relay     unix  -     -     n     -      -    smtp
#       -o smtp_helo_timeout=5 -o smtp_connect_timeout=5
showq     unix  n     -     n     -      -    showq
error     unix  -     -     n     -      -    error
local     unix  -     n     n     -      -    local
virtual   unix  -     n     n     -      -    virtual
lmtp      unix  -     -     n     -      -    lmtp
anvil     unix  -     -     n     -      1    anvil
#localhost:10025 inet  n     -     n     -      -      smtpd -o content
_filter=
#
--More--
```

8. Save any changes and close the file.
9. Open `/etc/postfix/main.cf` in a text editor.
10. Scroll down to the `mail_spool_directory` parameter and delete its value, as shown in Figure 7.24.

FIGURE 7.24
Editing the `/etc/postfix/main.cf` file.

```
html_directory=/usr/share/doc/packages/postfix/html
# manpage_directory: The location of the Postfix on-line manual pages.
manpage_directory=/usr/share/man
# sample_directory: The location of the Postfix sample configuration files.
# This parameter is obsolete as of Postfix 2.1.
sample_directory=/usr/share/doc/packages/postfix/samples
# readme_directory: The location of the Postfix README files.
readme_directory=/usr/share/doc/packages/postfix/README_FILES
mail_spool_directory=
canonical_maps=hash:/etc/postfix/canonical
virtual_maps=hash:/etc/postfix/virtual
relocated_maps=hash:/etc/postfix/relocated
transport_maps=hash:/etc/postfix/transport
sender_canonical_maps=hash:/etc/postfix/sender_canonical
masquerade_exceptions=root
masquerade_classes=envelope_sender, header_sender, header_recipient
myhostname=fs1.cle9.com
program_directory=/usr/lib/postfix
inet_interfaces=127.0.0.1 ::1
masquerade_domains=
mydestination=$myhostname, localhost.$mydomain
defer_transports=
disable_dns_lookups=no
-- INSERT --                                        570,1         97%
```

NOTE

This configures Postfix to *not* deliver messages to the local mail queue.

11. Scroll down to the `mailbox_transport` parameter.
12. Set the `mailbox_transport` parameter to the following value:

```
mailbox_transport=lmtp:unix:/var/lib/imap/socket/lmtp
```

NOTE

This parameter specifies that Postfix use LMTP to transfer mail messages to the Cyrus IMAP server socket `lmtp:unix:/var/lib/imap/socket/lmtp`, which you configured in the `cyrus.conf` file.

13. Add the `home_mailbox` parameter to the end of the file, but don't assign it a value.

NOTE

This also disables local mail delivery.

14. Save your changes and then close the file.
15. Restart Postfix by entering **`rcpostfix`** at the shell prompt.

You can also configure Postfix to use the Cyrus IMAP server using YaST. To do this, complete the following:

1. Start YaST.
2. When prompted, supply your root user *password*.
3. Select **Network Services, Mail Server**.
4. Enter the *password* for your LDAP administrative user.
5. Wait while the YaST Mail Server module is started.
6. In the left frame, select **Local Delivery**. The screen in Figure 7.25 is displayed.
7. Under Local Delivery Type, mark **Cyrus IMAP**.
8. (Optional but recommended) Under Security, mark **Enabled**.
9. Select **OK**.

That's all there is to it! By configuring SMTP authentication and integrating Postfix with the Cyrus IMAP server, your simple Postfix MTA can become a very powerful (yet inexpensive) email server solution.

However, the configuration I've presented here is a relatively simple Cyrus IMAP Server deployment. Notice that we configured both Postfix and Cyrus IMAP on the same server. Going beyond this basic configuration can become very complex.

FIGURE 7.25
Configuring Cyrus IMAP support.

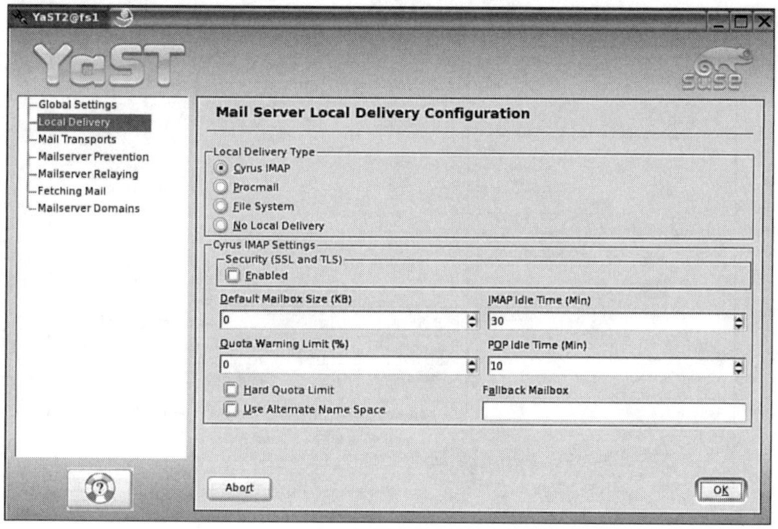

NOTE

If you want to learn more about deploying Cyrus IMAP, visit http://asg.web.cmu.edu/cyrus/imapd/.

If you want to implement a simpler POP3/IMAP deployment, consider using the WU-IMAP server. We'll talk about this service next.

IMPLEMENTING THE WU-IMAP SERVER

On your SLES 9 CDs is a POP3/IMAP service based on the WU-IMAP server. To use this service, you need to configure Postfix to deliver mail messages to the system mail queue in `/var/spool/mail`. The IMAP and/or POP3 daemons provided in the package will pull the messages from the queue and send them down to IMAP and/or POP3 email clients.

You install this server by installing the imap package, as shown in Figure 7.26.

If you've already got the Cyrus IMAP server installed (which is the default with SLES 9), you must first uninstall that package before installing imap.

FIGURE 7.26
Configuring the WU IMAP server.

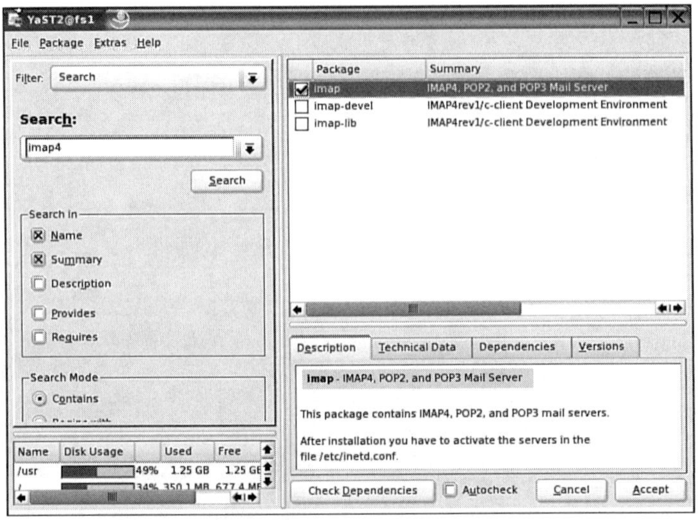

After the package is installed, you need to configure the service and then configure Postfix to support it. Complete the following steps:

1. Create security certificates for the WU-IMAP server to use:
   a. Open a terminal session and **su –** to root.
   b. At the shell prompt, enter **cd /etc/ssl/certs**.
   c. Enter **openssl req -new -x509 -nodes -out imapd.pem -keyout imapd.pem**.
   d. When prompted, provide the locality information needed for the certificate.
   e. When prompted for the Common Name, enter the DNS name or IP address of the Linux server.
   f. When prompted for an email address, enter the email address of your mail administrator.
   g. Enter **openssl req -new -x509 -nodes -out ipop3d.pem -keyout ipop3d.pem**.
   h. When prompted, provide the locality information needed for the certificate.
   i. When prompted for the Common Name, enter the DNS name or IP address of the Linux server.
   j. When prompted for an email address, enter the email address of your mail administrator.

2. Configure the POP3 and IMAP daemons by completing the following:
   a. Start YaST.
   b. When prompted, provide your root password.
   c. Select **Network Services**, **Network Services (inetd)**.
   d. From the list presented, select **pop3**; then select **Toggle Status**, as shown in Figure 7.27.

FIGURE 7.27
Enabling the POP3 service.

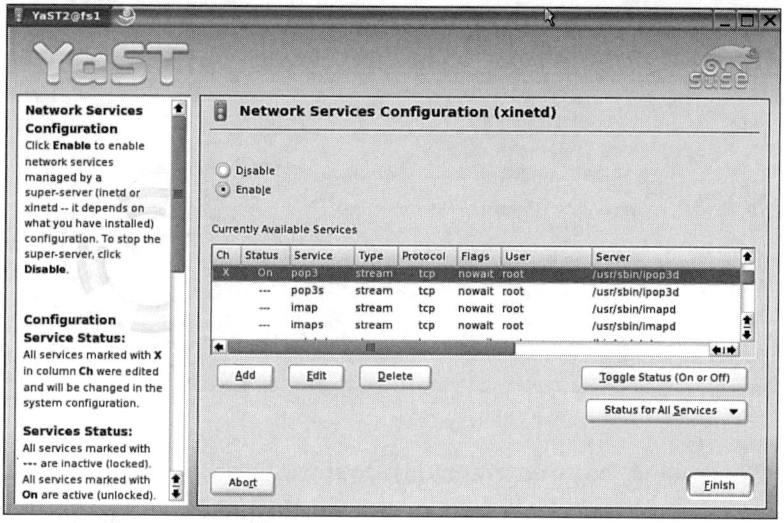

   e. Select **pop3s**; then select **Toggle Status**.
   f. Select **imap**; then select **Toggle Status**.
   g. Select **imaps**; then select **Toggle Status**.
   h. Select **Finish**.
   i. Open a terminal session.
   j. At the shell prompt, **su –** to root.
   k. At the shell prompt, enter **`rcxinetd restart`**.
3. Configure Postfix to integrate with the POP3 and IMAP services by completing the following:

a. In YaST, select **Network Services**, **Mail Server**.

b. When prompted, enter the password for your LDAP administrative user.

c. Select **Local Delivery**. The screen shown in Figure 7.28 is displayed.

FIGURE 7.28
Configuring Postfix for local delivery.

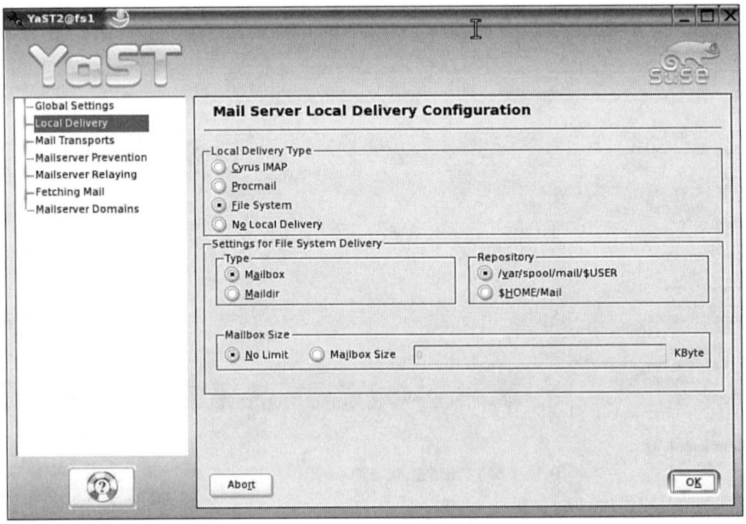

d. Under Local Delivery Type, ensure **File System** is marked.

e. Under Settings for File System Delivery, ensure **Mailbox** and **/var/spool/mail/$USER** are marked.

f. Select **OK**.

That's about all there is to it! Let's practice by setting up full email deployment on SLES 9 in Lab Exercise 7.1.

Lab Exercise 7.1: Configuring a Postfix Email Server

In this lab exercise, you will configure the Postfix service on your server as an MTA for the cle9.com domain. You will also configure authentication for SMTP users using Cyrus SASL. Then you will integrate your Postfix system with the WU-IMAP server.

To complete this exercise, you will need your SLES 9 server with all the services we've configured running. Complete the following:

1. Boot your SLES 9 server and authenticate as **tux** with a password of **SuSE789**.
2. Start YaST.
3. When prompted to provide your root password, enter **tuX123**.
4. Install the packages needed in this exercise by completing the following:
    a. Select **Software**, **Install and Remove Software**.
    b. In the Search field, enter **cyrus**; then select **Search**.
    c. Mark the **cyrus-sasl-plain** package.
    d. In the search field, enter **imap4**.
    e. Mark the **imap** package; then select **Accept**.
    f. When prompted that the imap package conflicts with cyrus-imapd, mark **Remove the Conflicting Package**.
    g. Select **OK—Try Again**.
    h. Insert SLES 9 CDs as prompted.
    i. Wait while the packages are installed.
5. Configure your DNS server with a mail server A record and an MX record for the cle9.com domain by completing the following:

NOTE

Because DDNS is running from a previous exercise, we'll have to turn it off before we can add the MX record.

a. In YaST, select **Network Services**, **DNS Server**.
b. Select **DNS Zones**.
c. Select your **cle9.com** zone; then select **Edit Zone**.
d. Deselect **Allow Dynamic Updates**.
e. Select **OK, Finish**.
f. In YaST, select **DNS Server** again.
g. In the DNS Server—Start-Up screen, mark **LDAP Support Active**.
h. Select **DNS Zones**.
i. Select your **cle9.com** zone; then select **Edit Zone**.
j. Select the **MX Records** tab.
k. In the Address field, enter **fs1.cle9.com**. This configures fs1 as the mail server for the cle9.com zone.
l. Select **Add, OK, Finish**.
m. When prompted for the LDAP server password, enter **`tuX123`**; then select **OK**.
n. (Optional) Select **DNS Server** and reenable DDNS.
o. Open a terminal session and rest the configuration by entering **`dig fs1.cle9.com`** at the shell prompt.
p. Verify that fs1.cle9.com resolves to your server's IP address.

6. Configure the Postfix configuration file by completing the following:
   a. At the shell prompt, **su –** to root.
   b. **`Enter vi /etc/postfix/main.cf`**.
   c. Scroll down to the myhostname parameter near the end of the file.
   d. Verify that this parameter to **fs1.cle9.com**.
   e. Insert a new line after the `myhostname` parameter.
   f. Add the following lines:
   ```
   mydomain=cle9.com
   myorigin=cle9.com
   ```
   g. Save your changes and close the file.
   h. At the shell prompt, enter **`rcpostfix restart`**.
   i. In YaST, select **Network Services**, **Mail Server**.

j. When prompted, for your LDAP administrative user password, enter **tuX123**.

k. In the left frame, select **Local Delivery**.

l. Under Local Delivery Type, mark **File System**.

m. Under Settings for File System Delivery, mark **Mailbox** and **/var/spool/mail/$USER**.

n. In the left frame, select **Mailserver Relaying**.

o. Mark **Require SASL Authentication**.

p. Mark **Use TLS Only for SASL Authentication**.

q. Select **OK**.

7. Configure saslauthd to automatically start on boot by completing the following:

   a. In YaST, select **System, Runlevel Editor**.

   b. Mark **Expert Mode**.

   c. Scroll down to and select **saslauthd**.

   d. Mark **runlevels** 3 and 5.

   e. Select **Start/Stop/Refresh**, **Start Now**.

   f. When prompted that the service has started successfully, select **OK**.

   g. Select **Finish**.

   h. When prompted that the changes will be saved, select **Yes**.

8. Create security certificates for the WU-IMAP server to use:

   a. At the shell prompt, enter **cd /etc/ssl/certs**.

   b. Enter **openssl req -new -x509 -nodes -out imapd.pem -keyout imapd.pem**.

   c. When prompted, provide the locality information needed for the certificate.

   d. When prompted for the Common Name, enter **fs1.cle9.com**.

   e. When prompted for an email address, enter **root@cle9.com**.

   f. Enter **openssl req -new -x509 -nodes -out ipop3d.pem -keyout ipop3d.pem**.

   g. When prompted, provide the locality information needed for the certificate.

   h. When prompted for the Common Name, enter **`fs1.cle9.com`**.
   i. When prompted for an email address, enter **`root@cle9.com`**.

9. Configure Postfix to work with the WU-IMAP server by completing the following:
   a. From the shell prompt, enter **`vi /etc/postfix/main.cf`**.
   b. Scroll down to the **`local_recipient_maps`** parameter near the end of the file.
   c. Comment out this parameter by placing a **#** in front of it.
   d. Save the changes and close the file.
   e. Restart Postfix by entering **`rcpostfix restart`**.
   f. In YaST, select **Network Service**, **Network Services (inetd)**.
   g. From the list presented, select **pop3**; then select **Toggle Status**.
   h. Select **pop3s**; then select **Toggle Status**.
   i. Select **imap**; then select **Toggle Status**.
   j. Select **imaps**; then select **Toggle Status**.
   k. Select **Finish**.
   l. At the shell prompt, enter **`rcxinetd restart`**.

10. Configure an MUA for the tux user by completing the following:
    a. From the tux user account (which you should be currently using), select **N, Internet, Email, KMail**.
    b. In the Tip of the Day screen, select **Close**.
    c. In the KMail window, select **Settings, Configure KMail**.
    d. Select **Identities**; then select **Modify**.
    e. In the Email Address field, enter **`tux@cle9.com`**; then select **OK**.
    f. Select **Network**.
    g. In the Sending tab, select **Add**.
    h. In the Transport screen, mark **SMTP**; then select **OK**.
    i. In the Name field enter **`CLE 9 Mail`**.
    j. In the Host field, enter **`fs1.cle9.com`**.
    k. Mark **Server Requires Authentication**.
    l. In the Login field, enter **`tux`**.

m. In the Password field, enter **SuSE789**.

n. Mark **Store SMTP Password in Configuration File**.

o. Select the **Security** tab; then select **Check What the Server Supports**.

p. When prompted that the server certificate test failed, select **Continue**; then select **Forever**. The client should have detected that your Postfix SMTP server uses PLAIN authentication using TLS.

TIP

This error is displayed because the certificate is self-signed. For what we're doing here, it's not important.

q. Select **OK**.

r. Mark **Send Messages in Outbox Folder on Check**.

s. Select the **Receiving** tab; then select **Add**.

t. In the Account Type field, mark **POP3**; then select **OK**.

u. Enter the following information:

- Name: **`CLE 9 Mail`**
- Login: **`tux`**
- Password: **`SuSE789`**
- Host: **`fs1.cle9.com`**

v. Mark **Store POP Password in Configuration File**.

w. Select the **Extras** tab.

x. Select **Check What the Server Supports**. The client should have detected that your server uses Clear Text authentication with TLS encryption.

y. Select **OK, OK**.

11. Send an email message to jcorry by completing the following:

a. Select **Message, New Message**.

b. In the To field, enter **`jcorry`**.

c. Add *text* to the Subject and the message body fields.

d. Select the **Send** icon. You should see a message in the status bar indicating that the message was sent successfully, as shown in Figure 7.29.

FIGURE 7.29
Message successfully sent via SMTP.

e. Close KMail.

f. Log out of the tux user account by selecting **N, Logout, Logout**.

12. Configure an MUA for the jcorry user by completing the following:

a. Log in as **`jcorry`** with a password of **`Annel`**.

b. Select **N**, **Internet,** Email, **KMail**.

c. In the Tip of the Day screen, select **Close**.

d. In the KMail window, select **Settings, Configure KMail**.

e. Select **Identities**; then select **Modify**.

f. In the Email Address field, enter **jcorry@`cle9.com`**; then select **OK**.

g. Select **Network**.

h. In the Send tab, select **Add**.

i. In the Transport screen, mark **SMTP**; then select **OK**.

j. In the Name field enter **`CLE 9 Mail`**.

k. In the Host field, enter **`fs1.cle9.com`**.

l. Mark **Server Requires Authentication**.

m. In the Login field, enter **`jcorry`**.

n. In the Password field, enter **`Annel`**.

o. Mark **Store SMTP Password in Configuration File**.

p. Select the **Security** tab; then select **Check What the Server Supports**.

q. When prompted that the server certificate test failed, select **Continue**; then select **Forever**. The client should have detected that your Postfix SMTP server uses PLAIN authentication with TLS encryption.

r. Select **OK**.

s. Mark **Send Messages in Outbox Folder on Check**.

t. Select the **Receiving** tab; then select **Add**.

u. In the Account Type field, mark **POP3**; then select **OK**.

v. Enter the following information:

- Name: **`CLE 9 Mail`**
- Login: **`jcorry`**
- Password: **`Annel`**
- Host: **`fs1.cle9.com`**

w. Mark **Store POP3 Password in Configuration File**.

x. Select the **Extras** tab.

y. Select **Check What the Server Supports**. The client should have detected that your POP3 server uses clear text authentication with TLS encryption.

z. Select **OK, OK**.

13. Click the **Check Mail** icon to download mail from the Cyrus IMAP server.

14. You should see the message sent from the tux user account.

TIP

If you experience problems, view the `/var/log/mail` log file. It contains invaluable troubleshooting information.

Congratulations! Your SLES 9 server has been configured as a powerful email server using Postfix, Cyrus SASL, and WU-IMAP.

Before we end this chapter, we need to address two more topics for your CLE 9 certification: preventing spam and viruses!

Securing Postfix Against Viruses and Spam

TEST OBJECTIVE COVERED:

1. Use SLES 9 as a mail server.

Unfortunately, as the popularity of email has risen over the years, many less-than-scrupulous individuals have figured out ways to manipulate the service to their own ends. Two of the biggest issues facing email administrators today are spam and viruses. Let's talk about these issues next.

Preventing Spam

If you have an email account, you probably already know what spam is. Some genius a few years ago figured out that email is a really fast, easy, and inexpensive way to try to sell stuff to people. Whether you are sending an email message to one person or ten thousand, the cost to the sender is the same (practically nothing).

Since then, spam has degenerated into the marketing medium of choice for disreputable vendors. As I receive spam mail, I often wonder to myself, "Who would be stupid enough to actually buy this stuff?" Then I watch the evening news and see stories about lots of people who did just that.

The problem is that people tend to be very trusting of email; especially those who are new to computers. So, when they receive an email message indicating they can have a share of a million dollars from an African government official if they just reply with their bank account number, they do it.

In addition to the human impact of spam, there's also a technological impact. Because spam is sent out by the thousands, it can really bog down the performance of your MTA. One email administrator I know indicated that around 80% of the mail that arrives at his server is spam. Imagine having to spend money to add capacity to a server just so it can handle a bunch of email messages nobody wants.

Can you fight back against spam? Kind of. Spammers are good at what they do. In the beginning, spammers spewed their email from their own systems. It didn't take long for system administrators to identify the systems where spam was originating and filter it out.

To get around the filters, spammers began using relay servers. Earlier in this chapter, we talked about how a relay server is one where the MTA accepts SMTP email requests from anyone who submits it. Spammers soon learned to bounce around from one relay server to another. This made it very difficult for email administrators to filter the spam out based on the origin of the messages. It started coming from many different systems, seemingly at random.

That's the situation we face today. Fortunately we have some tools to combat it. We're going to look at how to use these tools with Postfix in just a minute.

Before we do, be aware that these tools frequently end up filtering out legitimate email messages along with the spam. The stronger you choose to make your antispam measures, the more good messages you will end up rejecting. This will make your users even angrier than having a lot of spam. The point is, you have to use your own judgment in determining how tightly you're going to screen for spam, based on the values of your organization.

With that said, let's look at what we can do to fight spam. One of the best weapons in our arsenal are Realtime Blacklists (RBLs). Whenever someone identifies a spamming system, whether it's a spammer's own system or a relay server, it's cataloged into an RBL server's database.

NOTE

RBLs are also referred to as *DNS Black Lists (DNSBLs)*.

You can then configure Postscript to check incoming messages against the RBL database. Base on the results, spam messages can be identified and rejected.

There are free RBL servers on the Internet that you can use as well as some that require a subscription. Be aware that the free RBL servers may respond slowly during high-utilization periods. One of my favorite is spamcop.net. It's free and relatively fast.

There are two parameters in `main.cf` that you use to implement RBLs:

- `maps_rbl_domains`
- `smtpd_recipient_restrictions`

To implement an RBL with Postfix, you would set the value of `maps_rbl_domains` to the IP address or DNS name of the RBL server. For example, if you wanted to use spamcop.net's free service, you would set this parameter to `bl.spamcop.net`.

Then you need to configure a series of restrictions using the `smtpd_recipient_restrictions` parameter. You should consider including the following values (separated by a comma):

- `reject_maps_rbl`
- `reject_invalid_hostname`
- `reject_non_fqdn_recipient`
- `reject_non_fqdn_sender`
- `reject_unknown_recipient_domain`

- `reject_unknown_sender_domain`
- `reject_unauth_pipelining`

YaST provides a very nice interface for doing this, as well. To use YaST to configure antispam measures, complete the following:

1. Start YaST.
2. Select **Network Services**, **Mail Server**.
3. In the left frame, select **Mail Server Prevention**. The screen in Figure 7.30 is displayed.

FIGURE 7.30
Configuring antispam measures with YaST.

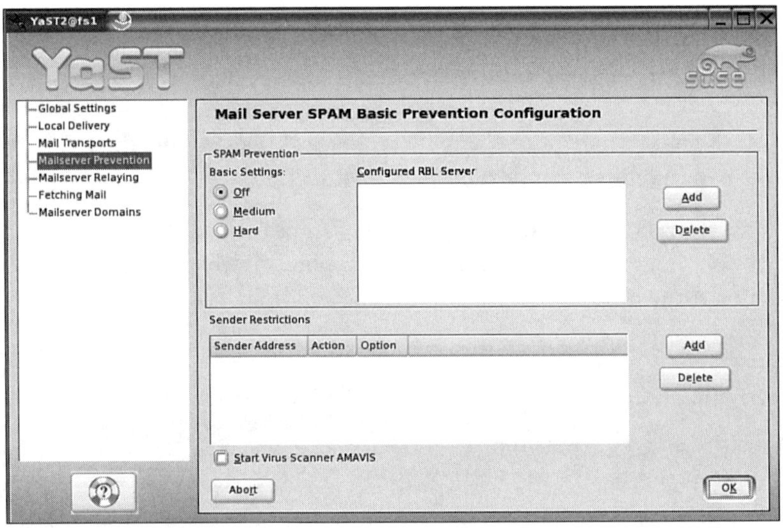

4. Under Basic Settings, select **Medium** or **Hard**; depending on how stringent you want to be.
5. To configure an RBL server, complete the following:
   a. Next to Configured RBL Server, select **Add**.
   b. In the New RBL Server field, enter the IP address or DNS name of the RBL server you want to use.
   c. Select **OK**.

6. To configure your own restrictions, complete the following:
   a. Select **Add** next to Sender Restrictions. The screen in Figure 7.31 is displayed.

FIGURE 7.31
Adding a sender restriction.

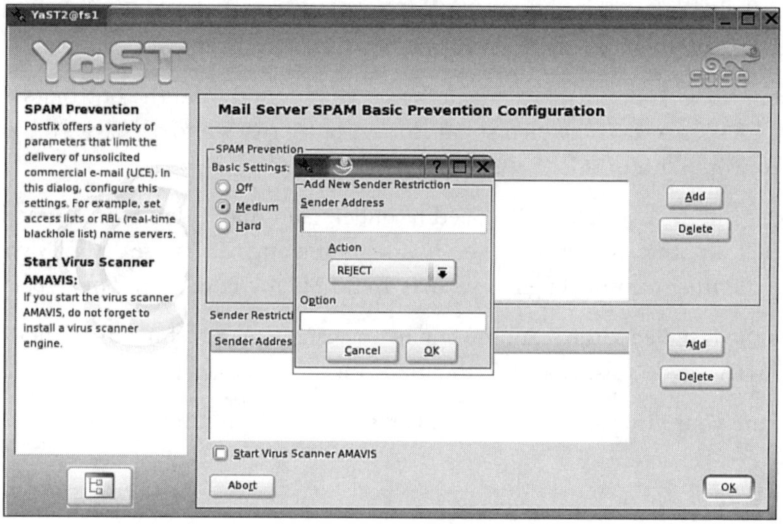

   b. In the Sender Address field, enter the *IP address* or *DNS name* of the sending system you want to set up a restriction for.
   c. In the Action drop-down list, select the *action* you want to take, such as REJECT or DISCARD.
   d. Select **OK**.
7. Select **OK**.

Spam is a bad thing for our mail servers. However, there's something, I think, that is worse: email viruses. Let's next discuss how to configure Postfix to scan attachments for viruses.

Combating Email Viruses

Viruses are the network administrator's worst nightmare. In 2003 and 2004, email-born worms and viruses caused some of the most severe disruptions we've seen in many years. How was it done? Through email attachments.

Although the Linux operating system itself is relatively immune to viruses, Windows clients that attach to it via SMTP, POP3, and IMAP are not, especially the Microsoft Outlook client. The disruptions in 2003 and 2004 were perpetrated by attachments that would read victims' address books and send a copy of themselves to everyone in it. This behavior nearly brought many organizations' networks to their knees.

As a means to halting the spread of viruses, you can integrate a virus scanning mechanism with Postfix to clean up email messages *before* they reach the client workstations.

There are many ways to do this, but one of the best I've found (and the one that's easily configured on SLES 9) is AMaViS (which stands for A Mail Virus Scanner). That's the package we're going to work with in this chapter.

Before we get going with AMaViS, you need to understand that AMaViS doesn't actually scan for viruses itself. In other words, it isn't a virus-scanning engine. To use AMaViS you must also install an actual virus scanning engine, such as Trend Micro's FileScanner or CyberSoft's Vfind.

AMaViS uses the installed virus scanning engine to scan email attachments as they arrive at your Postfix MTA. To do this, complete the following:

1. Make sure your virus scanning engine is installed and running.
2. Start YaST.
3. Select **Network Services**, **Mail Server**.
4. Provide your LDAP administrative user password.
5. Select Mailserver Prevention. The screen in Figure 7.32 is displayed.
6. Mark **Start Virus Scanner AMAVIS**.
7. Select **OK**.
8. Test your configuration by completing the following:
    a. Create a new file named **`eicar.com`**.

TIP

This file is a standardized virus-test file. It doesn't actually do anything. Your virus scanning engine should recognize this file as a test file. For more information, visit http://www.eicar.org/anti_virus_test_file.htm.

    b. In this file enter the following text:

```
X5O!P%@AP[4\PZX54(P^)7CC)7}$EICAR-STANDARD-ANTIVIRUS
➥-TEST-FILE!$H+H*
```

    c. Make the file executable.

d. Compose a new message to a *user* on your MTA where AMaViS is running.

e. Attach the `eicar.com` file you just created as an attachment.

f. Send the file.

FIGURE 7.32
Enabling AMaViS.

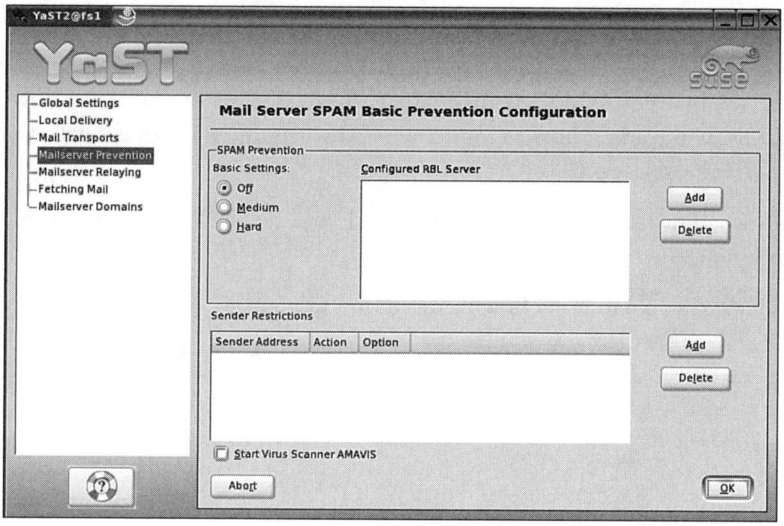

That's it for this chapter. Before we go to Chapter 8, "Using SLES 9 to Manage Network Traffic," let's review what you've learned.

Summary

In this chapter, you learned how to configure Postfix as a full-functioning email server. To do this, you first learned how email works from a generic standpoint. You learned about the roles of:

- MUAs
- MTAs
- MDAs

You then learned how email messages are processed through the Postfix MTA.

After that, you learned about the process you must go through to configure Postfix as an email server. First, you learned that you must create an MX record in your DNS zone for your mail server.

Then you must configure the Postfix configuration file: `main.cf`. You then learned that, by default, Postfix doesn't require SMTP users to authenticate before relaying their email messages. To fix this, you learned how to implement the Cyrus SASL server to keep unauthorized users from using your Postfix MTA.

Then you learned that Postfix doesn't include any means for remote MUAs to download messages. To fix this, you learned how to implement IMAP and POP3 support with the Cyrus IMAP server and the WU-IMAP server.

Finally, you learned how to protect your server and your network by implementing spam and virus prevention measures with Postfix.

In the next chapter, you will learn how to monitor and manage traffic on your network using Linux utilities. Stay tuned!

CHAPTER 8

Using SLES 9 to Manage Network Traffic

This chapter covers the following requirements for Novell's Certified Linux Engineer (CLE) 9 certification:

1. Use ntop and Nagios to monitor network traffic.
2. Use ethereal and tcpdump to troubleshoot network problems.
3. Use SNMP to monitor network devices.

As a network administrator, you wear many hats in your organization. Management expects you to be able to install and configure the latest hardware they just purchased. Users expect you to be able to figure out why they can't find their oh-so-important spreadsheet file.

In addition to these roles, you also are responsible for managing the traffic on your network. In this chapter, you will learn how to use SLES 9 to keep tabs on what's happening on the wire.

Let's begin by discussing ntop.

Using ntop to Manage Network Traffic

TEST OBJECTIVE COVERED:

1. Use ntop and Nagios to monitor network traffic.

Let's face it—deploying a network system is hard work. It takes hundreds of hours of planning, getting quotes from vendors, pulling wire, installing hardware, configuring server and workstation operating systems, testing, and troubleshooting the inevitable problems encountered. After this Herculean effort, we, as network administrators like to think the hard part is over. We envision ourselves with our feet propped up on our desk watching our network hum like a well-oiled machine.

Unfortunately, you and I know that isn't the case. Network deployment is only the beginning. During the planning phase of the deployment, you (hopefully) modeled your new network in a lab environment to work out as many of the kinks as possible before actually installing hardware and operating systems.

Try as you might, however, nothing you do during the planning phase can truly predict how your network will respond when you turn your users loose on it. The needs of your users can quickly tax the limits of your network deployment.

To be an effective administrator, you should regularly monitor traffic on your network. Doing so will allow you to identify systems or processes that are bandwidth hogs before they bring your system to a screeching halt.

One of the best utilities available for monitoring your network is `ntop`. From your CLP certification, you should already be familiar with the `top` utility on Linux, which is used to view, sort, and manage processes running on your local system. The ntop utility is similar to top, except that it is used to monitor systems on the network. Just as you can use top to identify a CPU hog on your Linux system, you can use ntop to monitor your network traffic and identify top bandwidth utilizers (among other things).

Let's talk about how ntop works and what we can do with it.

How ntop Works

The ntop utility is a web-based service that can be used to gain a bird's eye view of your network's performance. The ntop web interface is shown in Figure 8.1.

The ntop utility is unique in that it looks at your network holistically. Instead of testing communications from a point-to-point perspective (such as ping does), ntop monitors the entire network all at once.

One of the things that I love about ntop is that you can start by looking at a birds-eye view of the network. From this perspective, you can easily identify things that just don't look "right." From there, you can drill down to identify specific problems in the network.

Using ntop can make your life as a network administrator easier, and it can save your organization a lot of money. Instead of throwing more bandwidth at a network bottleneck (which is our usual response), ntop allow us to identify what is causing the bottleneck in the first place.

Fixing a system that's producing excessive network traffic is a lot easier than upgrading the entire network to the latest and greatest hardware.

FIGURE 8.1
The ntop web interface.

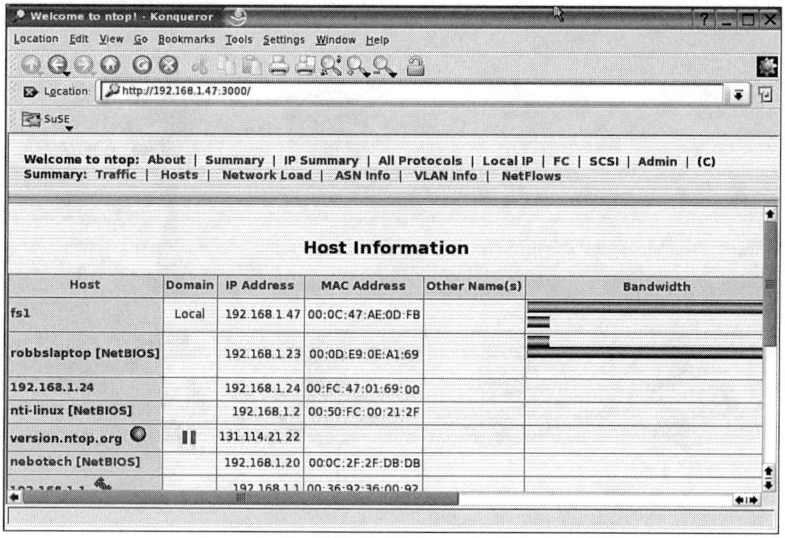

To provide this functionality, ntop is composed of the following five components, as shown in Figure 8.2:

- ntop host—The ntop host is the Linux system where ntop is running.
- ntop sniffer—The ntop sniffer component runs on the ntop host and captures all packets on the network wire. On an ethernet network, as you know, datagrams being transmitted are delivered to each host. Only the host to whom the datagrams are addressed accepts them. All other hosts discard the datagrams. The ntop sniffer breaks this rule. It accepts *all* datagrams transmitted on the network—even those not addressed to the local interface.

NOTE

The ntop utility is also compatible with Token Ring networks as well as Point-to-Point Protocol (PPP) connections. We're going to focus on ethernet networks in this chapter because that's what just about everyone uses these days.

FIGURE 8.2
ntop components.

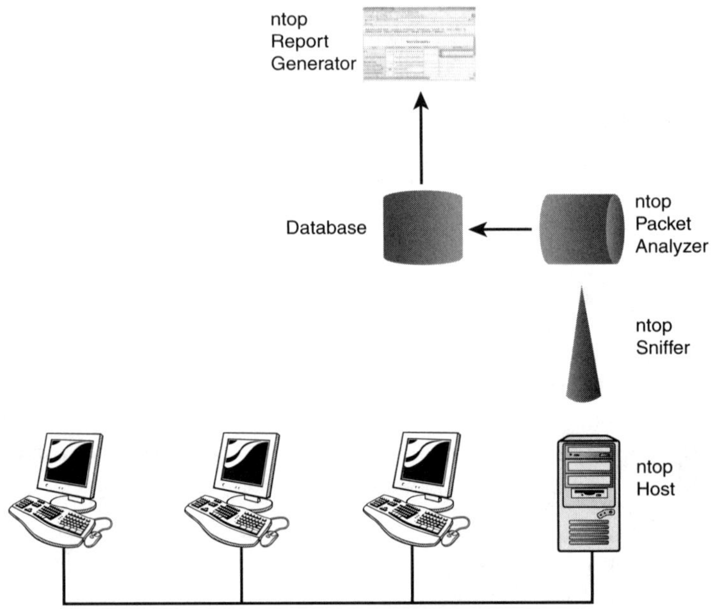

- ntop packet analyzer—The ntop packet analyzer is a key component in the ntop system. You need to understand that the data captured by the sniffer is totally and completely raw. You would fall asleep very quickly if you were to try to pour through it manually. Worse than that, the amount of data would be so enormous that you wouldn't be able to see the trends and issues occurring in the network. The job of the packet analyzer is to do just that—decode the data captured by the sniffer and organize it in a way that is meaningful to us humans.
- ntop database—After the packet analyzer has finished decoding the sniffed data from the network, it stores it in the ntop database. By default, ntop uses a simple memory buffer (called the cache) to store decoded captures. This buffer is fixed in size and gets cleaned out from time to time whenever it gets too full. On a very large network, this internal cache could be too small. To accommodate this situation, you can configure ntop to use a SQL database, such as MySQL, in addition to its memory buffer to store analyzed network data. Instead of flushing old data from its buffer, ntop will then move it into the database using an ODBC driver. By default, the ntop database files reside in `/var/lib/ntop`.

- ntop report generator—The ntop report generator is used to format the analyzed data in the ntop database and present it to the administrator in the web-based ntop interface. The ntop daemon provides its own HTTP server to provide this interface. It's not dependent on Apache or any other web server being present on the ntop host.

With this background in mind, let's now look at how you install and configure ntop on your SLES 9 system.

Installing and Configuring ntop on SLES 9

Like the other services we've covered in this course, you need to make sure the ntop package is installed on your server. To do this, complete the following steps:

1. From your SLES 9 desktop, select **YaST**.
2. When prompted, provide your root password.
3. In the left frame, select **Software**.
4. In the right frame, select **Install and Remove Software**.
5. In the Search field, enter **ntop**; then select **Search**.
6. Mark the ntop package as shown in Figure 8.3.

FIGURE 8.3
Installing the ntop package.

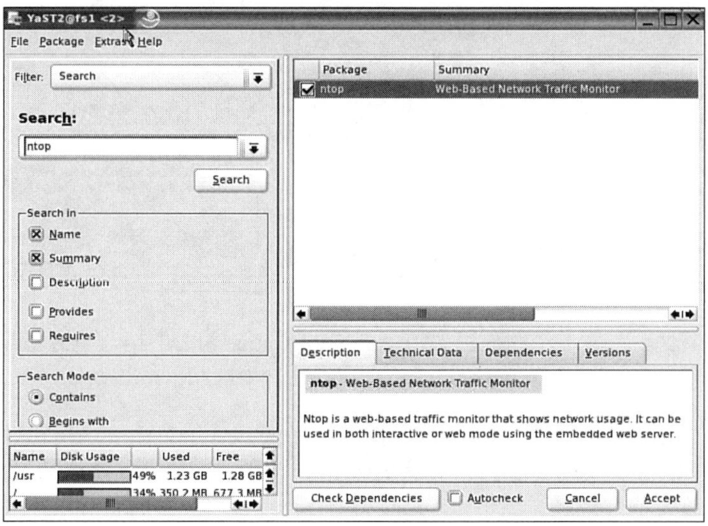

7. Select **Accept**.
8. When prompted, insert the appropriate CDs.
9. Wait while the packages are installed and SuSEconfig is run.
10. Close YaST by selecting **Close**.

As with the other products we've covered so far in this book, your SLES 9 system should already have the ntop package installed if you followed the steps in the lab exercises in Chapter 2.

To verify that it's there, open YaST and select **Software, Install and Remove Software**. In the Search field, enter **ntop**; then select **Search**. You should see the ntop package marked with a blue check mark; as shown in Figure 8.4.

FIGURE 8.4
The ntop package is already installed.

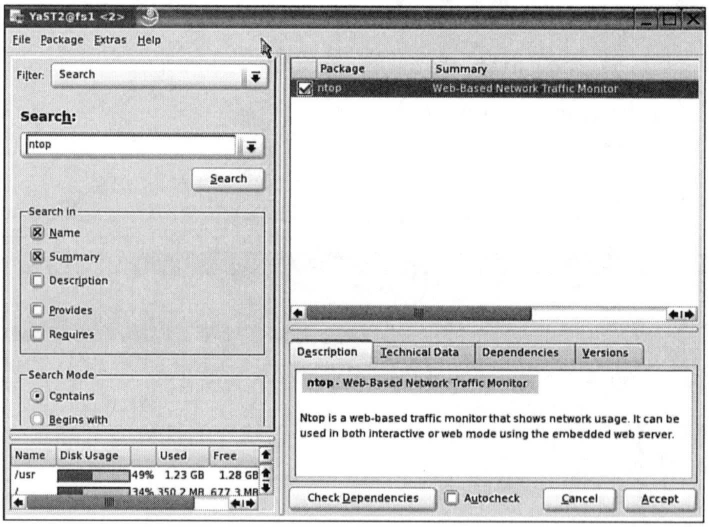

If, for some reason, the ntop package isn't installed on your SLES 9 system, follow the steps presented earlier to install it. After installation, the `/usr/bin/ntop` daemon is used to provide the ntop service, as shown in Figure 8.5.

The ntop service is started and stopped using the **ntop** init script in `/etc/init.d`, as shown in Figure 8.6.

FIGURE 8.5
The ntop daemon.

```
fs1:/usr/bin # ls ntop*
ntop
fs1:/usr/bin #
```

FIGURE 8.6
The ntop startup script.

```
fs1:/etc/init.d # ls nt*
ntop
fs1:/etc/init.d #
```

After installing the ntop package, the ntop daemon is configured using the `/etc/sysconfig/ntop` file shown in Figure 8.7.

FIGURE 8.7
The ntop configuration file.

```
## Path:           Network/Monitors/Ntop
## Description:    ntop startup parameters
## Type:           string(eth0)
## Default:        eth0
## Config:
## ServiceRestart: ntop
#
# Specifies the network interface used by ntop
#
NTOPD_IFACE="eth0"

## Type:        ip
## Default:     127.0.0.1:3000
#
# Supposing to start  ntop  at  the port  3000,
# the  URL  to  access  is http://hostname:3000/
#
# Please note that an HTTP server is NOT needed  in
# order to use the program in interactive mode.
#
NTOPD_PORT="127.0.0.1:3000"

## Type:        integer(0:65535)
./ntop lines 1-23/53 42%
```

In this file, you can configure the following ntop parameters:

- `NTOPD_IFACE`—This parameter is used to configure the network interface that ntop will use to capture packets. By default, this parameter is set to `eth0`.
- `NTOPD_PORT`—This parameter is used to configure the IP port that ntop will use to provide its web-based interface. By default, this is set to `3000` on the local loopback address.
- `NTOPD_SSL_PORT`—This parameter is used to configure the secure IP port that ntop will use to provide its web-based interface. The recommended port is `3001`; however, this option is disabled by default. To use a secure port, you must create an SSL certificate for the daemon to use. We'll talk about how to do this in just a minute.
- `NTOP_USER`—This parameter is used to configure the user account that ntop will run as. By default, ntop will run as `wwwrun`.

With your `/etc/sysconfig/ntop file` configured, you're almost ready to load the service on your server. However, be aware that before you can load the ntop daemon, you must first run the service from a shell prompt to configure the user account that ntop will use. (You need to complete this procedure only once.) To do this, complete the following steps:

1. Open a terminal session.
2. From the shell prompt, change to your root user.
3. At the shell prompt, enter **`ntop -A -u wwwrun`**. The screen in Figure 8.8 is displayed:

FIGURE 8.8
Configuring ntop.

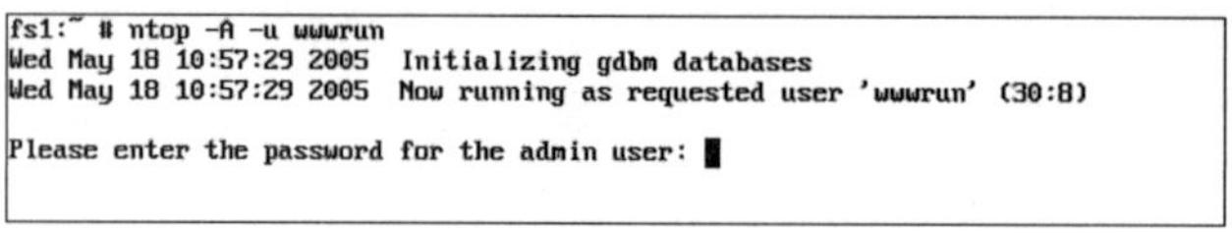

NOTE

The -A switch is used to set the admin user password. The -u switch sets the user account ntop will run as.

4. When prompted, enter your ntop administrative user's *password*.

In addition, if you enabled ntop to use a secure port, you must also generate a certificate for ntop to use. To do this, complete the following:

1. Open a terminal session.
2. At the shell prompt, switch to root.
3. At the shell prompt, **enter `openssl req -new -x509 -sha1 -extensions v3_ca -nodes -days 365 -out cert.pem`**. The screen shown in Figure 8.9 is displayed.

FIGURE 8.9
Creating a certificate for ntop.

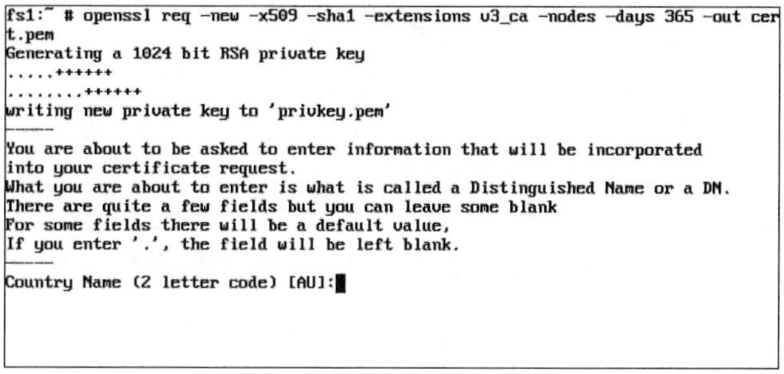

NOTE

We'll cover OpenSSL in Chapters 9, "Securing the SLES 9 Server," and 10, "Implementing Packet Filter Firewalls with SLES 9."

4. When prompted, provide the *locality* and *organizational information* requested.
5. When prompted for the Common Name, enter the *DNS name* of your server.
6. When prompted, provide your administrative user's *email address*.
7. At the shell prompt, enter **`cat privkey.pem cert.pem > /etc/ntop/ntop-cert.pem`**.
8. At the shell prompt, enter **`rm -f privkey.pem cert.pem`**.

The ntop daemon has now been properly configured. You can start the daemon using the `rcstart` command from a shell prompt. After starting the daemon, you should allow it to run for a while to capture enough network data for you to analyze. After that, you're ready to take a look at what ntop found. Let's talk about how to do this next.

Generating Reports with ntop

After ntop is running, you can view your network's performance by running a web browser and navigating to http://*IP_address*:3000. If you configured ntop to use a secure connection, enter **`https://ip_address:3001`** (assuming you specified the default secure port of 3001).

TIP

The `/etc/sysconfig/ntop` file specifies, by default, the localhost IP address (127.0.0.1). This is done for security reasons. In this configuration, the ntop web utility can be accessed only from the server's desktop. If you need to make your ntop page available to remote systems over the network, replace 127.0.0.1 in the NTOPD_PORT parameter with the *IP address* of server.

The screen in Figure 8.10 is displayed.

FIGURE 8.10
Accessing ntop.

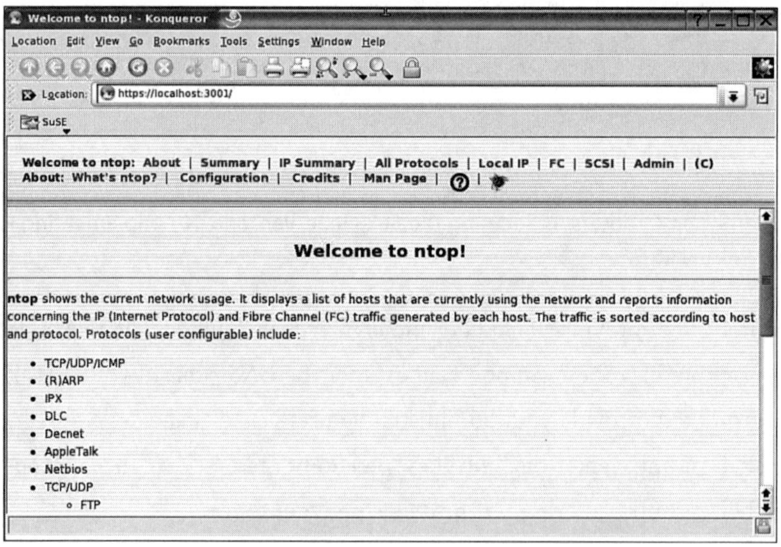

From this interface, you can view a veritable plethora of data gathered from your network. The ntop daemon can do the following:

- Provide detailed information about hosts on the network.
- Report current traffic statistics and bandwidth use.
- Identify hosts that are consuming the most network bandwidth.

- Report current active connections.
- Identify traffic between hosts on the local subnet as well as traffic between hosts on the local subnet and remote hosts.
- Report non-IP protocol usage.
- Identify protocols that are generating network traffic but aren't being used for meaningful work.
- Provide multicast traffic reports.

This list is just a smattering of what ntop can do. We're not going to spend extensive time here going through every last menu function in the interface; it would take about a hundred or so pages. It's better that you explore the utility on your own. However, we will go through a sampling of what you can do.

For example, if you wanted to see a graphical representation of the historical load on your network, you would do the following:

1. In the ntop interface, select **Summary, Traffic**.
2. Scroll down to the Network Load pie chart and select the **Historical Data** icon. The screen shown in Figure 8.11 is displayed.

FIGURE 8.11
Generating a Network Load Graph with ntop.

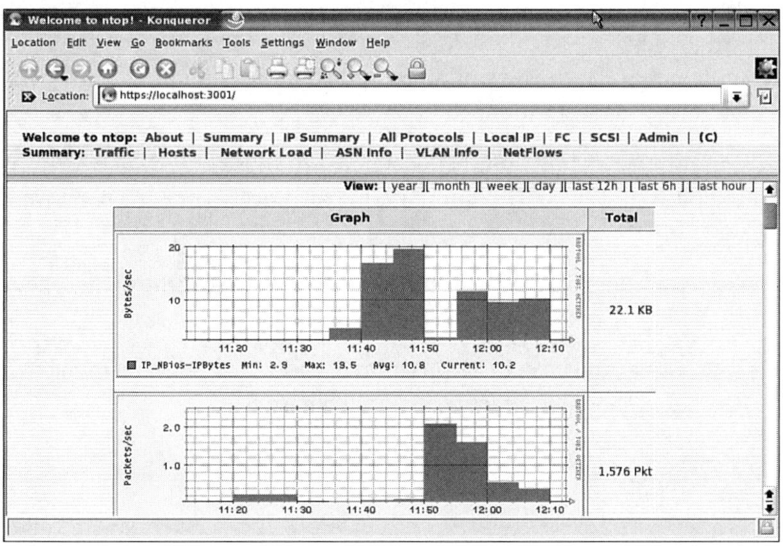

In this graphic, you can see a spike in activity shortly before 12:00. Perhaps everyone saved their work and checked their email before going to lunch.

3. You can also see a similar view by selecting **Summary**, **Network Load**. This option displays the graph shown in Figure 8.12.

FIGURE 8.12
An alternative view of the network load.

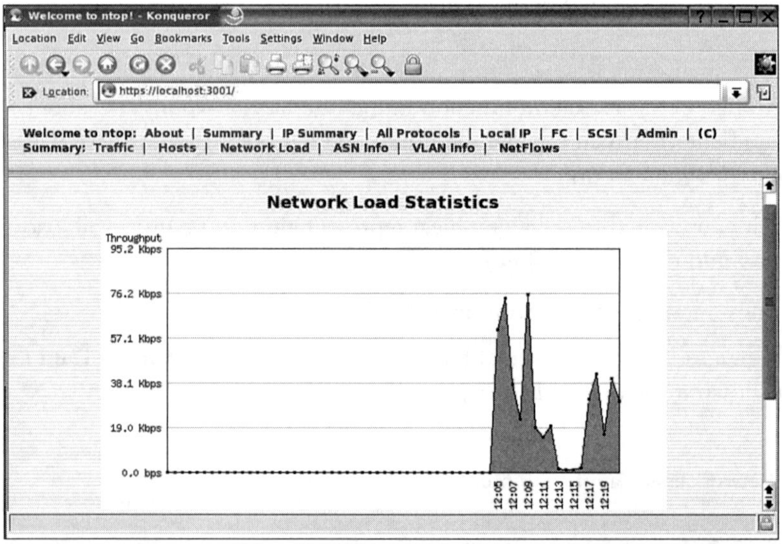

As you can see in Figure 8.12, the network load spiked around 5 minutes after 12:00 and then tapered off as everyone went to lunch.

If you wanted to view a list of hosts on the local network to identify which hosts are using the most bandwidth, you would select **IP Summary, Local, Local**. The screen shown in Figure 8.13 is displayed.

If you want to view your network's throughput statistics, select **All Protocols, Throughput**. The screen shown in Figure 8.14 is displayed:

That's all there is to it. As you can see, ntop is a pretty powerful network monitoring tool It's time for you to get some hands-on practice in Lab Exercise 8.1.

FIGURE 8.13
Viewing hosts on the local subnet.

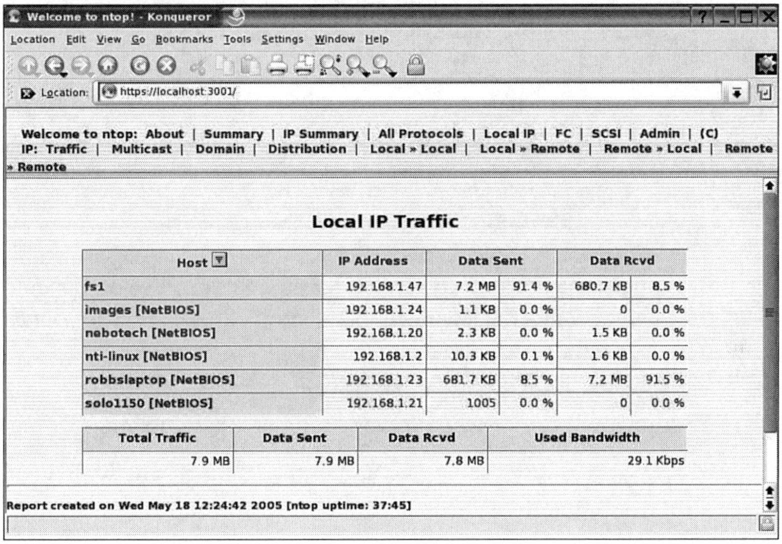

FIGURE 8.14
Viewing network throughput.

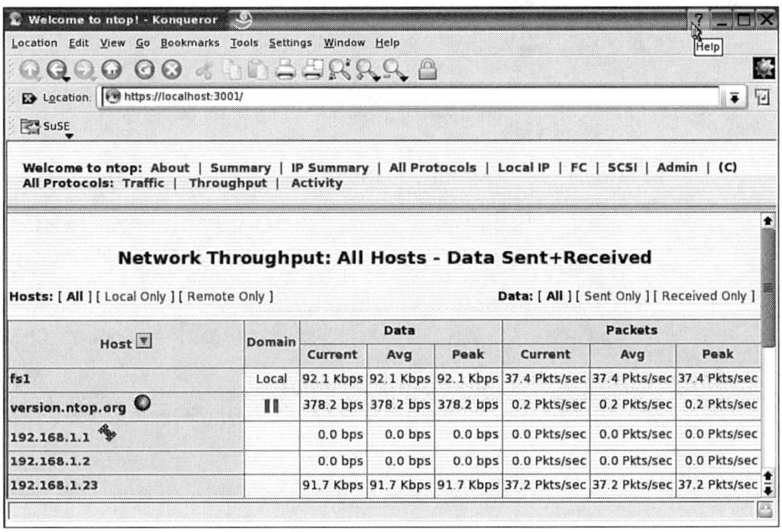

Lab Exercise 8.1: Configuring ntop

In this lab exercise, you will configure ntop on your SLES 9 system and use it to gather network traffic statistics. To complete this exercise, you will need your SLES 9 server with DNS, DHCP, Samba, Postfix, and CUPS running. If you're on an isolated lab segment (which is a very good idea), you may want to use an additional NLD or Windows workstation to generate some network traffic for ntop to capture.

TIP

Be careful if the network you are performing this exercise on is connected to the Internet with a DSL connection. The ntop utility can cause your DSL gateway to go offline.

To configure ntop on your server, complete the following:

1. Boot your SLES 9 server and authenticate as **tux** with a password of **SuSE789**.
2. Configure the ntop daemon by doing the following:
   a. Open a terminal session.
   b. At the shell prompt, enter **su -** and supply a password of **tuX123**.
   c. At the shell prompt, enter **vi /etc/sysconfig/ntop**.
   d. Press **Ins**.
   e. Scroll down to the NTOPD_SSL_PORT parameter and set it to a value of **"3001"**.
   f. Press **Esc**; then enter **:exit**.
   g. At the shell prompt, enter **openssl req -new -x509 -sha1 -extensions v3_ca -nodes -days 365 -out cert.pem**.
   h. When prompted, provide the *locality information* requested. When prompted for an organization name and unit, enter **CLE9** and **IS**, respectively.
   i. When prompted for the Common Name, enter the *DNS name* or *IP address* of your server.
   j. When prompted to provide your administrative user's email address, enter **root@cle9.com**.
   k. At the shell prompt, enter **cat privkey.pem cert.pem > /etc/ntop/ntop-cert.pem**.

l. At the shell prompt, enter **`rm -f privkey.pem cert.pem`**.

3. Run ntop for the first time by completing the following:
    a. At the shell prompt, enter **`ntop -A -u wwwrun`**.
    b. When prompted for a password for your ntop admin user, enter **`mycle9`**.
    c. Start the ntop daemon by entering **`rcntop start`** at the shell prompt.
    d. Let ntop run for a few minutes to gather packets. If necessary, fire up your workstation and generate some traffic by connecting to the Samba shares you created earlier.
4. View network statistics with ntop by completing the following:
    a. On your SLES 9 server desktop, start a web browser.
    b. In the Location field, enter **`https://localhost:3001`**.
    c. When prompted, accept the server certificate forever.
    d. In the ntop interface, select **Summary, Traffic**.
    e. Scroll down to the Network Load pie chart and select the **Historical Data** icon.
    f. What's your network's load?
    g. Select **Summary**, **Network Load**.
    h. How does the information in this screen compare to the statistics you recorded earlier?
    i. Select **IP Summary**, **Local**, **Local**.
    j. Which network host is consuming the most network bandwidth?
    k. Select **All Protocols**, **Throughput**.
    l. What's the overall bandwidth being used on your network segment?
    m. Explore the other functions provided in the ntop interface.

Congratulations! You now have a powerful network monitoring tool at your fingertips with ntop!

Now that you have ntop under your belt, we're going to continue our discussion of network monitoring and management by talking about Nagios.

Using Nagios to Manage Network Traffic

TEST OBJECTIVE COVERED:

1. Use ntop and Nagios to monitor network traffic.

Like ntop, Nagios is a network monitoring service that runs beautifully on SLES 9. What's the difference between them? Instead of monitoring network traffic, Nagios monitors specific network hosts and the critical services running on them.

With Nagios, you configure a series of checks that you want to run on your network. The Nagios daemon runs these checks and warns you when problems are detected. Like ntop, Nagios provides you with an intuitive web-based interface, shown in Figure 8.15:

FIGURE 8.15
The Nagios web interface.

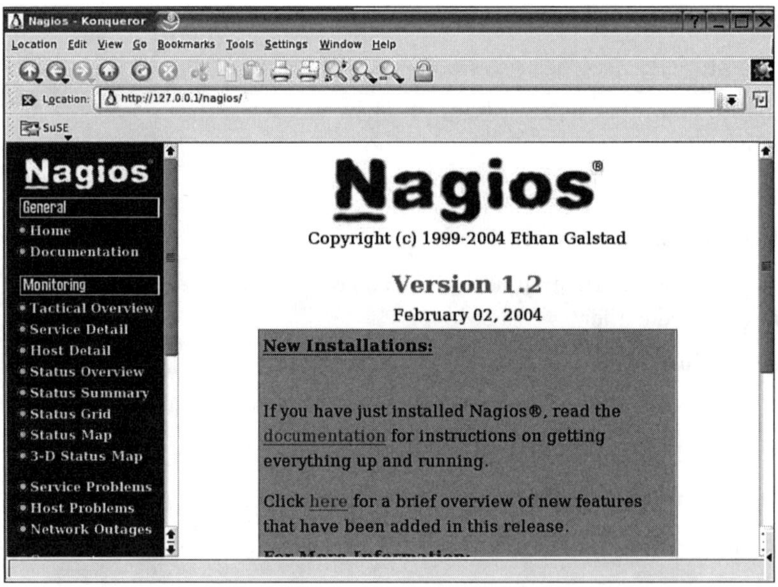

Nagios can do the following:

- Monitor services running on hosts in your network, such as web servers, FTP servers, and mail servers.
- Notify the network administrator (using email or instant messaging) when thresholds are exceeded.

- Implement redundant Nagios monitoring servers.
- Authenticate users and provide them with customized web views based on account restrictions.

Getting ntop up and running is a relatively easy process; getting Nagios going takes a little more work. You'll learn how you go about doing it next.

Installing and Configuring Nagios

The first thing you need to do is make sure the Nagios packages are installed on your system. Using the installation pattern we used in Chapter 2, the necessary software should already be installed on your SLES 9 server. These include the following (as shown in Figure 8.16):

FIGURE 8.16
Installing Nagios packages.

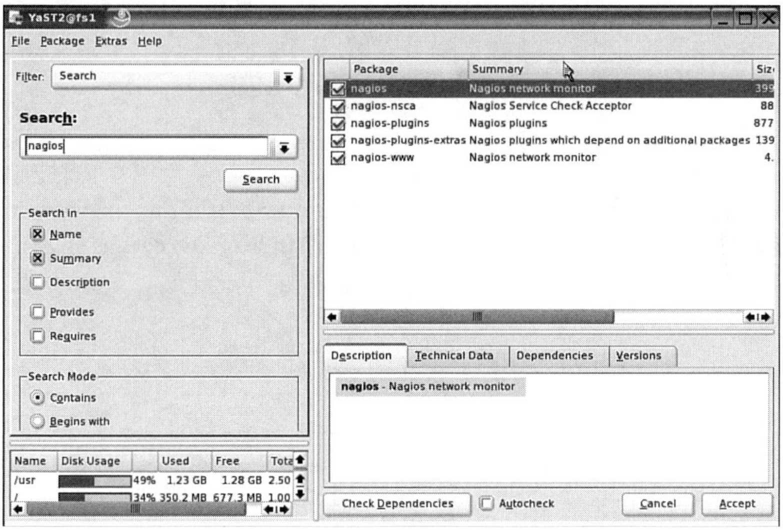

After installing these packages, the Nagios service is managed using the `/etc/init.d/nagios init` script, as shown in Figure 8.17.

However, before you start the service, you must complete a number of configuration tasks first. Specifically, you must

- Configure Apache to support Nagios.
- Configure the Nagios service.

FIGURE 8.17
The Nagios init script.

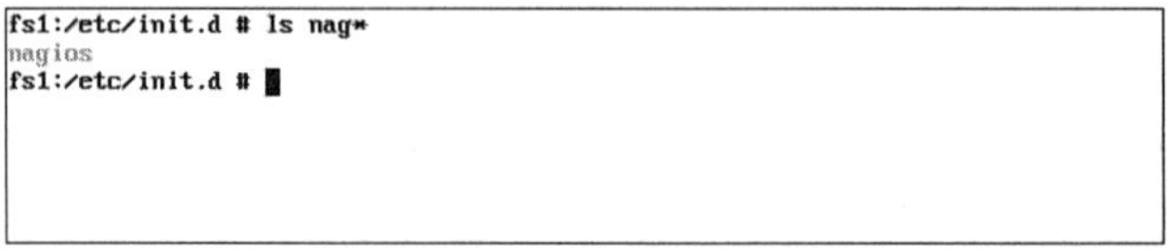

Let's start by configuring the Apache web server on your server to support Nagios.

CONFIGURING APACHE TO SUPPORT NAGIOS

The Nagios web interface is composed of a series of HTML files that are stored in /usr/share/nagios, as shown in Figure 8.18.

FIGURE 8.18
The Nagios web files.

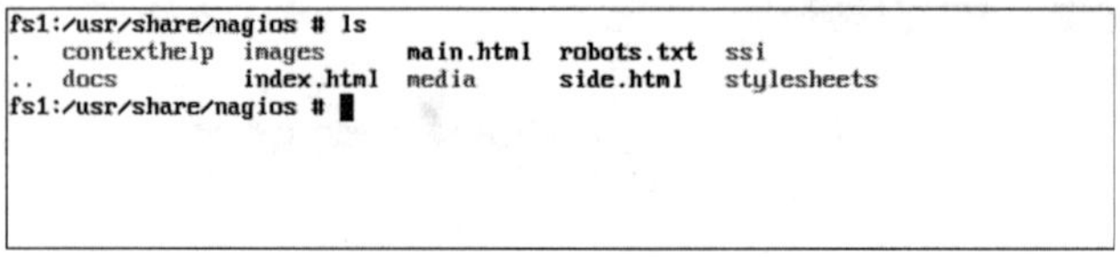

The Nagios service also uses a series of CGI scripts to provide real-time network information in your web browser. These scripts are stored in `/usr/lib/nagios/cgi`, as shown in Figure 8.19:

FIGURE 8.19
The Nagios CGI scripts.

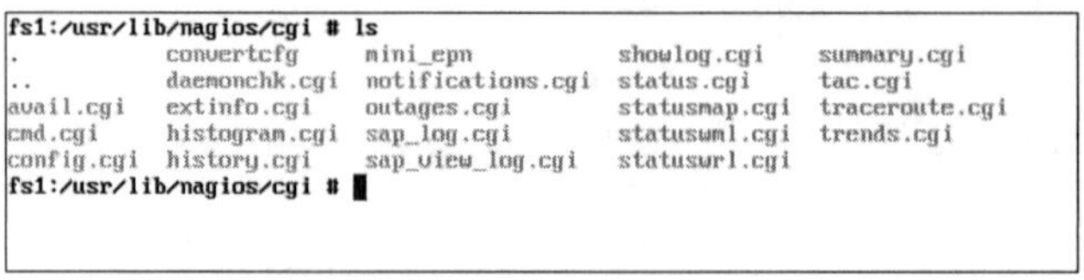

Notice that these directories reside outside the document directory of the Apache2 web server running on your server. To make these available in a web interface, you need to create an Alias for the Nagios web files and a ScriptAlias for the Nagios web files.

Although you could manually edit your **`httpd.conf`** file and add these directives, the folks at SUSE did a lot of the legwork for you. Inside of the `/etc/apache2/conf.d` directory is a file named `nagios.conf`; shown in Figure 8.20.

FIGURE 8.20
The `nagios.conf` File.

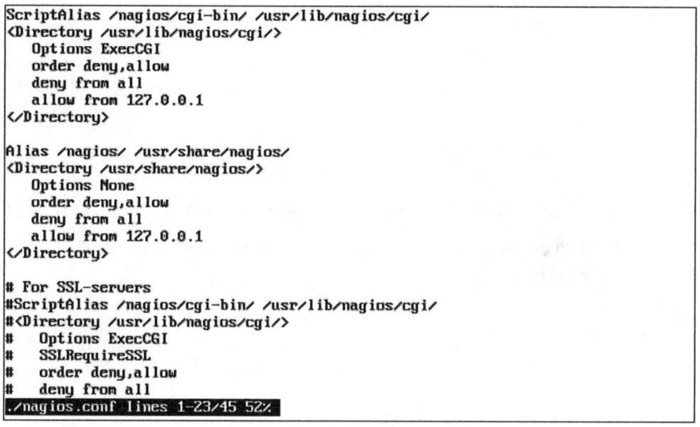

```
ScriptAlias /nagios/cgi-bin/ /usr/lib/nagios/cgi/
<Directory /usr/lib/nagios/cgi/>
   Options ExecCGI
   order deny,allow
   deny from all
   allow from 127.0.0.1
</Directory>

Alias /nagios/ /usr/share/nagios/
<Directory /usr/share/nagios/>
   Options None
   order deny,allow
   deny from all
   allow from 127.0.0.1
</Directory>

# For SSL-servers
#ScriptAlias /nagios/cgi-bin/ /usr/lib/nagios/cgi/
#<Directory /usr/lib/nagios/cgi/>
#    Options ExecCGI
#    SSLRequireSSL
#    order deny,allow
#    deny from all
./nagios.conf lines 1-23/45 52%
```

To integrate Nagios with your Apache2 web server, you specify the `nagios.conf` file as an include for your `httpd.conf` file. This is done by completing the following:

1. On your server, open a terminal session.
2. At the shell prompt, change to root.
3. At the shell prompt, enter **`vi /etc/sysconfig/apache2`**.
4. Scroll down to the `APACHE_CONF_INCLUDE_DIRS` directive, shown in Figure 8.21:

FIGURE 8.21
Configuring an include directory for Apache.

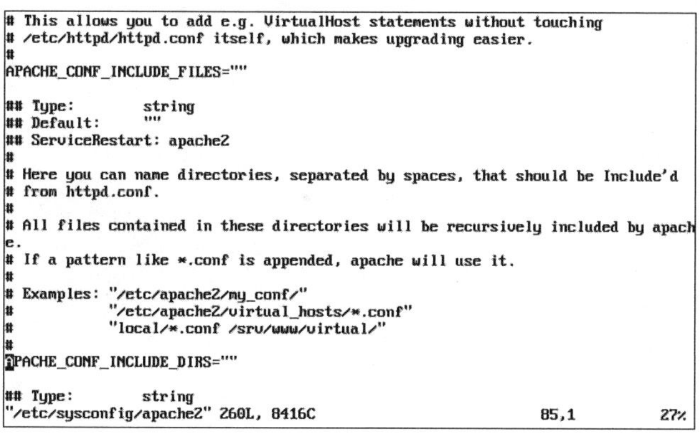

```
# This allows you to add e.g. VirtualHost statements without touching
# /etc/httpd/httpd.conf itself, which makes upgrading easier.
#
APACHE_CONF_INCLUDE_FILES=""

## Type:         string
## Default:      ""
## ServiceRestart: apache2
#
# Here you can name directories, separated by spaces, that should be Include'd
# from httpd.conf.
#
# All files contained in these directories will be recursively included by apach
e.
# If a pattern like *.conf is appended, apache will use it.
#
# Examples: "/etc/apache2/my_conf/"
#           "/etc/apache2/virtual_hosts/*.conf"
#           "local/*.conf /srv/www/virtual/"
#
APACHE_CONF_INCLUDE_DIRS=""

## Type:         string
"/etc/sysconfig/apache2" 260L, 8416C                        85,1          27%
```

TIP

If you haven't already done so, you should probably configure the `APACHE_SERVERADMIN` and `APACHE_SERVERNAME` directives while you're at it.

5. Set the value of `APACHE_CONF_INCLUDE_DIRS` to "**`/etc/apache2/conf.d/*.conf`**".

NOTE

Doing this will add all of the `.conf` files in `/etc/apache2/conf.d` to your Apache configuration. If you want to add only the `nagios.conf` file, you can specify it in the `APACHE_CONF_INCLUDE_FILES` directive (shown in Figure 8.21) instead.

6. Press **Esc**; then enter **`:exit`**.
7. At the shell prompt, enter **`SuSEconfig`**.
8. At the shell prompt, enter **`rcapache2 restart`**.
9. Test the configuration by opening a web browser window and navigating to `http://localhost/nagios/`. The screen shown in Figure 8.22 should be displayed:

FIGURE 8.22
The Apache includes for Nagios are configured correctly.

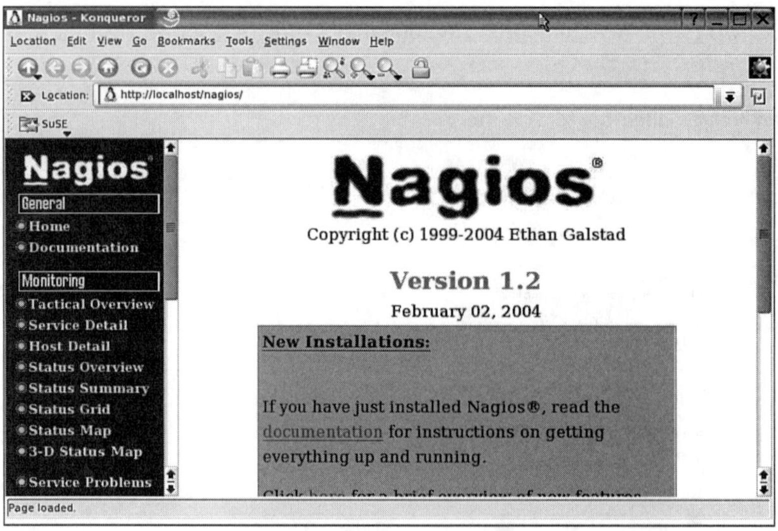

At this point, Nagios isn't actually doing anything. The actual Nagios daemon hasn't been configured, nor has it been started. Let's look at how to configure Nagios next.

CONFIGURING NAGIOS

The Nagios service is extremely flexible. You can customize its to exactly match your network. You can make it as simple or as complex as you want. However, be aware that this high degree of flexibility comes at a price. Configuring Nagios is no walk in the park.

In this part of this chapter, I'm going to present generic configuration steps for Nagios. Then, in Lab Exercise 8.2, you will implement a very basic Nagios configuration that checks the local Linux system. You will then need to customize and adapt what you learned to the specific needs of the network where you implement Nagios.

The Nagios service is configured using the files stored in `/etc/nagios`. These are shown in Figure 8.23:

FIGURE 8.23
Nagios configuration files.

```
fs1:/etc/nagios # ls
.                   contactgroups.cfg  hosts.cfg           resource.cfg
..                  contacts.cfg       minimal.cfg-sample  send_nsca.cfg
cgi.cfg             dependencies.cfg   misccommands.cfg    services.cfg
checkcommands.cfg   escalations.cfg    nagios.cfg          timeperiods.cfg
command.cfg         hostgroups.cfg     nsca.cfg
fs1:/etc/nagios #
```

To configure Nagios, you will need to do the following:

- Configure `nagios.cfg`.
- Configure an object configuration file.

Let's start with `nagios.cfg`.

CONFIGURING `nagios.cfg`

The `nagios.cfg` file is the master configuration file for Nagios. A sample `nagios.cfg` file is copied to `/etc/nagios` during installation of the package, as shown in Figure 8.24.

Before running the Nagios daemon, you need to edit this file and configure it for your network. Fortunately, most of the directives in the sample `nagios.cfg` file will work with most networks. There are actually about 100 directives that can be used in this file. We're going to cover only a couple of the most important ones here. If you want to learn about all of them (and there are a bunch), check out the documentation available in your Nagios browser window at `http://localhost/nagios/`.

FIGURE 8.24

The sample `nagios.cfg` configuration file.

```
###############################################################################
#
# NAGIOS.CFG - Sample Main Config File for Nagios
#
# Read the documentation for more information on this configuration
# file.  I've provided some comments here, but things may not be so
# clear without further explanation.
#
# Last Modified: 07-04-2002
#
###############################################################################


# LOG FILE
# This is the main log file where service and host events are logged
# for historical purposes.  This should be the first option specified
# in the config file!!!

log_file=/var/log/nagios/nagios.log



# OBJECT CONFIGURATION FILE(S)
./nagios.cfg lines 1-23/666 3%
```

You need to be most concerned with the following directives:

- `cfg_file`—This directive is used to configure the object configuration file that will be used. We're going to discuss what the object configuration file is later in this chapter. Each object configuration file should be referenced with its own separate **`cfg_file`** directive.

TIP

If you choose to use multiple object configuration files and they all reside in the same directory, you can use the `cfg_dir` directive instead. That way you won't have to create a separate `cfg_file` directive for each file.

- `log_file`—This directive is used to specify where you want the Nagios log file stored.
- `status_file`—This directive is used to specify the file that Nagios will use to store the current status of the system it's monitoring.
- `nagios_user`—This directive is used to specify the user that Nagios will run as on your server.
- `nagios_group`—This directive is used to specify the group Nagios will run as.
- `enable_notifications`—This directive is used to specify whether Nagios sends out event notifications. To enable this functionality, set this parameter to **1**.
- `execute_service_checks`—This directive is used to specify whether Nagios will run the checks you've configured it to make. To enable this (which you probably want to do unless the server is a backup Nagios server), set this directive to **1**.

- `check_external_commands`—This directive is used to specify whether you want to be able to send check commands manually through the web interface. Set this directive to a value of **1** if you want this functionality enabled.
- `use_syslog`—This directive is used to specify whether or not Nagios messages are logged to syslog on your server. If you want this enabled, set this parameter to **1**.
- `log_notifications`—This directive is used to specify whether notifications are written to a log file. Set this parameter to **1** if you want to enable this functionality.
- `enable_flap_detection`—This directive is used to suppress flap notifications. When a service or system being monitored is having a lot of problems, it can send out a barrage of notifications (called *flapping*). Enabling this option (by setting it to **1**) suppresses the barrage of notifications.
- `admin_email`—This directive is used to specify the email address of the local server's administrative user.
- `admin_pager`—This directive is used to specify the pager number or pager email gateway of the local server's administrative user.

After your `nagios.cfg` file has been configured, your next task is to create an object configuration file.

CONFIGURING AN OBJECT CONFIGURATION FILE

So far so good, right? Configuring the `nagios.cfg` file isn't much different from configuring any of the other services we've worked with so far. Well, here's where things get a little more complex. The next thing you need to do is to configure an object configuration file. This is the file that is specified by the `cfg_file` directive in `nagios.cfg`.

Refer back to Figure 8.23. Notice that there are a bunch of configuration files in `/etc/nagios` besides `nagios.cfg`. Most of the files you see are object configuration files. What's an *object*? It's any entity that you want to configure Nagios to work with. These objects can be defined either in a single, big file or in multiple files.

TIP

Regardless of which approach you choose, all object configuration files you want to use must be referenced in `nagios.cfg`.

For example, the following objects are defined by the files shown in Figure 8.23:

- Contact Groups (`contactgroups.cfg`)
- Contacts (`contacts.cfg`)

- Host Dependencies (**dependencies.cfg**)
- Service Escalations (**escalations.cfg**)
- Host Groups (**hostgroups.cfg**)
- Network Hosts (**hosts.cfg**)
- Commands (**miscommands.cfg**)
- Network Services (**services.cfg**)
- Time Periods (**timeperiods.cfg**)

If you want to use the multiple file approach, you can use the sample files in **/etc/nagios** as templates. If you want to use a single file that contains all object definitions, use the **minimal.cfg-sample** file in **/etc/nagios** as a template.

TIP

If you use minimal.cfg-sample as a template, be sure to rename it to **minimal.cfg** before using it.

Before we get going, we need to talk about some Nagios terminology. Within the various files we're going to work with, you're going to configure Nagios hosts and groups. These are in no way related to DNS hostnames or Linux groups, but are entries that you customize yourself specifically for Nagios, as you will see in just a minute. To configure your object configuration file(s), complete the following:

1. Define the *hosts* you want to monitor. This can be done in the **hosts.cfg** file or as a part of a single object configuration file. Add the following lines:

```
# Generic host definition template
define host{
    name                generic-host        notifications_enabled       1
    event_handler_enabled        1       flap_detection_enabled     1
process_perf_data       1         retain_status_information     1
retain_nonstatus_information     1    s

    register            0        }

#  host definition
define host{
    use            generic-host        ; Name of host template to use

    host_name        name_of_host_to_monitor
    alias            alias_name_for_host
    address         IP_address_of_host_to_monitor
```

```
    check_command         check-host-alive
    max_check_attempts    10
    notification_interval    120
    notification_period    24x7
    notification_options    d,u,r
    }
```

The first host definition is just a template; it doesn't actually define a host. It's called by the real host definition by the `use` directive. You can define multiple hosts, which can be computers, printers, network switches, and so on.

2. Add each *host* defined above to a *hostgroup*. This can be done in the `hostgroups.cfg` file or as a part of a single object configuration file. Add the following lines:

```
# host group definition
define hostgroup{
    hostgroup_name          name_of_hostgroup
    alias               hostgroup_alias
    contact_groups          name_of_contactgroup
    members         comma-separated_list_of_member_hosts
    }
```

Enter the hostname(s) you defined in the `hosts.cfg` file in the list of hosts in the `members` directive. You also need to specify the contactgroup that notifications will be sent to in the `contact_groups` directive. You can add multiple hostgroup definitions.

3. Configure the contactgroup definitions you specified earlier in the hostgroups.cfg file. This can be done in the `contactgroups.cfg` file in `/etc/nagios` or as a part of a single object configuration file. Add the following lines:

```
# contact group definition
define contactgroup{
    contactgroup_name     name_of_contactgroup
    alias             alias_for_contactgroup
    members         comma-separated_list_of_members
    }
```

For the contactgroup_name directive, use the *contactgroup name* you specified in `hostgroups.cfg`. In the members directive, specify the *contacts* that will be members of the contactgroup. You can add multiple contactgroup definitions.

4. Configure your contacts . This can be done in the `contacts.cfg` file or as a part of a single object configuration file. Add the following lines:

```
# contact definition
define contact{
    contact_name            contact_name
    alias               full_name_of_contact
```

```
    service_notification_period    workhours
    host_notification_period    workhours
    service_notification_options    c,r
    host_notification_options    d,r
    service_notification_commands    notify-by-email
    host_notification_commands    host-notify-by-email
    email                jdoe@localhost.localdomain
    }
```

For the contact_name directive, use the *contact name* you specified in the `contactgroups.cfg` file. You can add multiple contact definitions.

5. Configure the services that will be monitored by Nagios. This can be done in the `services.cfg` file or in a single object configuration file. Add the following lines:

```
# Generic service definition template
define service{
    name                generic-service        active_checks_enabled        1
      passive_checks_enabled    1        parallelize_check        1
obsess_over_service        1        check_freshness            0
notifications_enabled        1        event_handler_enabled        1
flap_detection_enabled        1        process_perf_data        1
retain_status_information    1        retain_nonstatus_information    1

    register            0        }

# Service definition
define service{
    use                generic-service        ;

    host_name            name_of_host
    service_description        service_to_be_monitored
    is_volatile            0
    check_period            24x7
    max_check_attempts        3
    normal_check_interval        3
    retry_check_interval        1
    contact_groups            name_of_contactgroup
    notification_interval        120
    notification_period        24x7
    notification_options        w,u,c,r
    check_command            plugin_to_be_used
    }
```

As you saw earlier, the first service definition is simply a template that is called by subsequent service definitions using the **use** directive. It configures default settings that can be used by subsequent service definitions in the file. For the **host_name** directive, use the *hostname* you specified when you defined your hosts.

For the service_description directive, create an intuitive *name* for the service that will be monitored. For the contactgroups directive, enter the name of the *contactgroup* you defined earlier.

For the check_command directive, enter the name of the Nagios plug-in you want to run against the host specified. A Nagios plug-in is an executable or a script that performs a specific function on a specified host. They are installed by the nagios-plugins and nagios-plugins-extra packages. They are stored in the `/usr/lib/nagios/plugins` directory on your server, as shown in Figure 8.25:

FIGURE 8.25
Nagios plug-ins.

```
fs1:/usr/lib/nagios/plugins # ls
.               check_ftp           check_mrtg      check_ping      check_tcp
..              check_hpjd          check_mrtgtraf  check_pop       check_time
check_breeze    check_http          check_mysql     check_procs     check_udp
check_by_ssh    check_ifoperstatus  check_nagios    check_radius    check_ups
check_dig       check_ifstatus      check_nntp      check_real      check_users
check_disk      check_imap          check_nt        check_rpc       check_vsz
check_disk_smb  check_ircd          check_ntp       check_sensors   check_wave
check_dns       check_ldap          check_nwstat    check_smtp      negate
check_dummy     check_load          check_oracle    check_snmp      urlize
check_flexlm    check_log           check_overcr    check_ssh       utils.pm
check_fping     check_mailq         check_pgsql     check_swap      utils.sh
fs1:/usr/lib/nagios/plugins #
```

For example, if you want to run a check on the remote host's FTP server, you would specify the `check_ftp` plug-in in the `check_command` directive.

As you've probably noticed, configuring Nagios takes a lot of preplanning and custom configuration on your part. However, I think you'll agree that after you're done, Nagios is worth the effort, especially if you're responsible for managing a very large network.

You're now ready to check your configuration and start the nagios daemon.

Checking Your Configuration and Starting Nagios

Because of its complex configuration, the nagios daemon provides a verification option that can be used to check your configuration and verify that everything will work correctly. You do this by entering the following command at a shell prompt:

```
nagios -v nagios.cfg |more
```

Rest assured, you will probably have to fix a number of items before you get everything right, especially the first time you set up Nagios.

After you've corrected the errors that were detected, you can start the daemon by entering **rcnagios start** at a shell prompt.

Let's give it a try in Lab Exercise 8.2.

Lab Exercise 8.2: Configuring Nagios

In this lab exercise, you will configure Nagios on your SLES 9 system and use it to monitor the DNS and Postfix SMTP services running locally.

NOTE

We're doing it this way because of lab constraints. You can customize the steps presented here to monitor a remote system, if you have one available.

To complete this exercise, you will need your SLES 9 server with DNS, DHCP, Samba, Postfix, and CUPS running. To configure Nagios on your server, complete the following:

1. Boot your SLES 9 server and authenticate as **tux** with a password of **SuSE789**.
2. Integrate Nagios with your Apache2 web server by completing the following:
   a. On your server, open a terminal session.
   b. At the shell prompt, enter **sux -** with a password of **tuX123**.
   c. At the shell prompt, enter **vi /etc/sysconfig/apache2**.
   d. Scroll down to the APACHE_SERVERADMIN directive.
   e. Set the value of APACHE_SERVERADMIN to **root@cle9.com**.
   f. Scroll down to the APACHE_SERVERNAME directive.
   g. Set the value of APACHE_SERVERNAME to "**fs1.cle9.com**".
   h. Scroll down to the APACHE_CONF_INCLUDE_DIRS directive.
   i. Set the value of APACHE_CONF_INCLUDE_DIRS to "**/etc/apache2/conf.d/*.conf**".
   j. Press **Esc**; then enter **:exit**.
   k. At the shell prompt, enter **SuSEconfig**.
   l. At the shell prompt, enter **rcapache2 restart**.
   m. Test the configuration by opening a web browser window and navigating to http://localhost/nagios/. The Nagios home page on your server should be displayed.

3. Configure your `nagios.cfg` file by completing the following:
   a. At the shell prompt, enter **`vi /etc/nagios/nagios.cfg`**.
   b. Verify that a `cfg_file=` directive exists for each of the following files. (The first two directives are found in the paragraphs above the main grouping of `cfg_file=` directives.)
      - `checkcommands.cfg`
      - `miscommands.cfg`
      - `contactgroups.cfg`
      - `contacts.cfg`
      - `dependencies.cfg`
      - `escalations.cfg`
      - `hostgroups.cfg`
      - `hosts.cfg`
      - `services.cfg`
      - `timeperiods.cfg`
   c. Scroll down to the `check_external_commands` directive and set it to a value of **`1`**.
   d. Scroll down to the `admin_email` directive and set it to **`root@cle9.com`**.
   e. Press **Esc**; then enter **`:exit`**.
4. Configure your `cgi.cfg` file by completing the following:
   a. At the shell prompt, enter **`vi /etc/nagios/cgi.cfg`**.
   b. Scroll down to the `use_authentication` line.
   c. Set the value of `use_authentication` to **`0`**.
   d. Press **Esc**; then enter **`:exit`**.

NOTE

Essentially, what we're doing here is allowing anyone using the browser on the localhost to view the monitor results.

If you want to use authentication, you will need to create an include file in `/etc/apache2/conf.d` that contains an `AuthOverride AuthConfig` statement for the `/usr/lib/nagios/cgi` directory.

You will then need to create an `.htaccess` file in this directory and create an `htpasswd` file to be used for authentication. For more information on how to do this, see the documentation available in your Nagios browser window.

5. Configure your `hosts.cfg` file by completing the following:
   a. At the shell prompt, enter **kate**.
   b. Select **File, Open**; then open the `/etc/nagios/hosts.cfg file`.

NOTE

We're going to use kate in this exercise to edit these files because of the amount of editing involved. If you would rather, feel free to use vi instead.

   c. Scroll down to the `novell1` host definition.
   d. Delete `novell1` host definition and each host definition after it.
   e. Add the following lines after the generic host definition:

```
#  'fs1' host definition
define host{
    use              generic-host

    host_name          fs1
    alias              Our CLE9 Server
    address          IP_address_of_fs1
    check_command            check-host-alive
    max_check_attempts     10
    notification_interval     120
    notification_period     24x7
    notification_options     d,u,r
    }
```

   f. Save your changes to the file.
6. Configure your hostgroups by completing the following:
   a. In kate, open `/etc/nagios/hostgroups.cfg`.
   b. Scroll down to the `novell-servers` group definition.
   c. Delete the `novell-servers` group definition and all group definitions that follow it.
   d. Add the following lines at the end of the file:

```
# 'CLE9-Servers' host group definition
define hostgroup{
```

```
hostgroup_name        CLE9-Servers
alias            CLE9 Lab Servers
contact_groups        CLE9-admins
members         fs1
}
```

   e. Save your changes to the file.

7. Configure your contactgroup by completing the following:

   a. In kate, open `/etc/nagios/contactgroups.cfg`.

   b. Scroll down to the `novell-admins` group definition.

   c. Delete the `novell-admins` group definition and all group definitions that follow it.

   d. Add the following lines at the end of the file:

```
# 'CLE9-admins' contact group definition
define contactgroup{
    contactgroup_name    CLE9-admins
    alias            CLE9 Administrators
    members         tux
    }
```

   e. Save your changes to the file.

9. Configure your contacts by completing the following:

   a. In kate, open `/etc/nagios/contacts.cfg`.

   b. Scroll down to the daemon contact definition.

   c. Delete the daemon definition and all contact definitions that follow it.

   d. Add the following lines at the end of the file:

```
# 'tux' contact definition
define contact{
    contact_name            tux
    alias                Nagios Admin
    service_notification_period    24x7
    host_notification_period    24x7
    service_notification_options    w,u,c,r
    host_notification_options    d,u,r
    service_notification_commands    notify-by-email
    host_notification_commands    host-notify-by-email
    email                tux@cle9.com
    }
```

   e. Save your changes to the file.

10. Configure nagios to monitor the DNS and SMTP services running on fs1 by completing the following:

a. In kate, open `/etc/nagios/services.cfg`.

b. Scroll down to the novell1 SMTP service definition (after the template definition).

c. Delete the novell1 SMTP service definition and all service definitions that follow it.

d. Add the following lines at the end of the file:

```
# Service definition
define service{
    use                     generic-service

    host_name               fs1
    service_description         DNS
    is_volatile             0
    check_period             24x7
    max_check_attempts         3
    normal_check_interval         3
    retry_check_interval         1
    contact_groups             CLE9-admins
    notification_interval         120
    notification_period          24x7
    notification_options          w,u,c,r
    check_command              check_dns
    }

# Service definition
define service{
    use                     generic-service

    host_name               fs1
    service_description         SMTP
    is_volatile             0
    check_period             24x7
    max_check_attempts         3
    normal_check_interval         3
    retry_check_interval         1
    contact_groups             CLE9-admins
    notification_interval         120
    notification_period          24x7
    notification_options          w,u,c,r
    check_command              check_smtp
    }
```

e. Save your changes to the file.

11. Open `/etc/nagios/dependencies.cfg` in kate.
12. Delete all the text from the file and save it.
13. Open `/etc/nagios/escalations.cfg` in kate.
14. Delete all the text from the file and save it.
15. In kate, select **File, Close All**.
16. Test your configuration by completing the following:
    a. At the shell prompt, change to the `/etc/nagios` directory.
    b. At the shell prompt, enter **`nagios -v nagios.cfg`**.
    c. You should receive a message indicating that no serious problems were identified, as shown in Figure 8.26:

FIGURE 8.26
Preflight check passed!

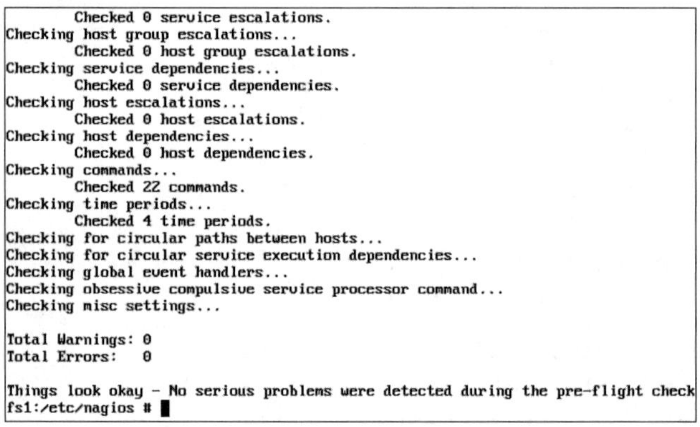

17. Start the nagios daemon by entering **`rcnagios start`** at the shell prompt.
18. Close your Nagios browser window; then restart your browser.
19. Access http://localhost/nagios/.
20. Explore the links provided under Monitoring. You should see output similar to that shown in Figure 8.27:

FIGURE 8.27
Monitoring with Nagios.

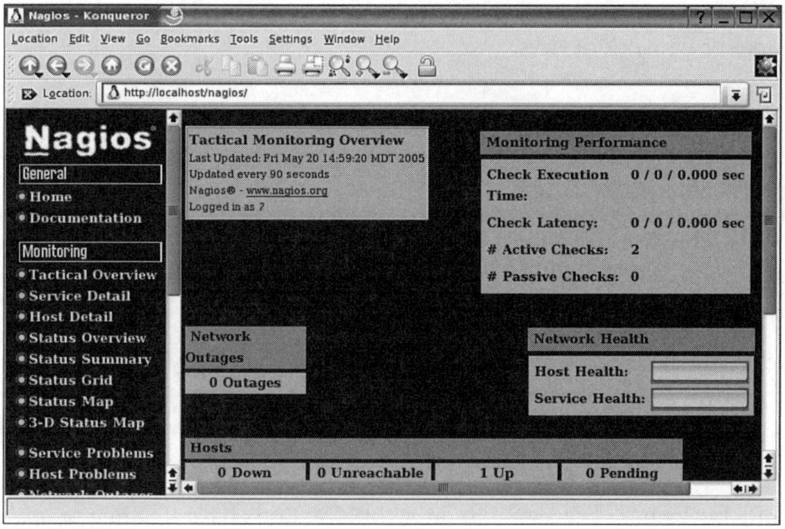

Congratulations! You now have a second powerful network monitoring tool at your fingertips: Nagios!

As I mentioned at the beginning of the exercise, this is only a very simple, single-host configuration. However, the general principles of using Nagios are there. You can take what you've learned and customize a Nagios solution for your network.

Now that you have Nagios behind you, we're ready to move on and talk about SNMP.

Using SNMP to Manage Network Traffic

TEST OBJECTIVE COVERED:

3. Use SNMP to monitor network devices.

SNMP stands for Simple Network Management Protocol. SNMP is one of the most powerful and widely implemented network management tools in use today. If you work in a large organization, you will probably work with SNMP.

One of the benefits of SNMP is that it has been around for long time. Nearly every operating system provides some form of SNMP support, including Linux, Windows, and NetWare. Because it has been around for so long, it's a mature, stable means of network monitoring.

Don't be fooled, however, by the name. Many new administrators mistakenly assume that because it's the *Simple* Network Management Protocol that it must, therefore, be simple to deploy. The term *Simple* refers to the way the protocol itself works.

Implementing SNMP is fairly complex. Like other services we've covered in this book, such as Postfix and CUPS, entire books have been written on SNMP. We don't have the time or space to pursue SNMP in its fullness here. Instead, we will cover the theoretical concepts behind SNMP; then we will discuss how to configure a basic SNMP implementation on your SLES 9 system.

With that disclaimer in mind, let's first discuss how SNMP works.

How SNMP Works

SNMP is a network protocol that's used to gather information from various network devices. Like Nagios, SNMP provides the administrator with a powerful overview of the health of the devices on the network. This information gives you the capability to spot a problem and rectify it *before* it causes an outage. In other words, SNMP helps you to be a proactive administrator rather than a reactive one; which is much better for your blood pressure.

To provide its network monitoring functionality, SNMP uses the components shown in Figure 8.28:

FIGURE 8.28
SNMP components.

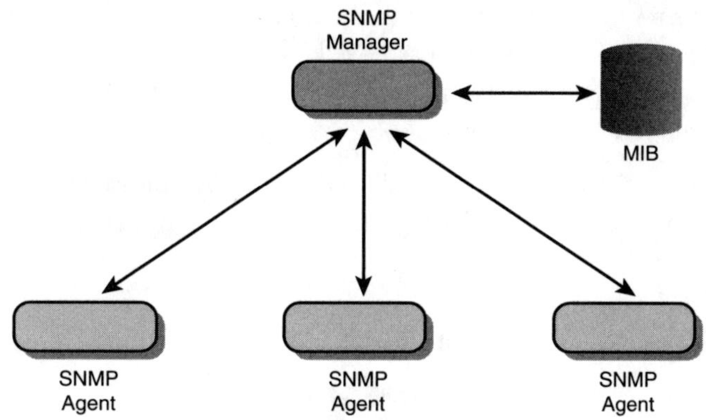

They do the following:

- SNMP Manager—The SNMP Manager is responsible for collecting data from network hosts that are being monitored via the SNMP protocol.
- SNMP Agents—The SNMP Agents are small software applications that run on a variety of network hardware, including servers, workstations, printers, routers, and switches. The SNMP Agents monitor their respective devices and provide status information to the SNMP Manager.
- Management Information Base (MIB)—The MIB defines the parameters that the SNMP Agents on the network will monitor for their respective devices. The SNMP Manager uses the MIB to determine what data it will gather from the SNMP Agents.

The MIB is fairly complex. To deploy SNMP, you need to understand how the MIB is organized. Before going any further, let's spend a few minutes reviewing the structure of the MIB.

HOW THE MIB IS ORGANIZED

The MIB is a hierarchical, structured definition of properties, similar to a database schema.

TIP

The MIB is not an actual database. It simply defines the structure of the information used by SNMP.

If you're familiar with DNS (which you should be by this point) or Novell's eDirectory, you're already familiar with how data can be arranged into a hierarchy.

In DNS, we have our root (.) and our TLDs (such as com, edu, org, and net). Within each TLD are organization-specific zones, such as novell.com, suse.com, and tldp.org. Within these zones, you could have individual network hosts or more subzones. Arranged in this manner, DNS is a hierarchical system.

The MIB uses a similar structure. It's top level is called iso. Within iso is org. Within org is dod. Within dod is internet. This top-level structure is shown in Figure 8.29:

FIGURE 8.29
SNMP MIB structure.

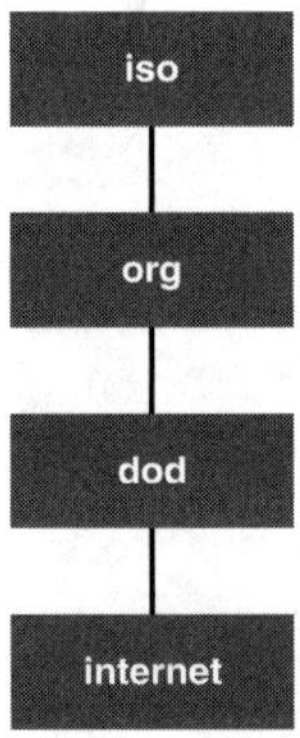

An important aspect of the MIB that you must understand is that the naming convention for referencing elements is reversed from the convention we use with DNS. With DNS (as well as eDirectory and LDAP), we start by referencing the specific object or element at the left. Then we reference all the levels of the hierarchy, separated by periods, up to the root.

With SNMP, however, we do it in just the opposite manner. For example, if we wanted to refer to internet, we would start with the topmost level at the left and then work our way down, resulting in a name of `iso.org.dod.internet`. In short, DNS, eDirectory, and LDAP all start at the bottom and work their way up. With an SNMP MIB, we start at the top and burrow our way down.

Also unlike DNS, eDirectory, or LDAP, the top four layers of the MIB hierarchy aren't used for much of anything in SNMP. They're just there. The layers below the internet layer are where we start actually organizing our information. It's also where things start to get kind of confusing.

Beneath internet are two subtrees: mgmt and private. Beneath mgmt are standard SNMP MIB elements, which are supported by most SNMP implementations. Underneath private are extensions to the standard SNMP MIB elements specific to particular vendors. IBM, CISCO, and Hewlett-Packard all have their own subtrees in the MIB under private that are used for their own custom MIB information.

There's also a subtree called ucdavis. This node will be important to us because it contains elements specific to the Net-SNMP package we will be using on our SLES 9 system. This hierarchy is shown in Figure 8.30:

FIGURE 8.30
Lower layers of the SNMP MIB structure.

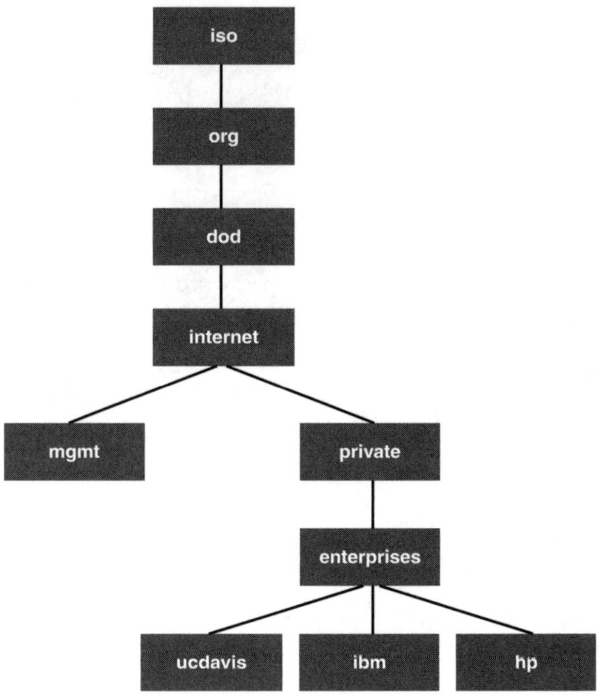

Sometimes, however, you will see references to elements in a MIB referred to using a numerical notation. At first glance, you may mistake this notation for an IP address, until you realize that there are way too many octets for an IP address. This numeric notation is also called the *Object ID (OID)*.

Each layer and each object in the MIB has a number assigned to it. Using OID, we replace the name of the particular object or layer with its associated number. The hard part is that there isn't much rhyme or reason to the numbers assigned. Following is a list of numbers for the upper layers:

- iso: **1**
- org: **3**
- dod: **6**
- internet: **1**
- mgmt: **2**
- private: **4**
- enterprises: **1**
- ucdavis: **2021**
- ibm: **2**
- hp: **11**

If you were to refer to the ucdavis node using OID, you would use **`1.3.6.1.4.1.2021`**.

Access to the MIB is controlled through a type of password called the *community name*. There are three community names:

- Read-Only Community Name
- Read/Write Community Name
- Trap Community Name

Each of these should use a different password, which allows you a form of access control based on the community name supplied.

Now that you know about the SNMP MIB, you next need to understand how communications take place using SNMP.

HOW SNMP COMMUNICATIONS WORK

Notice in Figure 8.28 that the lines are drawn with an arrowhead on each end. That's because SNMP communications can occur in two ways on your network. First, the SNMP Manager can periodically poll the SNMP Agents it has been configured to work with on the network.

Using the MIB, it queries them for specific information regarding their associated devices. The SNMP Manager consolidates this information and makes it available to the network administrator. This type of SNMP communications is referred to as *polled mode*. In polled mode, SNMP communicates using the IP protocol on UDP port 161.

In addition, SNMP can communicate using *traps*. With SNMP traps, you configure your SNMP Agents with thresholds for certain parameters. Whenever the Agent detects that its associated device has exceeded one of these thresholds, it sends an SNMP trap message to the SNMP Manager instead of waiting to be polled. Basically, think of a trap as an emergency notification. The Agent uses the IP protocol on UDP port **162** to send SNMP trap messages.

For the most part, most organizations today favor polled mode over traps. SNMP traps have some insecurities that make administrators sweat. Key among these is that it sends the community name unencrypted. If someone were able to sniff this information, they could cause a great deal of problems on your network.

Now that you have a high-level understanding of SNMP, let's talk about how to install and configure it on SLES 9.

Installing and Configuring SNMP on SLES 9

For the purposes of the CLE 9 certification, you need to understand how to deploy SNMP on a SLES 9 server using the Net-SNMP package. Be aware that this package isn't a full-blown SNMP suite. It's primarily designed to function as an SNMP Agent. It's capability to function as an SNMP manager is very limited.

If you need to implement an SNMP Manager, you will need to install an additional package. At this time, most of these packages are not open source, which means you will have to pay (and pay heavily) to obtain them. There is one open-source project in progress called OpenNMS; however, it hasn't been fully developed yet and isn't included in your SLES 9 distribution. If you want to learn more about OpenNMS, visit http://www.opennms.org.

The point of all this? We're going to focus on implementing Net-SNMP as an Agent in this chapter. Fortunately, this package includes some command-line utilities we can use to pull information gathered by SNMP, much like a full-blown manager package would.

With this in mind, let's first talk about installing Net-SNMP on your server.

INSTALLING NET-SNMP ON SLES 9

Before you can do much with SNMP on SLES 9, you have to install all the relevant packages. In YaST, run the Install and Remove Software module and search for snmp. Install the following packages, as shown in Figure 8.31:

FIGURE 8.31
Installing Net-SNMP Packages on SLES 9.

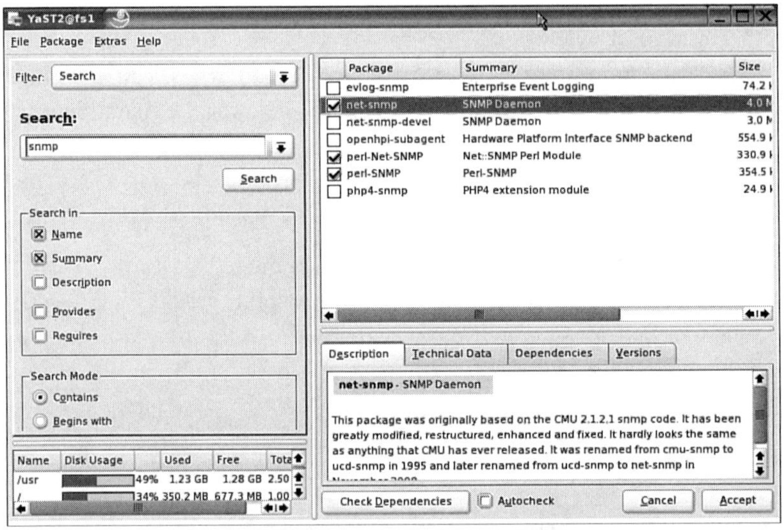

- net-snmp
- perl-Net-SNMP
- perl-SNMP

After installation, the Agent services are provided by the SNMP daemon (snmpd). This daemon is designed to operate in polled mode only, responding to requests from an SNMP Manager. It doesn't send traps.

To provide trap functionality, you must use the SNMP Trap daemon (snmptrapd). However, because of security issues with SNMP traps, snmptrapd and its associated init scripts and configuration files aren't fully implemented during installation of the net-snmpd package. In fact, the folks at SUSE recommend against using them at all.

If, for some reason, you need to use traps, you must manually enable the snmptrapd daemon. To do this, follow the steps contained in the `/usr/share/doc/packages/net-snmp/README.SuSE` file.

With the packages installed, let's now look at how you go about configuring an SNMP Agent on a SLES 9 server.

CONFIGURING AN SNMP AGENT ON SLES 9

Remember when I said that SNMP is anything but simple? Let me tell you—configuring an `snmp.conf` file for the first time can be a daunting experience. Fortunately, the authors of the net-snmp package included a script file that provides a simple wizard for creating your snmp.conf file called snmpconf.

I highly recommend that you use snmpconf the first time you try to configure an SNMP Agent. The wizard will configure your `snmpd.conf` file for you and also extensively comment it. From there, you can study the file and learn how each of the directives affects the way the Agent works.

To configure your `snmpd.conf` file with snmpconf, complete the following:

1. Open a terminal session.
2. From the shell prompt, change to root.
3. Change to the `/etc` directory.
4. At the shell prompt, enter **`snmpconf -r none -g basic_setup`**. The screen in Figure 8.32 is displayed:

FIGURE 8.32
Configuring SNMP with snmpconf.

```
fs1:/etc # snmpconf -r none -g basic_setup
************************************************
*** Beginning basic system information setup ***
************************************************
Do you want to configure the information returned in the system MIB group (conta
ct info, etc)? (default = y):
```

5. When prompted whether you want to configure the information returned in the system MIB group, enter **y**; then complete the following:
   a. When prompted to configure your system location, enter a *description of the physical location* of your server. The screen in Figure 8.33 is displayed:
   b. When prompted for contact information, enter the *email address*, *phone number*, or *address* of the SNMP administrator.
   c. When prompted to set the value of the sysServices.0 OID, enter **n**.
6. When prompted to set up the Agent's access controls, enter **y**.

FIGURE 8.33
Configuring SNMP contact Information with snmpconf.

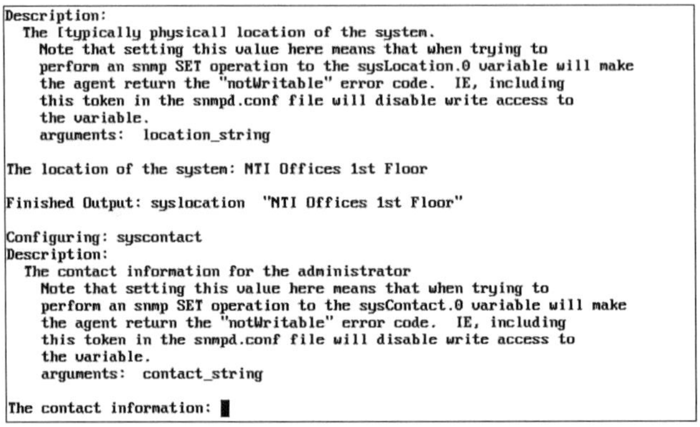

7. When prompted to set up SNMPv3 read-write user based access, enter **y**; then complete the following:

NOTE

To address many of the security issues associated with versions 1 and 2 of SNMP, version 3 implements user-based authentication. With versions 1 and 2, any user who had the correct community name could access SNMP information. With version 3, you can limit access to specific user accounts.

   a. When prompted to enter an SNMPv3 user that should have read-write access, enter a *username*.
   b. When prompted for a security level, enter **auth**.
   c. When prompted for OID that the community should be restricted to, press **Enter**.
   d. When prompted to create another read/write user, enter **y** if you want to add another user; otherwise, enter **n**.

8. When prompted to create a read-only user, enter **y**; then complete the following:
   a. When prompted, enter the *username* of the user you want to give read-only access.
   b. When prompted for the security level, enter **auth**.
   c. When prompted for OID that the community should be restricted to, press **Enter**.
   d. When prompted to create another read-only user, enter **y** if you want to add another user; otherwise, enter **n**.

9. When prompted whether you allow SNMPv1/v2c read-write community access, enter **y**; then complete the following:

NOTE

Doing this will allow read/write access to SNMP information to all users on the system you specify. If you don't want to do this, enter **n**.

a. When prompted, enter the ***community name*** (which is a form of password) for read/write access.

TIP

The industry convention is to use a default community name of private for r/w access. You should use something other than this for obvious security reasons. A password isn't secure if everyone knows it!

b. When prompted, enter the *IP address* or *hostname* of the system you want to allow r/w access from. If you want to lock down access, use **localhost**.

c. When prompted for the OID that this community should be restricted to, press **Enter**.

d. When prompted to define another r/w community, enter **n**.

10. When prompted to allow SNMPv1/v2c read-only community access, enter **y**; then complete the following:

a. When prompted, enter the *community name* for read-only access.

TIP

Again, the industry convention is to use a default community name of `public` for read-only access. You should use a value other than this!

b. When prompted, enter the *IP address* or *hostname* of the system you want to allow read-only access from. If you want to lock down access, use **localhost**.

c. When prompted for the OID that this community should be restricted to, press **Enter**.

d. When prompted to define another read-only community, enter **n**.

11. When prompted to configure traps, enter **n**.

12. When prompted to configure the Agent to monitor your system, enter **y**.

13. If you want to monitor processes running on the server, enter **y**; then complete the following:

    a. Enter the name of a process you want to monitor, as shown in Figure 8.34.

FIGURE 8.34
Configuring snmpd to monitor named.

```
n
****************************************
*** Beginning monitoring setup ***
****************************************
Do you want to configure the agent's ability to monitor various aspects of your
system? (default = y): y
Do you want to configure the agents ability to monitor processes? (default = y):
 y

Configuring: proc
Description:
  Check for processes that should be running.
      proc NAME [MAX=0] [MIN=0]

      NAME:  the name of the process to check for.  It must match
             exactly (ie, http will not find httpd processes).
      MAX:   the maximum number allowed to be running.  Defaults to 0.
      MIN:   the minimum number to be running.  Defaults to 0.

    The results are reported in the prTable section of the UCD-SNMP-MIB tree
    Special Case:  When the min and max numbers are both 0, it assumes
    you want a max of infinity and a min of 1.

Name of the process you want to check on: named
```

    b. When prompted, enter the *maximum number of processes* that should be running with the string you entered previously.

    c. When prompted, enter the *minimum number of processes* that should be running with the string you entered previously.

    d. When prompted, enter **y** to enter another process to monitor; otherwise, enter **n**.

14. If you want to monitor disk space on the host, enter **y** when prompted; then complete the following:

    a. When prompted, enter the mount point of the disk partition to be monitored, as shown in Figure 8.35.

    b. When prompted, enter the *minimum amount of free space* that should be available on the partition. This can be specified in bytes or as a percentage of the total space.

    c. When prompted, enter **y** to enter another partition to monitor; otherwise, enter **n**.

15. If you want to monitor the load on the system, enter **y** when prompted; then complete the following:

    a. When prompted, enter the *1 minute maximum load amount*, as shown in Figure 8.36.

FIGURE 8.35
Configuring snmpd to monitor /.

```
Minimum number of processes named 'named' that should be running [default = 0]:
1

Finished Output: proc  named 2 1
Do another proc line? (default = y): n
Do you want to configure the agents ability to monitor disk space? (default = y)
: y

Configuring: disk
Description:
  Check for disk space usage of a partition.
    The agent can check the amount of available disk space, and make
    sure it is above a set limit.

     disk PATH [MIN=100000]

     PATH:  mount path to the disk in question.
     MIN:   Disks with space below this value will have the Mib's errorFlag set.
            Can be a raw byte value or a percentage followed by the %
            symbol.  Default value = 100000.

    The results are reported in the dskTable section of the UCD-SNMP-MIB tree

Enter the mount point for the disk partion to be checked on: /
```

FIGURE 8.36
Configuring snmpd to monitor system load.

```
Enter the mount point for the disk partion to be checked on: /
Enter the minimum amount of space that should be available on /: 20%

Finished Output: disk  / 20%
Do another disk line? (default = y): n
Do you want to configure the agents ability to monitor load average? (default =
y): y

Configuring: load
Description:
  Check for unreasonable load average values.
    Watch the load average levels on the machine.

     load [1MAX=12.0] [5MAX=12.0] [15MAX=12.0]

     1MAX:   If the 1 minute load average is above this limit at query
             time, the errorFlag will be set.
     5MAX:   Similar, but for 5 min average.
     15MAX:  Similar, but for 15 min average.

    The results are reported in the laTable section of the UCD-SNMP-MIB tree

Enter the maximum allowable value for the 1 minute load average: 10
```

  b. When prompted, enter the *5 minute maximum load amount.*

  c. When prompted, enter the *15 minute maximum load amount.*

  d. When prompted to enter another load line, enter **n**.

16. If you want to monitor file sizes in the local file system, enter **y** when prompted; then complete the following:

a. When prompted, enter the *path* to the file whose size you want to monitor, as shown in Figure 8.37:

FIGURE 8.37
Configuring snmpd to monitor file size.

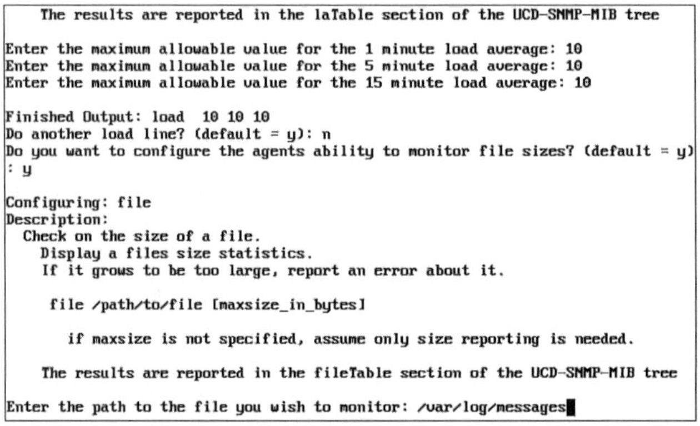

b. When prompted, enter the *maximum size* threshold for the file (in KB).

c. When prompted, enter **y** to enter another file to monitor; otherwise, enter **n**.

d. If prompted that an snmpd.conf file already exists in `/etc`, enter **`overwrite`**.

TIP

A sample snmpd.conf file is automatically created in `/etc` when you install the net-snmp package. You can safely overwrite it with the snmpconf utility.

In addition, notice that the wizard indicates that you need to copy the snmpd.conf file to `/usr/share/snmp`. On SLES 9, you don't need to do this. The `snmpd.conf` can reside in either `/usr/share/snmp` or in `/etc`.

17. Start the daemon by entering **`rcsnmpd start`** at the shell prompt.

At this point, you can monitor your system using a SNMP Manager. Before starting Lab Exercise 8.3, you first need to know about several command-line utilities that are included with net-snmp. These can be used to interact in various ways with the SNMP Agent running on your system. They include the following:

- snmptranslate—This utility is used to convert MIB OID names into OID numbers, and vice versa.

- snmpget—This utility is used to poll an SNMP Agent with **GET** commands. The Agent will respond with the value of the parameter requested.
- snmpwalk—This utility can be used to get the value of all the parameters located within a subtree of the MIB.
- snmpset—This utility is used to set the value of specified parameters on the Agent using SET commands.
- snmptest—This utility is used to test communications with an SNMP Agent.

You'll practice setting up the net-snmp Agent on your SLES 9 server in Lab Exercise 8.3.

Lab Exercise 8.3: Configuring SNMP

In this lab exercise, you will configure net-snmp on your SLES 9 system to deploy an SNMP Agent that will monitor your system.

NOTE

The SLES 9 distribution doesn't include any packages that can be used as an SNMP Manager. In this exercise, we'll configure an SNMP Agent and then use the `snmpget` command to simulate a poll request from an SNMP Manager.

To complete this exercise, you will need your SLES 9 server with DNS, DHCP, Samba, Postfix, and CUPS running. To configure net-snmp on your server, complete the following:

1. Boot your SLES 9 server and authenticate as **tux** with a password of **SuSE789**.
2. Install the net-snmp packages on your system by completing the following:
   a. Start YaST.
   b. When prompted for your root password, enter **tuX123**.
   c. Select Software, Install and Remove Software.
   d. In the Search field, enter **snmp**; then select **Search**.
   e. Mark the following packages (some may already be installed):
      - **net-snmp**
      - **perl-Net-SNMP**
      - **perl-SNMP**
   f. Select **Accept**.
   g. When prompted, insert the necessary CDs.
   h. Wait while the packages are installed and SuSEconfig is run.
3. Open a terminal session.
4. From the shell prompt, enter **su -** using a password of **tuX123**.
5. Change to the `/etc` directory.
6. At the shell prompt, enter **snmpconf -r none -g basic_setup**.

7. When asked if you want to configure the information returned in the system MIB group, enter **y**; then complete the following:
    a. When prompted to configure your system location, enter **CLE9 SNMP Agent Server**.
    b. When prompted for contact information, enter **root@cle9.com**.
    c. When prompted to set the value of the sysServices.0 OID, enter **n**.
8. When prompted to set up the Agent's access controls, enter **y**.
9. When prompted to set up SNMPv3 read-write user based access, enter **n**.
10. When prompted to create a read-only user, enter **n**.
11. When asked if you allow SNMPv1/v2c read-write community access, enter **y**; then complete the following:
    a. When prompted, enter a community name of **cle9private**.
    b. When prompted for the IP address or hostname of the system you want to allow read/write access from, enter **127.0.0.1**.
    c. When prompted for the OID that this community should be restricted to, press **Enter**.
    d. When prompted to define another read/write community, enter **n**.
12. When prompted to allow SNMPv1/v2c read-only community access, enter **y**; then complete the following:
    a. When prompted, enter a community name of **cle9public**.
    b. When prompted for the IP address or hostname of the system you want to allow read-only access from, enter **127.0.0.1**.
    c. When prompted for the OID that this community should be restricted to, press **Enter**.
    d. When prompted to define another read-only community, enter **n**.
13. When prompted to configure traps, enter **n**.
14. When prompted to configure the Agent to monitor your system, enter **y**.
15. When asked if you want to monitor processes running on the server, enter **n**.
16. When asked if you want to monitor disk space on the host, enter **y**; then complete the following:

   a. When prompted for the mount point of the disk partition to be monitored, enter **/**.
   b. When prompted for the minimum amount of free space that should be available on the partition, enter **20%**.
   c. When prompted to enter another partition to monitor, enter **n**.
17. When asked if you want to monitor the load on the system, enter **y**; then complete the following:
   a. When prompted for the 1 minute maximum load amount, enter **10**.
   b. When prompted for the 5 minute maximum load amount, enter **15**.
   c. When prompted for the 15 minute maximum load amount, enter **20**.
   d. When prompted to enter another load line, enter **n**.
18. When asked if you want to monitor file sizes in the local file system, enter **y**; then complete the following:
   a. When prompted, enter **/var/log/messages**.
   b. When prompted for the maximum size threshold for the file, enter **500000**.
   c. When prompted to enter another file to monitor, enter **n**.
19. If prompted that an snmpd.conf file already exists in `/etc`, enter **overwrite**.
20. Start the daemon by entering **rcsnmpd start** at the shell prompt.
21. Verify that snmpd started properly by completing the following:
   a. At the shell prompt, enter **less /var/log/snmpd.log**.
   b. Verify that no startup errors were logged.
   c. Press **q**.
22. Review the `snmpd.conf` file created by snmpconf by completing the following:
   a. At the shell prompt, enter **less /etc/snmpd.conf**.
   b. Scroll through the various directives you configured. You should see the following directives in the file:

```
rocommunity  cle9public 127.0.0.1
rwcommunity  cle9private 127.0.0.1
disk  / 20%
load  10 15 20
file  /var/log/messages 500000
syslocation  "CLE9 SNMP Agent Server"
syscontact  root@cle9.com
```

c. In particular, read the comments included in the file for each directive.

TIP

The directives shown in this basic file are only a very small subset of all that are available. To explore all the options, view the man page for `snmpd.conf`.

d. When you're finished, press **q**.

23. View the nodes beneath ucdavis in the MIB by entering **`snmptranslate -Tp .1.3.6.1.4.1.2021 | more`**.

24. View system information about your server from the Agent by completing the following:

a. At the shell prompt, enter **`snmpget -v2c -c cle9public localhost system.sysDescr.0`**. The Agent should return system information about your SLES 9 server, as shown in Figure 8.38:

FIGURE 8.38
Using snmpget to poll the SNMP Agent.

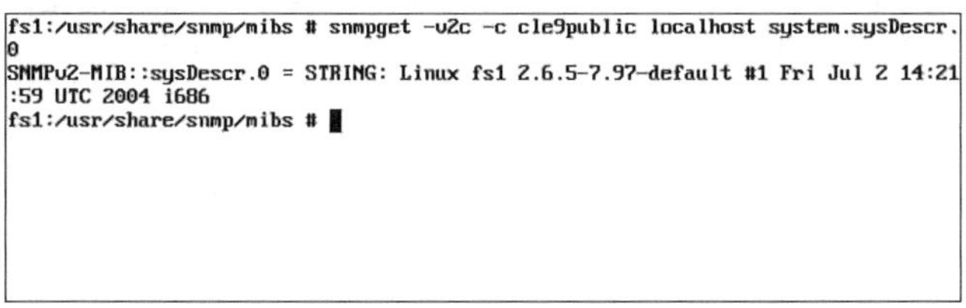

b. At the shell prompt, enter **`snmpget -v2c -c cle9public localhost system.sysContact.0`**. The Agent should return the contact information you configured earlier in the exercise.

c. At the shell prompt, enter **`snmpget -v2c -c cle9public localhost system.sysUpTime.0`**. The Agent should report how long your server has been up.

d. At the shell prompt, enter **snmpget -v2c -c cle9public localhost system.sysLocation.0**. The Agent should return the location information you entered earlier in the exercise.

TIP

View the `/usr/share/snmp/mibs/SNMPv2-MIB.txt` file for a list of other system parameters you can poll the Agent for with snmpget. You can also view the `/usr/share/snmp/mibs/UCD-SNMP-MIB.txt` file to see nodes in the ucdavis branch of the MIB.

25. Check your system load using the snmpget utility by completing the following:

    a. At the shell prompt, enter **snmpget -v2c -c cle9public localhost laLoad.1**. The Agent should return the 1 minute load average.

    b. Repeat this command to get the value of `laLoad.2` and `laLoad.3` (the 5 minute and 15 minute load average).

26. Check your disk percent free parameter by entering **snmpget -v2c -c cle9public localhost dskPercent.1**. The Agent should return the percentage of free disk space on the / partition.

27. Check the size of `/var/log/messages` by entering **snmpget -v2c -c cle9public localhost fileSize.1**. The Agent should return the size of the file.

28. View the value of all variables under the ucdavis node in your MIB by entering **snmpwalk -v2c -c cle9public localhost ucdavis |more**. The Agent should return values for all the variables.

Congratulations! You now know how to configure and test an SNMP Agent!

As we said earlier, to implement a full SNMP deployment, you would also need to deploy an SNMP Manager package; which would be used to poll all the SNMP Agents deployed in the network.

Before ending this chapter, we have one more topic to talk about: troubleshooting network problems. To do this, we will learn how to use ethereal and tcpdump.

Using ethereal and tcpdump to Troubleshoot Network Problems

TEST OBJECTIVE COVERED:

2. Use ethereal and tcpdump to troubleshoot network problems.

The life of a network administrator has often been characterized as weeks of total boredom accompanied by minutes of absolute terror. My experience has been that this is a pretty accurate assessment. When the network is working properly, life is uneventful. When problems happen, however, panic can set in very quickly.

The key to managing network problems is knowing how to respond. We're not going to spend a lot of time talking about troubleshooting models and steps in this chapter. I'm assuming you already have an understanding of these concepts. Instead, we're going to spend time discussing two tools you can use to troubleshoot network problems when they appear. As you know, identifying the source of a network problem is one of the first steps you must take when issues arise. The tcpdump and ethereal utilities can be a great help in do this.

Let's talk about tcpdump first.

Using tcpdump

The tcpdump utility can be exceptionally useful when troubleshooting network communication problems. tcpdump is a capture tool that grabs packets off the network wire and prints the headers of each packet on screen for you to analyze. If you're having trouble, tcpdump can help you track down the source.

For example, if a network client is having trouble mounting a Samba share, you can use tcpdump to capture the SMB blocks as they are exchanged between the server and the workstation. This will allow you to see exactly what's happening during the exchange.

In addition, tcpdump can be configured to save the captures to a file. I love this feature of tcpdump. Many times I've run a capture, analyzed it, got flustered, thought about it for a while, and then realized something I overlooked. In these circumstances, it's really helpful to come back to the original capture instead of having to set everything up again to recapture packets. tcpdump can be configured to load the existing capture file instead of capturing new data—allowing you to verify your troubleshooting epiphany.

To start capturing packets, enter **`tcpdump -i eth0`** at a shell prompt. The `-i` option specifies the interface that tcpdump should capture on. You can, of course, use interfaces other than eth0 if you have multiple network boards installed in the system.

NOTE

Like other system utilities, you must have root privileges to run tcpdump.

This command will capture all packets sent on the network segment, regardless of where they originated or where they are being sent. In Figure 8.39, tcpdump has been used to capture packets being exchanged during a VNC connection between my SLES 9 server and a browser on my notebook system:

FIGURE 8.39
Capturing packets with tcpdump.

```
ack 1001 win 5840
14:06:06.488754 IP 192.168.1.23.ipcd3 > fs1.cle9.com.5901: . ack 610008 win 1752
0
14:06:06.489686 IP fs1.cle9.com.5901 > 192.168.1.23.ipcd3: P 612052:612191(139)
ack 1001 win 5840
14:06:06.490791 IP fs1.cle9.com.5901 > 192.168.1.23.ipcd3: P 612191:612354(163)
ack 1001 win 5840
14:06:06.491764 IP fs1.cle9.com.5901 > 192.168.1.23.ipcd3: P 612354:612416(62) a
ck 1001 win 5840
14:06:06.492236 IP 192.168.1.23.ipcd3 > fs1.cle9.com.5901: . ack 610388 win 1714
0
14:06:06.496806 IP 192.168.1.23.ipcd3 > fs1.cle9.com.5901: . ack 610743 win 1678
5
14:06:06.501055 IP 192.168.1.23.ipcd3 > fs1.cle9.com.5901: . ack 611163 win 1636
5
14:06:06.504390 IP 192.168.1.23.ipcd3 > fs1.cle9.com.5901: . ack 611552 win 1752
0
14:06:06.504961 IP 192.168.1.23.ipcd3 > fs1.cle9.com.5901: . ack 611860 win 1721
2
14:06:06.507721 IP 192.168.1.23.ipcd3 > fs1.cle9.com.5901: . ack 612191 win 1688
1
14:06:06.509147 IP 192.168.1.23.ipcd3 > fs1.cle9.com.5901: . ack 612416 win 1665
6
```

Each line in the tcpdump output represents the data from the header of a single packet. Figure 8.40 identifies the different elements contained in a sample line of tcpdump output:

Each header contains the following information (refer to Figure 8.40):

- The date the packet was sent
- The protocol used by the packet
- The packet's source address
- The packet's destination address
- The header flag
- The packet's sequencing number
- The ACK bit and sequencing number of the next expected packet
- The receive buffer size

FIGURE 8.40
Interpreting tcpdump output.

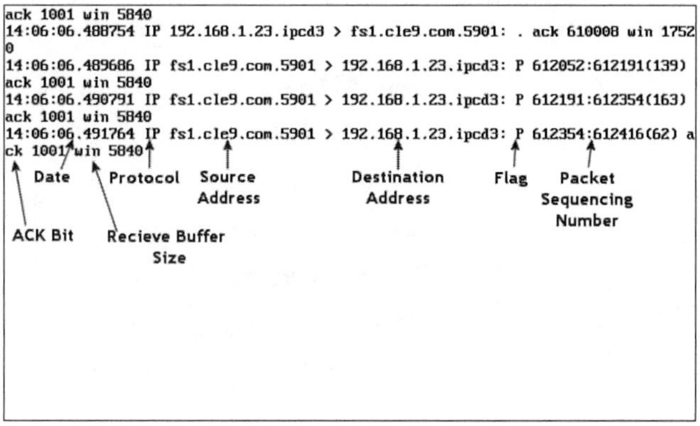

Using the command specified previously, tcpdump will run continuously until you press **Ctrl+C**. When you do, tcpdump will display the number of packets captured, the number of packets that made it through any filters you established, and the number of packets that were dropped (which usually happens when your buffer gets full). These are shown in Figure 8.41:

FIGURE 8.41
Packets captured and packets dropped by tcpdump.

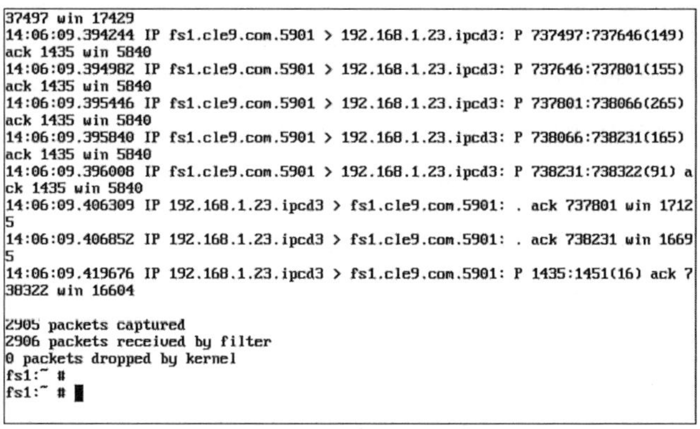

If you want tcpdump to automatically stop capturing after a specified number of packets have been sent, you can use the **`-c`** ***`number_of_packets`*** option. If you want more detail in your capture, you can use the **`-v`** option. If you want less detail, use the **`-q`** option.

Using the simple command specified earlier, the packets captured are discarded as soon as they are processed. If you want to come back and review your capture later (a very useful thing to do), include the **-w *file_name*** otion. You can then use tcpdump later to open the capture file by using the **-r *file_name*** option.

If you're a graphically oriented type of person, you may want to consider using ethereal. Let's look at this utility next.

Using ethereal

The ethereal utility performs essentially the same functions as the tcpdump utility, but graphically. The ethereal utility can do the following:

- Capture data from the network like tcpdump.
- Save captures to a file.
- Read captures from a file (its own or those produced by tcpdump).
- Capture data from Ethernet, Token Ring, ATM, FDDI, and PPP networks.
- Display data in an X-Windows GUI or at the shell prompt using the ethereal utility.
- Format captures as PostScript files.
- Filter data.

To use ethereal, you must first install the ethereal package, as shown in Figure 8.42.

You should have installed this package as a part of an exercise in Chapter 2 of this book. If not, be sure to do so before continuing.

After installing the package, you can use ethereal by completing the following:

1. Open a terminal session.
2. At the shell prompt, use the **sux -** command to change to root.
3. At the shell prompt, enter **ethereal**. The ethereal interface is displayed, as shown in Figure 8.43.
4. To start a capture, select **Capture, Start**. The screen in Figure 8.44 is displayed.

FIGURE 8.42
Installing the ethereal package.

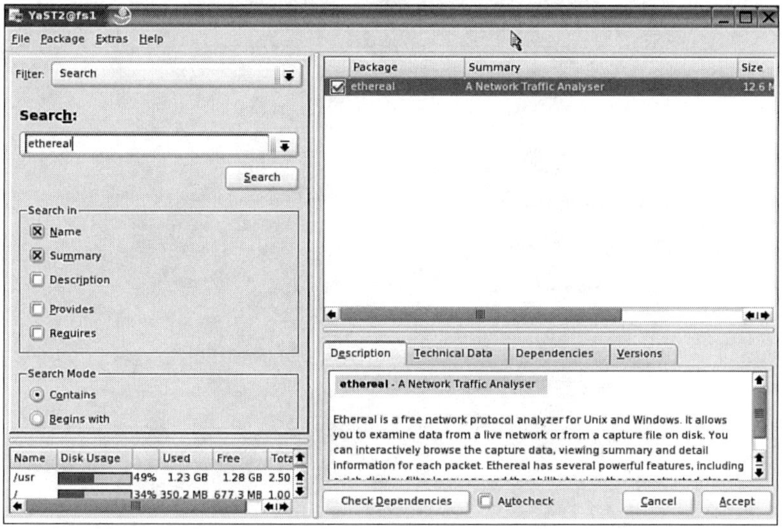

FIGURE 8.43
The ethereal interface.

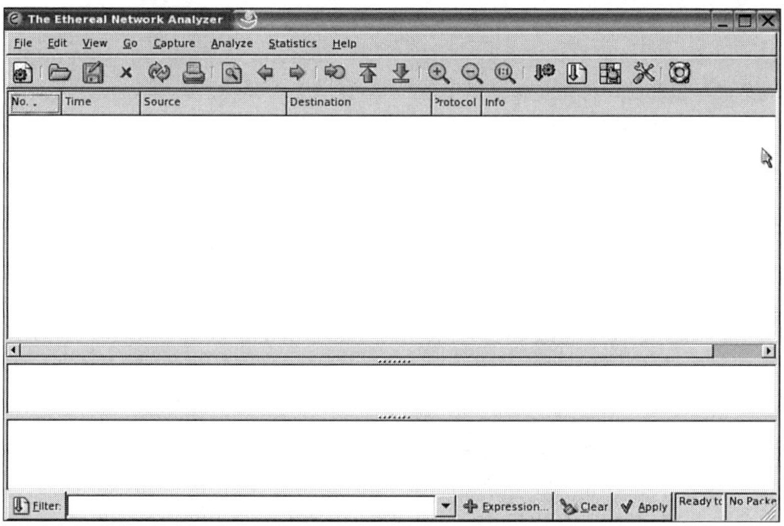

FIGURE 8.44
Starting a packet capture in ethereal.

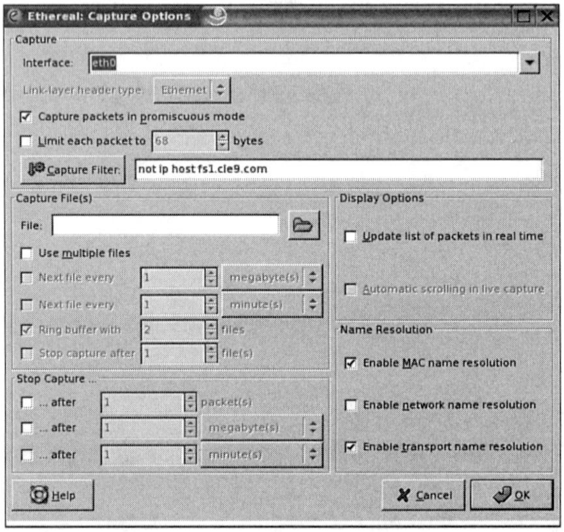

5. In the Capture Options screen, configure the following options:
   - Which interface should be used for capturing.
   - Whether to use promiscuous mode.
   - The capture filter.
   - The file to save the capture in.
   - Set limits to stop the capture.
   - Whether to display the capture in real time on screen.
   - Whether to use name resolution.

6. Select **OK**.
7. If you want to see the details of a particular packet, select it in the top window. Its details are displayed in the bottom windows.

I think you'll agree that ethereal provides a very powerful and very flexible interface for analyzing network traffic. Call me a GUI wimp, but I've pretty much moved over to ethereal from tcpdump. I like having all the information ethereal provides at my fingertips.

You'll practice using tcpdump and ethereal in Lab Exercise 8.4.

Lab Exercise 8.4: Using ethereal and tcpdump

In this lab exercise, you will use tcpdump and ethereal to capture and analyze transmission on your network.

To complete this exercise, you will need your SLES 9 server with DNS, DHCP, Samba, Postfix, and CUPS running. You will also need a second system to generate traffic with. Although you can configure these utilities to use the lo interface, the results just aren't terribly interesting.

Complete the following:

1. Boot your SLES 9 server and authenticate as **tux** with a password of **SuSE789**.
2. Capture network traffic with tcpdump by completing the following:
   a. Open a shell prompt and enter **sux -** using a password of **tuX123**.
   b. At the shell prompt, enter **tcpdump -i eth0 -c 1000 -w /tmp/testcapture1**.
   c. From your second system, generate network traffic by mounting your SMB share, pinging your SLES 9 system, or sending a print job to your CUPS printer.
   d. Wait while the capture completes. You may have to generate additional traffic to reach 1,000 packets.
   e. Read the results of the capture by entering **tcpdump -r /tmp/testcapture1 |more**.
   f. Analyze the results of the capture.
3. Capture traffic with ethereal by completing the following:
   a. Using the YaST Install and Remove Software module, verify that the ethereal package has been installed on your system.
   b. At your shell prompt, enter **ethereal**.
   c. Select **Capture, Start**.
   d. Verify that eth0 is listed in the Interface field.
   e. Erase the text in the Capture Filter field.
   f. In the File field, enter **/tmp/testcapture2**.

g. In the Stop Capture field, configure ethereal to stop capturing after **`1 minute`**.

h. Under Display Options, mark **Update List of Packets in Real Time**.

i. Under Name Resolution, mark **Enable Network Name Resolution**.

j. Select **OK**.

k. Generate network traffic using your second system.

l. Wait while the capture occurs.

m. When complete, explore the packets that were captured.

n. View the testcapture1 file in ethereal by selecting **File, Open**; then browse to and select **/tmp/testcapture1**.

That's it! You now have two powerful network troubleshooting tools in your administrator's toolbelt.

That's it for this chapter. We covered a lot of ground. Before we go to Chapter 9, let's review what you've learned.

Summary

In this chapter, you learned many ways of monitoring traffic and hosts on your network. You first learned how to implement ntop on your SLES 9 system to monitor traffic on your network. You learned that ntop is particularly useful when trying to identify hosts on your network that are consuming excessive bandwidth.

After that, you learned how to implement Nagios on your SLES 9 system. You learned that Nagios can be configured to monitor specific hosts and the services they offer on your network. You learned that Nagios can be configured with various thresholds that will trigger a notification to be sent if they are exceeded.

Next, you ventured into the world of SNMP. You learned about the roles of Master and Agent, as well as how the MIB is used to define data that the Agent gathers. You then learned how to implement an SNMP Agent on your SLES 9 system using the net-snmp package. You also learned how to use various SNMP tools in the package, such as snmpget.

Finally, you learned how to troubleshoot network communication problems using two excellent traffic analyzers: tcpdump and ethereal. You have to be humble when you know this much!

Stay tuned; in Chapter 9, we're going to discuss how to establish a security policy for your network as well as how to detect intruders.

CHAPTER 9

Securing the SLES 9 Server

This chapter covers the following requirements for Novell's Certified Linux Engineer (CLE) 9 certification:

1. Configure Linux host security.
2. Configure cryptography.
3. Configure Linux network security.
4. Detect intruders.

In today's networking world, security has become a huge issue. As a network administrator, it is your job to ensure that your network stays secure—especially your network servers.

In the early days of networking, we didn't worry all that much about security issues. Yes, the concern was always there, lurking in the back of our minds. However, break-ins were relatively rare. Our complacency was born of the fact that most networks back then were relatively small and usually isolated.

In fact, in the late 1980s, our biggest security concerns were viruses that were spread by floppy disks. During my freshman year in college, the computer labs at the university I attended each had an isolated system located at the front desk. Before you could insert any floppy in any of the networked lab systems, you had to run it through this isolated system and run a virus scan.

My how things have changed. Back in the "old days," not many organizations connected their networks to the Internet, the exception being universities and some colleges. It wasn't until much later that companies and public schools connected their networks to the Internet. For example, my first job out of college in the early 1990s was managing networks for a local high school. The school's networks were confined to three computer labs. Each lab had its own isolated segment.

My fellow administrators and I had our wildest dreams come true in 1994 when the state granted the school extra funds that we used to connect our little networks together, run wire to every classroom, and connect the entire school to the Internet through a T-Carrier line. We were on the bleeding edge (at least in our own minds) and puffed out our chests accordingly.

Unfortunately, as soon as we did, security became a stingingly critical issue. Problems we had never even thought of before became daily occurrences. From that experience, I've decided that there's no better network security laboratory in the world than a high school. The place is filled with up-and-coming hackers that will keep you on your toes from the minute you get to work until they finally go home in the afternoon.

The problem wasn't unique to my school network. Most organizations, as soon as they connected their networks to the Internet in the early 1990s, became painfully aware that network security is a major issue.

There are many ways your system can be attacked. As we go through this chapter, we'll discuss how you can secure your server against attacks by creating a security plan for your SLES 9 system. Then we'll discuss how to monitor your system to detect attacks as they occur. Let's talk about how you go about developing and implementing your server security plan.

Implementing a SLES 9 Server Security Plan

TEST OBJECTIVE COVERED:

1. Configure Linux host security.
2. Configure cryptography.
3. Configure Linux network security.

You've heard the old axiom "Those who fail to plan, plan to fail." The same principle holds true for server security. A good administrator takes a proactive approach to network security. Simply put, you're much better off if you can head off attacks before they occur. Responding after the fact isn't nearly as effective (and is much worse for your blood pressure).

To take this proactive approach, you should implement a server security plan. This plan should include the following components:

- Keeping abreast of current security threats
- Patching your server
- Documenting your SLES 9 system
- Physically securing your server
- Securing services on your server
- Securing access to the server

Let's begin by discussing the first topic: keeping abreast of current threats.

Stay Abreast of Current Security Threats

One of the biggest problems with network security is that we, as administrators, are always one step behind the bad guys. As soon as we work out a way to shield our networks from the latest exploit, they hit us with a new one.

As a network administrator, it's critical that you stay current with the latest network threats because they change from week to week. The only way you can keep your network safe is to be aware of what the latest threats are.

How do you do that? The best way is to visit several of the most important security-related web sites regularly. There you can learn about the latest exploits and how you can defend your network against them. Some of the best sites to visit include:

- http://www.cert.org—The Computer Emergency Response Team (CERT) website is maintained by the Carnegie Mellon Software Engineering Institute. It's one of the best places to stay up-to-date with current threats. The CERT web page contains links for the latest advisories, as shown in Figure 9.1.
- http://www.us-cert.gov—Maintained by the government of the United States, the US-CERT website also contains a great deal of information about cyber attacks. Sample US-CERT security vulnerability bulletins are shown in Figure 9.2.
- http://www.novell.com/linux/security/securitysupport.html—The two websites listed previously deal with network security threats in general. For SUSE LINUX-specific threats, you should frequently visit Novell's Linux security web page at this URL. There you can see a list of the latest security announcements for your SLES 9 system, as shown in Figure 9.3.

FIGURE 9.1
CERT advisories and incidents.

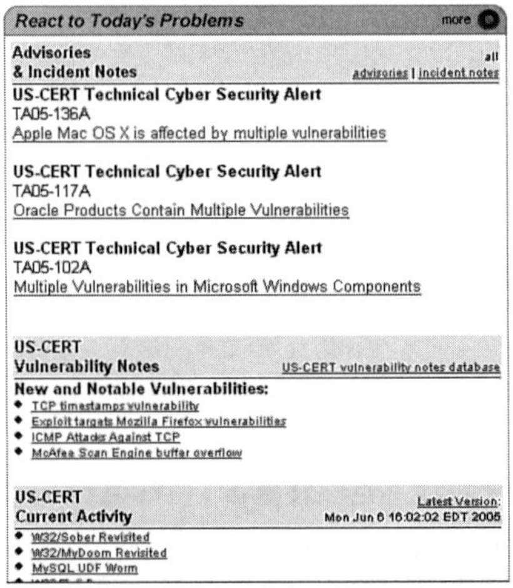

FIGURE 9.2
US-CERT security bulletins.

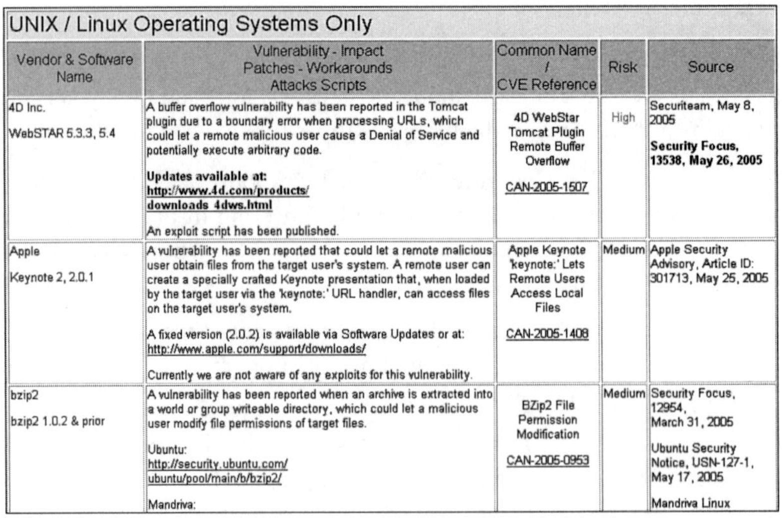

UNIX / Linux Operating Systems Only

Vendor & Software Name	Vulnerability - Impact Patches - Workarounds Attacks Scripts	Common Name / CVE Reference	Risk	Source
4D Inc. WebSTAR 5.3.3, 5.4	A buffer overflow vulnerability has been reported in the Tomcat plugin due to a boundary error when processing URLs, which could let a remote malicious user cause a Denial of Service and potentially execute arbitrary code. **Updates available at: http://www.4d.com/products/downloads_4dws.html** An exploit script has been published.	4D WebStar Tomcat Plugin Remote Buffer Overflow CAN-2005-1507	High	Securiteam, May 8, 2005 **Security Focus, 13538, May 26, 2005**
Apple Keynote 2, 2.0.1	A vulnerability has been reported that could let a remote malicious user obtain files from the target user's system. A remote user can create a specially crafted Keynote presentation that, when loaded by the target user via the 'keynote:' URL handler, can access files on the target user's system. A fixed version (2.0.2) is available via Software Updates or at: http://www.apple.com/support/downloads/ Currently we are not aware of any exploits for this vulnerability.	Apple Keynote 'keynote:' Lets Remote Users Access Local Files CAN-2005-1408	Medium	Apple Security Advisory, Article ID: 301713, May 25, 2005
bzip2 bzip2 1.0.2 & prior	A vulnerability has been reported when an archive is extracted into a world or group writeable directory, which could let a malicious user modify file permissions of target files. Ubuntu: http://security.ubuntu.com/ubuntu/pool/main/b/bzip2/ Mandriva:	BZip2 File Permission Modification CAN-2005-0953	Medium	Security Focus, 12954, March 31, 2005 Ubuntu Security Notice, USN-127-1, May 17, 2005 Mandriva Linux

FIGURE 9.3
SUSE Linux security announcements.

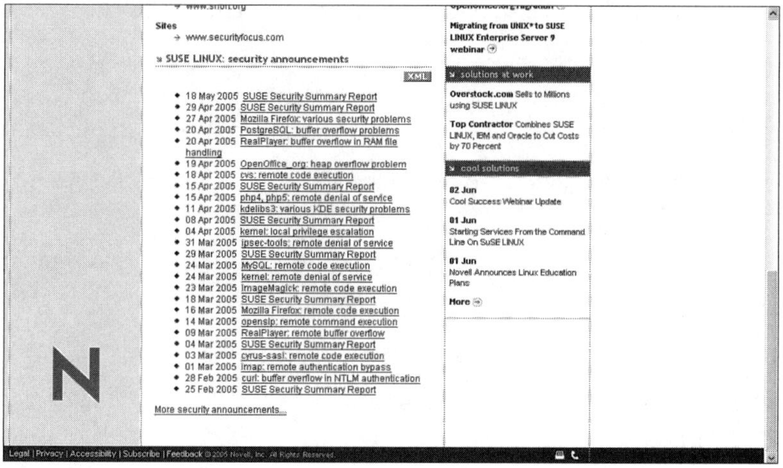

- http://www.suse.com/en/business/mailinglists.html—The SUSE Mailing Lists site provides you with links for subscribing to SUSE security-related mailing lists; such as suse-security and suse-security-announce. These are shown in Figure 9.4.

FIGURE 9.4
Subscribing to SUSE LINUX security mailing lists.

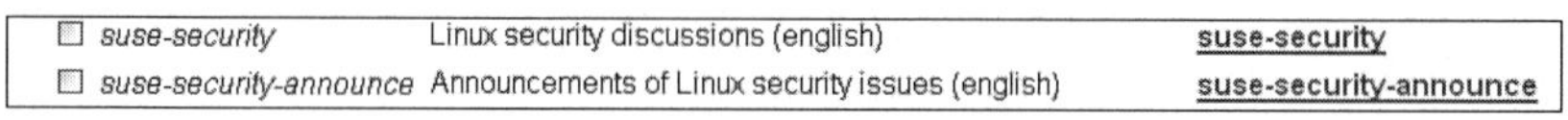

By all means, this isn't an all-encompassing list. There are hundreds of security-related websites out there. However, those previously listed are among the most authoritative sites around. Many other security-related sites get a good portion of their content from the sites we've listed here. If you visit these sites and read these mailing lists regularly, you can stay abreast of what's happening in the security world and, potentially, head off an attack on your own network.

In addition to staying current with these sites, another key component in your security plan should be to keep your SLES 9 system software up-to-date. Let's talk about how to do that next.

Keep Your System Software Up-to-Date with YOU

As security vulnerabilities are discovered in the software running on your sever, updates are made available that you can download and apply. This is done using YOU.

As you should have learned in the prerequisite courseware for this book, YOU stands for *YaST Online Update*. It's a YaST module you can use to automatically download and install SLES 9 updates and patches on your server. To do this, you need to do the following:

1. From within a browser, navigate to http://portal.suse.com and register your SLES 9 server.
2. Using the information you used to register, complete the following to configure YOU:
    a. Start YaST.
    b. When prompted, provide your root password.
    c. In YaST, select **Software, Online Update**. The screen shown in Figure 9.5 is displayed:

FIGURE 9.5
Configuring a server update with YOU.

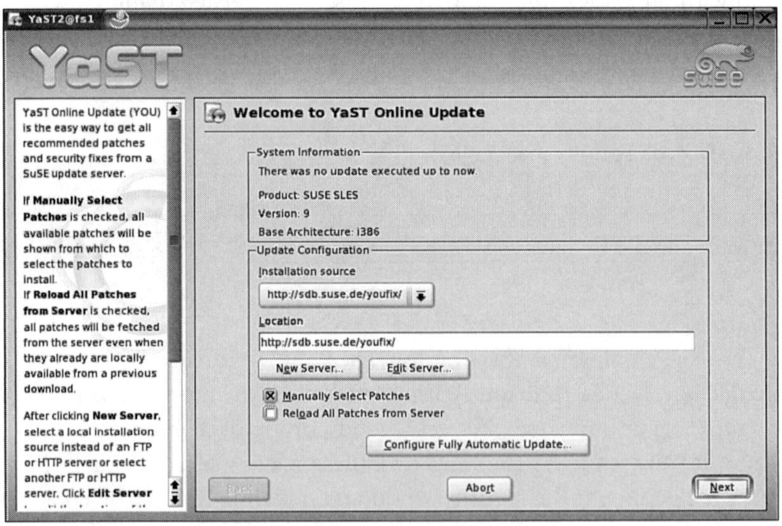

    d. Select **Configure Fully Automatic Update**.
    e. Mark **Enable Automatic Update**, as shown in Figure 9.6.

FIGURE 9.6
Configuring YOU to update the server automatically.

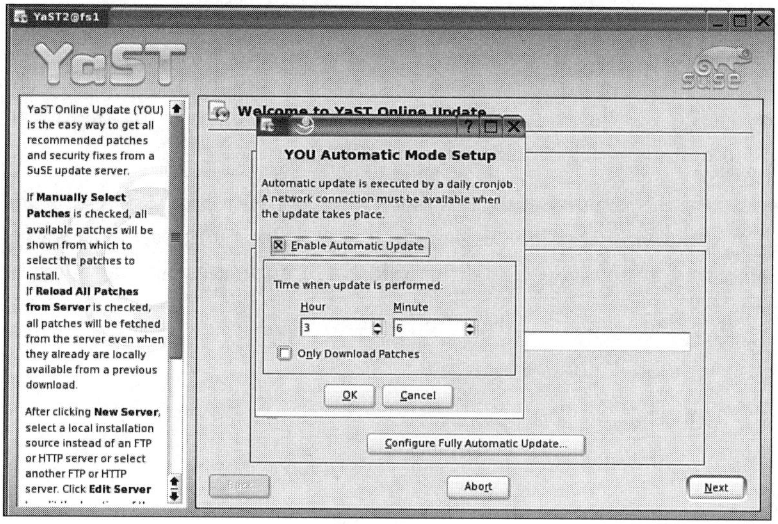

f. Configure when the update will occur; then select **OK**.

g. Select **Next**.

h. Select the **YOU HTTPS** patch; then select Accept.

NOTE

This YOU patch must be installed before you can install any system patches.

i. When prompted that the patches have been installed, select **Finish**.

j. Wait while SuSEconfig runs.

k. In YaST, select **Software, Online Update**.

l. In the Welcome screen, select Next.

m. When prompted, authenticate using the username and password you received in step 1.

n. Select the patches you want to download and install; then select **Accept**.

o. Wait while the patches are downloaded and installed.

p. When finished and SuSEconfig has been run, close YaST.

After you have this component of your server security plan taken care of, you need to move on to the next component, which is to document your system.

Document the Server

Let's all just admit it right up front—we hate documenting anything. It's tedious and it's boring. There's no getting around it. However, documenting your server may help you prevent an attack and it will definitely help you recover should one occur.

So how do you go about documenting your server? It's actually pretty simple. Just record various information about your server. This can be done with pen and paper or using a word processor. Either way, you should record the following information about your system:

- Purchase date and vendor contact information.
- System make, model, and serial number.
- System CPU model and specs.
- Memory configuration.
- Disk interfaces.
- Installed disks.
- Disk partitions and mount points from `/etc/fstab`.
- RAID configuration information.
- Installed network interfaces and associated parameters (IP address, subnet mask, sect).
- SLES version information.
- A list of installed packages and their version numbers.
- Backups of your `.conf` files from `/etc`.

Again, I know that this information isn't very interesting to compile. However, it can really save your hide in an emergency.

After you get your server documented, you next need to ensure that your server is physically secured.

Physically Secure the Server

A key point you need to remember is that all the virus scanners, intrusion detection systems, and firewalls in the world won't do you much good if your server is placed in a physical location where folks (such as employees, contractors, or visitors) have easy access to it. You need to make your server hardware as *inaccessible* as possible. A locked room that only a limited number of trusted people have keys to would be ideal.

My experience has been that larger organizations usually understand this principle very well. Their servers are locked away where only a select few can get at them. However, smaller companies tend to violate this principle all the time.

In my line of work, I visit a lot of different companies. I can't tell you how many times I've walked into a small organization's office and have discovered that they keep their server in an unoccupied cubicle, usually away from everyone else. One office I recently visited had their server sitting on the front desk next to the receptionist!

Why is this a problem? First of all, remember that your server probably contains your organization's most critical and valuable data. Consider the example I just gave you of a server sitting at the front desk next to the receptionist. How hard would it be for someone (such as a competitor, a corporate spy, or a plain old thief) to walk in, grab the whole system, and run out the door? It would be very easy; especially if the receptionist were away from the desk at the time.

In addition to the "smash and grab" scenario, locating your server in an easily accessible location makes it very easy for someone to access the terminal and keyboard. Now, we're all supposed to be good administrators and consistently log out whenever we leave the system, right? Well, you and I both know that this rule gets broken all the time. We're working along and find ourselves in need of a bathroom break and/or a caffeine fix. Rather than log out, we leave our system running and go take care of business, right? Admit it, you've done it!

Unfortunately, this practice makes it very easy for someone to wreak all kinds of havoc with your system. They could destroy data, steal data, load mischievous applications, steal password files, and alter log files to hide their tracks.

NOTE

In the Novell NetWare world, this can be a real problem because the server console prompt, by default, doesn't require any kind of authentication to load applications and services.

A few years ago, there was an application floating around the Internet called burglar.nlm that, when loaded, would create a hidden supervisor account that an intruder could use to gain full access to the system. All you needed was about three seconds of access to the console prompt to execute this attack.

The best way to keep this from happening is to keep your server in a locked, air-conditioned room that only you and a few others have keys to.

The practice I mentioned earlier of keeping the server in an unoccupied cubicle is really a bad idea. First, there's no door on the cubicle. Anyone, including employees, visitors, or contractors, has easy access to the system. In addition, when you put the server in a cubicle, it's easy for the intruder to stay hidden while they do their dirty work. Because no one works in the cubicle, no one looks in the cubicle (you know how cubicle life is). Intruders can easily work their mischief without drawing attention.

In addition to locking up the server, you should also consider implementing a GRUB password on the system. With a GRUB password in place, you must authenticate before the GRUB boot menu is displayed. This denies an intruder the ability to specify custom boot options in the GRUB boot menu. To do this, complete the following:

1. Open a terminal session and change to root.
2. At the shell prompt, enter **grub**.
3. Encrypt the password in the GRUB shell by entering **`md5crypt`** at the grub prompt.
4. At the password prompt, enter the GRUB password you want to use. You will be presented with a hashed version of the password, as shown in Figure 9.7.

FIGURE 9.7
Encrypted GRUB password.

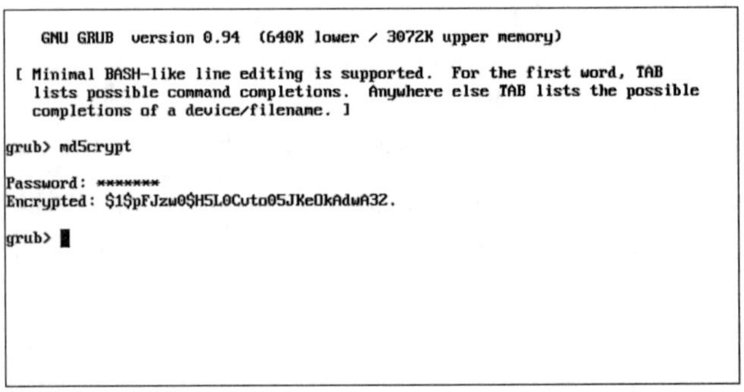

5. Start YaST and authenticate as your root user.
6. Select **System, Boot Loader Configuration**.
7. In the Boot Loader Setup screen, select **Edit Configuration Files**.
8. In the File Name drop-down list, ensure **`/boot/grub/menu.1st`** is selected.
9. Beneath the gfxmenu directive, add the following:

   ```
   password -md5 encrypted_password
   ```

   If possible, you should use the Copy/Paste functions of your system to avoid errors when entering the encrypted password portion of the directive. An example is shown in Figure 9.8.

FIGURE 9.8
Configuring a password in menu.lst.

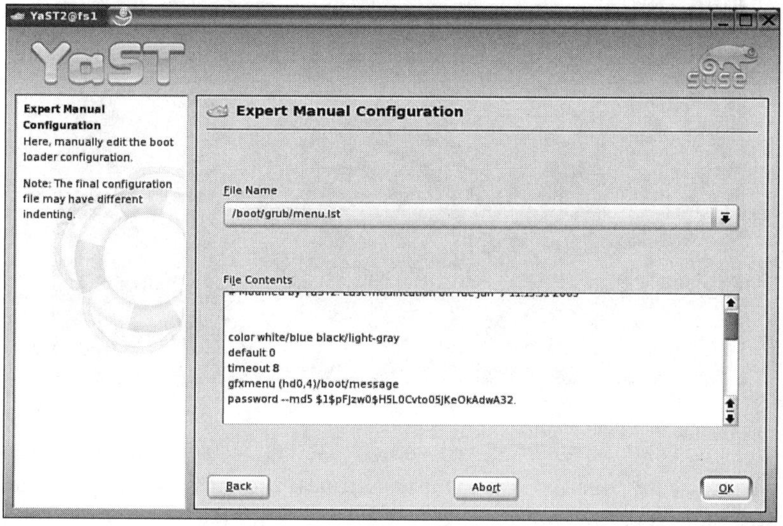

In this configuration, the system will boot as per normal. However, you will have to press **p** and enter a password in the GRUB menu screen to configure any boot options.

10. (Optional) If you want to require a password to boot from any GRUB menu option, add the **`lock`** to the end of every menu item you want to lock down, as shown next:

```
title linux
kernel (hd0,4)/boot/vmlinuz root=/dev/sda5 vga=791
initrd (hd0,4)/boot/initrd
lock
```

TIP

Use the lock directive with discretion. Although it does keep intruders out, it also makes it so that your system won't fully reboot without manual intervention.

11. Select **OK**, **Finish**.
12. Reboot your system. You should see a screen similar to that shown in Figure 9.9.

FIGURE 9.9
Password-protected GRUB menu.

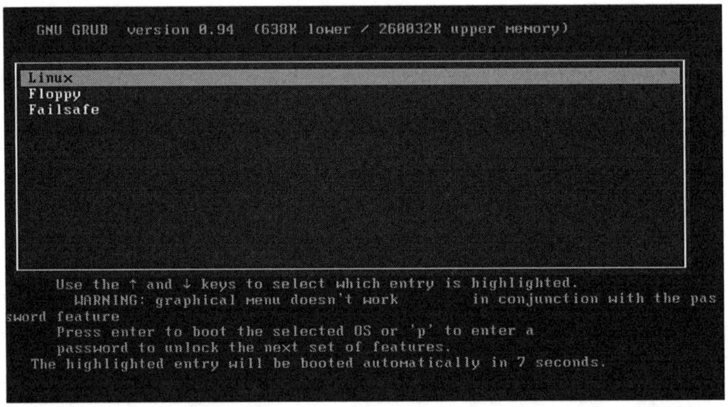

In addition to using a GRUB password, you should also jealously guard your root password. As you've probably heard over and over, you should never log in to your system directly as root. Why? For the reason I mentioned earlier. We should all remember to log out before we leave our desk, but the reality is that we just don't. We're in a hurry, we've got a lot to do, and we'll only be gone for a second anyway, right?

Leaving your desk while logged in as root is an open invitation to the mischievous or the malicious. Always log in as a regular user and use **su** or **sux** to change to root only when necessary. Before you leave your desk for any length of time, be sure to exit any root sessions you may have running. Better yet, log off completely.

Although we're talking about passwords and intruders, part of keeping your server physically secure is to implement a secure password policy. To get easy access to a server, intruders are always looking for passwords. You need to make their hunt as difficult as possible. Here's some things you should do:

- Educate your users about password security. The best password policy in the world is almost worthless if your users write down their passwords on a Post-It note and stick it to the monitor. This is another security issue I see over and over as I visit various companies. Anyone walking through some companies could gather a whole bunch of passwords by simply glancing at user workstations as they walk down a row of cubicles.
- Educate your users about social engineering security issues. Social engineering has become quite popular lately as an effective way to get passwords. Instead of mounting a sophisticated technological attack at the intended system, they call an employee on the

phone and pretend to be a fellow co-worker who has lost or forgotten his or her password. Most folks want to be a team player and help out, so they are quick to give out passwords. Any calls such as this should be forwarded to you or your help desk where the identity of the caller can be established.

- Educate your users about dumpster diving. This goes back to the sticky note issue. If your users swear off their monitor-mounted sticky notes and throw them in the trash, your network can still be at risk. Many intruders will sift through mountains of corporate garbage, looking for gold nuggets that provide them with the information they need to invade the network. Have your users shred any sensitive information instead of throwing it in the trash, especially those little yellow sticky notes with their passwords written on them!
- Educate your users about secure passwords. Users should never pick passwords that somehow relate to themselves. For example, they should never use their first name, their middle name, their spouse's name, their kid's name, their pet's name, or their birth date as a password. That kind of information is really easy to dig up. If an intruder wanted to break into their account, most likely they will start throwing all of the preceding passwords at the system to see if one will let him or her in.
- In addition to the previous point, train your users to use passwords that aren't in the dictionary. More sophisticated intruders will use *dictionary attacks* to compromise a system. These attacks simply throw words from the dictionary at the system to see if one will be accepted as a password. Your users should use a nondictionary term that includes both upper- and lowercase letters as well as numbers for a password. The problem with this approach is that these passwords are hard to remember. When you implement this policy, don't be surprised if you see those yellow sticky notes start to appear on monitors again!

With these tips in mind, let's shift gears and discuss securing services—the next element in your server security plan.

Secure Services on the Server

The network services we install and run are the reason we implement servers in the network in the first place. These provide the file, print, mail, web, FTP, and name resolution service that we need to make users productive. Unfortunately, many of them also introduce security holes into the server system.

Herein lies one of the great paradoxes of modern computer networking. I've often heard it said that it's really easy to create a perfectly secure server. First, you remove the network board, floppy drive, CD/DVD drive, and keyboard. Then, you lock it in a closet and destroy the key. That server is now truly secure! However, it's also completely useless.

One of your jobs as a network administrator is to decide whether the particular service you want to deploy is worth the security risks it brings with it. In some cases it is; in others, it isn't. If you do decide to deploy a particular service, you need to be aware of the vulnerabilities it introduces as well as the measures you can take to reduce the risk as much as possible. In this part of this chapter, we're going to look the following topics:

- Analyzing existing packages and services.
- Implementing encryption.

Let's look first at analyzing existing packages.

ANALYZE EXISTING PACKAGES AND SERVICES

One of the key problems with installing just about any Linux distribution is that it installs a whole bunch of default services, many of which you're not aware of nor do you need. In addition, some of these can introduce security risks.

For example, most distributions install some type of email MTA by default on the system. On Red Hat and other distributions, you get Sendmail installed. On SLES 9, you get Postfix. These MTAs seem relatively harmless, however, they can be used by an intruder against you.

My nephew is the Director of Security at a large ISP. He told me of an occasion where an intruder was able to hijack a root-user telnet session (we'll talk about the problems with telnet in just a minute) for one of the servers they host. The intruder knew that he would lose the connection as soon as the ISP figured out what had happened, so he used the Sendmail MTA to email the `/etc/passwd` and `/etc/shadow` to himself. This would allow him to use a cracker against them to extract the user account passwords, giving him easy access to the system in the future.

In this case, the customer using the hosted server didn't even need the Sendmail MTA. It was there by default and nobody did anything about it. The only reason the intruder in this case was caught was that my nephew intercepted the hijacked telnet session and observed what the intruder was doing.

The point is, one of the first things you should do is look at your system and see what services have been installed and decide whether you need them. One of the easiest ways to do this is to use the YaST Runlevel Editor module in Expert Mode, shown in Figure 9.10.

FIGURE 9.10
Viewing installed services in YaST.

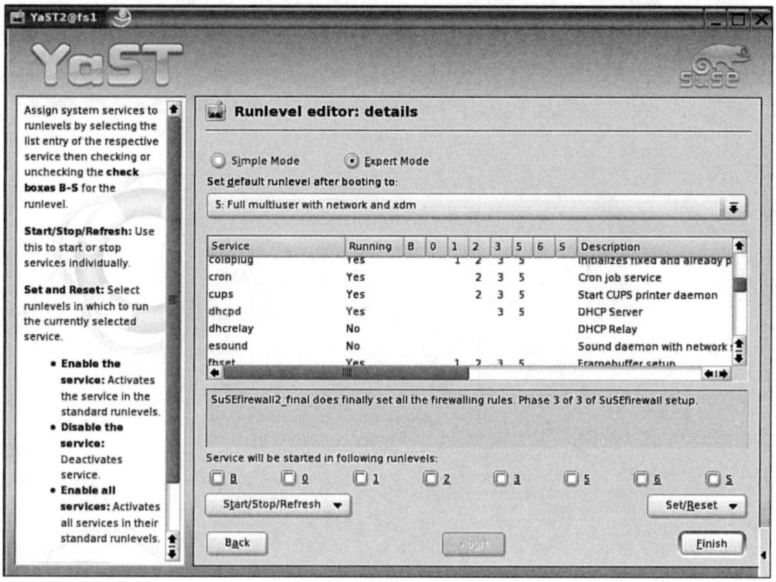

If you see a service running that you don't need, disable the service using the runlevel configuration settings. Better yet, uninstall the associated package.

In addition to this, you should also use the *nmap* utility to identify the ports that are being used on your server by the services running on it. The nmap utility is a powerful port scanner that will scan your server and let you know what IP ports are in use.

NOTE

If you want to learn more about nmap, visit http://www.insecure.org.

To use nmap, complete the following:

1. Using YaST, install the **nmap** and **nmap-gtk** packages on your server, as shown in Figure 9.11.
2. Start nmap completing the following:
   a. Open a terminal session and **sux –** to root.
   b. At the shell prompt, enter **nmapfe**. The nmap graphical interface is displayed, as shown in Figure 9.12.

FIGURE 9.11
Installing nmap packages.

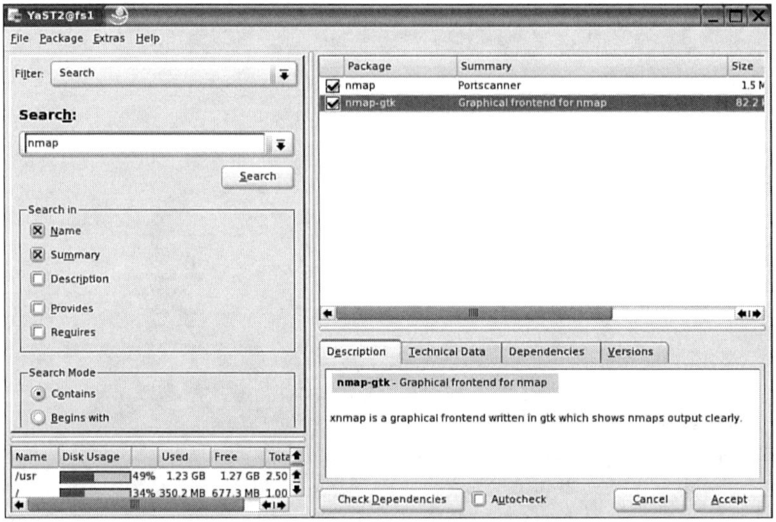

FIGURE 9.12
Using nmap.

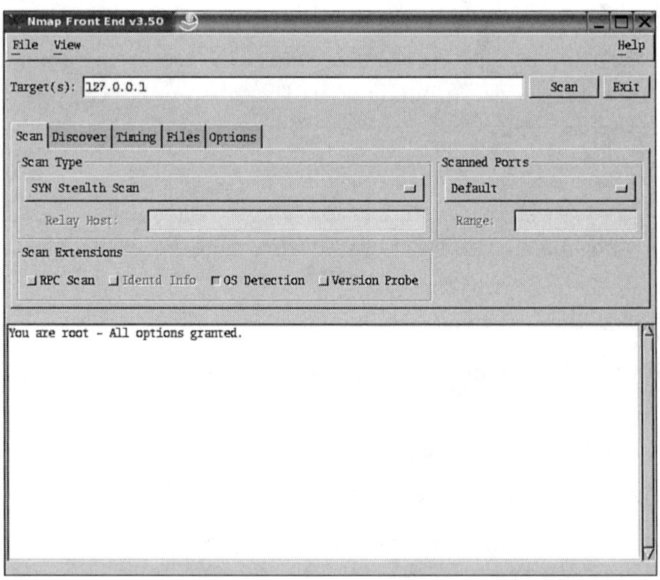

TIP

The nmap utility can also be run from a shell prompt. See the nmap man page for the available options.

3. Run a TCP port scan by completing the following:
   a. In the Target field, enter the *IP address* of your server.
   b. In the Scan Type drop-down list, select **Connect Scan**.
   c. In the Scanned Ports drop-down list, select **All**.
   d. Select **Scan**.
   e. Wait while ports are scanned (this may take a few minutes).
   f. Note the open TCP ports; as shown in Figure 9.13.

FIGURE 9.13
TCP port scan results.

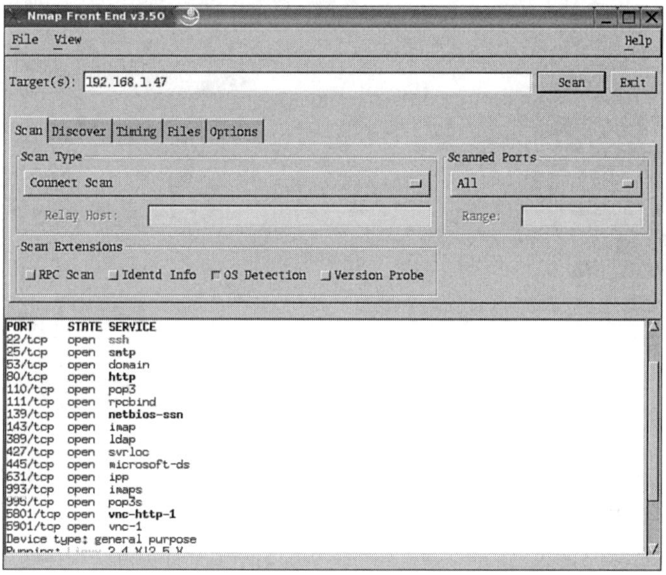

As you can see, many daemons are running on the server in Figure 9.13 because of all the products we've been configuring. For example, you can see the SMTP (port 25), DNS (port 53), POP3 (port 110), IMAP (143), NetBIOS (port 139), and IPP (port 631) services running in the nmap output.

4. Complete a UDP port scan by completing the following:
   a. In the Scan Type drop-down list, select **UDP Port Scan**.
   b. In the Scanned Ports drop-down list, select **All**.
   c. Select **Scan**.
   d. Wait while ports are scanned.
   e. Note the open UDP ports, as shown in Figure 9.14.

FIGURE 9.14
UDP port scan results.

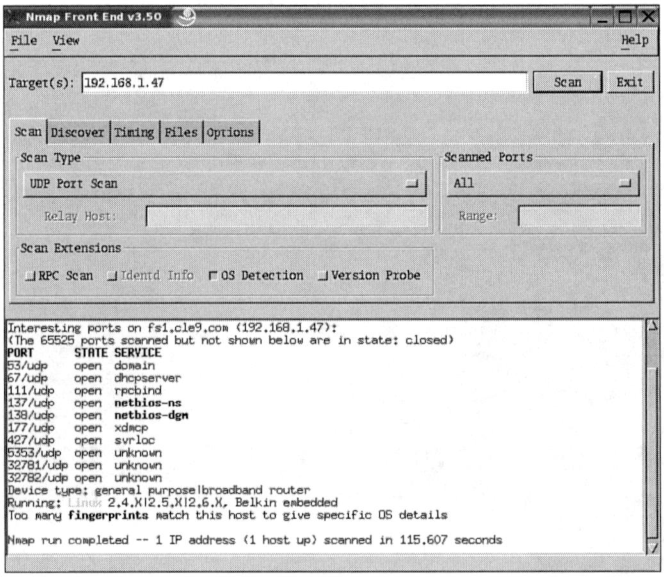

Using nmap, you can see that DNS (port 53), DHCP (port 67), and NetBIOS (ports 137 and 138) UDP ports are in use on the server in Figure 9.14.

Using nmap, you should analyze and document what ports are in use on your server. In addition, you should also review the packages installed on your server. This can be done using the YaST Install and Remove Software module with the Filter set to Selections, as shown in Figure 9.15.

FIGURE 9.15
Viewing installed packages in YaST.

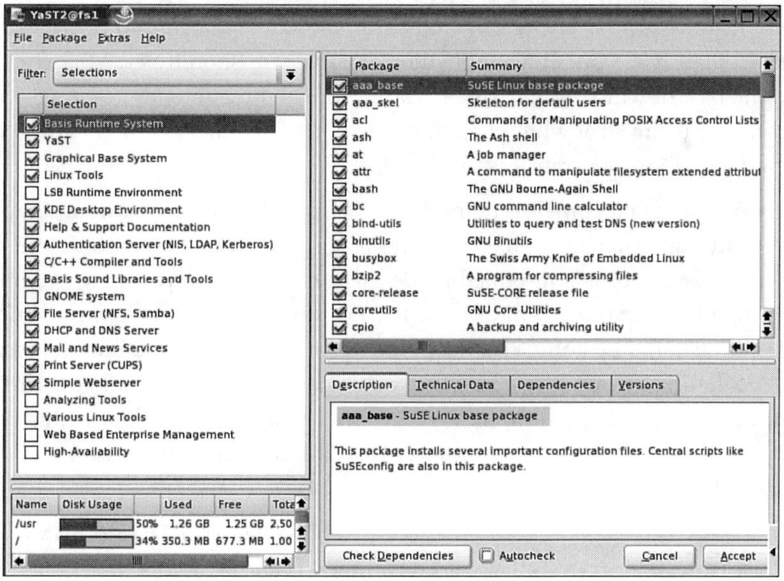

In the Selection field on the left, select each Selection and view the packages that it has installed on the right. If you see a package that you don't need or want, uninstall it. It will save space on your server and it may potentially reduce your security exposure.

When that is done, you should next review the services running on your system that you do, in fact, need and become familiar with the various security issues surrounding them. For example:

- telnet—In the old days, most Linux distributions installed the telnetd daemon by default during installation. The daemon was usually configured to run at most runlevels. The problem with this is that telnet is notoriously insecure. Everything you do with telnet is done clear-text, including login. Anyone running a sniffer, such as we covered in the previous chapter, could easily watch your entire session. They could capture your user login and password as well as your root user password if you used su - to change to root in the telnet session. For these reasons, telnet is usually *not* enabled by default in most Linux distributions today. If you need the type of remote access telnet provides, you should use ssh instead.

- FTP—Like telnet, FTP is very useful and very insecure. Just as with telnet, the FTP protocol transfers everything clear-text, including your username and password. If you need FTP functionality, you should consider disabling user-based logins via FTP and provide only anonymous access. The anonymous user should be allowed to download only, not upload. Obviously, if you allow anonymous logins, you should *never* place any sensitive data in the FTP download directory. If you need FTP functionality to move sensitive data, consider using sftp, which is part of the OpenSSH package. This utility provides encrypted FTP-like data transfers.
- SNMP—We discussed some of the problems with SNMP in the previous chapter. First of all, SNMP traps are considered insecure. If possible, you should configure your SNMP manager to operate in polled mode instead of using traps. As well, remember that community strings are sent as clear-text. If someone were to capture your read/write community string, they could use the SNMP service running on a remote host to change various configuration settings. The latest version of SNMP (version 3) uses a stronger authentication system. If you need SNMP functionality, you should use this version of the protocol. You should also block ports 161 and 162 on your firewall (we'll discuss how to do that in the next chapter).
- NIS—Ah, what can we say about good old NIS? Like telnet, FTP, and SNMP, NIS is notoriously insecure. Frankly, I would recommend not using it at all. It offers much more exposure to system passwords than I'm comfortable with. If you need distributed, replicated user-account functionality, go with OpenLDAP or (better yet) Novell's eDirectory instead.
- SMTP—Like many of the services we've talked about so far, your Postfix SMTP daemon uses no encryption or authentication by default. Fortunately, as we discussed earlier in this book, you can add the Cyrus saslauthd daemon to the system to rectify this problem.
- POP3 and IMAP—When implementing a POP3/IMAP service on your server, you should be sure to use a package that provides secure versions of these protocols. If you don't, user names and passwords are transferred clear-text. The Cyrus-IMAP and the WU-IMAP packages, which we implemented in an earlier chapter, both offer encrypted POP3 and IMAP services (which run on ports 995 and 993, respectively).

When you're done, you next need to perform a computer-based vulnerability analysis of your system that will inform you of any weaknesses in the current configuration of your SLES 9 system. To do this, you can use the *nessus* utility. This utility is a vulnerability scanner that can be run against your system to identify potential problems. To do this, complete the following:

1. Using YaST, install the nessus-core, libnasl, and nessus-libraries packages on your server; as shown in Figure 9.16.

FIGURE 9.16
Installing nessus on SLES 9.

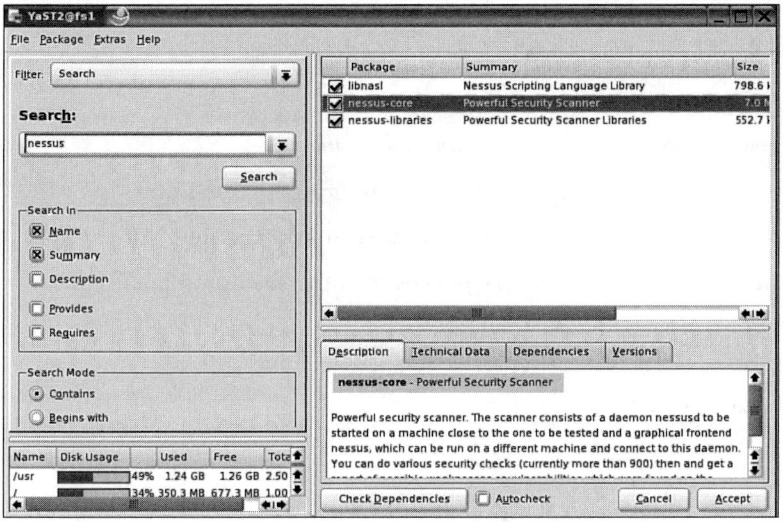

2. Open a terminal session and use **sux –** to change to root.
3. Create a nessus user by completing the following:
   a. At the shell prompt, enter **nessus-adduser**.
   b. At the login prompt, enter the *user account* you want to use for the nessus user.
   c. At the Authentication prompt, press **Enter**.
   d. When prompted, enter the password for the user account you just entered.
   e. When prompted to create a set of rules, press **Ctrl+d**.

TIP

Rules in nessus are used to restrict what the user can do on remote systems begin tested. To learn how to create nessus rules, see the nessus man page or visit http://www.nessus.org. There's also a great introduction to nessus available at http://www.securityfocus.com/infocus/1741.

   f. When prompted whether the configured parameters are OK, enter **y**.

4. Generate a nessus security certificate by completing the following:
   a. At the shell prompt, enter **nessus-mkcert**.
   b. When prompted, enter the CA certificate life time in *days*.
   c. When prompted, enter the server certificate life time in *days*.
   d. When prompted, enter your 2-character *country code*.
   e. When prompted, enter your *state* or province.
   f. When prompted, enter your *location*.
   g. When prompted, enter your *organization name*.
   h. When prompted that your certificate was created, press **Enter**.
5. Start the nessus daemon by entering **rcnessusd start** at the shell prompt.
6. Start the nessus client by entering **nessus &** at the shell prompt. The nessus interface is displayed, as shown in Figure 9.17.

FIGURE 9.17
Using the nessus client interface.

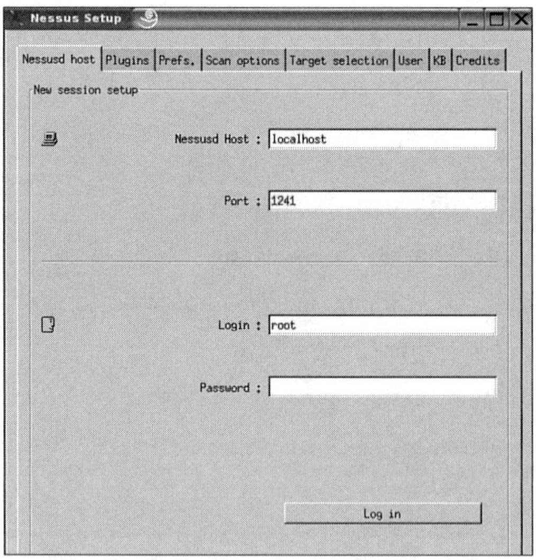

7. Configure a scan by completing the following:
   a. In the Login and Password fields, authenticate to the nessus server as the *user* you created previously.
   b. In the SSL Setup screen, mark **Display and Remember the Server Certificate**; then select **OK**.

c. When prompted, accept the SSL certificate by selecting **Yes**.

d. When prompted that some plug-ins have been disabled, select **OK**.

e. Select the **Prefs** tab. Notice that nessus can be configured to run nmap scans, as shown in Figure 9.18.

FIGURE 9.18
nmapintegration with nessus.

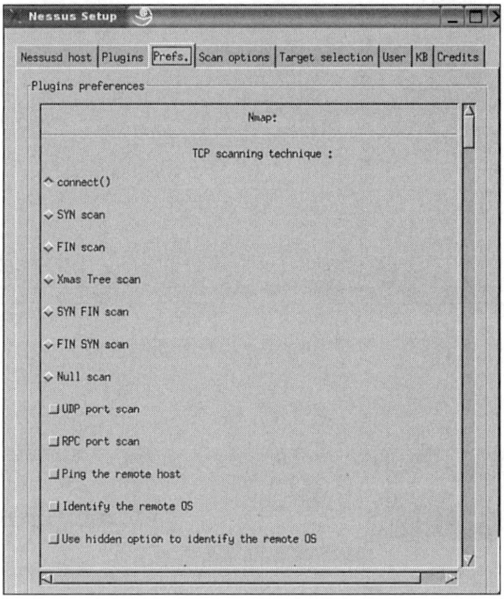

f. Select the *nmap options* you want to run.

g. Select the **Target Selection** tab.

h. In the Target(s) field, enter the *IP address* of the host you want to scan.

i. Start the scan by selecting **Start the Scan** at the bottom of the nessus window.

j. Wait while the scan is run. This may take up to 15 minutes to complete. When it's done, the screen in Figure 9.19 is displayed.

k. To view the results, select your *subnet* in the Subnet field; then select the *host* you scanned in the Host field. A list of warnings and notes will appear in the Port field.

l. In the Port field, select the *item* you want to view; then select the *item* in the Severity field. The text of the note or warning is displayed, as shown in Figure 9.20.

FIGURE 9.19
The nessus report.

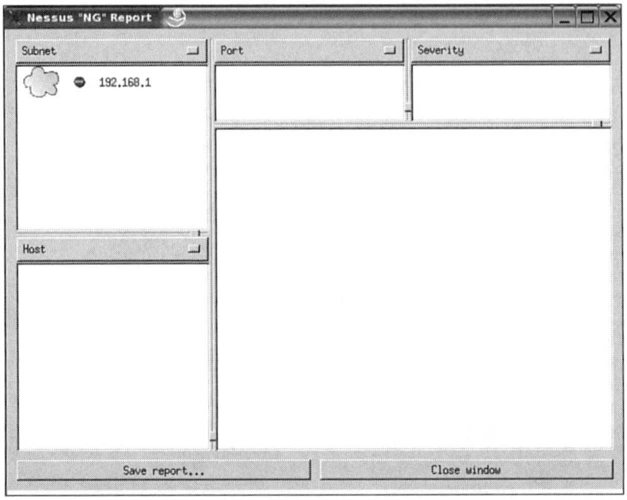

FIGURE 9.20
The nessus report detail.

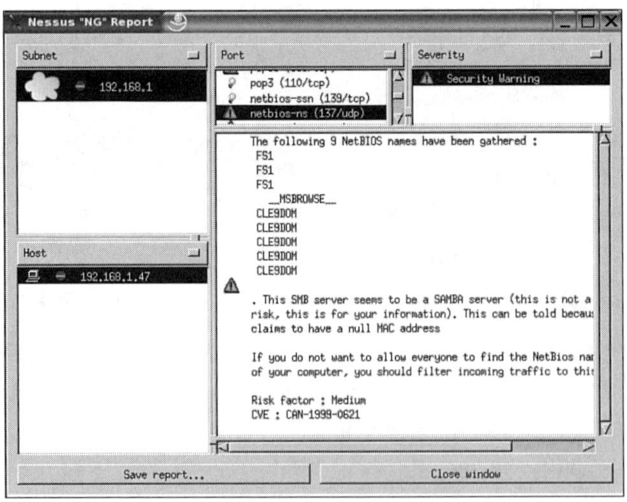

As you've probably noticed, one of the key weaknesses associated with many of the services we've discussed in the chapter is that they transfer data clear-text. For many protocols, we can add a layer of security using encryption. Let's discuss how encryption works next.

IMPLEMENT ENCRYPTION

Hearken back with me, if you will, to your grade-school days. Did you ever pass notes to your friends? I know that in the modern era of wireless phones with text messaging this may seem archaic; but when I was a kid, notes were a vital means of communication at school.

After all, you had important business to conduct, right? You needed to determine where you were going to meet to play football and who was going to get to choose teams. Recess was only 20 minutes long and you had to have all these things ironed out before the bell rang!

If your school was like mine, these extracurricular forms of communication were strictly forbidden in class. If a teacher intercepted a poorly handled note pass, you could be sure it would be read in front of the class, which could be a fate worse than death.

To prevent this, my buddies and I developed codes to encrypt our notes. In the event that one of them was intercepted, we could rest assured that the teacher wouldn't be able to read it to the rest of the class. Being in the fourth and fifth grades, our encoding mechanisms were somewhat primitive. For the most part, we used two codes. The first one involved skewing the alphabet down a couple of letters, as shown next:

```
Z A B C D E F G H I J K L M ....
A B C D E F G H I J K L M N ....
```

We would use the bottom line for the clear text and the top line for the cypher text. For example, the word "JAKE" would come out "IZJD" when coded.

If the teacher started getting wise to this code, we would switch to a different code using numbers and letters, as shown next:

```
26 1 2 3 4 5 6 7 8 9 10 11 ....
A  B C D E F G H I J  K  L ....
```

Using this code, my friend Jake's name would be encoded as 9-26-10-4. This basic concept can be used to encode network communications as well. Let's talk about how this is done next.

HOW ENCRYPTION WORKS

In today's world of computing, the need to scramble the contents of network communications is preeminent. Using the network monitoring tools discussed in the previous chapter, it's relatively easy for a mischievous individual to sniff out network transmissions and read them. If they contained sensitive information, such as usernames, passwords, financial data, credit card numbers, or personal information, we could have a real problem on our hands.

To protect this information, we need to encrypt critical network communications. Unlike the simple codes I used in the fourth grade, network cryptography today uses much more sophisticated encoding mechanisms. There are two general approaches to doing this:

- Symmetric Encryption—For my fourth grade encryption system to work, my buddies and I all had to have the same key to encrypt and decrypt our messages. This is called *symmetric encryption*. The same key is used to encrypt and decrypt the message. That means the sender and the receiver both need to have the same key. One of the difficulties with symmetric encryption is how to securely distribute the key to all the parties needing to communicate with each other. For example, if you've ever configured a WEP key on a wireless network, you know that you must generate the key on the wireless access point, copy it to a disk or a USB thumb drive, sneaker-net it to the wireless client, and paste the WEP key in the configuration of the wireless NIC. Examples of cryptographic standards that use symmetric encryption include the Data Encryption Standard (DES), Advanced Encryption Standard (AES), and Blowfish.
- Asymmetric Encryption—Unlike symmetric encryption, asymmetric encryption uses two keys instead of one: the *public* key and the *private* key. Data that has been encoded with the private key can be decoded only with the public key, and vice versa. For this reason, asymmetric encryption is frequently referred to as *public key cryptography*. Rivest Shamir Adleman (RSA) and the Digital Signature Algorithm (DSA) are examples of cryptographic standards that use asymmetric encryption. This type of encryption is used to encrypt the contents of network communications as well as generate digital signatures. In a *digital signature*, the contents of a message aren't encrypted. Instead, the private key is used by the sender to create an encrypted *hash* of the message. This hash is sent along with the message to the recipient. The recipient generates its own hash of the message. Then it uses the public key to decrypt the hash sent with the message. If the hashes are the same, the recipient can be assured that the message arrived without being altered en route.

An important factor to keep in mind when selecting any encryption scheme is the number of bits used to encode the data. Older encryption schemes used 40 or 56 bits to encode data. In today's computing world, this simply isn't strong enough. A fast Pentium IV PC from your local discount retail store can crack 40-bit encryption in a relatively short amount of time. When selecting an encryption scheme, you should pick one that supports a minimum of 128 bits.

Because of its flexibility, public key cryptography is the most widely used method for encrypting data. It allows us to easily scramble and send sensitive information over a public network, such as the Internet. If you've ever bought anything online from an e-commerce web site, you've used public key cryptography. When you sent your credit card number, the vendor's web site should have used secure HTTPS to encrypt your data so that prying eyes would be unable to read it.

One of the problems associated with public key cryptography is the issue of how to verify that the public key is legitimate. To do that, we use a certificate authority (CA). Let's talk about how CAs work next.

HOW CAS WORK

The CA is a network service that is responsible for issuing and managing encryption keys. When a key pair is requested from a CA, it generates a public and private key simultaneously, using a specified encryption scheme, such as RSA or DSA.

The private key in the pair is given only to the requesting entity. It is not shared with anyone else. The public key in the pair, on the other hand, is made available to anyone who needs it. The key role of the CA is to verify that parties involved in an encrypted exchange are who they say they are.

CAs do this by issuing *public key certificates*. A public key certificate is a digital message signed with the private key that provides a cryptographic binding between the public key and the organization that owns the private key. A certificate contains the following information:

- The name of the organization.
- The public key of the organization.
- The expiration date of the certificate.
- The certificate's serial number.
- The name of the CA that signed the certificate.
- A digital signature from the CA.

In this regard, there are two types of CAs that you will encounter:

- Internal CAs—An internal CA is one that is maintained by an organization for internal use. When you installed your SLES 9 server, the OpenSSL package was used to create a CA on your system. This CA is used to create keys and issue certificates for services running on the server. If you will recall the Postfix exercise you completed earlier in this book, the KMail client issued a warning when you accessed your WU-IMAP server over a secure connection. It said the certificate it received was valid, but it didn't come from a trusted CA. That's because the certificate came from the CA on your own server. For internal communications, this doesn't represent a serious issue. We trust ourselves.
- External CAs—If you're going to be dealing with external parties, such as with an e-commerce website, an internal CA won't suffice. External parties need assurance from a trusted, objective third party that the certificates they are receiving are legitimate and that you are who you say you are. This is done by using an external CA, such as

VeriSign or GTECyberTrust. These organizations perform the same functions as an internal CA. However, they are globally trusted. For example, suppose you were to access a secure website on the Internet using the Firefox web browser. If the site is using an external CA, you won't be presented with the warning that you saw when using your internal CA. That's because your browser has been preconfigured with a list of trusted CAs, as shown in Figure 9.21.

FIGURE 9.21
Trusted CAs in Firefox.

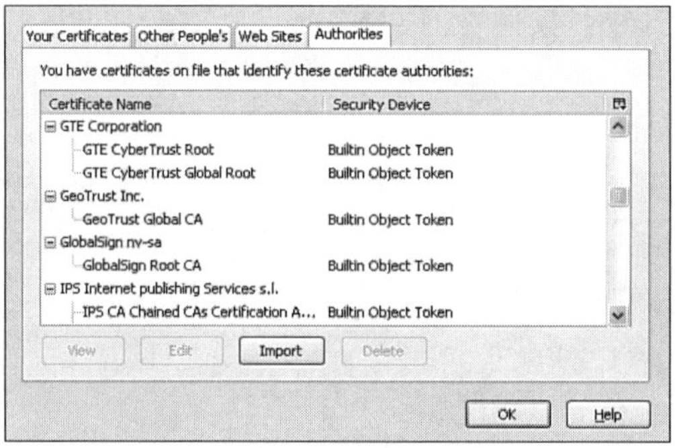

Right about now your head is probably swimming. My experience has been that cryptography is one of the most difficult concepts to teach. Let's look at an example to clear the fog.

Suppose you're using a web browser to visit www.hotcomputerparts.com and you've found a super-fast wireless access point that you just can't live without. You've put it in your shopping cart and are in the process of checking out from the online store. The process shown in Figure 9.22 occurs as you submit your credit card information to the e-commerce web server.

As you enter your credit card information in the browser window and click Submit, the following happens:

1. Your browser requests the public key for www.hotcomputerparts.com from the external CA.
2. The CA returns the public key to the browser, which then encrypts the submission.
3. The browser sends the encrypted message to www.hotcomputerparts.com.
4. The web server at the other end then uses its private key to decrypt the transmission.

FIGURE 9.22
How public key encryption works.

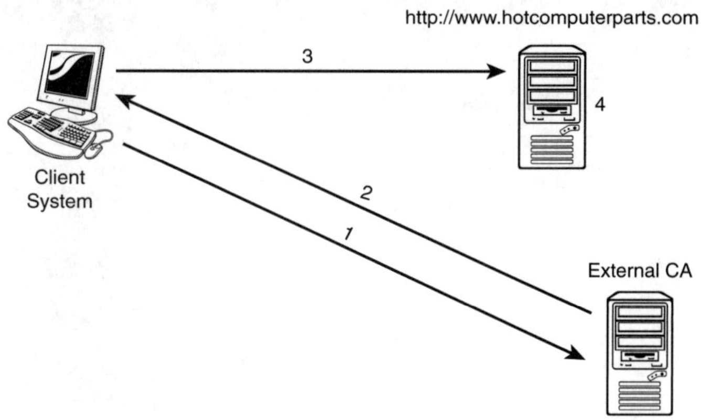

The whole reason this process works is because only the private key can decrypt a message encoded by the public key. Sure, anyone, including a hacker, could get the public key for the transaction in Figure 9.22; that's how the system works. However, they couldn't decrypt the credit card transmission even if they had it. That can be done only by the private key, which is never openly transmitted.

Let's now look at how you can use OpenSSL on SLES 9 to manage certificates for your system.

MANAGING CERTIFICATES ON SLES 9

When you installed your SLES 9 system, a CA was automatically created on the server; as shown in Figure 9.23.

This is an internal CA. You can use it to encrypt communications with the server. However, as we mentioned earlier, most clients, such as KMail or Firefox, will not see this CA as a trusted CA. Therefore, it will accept the certificates generated by your CA, but not without generating a warning.

Notice that the YaST screen in Figure 9.23 uses the term "Root CA." That's because CAs can be arranged into a hierarchy. You can create subordinate CAs below the root CA. However, the root CA still signs all certificates created by its subordinate CAs. One of the things you need to know how to do for your CLE 9 certification exam is create a subordinate CA.

FIGURE 9.23
The CA on your SLES 9 server.

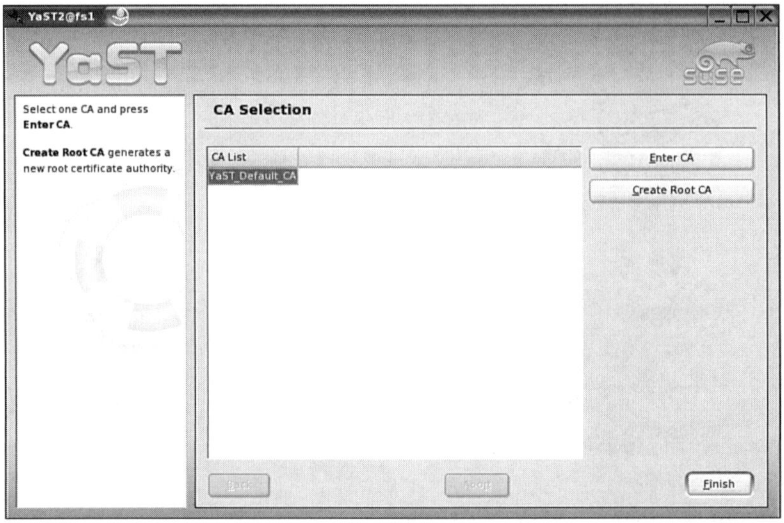

To do this, you would complete the following:

1. In YaST, select **Security and Users, CA Management**. The screen in Figure 9.23 is displayed.
2. In the CA List, select the *root* CA for which you want to create a subordinate CA.
3. Select **Enter CA**.
4. When prompted for your CA password, enter your *root password*. The screen in Figure 9.24 is displayed.
5. Select **Advanced, Create SubCA**. The screen in Figure 9.25 is displayed.
6. In the CA Name and Common Name fields, enter the *name* of the CA.
7. Next to the Add button, enter the *email address* of the server administrator; then select **Add**.
8. Enter your *organization* and *locality information* in the respective fields.
9. Select **Next**. The screen in Figure 9.26 is displayed.

FIGURE 9.24
Viewing the root CA.

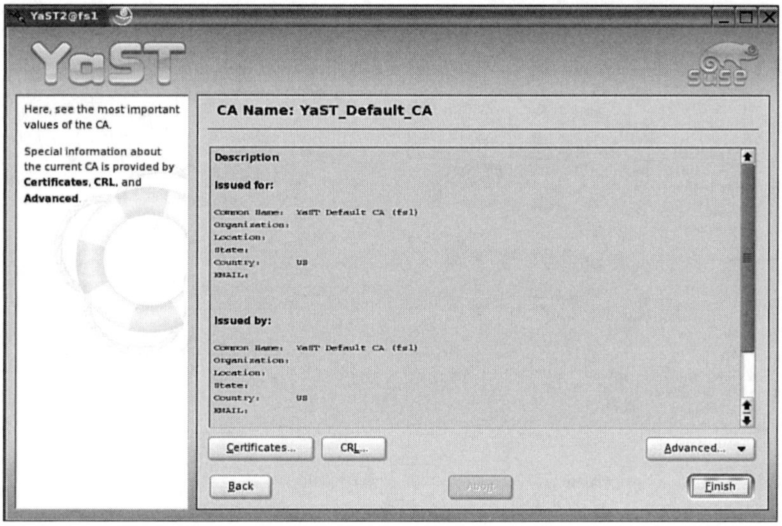

FIGURE 9.25
Creating a subordinate CA, part 1.

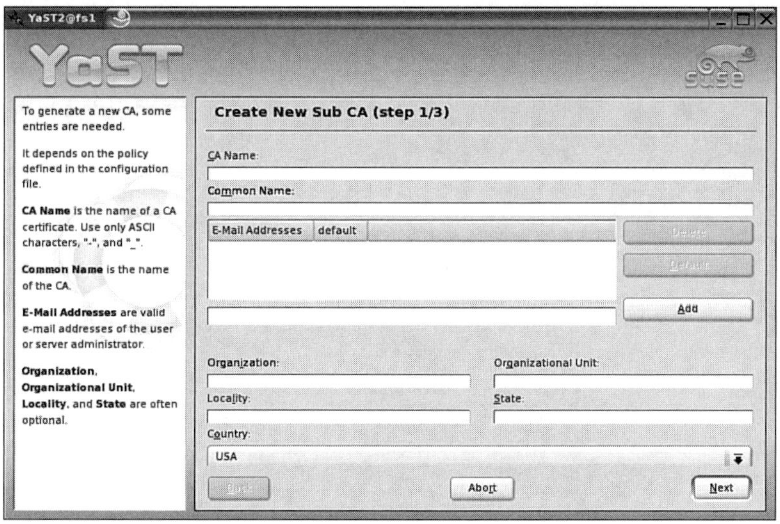

FIGURE 9.26
Creating a subordinate CA, part 2.

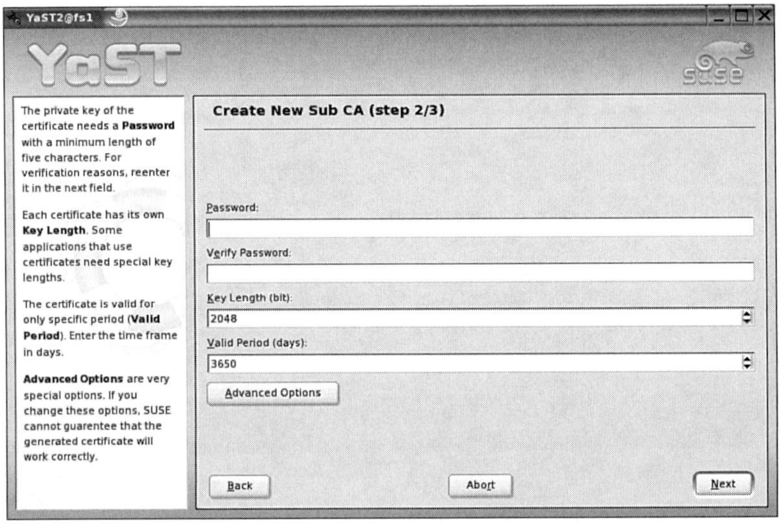

10. In the Password fields, enter a *password*.
11. Select **Next**. The screen in Figure 9.27 is displayed:

FIGURE 9.27
Creating a subordinate CA, part 3.

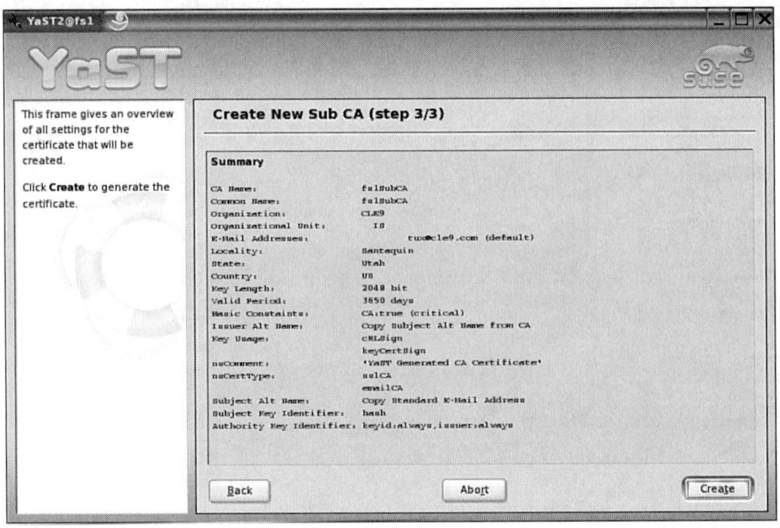

12. Select **Create**.
13. Select **Finish**.

You can also create a second root CA. This is done by selecting the **Create Root CA** option, shown in Figure 9.23. The steps for creating the root CA are the same from there as for creating a subordinate CA.

After you have your CAs in place, you can use them to generate certificates that services running on your server can use to encrypt data. In fact, you've already done this several times in earlier exercises in this course. Remember those long `openssl` commands? You can accomplish the same task in YaST (and it is a lot easier). To do this, complete the following:

1. Start YaST.
2. Select **Security and Users, CA Management**.
3. In the CA List, select the *CA* you want to use to generate the certificate.
4. Select **Enter CA**.
5. When prompted, enter your CA *password*.
6. In the CA Properties screen, select **Certificates**. The screen in Figure 9.28 is displayed:

FIGURE 9.28
CA properties.

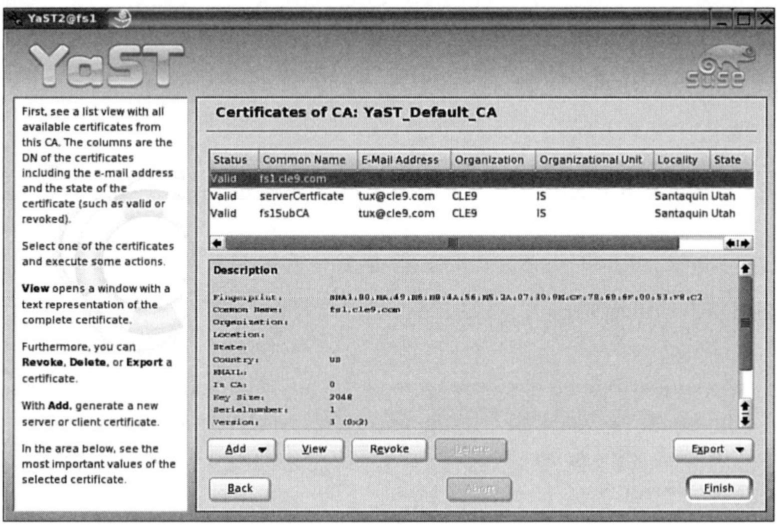

7. Select **Add, Add Server Certificate**.
8. In the Common Name field, enter a *name* for the certificate.
9. Next to the Add button, enter the *email address* of the server administrator; then select **Add**.
10. Enter your *organization* and *locality information* in the respective fields.
11. Select **Next**.
12. In the Password fields, enter a *password*.
13. Select **Next**. The screen in Figure 9.29 is displayed:

FIGURE 9.29
Creating a new server certificate.

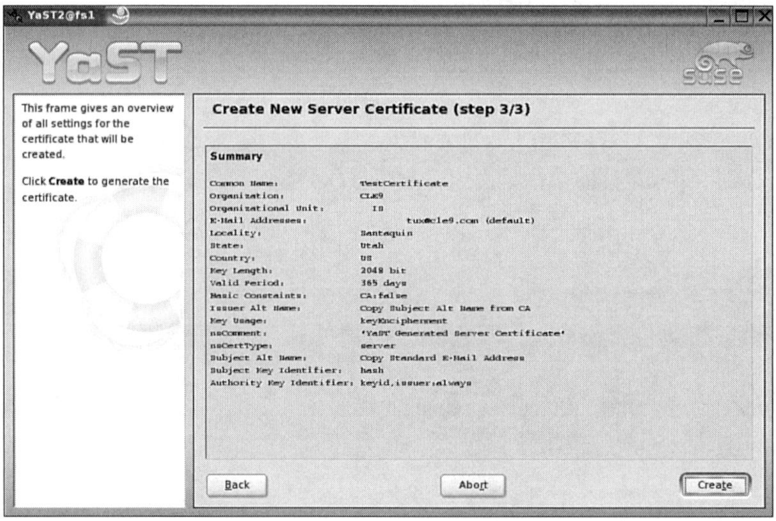

14. Select **Create**.
15. Select **Finish, Finish, Finish**.

With cryptography under our belts, we now need to shift our focus for the remainder of this chapter. Up to this point, we've been talking about preventative measures you can take to protect your server by creating a server security plan. Now we need to talk about how to monitor the system to detect intruders.

Monitoring the Server

TEST OBJECTIVE COVERED:

4. Detect intruders.

After you've got your system up and secured using your server security plan, you need to keep an eye on things to try to detect any attacks on your system. Whenever I introduce the topic of intrusion detection, many people get really excited, thinking we're going to talk about some high-tech, super-sleuthing gadget that will catch intruders in their tracks.

In reality, however, most of the intrusion detection process involves relatively simple and sometimes mundane legwork on your part. It also takes a great deal of intuition as you try to identify something that appears out of place or unusual. I can help teach you the first part. However, the second part is completely up to you. How do you develop the intuition? Observation and practice!

In this part of the chapter, we're going to discuss how we can detect intruders by doing the following:

- Analyzing log files.
- Implementing an intrusion detection system (IDS).

Let's start by talking about how to analyze log files.

Analyzing Log Files

Much like a crime scene, detecting intruders involves looking for clues they left behind. One of your best resources in this regard is the voluminous log files your SLES 9 system maintains. The big question is what to look for.

In this chapter, I can give you a list of log files to look at as well as recommend some tools that you can use to sift through all the information in them. However, much like a crime detective, you have to develop your own intuition that tells you when something looks suspicious. The best way to develop this intuition is to spend a lot of time reviewing your log files. This will help you develop a sense of what is normal for your network, helping you spot that which is not. With that in mind, let's look at four log files you can analyze to identify suspicious activity:

- `/var/log/wtmp`—This file contains a list of all the users who have authenticated to the system. The file itself is a binary file. To view it, use the `last` utility from a shell prompt. Sample output from last is shown in Figure 9.30.

FIGURE 9.30
Analyzing logins with last.

```
fs1:/var/log # last -a |more
tux      :0          Tue Jun  7 11:41   still logged in    console
reboot   system boot Tue Jun  7 11:38          (23:15)     2.6.5-7.97-default
tux      :0          Tue Jun  7 11:28 - 11:33  (00:04)     console
reboot   system boot Tue Jun  7 11:25          (00:08)     2.6.5-7.97-default
tux      :0          Mon May 30 15:25 - 11:22 (7+19:57)    console
reboot   system boot Mon May 30 15:23         (7+19:59)    2.6.5-7.97-default
tux      :0          Mon May 30 15:18 - 15:19  (00:01)     console
tux      :1/fs1      Wed May 25 17:45 - 17:53  (00:08)     fs1.cle9.com
tux      :1/fs1      Tue May 24 15:59 - 16:12  (00:12)     fs1.cle9.com
tux      :2/fs1      Tue May 24 15:47 - 15:58  (00:11)     fs1.cle9.com
tux      :1/fs1      Tue May 24 14:04 - 15:54  (01:49)     fs1.cle9.com
tux      :0          Tue May 24 09:26 - 15:17 (6+05:51)    console
tux      :1/fs1      Thu May 19 09:49 - 13:04 (1+03:15)    fs1.cle9.com
tux      :1/fs1      Thu May 19 09:42 - 09:48  (00:06)     fs1.cle9.com
tux      :1/fs1      Thu May 19 09:31 - 09:41  (00:10)     fs1.cle9.com
tux      :2/fs1      Wed May 18 13:59 - 14:03  (00:03)     fs1.cle9.com
tux      :1/fs1      Wed May 18 13:56 - 13:59  (00:02)     fs1.cle9.com
tux      :1/fs1      Wed May 18 12:59 - 13:40  (00:40)     fs1.cle9.com
jcorry   :0          Mon May 16 13:59 - 09:25 (7+19:26)    console
reboot   system boot Mon May 16 13:57        (14+01:22)    2.6.5-7.97-default
jcorry   :0          Mon May 16 13:26 - 13:55  (00:28)     console
tux      :1/fs1      Wed May  4 14:48 - 16:35  (01:46)     fs1.cle9.com
--More--
```

This utility displays the users who authenticated, when they logged in, when they logged out, and where they logged in from. Review this file and look for anything that appears unusual, such as logins that occurred in the middle of the night or rapid, multiple logins.

- `/var/log/faillog`—This log file contains a list of users whose authentication attempts have failed at some point. This is a very useful file for detecting dictionary attacks, which spew tons of dictionary terms as passwords. Like the wtmp file, faillog is a binary file. To view it, you need to use the **`faillog`** utility. Sample output from the faillog file is shown in Figure 9.31.

FIGURE 9.31
Analyzing failed logins with faillog.

```
fs1:~ # faillog
Username    Failures  Maximum  Latest
root               1        0  Wed Jun  8 11:15:35 -0600 2005 on tty2
dcoughanour        1        0  Wed Jun  8 11:15:45 -0600 2005 on tty2
jcorry             1        0  Wed Jun  8 11:15:53 -0600 2005 on tty2
fs1:~ #
```

This utility displays users who tried to authenticate, how many times they failed to login, and when the last unsuccessful attempt occurred. Review this file and look for anything that appears unusual, such as an abnormally high number of failed logins. Pay special attention if this occurred late at night.

- `/var/log/lastlog`—This log file contains a list of all the users in the system and when they last logged in. Like the wtmp file, lastlog is a binary file. To view it, you use the **`lastlog`** utility from the command line. Sample output from lastlog is shown in Figure 9.32.

FIGURE 9.32
Analyzing logins with lastlog.

```
fs1:/var/log # lastlog |more
Username         Port     From             Latest
root             :0       console          Wed Apr  6 09:20:28 -0600 2005
bin                                        **Never logged in**
daemon                                     **Never logged in**
lp                                         **Never logged in**
mail                                       **Never logged in**
news                                       **Never logged in**
uucp                                       **Never logged in**
games                                      **Never logged in**
man                                        **Never logged in**
at                                         **Never logged in**
wwwrun                                     **Never logged in**
squid                                      **Never logged in**
ftp                                        **Never logged in**
named                                      **Never logged in**
postfix                                    **Never logged in**
vscan                                      **Never logged in**
pop                                        **Never logged in**
sshd                                       **Never logged in**
mailman                                    **Never logged in**
ntp                                        **Never logged in**
ldap                                       **Never logged in**
--More--
```

- `/var/log/messages`—Yep, you can also use the good old messages log file to try to identify intrusion attempts. As you know, this file is loaded with good stuff, only some of which is related to authentication. If you want to find only failed login attempts, use grep to isolate the relevant entries. For example, entering **`less /var/log/messages | grep login`** would produce the output shown in Figure 9.33.

FIGURE 9.33
Analyzing logins with messages.

```
fs1:~ # less /var/log/messages |grep login
Jun  8 11:15:35 fs1 login[3720]: FAILED LOGIN 1 FROM /dev/tty2 FOR root, Authent
ication failure
Jun  8 11:15:45 fs1 login[3720]: pam_ldap: error trying to bind as user "uid=dco
ughanour,ou=people,dc=cle9,dc=com" (Invalid credentials)
Jun  8 11:15:45 fs1 login[3720]: FAILED LOGIN 2 FROM /dev/tty2 FOR dcoughanour,
Authentication failure
Jun  8 11:15:53 fs1 login[3720]: pam_ldap: error trying to bind as user "uid=jco
rry,ou=people,dc=cle9,dc=com" (Invalid credentials)
Jun  8 11:15:53 fs1 login[3720]: FAILED LOGIN SESSION FROM /dev/tty2 FOR jcorry,
 Authentication failure
fs1:~ #
```

The log files listed previously are great for detecting unauthorized access that happened in the past. If you need to check on what's happening right now on your system, you can use the **who** command from a shell prompt to see who is currently logged in to your system, as shown in Figure 9.34.

FIGURE 9.34
Analyzing currently logged-in users with who.

```
fs1:~ # who -H
NAME     LINE         TIME             COMMENT
tux      :0           Jun  8 11:11 (console)
fs1:~ #
```

You can also use `finger` to see who's currently logged in to the system, as shown in Figure 9.35.

FIGURE 9.35
Analyzing currently logged-in users with finger.

```
fs1:~ # finger
Login     Name            Tty      Idle  Login Time   Where
tux       Tux Penguin     :0       342d     Wed 11:11 console
fs1:~ #
```

If you're dealing with an inexperienced intruder, he or she will leave footprints all over in these log files. However, smart intruders will, once authenticated to the system, try to erase their tracks by altering the log files. If you're dealing with this type of intruder, you may never notice their attack unless you take steps to make your log files inaccessible. You can do this by redirecting logging to a different Linux server on your network. To accomplish this, complete the following:

1. On your server, open a terminal session and use **su –** to switch to root.
2. Open `/etc/syslog.conf` in a text editor, such as vi.
3. Add a line to the beginning of the file that reads as follows:
   ```
   *.*                    @IP_Address_of_loghost
   ```

   For example, in Figure 9.36, all messages logged by the syslogd daemon are being redirected to a host with an IP address of 192.168.1.48:

FIGURE 9.36
Redirecting log files.

```
# /etc/syslog.conf - Configuration file for syslogd(8)
#
# For info about the format of this file, see "man syslog.conf".
#
*.*                                  @192.168.1.48
#
#
```

4. Restart syslogd.
5. To configure the remote system to receive logs, complete the following:
   a. In a text editor, open `/etc/sysconfig/syslog`.
   b. Scroll down to the SYSLOGD_PARAMS directive.
   c. Set the value of the SYSLOGD_PARAMS directive to **"-r"**, as shown in Figure 9.37.

FIGURE 9.37
Configuring a remote host to receive log files.

```
## Path:                System/Logging
## Description:         System logging
## Type:                list(0,1,2,3,4,5,6,7)
## Default:             1
## Config:              ""
## ServiceRestart:      syslog
#
# Default loglevel for klogd
#
KERNEL_LOGLEVEL=1

## Type:                string
## Default:             ""
## Config:              ""
## ServiceRestart:      syslog
#
# if not empty: parameters for syslogd
# for example SYSLOGD_PARAMS="-r -s my.dom.ain"
#
SYSLOGD_PARAMS="-r"

## Type:                string
## Default:             -2
-- INSERT --                                        20,20        Top
```

   d. Save the changes and exit the file.
   e. Run SuSEconfig to apply the changes
   f. Restart syslogd.

In addition to analyzing log files, you can also implement an Intrusion Detection System (IDS) on your server to catch intruders as they try to infiltrate your system. Let's talk about how to implement IDS next.

Implementing an IDS

The concept of IDS is somewhat new in the networking world. However, IDSs are becoming extremely popular. Basically, an IDS works in a manner similar to antivirus software you may already be familiar with. Antivirus software works by looking for patterns in files known to indicate the presence of a virus.

A network IDS operates by monitoring network traffic, looking for patterns in the transmissions that indicate suspicious activity is under way. Just as virus definitions need to be updated regularly, most IDS packages also require their attack definitions to be updated regularly. Most IDS packages can detect the following:

- Unauthorized access attempts
- Denial of Service (DoS) attacks
- Network reconnaissance

TIP

Other IDSs don't use predefined patterns. Instead, they monitor the network for a period of time, developing a baseline. Then they look for traffic that doesn't fit the baseline and analyze it to see if an attack is under way.

Some IDSs can be linked into your network firewall. When these systems detect an attack or an intrusion, they can be configured to contact your firewall and immediately shut down the errant communications. Pretty cool, huh?

IDSs, because they are so new, are frequently overlooked by many companies. The problem is that attacks on networks are so stealthy these days that administrators don't even realize they are happening. Hence, many system administrators don't think they need an IDS. Frequently, if they do go ahead and implement one, they are shocked and amazed at how many attacks are detected on their network each day.

IDS is usually implemented on a dedicated system. It can be placed in a variety of places in the network. For example, many organizations use a basic IDS configuration by placing their IDS in their demilitarized zone (DMZ); as shown in Figure 9.38.

NOTE

DMZs will be discussed in depth in the next chapter.

FIGURE 9.38
Placing an IDS in the DMZ.

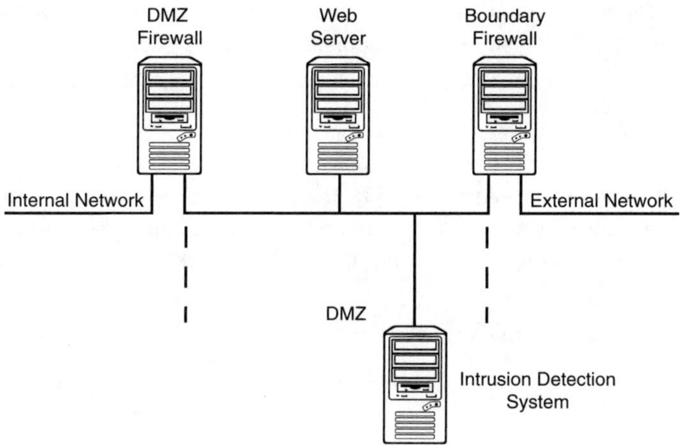

Here, it can detect attacks that might initially make it through the organization's firewall. Folks who are more serious about intrusion detection will place an IDS in the DMZ and additional IDSs on each segment in their network, as shown in Figure 9.39.

FIGURE 9.39
Extensive IDS placement.

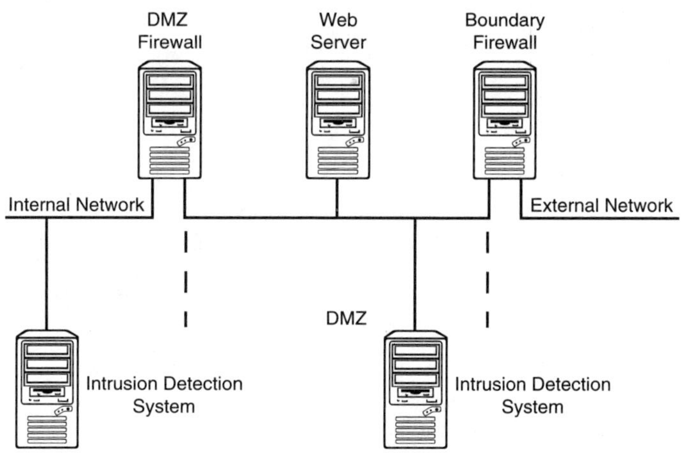

Some organizations will even place an IDS *outside* their firewall! Your choice of placement depends on how worried you are about attacks.

A variety of IDS packages are available today. Some, from companies such as Cisco, are completely hardware based. Others, such as the open source Snort package, are software based. In this chapter, we're going to focus on implementing Snort on your SLES 9 system.

NOTE

Several other open source IDS packages are available, such as AIDE, which checks for altered files on your Linux system, arpwatch, which watches arp traffic to detect new hosts attaching to the network, and Argus, which monitors connections between network hosts.

To implement Snort, you need to complete the following:

1. Install Snort on your system by installing the Snort package on your server, as shown in Figure 9.40.

FIGURE 9.40
Installing Snort.

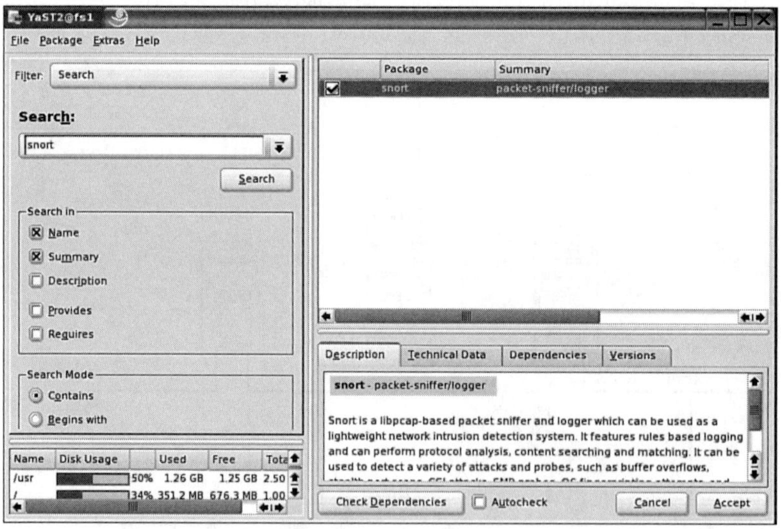

2. Open `/etc/sysconfig/snort` in a text editor.
3. Configure the following directives:

- SNORT_INTERFACE—This is the interface Snort will monitor on.
- SNORT_ACTIVATE—This specifies whether you want Snort to automatically run whenever the interface it's monitoring comes up. The default is no.
- SNORT_AUTO—This directive specifies whether you want the `HOME_NET` variable set to the IP address of the Snort interface previously configured. The default value is yes.
- SNORT_PROMISC—This directive configures Snort to run in promiscuous mode. The default value is no.
- SNORT_EXTRA_OPTIONS—This option is used to include switches with the Snort startup command. It's important that you understand that Snort can be run in three modes: Sniffer, Packet Logger, and Network Intrusion Detection (NDIS). To configure Snort to run in NDIS mode, set the value of this directive to **"-d -h your_subnet/your_mask"**. For example, if your subnet is 192.168.2.0 with a mask of 255.255.255.0, you would enter **"-d -h 192.168.2.0/24"**. This configures Snort to monitor the network and log packets that match the rules contained in the various rule files in `/etc/snort`.

TIP

You can download the latest sets of rules from http://www.snort.org. You can also view the Snort documentation at this URL to learn about all the configuration options Snort can use.

4. Run SuSEconfig to implement your changes.
5. Run Snort by entering **`rcsnort start`** at the shell prompt.

In this configuration, Snort will monitor the network and dump suspicious packets into the Snort log files located in `/var/log/snort`.

TIP

If you include the -v option in the SNORT_EXTRA_OPTIONS directive above, it will also write notifications to the screen when a suspicious packet is encountered.

Snort is a very powerful and very extensive tool. We don't have time nor space here to provide an exhaustive review of all the options. If you're serious about using Snort as an IDS, check out the Snort documentation at http://www.snort.org.

People who have implemented an IDS agree that they are worth the effort, but they aren't perfect by any means. Intruders will, of course, find ways to circumvent them. However, they can make your life as a system administrator much easier by letting you know when an attack is occurring. This gives you the ability to head off an attack in progress instead of learning about it after the fact in a log file.

With that in mind, let's practice some of the security techniques you learned about in this chapter in Lab Exercise 9.1.

Lab Exercise 9-1: Practicing With Security Tools

In this lab exercise, you will practice using some of the security tools we've reviewed in this chapter. To complete this exercise, you will need your SLES 9 server with named, dhcpd, Samba, Postfix, and CUPS running.

Complete the following:

1. Boot your SLES 9 server and authenticate as **tux** with a password of **SuSE789**.
2. Implement a GRUB password by completing the following:
   a. Open a terminal session and enter **su -** to change to root.
   b. At the shell prompt, enter **grub**.
   c. Encrypt the password in the GRUB shell by entering **md5crypt** at the grub prompt.
   d. At the password prompt, enter a GRUB password of **c1e9**. You will be presented with a hashed version of the password.
   e. Highlight the hash with your mouse cursor.
   f. Right-click; then select **Copy**.
   g. Start YaST.
   h. When prompted for your root password, enter **tuX123**.
   i. Select **System, Boot Loader Configuration**.
   j. In the Boot Loader Setup screen, select **Edit Configuration Files**.
   k. In the File Name drop-down list, ensure /boot/grub/menu.lst is selected.
   l. Beneath the gfxmenu directive, add the following:

      ```
      password –md5
      ```

   m. Place the cursor after —md5; then right-click and select **Paste**.
   n. Scroll down to the linux entry in the file.
   o. Add a line after the initrd line and enter **lock**.
   p. Repeat this process for the Floppy and Failsafe entries in the file.
   q. Select **OK, Finish**.

r. Reboot your system.

s. In the GRUB menu, press **p**; then enter a password of **cle9**.

t. Select **Linux** from the boot menu. The system should boot normally.

3. Run a TCP and a UDP port scan with nmap by completing the following:

a. Using YaST, install the nmap, nmap-gtk, nessus-core, libnasl, nessus-libraries, and snort packages on your server.

b. Open a new terminal session and enter **sux -** to change to root using a password of **tuX123**.

c. At the shell prompt, enter **nmapfe**.

d. In the Target field, enter the *IP address* of your server.

e. In the Scan Type drop-down list, select **Connect Scan**.

f. In the Scanned Ports drop-down list, select **All**.

g. Select **Scan**.

h. Wait while ports are scanned (this may take a few minutes).

i. Note the open TCP ports on your server.

j. In the Scan Type drop-down list, select **UDP Port Scan**.

k. In the Scanned Ports drop-down list, select **All**.

l. Select **Scan**.

m. Wait while ports are scanned.

n. Note the open UDP ports on your server.

o. Close the Nmap front-end by selecting **Exit**.

4. Use nessus to run a vulnerability scan on your sever by completing the following:

a. Create a nessus user by entering **nessus-adduser** at a shell prompt.

b. At the Login prompt, enter **tux**.

c. At the Authentication prompt, press **Enter**.

d. When prompted for a password, enter **SuSE789**.

e. When prompted to create a set of rules, press **Ctrl+d**.

f. When asked if the configured parameters are OK, enter **y**.

g. Generate a nessus security certificate by entering **nessus-mkcert** at a shell prompt.

h. When prompted for the certificate lifetime, press **Enter**.

i. When prompted for the server certificate lifetime, press **Enter**.

j. When prompted, enter your 2-character *country code*.

k. When prompted, enter your *state* or *province*.

l. When prompted, enter your *location*.

m. When prompted for your organization name, enter **CLE9**.

n. When prompted that your certificate was created, press **Enter**.

o. Start the nessus daemon by entering **rcnessusd start** at the shell prompt.

p. At the sux shell prompt, start the nessus client by entering **nessus &**.

q. In the Login and Password fields, authenticate to the nessus service as **tux** with a password of **SuSE789**.

r. In the SSL Setup screen, mark **Display and Remember the Server Certificate**; then select **OK**.

s. When prompted, accept the SSL certificate by selecting **Yes**.

t. When prompted that some plug-ins have been disabled, select **OK**.

u. Select the **Prefs** tab.

v. Select the *nmap options* you want to run.

w. Select the **Target Selection** tab.

x. In the Target(s) field, enter the *IP address* of your server.

y. Start the scan by selecting **Start the Scan** at the bottom of the nessus window.

z. Wait while the scan is run. This may take up to 15 minutes to complete. When done, the Report window will be displayed.

aa. To view the results, select your *subnet* in the Subnet field; then select *your server* in the Host field. A list of warnings and notes appears in the Port field.

bb. In the Port field, select the *item* you want to view; then select the *item* in the Severity field. The text of the note or warning is displayed.

cc. Close the Nessus "NG" Report window; then select **Quit** from the Nessus Setup window.

5. Configure and run Snort on your server by completing the following:

   a. Open `/etc/sysconfig/snort` in a text editor.

   b. Configure the following directives:

      - SNORT_INTERFACE—Verify that this is set to **eth0**.
      - SNORT_ACTIVATE—Verify that this is set to **no**.

TIP

In the "real world," you would probably want to set this directive to **yes.**

      - SNORT_AUTO—Verify that this is set to **yes**.
      - SNORT_PROMISC—Set this to **yes**.
      - SNORT_EXTRA_OPTIONS—Set this to **-d -h *your_subnet/your_mask***.

   c. Save your changes and exit the file.

   d. At the shell prompt, enter **SuSEconfig**.

   e. Run Snort by entering **rcsnort start** at the shell prompt.

   f. Verify that Snort started properly by entering **tail /var/log/messages** at the shell prompt. You should see a line indicating that Snort initialized successfully.

Watch Snort for a while. However, unless you actually have an attack happen, Snort won't detect anything. When you're done, be sure to enter **rcsnort stop** at the shell prompt to shut it down.

If time permits, experiment with last, lastlog, and faillog as well. You may need to deliberately fail authentication attempts several times first to see any meaningful results.

Summary

We talked about a variety of security topics in this chapter. First, we talked about how to implement a SLES 9 server security plan. We then reviewed the various components of this plan, which included the following:

- Staying abreast of current security threats.
- Keeping your system software up-to-date using YOU.
- Documenting your server system.
- Physically securing the server in a locked room.
- Employing GRUB passwords.
- Teaching users about password security.
- Analyzing services and packages running on the server.
- Using nmap to run port scans.
- Being aware of vulnerabilities associated with services you're running on your server.
- Running a vulnerability scan with nessus.
- Implementing encryption on your server to secure communications.

After discussing your server security plan, we then turned to a discussion of how to monitor your server to detect suspicious behavior. We first discussed how to review log files to identify possible intrusion attempts. We also discussed how to redirect log files to a different server on the network to prevent intruders from erasing their tracks.

Finally, we discussed how to implement an IDS system on your server to detect intruders. We reviewed how to complete a basic configuration of Snort to do this.

If you've been around networking awhile, you probably noticed that we didn't cover one very important security topic in this chapter. One of the most critical aspects of your network's security is the use of firewalls. In Chapter 10, " Implementing Packet Filter Firewalls with SLES 9," we're going to spend a lot of time discussing packet filtering firewalls as well as application-level gateways. Stay tuned!

CHAPTER 10

Implementing Packet Filter Firewalls with SLES 9

This chapter covers the following requirements for Novell's Certified Linux Engineer (CLE) 9 certification:

1. Describe how firewalls work.
2. Implement a packet-filtering firewall on SLES 9.
3. Implement an application-level gateway on SLES 9.

As a network administrator, one of your most important roles is to keep your network safe from intruders. Intruders can threaten your system from a variety of vantage points using a wide array of tools, as we discussed in the previous chapter.

One of the key vulnerabilities in your network that you need to protect is its interface with any public network. To do this, you need to implement and manage network firewalls. In this chapter, we'll discuss how you can use SLES 9 to provide a network firewall. Specifically, we'll discuss the following:

- How firewalls work.
- Implementing a packet-filtering firewall.
- Implementing Network Address Translation (NAT).
- Implementing an application-level gateway with Squid.

Let's begin by discussing the first topic—how firewalls work.

How Firewalls Work

TEST OBJECTIVE COVERED:

1. Describe how firewalls work.

Today, most of the computer networks you will be responsible for will probably be connected to the Internet in some form or fashion. We all pretty much take it for granted. Users expect to be able to access the Web from their desktops and to be able to send and receive email over the Internet.

However, this Internet connectivity represents a great risk to the security of your network. You absolutely must take measures to ensure that a malicious user on the Internet can't compromise your network. If you don't, you're asking to get hacked or attacked. One of the most important things you can do is erect a barrier between your network and the public network in the form of a firewall.

As a network administrator, you are probably already aware of the importance of firewalls. You don't need to be sold on the idea. However, be aware that many organizational decision-makers may not share your level of concern. To many of these folks, a network firewall is an expensive "network thingy" that isn't necessary.

Let me give you an example. About a year ago, I visited a potential client to work up a bid for a small business network deployment. In discussing various options, the business owner was dead set against implementing any form of wireless networking in his offices. He'd seen a television news report about unencrypted home wireless networks being hijacked and had decided there was no way he would allow them in his business. He refused to accept my explanation that 802.11x transmissions could be protected with encryption. Too bad.

On the topic of firewalls, however, he was pretty sure he didn't need one on his network. I was absolutely dumbfounded. His network would be connected to a backbone segment (that was shared by all the tenants in the office complex) which itself was connected to the Internet using a T3 line. No matter how hard I tried, I couldn't convince him that this was a much more serious threat to his network than using wireless connectivity. Consequently, I didn't take the job. Even though I certainly would have liked to have had the money, I didn't want the responsibility for a network that would surely be compromised.

Enough war stories; let's talk about what a firewall does.

The Role of a Firewall

So what exactly is a firewall? A firewall is a combination of hardware and/or software that sits between your network and another network. It has one network interface connected to the internal network and a second interface connected to the public network. At first glance, you may say, "That sounds more like a gateway or a router." Although a firewall is frequently implemented in conjunction with a gateway/router, its role in the network is very different.

The job of a firewall is to monitor the traffic—both inbound and outbound—that flows between the networks. As the administrator, you configure the firewall with a set of rules that define what kind of traffic is allowed through it. Any network traffic that violates the rules is not allowed through, as shown in Figure 10.1.

FIGURE 10.1
The role of a firewall.

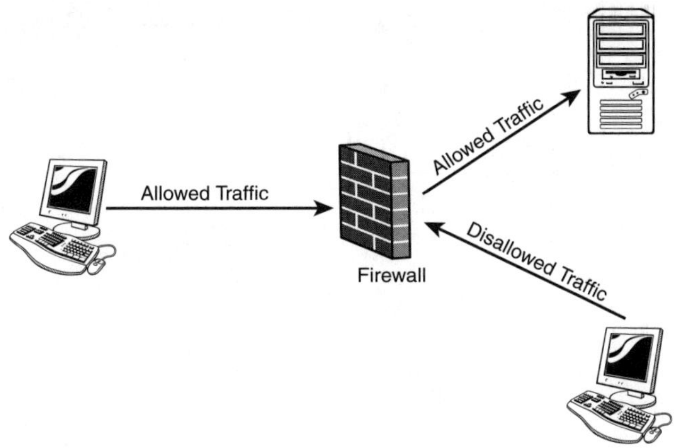

So why do we call this kind of device a *firewall*? The term actually comes from several non-technical fields. A traditional firewall is designed to prevent the spread of fire from one place to another. For example, your automobile uses a firewall. It's situated between the passenger compartment and the engine compartment. Its job is to prevent a fire in the engine from spreading into the passenger area.

A network firewall is designed to do a similar thing—hence the use of the *firewall* metaphor. Its job is prevent the spread of damage caused by unauthorized access or attacks in your network.

The way firewalls accomplish this task varies. There are several types of firewalls. The first type you need to be familiar with is the *packet-filtering* firewall.

HOW PACKET-FILTERING FIREWALLS WORK

A packet-filtering firewall operates at the Network and Transport layers of the OSI model. Like all firewalls, it has one interface connected to the private internal network and another to the public external network.

NOTE

Although we say that a packet-filtering firewall operates at both the Network and the Transport layers of the OSI model, its functionality at Layer 4 is limited to TCP and UDP ports.

A packet-filtering firewall operates in a manner just as its name implies. All traffic moving between the private and the public network must go through the packet-filtering firewall. As it does, the firewall captures *all* packets, both incoming and outgoing, and compares them against a set of rules configured by the administrator.

A packet-filtering firewall can filter packets based on origin address, destination address, origin port, destination port, the protocol used, and the type of packet. If a packet meets the specified criteria, it is forwarded on to the next network. If it doesn't it's dropped, as shown in Figure 10.2.

FIGURE 10.2
How a packet-filtering firewall works.

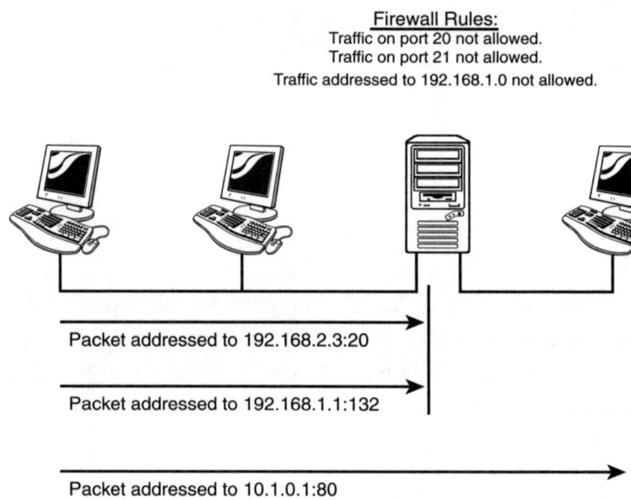

NOTE

Packet-filtering firewalls don't necessarily have to be implemented between your private network and a public network, such as the Internet. They can also be implemented between a particular network segment and a WAN link or a backbone segment. Doing this really beefs up your internal network security.

Packet-filtering firewalls are very commonly implemented. Generally speaking, they cost less than other types of firewalls. In fact, many hardware routers include some form of packet-filtering firewall functionality.

For example, in my office at home I have a simple little router that I purchased for less than $60.00 at a big-box computer store. I use it to connect my home office network to a DSL Internet connection through a local ISP. This great little router includes a simple packet-filtering firewall. I can set up rules blocking specified protocols, ports, or IP addresses, as shown in Figure 10.3.

FIGURE 10.3
Configuring a simple packet-filtering firewall.

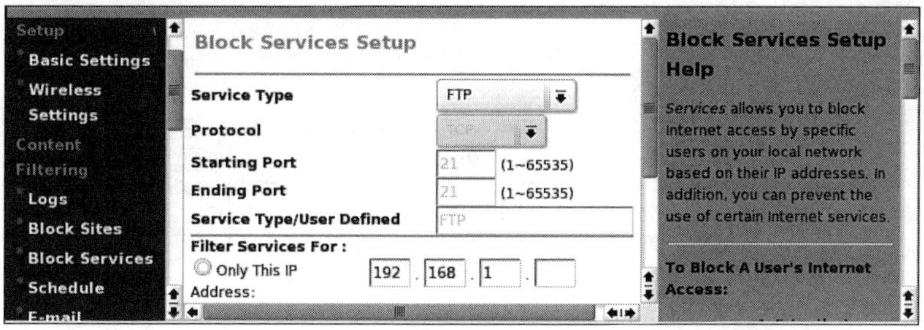

In addition to being inexpensive, packet-filtering firewalls are very robust in comparison with other types of firewalls. Packet-filtering requires relatively little processing, so data moves very quickly through the firewall.

Unfortunately, packet-filtering firewalls also have a number of weaknesses. Key among these is that your configuration options are limited. Because you're working at the Network and Transport layers of the OSI model, you can't configure rules based on protocols or features associated with upper layers of the OSI model.

Accordingly, packet-filtering firewalls don't protect your network from attacks associated with higher layers of the OSI model. Attacks have been known to happen by exploiting open ports on the packet-filtering firewall. The attacker sends what appear to be legitimate packets, according to the firewall's IP address and port rules. However, the contents of the packets contain mischievous stuff that can compromise the internal host behind the firewall. Packet-filtering firewalls have no way to defend against this.

Packet-filtering firewalls also don't provide any means of user authentication before processing packets. All packets arriving at the firewall are processed according to the rules you've configured, regardless of who sent them.

If you want to implement a more sophisticated firewall, you have to move up higher in the OSI model. Let's do just that and talk about stateful firewalls next.

HOW STATEFUL FIREWALLS WORK

Stateful firewalls operate up one layer from packet-filtering firewalls at the Transport and Session layers of the OSI model. A stateful firewall doesn't filter individual data packets as a packet-filtering firewall does. Instead, it monitors protocol sessions. To understand this concept, let's take a look at a sample TCP connection.

As you know, when two systems set up a TCP connection, a three-way handshake occurs, as shown in Figure 10.4.

FIGURE 10.4
A TCP three-way handshake.

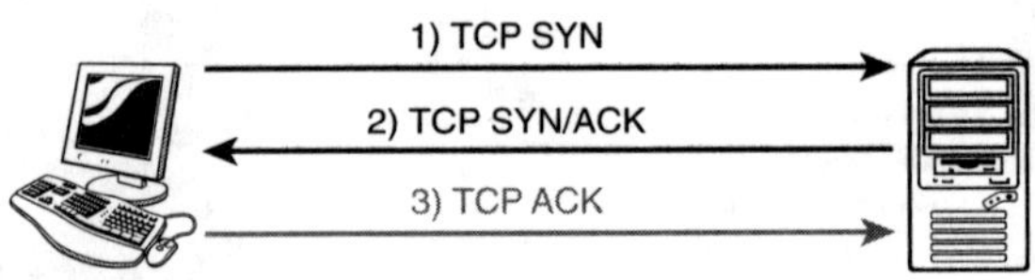

First, the originating host sends a ***TCP SYN*** message to the destination host. The SYN message originates from a random IP port above port number 1024 on the source host and is sent to the IP port used by the desired service on the destination host.

Upon receipt, the destination host responds with a ***TCP SYN/ACK*** message sent back to the same IP port on the source host where the first message originated. The source host then responds with a ***TCP ACK*** message to the destination host and the connection is established.

The problem with packet-filtering firewalls is that they don't understand any of this. This leaves your network open to attacks based on the TCP handshake, as shown in Figure 10.5.

How do you get around this situation? You use a stateful firewall. Instead of monitoring individual packets, as a packet-filtering firewall does, a stateful firewall monitors the connection itself.

With a stateful firewall, TCP SYN messages are logged in the firewall's *state table*. When TCP SYN/ACK messages return from the destination host, the stateful firewall checks its state table to see if the message is a legitimate response to a SYN message that originated from within the protected network. If so, the stateful firewall allows the message to go through. If not, the message is assumed to be bogus and is dropped. This process is shown in Figure 10.6.

FIGURE 10.5
A bogus SYN/ACK message.

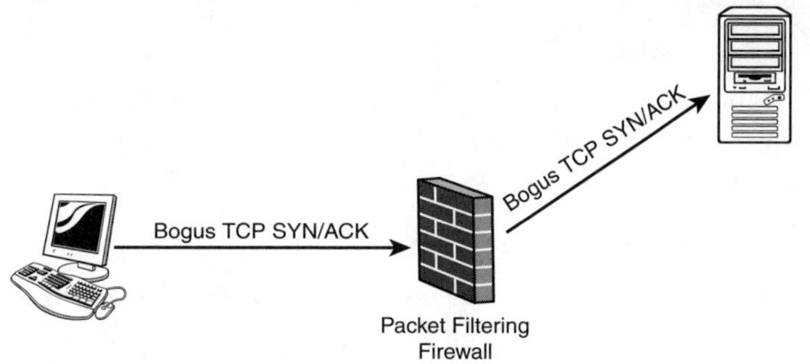

FIGURE 10.6
How a stateful firewall works.

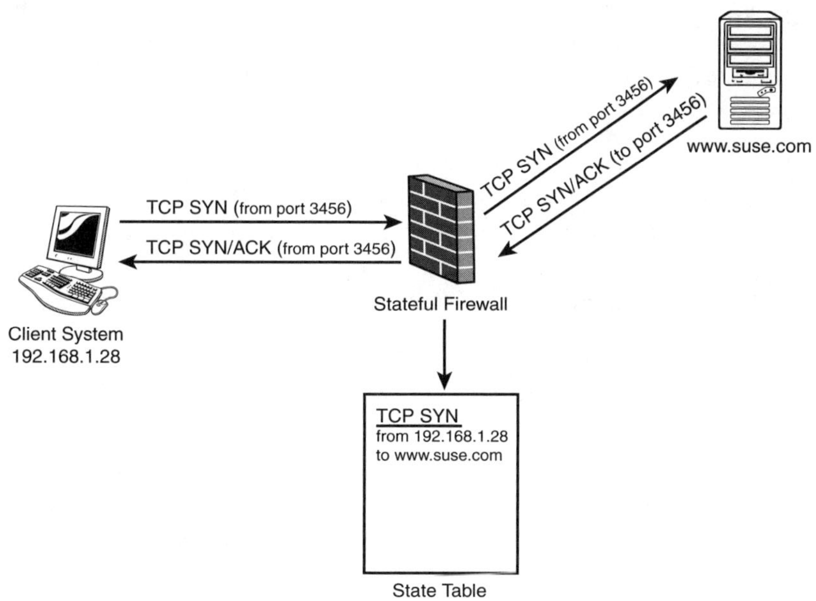

Not only does this allow your hosts to access resources on the public network without opening up an unholy number of ports on your firewall, it also prevents bogus TCP connection messages from entering the network. In today's world of Denial of Service attacks, this is a very useful aspect of stateful firewalls.

Unfortunately, like packet-filtering firewalls, stateful firewalls have some shortcomings. Because they are more complex than a packet-filtering firewall, they require more CPU processing, especially if the state table gets large (which tends to happen quickly on a big network).

In addition, stateful firewalls don't authenticate users, nor can they filter content. If you want this level of security, you have to move up the OSI model to the Application layer and implement an application-level gateway.

HOW APPLICATION-LEVEL GATEWAYS WORK

Application-level gateways, also called *proxy servers*, operate at the Application layer of the OSI model. Usually, they are associated with a specific Layer 7 protocol, such as HTTP. That means a given application-level gateway is concerned only with managing traffic for the protocol it's designed to support. However, generic application-level gateways are also available that aren't protocol-specific. We'll talk more about them later in the chapter.

They also do the one thing packet-filtering firewalls and stateful firewalls can't: authenticate users. This allows application-level gateways to provide you with a great deal of control over how data flows between your LAN and the external network. In addition, some can also filter content requested by users.

An application-level gateway is usually implemented as an intermediary between users on your network and hosts on a public network, such as the Internet. Usually, a packet-filtering or stateful firewall is configured so that individual user's workstations aren't allowed to directly access hosts on the public network. Instead, the requests for resources on the public network (such as an HTML page from a web server) are redirected to the application-level gateway.

The application-level gateway then requires the user to supply a valid username and password. After authentication, the application-level gateway then examines the request to see if it meets the rules the administrator has established.

If it passes the test, the request is then forwarded on to the host on the public network. The cool thing here is that the remote host on the public network sees the request as originating from the application-level gateway. It has no idea that the request originated from a workstation behind the firewall.

The application-level gateway retrieves the resource from the remote host and then forwards it to the host on the internal network that originally requested it.

NOTE

If you implement an HTTP caching proxy server, the server will check to see if the requested web page exists in its cache before requesting the page from the remote web server. If it's there, it pulls it out of cache and sends it to the requesting workstation.

This eliminates the need for the application-level gateway to pull the page down every time it's requested. A caching proxy server can dramatically reduce traffic on your Internet connection as well as increase response time, especially if pages are accessed frequently by a large number of users in your network.

If the requested page isn't in its cache, it forwards the request to the remote web server and pulls the page down. When it does, it keeps a copy of the page in its cache. That way, it can use the cached copy the next time the page is requested.

This process is depicted in Figure 10.7.

FIGURE 10.7
How an application-level gateway works.

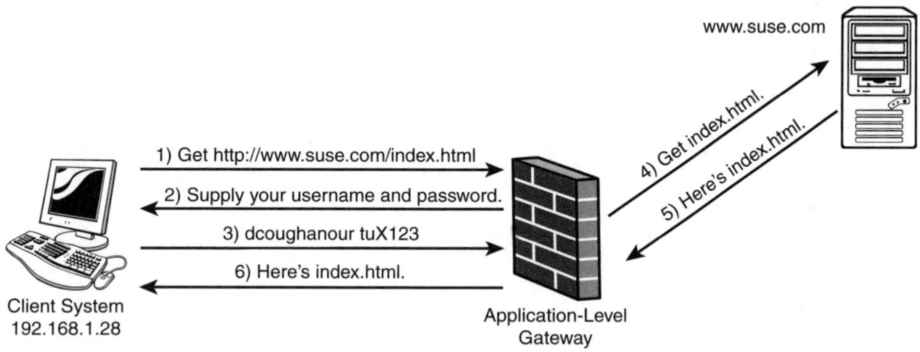

In this example, the user dcoughanour sends a request for http://www.suse.com/index.html to his organization's HTTP application-level gateway. The gateway then challenges the user for a username and password, which the user supplies.

The gateway then sends a request for index.html to www.suse.com. The SUSE web server responds with the file. The gateway then forwards the page back to dcoughanour.

Most application-level gateways can also be configured to examine the contents of the traffic it receives, making sure that it's legitimate and meets the rules established by the administrator.

Application-level gateways sound great—and they really are. Most organizations that I've been associated with implement some form of an application-level gateway. However, they do come at a price. Because of their complexity, they require a great deal of processing horsepower, usually requiring dedicated hardware.

So now you know about the three general types of firewalls: packet filtering, stateful, and application-level gateway. What do you use where? Should one be used over another? To answer these questions, let's discuss some general guidelines for implementing firewalls.

Designing a Firewall Implementation

You've probably heard the old maxim "Measure twice; cut once." This phrase holds as true with implementing a firewall solution as it does with carpentry. Before you go off willy-nilly installing firewalls on your network, you should sit down and plan out how you will place and configure your firewall(s). If you don't, there's a good chance you'll end up filtering out legitimate traffic and/or allowing unauthorized traffic in. Here's what you should do:

- Define a security policy.
- Plan your boundary firewall.
- Plan your demilitarized zone (DMZ).
- Plan your internal firewalls.

Let's start by discussing your security policy.

DEFINING A SECURITY POLICY

The very first thing you should do when implementing a firewall is define a security policy for your organization's network, if one hasn't been created already.

However, understand that, depending on your organization, you may have total, little, or no control over this security policy. In a large, bureaucratic organization, you will probably have to get "buy-off" from many organizational leaders before you can start implementing your policy. In a small, start-up organization, you will probably be given full and complete control over the security policy.

Either way, this policy must be defined before you implement your firewalls. What should be in this policy? Again, that depends on your organization. Some organizations are very strict about what is allowed with regard to the network; others are relatively lax.

NOTE

With all of the security breaches we've been experiencing in recent years, I've noticed that most of the organizations I have dealings with are gravitating toward the strict side of the spectrum. The costs associated with a network breach, in terms of lost productivity and even litigation, are pushing most organizations to lock things down as tightly as possible.

With that in mind, your security policy should include, at a minimum, the following elements:

- An "Acceptable Use" statement that defines what internal users are allowed to do with their workstations and with the network in general.

CREATING AN ACCEPTABLE USE POLICY

There's a couple of points you should keep in mind when creating your Acceptable Use statement. These are things that I've observed over the years working for several high-tech companies.

First, don't be hard-headed and inflexible. Remember that the network is there to facilitate the work of the organization. If your acceptable use policy becomes an impediment, the whole purpose of the network has been defeated.

Let me give you an example of what I mean. Back in the early 1990s, I was hired by a high-tech corporation to create some web-based multimedia training materials for employees and customers.

However, after I was hired, the IS department wouldn't let me install the development software I needed to do the job. (They wouldn't even allocate a PC to me for the first six weeks I was there.) They also refused to allocate the network storage space needed to deploy the materials (were I ever able to create them). What a fun place to work—NOT!

Second, make your Acceptable Use statement easily accessible. Better yet, give each user a copy to read and sign.

Another high-tech company I worked for in the 1990s had a problem with this. They had an Acceptable Use statement, but they kept changing it and guarded it jealously. The result? You had no idea what you could and couldn't do as an employee. In addition, managers had no idea what was allowable and what wasn't, which results in uneven enforcement.

For example, a good friend of mine at the company got into a great deal of hot water with his manager for sending instant messages to his friends. He had no idea this was unacceptable. In fact, it may not have been. Because the Acceptable Use statement was so hard to obtain, nobody really knew.

Case in point: Just a few cubicles down from my friend sat another employee (who had a different manager). On several occasions, when I walked into his cubicle, he had pages open in his web browser that were so offensive that it would make any normal, balanced person gag. His manager didn't say a word about it. Talk about a hostile environment lawsuit just waiting to happen!

The point is, establish an Acceptable Use statement and make it freely available for everyone so there's no misunderstanding of what is and what is not allowed.

- A diagram that identifies all entry points into the network, such as T-Carrier connections, WAN links, and modem banks.
- A list of services on the network that must be made available to anonymous users on the public network, such as web and FTP servers.
- A list of services on the network that must be made available to trusted users on the external network, such as mobile salespeople, contractors, and partners.
- A list of services on the network that must be available to internal users but must not be accessible by users on the external network.
- A network diagram that identifies which internal network segments need to be protected from other segments within the network. For example, you may want to protect the network segment used by the Accounting/Payroll department from all other users on the internal network.
- A list of protocols that will be allowed out of the internal network to the external network.
- A list of protocols that will be allowed to enter the internal network from the external network.

Again, this is a suggested list of items to include in your security policy. Your organization's values will dictate what is important and what is not.

After you've established your security policy, the next step is to plan your boundary firewall.

PLANNING YOUR BOUNDARY FIREWALL

With your security policy in hand, you're ready to plan your firewall deployment. As with the security policy, there are a number of different ways to configure the firewalls on your network. Each way can be valid, depending on your organization's security policy.

A key element in planning your firewalls should be the notion of hedgerows. What on earth do hedgerows have to do with firewalls? Let me explain.

Between my back yard and my neighbor's back yard I planted an evergreen hedge to form a natural fence. I like things nice and open, so I was resistant to the idea of a fence initially. However, my neighbors love animals—*lots* of animals. Chickens, rabbits, dogs, turkeys—you name it and they have it.

I like animals, too—just not as much as they do. I had to do something to keep the animals out of my yard. So, in went the hedge. Now, if you've ever planted a hedge, you know that it's not a single plant. The hedge is actually composed of multiple evergreens planted in a long line. It makes a great fence. It's prickly, so animals don't like to crawl through it.

The hedge worked great for a while. Then a couple of things happened. First, some very intrepid little animals found some weak spots in the hedge and started burrowing in the dirt beneath it. Soon, the little holes they dug got bigger and bigger as larger and larger animals started using them. Then some of the plants that made up the hedge started to die. Not many—just one here and one there. The point? Pretty soon my beautiful natural fence was completely porous. It no longer did its job.

Fortunately, my neighbor decided to erect a real fence on his side of the property. Now we have two layers of defense; a vinyl fence accompanied by my evergreen hedge. The incursions into my back yard by the neighbor's animals have dramatically decreased. Occasionally, a rabbit or two still works its way through, but for the most part, their backyard migration habits have been thwarted.

What do fences and rabbits have to do with firewalls? Actually, we can learn quite a bit from this experience. The key thing is that a single defensive barrier isn't enough. Certainly, it's better than nothing at all. However, as soon as that defense is breached, everything can come through. It's true with my backyard fence; it's true with your network firewalls.

Implementing a single firewall to protect your network is like my evergreen hedge. It works for a while, but as soon as one intruder gets through, they have full rein to your entire network.

Therefore, when planning your firewall deployment, you should be thinking in terms of barrier behind barrier behind barrier. In my backyard, if an animal manages to get beneath my neighbor's fence, it finds itself faced with yet another fence (my hedgerow). You want intruders in your network to face the same obstacles. If they manage to defeat one firewall, they should find themselves faced with yet another firewall, as shown in Figure 10.8.

FIGURE 10.8
Facing barrier after barrier.

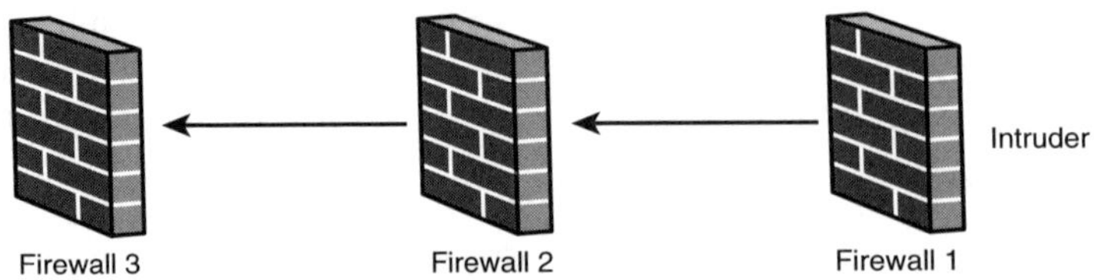

The first element in your firewall plan should be what is referred to as your *boundary* firewall. This firewall connects the internal network to the public network and is shown in Figure 10.9.

FIGURE 10.9
Planning the boundary firewall.

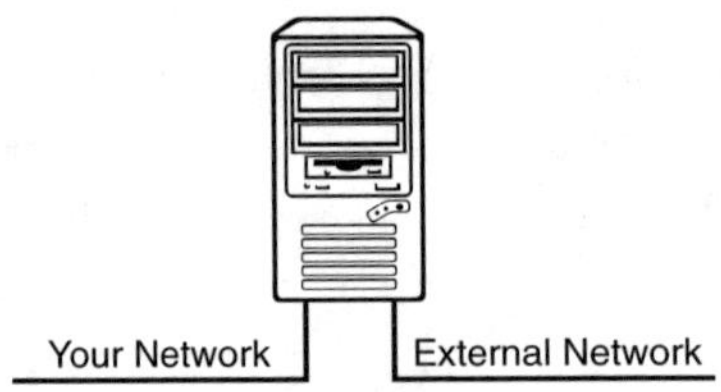

NOTE

In Figure 10.9, I've drawn the firewall as a server box. That's because in this chapter, we're going to implement our firewalls as software on a SLES 9 server. You could also use a hardware-based firewall.

The boundary firewall's job is to serve as the first line of defense against attack or intrusion. It's really not intended to authenticate users or monitor content. Its job is to filter the raw traffic going in and out of the network. Therefore, the boundary firewall is usually implemented as a packet-filtering or stateful firewall.

Because the boundary firewall is frequently a packet-filtering firewall, you need to include the following elements in your firewall design:

- Will you allow all incoming traffic by default, establishing rules for specific types of traffic that you don't want to allow in?
- Will your firewall deny all incoming traffic except for specific types of traffic that you want to allow?

NOTE

When I first started working with firewalls back in the 1990s, the first option in the preceding list tended to be the default strategy that everyone used. We were much more trusting back then. Nowadays, the second option is the default. I suspect that you may never see a firewall configured using the first option.

- Will you allow all outgoing traffic by default, blocking only specific types or destinations?
- Will you block all outgoing traffic except for specific types or destinations?
- What ports must be opened on the firewall to allow traffic through from the outside? For example, are you going to implement a web server that needs to be publicly accessible behind the firewall? If so, you will need to open up ports 80 and probably 443 on your boundary firewall.

Again, how you decide to configure your boundary firewall is up to you and your organization. However, I recommend that you err on the side of caution. Given a choice, I'd rather deal with an employee inside the network who's upset because my firewall won't let him run his music sharing app through to the Internet than deal with a major attack that made its way into the network.

After you have your boundary firewall planned, you next need to plan your demilitarized zone (DMZ).

PLANNING YOUR DMZ

If you're not familiar with firewalls, you may be asking what on earth a DMZ is. Here's the issue: Suppose you manage networks for a small company of about 500 employees. The company's main means of marketing and selling its products is through a website.

If you locate the web server running your company's website on the public side of the boundary firewall, you've got a major security issue. There's very little to prevent anyone on the public network from hacking into the web server box. You don't want that.

What happens, then, if you put it behind the boundary firewall? Unless you open up ports 80 and 443 on the firewall, no one is going to be able to get to your web server from the Internet. If that happens, your company will close its doors and you'll be out of a job.

If you open ports 80 and 443, users from the Internet will be able to get to your website. However, you will also have opened up two small holes into your entire network, as shown in Figure 10.10.

FIGURE 10.10
Opening ports in the boundary firewall.

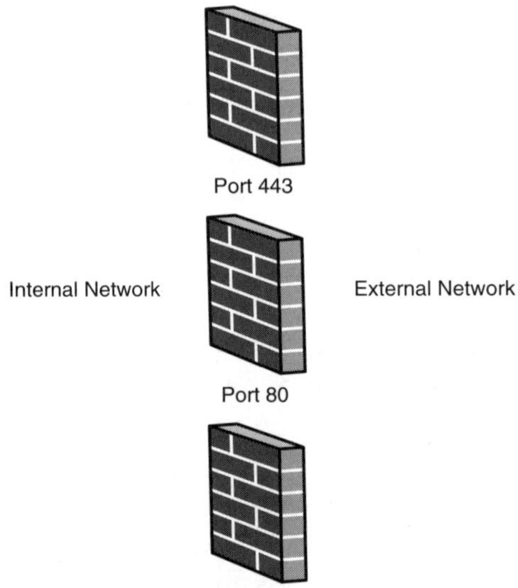

This can be a bad thing, especially when dealing with web servers. A ton of exploits take advantage of this very scenario—gaining access to the web server through the firewall on port 80 and then using a variety of exploits to use the web server do all kinds of damage.

So what do you do? You need to protect your network and your web server, but you also need to make the web server available to Internet users. You can do this by creating a demilitarized zone (DMZ).

How do you do this? First of all, you have to accept the fact that you have to open up ports on the boundary firewall to let Internet users in to use your web server. It's a painful fact of life. As we've just discussed, this creates a relatively insecure area on your network.

The key is to contain the area of low security by implementing a *second* firewall on your internal network behind the boundary firewall, as shown in Figure 10.11.

By doing this, you create two zones in your network. Because your web server resides on a network segment behind the boundary firewall with several ports opened up, we say it resides in the *DMZ*. The DMZ is a zone of low security on your network segment. You don't put anything in the DMZ that doesn't absolutely have to be there. The DMZ is not the place for your payroll or R&D servers!

FIGURE 10.11
Creating a DMZ.

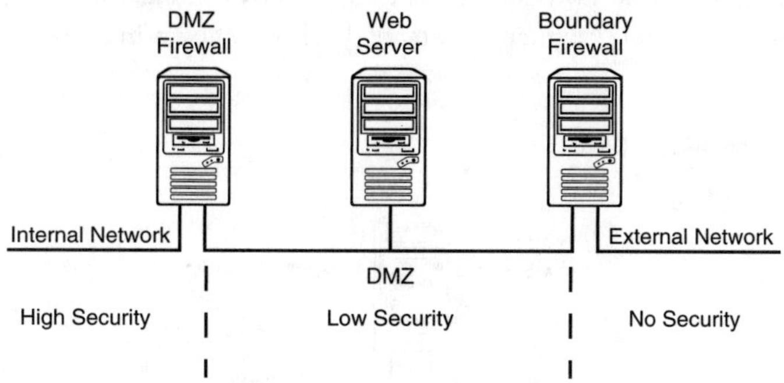

However, a publicly accessible web server should be placed there. You may be asking, "What if the web server hosts an e-commerce website?" This is a serious issue. This server is a goldmine for the hacker; it needs additional protection because of the low level of security in the DMZ. How do you do this? You configure the server with its own host-based firewall. This firewall runs on the server and is used to protect itself.

Because you implemented a second, internal firewall behind the boundary firewall, you've contained the low security area of your network to a single segment. The second, internal firewall behind the DMZ can be a packet-filtering or a stateful firewall, depending on your organization's needs. The rest of your network is hiding behind this second firewall. Remember what I said about hedgerows earlier in the chapter? Here it is in action. No backyard migrations!

The general rule you should follow when planning your firewall rules is that traffic originating in the secured internal network should be allowed into and through the DMZ.

For example, users should be able to access the Internet with a browser. As well, if the web server in the DMZ uses a database, the database should be able to reside in the high-security area of the network while the web server remains in the low security area.

However, traffic originating in the low or no security areas must not be allowed to travel to the high security area.

You can implement a DMZ in two ways. The first is the one shown in Figure 10.11. In this configuration, two firewalls are used: one on the boundary and a second one behind the DMZ. You can also create a DMZ using a single firewall. One interface is connected to the internal network and one is connected to the public network, just like we discussed before.

However, to create the DMZ, we add a third network interface to the firewall. The DMZ is created with this single segment. High-security firewall rules are established for the interface connected to the internal network. Low-security rules that allow public access are established for the interface to which the DMZ segment is attached. This is shown in Figure 10.12.

FIGURE 10.12
An alternative way of creating a DMZ.

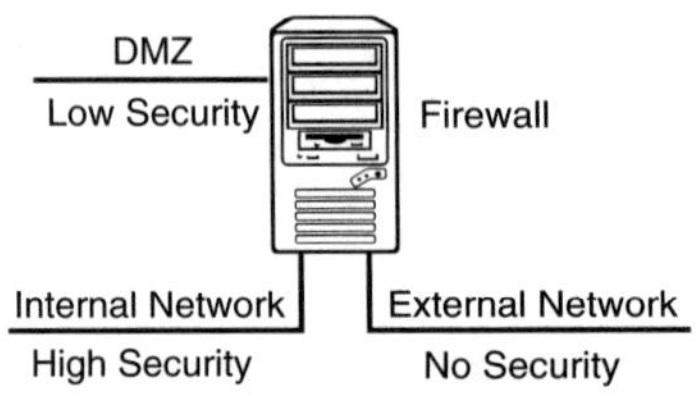

Which way is the best? Neither. Each has it strengths and its weaknesses. The two firewall systems discussed first requires more hardware and requires you to administer two separate firewall systems. However, an attack on the boundary firewall has absolutely no effect on the internal firewall. Everything inside the network could be functioning swimmingly while the boundary firewall is out on the front lines fighting a pitched life-or-death battle with a Denial of Service attack.

The single-firewall-with-three-interfaces system requires less hardware and requires you to maintain only a single system. It allows you to create multiple DMZs by adding additional interfaces. However, it also introduces a single point of failure. If the firewall goes down, everything else goes down with it.

After you have your DMZ planned, the next thing you need to do is plan your internal firewalls.

PLANNING INTERNAL FIREWALLS

Internal firewalls? Aren't firewalls supposed to protect your network from external threats? Yep, and they also do a great job of securing your network internally. It all goes back to the hedgerow analogy I presented earlier. The more barriers that intruders or attackers have to go through, the better off you are.

In addition, remember from the previous chapter that many of the threats your network faces come from *inside*. Whether you're dealing with disgruntled employees who want to cause problems, employees who are on the take trying to damage or steal from their own company, or simply mischievous employees who want to see what they can do, using internal firewalls can protect your internal network just like your boundary firewall protects you from external threats.

So how do you plan to implement internal firewalls? Recall earlier that I suggested that your security policy should define which areas of your internal network need to be secured from other areas of your internal network. These could include departments that deal with finances, human resources, or R&D. If the network contains sensitive data that needs to be protected internally, you should consider implementing internal firewalls. A sample is shown in Figure 10.13.

FIGURE 10.13
Implementing internal firewalls.

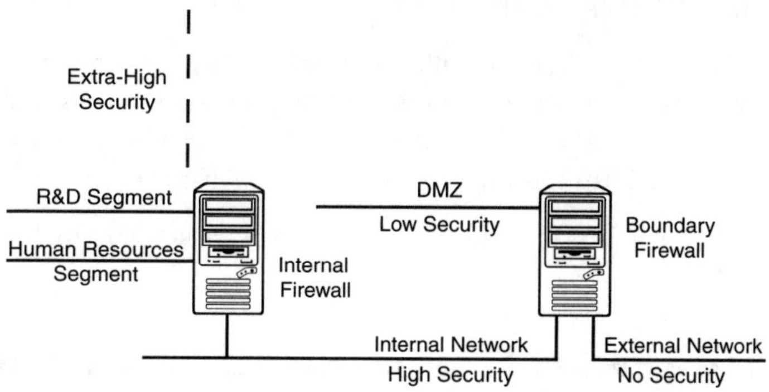

In this example, an internal firewall has been implemented on the internal network. This firewall has been configured with rules that protect the R&D network segment as well as the Human Resources network segment.

That was a lot of firewall theory. Thanks for hanging in there. Unfortunately, time and space won't permit a thorough exploration of firewalls in detail. Like most of the topics we hit in the book, we can touch on only the most critical points. If you want a more thorough treatment of firewalls, a number of titles are completely devoted only to that topic.

Let's shift gears a bit and get our hands dirty. Let's next talk about how to implement a packet-filtering firewall on SLES 9.

Implementing a Packet Filtering Firewall on SLES 9

TEST OBJECTIVE COVERED:

2. Implement a packet filtering firewall on SLES 9.

Recall that earlier in this chapter, I mentioned that firewalls can be implemented using either a dedicated hardware firewall or using standard server hardware combined with software.

For your CLE 9 certification, you need to know how to implement a packet filtering firewall on an SLES 9 server. As with many of the other services we've covered in this book, there are two ways to do this. You can configure a firewall using the iptables command-line utility as well as using the YaST Firewall module.

Just as we've done before, we're going to talk about how to do this both ways. I know I sound like a broken record, but I really think it's important that you know what's going on behind the scenes of a GUI interface. After you do, however, why spend all that time typing when you can use YaST to accomplish the same task with a few mouse clicks?

With that in mind, let's first talk about how to implement a packet-filtering firewall on SLES 9 using iptables.

Implementing a Packet-Filtering Firewall with iptables

The heart of the Linux firewall is a package called iptables, which has been available since the introduction of version 2.4 of the Linux kernel. This package is included within your SLES 9 distribution as well as from http://www.netfilter.org, as shown in Figure 10.14.

The YaST Firewall module, which is an optional way of implementing a packet-filtering firewall on SLES 9, is simply a GUI front-end for configuring iptables on the system.

TIP

The YaST Firewall module, although it uses iptables, doesn't provide the same degree of flexibility that manually configuring iptables does. However, it makes the initial configuration of the firewall much faster!

Older versions of the Linux kernel didn't use iptables to create firewalls. Instead, version 2.0 used ipfwadm and version 2.2 used ipchains. If you access the Linux Documentation Project at http://www.tldp.org, you'll see that many of the firewall HOWTOs available are written to these older packages.

FIGURE 10.14
Packet filtering with the iptables package.

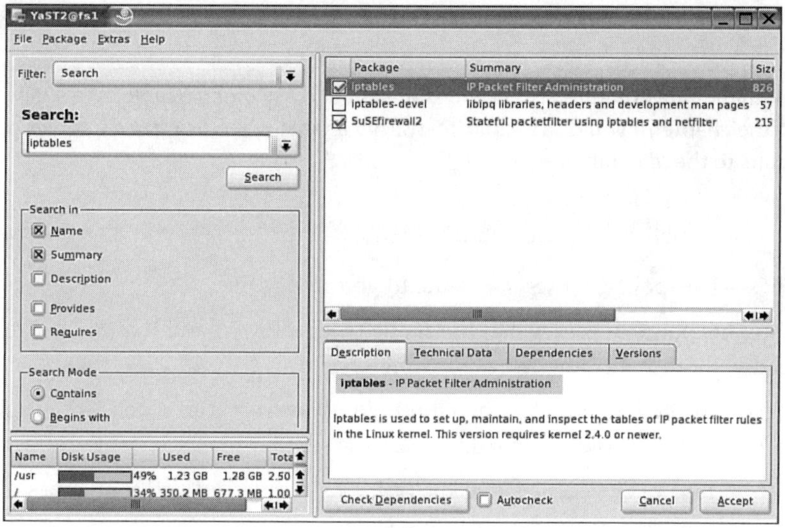

Packet filtering under Linux is done by the Linux kernel itself. To use iptables on your server, the kernel must have been compiled with the *netfilter* infrastructure included. This infrastructure is what allows the kernel to perform the firewalling functions we want. This infrastructure is included by default when installing SLES 9. To configure the way the kernel actually filters packets, you use the iptables utility.

The iptables utility on your SLES 9 is used to configure the firewalling rules your Linux kernel will use to carry out packet filtering functions. iptables communicates with the kernel and, using the rules you configure, tells the kernel what packets should be allowed through the firewall and which should be dropped.

The netfilter infrastructure in your Linux kernel uses the concept of *tables* and *chains* to create firewall rules. These terms sound kind of confusing; however, a chain is a rule that you implement to determine what the Linux kernel will do with an incoming packet. The netfilter infrastructure uses the *filter* table to configure simple packet filtering rules. Within the filter table are three default chains:

- FORWARD—The FORWARD chain is a list of rules for packets being transferred between networks through interfaces in the Linux system.
- INPUT—The INPUT chain contains rules for packets that are addressed to the local system.

- OUTPUT—The OUTPUT chain contains rules for packets that originate from the local system.

NOTE

The default netfilter infrastructure also includes the *nat* and the *mangle* tables. We'll talk about those later in the chapter. If you don't explicitly specify a table when using the iptables command, it defaults to the *filter* table.

Each chain has four policies that you can configure:

- ACCEPT—This policy allows the traffic to go through.
- DROP—This policy specifies that the traffic be disallowed and that the packets be dropped without informing the originating system.
- QUEUE—This policy puts the traffic on hold, delivering it to a defined location where it can be inspected or even modified.
- REJECT—This policy specifies that the traffic be disallowed and that a message indicating this be sent back to the originating system.

Using iptables, you can create rules within a chain. These rules specify a set of conditions and what action the kernel is to take if the given packet meets these conditions. You can add multiple rules to a chain. Each rule you add is assigned a number. For example, the first rule you add is assigned the number 1. Using iptables, you can add rules, delete rules, insert rules, and append rules. The basic syntax for using iptables is as follows:

```
iptables -t table_name command chain options
```

The commands you can use with iptables include the following:

- -L—List all rules in the chain.
- -N—Create a new chain.

NOTE

You can create your own chain by entering **`iptables -N`** ***`chain_name`***. You can then add rules to the chain by using the -A option, just as you would with one of the default chains. You can then call the custom chain using the `-j` option.

- -A—Appends a rule to the chain.
- -I—Inserts a rule into the chain.
- -R—Replaces a rule in the chain.
- -D—Deletes a rule from the chain.
- -F—Deletes all the rules from the chain (also called flushing).
- -P—Sets the default policy for the chain.

The options you can configure with iptables include the following:

- -p—Specifies the protocol to be checked by the rule. You can specify all protocols, tcp, udp, or icmp. If you specify tcp or udp, you can also use the following extensions for matching:
  - `-sports`—Specifies the source port to match on.
  - `-dports`—Specifies the destination port to match on.

NOTE

If you specify tcp, you can also use -tcp-flags to specify which type of TCP packets be monitored, such as SYN, ACK, FIN, and so on.

- `-s ip_address/mask`—Specifies the source address to be checked. You can specify a hostname, a specific IP address, or a network IP address. If you want to specify all IP addresses, use 0/0.
- `-d ip_address/mask`—Specifies the destination address to be checked. You can specify a hostname, a specific IP address, or a network IP address. If you want to specify all IP addresses, use 0/0.
- `-j target`—Specifies what to do if the packet matches the rule. You can specify ACCEPT, REJECT, DROP, or LOG actions. You can also create your own custom chain and call it using -j.
- `-i interface`—Specifies the interface where a packet is received. This applies only to INPUT and FORWARD chains.
- `-o interface`—Specifies the interface where a packet is to be sent. This applies only to OUPUT and FORWARD chains.

NOTE

The options presented here are only a subset of what's possible with iptables. To see all options you can use, view the iptables man page.

For example, if you want to set a default policy for the INPUT chain that would drop all incoming packets, enter

iptables -P INPUT DROP

To configure your FORWARD chain to drop all packets, enter

iptables -P FORWARD DROP

To configure your kernel to disregard incoming PING packets intended for the local system, enter

iptables -A INPUT -s 0/0 -p icmp -j DROP

To configure your firewall so that HTTP replies from any web server are allowed, enter

iptables -A FORWARD -p tcp -s 0/0 --sport 80 -j ACCEPT

If you want to configure your firewall so that all incoming packets on eth0 coming from the 192.168.2.0 network segment are dropped, enter

iptables -A INPUT -i eth0 -s 192.168.2.0/24 -j DROP

If you simply want to list the rules, enter the following:

iptables -L

By default, your SLES 9 system has no rules defined, as shown in Figure 10.15.

FIGURE 10.15
Displaying iptables rules.

```
fs1:/ # iptables -L
Chain INPUT (policy ACCEPT)
target     prot opt source               destination

Chain FORWARD (policy ACCEPT)
target     prot opt source               destination

Chain OUTPUT (policy ACCEPT)
target     prot opt source               destination
fs1:/ #
```

If you want to delete the first rule in the FORWARD chain, enter

iptables -D FORWARD 1

If you want to delete all rules from the filter table, enter

`iptables -t filter -F`

Using the syntax described previously, you can use iptables to create an amazing array of rules that will determine how data flows through your firewall. Use your organizational security policy to determine what traffic is allowed and what isn't.

A general model you could follow would be to first use *`-P`* with iptables to set up your kernel's default filtering behavior. After the default behavior is set, use iptables to configure rules that are exceptions to the default behavior needed by your network.

For example, suppose you are using your SLES 9 system as a packet filtering firewall between an internal network segment and a segment connected to the Internet. Your internal network address is 192.165.1.0 and your organization's DNS server is on a different segment with an IP address of 192.165.2.254.

You want to lock out all traffic except for HTTP requests and responses as well as DNS queries and responses. You could configure the following rules:

- `iptables -P FORWARD DROP`—This command configures the filter to lock down all routed traffic by default. Nothing gets through the filter.
- `iptables -A FORWARD -m tcp -p tcp -s 192.165.1.0/24 -d 0/0 --dport 80 -j ACCEPT`—This command configures the filter to allow outbound HTTP requests to any web server on port 80.
- `iptables -A FORWARD -m tcp -p tcp -s 0/0 --sport 80 -d 192.165.1.0/24 -j ACCEPT`—This command configures the filter to allow inbound HTTP responses coming from any web server on port 80.
- `iptables -A FORWARD -p udp -s 192.165.1.0/24 -d 192.165.2.254/24 --dport 53 -j ACCEPT`—This command configures the filter to allow outbound DNS queries from the internal network to the DNS server at 192.165.2.254 on port 53.
- `iptables -A FORWARD -p udp -s 192.165.2.254/24 --sport 53 -d 192.165.1.0/24` *`-j ACCEPT`*—This command configures the filter to allow inbound DNS responses from the DNS server at 192.165.2.254 on port 53.

In addition to protocols, addresses, and ports, you can use iptables to define rules that apply to packet states, allowing you to create a type of stateful firewall. This is done using the *`-m state`* option, which enables you to create rules using the following states:

- `NEW`—This state relates to a packet that initiates a new connection. For example, for a TCP connection, this would be the TCP SYN packet.

- `ESTABLISHED`—This state relates to packets that are being exchanged as part of an established connection.
- `RELATED`—This state relates to packets that are part of a connection that is itself related to another connection. For example, an FTP session will establish two connections: the data connection and the control connection. The FTP data connection is related to the FTP control connection for any given FTP session.
- `INVALID`—This state relates to stray packets that aren't known to be part of an established connection.

For example, if you want to create a stateful rule that disallows all invalid packets trying to pass through the router, enter

```
iptables -A FORWARD -m state --state INVALID -j DROP
```

It's important to remember that any rules you create with iptables are *not* persistent. If you reboot the system, they are lost forever! If you were to implement a very complex system of rules, this could make you utter things that your mother doesn't want you to say.

To preserve your rules, you can use the `iptables-save` command to write your tables out to a file. You can then use the `iptables-restore` command to restore the tables from the file you created.

Let's practice a bit with iptables in Lab Exercise 10.1:

Lab Exercise 10.1: Creating a Packet Filtering Firewall with iptables

In this lab exercise, you will configure a very simple packet-filtering firewall on your SLES 9 system using iptables. To complete this exercise, you will need your SLES 9 server with DNS, DHCP, Samba, Postfix, and CUPS running. You will also need an additional NLD or Windows workstation to test the firewall.

To configure a simple firewall with iptables on your server, complete the following:

1. Boot your SLES 9 server and authenticate as **tux** with a password of **SuSE789**.
2. From your NLD or Windows XP system, do the following:
   a. Ping your SLES 9 server and verify that it responds.
   b. Run nslookup from a command prompt and verify that you can use your SLES 9 system to resolve domain names.
   c. Open a web browser and verify that you can open the default web page (`http://fs1.cle9.com`) from the Apache web server running on your SLES 9 system.
3. Configure the kernel to use the iptables filter by completing the following:
   a. Open a terminal session.
   b. At the shell prompt enter **su -** to change to root with a password of **tuX123**.
   c. At the shell prompt, enter **modprobe iptable_filter**.
   d. At the shell prompt, list the currently configured rules for the filter table by entering **iptables -t filter -L**. There should be no rules defined.
4. Configure a firewall rule by completing the following:
   a. At the shell prompt, enter **iptables -t filter -A INPUT -s 0/0 -p icmp -j DROP**. This command specifies that all incoming packets using the icmp protocol from any source destined for the local system are to be dropped.

b. View your rule by entering **`iptables -t filter -L`** at the shell prompt. You should see output similar to that shown in Figure 10.16.

FIGURE 10.16
INPUT rule dropping all ICMP packets.

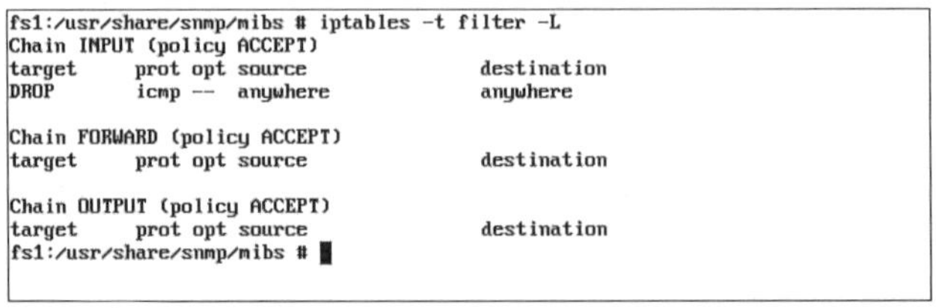

Using your NLD or Windows XP system, ping your server's IP address. The packets should be dropped, as shown in Figure 10.17.

FIGURE 10.17
No ping response.

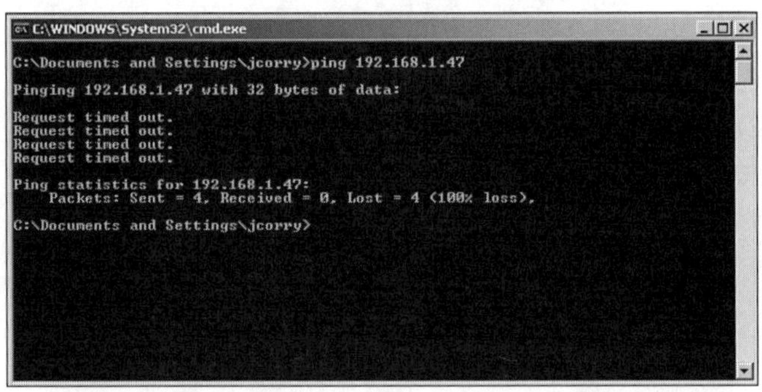

5. Block web server traffic by entering **`iptables -t filter -A INPUT -s 0/0 -p tcp --dport 80 -j DROP`**.
6. View your rule by entering **`iptables -t filter -L`** at the shell prompt. You should see a new rule added that drops tcp packets destined for port 80 on the server.
7. On your NLD or Windows XP system, try to access the Apache web server on your server. The page should fail to load.

8. Block DNS traffic by entering **iptables -t filter -A INPUT -s 0/0 -p tcp --dport 53 -j DROP**.
9. Block DNS traffic by entering **iptables -t filter -A INPUT -s 0/0 -p udp --dport 53 -j DROP**.
10. View your rule by entering **iptables -t filter -L** at the shell prompt. You should see a new rule added that drops tcp packets destined for port 53 on the server.
11. From your NLD or Windows XP system, run nslookup and try to resolve `fs1.cle9.com`. The resolution should fail.
12. Clear your rules by entering **iptables -F**.
13. At the shell prompt, enter **iptables -t filter -L**. You should see all rules removed.
14. From your NLD or Windows XP system, try to ping your server, run nslookup, and open a web page from your SLES 9 system. Everything should work again.

Notice in this exercise that we operated from a "wide-open door" perspective on our very simple firewall. In Figure 10.16, you'll see that the default policy for all chains is ACCEPT. In essence, this firewall is configured to accept all traffic and then filter out the exception.

If time permits, try re-creating the firewall from the opposite perspective. Start by setting the default policy on all chains to DROP with the `-P` command. Then reconfigure the rules to allow specific types of traffic and test their effect. Remember, if you get completely messed up, you can always clean out your rules by entering **iptables -F** and start fresh.

Let's now turn to a discussion of how to implement a packet filtering firewall with YaST.

Configuring a Packet Filtering Firewall with YaST

There's no question that iptables is a powerful tool for creating packet-filtering firewalls. It provides you with the ultimate in customization and flexibility.

The problem with iptables, however, is that you create your rules one at a time. Even when you use `-P` to establish default policies, configuring even a moderately complex firewall could require manual configuration of rule after rule after rule. The risk of making a mistake is high, requiring grueling hours of troubleshooting trying to identify which line is causing the problems.

That's where good old YaST comes into the picture. Like the other services we've configured, YaST makes tedious processes on SLES 9 faster and easier while eliminating mistakes. The options provided in YaST allow you to configure a fairly advanced firewall using commonly used options. When you're done, you can always use iptables to edit the chains YaST created for you, customizing them in a manner that suits your network.

The YaST Firewall module is used to configure the `/etc/sysconfig/SuSEfirewall2` file, which SuSEconfig uses to configure iptables.

To use YaST to configure your packet-filtering firewall with iptables, complete the following:

1. On your SLES 9 server, start YaST.
2. When prompted, provide your root user password.
3. Select **Security and Users, Firewall**. The screen in Figure 10.18 appears.
4. In the External Interface drop-down list, select the interface connected to the external network.
5. In the Internal Interface drop-down list, select the interface connected to the internal network.
6. Select **Next**. The screen in Figure 10.19 is displayed:
7. Mark the services on your server that should be made available to the external network through the firewall.
8. Select **Expert**. The screen in Figure 10.20 is displayed:
9. In the Additional TCP Services field, enter the port numbers, separated by spaces, of services on your server that should be made available to the external network through the firewall.
10. Select **OK**.
11. Select **Next**. The screen in Figure 10.21 is displayed:

FIGURE 10.18
Selecting the interfaces to be used for a firewall.

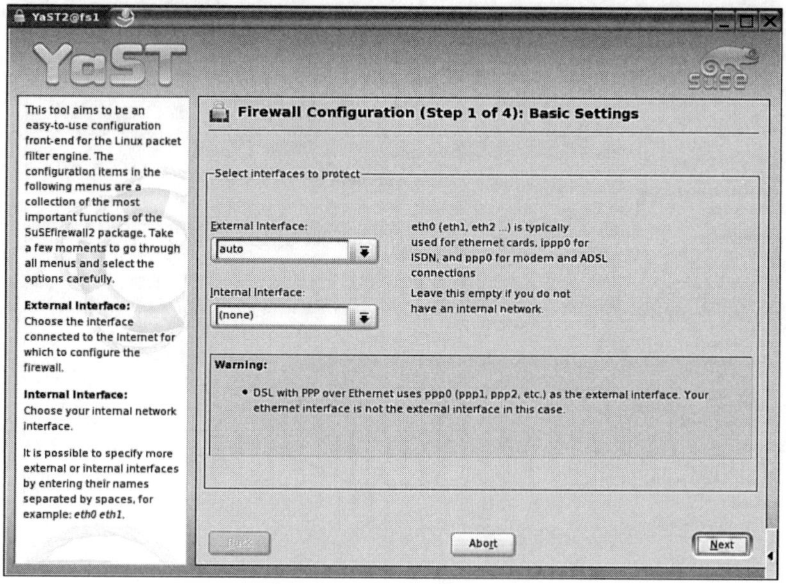

FIGURE 10.19
Selecting services to be allowed through the firewall.

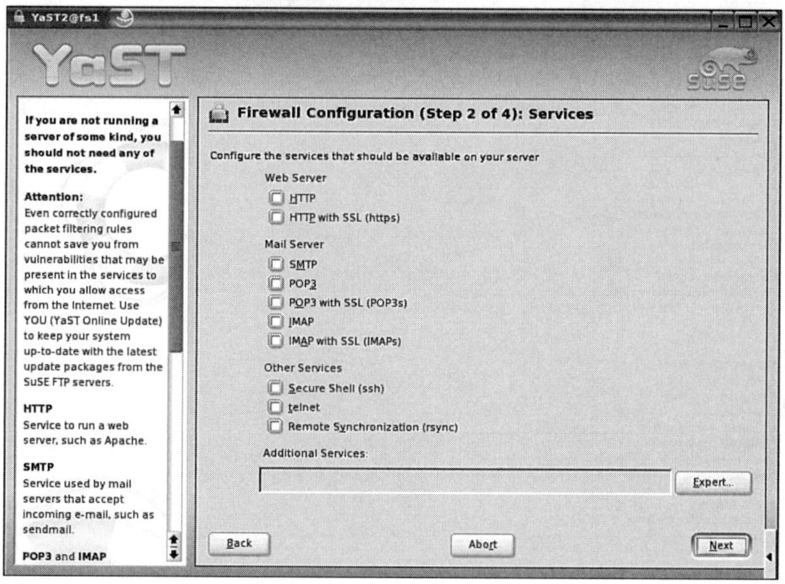

FIGURE 10.20
Adding additional services to be allowed through the firewall.

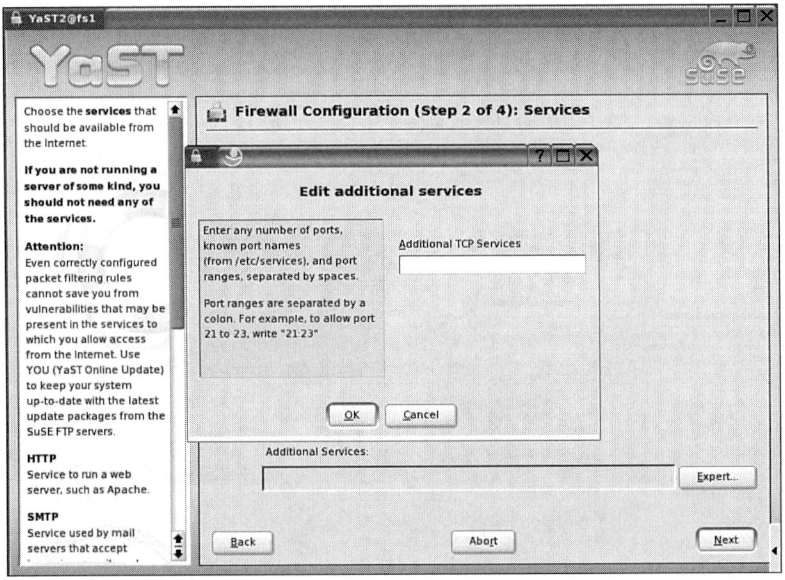

FIGURE 10.21
Configuring firewall features.

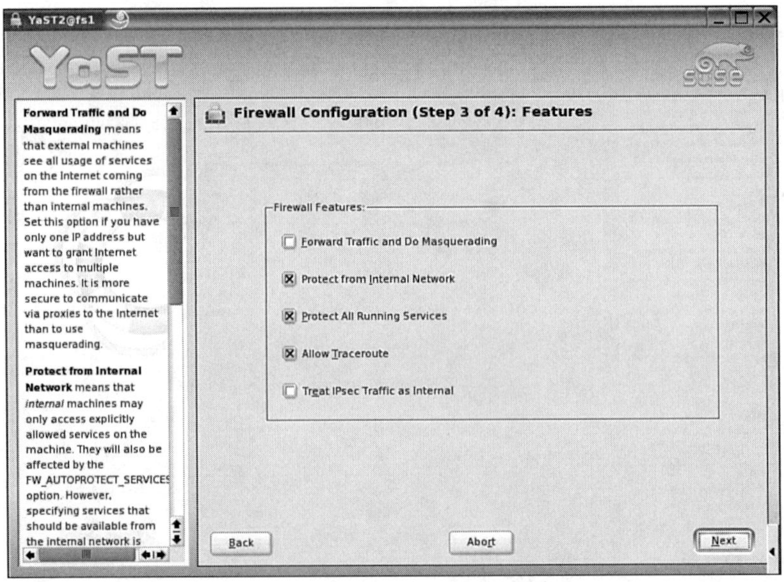

12. Select from the following:

- Forward Traffic and Do Masquerading—This option enables Network Address Translation on your system. We'll talk about NAT later in this chapter.
- Protect from Internal Network—This option, if selected, specifies that hosts on the internal network can use only the services explicitly made available to them.
- Protect All Running Services—This option, if selected, configures the firewall so that access to all TCP and UDP services running on the server is denied except for those you marked in the previous screen.
- Allow traceroute—Selecting this option allows your server to respond to ICMP messages.
- Treat IPsec Data Traffic as Internal—This option configures the firewall to treat successfully decrypted IPsec packets as if they came from the internal network.

13. Select **Next**. The screen in Figure 10.22 is displayed:

FIGURE 10.22
Configuring firewall logging options.

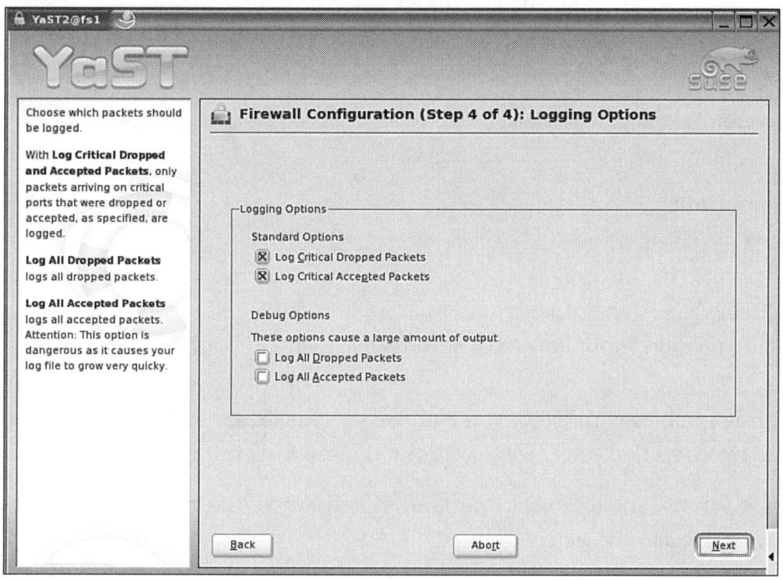

14. Configure your logging and debugging options and then select **Next**. The screen in Figure 10.23 is displayed:

FIGURE 10.23
Activating the firewall.

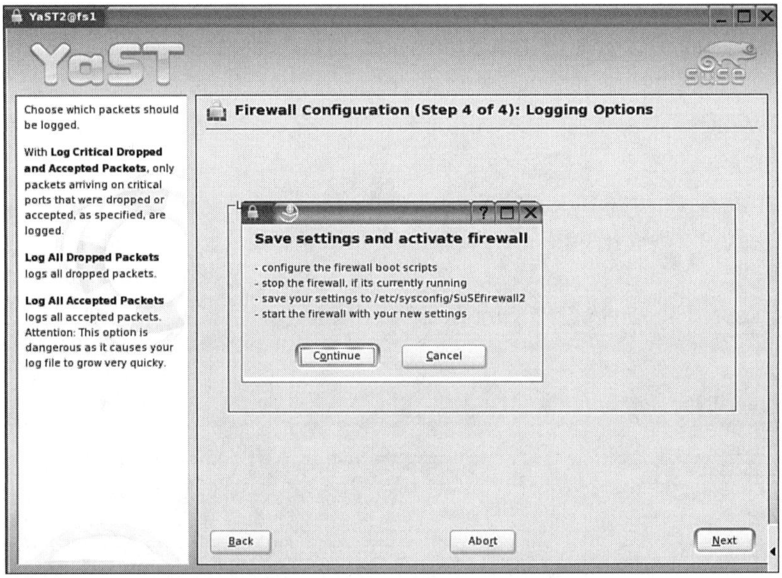

15. Select **Continue**.

TIP

Notice that YaST configures your firewall to automatically start at boot.

After configuring iptables with YaST, you can use the **`iptables -L -v`** command from a shell prompt to see the rules that have been configured, as shown in Figure 10.24.

From here, you can use the iptables command to edit any of the rules to meet the requirements of your organization's security policy.

Before practicing setting up a firewall with YaST, we need to discuss one more topic: configuring Network Address Translation (NAT).

FIGURE 10.24
iptables rules configured by YaST.

```
fs1:/etc/sysconfig # iptables -L -v |more
Chain INPUT (policy DROP 0 packets, 0 bytes)
 pkts bytes target     prot opt in     out     source               destination

   22  2064 ACCEPT     all  --  lo     any     anywhere             anywhere

    0     0 ACCEPT     udp  --  eth1   any     anywhere             255.255.255.
255      state NEW,ESTABLISHED udp spt:bootpc dpt:bootps
    2   477 ACCEPT     udp  --  eth1   any     anywhere             anywhere
         state NEW,RELATED,ESTABLISHED udp dpts:netbios-ns:netbios-dgm
    0     0 DROP       all  --  eth0   any     anywhere             255.255.255.
255
   11  2191 DROP       all  --  eth0   any     anywhere             192.168.1.25
5
    6   850 input_ext  all  --  eth0   any     anywhere             anywhere

    6  1044 input_int  all  --  eth1   any     anywhere             anywhere

    0     0 LOG        all  --  eth1   any     anywhere             fs1.cle9.com
         LOG level warning tcp-options ip-options prefix `SFW2-IN-ACC_DENIED_INT
'
    0     0 DROP       all  --  eth1   any     anywhere             fs1.cle9.com

--More--
```

Implementing Network Address Translation (NAT) on SLES 9

NAT is an exceptionally useful feature that can be implemented on SLES 9.

NOTE

Most other server operating systems, such as Windows and NetWare, also provide NAT functionality.

NAT allows you to hide your network behind a router. When packets flow through the router from the internal private network to the external network, NAT strips off the source address and substitutes its own external IP address. Systems on the external network see all traffic as coming from the router system itself, not from a host within the internal network. When the response packets are received, the destination address is removed by NAT and replaced with the original requesting host's IP address on the internal network.

Let's look at some of the benefits of using NAT in your network.

THE BENEFITS OF NAT

NAT solves a number of key problems network administrators must deal with. First is the shortage of IP addresses. As you probably know, any IP host that is going to participate on a public network must have a globally unique registered IP address. No two hosts can have the same registered address.

This presents several problems. Because of the acute shortage of available registered IP addresses, most of the Class A and B address ranges have been long taken. Depending on the size of the organization you work for, there's a pretty good chance you will have one or more Class C address ranges, which allow for only 254 hosts per network.

In addition, registered IP addresses are somewhat expensive. Recently, organizations have had to start paying yearly for their registered IP addresses. If you have a lot of users, the cost can add up fast.

NAT can be a real lifesaver in this respect. With NAT, you need only one registered IP address to connect an entire network segment to the external network. All the hosts within the internal network can use whatever IP addresses they want. It doesn't matter because all traffic on the external network (where registered addresses are required) appears to be coming from the one registered address on the external interface of the NAT router.

Although you can use any address range you want behind a NAT router, you should use one of three nonroutable private IP address ranges defined in RFC 1918 and reserved by the Internet Assigned Numbers Authority (IANA) specifically for this purpose. These include

- Class A: 10.0.0.0 – 10.255.255.255.255
- Class B: 172.16.0.0 – 172.31.255.255
- Class C: 192.168.0.0 – 192.168.255.255

Anyone can use any of the addresses in these ranges without registering them. For example, in Figure 10.25, a NAT router has been configured between an internal network segment and an external network segment where registered IP addresses are required.

FIGURE 10.25
A basic NAT configuration.

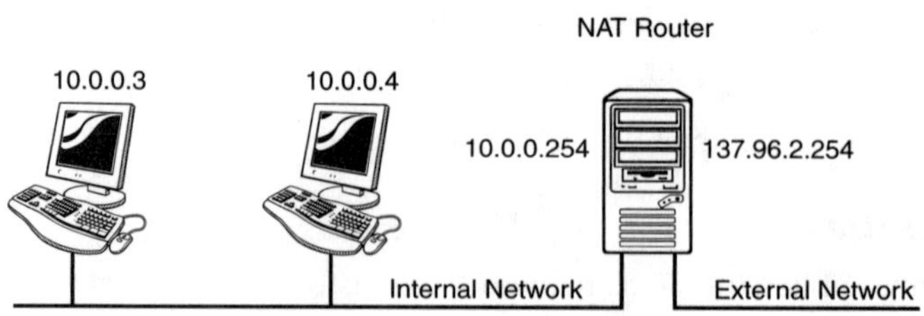

The NAT router has two interfaces—one connected to the internal network, the other to the external network. The interface connected to the external network has a registered IP address of 137.96.2.254 assigned to it. The internal interface has an IP address of 10.0.0.254 assigned to it. Hosts on the internal network use the private IP addressing scheme of 10.0.0.0 (sometimes called *ten-net*).

Using this configuration, whenever a host on the internal network accesses a resource on the external network, the request is seen as coming from 137.96.2.254, not 10.0.0.*x*. This means that this entire network segment, which could have hundreds of hosts on it, consumes only a single registered IP address.

The second benefit of NAT is that it hides the internal network. Even though NAT is primarily concerned with routing, it creates a firewall at the Network layer of the OSI model. Because of the way NAT works, hosts on the external network have no way to access hosts on the internal network segment. Talk about security!

TIP

There is a way to make hosts behind the NAT router available to hosts on the external network—for example, if you had a web server inside the internal network that needs to be publicly accessible.

To do this, you must either add an additional external interface to the NAT router or multihome the existing interface with a second registered IP address. Then you create a static, one-to-one NAT mapping between the second registered IP address and the internal IP address of the host you want to make publicly accessible.

Basically, with NAT you get conservation of registered IP addresses along with a powerful firewall. Not too shabby! Let's now explore how NAT works in a little more depth.

HOW NAT WORKS

When I first learned about NAT, my first thought was, "How in the world does the NAT router keep track of which response is intended for which internal host?" If you think about it, a NAT router on a heavily utilized network segment may have hundreds of requests each second coming through from the internal network to hosts on the external network. The NAT router has to keep track of all the response packets it receives from the external network, associating them with the originating internal hosts. To do this, NAT uses port numbers, as shown in Figure 10.26.

FIGURE 10.26
How NAT works.

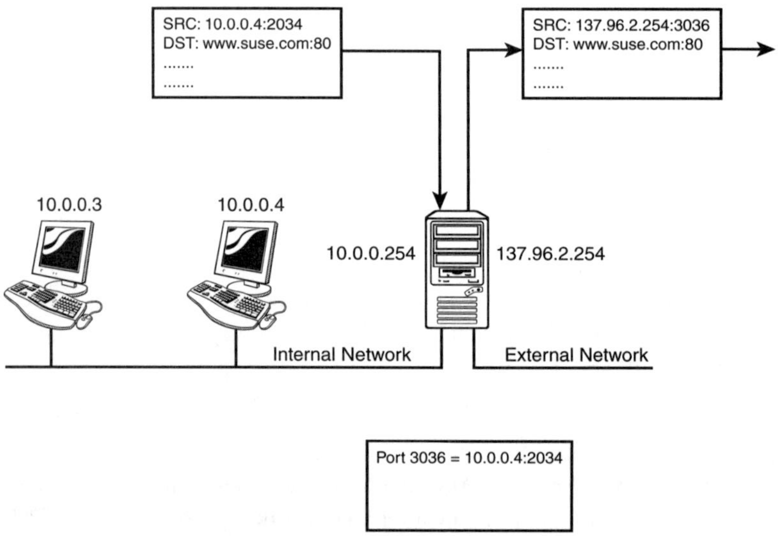

Here's how it works:

First, a host on the internal network generates an IP packet that gets sent to the NAT router. NAT removes the internal IP address from the packet and replaces it with the registered IP address assigned to its external interface.

Then, the NAT router selects a random high port number on its external interface to forward the packet from. The NAT router keeps a table in memory that maintains a list of each internal IP address it has received packets from and the corresponding port number it used to forward the request to the external network.

The NAT router then forwards the packet to the destination host on the external network. When the external host responds, the NAT router refers to the table to determine where the packet should go. When that is determined, the NAT router replaces the destination address of the packet with the IP address of the internal host that originated the request and forwards the packet to it. When the communication is complete, the port the NAT router used is returned to its pool of unused ports, ready to be reassigned again as needed.

To provide this functionality, the NAT router maintains a pool of 5,000 ports available for TCP connections, a pool of 5,000 ports available for UDP connections, and a pool of 5,000 ports available for ICMP connections.

As you can see, there is a theoretical limit to how many concurrent connections a NAT router can handle. After the 5,000 connection limit is reached, the NAT router has to make a hard decision. It doesn't want to get bogged down with new requests queued up waiting for ports to be freed.

Therefore, to make sure data keeps flowing, the NAT router will drop the oldest port-to-address mappings in its table, allowing new traffic to use the freed ports. Specifically, the router looks for the following:

- Any connection that has been inactive for more than 8 hours.
- Any connection attempt that has been waiting more than 2 minutes for the 3-way TCP handshake to be completed.

With this NAT theory in mind, let's look at how NAT is implemented on SLES 9.

HOW NAT IS IMPLEMENTED ON SLES 9

The nice thing about NAT on SLES 9 is that it's implemented using the netfilter kernel infrastructure and iptables. Recall our earlier discussion of packet-filtering firewalls. We mentioned that this type of firewall is configured using the filter table. NAT is implemented using the *nat* table. The chains in the nat table are shown in Figure 10.27.

FIGURE 10.27
The chains in the nat table.

```
fs1:~ # iptables -t nat -L
Chain PREROUTING (policy ACCEPT)
target     prot opt source               destination

Chain POSTROUTING (policy ACCEPT)
target     prot opt source               destination

Chain OUTPUT (policy ACCEPT)
target     prot opt source               destination
fs1:~ #
```

Notice that these tables are somewhat different than those used in the filter table. Instead of INPUT, FORWARD, and OUTPUT, the nat table uses the PREROUTING, POSTROUTING, and OUTPUT chains. The PREROUTING chain contains rules that are applied to incoming packets. The POSTROUTING chain contains rules that are applied to routed outgoing packets.

NOTE

The POSTROUTING chain is the one we will be most concerned with when implementing NAT.

Like the filter table, the OUTPUT chain in the nat table is applied to outgoing packets that originated from the system itself.

To use the nat table, you must add the `iptable_nat` module to the kernel using modprobe. After that, you can use iptables to add a simple rule to the POSTROUTING chain in the nat table to turn on NAT.

For example, suppose we have a SLES 9 system with two interfaces. The eth0 interface is connected to the external network, and the eth1 interface is connected to the internal network. To enable NAT on this system, enter the following:

```
iptables -t nat -A POSTROUTING -o eth0 -j MASQUERADE
```

In the Linux world, you will often hear NAT referred to as *masquerading* because of the iptables action used to accomplish it. After issuing this command, the POSTROUTING rule appears as shown in Figure 10.28:

FIGURE 10.28
Configuring MASQUERADE in the POSTROUTING chain.

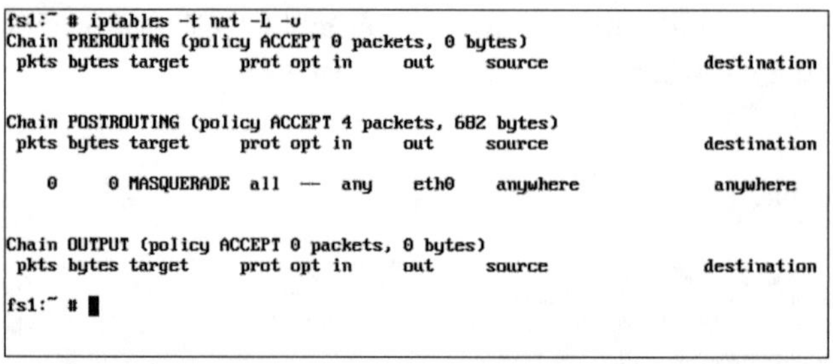

You will also need to enable IP forwarding. You can do this by editing `/etc/sysconfig/sysctl` and setting IP_FORWARD to **yes**. This is shown in Figure 10.29.

This can also be done by entering **`echo 1 > /proc/sys/net/ipv4/ip_forward`** at the shell prompt.

When you're done, save your changes to the file and run SuSEconfig to implement the change. After doing so, your server can function as a NAT router. Of course, all other packet-filter firewalling capabilities aren't enabled unless you previously configured them.

Next, you need to configure all the hosts on the internal network to use the IP address of the internal interface of the NAT router as the default gateway address. After that, your internal hosts will be able to communicate with outside hosts through the NAT router.

FIGURE 10.29
Enabling IP forwarding.

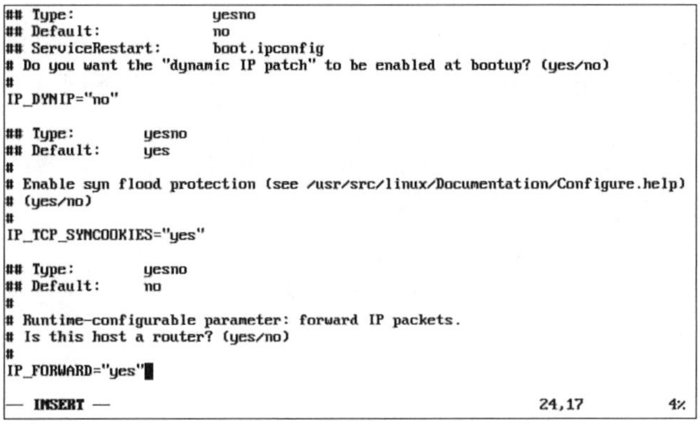

For example, in Figure 10.30, a SLES 9 system has been configured to masquerade between two network segments. The eth0 interface is connected to the external network. Its IP address is 192.168.1.47. The eth1 interface is connected to the internal network with an IP address of 10.0.0.254.

FIGURE 10.30
Pinging through a SLES 9 NAT router.

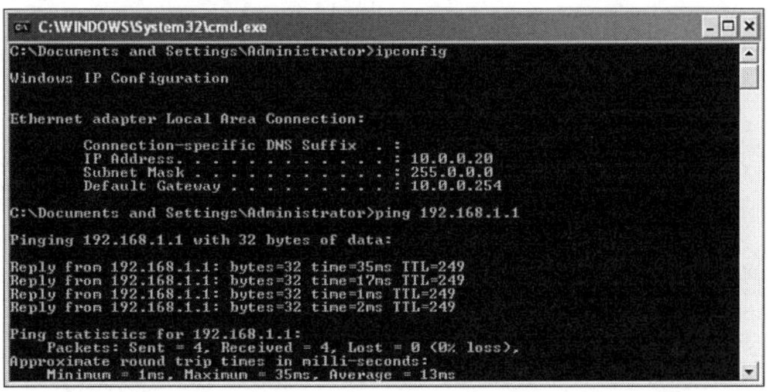

A Windows XP system has been configured on the internal network segment with an IP address of 10.0.0.20. The default route has been configured to the IP address of the internal network side of the SLES 9 system: 10.0.0.254. The workstation is able to ping through the NAT router to a host on the external network—in this case, 192.168.1.1.

Again, hosts on the external network see all this traffic as coming from the external interface of the NAT router. In this case, 192.168.1.1 has no idea that 10.0.0.20 actually sent the pings. It thinks they came from 192.168.1.47.

This begs the question, then, of whether you can have rules on the filter table and the nat table and run both at the same time. In other words, can you run a packet-filtering firewall and a NAT router at the same time? You bet you can. The two can coexist very well. Configure your packet-filtering rules in the filter table; then configure masquerading using the POSTROUTING chain in the nat table.

Because the translation process occurs at the very end of the netfilter process, all firewalling rules are applied first. Then the nat table rules are applied right before the packet leaves the server. Pretty slick, huh?

Before we start on Exercise 10.2, I want you to understand that you really need to know firewalling and NAT. In the course of my day-to-day work, I've had the opportunity to visit the sites of many clients. Every single client I work with has a firewall protecting its network and has deployed at least one NAT router in the network. If you're going to work in the IT industry, you will more than likely be working with both NAT routers and firewalls extensively.

Now, just as with firewalls, you can also use YaST to configure NAT on your system. All it takes is a single click. You'll learn how this done in Exercise 10.2. In this exercise, you will create a more advanced packet-filtering firewall using YaST as well as enable masquerading.

Lab Exercise 10.2: Creating a Packet-Filtering Firewall and a NAT Router with YaST

In this lab exercise, you will configure a more complex packet filtering firewall on your SLES 9 system using YaST. You will also enable NAT routing on the system.

To complete this exercise, you will need your SLES 9 server with DNS, DHCP, Samba, Postfix, and CUPS running. You will also need a second network interface card to install in your SLES 9 server. Finally, you will need an additional NLD or Windows workstation to test the firewall with. Complete the following:

1. Down your SLES 9 server.
2. Install a second network interface card in your SLES 9 server.

TIP

If you're using VMware, this is really easy to do. Just add a second network adapter to the virtual machine. Make sure the external segment adapter is configured in Bridged mode and that the internal segment adapter is configured in Host-Only mode. Then configure the adapter in your workstation to Host-Only.

3. Reconfigure your network cabling as shown in Figure 10.31.

FIGURE 10.31
Setup for Lab Exercise 10.2.

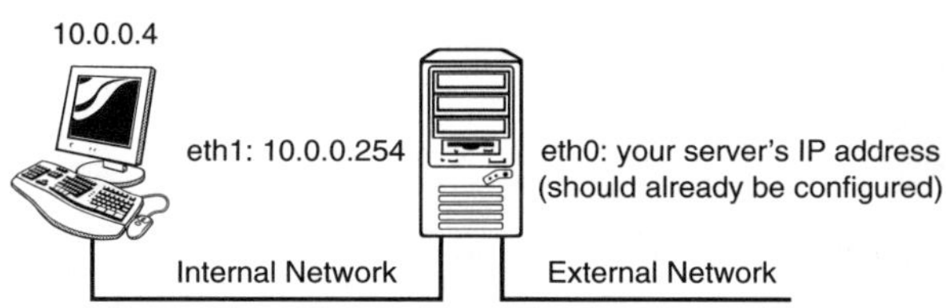

NOTE

Basically, I'm having you move your NLD or Windows workstation on to the internal network segment. You can create this segment using a network hub/switch, or you can use a crossover cable to connect the NIC in the workstation with the NIC in the server. See the preceding tip if you're using VMware.

4. Change the IP address of your NLD or Windows workstation to 10.0.0.4 with a subnet mask of 255.0.0.0.

   If you're already using 10.x.x.x on eth0, use 192.168.1.4 instead. If you do, adjust the remaining steps accordingly, using 192.168.1.254 for the eth1 interface on your server as well as for the default route on the workstation.

5. Change the default route of your NLD or Windows workstation to 10.0.0.254.

6. Boot your SLES 9 server and authenticate as **tux** with a password of **SuSE789**.

7. When prompted to configure your new network board, select **Yes**; then complete the following:

   a. When prompted, enter a root password of **tuX123**.

   b. Under Network Cards to Configure, mark your new adapter; then select **Configure**.

   c. In the Network Address Setup screen, write down the Network Device ID.

   d. Under Choose the Setup Method, mark **Static Address Setup**.

   e. In the IP Address field, enter **10.0.0.254**.

   f. In the Subnet Mask field, enter **255.0.0.0**.

   g. Select **Finish**.

8. Configure your firewall by completing the following:

   a. In YaST, select Security and Users > Firewall.

   b. In the External Interface drop-down list, select the interface connected to the external network.

TIP

If you can't remember which is which, use the ifconfig command from a shell prompt. Be sure to configure eth0 as the external interface and eth1 as the internal interface.

c. In the Internal Interface drop-down list, select the interface connected to the internal network; then select **Next**.

d. Mark the following services:
   - **HTTP**
   - **HTTP with SSL**
   - **SMTP**
   - **POP3**
   - **POP3 with SSL**
   - **IMAP**
   - **IMAP with SSL**

e. Select **Expert**.

f. In the Additional TCP Services field, enter **`3000 3001 domain ipp netbios-dgm netbios-ns netbios-ssn snmp snmptrap`**.

TIP

The names you can use for ports are found in `/etc/services`.

g. Select **OK**; then select **Next**.

h. Mark the following:
   - Forward Traffic and Do Masquerading
   - Allow traceroute
   - Protect All Running Services

i. Deselect Protect from Internal Network.

TIP

If you don't deselect this option, internal network packets won't be allowed to reach the NAT router.

   j. Select **Next**.

   k. In the Logging Options screen, accept the default by selecting **Next**.

   l. When prompted to save the settings and activate the firewall, select **Continue**.

9. Customize the installation to support DHCP, DNS, and Samba by completing the following:

   a. Open a terminal session and enter **`sux -`** to change to root using a password of **`tuX123`**.

   b. At the shell prompt, enter **`kate`**.

   c. In Kate, open `etc/sysconfig/SuSEfirewall2`.

   d. Scroll down to the FW_SERVICES_EXT_TCP parameter.

   e. Select the *value* of FW_SERVICES_EXT_TCP and copy it to the clipboard.

   f. Scroll down to the FW_SERVICES_INT_TCP parameter and paste the contents of the clipboard for its value.

   g. Scroll down to the FW_SERVICES_INT_UDP parameter and paste the contents of the clipboard for its value.

   h. Scroll down to the FW_ALLOW_INCOMING_HIGHPORTS_TCP parameter and set it to **domain**.

   i. Scroll down to the FW_ALLOW_INCOMING_HIGHPORTS_UDP parameter and set it to **domain**.

   j. Scroll down to the FW_SERVICE_DNS parameter and set it to **yes**.

   k. Scroll down to the FW_SERVICE_DHCPD parameter and set it to **yes**.

   l. Scroll down to the FW_SERVICE_SAMBA parameter and set it to **yes**.

   m. Save the changes and exit Kate.

   n. At the shell prompt, enter **`SuSEconfig`**.

   o. At the shell prompt, enter **`rcSuSEfirewall2 restart`**.

10. Test your configuration by completing the following:

  a. From your NLD or Windows workstation, verify that you can ping the internal network interface of your server by pinging 10.0.0.254.

  b. Ping a host on the external network segment by its *IP address*. Verify that the remote host responds.

  c. Open a web browser and verify that you can open the default Apache web server page from your SLES 9 server using the internal IP address and the external IP address.

  d. From your NLD or Windows workstation, open an ssh session through both the external and internal interfaces and verify that you are able to authenticate as root.

  e. If you have access to a Linux workstation that you can set up on the external network, try opening an ssh session to your SLES 9 server.

11. Turn off the firewall by entering **`rcSuSEfirewall2 stop`** at the shell prompt on the server.

That's it! You now know how to configure a powerful packet filtering firewall on your server.

If you're interested in creating a DMZ, read through the comments in the `/etc/sysconfig/SuSEfirewall2` file. You'll find everything you need to create a DMZ. It's really pretty easy. Essentially you just add a third interface to the server and then configure an additional set of firewall rules for the DMZ segment as well as the internal network.

Before we end this chapter, we need to cover one more topic. Recall that we talked earlier about application-level gateways. For your CLE exam, you need to know how to configure Squid on your SLES 9 system to create an application-level gateway. Let's talk about how to do this next.

Implementing Application-Level Gateways on SLES 9

TEST OBJECTIVE COVERED:

3. Implement an application-level gateway on SLES 9.

Up to this point, we've configured our SLES 9 system with two network interfaces, configured a packet-filtering firewall, and enabled masquerading. This system works fine as it is. In fact, I've seen many organizations that use just this type of configuration.

However, it could be made better. There's two problems with our current network. First of all, every workstation on our internal network has full and unfettered access to the external network (including the Internet). Aside from some packet-filtering firewall rules, we don't have many controls on what the users can access.

Second, our packet-filtering firewall looks only at Layer 3 and a little bit of Layer 4 for filtering. It's possible for an intruder or attacker to send legitimate-looking packets at our firewall and use malicious content in the packets themselves to cause all kinds of problems.

We need to fix these problems. We need to implement an application-level gateway (also called a *proxy*) that will force all users on the internal network to go through it to reach the Internet. Doing this will decrease our network traffic (through caching), give us more control over what users can access on the Internet, and add Layer 7 protection to our firewall solution.

In this part of this chapter, we're going to look at proxies in greater depth. Specifically, we're going to cover:

- Types of proxies
- Caching hierarchies
- Generic proxies
- Protocol-specific proxies

Let's start by looking at the various types of proxies you may encounter as a network administrator.

Types of Proxy Servers

In discussions about proxy servers, you will probably hear them referred to using a dizzying array of terms. We're going to spend a few pages up front sorting all these terms out.

Let's start by talking about the difference between *generic* proxies and *protocol-specific* proxies.

GENERIC VERSUS PROTOCOL-SPECIFIC PROXIES

So far in this chapter, all the proxies we've been discussing are protocol-specific proxies. That is, the proxy server is designed to provide application-level gateway services for a specific protocol, such as HTTP/HTTPS or FTP.

There's also another type of application-level gateway called a *generic* proxy. As the name would imply, a generic proxy is not concerned with a specific application. Instead, it provides application-level gateway functionality for TCP or UDP connections.

When you look at that, you're probably saying, "Wait a minute! Those are not application-layer protocols!" You're right. Even though a generic proxy is technically an application-level gateway, it operates much lower in the OSI model than a protocol-specific proxy.

When a client sends a request for a network resource, the client first connects to the generic proxy server. The generic proxy then establishes a connection with the server hosting the resource on behalf of the client. It then relays the data between the client and the server. As with a protocol-specific proxy, the server providing the resource sees the connection originating from the generic proxy. It has no idea that the request is actually coming from a different system.

The advantage of a generic proxy is that it isn't application specific. With a protocol-specific proxy, you must implement a separate proxy for each upper-layer protocol you want to provide an application-level firewall for. A generic proxy, on the other hand, because it works with TCP and UDP, can work with all application-layer protocols.

The disadvantage of generic proxies is that, because they operate lower in the OSI model, they can't provide the same degree of functionality we associate with protocol-specific proxies. Some do provide user-authentication capabilities (such as Dante, which uses the SOCKS protocol); however, they can't filter or cache content.

In addition to generic proxies, there's another type of application-level gateway that you need to be aware of: *transparent proxies*.

TRANSPARENT PROXIES

With a traditional application-level gateway, the client system must be configured to use the proxy. For example, if you implement an HTTP proxy, your users' web browsers must be configured to use it.

However, you can use your network router to create a transparent proxy. Instead of configuring each client to use the proxy server, with a transparent proxy, you configure your network router to automatically redirect traffic of a specific type to the proxy.

If you're using a Linux system as your NAT router and proxy server, you can easily do this using good old iptables. To create a transparent proxy, you will need to intercept packets when they first arrive at the router, before they are processed and forwarded.

Therefore, you need to set a rule on the PREROUTING chain in the NAT table that matches traffic on a specific port and then redirects it. For example, if you want to redirect HTTP traffic (on port 80) when it arrives at the NAT router to the proxy service on the same server, enter the following command:

```
iptables -t nat -A PREROUTING -p TCP -dport 80 -j REDIRECT -to-port
proxy_server_port
```

Transparent proxies can reduce the amount of configuration work required on your part to get your users' workstations to work with the proxy server. The downside of transparent proxies is that they don't work with all application-layer protocols (although they work great with HTTP traffic).

With these concepts in mind, let's now talk about *caching hierarchies*.

Caching Hierarchies

With many caching proxy servers, you can configure multiple caching proxies into a caching hierarchy. In a caching hierarchy, you configure multiple caching proxy servers in your network in parent/child relationships. The goal is to prevent a single proxy cache server from having to handle all the requests from users in the network.

NOTE

Remember that application-level gateways (proxies) require a lot of processing horsepower. Funneling all web traffic through a single proxy in a large organization would bring the server to its knees.

An example of a caching hierarchy is shown in Figure 10.32.

In this example, a single *parent* proxy has three *child* proxies. Each of the children is called a *sibling*. Suppose the client system in Figure 10.32 sends a request for a web page from a remote web server to the proxy server it has been configured to use.

As proxy servers do, it checks its own cache first to see if it has the requested page. If it has it, then it returns it to the requesting system. However, if it doesn't, it uses the caching hierarchy to avoid going out on the Internet to get the requested page.

Before doing that, it checks the cache of each of its sibling caches first. This is done using the Internet Cache Protocol (ICP), which is an upper-layer protocol that runs on top of UPD/IP. Each of the siblings responds via ICP as to whether they have the requested page.

FIGURE 10.32
A sample caching hierarchy.

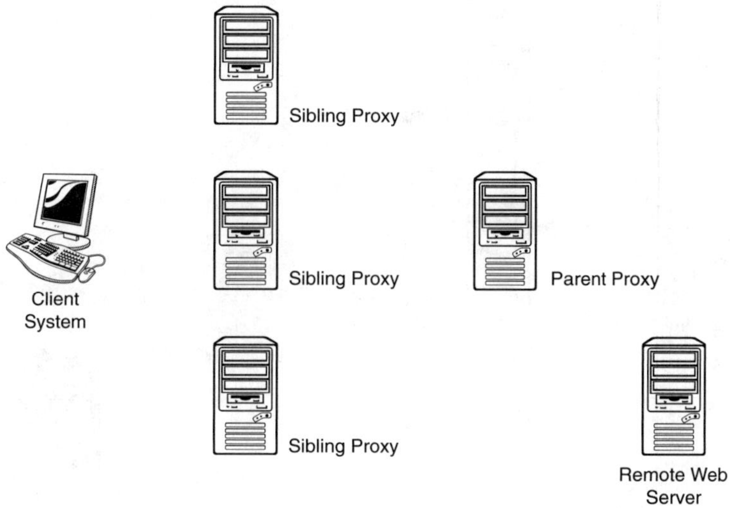

If the responses are positive, the original proxy then decides which sibling cache to pull the resource from. If there are positive responses from more than one sibling, the original proxy will use ICP to determine which sibling has the fastest response time and pull the requested resource from it via the Hypertext Caching Protocol (HTCP).

For an example, refer to Figure 10.33.

In this example, the following occurs:

1. The client system sends a request for http://www.suse.com/index.html to its proxy server.
2. The proxy server doesn't have the resource in its cache, so it sends a request to its siblings via ICP.
3. One of the sibling proxies doesn't have the page requested and responds in the negative.
4. The other sibling proxy has the requested resource and responds in the affirmative. The page is transferred from its cache via HTTP to the original proxy server.
5. The page is transferred to the requesting client system.

If none of the siblings have the requested resource, the original proxy then contacts the parent proxy via ICP. If the parent has the requested page in its cache, it pulls it out and sends to back to the original proxy. If not, the parent proxy contacts the actual web server on the Internet for the page and pulls it down for the requesting system, as shown in Figure 10.34.

FIGURE 10.33
A caching hierarchy in action.

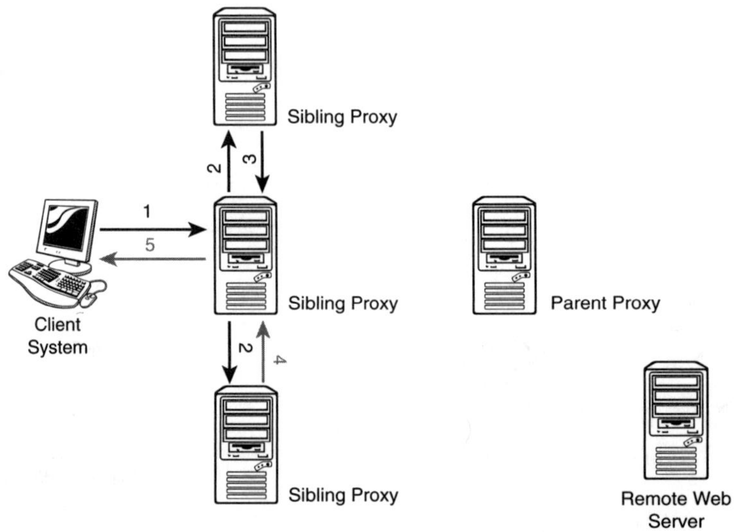

FIGURE 10.34
Contacting the parent cache.

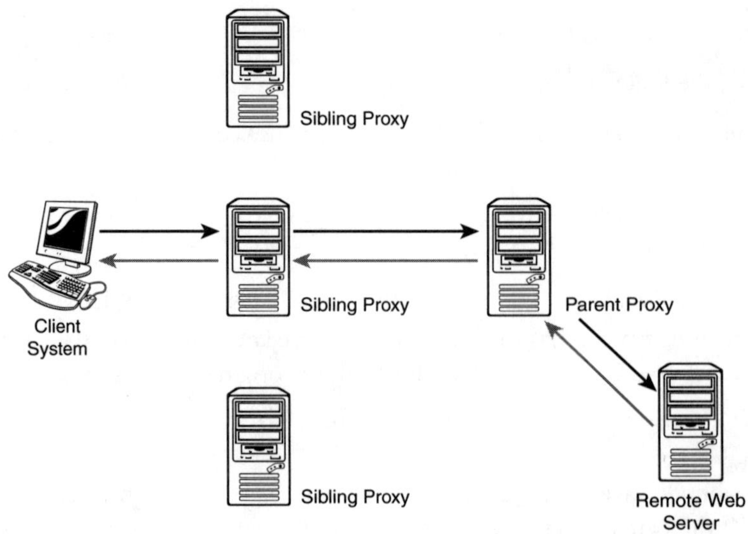

As you can see, using a caching hierarchy can really decrease the traffic on your network, especially your connection to the Internet. It also reduces the load on your main proxy cache server and increases response time and throughput.

The general rule for implementing caching hierarchies is to implement sibling proxy caches on each subnet in your organization and then set up one parent proxy cache server for all the siblings you configured.

With all this background information in mind, let's now shift gears and start working with specific proxy packages. Let's start by looking at a couple of generic proxy server packages.

Implementing Generic Proxy Servers

For your CLE 9 certification, you need to be familiar with both generic and protocol-specific proxy servers. However, the emphasis in the certification is on protocol-specific proxies, so we're going to briefly talk about a couple of generic proxies first; then we'll spend the rest of the chapter working with Squid in detail.

Let's start by working with rinetd.

USING RINETD AS A GENERIC PROXY

The rinetd is a basic, TCP-based generic proxy daemon that you can install on your SLES 9 system. To use it, you must first install the rinetd package on your server, as shown in Figure 10.35.

FIGURE 10.35
Installing the rinetd daemon.

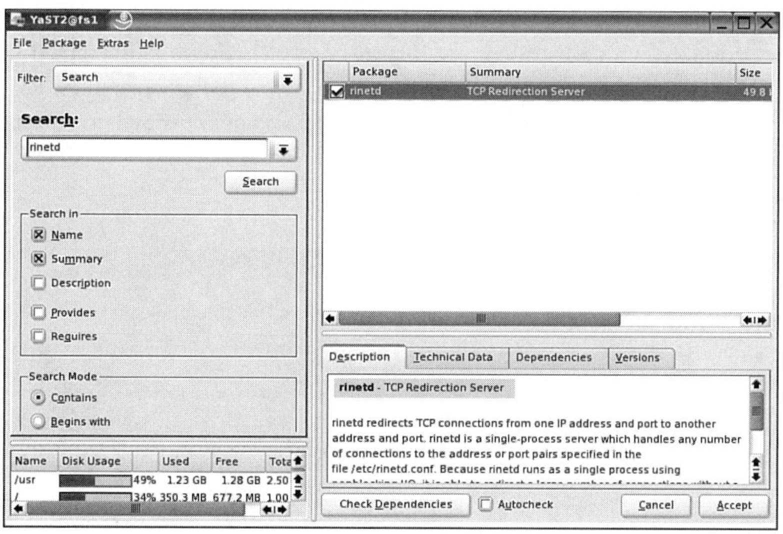

After it is installed, the rinetd daemon is configured using the `/etc/rinetd.conf` file. However, this file is not created during installation. A sample `rinetd.conf` file, shown in Figure 10.36, is provided by the package in `/usr/share/doc/packages/rinetd` that you can edit and then copy to `/etc`.

FIGURE 10.36
The sample *rinetd.conf* file.

```
# This is a sample configuration file for rinetd
# Please refer to the rinetd manual page, adjust it to your personal needs
# and copy it to /etc/rinetd.conf

# FORWARDING RULES

# A simple forwarding rule
#
# Format: <bindaddress> <bindport> <connectaddress> <connectport>
#
# This would redirect all connections to port 80 of the "real" IP address
# 206.125.69.81, which could be a virtual interface, through rinetd to port
# 80 of the address 10.1.1.2, which would typically be a machine on the
# inside of a firewall which has no direct routing to the outside world.
# Service names can be specified instead of port numbers. On most systems,
# service names are defined in the file /etc/services.
# Both IP addresses and hostnames are accepted for bindaddress and
# connectaddress.
# Optionally another column <sourceaddress> can be given to specify
# a local address to bind to specifically on outgoing connections.

206.125.69.81 80 10.1.1.2 80

./rinetd.conf.sample lines 1-23/68 35%
```

Within this file you can configure ALLOW rules, DENY rules, and FORWARD rules. At this point, you need to understand that, like rules in a netfilter chain, the rules you define in `/etc/rinetd.conf` are order specific.

For example, if you define an ALLOW rule at the beginning of the file (before any FORWARD rule), it is applied globally to all subsequent forwarding rules. If you define an ALLOW rule after a FORWARD rule, then the ALLOW rule applies only to the associated FORWARD rule. Read the sample `rinetd.conf` file in `/usr/share/doc/packages/rinetd` for more details on how this works.

The syntax for ALLOW and DENY rules are as follows:

```
ALLOW IP_address

DENY IP_address
```

TIP

You can't use hostnames in an ALLOW or DENY rule.

Within the IP_address parameter, you can use ? and * characters to specify address or host ranges. For example, if you want to allow all traffic from the 192.168.1.0 subnet, add a rule like the following:

```
ALLOW 192.168.1.*
```

Likewise, if you want to deny traffic from the same subnet, add a rule like the following:

```
DENY 192.168.1.*
```

Within the `/etc/rinetd.conf` file, you also configure FORWARD rules. These are the most important rules within the configuration file. They are used to specify where TCP traffic arriving at a specific interface is to be forwarded to. The syntax for a FORWARD rule is as follows:

```
local_IP_address port remote_host_IP_address port
```

For example, suppose the IP address of the interface in the server running rinetd is 192.168.1.47. You want all incoming HTTP traffic arriving at this host to be forwarded to a web server in your DMZ that has an IP address of 192.168.2.1. You would create the following rule:

```
192.168.1.47 80 192.168.2.1 80
```

You can also specify the location of the rinetd log file in the rinetd.conf file by adding a line that reads:

```
logfile path
```

Pretty straightforward, isn't it? After you've configured your rules, you can manage the daemon using the **rcrinetd start|stop** commands.

Now that you've got rinetd under your belt, let's look at another generic proxy: Dante.

IMPLEMENTING DANTE

The rinetd daemon is a robust, yet relatively basic, generic proxy service. If you need to implement a generic proxy that provides a more extensive feature set (such as authenticating proxy users), you may want to consider the Dante package.

Dante is a generic proxy that uses the SOCKS protocol. This protocol is used by proxy servers to accept requests from SOCKS clients and forward them through the network to hosts on the external network (including the Internet). The SOCKS protocol uses *sockets* to keep track of client connections.

NOTE

A *socket* is an endpoint for a connection between the server and the client. If you establish a client/server connection, a socket is created on the server and on the client.

Like other application-level gateways, the Dante SOCKS proxy server handles requests from clients from the internal network and either allows or rejects them based on a set of rules you configure. Allowed requests are forwarded on, appearing to remote hosts to have originated from the proxy server itself.

Like the rinetd daemon, the Dante daemon (sockd) operates at the Transport layer of the OSI model, working with TCP and UDP packets. As such, it can be used to manage any upper-layer protocols. However, just like rinetd, the Dante proxy is limited by the same general shortcomings as other generic proxies. For example, it can manage forwarding and even authenticate users, but it can't filter content nor can it cache content.

To use the Dante proxy server on your SLES 9 system, you need to install the software on your server. This is done by installing the dante-server package, as shown in Figure 10.37.

FIGURE 10.37
Installing Dante.

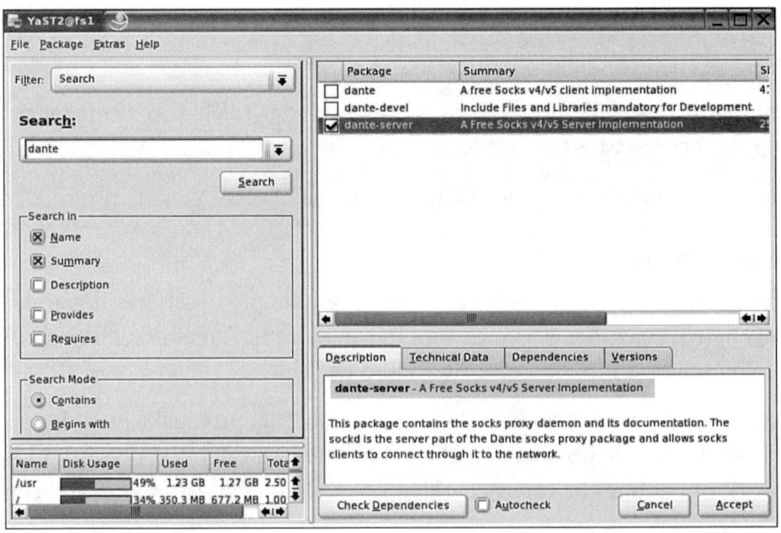

After it is installed, the sockd daemon is configured using the `/etc/sockd.conf` file, shown in Figure 10.38.

FIGURE 10.38
The `/etc/sockd.conf` file.

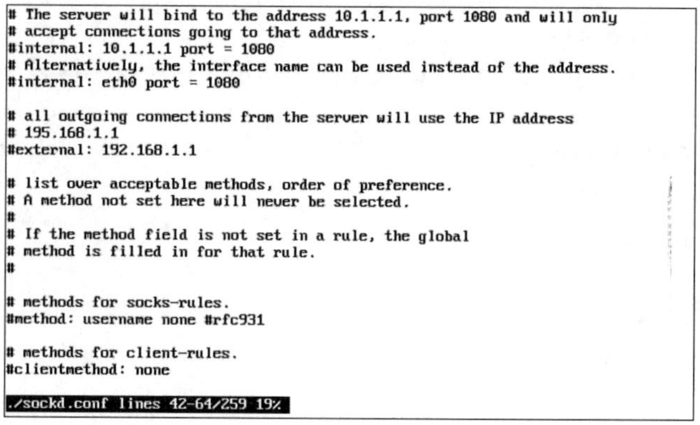

```
# The server will bind to the address 10.1.1.1, port 1080 and will only
# accept connections going to that address.
#internal: 10.1.1.1 port = 1080
# Alternatively, the interface name can be used instead of the address.
#internal: eth0 port = 1080

# all outgoing connections from the server will use the IP address
# 195.168.1.1
#external: 192.168.1.1

# list over acceptable methods, order of preference.
# A method not set here will never be selected.
#
# If the method field is not set in a rule, the global
# method is filled in for that rule.
#

# methods for socks-rules.
#method: username none #rfc931

# methods for client-rules.
#clientmethod: none

./sockd.conf lines 42-64/259 19%
```

The `sockd.conf` file is divided into several sections—Server Configuration and Rules. In the Server Configuration section you configure how the sockd daemon itself functions. In this part of `sockd.conf`, you can configure the following parameters:

- `connecttimeout`—This parameter specifies the number of *seconds* within which a client must send its request after a connection is established before being closed. You can disable this function by setting this option to **0**.
- `external`—This parameter configures the IP address or interface in the server that will be used for outgoing connections.
- `internal`—This parameter configures the IP address or interface in the server that will be allowed to accept incoming connections.
- `iotimeout`—This parameter sets the number of seconds an established connection can be idle before it is closed. You can disable this function by setting this option to **0**.
- `method`—This parameter is used by socks rules (which we'll discuss in a minute) to specify the method used to authenticate users. You can specify a list of methods in order of preference. You can specify **username**, **none**, **rfc931**, and/or **pam**.
- `clientmethod`—This parameter is used by client rules (which we'll discuss in a minute) to specify authentication methods; listed in order of preference. You can specify **none**, **rfc931**, and **pam**.
- `user.privileged`—Specifies the user account the daemon will use when performing privileged operations.

- **user.notprivileged**—Specifies the user account that the daemon will run as by default.

For example, suppose your Dante daemon is running on a SLES 9 server that has two interfaces. The internal interface has been assigned an IP address of 192.168.2.254; the external interface has been assigned an IP address of 23.5.67.1. You want users to be authenticated via PAM. You could configure a simple Server Configuration section in **sockd.conf** as shown:

```
internal: 192.168.2.254 port =1080
external: 23.5.67.1
method: pam
clientmethod: pam
user.privileged: root
user.notprivleged: dante
```

After you've configured the Server Configuration portion of **sockd.conf**, you next need to configure the Rules section. This section is itself divided into two parts:

- Client Rules—This section is used to set rules for allowing users to connect to the proxy.
- Socks Rules—This section is used to set rules that define what actions to take after users have authenticated. Users must have been accepted by the Client Rules for the Socks Rules to be applied.

Client rules begin with **client pass** or **deny**. Socks rules begin with **pass** or **deny**. These keywords tell the sockd daemon what to do with a connection if the specified rule is met. With both types of rules, you can specify the source and destination IP addresses to match on using the **from** and **to** keywords.

Under client rules, the **from** keyword specifies the IP address of the client system making the connection. The **to** parameter specifies the IP address the sockd daemon is running on (where client requests are accepted).

Under socks rules, the **from** keyword also specifies the IP address of the client system making the connection. However, the **to** keyword specifies the IP address of the remote host client systems are trying to contact.

That probably makes no sense to you, so let me give you some examples. Suppose you want to establish a rule for your Dante server that will constrain the server to accept connections only from hosts that reside on the 192.168.2.0 subnet. You want Dante to accept the connection on any interface it's listening on. You also want users to be forced to authenticate upon connection. To do this, you create a client rule formatted as follows:

```
client pass {
    from: 192.168.2.0/24 port 1-65535 to: 0.0.0.0/0
    method: pam
}
```

Let's further assume that there's a worm-laden website that you want to keep your users from using. Its IP address is 205.172.1.45. You could block access to the site by configuring a socks rule as follows:

```
block {
    from: 0.0.0.0/0 to: 205.172.1.45
}
```

Let's also suppose you've got a problem with users spending too much time at work playing multiplayer Quake over the Internet. You want to completely block off the IP port used by the Quake game. To do this you could add a socks rule as follows:

```
block {
    from: 0.0.0.0/0 to: 0.0.0.0/0
    port: 27660
}
```

You can use a wide array of options in your client and socks rules; many more than we have space to cover here. Have a look at the `sockd.conf` man page for a listing of all the keywords you can use in your rules.

After you have your rules configured, you can start the Dante service on your server by entering **`rcsockd start`** from a shell prompt.

After sockd is running, you will need to configure your client applications to use the proxy. Most browsers now support SOCKS-based proxy servers such as Dante. Check the browser's proxy configuration to see if it will. For example, the Konqueror browser's proxy configuration tab provides an option to enable SOCKS and specify the Dante proxy server, as shown in Figure 10.39.

Well, that's it for generic proxies. It's now time to turn our attention to application-specific proxy servers. The package you need to know for your CLE 9 certification is Squid.

Implementing an Application-Specific Proxy with Squid

Squid is a very popular application-specific proxy server. It's included with just about every Linux distribution I've worked with. Squid functions as an HTTP proxy with caching capabilities.

FIGURE 10.39
Configuring Konqueror to use the Dante SOCKS proxy.

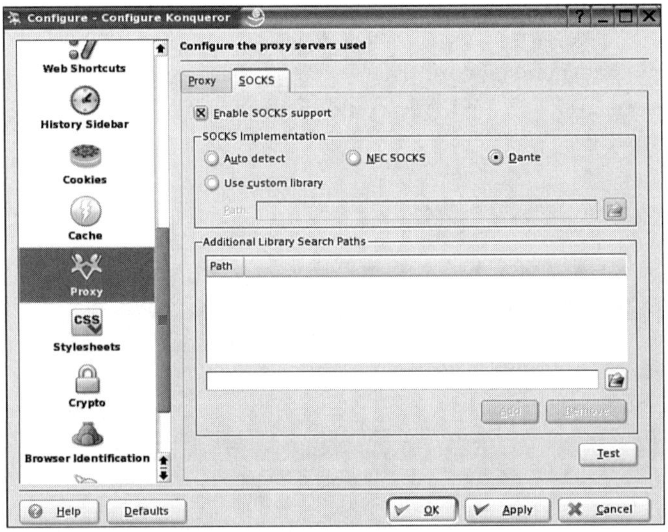

Now, whenever I discuss Squid in class or in conversation, someone pipes up with an assertion to the effect of "What? Why would you run your proxy cache on top on server hardware? I will only use a proxy cache appliance from XYZ Corporation."

These folks have a valid point from the standpoint of performance. Admittedly, a proxy cache appliance running on dedicated hardware will probably have a slight edge in performance over Squid running on typical server hardware. My response, however, is "How much is that slight performance edge worth to you?" Proxy cache appliances are expensive! Squid, on the other hand, costs next to nothing. In addition, the hardware Squid runs on is easily upgradeable. Need a faster CPU? No problem. Need a faster hard drive? No problem. Need more memory? Again, no problem. Try that with most hardware proxy servers! Given a choice, I'll take a Squid proxy any day.

Enough lecturing; let's get back to talking about Squid. Squid has been around since the mid-1990s. Because it has been around a while, Squid is rock solid and feature rich; making it an excellent choice for a proxy cache solution.

Just like any other application-level gateway, the Squid proxy server is very demanding in terms of hardware. You should consider using very high-end hardware if your system is going to shoulder a heavy load of proxy traffic. Because of the size of the files stored in the cache, you should use a RAID solution that employs some form of striping with very small block sizes. Don't skimp on disk size either. You want to allocate plenty of disk space for caching. Depending on your network, I wouldn't allocated anything less than about 40GB for caching (yes, I said 40GB!)

You should also use the fastest processor you can afford. The gateway functions provided by Squid use up a lot of CPU cycles. RAM is also an important consideration. Okay, it's not just important, it's absolutely critical. If available memory drops too low, Squid's throughput goes down the tubes. That's because Squid caches entries in the hard drive cache in memory for faster access.

The general rule is that Squid consumes about 32MB of RAM for each GB of hard disk space used for cache. That may not sound like much, but remember that a heavily used proxy server will consume about 5GB of disk cache *every day*. If you've configured 40GB of disk storage for cache, you could potentially need 1280MB of RAM just for Squid! Be sure to plan your deployment according.

INSTALLING SQUID

Of course, you must install Squid on your server before you can use it. Under SLES 9 this is most easily done with good old YaST. Select **Software, Install and Remove Software**. In the Search field, enter **`squid`**; then mark the squid package as shown in Figure 10.40.

FIGURE 10.40
Installing Squid.

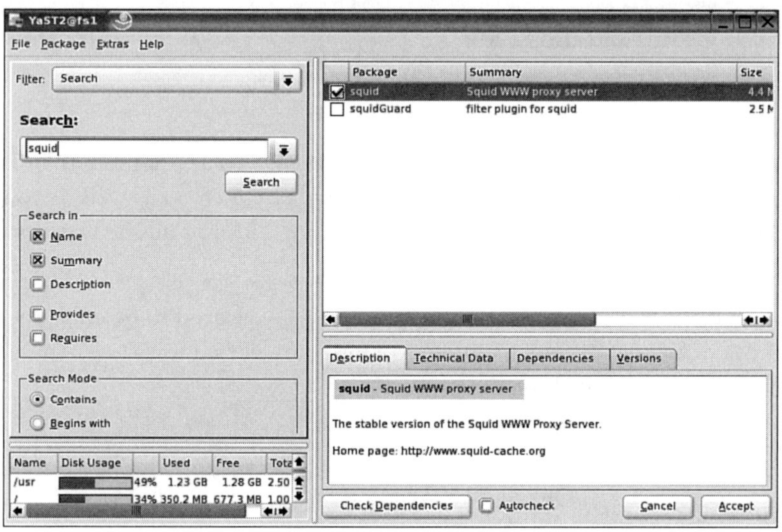

In Figure 10.40, you'll notice there's another Squid package available in the SLES 9 distribution called squidGuard. I highly recommend this package as well as the basic Squid server. squidGuard is a plug-in for Squid that enables you to create complex content filtering rules.

Click **Accept** to install the package. With Squid installed, you need to do some heavy-duty configuration work to get your proxy cache server working. Let's talk about how to do that next.

CONFIGURING SQUID USING `squid.conf`

After installing Squid, you configure it using the `/etc/squid/squid.conf` file shown in Figure 10.41.

FIGURE 10.41
The `/etc/squid/squid.conf` file.

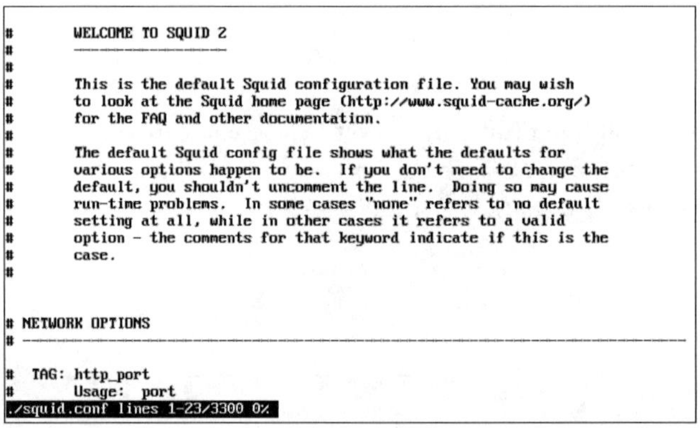

```
#       WELCOME TO SQUID 2
#       ------------------
#
#       This is the default Squid configuration file. You may wish
#       to look at the Squid home page (http://www.squid-cache.org/)
#       for the FAQ and other documentation.
#
#       The default Squid config file shows what the defaults for
#       various options happen to be.  If you don't need to change the
#       default, you shouldn't uncomment the line.  Doing so may cause
#       run-time problems.  In some cases "none" refers to no default
#       setting at all, while in other cases it refers to a valid
#       option - the comments for that keyword indicate if this is the
#       case.
#

# NETWORK OPTIONS
# -----------------------------------------------------------------------------

#  TAG: http_port
#       Usage:  port
./squid.conf lines 1-23/3300 0%
```

I'll warn you right up front that this file can be intimidating. There are more than 200 different directives you can use. Fortunately, the file is heavily commented as well. If you want to learn Squid, one of the best things you can do is sit down and read all the way through this file. We don't have the space here to cover everything.

However, let's look at some of the most important options you need to be concerned with in `squid.conf`. Inside the `squid.conf` file, these options are referred to as *tags*. These are organized into logical groupings, which include

- Network Options
- Neighbor Selection Algorithm
- Cache Size
- Logfile Paths and Cache Directories
- Administrative Parameters

As an example, the Network Options section is shown in Figure 10.42.

FIGURE 10.42
The Network section in /etc/squid/squid.conf.

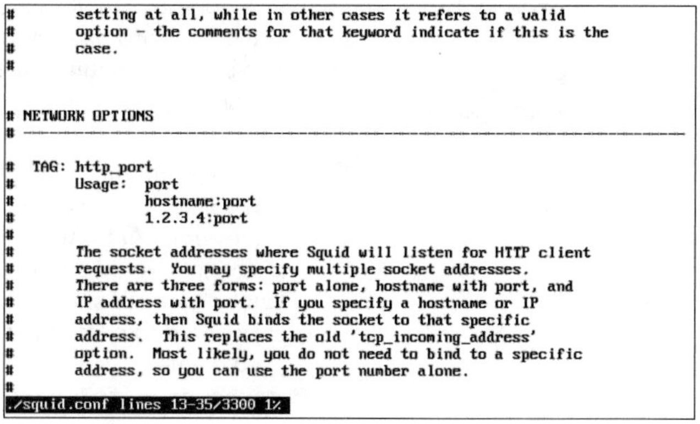

```
#       setting at all, while in other cases it refers to a valid
#       option - the comments for that keyword indicate if this is the
#       case.
#


# NETWORK OPTIONS
# -----------------------------------------------------------------------

#  TAG: http_port
#       Usage:  port
#               hostname:port
#               1.2.3.4:port
#
#       The socket addresses where Squid will listen for HTTP client
#       requests.  You may specify multiple socket addresses.
#       There are three forms: port alone, hostname with port, and
#       IP address with port.  If you specify a hostname or IP
#       address, then Squid binds the socket to that specific
#       address.  This replaces the old 'tcp_incoming_address'
#       option.  Most likely, you do not need to bind to a specific
#       address, so you can use the port number alone.
#
./squid.conf lines 13-35/3300 1%
```

The good news is that most tags have default values associated with them. Most of these will work for a basic installation. We're going to work extensively with many portions of the `squid.conf` file. First, we need to look at some basic configuration parameters.

BASIC SQUID CONFIGURATION TAGS

When configuring Squid, you first need to set several basic tags that will control how the service operates. Again, there are a ton of them; however, the default values for the majority of them will serve our purposes. Those you may need to customize (and the ones you need know for your CLE 9 certification) are shown in Table 10-1:

TABLE 10.1
Important Squid Tags

SECTION	TAG	DESCRIPTION
Network Options	*http_port*	The port Squid will listen on for clients. You can specify the port alone or an IP address and a port (if you have multiple interface installed). The default port is 3128. You can configure Squid to listen on multiple ports by adding additional *http_port* tags in the file.
	icp_port	The port Squid will use to listen for and send ICP messages to other proxy servers. The default value is 3130.
	htcp_port	The port Squid will use to pull content from the caches of sibling or parent proxy servers. The default is 4827.
Neighbor Selection Algorithm	*cache_peer*	Used to set up a caching hierarchy. The syntax is `cache_peer host type port icp_port options` For example, if I wanted to configure fs2 as a sibling, I would enter **`cache_peer fs2 sibling 3128 3130`** If I wanted to configure fs2 as a parent, I would enter **`cache_peer fs2 parent 3128 3130`**
Cache Size	*cache_mem*	Specifies the amount of RAM (in bytes) to used for processing objects stored in the disk cache. The default is 8MB.
	cache_swap_low and *cache_swap_high*	Specifies the low and high water marks (in percentage) for disk cache usage. When the *cache_swap_low* amount is reached, Squid will start dumping old files out of the cache. When the *cache_swap_high* amount is reached, Squid will really start going to town dumping old content out of cache. Defaults: cache_swap_low: 90 cache_swap_high: 95
	maximum_object_size	Specifies the maximum size (in KB) for files stored in the disk cache. Anything larger will not be saved. The default value is 4096KB.
	minimum_object_size	Specifies the minimum size (in KB) for files stored in the disk cache. Anything smaller will not be saved. The default value is 0KB.

SECTION	TAG	DESCRIPTION
	maximum_object_size_in_memory	Specifies the maximum size (in KB) for files stored in the RAM cache. Anything larger will not be kept in RAM. The default value is 8KB.
Logfile Paths and Cache Directories	*cache_dir*	Specifies the directory used in the file system to store cached files. The syntax is as follows: `cache_dir type path size L1 L2` The *type* option specifies the storage format to be used by Squid. The default is ufs. The *path* option specifies the directory where the cache will reside. The default is */var/squid/cache*. The *size* option specifies the amount of space you want to allocate to the cache. The default is 100MB (much too small). The *L1* option specifies the number of first-level subdirectories that will be created in the cache directory. The default is 16. The *L2* option specifies the number of second-level subdirectories that will be created in the cache directory. The default is 256.
	cache_access_log	Specifies the location and name of the Squid access log file. The default is */var/log/squid/access.log*.
	cache_log	Specifies the location of the Squid log file. The default is */var/log/squid/cache.log*.
Administrative Parameters	*cache_mgr*	Specifies the email address of the person responsible for managing Squid.
	cache_effective_user	If the root user starts Squid, this parameter defines the user account Squid will run as. If a nonroot user starts Squid, this parameter is ignored and Squid runs as the user who started it. The default value is *squid*.
	cache_effective_group	If the root user starts Squid, this parameter defines the group Squid will run as. If a nonroot user starts Squid, this parameter is ignored and Squid runs as the group associated with the user who started it. The default value is *nogroup*.

After you have these basic tags configured, you need to configure who can and who can't use the proxy server. Let's look at how to do that next.

CONFIGURING SQUID ACLS

Squid access control lists (ACLs) are also configured in the **squid.conf** file. These are listed under the Access Controls heading, shown in Figure 10.43.

FIGURE 10.43

The Access Controls section in /etc/squid/squid.conf.

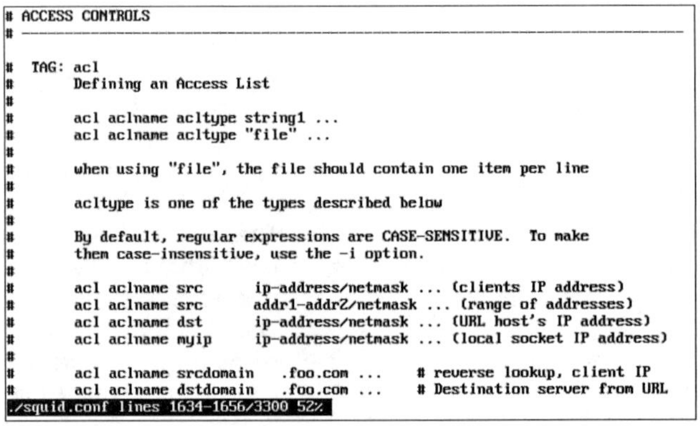

```
# ACCESS CONTROLS
# -----------------------------------------------------------------------------

#  TAG: acl
#       Defining an Access List
#
#       acl aclname acltype string1 ...
#       acl aclname acltype "file" ...
#
#       when using "file", the file should contain one item per line
#
#       acltype is one of the types described below
#
#       By default, regular expressions are CASE-SENSITIVE.  To make
#       them case-insensitive, use the -i option.
#
#       acl aclname src      ip-address/netmask ... (clients IP address)
#       acl aclname src      addr1-addr2/netmask ... (range of addresses)
#       acl aclname dst      ip-address/netmask ... (URL host's IP address)
#       acl aclname myip     ip-address/netmask ... (local socket IP address)
#
#       acl aclname srcdomain   .foo.com ...    # reverse lookup, client IP
#       acl aclname dstdomain   .foo.com ...    # Destination server from URL
./squid.conf lines 1634-1656/3300 52%
```

This section begins roughly halfway through the **squid.conf** file. In this section, you define rules that identify who can and who can't use the Squid proxy. These rules are defined in two parts.

The first part uses the acl tag. The acl tag defines a specific condition that is used for matching. It doesn't, however, define the actual rule; it just says who a rule may be applied to. The syntax for the acl tag is as follows:

```
acl name type condition
```

The *name* option is a name you define for the acl. As you will see in just a minute, you will use the acl name in a second tag later in the file to reference who a rule applies to.

The *type* option is used to specify what type of condition is being used to define the acl. The types you can use include:

- src—This specifies the client's IP address.
- dst—This specifies the IP address of the host being accessed by the client.

- myip—This specifies the IP address of the local socket being used by Squid.
- port—This specifies the port being accessed on the destination host.
- myport—This specifies the port where Squid received a request.
- srcdomain—This specifies the domain of the client.
- dstdomain—This specifies the domain of the host being accessed by the client.
- method—This specifies the type of HTTP request, such as GET, POST, or PUT.
- proto—This specifies the protocol specified in the URL, such as http, https, ftp, gopher, urn, whois, and cache_object.
- browser—This specifies the type of browser the client issued the request from.
- time—This specifies a timeframe for the acl. The syntax for the conditions with the time type is *days time*. For example, you could create an acl tag that reads acl BusinessHours MTWHF 07:30-18:00.
- req_mime_type—This specifies a match based on the mime type, which is contained in the header of an HTTP request received by Squid.

The condition you specify is dependent on the type included in the acl tag. Consider the following example acl tag:

```
acl MySubnet src 192.168.1.0/24
```

This tag defines an acl named MySubnet. The type of acl is the source systems' IP addresses. The condition is any system running on the 192.168.1.0 subnet with a mask of 255.255.255.0. Notice that the acl doesn't say what to do, it only defines the condition.

TIP

You can specify multiple values as a part of the condition. Just leave a space between them. You can also use multiple acl tags for the same acl name to define multiple values for the conditions portion of the acl.

To specify what to do with the acl, you use the http_access tag. This tag is used to define the actual rules that will be applied to the acls you defined. The syntax for the `http_access` tag is as follows:

```
http_access allow|deny acl_name
```

Essentially, you use the acl tag to define an acl, and then use the http_access tag to specify what to do if the condition in the referenced acl is met. For example, suppose I entered the following in my `squid.conf` file:

```
acl MySubnet src 192.168.1.0/24
http_access allow MySubnet
```

This would configure Squid to allow access to any system accessing the proxy that has an IP address of 192.168.1.*x* with a subnet mask of 255.255.255.0.

When working with acl and http_access tags, it is critical that you understand that the ordering of acl tags in the `squid.conf` file is unimportant. You could put them anywhere you want in the file in any order you want as long as they come *before* your http_access tags.

However, the ordering of http_access tags in the `squid.conf` file is absolutely important. In fact, it's critical. That's because Squid, when it receives incoming traffic from clients, processes the http_access tags in the order they appear in the file.

As soon as Squid finds a matching http_access tag, it stops and doesn't process the remaining http_access tags in the file. To save processing time, you should place your most commonly used http_access rules first and your more obscure http_access rules later.

TIP

If Squid processes all the http_access rules and doesn't find any matches, it will apply the exact *opposite* of the last http_access rule in the file. Therefore, you should always include a *deny all* or an *allow all* rule at the end of the list to ensure unauthorized traffic doesn't make its way through.

The `squid.conf` file includes a default set of acls and rules. You should probably leave these intact as they set up the initial environment. These defaults are shown next:

```
#Recommended minimum configuration:
acl all src 0.0.0.0/0.0.0.0
acl manager proto cache_object
acl localhost src 127.0.0.1/255.255.255.255
acl to_localhost dst 127.0.0.0/8
acl SSL_ports port 443 563
acl Safe_ports port 80        # http
acl Safe_ports port 21        # ftp
acl Safe_ports port 443 563    # https, snews
acl Safe_ports port 70        # gopher
acl Safe_ports port 210        # wais
acl Safe_ports port 1025-65535    # unregistered ports
acl Safe_ports port 280        # http-mgmt
acl Safe_ports port 488        # gss-http
acl Safe_ports port 591        # filemaker
acl Safe_ports port 777        # multiling http
acl CONNECT method CONNECT
```

```
#Recommended minimum configuration:
# Only allow cachemgr access from localhost
http_access allow manager localhost
http_access deny manager
# Deny requests to unknown ports
http_access deny !Safe_ports
# Deny CONNECT to other than SSL ports
http_access deny CONNECT !SSL_ports
http_access allow localhost
# And finally deny all other access to this proxy
http_access deny all
```

Notice that this configuration defines the following acls:

- all
- manager
- localhost
- Safe_ports
- CONNECT

The CONNECT acl may be a bit confusing. Notice that it specifies a method called CONNECT. Squid uses this method to directly connect secure HTTP requests through the proxy server. Because of the sensitive nature of HTTPS communications, Squid doesn't cache them. Instead, it simply passes them directly through.

The `http_access deny CONNECT !SSL_ports` rule denies all attempts to connect directly through the proxy server except for those defined in the SSL_ports acl (acl SSL_ports port 443 563), which specifies ports 443 and 563 on the destination host.

Also, notice that the rules defined for these acls do the following tasks in the following order:

- The cache administrator can access the proxy only from the local host.
- Requests to unknown ports are denied. Notice that this is done by placing a ! before the Safe_ports acl name in the http_access tag. This character specifies NOT. Therefore, this rule specifies DENY to any port NOT included in the Safe_ports acl.
- Access to SSL ports is allowed.
- Access from the local host is allowed.
- All other traffic is denied.

TIP

Remember that the last rule should be a deny all or an allow all so that unauthorized traffic doesn't weasel its way through.

If you read these rules carefully, you'll notice that, out of the box, Squid is pretty much locked down. Only a user on the local machine is allowed access. Therefore, to get Squid running in a networked situation, you would need to add the following acl to `squid.conf`:

```
acl our_networks src your_subnet/your_mask
```

For example, if the network segment you want to provide access to is 192.168.2.0 with a subnet mask of 255.255.255.0, you would enter

```
acl our_networks src 192.168.2.0/24
```

That sets up the acl; next you need to configure the rule. If you scroll down about halfway through `squid.conf`, you'll see a line that indicates a good spot to insert a rule to allow access, as shown in Figure 10.44:

FIGURE 10.44
Inserting a rule to allow access.

```
# Deny requests to unknown ports
http_access deny !Safe_ports
# Deny CONNECT to other than SSL ports
http_access deny CONNECT !SSL_ports
#
# We strongly recommend to uncomment the following to protect innocent
# web applications running on the proxy server who think that the only
# one who can access services on "localhost" is a local user
#http_access deny to_localhost
#
# INSERT YOUR OWN RULE(S) HERE TO ALLOW ACCESS FROM YOUR CLIENTS

# Example rule allowing access from your local networks. Adapt
# to list your (internal) IP networks from where browsing should
# be allowed
#acl our_networks src 192.168.1.0/24 192.168.2.0/24
#http_access allow our_networks
http_access allow localhost

# And finally deny all other access to this proxy
http_access deny all

#  TAG: http_reply_access
./squid.conf lines 1809-1831/3300 58%
```

Notice that the file already contains an http_access tag all ready and waiting for you. Simply uncomment the line that reads

```
http_access allow our_networks
```

After that is done, you can restart Squid with the **rcsquid restart** command and you have a basic system ready to go. However, notice that this configuration isn't much different from the generic proxies we covered earlier in this chapter. Access is being controlled based on IP address and port number. What's missing? Authentication! Let's talk about this next.

CONFIGURING SQUID AUTHENTICATION

One of the key benefits of using an advanced proxy server like Squid is that you can make users provide a username and password before being allowed to use the proxy. This provides you with a great deal of control over who can and who can't have access through the proxy server.

Authentication mechanisms used by Squid are configured in `squid.conf` in the Options for External Support Programs section. Squid can use either Basic authentication, which uses your system user account store, Digest authentication, using its own user account database, or Microsoft's NTLM authentication process. The `squid.conf` file includes sample code that you can uncomment and use to configure user authentication. These lines are shown in Figure 10.45.

FIGURE 10.45
Sample authentication configuration lines.

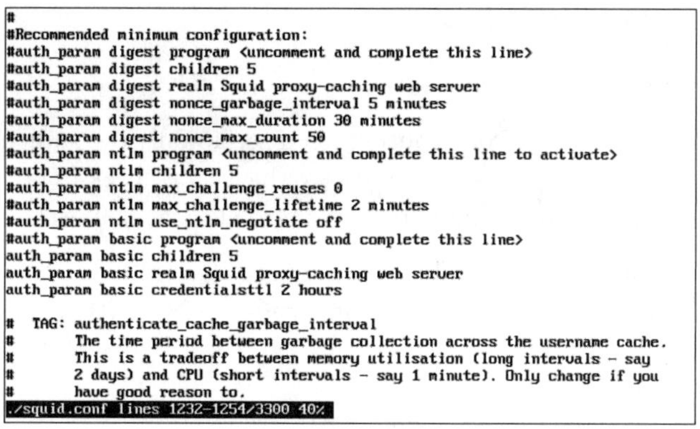

```
#
#Recommended minimum configuration:
#auth_param digest program <uncomment and complete this line>
#auth_param digest children 5
#auth_param digest realm Squid proxy-caching web server
#auth_param digest nonce_garbage_interval 5 minutes
#auth_param digest nonce_max_duration 30 minutes
#auth_param digest nonce_max_count 50
#auth_param ntlm program <uncomment and complete this line to activate>
#auth_param ntlm children 5
#auth_param ntlm max_challenge_reuses 0
#auth_param ntlm max_challenge_lifetime 2 minutes
#auth_param ntlm use_ntlm_negotiate off
#auth_param basic program <uncomment and complete this line>
auth_param basic children 5
auth_param basic realm Squid proxy-caching web server
auth_param basic credentialsttl 2 hours

#  TAG: authenticate_cache_garbage_interval
#       The time period between garbage collection across the username cache.
#       This is a tradeoff between memory utilisation (long intervals - say
#       2 days) and CPU (short intervals - say 1 minute). Only change if you
#       have good reason to.
./squid.conf lines 1232-1254/3300 40%
```

If Squid is running on the same server where user accounts are stored, you can configure Basic authentication to use PAM on the local host to authenticate users.

To do this, you first need to uncomment the line that reads:

```
auth_param basic program <uncomment and complete this line>
```

This line defines what program the Basic authentication mechanism will to use to authenticate users. To use PAM, we need to specify that Squid use the pam_auth program. You need to edit the preceding line so that it reads as follows:

```
auth_param basic program /usr/sbin/pam_auth
```

Next, you need to specify how many background authentication processes should be running concurrently. Generally speaking, five processes are enough; however, you may need to increase this if your proxy server is heavily utilized. The line needed to do this is in your `squid.conf` file and is already uncommented. It reads as follows:

```
auth_param basic children 5
```

Next, we must define the realm that authentication will service. This sounds confusing at first, but it really isn't. The realm is simply the service that authentication will be provided for. In this case, it's Squid proxy-caching web server. The line needed to do this is in your `squid.conf` file and is already uncommented. It reads as follows:

```
auth_param basic realm Squid proxy-caching web server
```

Next, you need to specify how long credentials supplied by the user will be valid in the Squid system. The line needed to do this is in your squid.conf file and is already uncommented. It reads as follows:

```
auth_param basic credentialsttl 2 hours
```

The default value of 2 hours is usually sufficient.

Your work isn't done yet. The tags you've just entered set up only the authentication system. They don't actually authenticate users. To do this, we have to go back to our acls and our rules section in `squid.conf` and configure the system to authenticate users.

First, we need to create an acl that lists the users that are allowed to use the proxy. This is done using the proxy_auth type. The syntax is `acl name proxy_auth REQUIRED`. For example:

```
acl MyUsers proxy_auth REQUIRED
```

NOTE

The REQUIRED condition is used to specify that all users in the account store be used. If you want only certain users to be able to authenticate and use the proxy, you can replace REQUIRED with a list of specific users (separated by a space), such as **`jcorry dcoughanour tux`**.

Last, you need to add a rule that specifies that authenticated users are allowed access to the proxy. This is done in the same manner as discussed earlier. For example, using the above acl, you would enter:

```
http_access allow MyUsers
```

Remember that http_access rules are processed in the order that they appear in the file. You probably want to check for authentication early on, so the above rule should probably come first (or near first) in your list of rules.

The last element of Squid configuration that we're going to discuss here is how to filter content. Let's do that next.

FILTERING CONTENT WITH SQUID

In addition to user authentication, the other significant advantage of protocol-specific proxies over generic proxies is that they can filter content that passes through proxies. This is especially useful and important with HTTP proxies.

Filtering is becoming more and more of an issue in the workplace. Back in the early 1990s, when user desktops first started getting connected to the Internet, the general acceptable-use strategy of most organizations was to tell their employees to make sure they used it only for work-related purposes. Basically, it was the honor system.

My, how things have changed. Today's IT environment is much different. We soon discovered that the Internet provided too much of a temptation for most folks to handle. Some users were spending the better part of their workday perusing sites that had nothing to do with their jobs. The idea behind providing Internet access was to enhance employee productivity. In reality, it proved to have just the opposite effect.

In addition, the late 1990s saw a surge in "hostile workplace" lawsuits. The result of these suits was that employers became the primary parties responsible for making sure one employee didn't create a hostile working environment for any other employees.

That responsibility extended to Internet access. Earlier in this chapter, I told you about the time I walked into a co-worker's cubicle and saw stuff on his PC screen that I really didn't want to see. Therein lies the problem. Most likely, when you go to work for a particular organization, you will be responsible for ensuring that employees can't access Internet content that would create a hostile environment.

This is one of the areas in which Squid really shines. Using our **squid.conf** file, we can create acls and rules that filter out sites we want to block. This is done using the url_regex and the urpath_regex acl types.

The url_regex type is used to match against a specific URL. The urpath_regex type is used to match against the path specified after a URL. It doesn't match against the URL itself.

For example, suppose you want to block out a website named www.restrainingorderwaitingto-happen.com. To do this, you would create an acl using the url_regex type, such as the following:

```
acl DontGoThere url_regex -i restrainingorderwaitingtohappen.com
```

The `-i` option specifies that the acl isn't case sensitive. Obviously, creating acls for every site you want to block could become an unwieldy task. Fortunately, there are folks who have done the work for you. If you go to http://www.squidguard.org/blacklist/, you can download a pre-compiled blacklist of websites. Then, instead of manually entering in every single site you want to block, you can tell Squid to use the blacklist file from **squidguard.org**.

TIP

The folks at squidguard.org also produce a Squid plug-in called squidGuard that you can use to filter content.

To do this, you would create an acl such as the following:

```
acl DontGoThere url_regex -i "/etc/squid/name_of_file"
```

Then you must create a rule that specifies what to do if the acl is matched. We want to block anything in the DontGoThere acl we created, so we need to create a rule such as

```
http_access deny DontGoThere
```

Give Squid a try on your SLES 9 server in Exercise 10.3.

Lab Exercise 10.3: Implementing Squid on SLES 9

In this lab exercise, you will configure a Squid HTTP proxy server on your SLES 9 system. To complete this exercise, you will need your SLES 9 server with DNS, DHCP, Samba, Postfix, CUPS, and NAT running.

This exercise assumes you have already completed exercise 10.2. If not, it will still work, but you may have to customize some of the steps. You will also need an additional NLD or Windows workstation to test the proxy server with. Complete the following:

1. Boot your SLES 9 server.
2. Authenticate as **tux** with a password of **SuSE789**.
3. Install calamaris on your server by completing the following:
   a. Start YaST.
   b. Authenticate as root using a password of **tuX123**.
   c. Select Software, Install and Remove Software.
   d. In the search field, enter **calamaris**; then select **Search**.
   e. Mark **calamaris**; then select **Accept**.
   f. Insert CDs as prompted.
   g. Wait while the packages are installed.
4. Configure the Squid administrator's email address by completing the following:
   a. Open a terminal session and enter **su -** to change to root with a password of **tuX123**.
   b. At the shell prompt, enter **vi /etc/squid/squid.conf**.
   c. Scroll down to the cache_mgr tag (located about three-fifths of the way down in the Administrative Parameters section).
   d. Press **Ins**.
   e. Delete the # from in front of the cache_mgr tag.
   f. Change the value of cache_mgr to **root@cle9.com**.

5. Configure Squid to allow hosts on your private network to access the proxy by completing the following:
   a. Scroll up to the list of acls.
   b. Insert the following acl after the acl CONNECT line:
      `acl our_networks src 10.0.0.0/8`

      Be sure to place an underscore (_) between *`our`* and *`networks`*.
   c. Scroll down to the #http_access allow our_networks rule and remove the # from in front of the line.
   d. Press **Esc**; then enter **`:exit`**.
6. Start the server by entering **`rcsquid start`** at the shell prompt.
7. From the shell prompt, enter **`less /var/log/squid/cache.log`**.
8. Read through the entries and verify that the server started without any errors.
9. Configure the browser on your workstation to use the proxy by completing the following:
   a. Boot your workstation.
   b. If you're using Windows XP, do the following:
      i. Start Internet Explorer.
      ii. Select Tools, Internet Options, > Connections.
      iii. Select **LAN Settings**.
      iv. Mark Use a Proxy Server.
      v. In the Address field, enter **`10.0.0.254`**.
      vi. In the Port field, enter **`3128`**.
      vii. Select **OK, OK**.
   c. If you're using Konqueror, do the following:
      i. Select Settings, Configure Konqueror.
      ii. Select **Proxy**.
      iii. Select Manually Specify the Proxy Settings.
      iv. Select **Setup**.
      v. In the HTTP field, enter **`10.0.0.254`**.
      vi. In the Port field, enter **`3128`**.

vii. Mark Use the Same Proxy Server for All Protocols.

viii. Select **OK**, **OK**.

10. Test the proxy by opening a browser on your workstation and navigating to http://www.suse.com. Novell's SUSE home page should load.

11. Close your browser window.

12. Check your log files by completing the following:

a. At the shell prompt, enter **`less /var/log/squid/store.log`**. Scroll through the entries created when you accessed www.suse.com.

b. Press **q**.

c. At the shell prompt, enter **`less /var/log/squid/access.log`**. Scroll through the entries created when you accessed www.suse.com.

d. Press **q**.

13. Configure Squid to authenticate users by opening `/etc/squid/squid.conf` in vi and completing the following:

a. Scroll down to the recommended minimum configuration for authentication section.

b. Remove the # from in front of the line that reads #auth_param basic program <uncomment and complete this line>.

c. Edit the line to read as follows:

```
auth_param basic program /usr/sbin/pam_auth
```

d. Scroll down to your list of acls.

e. Add the following acl:

```
acl MyUsers proxy_auth REQUIRED
```

Remember to insert an underscore (_) between *`proxy`* and *`auth`*.

f. Scroll down to the line where it reads *`INSERT YOUR OWN RULES HERE....`*

g. Add the following rule *before* the "... allow our_networks" rule:

```
http_access allow MyUsers
```

h. Press **Esc**; then enter **`:exit`**.

i. Restart Squid by entering **rcsquid restart**.

j. Test the configuration by opening a browser on your workstation and accessing http://www.google.com.

k. You should be prompted to enter a Squid *username* and *password*, as shown in Figure 10.46.

FIGURE 10.46
Authenticating to the proxy server.

l. In the User Name field, enter **jcorry**.

m. In the Password field, enter **Annel**.

n. Select **OK**. The Google home page should be displayed.

14. Configure content filtering by completing the following:

a. At the shell prompt, enter **vi /etc/squid/squid.conf**.

b. Scroll down to your list of acls.

c. Press **Ins**.

d. Add a new acl that reads as follows:

```
acl DontGoThere url_regex -i novell.com
```

Be sure to remember the underscore.

e. Scroll down to where it reads **INSERT YOUR OWN RULES HERE...**.

f. Before your allow MyUsers rule, add the following rule:

```
http_access deny DontGoThere
```

g. Press **Esc**; then enter **:exit**.

h. At the shell prompt, enter **rcsquid restart**.

TIP

In a production environment, you would enter **rcsquid reload**. The *restart* option clears all current connections. The *reload* option doesn't.

i. Test your configuration by opening http://www.novell.com from your workstation. You should see an Access Denied page displayed, as shown in Figure 10.47.

FIGURE 10.47
Access blocked by Squid.

15. Analyze your Squid log files with the calamaris utility by completing the following:

a. At the shell prompt, switch to the */var/log/squid* directory.

b. At the shell prompt, enter cat **./access.log | calamaris -a -F > access.html**.

c. From the kicker panel at the bottom of the screen, select **N, Run Command**.

d. In the Run Command dialog box, select **Options**.

e. Mark Run as Different User.

f. Ensure that root is in the Username field.

g. Enter **tuX123** in the Password field.

h. In the Command field, enter **kfmclient openProfile webbrowsing**; then select **Run**.

i. In Konqueror, open the **/var/log/squid/access.html** file. The page in Figure 10.48 is displayed:

FIGURE 10.48
calamaris proxy report.

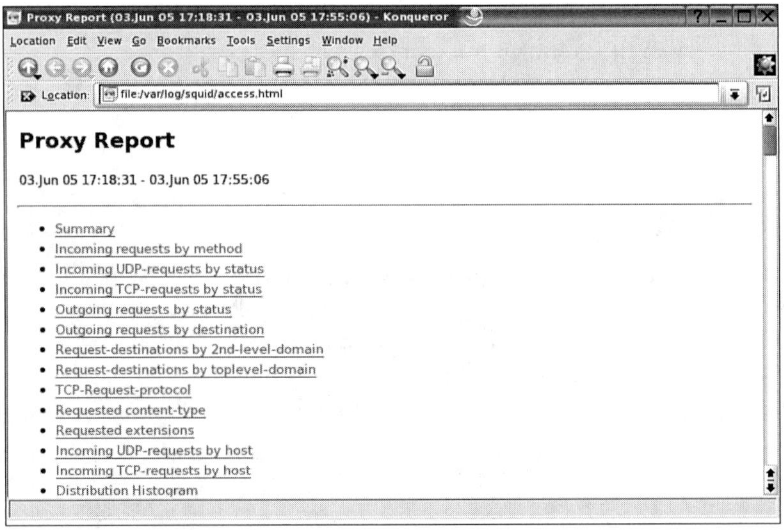

j. Scroll through the report to view statistics from your Squid proxy server.

That's it! You've now got a powerful proxy server running on your SLES 9 system.

This was a packed chapter. I'll bet your head is hurting! Let's review what you learned.

Summary

We talked about a wide variety of topics in this chapter. First we discussed the role of firewalls in general. Then we talked about how packet filtering firewalls work—filtering packets based on IP address and port number. You learned that this type of firewall operates primarily at the Network layer of the OSI model.

Then we talked about how stateful firewalls work. You learned that this type of firewall operates at the Transport and Session layers of the OSI model. There it monitors the actual protocol session itself instead of just source and destination IP addresses and ports.

We then talked about application-level gateways (also called proxies). You learned that this type of firewall operates high in the OSI model at the Application layer. This type of firewall can actually filter content and authenticate users—something packet filtering firewalls can't do.

After discussing firewalls in general, we talked about how to design a firewall implementation. We said the first step is to define an organizational security policy. Then you should plan your boundary firewall. Then you should plan your DMZ. Finally, you should plan your internal firewalls.

Then we entered the world packet filtering firewalls. You learned how to use iptables to implement a simple packet filtering firewall on SLES 9. You built on that knowledge to create a NAT router using iptables as well. To round off the discussion of packet filtering firewalls, you used YaST to configure a much more advanced firewall.

After learning about packet filtering firewalls, we turned our attention to application-level gateways. We began by discussing all the different types of application-level gateways. Then we discussed proxy caching hierarchies.

With the theory and terminology behind you, you then looked at how to configure two generic application level gateways: rinetd and Dante.

With those out of the way, we spent the rest of the chapter talking about Squid. You learned how to configure Squid acls and rules, how to configure authentication, and how to configure content filtering.

Hang in there; you've got two more chapters to go! Next, you'll learn about creating Virtual Private Networks (VPNs) in Chapter 11, "Implementing Virtual Private Networks with SLES 9."

CHAPTER 11

Implementing Virtual Private Networks with SLES 9

This chapter covers the following requirements for Novell's Certified Linux Engineer (CLE) 9 certification:

1. Implement a VPN on SLES 9.

With SLES 9, you can implement Virtual Private Networks (VPNs), which enable you to use the Internet instead of an expensive leased line for your WAN and remote access needs. In this chapter, we'll discuss how to use your SLES 9 server to provide VPN services. Specifically, we'll discuss

- How VPNs work.
- Configuring a VPN on SLES 9.

Let's begin by discussing the first topic—how VPNs work.

How VPNs Work

TEST OBJECTIVE COVERED:

1. Implement a VPN on SLES 9.

A VPN is a slick piece of technology. To understand what a VPN is and why it is so useful, we first need to take a step back and look at the traditional methods organizations used to implement WANs and provide remote user access.

Traditional WAN and Remote Access

Smaller organizations usually don't have a great deal of need for WANs or remote user access. However, as an organization grows, these needs can become pressing. Let's take a look at a hypothetical company: XYZ Wholesale Auto Body Parts. XYZ started small in a rented warehouse in Silver Spring, MD. Its primary business is importing aftermarket auto-body parts in quantity from Taiwan and reselling them to local auto-body repair shops.

Business has been good and XYZ has grown considerably. In fact, the company decided to open additional warehouse locations around the northeastern United States to provide aftermarket parts to auto-body repair shops around the region.

Because of its large inventory, XYZ, early on, implemented an inventory database system on its Linux servers to keep track of everything. When it was a one-warehouse shop, this was relatively easy to do. Now that XYZ expanded to multiple sites that are geographically dispersed, the company has a problem. It either must maintain separate inventory databases at each site (not a good idea) or it needs to figure out a way to implement an interconnected network between all the sites.

In addition, the lifeblood of XYZ is its sales team. These individuals travel around the region visiting the auto-body repair shops in their territories to hawk XYZ's parts. When they make a sale, they need a way to submit the order to the respective warehouse and process all the accompanying paperwork.

In the company's early days, the sales team relied on hand-written orders on preprinted forms and fax machines to do this. However, the volume of business they do now is bringing the fax machine to its knees. Salespeople are constantly getting a busy signal now as they try to submit their orders this way.

To solve these problems, XYZ needs to do two things. First, it needs to connect all its warehouses such that a central inventory database can be maintained. Second, it needs to implement a way that its on-the-road sales force can gain access to the home network so they can process orders and take care of paperwork without waiting for the fax machine.

One of the methods commonly used to fix the first problem is to implement a wide area network (WAN). To do this, XYZ must contact its local telecommunications provider and arrange for some kind of leased line that it can use to interconnect all its warehouses, as shown in Figure 11.1.

To fix the second problem, a common solution used by many organizations is to provide remote access using a bank of modems. When a remote user needs to access the network, he or she finds a telephone jack, plugs in a modem, and dials into the modem bank. The modem bank is managed by a Remote Access Server (RAS), which authenticates users and provides them with access to the network. This configuration is shown in Figure 11.2.

FIGURE 11.1
A typical WAN.

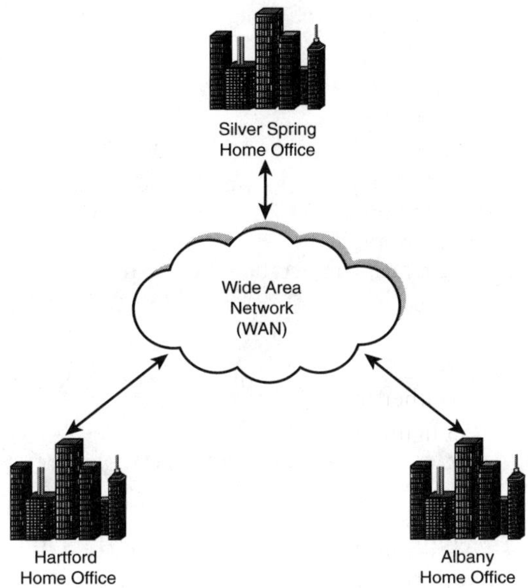

FIGURE 11.2
A typical remote access solution.

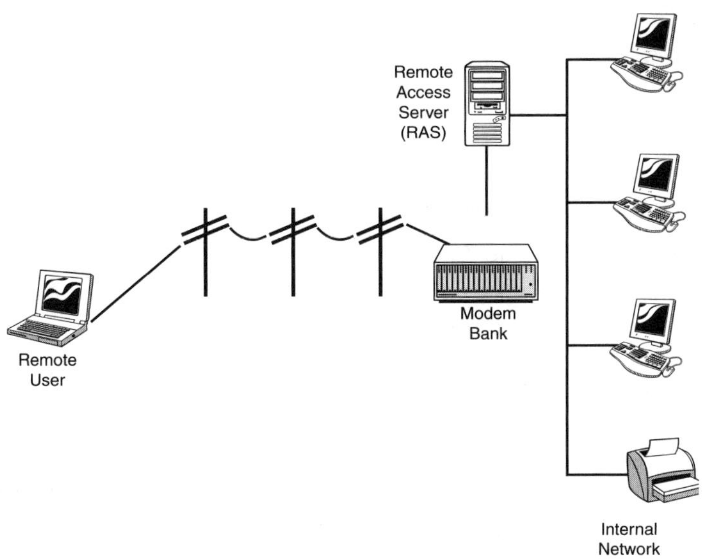

Both of these solutions have been around for some time and are very commonly implemented. However, they have some distinct drawbacks:

- Leased lines for WAN links can be very expensive.
- Leased lines require expensive hardware at each end that is not easy to set up and configure.
- Modem banks are expensive and difficult to configure and maintain.
- Concurrent connections are limited by the number of incoming phone lines and the number of modems in the bank.
- Long-distance telephone charges will accrue when remote users are geographically distant.

That's where VPNs come into the picture. Let's look at what a VPN can do for XYZ.

Using VPNs to Provide WAN Connectivity and Remote Access

A VPN can be used to eliminate the leased line required for the WAN link as well as the modem and telephone lines required for remote access. How does it do this? A VPN extends an organization's private network across a public network such as the Internet.

For example, let's review XYZ's need for WAN connectivity. Instead of leasing a line from a telecommunications provider, XYZ could connect the networks at each warehouse to the Internet, as shown in Figure 11.3.

Whenever a host at the branch office needs to communicate with a host at the home office (or vice versa), it can simply transmit the data over the Internet.

VPNs can also be used to provide remote users with network access through the Internet. Let's go back to XYZ's situation. Instead of maintaining a bank of modems, paying for multiple phone lines, and incurring long-distance charges, XYZ could use a VPN solution to allow users to connect to the home network through the Internet, as shown in Figure 11.4.

FIGURE 11.3
Using a VPN as a WAN.

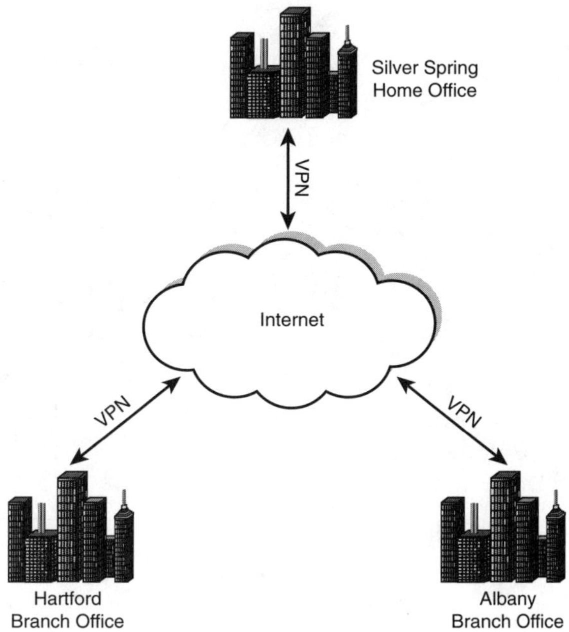

In this example, the traveling salesperson uses the wireless Internet access provided by her hotel to connect to the home office network through the Internet. With this connection, she can work on paperwork, submit orders, and send print jobs the same as if she were at her desk at company headquarters.

She wouldn't be limited to hotels with wireless access, either. If she works from home, she could also use a modem and her personal dial-up ISP account to access the office network through the Internet.

VPNs have the following advantages over the traditional solutions we discussed earlier:

- The costs associated with implementing a VPN versus implementing a traditional WAN leased line are considerably less.
- The costs associated with maintaining a VPN versus a traditional WAN leased line are also considerably less.
- If the company grows, the VPN can easily scale to accommodate additional sites without requiring additional leased lines. Everything goes through the Internet.

FIGURE 11.4
Using a VPN for remote access.

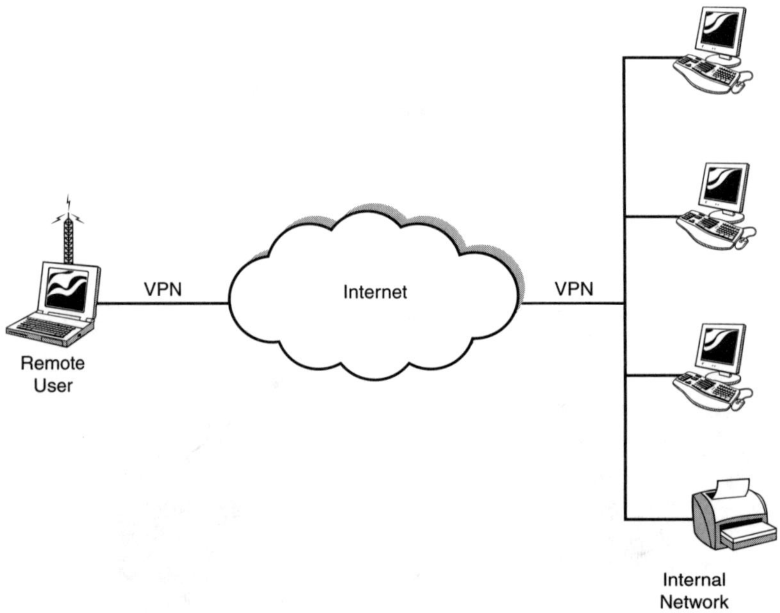

- VPNs can also easily scale to support more uses as the company grows. It's not limited by the number of phone lines available or the number of modems in the modem bank.
- The costs of implementing and maintaining a VPN are considerably less than for a modem bank and RAS server solution.
- VPNs eliminate long distance charges incurred when remote users dial in to a modem bank.

These advantages make VPNs an attractive WAN and remote access solution. However, they do have a couple of drawbacks you should be aware of:

- VPNs create a situation where your network is dependent on a component you have no control over: the Internet. If, as happened back in 2003 and 2004, massive worm or DoS attacks are going on, transmission speeds could be slowed way down and there's nothing you can do about it.
- VPNs require additional data processing that may impact performance to an extent.

From what you learned in the two preceding chapters, however, you may be saying "Hold on! I see another weakness! Couldn't someone intercept my VPN data on the Internet and use it to break into my network?" No need to worry; VPNs have got it covered. Next, let's discuss how they deal with this issue.

VPNs and Security

Obviously, you don't want your organization's sensitive data being transmitted clear-text over the Internet. To keep data secure, VPNs employ a high degree of security to render your data useless to anyone who tries to grab it. A key component of VPNs is the concept of *tunneling*.

Two VPN hosts are needed to create a VPN tunnel. Each host serves as an endpoint for the tunnel. When you tunnel data through the Internet with a VPN, you encapsulate your internal network data within standard IP packets. Hosts and routers on the Internet have no idea that the IP packets they process as you move data between points in a VPN actually contain packets from your internal network. This process is depicted in Figure 11.5.

FIGURE 11.5
Tunneling data in a VPN.

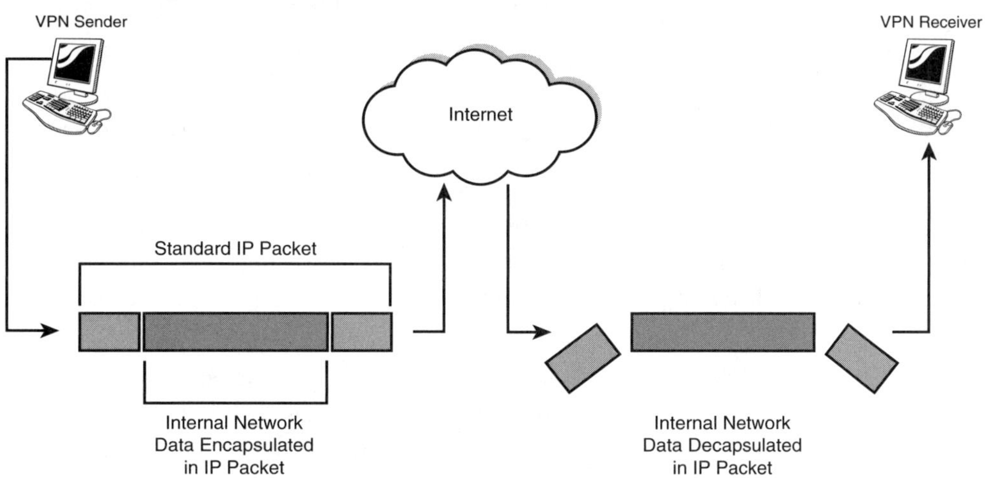

The sending VPN system encapsulates its network data in a standard IP packet and sends it across the Internet to the receiving VPN system. This system decapsulates the original network data from the IP packet and processes it just as if it originated on the internal network. Pretty cool!

You can use a variety of protocols with a VPN to tunnel data through the Internet. These include the following:

- PPTP—PPTP stands for Point-to-Point Tunneling Protocol. The PPTP protocol is used primarily on Microsoft Windows networks to create VPNs. It performs tunneling operations at the Data Link layer of the OSI model.
- L2TP—L2TP stands for Layer 2 Tunneling Protocol. L2TP is a tunneling protocol implemented by Cisco VPN systems. L2TP is an extension of the PPTP protocol discussed previously. L2TP operates at the Data Link layer of the OSI model. It encapsulates Point-to-Point Protocol (PPP) frames in IP packets for transmission across the Internet.
- IPsec—IPsec stands for IP Security. IPsec is an open tunneling standard that operates at the Network layer of the OSI model. IPsec is a very commonly implemented VPN tunneling protocol. IPsec offers two tunneling protocols: The Authentication Header (AH) protocol provides a means to authenticate the VPN sender. The Encapsulating Security Payload (ESP) protocol provides a means to both authenticate the sender and encrypt the data in the transmission. IPsec also provides the Internet Key Exchange protocol, which is used to coordinate the exchange of security keys between VPN hosts.

With this in mind, let's now look at the components you need to set up a VPN.

VPN Components

To set up a VPN solution, you need to have several critical components in place. These are shown in Figure 11.6.

You need the following:

- The VPN server—The VPN server's job is to establish VPN connections with other VPN servers or VPN clients. It provides user authentication, encryption, and encapsulation services.
- The VPN client—The VPN client is software running on a host operating system. This software is used to create a VPN tunnel with a VPN server, authenticate users to the VPN server, and encapsulate/decapsulate VPN data through the tunnel.
- The VPN tunnel—This is the point-to-point connection established using the tunneling protocols discussed earlier.

Put all these together and you've got a VPN. Be aware that specialized VPN routers are frequently used in place of the traditional firewall/router depicted in Figure 11.6. These are optimized and tuned specifically to work with VPN traffic, which can really enhance your tunnel throughput.

FIGURE 11.6
VPN components.

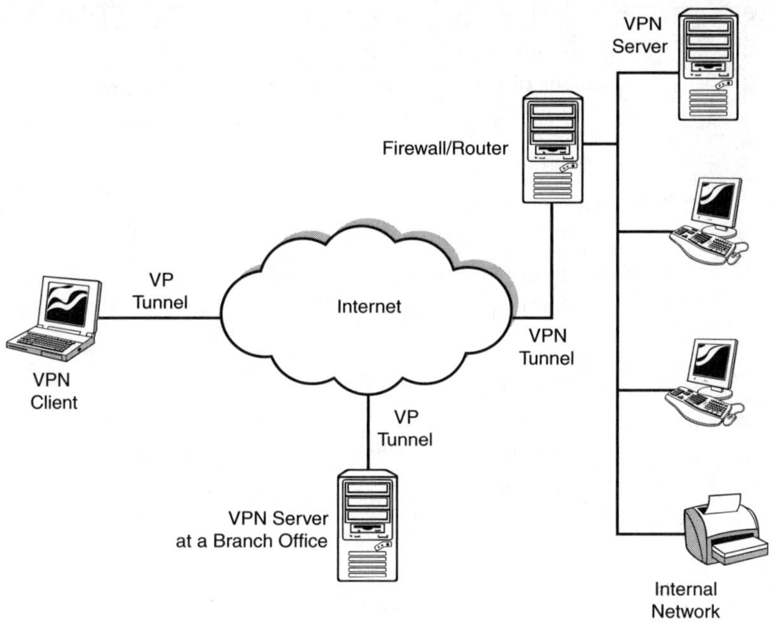

This is important because one of the biggest complaints I hear about VPNs is that the overhead added by the tunneling protocols really slows things down, especially on large networks with a lot of traffic. However, the low cost and ease of implementation of VPNs are usually enough to justify the impaired data rates.

I know this design may look somewhat complicated, but VPNs are fairly straightforward to implement. You'll learn how to do that next.

Implementing a VPN Server on SLES 9

TEST OBJECTIVE COVERED:

1. Implement a VPN on SLES 9.

Configuring a VPN server is a little more complex than the other services we've been working with in this book, but not much. Before you can begin, you need to install the necessary packages on your server. To do this, run the YaST Install and Remove Software module and search for ipsec. Install the freeswan, ipsec-tools, and yast2-ipsec packages; as shown in Figure 11.7.

FIGURE 11.7
Installing VPN packages.

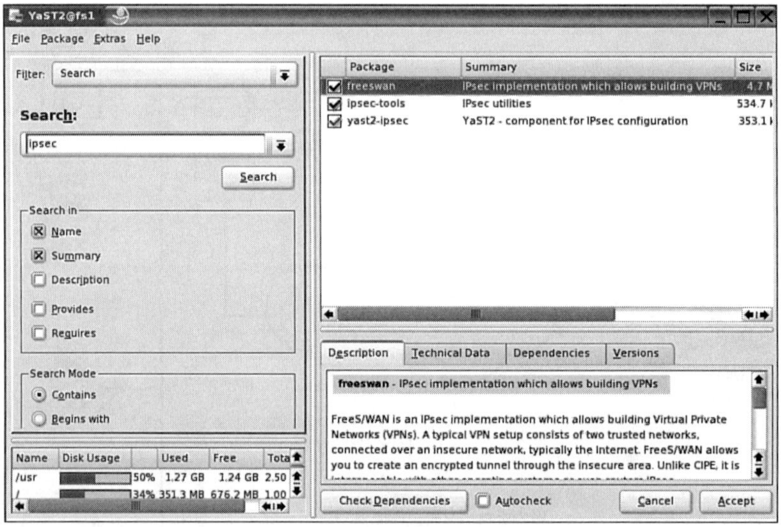

The base of the VPN service we're going to work with in this chapter is the FreeS/WAN package, shown in Figure 11.7. FreeS/WAN is an acronym for Free Secure Wide Area Network. FreeS/WAN is an open-source implementation of IPsec FreeS/WAN is composed of the following components:

- Kernel IP Security (KLIPS)—This component is an extension to the Linux kernel. It's responsible for encapsulation/decapsulation.
- pluto—This component is a daemon that is responsible for exchanging keys in a VPN connection and authenticating VPN users.

With the necessary packages installed on your server, you're ready to start the configuration process. To get a VPN server running on SLES 9, you need to do the following:

- Create and export security certificates.
- Configure `/etc/ipsec.conf`.

Just as you've done all the way along, you'll first spend some time looking at the `.conf` file for your VPN server. Then you'll learn how to do the same thing much faster in YaST. Let's begin by learning how to export certificates for your VPN server to use.

Creating and Exporting Certificates

As we've discussed, a VPN tunnel uses encryption to keep prying Internet eyes from seeing our private data. Accordingly, you need to create and export certificates for the hosts at each end of the tunnel. These will be used to encrypt VPN traffic.

TIP

When you install the ipsec packages, private and public keys are automatically generated for you and saved in the `/etc/ipsec.secrets` file. However, these are used only for authentication. After authentication, you need the certificates we're going to generate here to encrypt the actual contents of the VPN transmissions.

To do this, complete the following:

1. Open a terminal session and use **`su -`** to switch to root.
2. Create your key directory structure by completing the following:
    a. Change to the **`/etc`** directory.
    b. At the shell prompt, enter **`mkdir`** ***`directory`***.

TIP

I like to use a directory name that helps me keep track of which side of the VPN tunnel I'm working with, such as ca-left or fs1-left. As you will see in a minute, you have to complete this process on both ends of the VPN tunnel. It can be a real pain in the neck if you forget which certificates belong to which server.

Whatever you decide to name these directories, be sure to set permissions on them so that no one else can get at them!

    c. Create the following directories:
        - **`certs`**
        - **`newcerts`**
        - **`private`**
        - **`crl`**
3. Configure your OpenSSL defaults by completing the following:
    a. At the shell prompt, enter **`vi /etc/ssl/openssl.cnf`**.
    b. Scroll down to the HOME directive and set it to `/etc/`*`directory`*.
    c. Scroll down to the dir directive under [CA_default].
    d. Set the value of dir to `/etc/`*`directory`*.

e. Save the your changes and close the file.
f. Verify that the current directory is `/etc/`*`directory`*.
g. Create a self-signed root certificate by entering **`openssl req -newkey rsa:2048 -x509 -days 365 -keyout private/cakey.pem -out cacert.pem`** at the shell prompt.
h. When prompted, enter a *passphrase* for the private key.
i. When prompted, enter your *locality information*.
j. When prompted, enter your *organizational information*.
k. When prompted, enter your *personal information*.
l. At the shell prompt, enter **`touch index.txt ; echo 01 > serial`**.
m. Create a certificate signing request by entering **`openssl req -new -keyout private/ca_prv_key.pem -out certs/ca_req.pem -days 365`** at the shell prompt.
n. When prompted, enter a *passphrase*.
o. When prompted, enter your *locality information*.
p. When prompted, enter your *organizational information*.
q. When prompted, enter your *personal information*.
r. When prompted, enter a *challenge password* for the certificate.
s. When prompted for an optional company name, press Enter.
t. Sign the certificate-signing request by entering **`openssl ca -policy policy_anything -notext -out certs/newcert.pem -infiles certs/ca_req.pem`**.
u. When prompted, enter a *passphrase*.
v. When prompted to sign the certificate, enter **`y`**.
w. When prompted to commit, enter **`y`**.

4. Repeat these steps to generate certificates on the other host that will participate in the tunnel.

With your keys generated, you're ready to edit your VPN configuration file. Let's talk about how to do that next.

Configuring `/etc/ipsec.conf`

The behavior of your VPN server is configured using the `/etc/ipsec.conf` file, a portion of which is shown in Figure 11.8.

FIGURE 11.8
The `/etc/ipsec.conf` file.

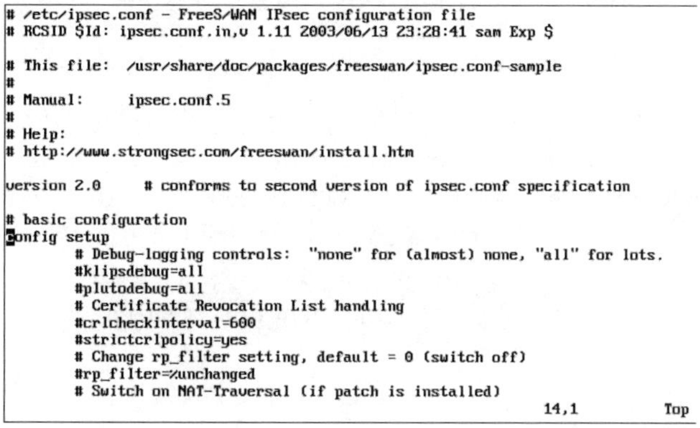

```
# /etc/ipsec.conf - FreeS/WAN IPsec configuration file
# RCSID $Id: ipsec.conf.in,v 1.11 2003/06/13 23:28:41 sam Exp $

# This file:  /usr/share/doc/packages/freeswan/ipsec.conf-sample
#
# Manual:     ipsec.conf.5
#
# Help:
# http://www.strongsec.com/freeswan/install.htm

version 2.0     # conforms to second version of ipsec.conf specification

# basic configuration
config setup
        # Debug-logging controls:  "none" for (almost) none, "all" for lots.
        #klipsdebug=all
        #plutodebug=all
        # Certificate Revocation List handling
        #crlcheckinterval=600
        #strictcrlpolicy=yes
        # Change rp_filter setting, default = 0 (switch off)
        #rp_filter=%unchanged
        # Switch on NAT-Traversal (if patch is installed)
                                                              14,1          Top
```

Within this file there are four sections:

- Basic Configuration—This section of the file contains basic parameters used to configure the pluto daemon. This section is shown in Figure 11.8.
- Default Connection Settings—This section of the file is used to configure default parameters for VPN connections. These parameters apply to all connections defined later in the file. These can be overridden for specific connections by declaring the parameter again in the connection definition and supplying a new value.
- Opportunistic Encryption—This section configures the opportunistic encryption functionality included in the freeswan package. Opportunistic encryption is disabled by default on SLES 9. See http://www.freeswan.org/freeswan_trees/freeswan-1.91/doc/toc.html for more information on this topic.
- Connection Definitions—This section of the file is used to define and configure VPN connections. We're going to spend most of our time in this chapter working with this part of the `.conf` file.

Before we get too far into this file, we need to spend some time discussing the terminology and syntax used in it. You should be familiar with the following terms:

- Gateway-to-Gateway VPN—This term refers to a VPN configuration option where you connect one gateway to another using a VPN tunnel. You could use this type of configuration to connect a branch office, for example, to a home office network. The gateways are assumed to have static IP addresses and are configured as VPN servers. In this capacity, they function as endpoints for the VPN tunnel. The gateways are responsible for encapsulation and decapsulation of packets flowing between the local network and the VPN tunnel. The two networks they connect through the tunnel function as though they were a single network.

- Road Warriors—This term refers to an alternative VPN configuration where a remote user connects to a VPN server using VPN client software on a notebook or home PC (the Road Warrior client). In this configuration, the VPN client and the VPN server each function as endpoints in the VPN tunnel. However, the road warrior system probably uses a dynamic IP address provided by an ISP. In addition, it's very likely that the ISP is using a NAT router somewhere in its network to hide its customers.
- Left and Right—Throughout the `ipsec.conf` file, you will see the terms *left* and *right* used. These refer to the endpoints of the VPN tunnel. If you drew a diagram of your tunnel, left would refer to the left host and right would refer to the right host. Unfortunately, real life isn't that cut and dried. The generally accepted convention is to use left to refer to your own VPN system (client or server) and right to refer to the host at the other end of the VPN tunnel.
- Manual Keying—With manual keying, the two hosts at the end of the VPN tunnel share a common key to encrypt their messages. In order to do this, you have to manually (and securely!) copy the common key between the hosts before setting up the tunnel.
- Automatic Keying—With automatic keying, the two hosts at the end of the VPN tunnel authenticate each other and then automatically exchange keys.

The `/etc/ipsec.conf` file comes with a sample connection predefined for you to use as a template. This is shown in Figure 11.9:

FIGURE 11.9
The sample connection definition.

```
        auto=ignore

#conn OEself
#       auto=ignore

# Add connections here.

# sample VPN connection
#sample#        conn sample
#sample#                # Left security gateway, subnet behind it, next hop towa
rd right.
#sample#                left=%defaultroute
#sample#                leftcert=myCert.pem
#sample#                leftsubnet=172.16.0.0/24
#sample#                # Right security gateway, subnet behind it, next hop tow
ard left.
#sample#                right=10.12.12.1
#sample#                rightid="<Distinguished name of right security gateway>"
#sample#                rightsubnet=192.168.0.0/24
#sample#                # To authorize this connection, but not actually start i
t, at startup,
#sample#                # uncomment this.
#sample#                #auto=start
                                                        62,1          Bot
```

To configure a connection, you need to understand the following elements of the connection definition:

- left—Specifies the IP address of the left end of the tunnel. If you have only one interface in the system, you can set this to `%defaultroute` to use the IP address of the default route interface.
- leftcert—Specifies the certificate file to be used for VPN.
- leftsubnet—If the VPN server is also a router, this parameter specifies the subnet on the other side of the router using the syntax *ip_address/mask*.
- leftnexthop—This parameter is used to specify the IP address of the default gateway. If you use `%defaultroute` for left, you don't need this parameter.
- leftid—Specifies the identity of the left host. In SLES 9, this is acquired from the certificate file used to encrypt data, as you will see in a minute.
- leftrsasigkey—Specifies the public key used by the left host. The `%cert` value causes ipsec to extract the key from the certificate.
- right—Specifies the IP address of the right end of the tunnel. You can use `%any` to indicate that any host can be the right end of the tunnel.
- rightsubnet—If the right host is a router, this parameter specifies the subnet on the other side of the router using the syntax *`ip_address/mask`*.
- rightcert—Specifies the certificate file to be used for VPN.
- rightnexthop—This parameter is used to specify the IP address of the default gateway. If you use `%defaultroute` for right, you don't need this parameter.
- rightid—Specifies the identity of the right host. In SLES 9, this is acquired from the certificate file used to encrypt data, as you will see in a minute.
- rightrsasigkey—Specifies the public key used by the right host. The `%cert` value causes ipsec to extract the key from the certificate.
- auto—This parameter can be set to `add` or `start`. When set to `add`, ipsec will load the configuration but won't establish a connection. If set to `start`, ipsec will load the configuration and try to establish a connection.

Let's take a look at the sample connection definition:

```
conn server2server
    authby=rsasig
    auto=add
    esp=aes,3des
    keyingtries=3
    left=192.168.1.47
    leftcert=/etc/ipsec.d/certs/newcert.pem
    leftid=emailAddress=root@cle9.com,CN=fs1,OU=IS,O=NTI,L=Sq,ST=Utah,C=US
```

```
leftrsasigkey=%cert
leftsubnet=10.0.0.0/8
pfs=yes
right=192.168.1.48
rightcert=/etc/ipsec.d/certs/cert_01.pem
rightid=emailAddress=root@cle9.com,CN=fs2,OU=IS,O=NTI,L=Sq,ST=Utah,C=US
rightrsasigkey=%cert
```

In this example, the host at the left end of the VPN tunnel has an IP address of 192.168.1.47. It's a router that has subnet with an address of 10.0.0.0 behind it. The host at the right end of the tunnel has an IP address of 192.168.1.48. It's not a router and doesn't have a subnet behind it. The rightid and leftid values are pulled from the respective certificate files for each host. Also notice that the public key (leftrsasigkey and rightrsasigkey) is pulled from the respective certificate files.

To set up the VPN tunnel, you need to copy this file to both the right and the left hosts, copy the appropriate certificate and key files to the locations listed, and start ipsec on both hosts by entering **`rcipsec start`**.

You can also configure a VPN on SLES 9 using YaST. Let's look at how to do that next.

Configuring VPNs with YaST

The YaST VPN module is used to configure each end of the VPN tunnel on SLES 9. To do this, complete the following:

1. Distribute your certificates and keys between the left and right hosts by completing the following:
    a. Prepare a floppy disk drive.
    b. Create a directory on the disk named **`rightCert`**.
    c. Copy the right host's certificate and key files to this directory.
    d. Create another directory on the disk named **`leftCert`**.
    e. Copy the left host's certificate and key files to this directory.
2. Start YaST on the left host.
3. Select **Security and Users, VPN**. The screen in Figure 11.10 is displayed.
4. Select Enable VPN Services.
5. When prompted to select certificates, select Yes. The screen in Figure 11.11 is displayed.

FIGURE 11.10
The Initial YaST VPN Screen.

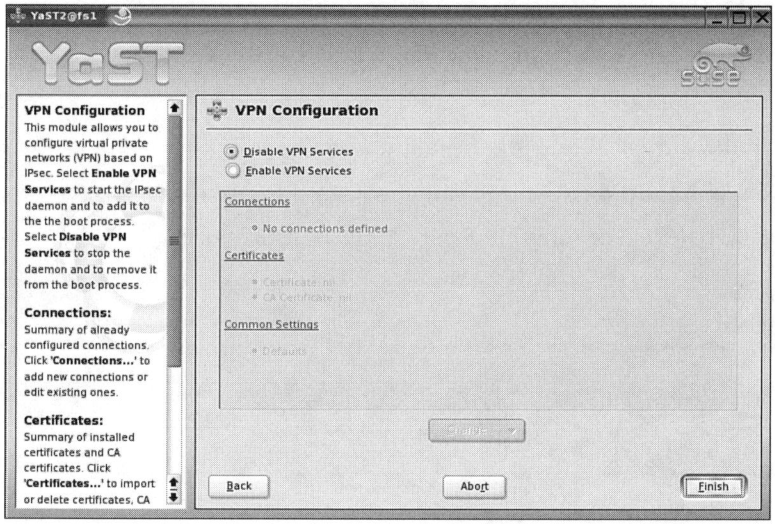

FIGURE 11.11
Configuring VPN certificates.

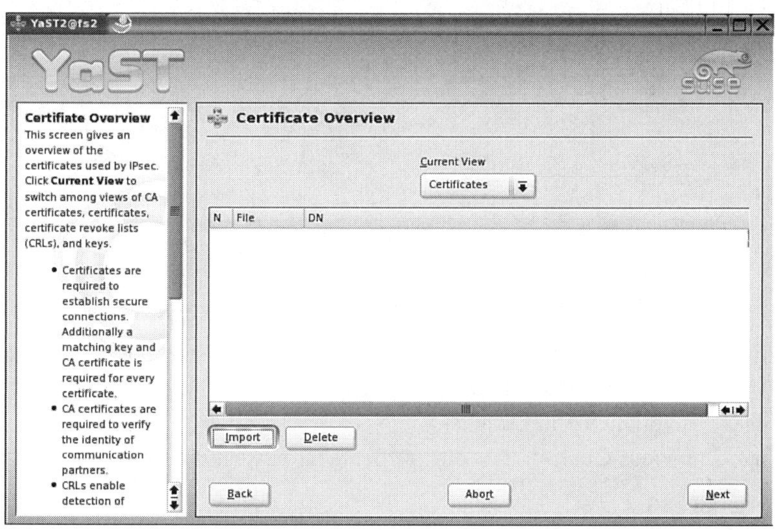

6. Configure your VPN certificates by completing the following:
   a. In the Current View drop-down list, select **CA Certificates**.
   b. Select **Import**; then browse to and select your *CA certificate*.
   c. In the Current View drop-down list, select **Certificates**.
   d. Select **Import**; then browse to and select your *certificate*.
   e. In the Current View drop-down list, select **Keys**.
   f. Select **Import**; then browse to and select your *private key*.
   g. Select **Next**. The screen in Figure 11.12 is displayed:

FIGURE 11.12
Configuring VPN roles.

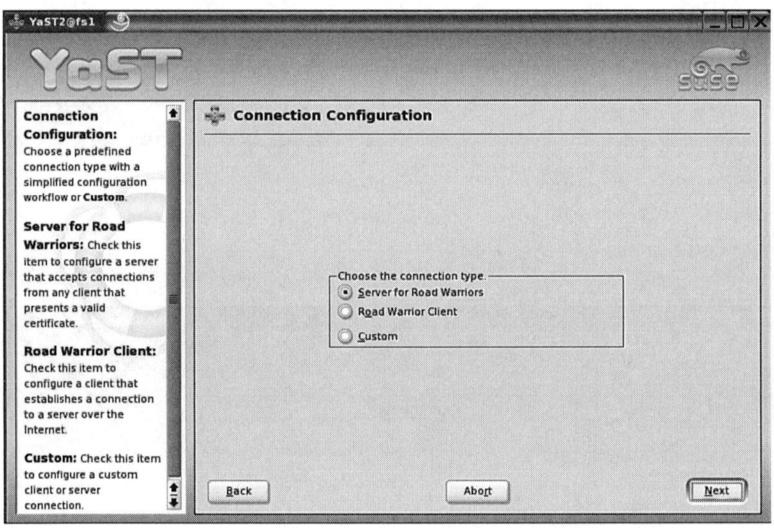

7. Configure your VPN connections by completing the following:
   a. If you're configuring a VPN server for remote clients, select **Server for Road Warriors**. If you are configuring the system as a VPN client, select **Road Warrior** client. If you are connecting two VPN servers together (in a branch/home office scenario), choose **Custom**. For our purposes here, we'll go through the Custom steps.
   b. Select **Next**.
   c. When prompted, enter a *name* for the connection; then select **OK**. The screen in Figure 11.13 is displayed:

FIGURE 11.13
Configuring the left VPN host.

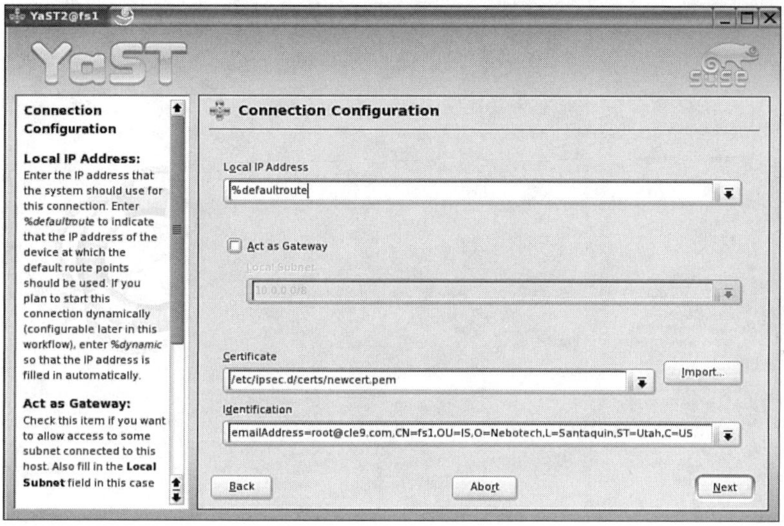

d. In the Local IP Address drop-down list, select the left server's *IP address* (or use `%default`).

e. If the system is acting as a gateway between subnets, mark **Act as Gateway**; then select the *subnet* behind the gateway in the Local Subnet drop-down list.

f. In the Certificate field, ensure that your left host's *certificate file* has been selected.

g. Verify that the *host ID* from the certificate file is displayed in the Identification field; then select **Next**. The screen in Figure 11.14 is displayed.

h. In the Remote Address drop-down list, do one of the following:

   - If you're configuring a Road Warrior server, select **%any**.
   - If you're configuring a server to server connection, enter the remote server's *IP address*.

i. If the remote server will act as a gateway for another subnet, mark **Act as Gateway**; then select its ***subnet*** from the Remote Subnet drop-down list.

j. In the Certificate field, select **Import, Import**.

k. Browse to and select the right host's *certificate file* from your floppy disk.

FIGURE 11.14
Configuring the right VPN host.

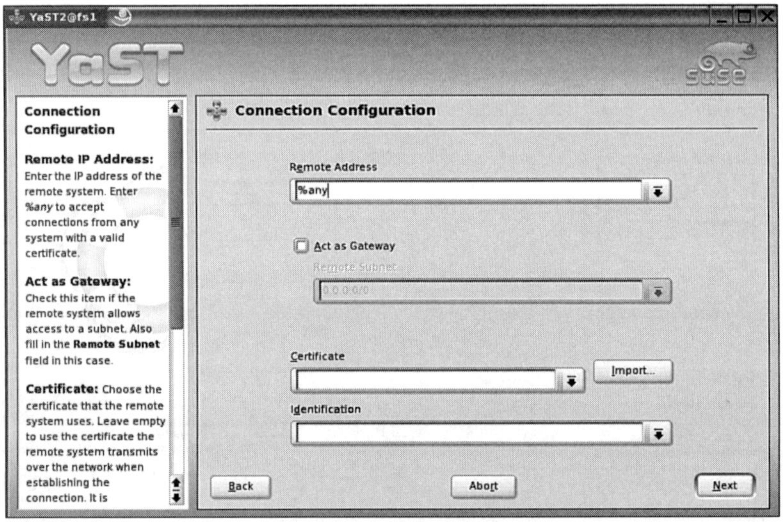

l. Select **Next**.

m. In the Certificate drop-down list, select the *certificate* you just imported.

n. Verify that the right host's *ID* was pulled correctly from the certificate in the Identification field.

o. Select **Next**.

p. In the During Boot drop-down list, select one of the following:

- Initiate Connection—This option configures ipsec to immediately try to connect to the remote system. If the remote host isn't available, it will cause the connection to fail.
- Prepare Connection—This option will open the configuration and listen for incoming connection requests. (This is the best option in most cases.)
- Ignore Connection—This option will cause the connection to not be loaded.

q. Select **OK**.

r. Select **Finish**.

At this point, the left end of the VPN tunnel has been established. Now you need to configure the right end of the tunnel. Complete the following:

1. Start YaST on the right host.
2. Select **Security and Users, VPN**.
3. Select **Enable VPN Services**.
4. When prompted to select certificates, select **Yes**.
5. Configure your VPN certificates by completing the following:
    a. In the Current View drop-down list, select **CA Certificates**.
    b. Select **Import**; then browse to and select your CA *certificate*.
    c. In the Current View drop-down list, select **Certificates**.
    d. Select **Import**; then browse to and select your *certificate*.
    e. In the Current View drop-down list, select **Keys**.
    f. Select **Import**; then browse to and select your *private key*.
    g. When prompted, enter your *RSA key password*.
    h. Select **Next**.
6. Configure your VPN connections by completing the following:
    a. Configure the type of connection you are creating (we're going to assume **Custom** here).
    b. Select **Next**.
    c. When prompted, enter a *name* for the connection; then select **OK**.
    d. In the Local IP Address drop-down list, select the right server's *IP address* (or use `%default`).
    e. If the system is acting as a gateway between subnets, mark **Act as Gateway**; then select the *subnet* behind the gateway in the Local Subnet drop-down list.
    f. In the Certificate field, ensure your right host's *certificate file* has been selected.
    g. Verify that the *host ID* from the certificate file is displayed in the Identification field; then select **Next**.
    h. In the Remote Address drop-down list, enter the left server's *IP address*.
    i. If the remote server will act as a gateway for another subnet, mark **Act as Gateway**; then select its *subnet* from the Remote Subnet drop-down list.
    j. In the Certificate field, select **Import, Import**.
    k. Browse to and select the left host's *certificate file* from your floppy disk.

l. Select **Next**.

m. In the Certificate drop-down list, select the *certificate* you just imported.

n. Verify that the left host's *ID* was pulled correctly from the certificate in the Identification field.

o. Select **Next**.

p. In the During Boot drop-down list, select one of the following:

- **Initiate Connection**
- **Prepare Connection**
- **Ignore Connection**

q. Select **OK**.

r. Select **Finish**.

If you're doing this for the first time, I highly recommend that you use YaST to set up the connection on the two hosts. After you do, carefully review the `ipsec.conf` files on both systems to see how YaST formatted the connection definitions.

As well, review the changes made to your `ipsec.secrets` file. You should see an entry added at the end that specifies the location of the private key along with its passphrase, as shown in Figure 11.15.

FIGURE 11.15
Changes made to `ipsec.secrets`.

```
a543935676ae1422d7249fb7ab5d79c61b8bb449cd63bc5b2082c0d6e116915ebe9e9e66ed99d2de
6ae1d1023b740d50a364fa1315d02b8ae7d11f07967e61f3ceda0113fb4155608a1348cbbb4330e7
e4a0601c0ef203cbdc386f74531955b4f3
        Prime2: 0xb049f41b0c1f6787421cbe7147069ab82171f84b66b5dc87343b1956316aa7
e00f2bd96799ec7e6802bd19ae07c67e1d4dce4708d86460ea085ec67ff8859c1530ad6c3bd41919
3137223944ce0579774b978667a1b588d64b7bcffb641bd8b0140079008dd4e7a075e7d95094401f
45fff82d2042149a5baec01f22475f8371
        Exponent1: 0x98dab9556dd85ce8f3f2a0bad581c06b79d6d1233b97c2569c1b32df6e7
591c3826239a4740d6c8f6dbfcfc793a684125d22dbde427d9215ac808f40b9b63f29bf14449e668
c94474136017cf808e06cedfc0cb935725c9a8b6a050efeebf7df3c00b7fcd638eb06b785dd27822
09a986aeabd5f4c0287e8259fa2e210e3cdf7
        Exponent2: 0x7586a2bcb2bf9a5a2c1329a0da0467256ba1503244793daf7827663976471a955f7290efbbf2fef001d36674052efebe33deda05e598409c05948455505912b8cb1e4827e2b
b6620cf6c262ddeae50fa32650445167905e432528aa79812907562aafb55b3e34515a3efe635b82
abf83fffac8c02c0dbc3d1f2abf6c2f95024b
        Coefficient: 0x6c6a4242da52d053e56b824cdef5df141cbd49352769d53d861e3cb74
0bc557593e4675c6fa02f62bde05a79c83c6cdef3f040c3a3a8a5553502d20bb521622a0abfc22aa
2cf9788b44db6de66ea962690b1d76072972ca9193ff4f292cc4c722c6b8d37ae23a5d077942fbe4
e263cdb6d80bf8cfa8d47a3cf34acb83c0ddec9
        }
# do not change the indenting of that "}"
: RSA /etc/ipsec.d/private/key_01.pem "tuX123"

/etc/ipsec.secrets lines 12-20/20 (END)
```

For security reasons, you should make sure this file is kept secure.

Let's practice setting up a VPN connection between two hosts in Lab Exercise 11.1.

Lab Exercise 11.1: Creating a VPN with YaST

In this lab exercise, you will create a VPN connection between two hosts using YaST. To complete this exercise, you will need your SLES 9 server along with your NLD system. We're going to tweak YaST in NLD with the ipsec module from your SLES 9 system. Complete the following:

1. Configure the YaST ipsec module on your NLD system by completing the following:
   a. Boot your NLD system and authenticate.
   b. Insert your SLES 9 CD 2 into the CD drive of your NLD system.
   c. Change to the `/media/cdrom/suse/noarch directory`.
   d. Copy the `yast2-ipsec-2.9.13-1.2.noarch.rpm` file to `/tmp` on your workstation.
   e. Remove the SLES 9 CD 2.
   f. Select **System, Administrator Settings**.
   g. When prompted supply your root *password*.
   h. Select **Software, Change Source of Installation**.
   i. In the Software Source Media screen, select **Add, Local Directory**.
   j. In the Directory Path field, enter `/tmp`; then select **OK**.
   k. When prompted that there's no product information in `/tmp`, select **Continue**.
   l. Select **Finish**.
   m. Select **Install** and **Remove Software**.
   n. In the Search field, enter **`ipsec`**; then select **Search**.
   o. Mark the freeswan, ipsec-tools, and yast2-ipsec packages; then select **Accept**.
   p. In the Automatic Changes screen, select **Continue**.
   q. Install CDs as prompted.
   r. When complete, close YaST.

2. Prepare your SLES 9 server by completing the following:
   a. Boot your SLES 9 server and authenticate as **tux** with a password of **SuSE789**.
   b. Open a shell prompt and use **sux –** to change to root with a password of **tuX123**.
   c. At the shell prompt, enter **rcsquid stop**.
   d. At the shell prompt, enter **rcSuSEfirewall2 stop**.
   d. At the shell prompt, enter **iptables -t nat -F**.
   e. At the shell prompt, enter **iptables -F**.
   f. Verify that both tables are empty using the `-L` option with iptables.
   g. Enable forwarding by entering **echo 1 > /proc/sys/net/ipv4/ip_forward** at the shell prompt.
3. Generate certificates and keys on your SLES 9 server by completing the following:
   a. At the shell prompt, change to the `/etc` directory.
   b. At the shell prompt, enter **mkdir ca-left**.
   c. Change to the `/etc/ca-left` directory.
   d. Create the following directories:
      - **certs**
      - **newcerts**
      - **private**
      - **crl**
   e. At the shell prompt, enter **vi /etc/ssl/openssl.cnf**.
   f. Scroll down to the HOME directive and set it to **/etc/ca-left**.
   g. Scroll down to the dir directive under [CA_default].
   h. Set the value of dir to **/etc/ca-left**.
   i. Press **Esc**; then enter **:exit**.
   j. Verify that the current directory is `/etc/ca-left`; then create a self-signed root certificate by entering **openssl req -newkey rsa:2048 -x509 -days 365 -keyout private/cakey.pem -out cacert.pem** at the shell prompt.
   k. When prompted, enter a passphrase of **test** for the private key.

- **l.** When prompted, enter your *locality* and *organizational information*.
- **m.** When prompted for the Common Name, enter the *DNS name* or *IP address* of your server.
- **n.** When prompted for an email address, enter **`tux@cle9.com`**.
- **o.** At the shell prompt, enter **`touch index.txt ; echo 01 > serial`**.
- **p.** Create a certificate signing request by entering **`openssl req -new -keyout private/ca_prv_key.pem -out certs/ca_req.pem -days 365`** at the shell prompt.
- **q.** When prompted, enter a passphrase of **`test`**.
- **r.** When prompted, enter your *locality* and *organizational information*.
- **s.** When prompted for the Common Name, enter the *DNS name* or *IP address* of your server.
- **t.** When prompted for an email address, enter **`tux@cle9.com`**.
- **u.** When prompted, enter a challenge password of **`test`** for the certificate.
- **v.** When prompted for an optional company name, press **Enter**.
- **w.** Sign the certificate signing request by entering **`openssl ca -policy policy_anything -notext -out certs/newcert.pem -infiles certs/ca_req.pem`**.
- **x.** When prompted, enter a passphrase of **`test`**.
- **y.** When prompted to sign the certificate, enter **`y`**.
- **z.** When prompted to commit, enter **`y`**.

4. Insert a disk into your SLES 9 server's floppy drive and mount it.

5. Copy the **`/etc/ca-left`** directory to the floppy disk; then umount the diskette.

6. Generate certificates and keys on your NLD workstation by completing the following:

- **a.** Open a terminal session and use **su -** to change to root.
- **b.** Change to the `/etc` directory.
- **c.** At the shell prompt, enter **`mkdir ca-right`**.
- **d.** Change to the **`ca-right`** directory.

e. Create the following directories:
   - **certs**
   - **newcerts**
   - **private**
   - **crl**

f. At the shell prompt, enter **vi /etc/ssl/openssl.cnf**.

g. Scroll down to the HOME directive and set it to **/etc/ca-right**.

h. Scroll down to the dir directive under [CA_default].

i. Set the value of dir to **/etc/ca-right**.

j. Press **Esc**; then enter **:exit**.

k. Verify that the current directory is `/etc/ca-right`; then create a self-signed root certificate by entering **openssl req -newkey rsa:2048 -x509 -days 365 -keyout private/cakey.pem -out cacert.pem** at the shell prompt.

l. When prompted, enter a passphrase of **test** for the private key.

m. When prompted, enter your *locality* and *organizational information*.

n. When prompted for the Common Name, enter the *IP address* or *DNS name* of your NLD workstation.

o. When prompted for an email address, enter **tux@cle9.com**.

p. At the shell prompt, enter **touch index.txt ; echo 01 > serial**.

q. Create a certificate signing request by entering **openssl req -new -keyout private/ca_prv_key.pem -out certs/ca_req.pem -days 365** at the shell prompt.

r. When prompted, enter a passphrase of **test**.

s. When prompted, enter your *locality* and *organizational information*.

t. When prompted for the Common Name, enter the *IP address* or *DNS name* of your NLD Workstation.

u. When prompted for an email address, enter **tux@cle9.com**.

v. When prompted, enter a challenge password of **test** for the certificate.

w. When prompted for an optional company name, press **Enter**.

x. Sign the certificate signing request by entering **openssl ca -policy policy_anything -notext -out certs/newcert.pem -infiles certs/ca_req.pem**.

y. When prompted, enter a passphrase of **test**.

z. When prompted to sign the certificate, enter **`y`**.

aa. When prompted to commit, enter **`y`**.

7. Insert your disk into your NLD workstation's floppy drive and mount it.
8. Copy the **`/etc/ca-right`** directory to the floppy disk; then umount the disk.
9. Configure the left end of the tunnel on your SLES 9 system by completing the following:
   a. Insert your disk into the floppy drive of your SLES 9 server.
   b. Mount the floppy by entering **`mount -t vfat /dev/fd0 /media/floppy`** at the shell prompt.
   c. Start YaST on your SLES 9 server.
   d. When prompted supply a root password of **`tuX123`**.
   e. Select **Security and Users, VPN**.
   f. If prompted that FreeS/WAN needs to be installed, select **Continue**; then insert CDs as prompted.
   f. Select **Enable VPN Services**.
10. Configure VPN certificates by completing the following:
    a. When prompted to import certificates, select **Yes**.
    b. In the Current View drop-down list, select **CA Certificates**.
    c. Select **Import**; then browse to and select **`/etc/ca-left/cacert.pem`**.
    d. In the Current View drop-down list, select **Certificates**.
    e. Select **Import**; then browse to and select **`/etc/ca-left/certs/newcert.pem`**.
    f. In the Current View drop-down list, select **Keys**.
    g. Select **Import**; then browse to and select **`/etc/ca-left/private/cakey.pem`**.
    h. When prompted for the RSA password, enter **`test`**; then select **Next**.
11. Configure a connection definition by completing the following:
    a. When prompted to define connections, select **Yes**.
    b. Under Choose the Connection Type, select **Custom**; then select **Next**.

c. When prompted enter **`host2host`** for the connection name.

d. In the Local IP Address drop-down list, select your server's *IP address*.

e. Mark **Act as Gateway**; then select the **10.0.0.0/8 subnet in the Local Subnet** drop-down list.

f. In the Certificate field, ensure that your left host's certificate file has been selected.

g. Verify that the *host ID* from the certificate file is displayed in the Identification field; then select **Next**.

h. In the Remote Address drop-down list, enter the *IP address* of your NLD workstation.

i. In the Certificate field, select **Import**, **Import**.

j. Browse to and select the right host's certificate file **`/media/floppy/ca-right/certs/newcert.pem`**.

k. Select **Next**.

l. In the Certificate drop-down list, select the *certificate* you just imported. Usually it will be named `cert_02.pem`.

m. Verify that the *right host's ID* was pulled correctly from the certificate in the Identification field; then select **Next**.

n. In the During Boot drop-down list, select **Prepare Connection**.

o. Select **OK**; then select **Finish**.

At this point, the left end of the VPN tunnel has been established. Now you need to configure the right end of the tunnel on your NLD workstation.

1. Configure VPN on your NLD workstation by completing the following:

   a. Start YaST on your NLD workstation.

   b. When prompted, supply your root *password*.

   c. Select **Security and Users, VPN**.

   d. Select **Enable VPN Services**.

   e. When prompted to import certificates, select **Yes**.

2. Configure your VPN certificates by completing the following:

   a. In the Current View drop-down list, select **CA Certificates**.

   b. Select **Import**; then browse to and select **`/etc/ca-right/cacert.pem`**.

c. In the Current View drop-down list, select **Certificates**.
d. Select **Import**; then browse to and select **/etc/ca-right/certs/newcert.pem**.
e. In the Current View drop-down list, select **Keys**.
f. Select **Import**; then browse to and select **/etc/ca-right/private/cakey.pem**.
g. When prompted for your RSA key password, enter **test**.
h. Select **Next**.

3. Configure your VPN connection by completing the following:
   a. When prompted to define connections, select **Yes**.
   b. Select **Custom**; then select **Next**.
   c. When prompted for a connection name, enter **host2host**; then select **OK**.
   d. In the Local IP Address drop-down list, select your workstation's *IP address*.
   e. In the Certificate field, ensure that your right host's certificate file has been selected.
   f. Verify that the *host ID* from the certificate file is displayed in the Identification field; then select **Next**.
   g. In the Remote Address drop-down list, enter the *IP address* of your SLES 9 server.
   h. Mark **Act as Gateway**; then enter **10.0.0.0/8** in the Remote Subnet drop-down list.
   i. In the Certificate field, select **Import, Import**.
   j. Browse to and select **/media/floppy/ca-left/certs/newcert.pem**.
   k. Select **Next**.
   l. In the Certificate drop-down list, select the *certificate* you just imported. Usually it will be named `cert_02.pem`.
   m. Verify that the *left host's ID* was pulled correctly from the certificate in the Identification field.
   n. Select **Next**.
   o. In the During Boot drop-down list, select **Initiate Connection**.

   p. Select **OK**.

   q. Select **Finish**.

4. At both systems, enter **`rcipsec restart`**.
5. At the shell prompt of either system, enter **`tcpdump -i eth0 -n`**. You should see IP traffic being exchanged between hosts on port 500, as shown in Figure 11.16.

FIGURE 11.16
Viewing VPN traffic with tcpdump.

```
nld:~ # tcpdump -i eth0 -n
tcpdump: verbose output suppressed, use -v or -vv for full protocol decode
listening on eth0, link-type EN10MB (Ethernet), capture size 96 bytes
13:04:46.749631 IP 192.168.1.47.500 > 192.168.1.50.500: isakmp: phase 1 ? ident
13:04:46.832930 IP 192.168.1.50.500 > 192.168.1.47.500: isakmp: phase 1 ? inf
13:04:47.841058 IP 192.168.1.50.500 > 192.168.1.47.500: isakmp: phase 1 ? ident
```

NOTE

If you do not see communications between the 2 systems over port 500, use the YaST runlevel editor to make sure your SuSEfirewall2 services are all disabled. Then restart the network service by entering rcnetwork restart. After doing so, make sure each system can ping the other. Then restart the VPN tunnel by entering rcipsec restart.

That's it! You'll probably find that after you set up a few VPN connections with IPsec, the VPN configuration process starts to become second nature. Again, I strongly recommend that you review the `ipsec.conf` file generated by YaST so you understand what it did in setting up the right and left connections.

You may also want to try using YaST to set up your SLES 9 system as a Road Warrior server and your NLD workstation as a Road Warrior client. Examine the differences between the connection definitions you created in this exercise with those created by the Road Warrior definitions.

That's it for this chapter. We've touched only the surface of VPN here. If you want to become a VPN expert, spend some time studying the freeswan documentation available at http://www.freeswan.org/freeswan_trees/freeswan-1.91/doc/toc.html. It's well worth the time. Let's review what we learned in this chapter.

Summary

In this chapter we introduced you to the concept of VPNs and how to implement them with SLES 9. To do this, we first discussed traditional WAN and remote access solutions. Then we related how VPNs can be used to provide the same functionality using the Internet instead of leased lines or modem banks.

Then we spend some time discussing how VPN works. You learned that VPN encapsulates LAN data within IP packets and tunnels them through the Internet to the remote site. The PPTP, L2TP, and IPsec protocols are used to do this.

We then discussed how to implement VPNs on SLES 9. We first discussed how to configure the `/etc/ipsec.conf` file. Then we did the same thing in YaST.

You're almost done! In the next chapter, we'll cover the last couple of topics you need to be familiar with for your CLE 9 certification exam.

CHAPTER 12

Putting It All Together: Adding OpenSLP and Tomcat to Your Server

This chapter covers the following requirements for Novell's Certified Linux Engineer (CLE) 9 certification:

1. Configure OpenSLP on SLES 9.
2. Configure Tomcat on SLES 9.

Welcome to the last chapter in this book! We've covered a lot of ground to get to this point. Before we end, there are two more topics you need to be familiar with for your CLE 9 certification exam: OpenSLP and Tomcat. In this chapter, we're going to spend some time with each of these services to round out your CLE 9 knowledge.

Let's start by learning about OpenSLP.

Implementing OpenSLP on SLES 9

TEST OBJECTIVE COVERED:

1. Configure OpenSLP on SLES 9.

OpenSLP is a Linux-based implementation of the Service Location Protocol (SLP). Novell was one of the key drivers behind the development of SLP in the mid 1990s. The purpose of SLP is to provide a level of automated service discovery for an IP network similar to that provided by other networking protocols, such as the Internetworking Packet Exchange (IPX) protocol or NetBIOS—in other words, how to make it as easy as possible for hosts on the network to locate the services they need to use.

To understand the need for SLP on an IP network, we have to first take a few steps back in time and take a look at how services were advertised using on an IPX-based network. This was done with the *Service Advertisement Protocol (SAP)*.

Advertising Services with SAP

Back in the "old days" of the late 1980s and early 1990s, the IPX protocol was one of the most widely deployed networking protocols around, mostly because Novell's NetWare server operating system ran on it. IPX was a very easy-to-use protocol. Like NetBIOS, which we discussed earlier in this book, all you had to do was plug your server or workstation into the network jack, and the protocol would automatically configure itself. You didn't need DHCP to dynamically assign addresses. You didn't need a DNS server to resolve hostnames into network addresses. That's because IPX used (and still uses) the Service Advertisement Protocol (SAP).

When an IPX-based server was booted, all the services it provided, such as file, print, or directory services, were advertised using the SAP protocol. Regardless of whether anyone else on the network wanted to use them, the server would periodically send out IPX broadcasts to the entire network describing the services it had to offer as well as its network address. If a service was shut down, the server would stop advertising it. If a new service was started, the server began advertising it. In essence, SAP provided a very dynamic, easy-to-use means of locating services on the network.

By way of analogy, imagine that you are sitting in a classroom. At 60-second intervals, each student in the class stands up and announces his or her name and the desk they are currently sitting in and then sits back down. Essentially, this is how SAP works.

This strategy works very well. If you've ever used Novell's Client software on a Windows workstation to log in to an IPX server, you know that you can browse the network to locate the server you want to log in to. The Novell Client software generates the list of trees and servers by listening on the network wire for SAP broadcasts, as shown in Figure 12.1.

For the most part, SAP was a joy for network administrators because little or no manual configuration was involved. Everything just "worked." There are, however, two problems associated with SAP. First, SAP can be a real bandwidth hog. Referring to Figure 12.1, imagine what would happen if there were hundreds of servers and clients on the network. Every service advertises its availability regardless of whether anyone wants to use it. A very large portion of your network bandwidth can be used up by traffic that isn't even necessary.

FIGURE 12.1
SAP broadcasts with IPX.

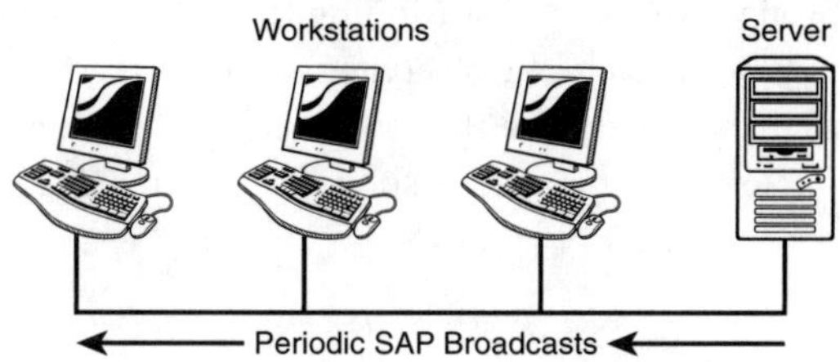

The second problem is that SAP is completely dependent on the IPX protocol. If you want to use IP (which is the norm today), you can't use SAP. With a traditional IP-based network, we had three options for locating services on the network:

- Using the hosts file—We discussed this option at length earlier in this book. Although using `/etc/hosts` in a very small network may be a viable option for locating network services, it can become completely unmanageable if the network has more than about 10 hosts.
- Using DHCP—Another option for locating network services is to deliver DHCP options to DHCP clients that contain the name of the service and its IP address. This strategy works and is frequently implemented. The drawback to this strategy is that it doesn't contain any state information. In other words, the DHCP server delivers the service name and IP address regardless of whether the service is up and running.
- Using DNS—This is another option frequently implemented in IP networks to locate services. Using DNS, you can create an A record for a given service that resolves to the IP address of the host providing the service. This strategy has the same drawbacks as using DHCP. The DNS server resolves the service hostname regardless of whether the service is actually available. In essence, it lacks the dynamic nature of SAP (which makes life so nice for administrators).

To provide this dynamic service discovery associated with IPX on an IP network, Novell worked with several other industry vendors to author RFC 2165 and RFC 2608, which define the Service Location Protocol (SLP).

SLP provides a level of automation on an IP network similar to that provided by SAP on an IPX network. It also eliminates some of the problems associated with SAP. Because of the way SAP broadcasts service availability, it is usually categorized as a *push* protocol, whereas SLP is categorized as a *pull* protocol.

Let's take a closer look at how SLP provides network service discovery without using large amounts of bandwidth the way SAP does.

How SLP Works

SLP uses software *agents* that run on both the network servers and on the workstations. When an SLP-aware service is brought up on a host running the slpd daemon, it registers itself with the SLP agent. When a host needs to locate a service, its agent sends out a request with a description of the service. Agents that have the requested information respond to the request with the necessary information. This process is shown in Figure 12.2.

FIGURE 12.2
Finding services with SLP.

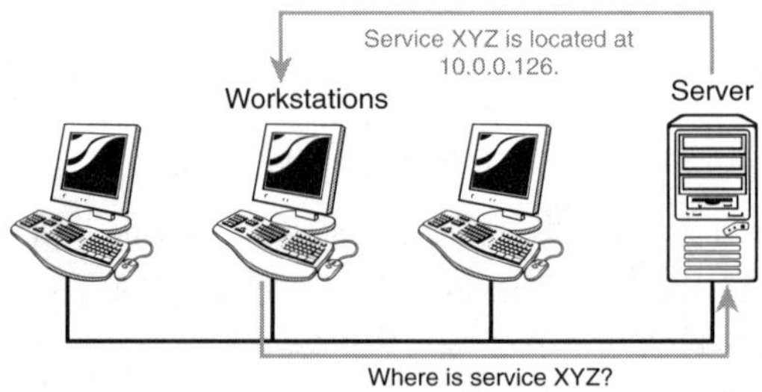

SLP responses are sent in the form of a URL. The format of the URL is slightly different from the URLs you use in a web browser. The general format of the URLs is as follows:

```
service:service_name:///service_address_or_hostname
```

For example, the SLP URL for an LDAP service running a network host that has an IP address of 192.168.1.100 is the following:

```
service:ldap:///192.168.1.100:389
```

Earlier, I mentioned that SLP is a pull protocol. That's because SLP doesn't use the network-wide service-announcement broadcasts that SAP uses.

NOTE

SAP is classified as a push protocol because it sends everyone its service information whether they want it or not.

With SLP, service information is sent only when it is requested. In addition, the requested information is sent only to the host that requested it. By implementing SLP in this way, the high bandwidth usage associated with SAP on an IPX network is dramatically reduced.

Next, let's review the different types of agents used by SLP.

SLP AGENTS

Three types of agents are used by the SLP protocol:

- User Agent (UA)—UAs are used by applications or services to locate services on the network. UAs query Service Agents or Directory Agents to retrieve URLs containing information about the requested service. UAs are always implemented with SLP and automatically start when the SLP service is started.
- Service Agent (SA)—SAs are run on service providers (servers). As with UAs, SAs are always implemented and are automatically loaded when the SLP service is started. When an SLP-aware application or service is run on the server, it registers itself with the SA. The SA keeps a list of all currently available services on the local server. If a service is shut down, it deregisters itself with the SA. By doing this, the SA keeps a dynamic list of services on the host. The SA listens for requests from UAs. If the SA knows about the service a particular UA is requesting, it responds with the service name and address. SAs can also be configured to register their services with a Directory Agent.
- Directory Agent (DA)—DAs are centralized storehouses for service information on a network. By default, DAs are not automatically loaded as SAs and UAs are. You must manually implement them. When deployed, SAs register the services they know about with the DA. In this configuration, SAs no longer respond to UA requests. Instead, UAs query the DA directly to locate service information.

SLP can also be configured to use *scopes*. An SLP scope is a grouping of network services associated with one or more Directory Agents. In essence, scopes are a means for you to organize resources on your network. Scopes are useful when you are deploying SLP in a very large or geographically dispersed organization.

For example, suppose your organization is composed of several divisions that function as separate business units. You have a paper products division, a light bulb division, and a DVD player division. You can configure a scope for each business unit so that users in the paper products division see, through SLP, only network resources in that division.

Likewise, users in the light bulb and DVD player divisions have their own scopes that contain only network resources specific to their divisions. If network resources are used across divisions, you can create a scope that includes those resources as well.

Scopes are also useful if your organization is geographically dispersed. Suppose your organization has three offices located in different areas of the country. Instead of requiring SLP requests to cross WAN links to access a remote DA, you can set up a DA in each location and configure each of those DAs with a scope that is limited to local network resources.

With this information in mind, you're ready to learn about the different ways SLP can operate on your network.

SA-ONLY MODE

The default mode for SLP is SA-Only mode. In this mode, there are no DAs configured in the network. Each server runs an SA and a UA. Each client workstation runs a UA. This configuration is shown in Figure 12.3.

FIGURE 12.3
Using SLP in SA-Only mode.

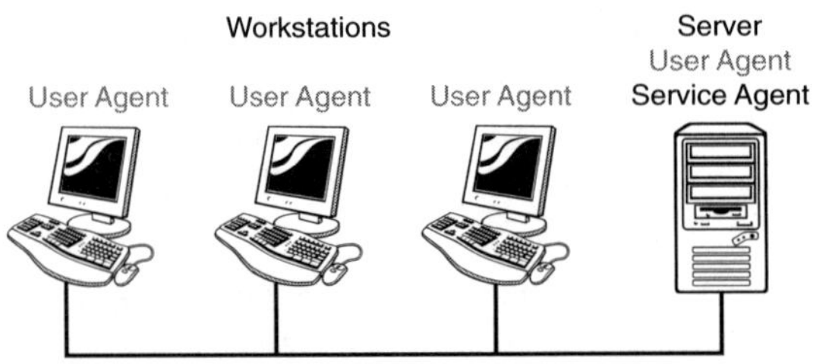

In this configuration, SLP-aware services on the local host register themselves with the local SA. The SA maintains a list of all services it knows about on the local server. For example, if the Postfix daemon were to be started on the server, it would immediately be registered with the SA.

NOTE

When a service is stopped, it deregisters itself from the SA.

The SA doesn't broadcast this service information. Instead, it waits passively for requests from UAs. When an application on a client workstation needs to use a network service, the application sends the request to the local UA. The UA then sends out a multicast to the entire network asking for the location of the specified service.

Before proceeding, we need to discuss the concept of a *multicast*. Although a multicast sounds similar to a broadcast, they are quite different. A network *broadcast* is a network transmission that is addressed to all hosts. Every host on the network accepts the broadcast packets and processes them.

A multicast, on the other hand, is a message from a single source host that is sent to multiple recipient hosts. Unlike a broadcast, however, the transmission isn't sent to all network hosts. Instead, it is sent only to hosts who are configured to listen for multicasts. Hosts configured to listen for multicasts are members of a multicast group. By using multicasting instead of broadcasts, SLP uses considerably less network bandwidth than SAP does.

In the SLP configuration we've been discussing, all SAs are members of the multicast group. When the UA sends its multicast requesting information about the specified service, all the SAs receive it and process the query. If an SA recognizes the service and has the information being requested, it responds with a unicast response to the requesting UA.

NOTE

A unicast is a network transmission that is sent from a single host to a single recipient host—in this case, the host running the UA making the request.

If the SA doesn't have any information about the requested service, it ignores the request and doesn't respond to the UA. This process is depicted in Figure 12.4.

FIGURE 12.4
Requesting service locations from Service Agents.

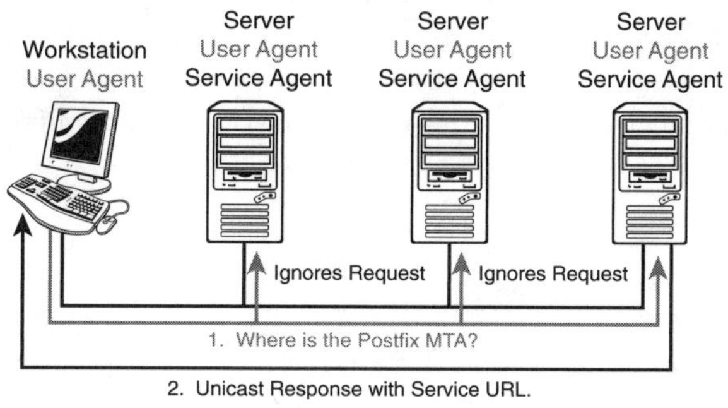

In Figure 12.4, the workstation UA makes a request for the location of the Postfix MTA. All server SAs in the multicast group receive and process the request. The first two SAs don't know anything about the requested service, so they ignore the request. The third SA, however, has information about the MTA, so it sends the appropriate URL back to the UA using a unicast transmission.

This is the default configuration when implementing SLP. It works acceptably well for small networks that have fewer than about 25 or so servers and a couple hundred clients. For networks larger than this, however, it may not be the best option. Even though SLP uses multicasts instead of broadcasts, the traffic from the multicast requests can still use excessive amounts of your network bandwidth on a large network.

In this case, you may need to configure one or more DAs.

DA MODE

By implementing one or more DAs on your network, you can significantly reduce SLP traffic on your network. As discussed earlier, a DA acts as a central repository for SLP information. As in SA-Only mode, each server in the network runs a UA and an SA. Each client workstation runs a UA. In DA mode, however, you select one or more servers to run a DA as well as an SA and a UA.

When you do this, the SAs on the network change their behavior. They still register SLP-aware applications and services on their individual servers, but they no longer respond to requests from UAs.

In DA mode, SAs send out a *DA discovery* multicast packet when the SA is first started. If a DA responds, the SA, using unicast transmissions, will register all the services it knows about with the DA. After that, the SA will no longer respond to UA requests. If the SA does not discover a DA, it will default to SA-Only mode and will respond to UA requests.

In DA mode, you configure your client workstation UAs with the IP address of the DA (or DAs) you want them to send their requests to. When a UA needs to locate a service, it sends a unicast request directly to the configured DA. The DA processes the query and responds with the requested information, again using unicast transmissions. This configuration is shown in Figure 12.5.

FIGURE 12.5
Requesting services from a Directory Agent.

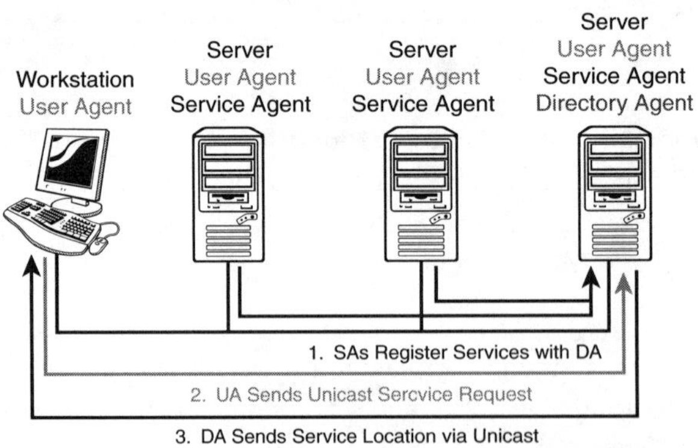

When a service is shut down, the local SA deregisters the service with the DA.

As you can see from Figure 12.5, using a DA requires more work on the part of the network administrator to configure. The bandwidth savings in larger organizations, however, is usually worth the effort.

DA mode also prevents other problems. Recall that SA-Only mode is heavily dependent on multicast transmissions. Most hardware and software routers, however, are configured by default to not allow multicast traffic to cross between network segments. If the servers in your organization lie on different network segments separated by routers, you must enable multicast routing to use SLP in SA-Only mode.

As a better alternative, Novell recommends that you implement DAs on each side of the router. I mentioned earlier that SAs still rely on multicast transmissions to discover DAs by default. You can, however, manually configure each SA with the IP address of the DAs that you want them to register their services with. By doing this, multicast traffic is all but eliminated. We'll discuss how to do this a little later in this chapter when we explore the SLP daemon's configuration file.

Now that you understand the conceptual architecture of SLP, you need to learn how to implement and configure the slpd daemon.

Configuring OpenSLP

The OpenSLP service offers a full SLP daemon that includes a UA, an SA, and a DA. To implement it on your server, you need to install the packages shown in Figure 12.6.

FIGURE 12.6
Installing SLP packages.

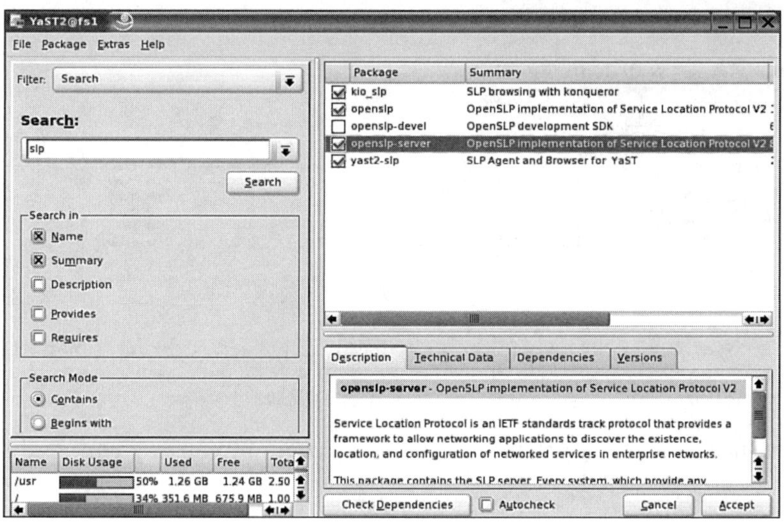

These packages do the following:

- openslp-server—This package installs the full OpenSLP server package providing DA functionality.
- openslp—This package provides an SLP client.
- kio_slp—This optional package is used to integrate SLP browsing functionality into your Konqueror web browser.
- yast2-slp—This package provides a YaST module you can use to browse SLP services registered on your server.

After you've installed the appropriate packages, you next need to enable multicasting on your Linux server.

CONFIGURING MULTICAST ROUTING

Depending on the mode you select, you will need some level of multicast support on your servers. By default, most Linux distributions have multicasting support disabled. To check, open a terminal session and enter **netstat -nr** at the shell prompt. If you see a route listed with a destination of 224.0.0.0, multicast routing has been enabled. If not, you need to enable it.

Output from netstat on a system where the multicast route has not been added is shown in Figure 12.7.

FIGURE 12.7
Output from netstat –nr with no multicast route.

```
fs1:~ # netstat -nr
Kernel IP routing table
Destination     Gateway         Genmask         Flags   MSS Window  irtt Iface
192.168.1.0     0.0.0.0         255.255.255.0   U         0 0          0 eth0
169.254.0.0     0.0.0.0         255.255.0.0     U         0 0          0 eth0
10.0.0.0        0.0.0.0         255.0.0.0       U         0 0          0 eth1
127.0.0.0       0.0.0.0         255.0.0.0       U         0 0          0 lo
0.0.0.0         192.168.1.1     0.0.0.0         UG        0 0          0 eth0
fs1:~ #
```

Output from netstat on a system where the route has already been added is shown in Figure 12.8.

If you need to add the multicast route, complete the following steps:

1. From a shell prompt, change to the root user account by entering **su -** and entering your root user password.
2. Enter the following:

   `route add -net 224.0.0.0 netmask 240.0.0.0 dev eth0`

3. Enter **netstat -nr** again to verify that the multicast route has been added.

FIGURE 12.8
Output from netstat –nr with the multicast route added.

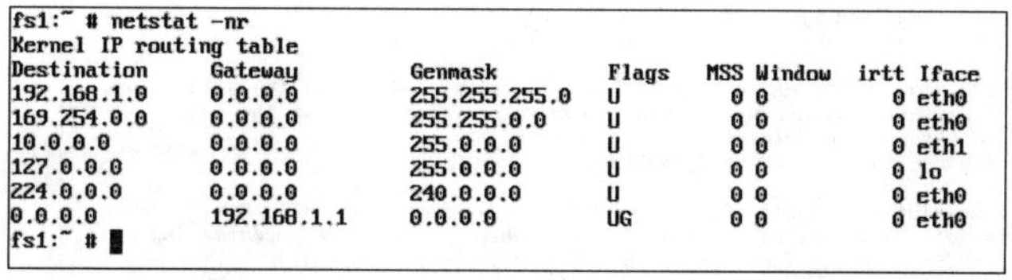

```
fs1:~ # netstat -nr
Kernel IP routing table
Destination     Gateway         Genmask         Flags   MSS Window  irtt Iface
192.168.1.0     0.0.0.0         255.255.255.0   U         0 0          0 eth0
169.254.0.0     0.0.0.0         255.255.0.0     U         0 0          0 eth0
10.0.0.0        0.0.0.0         255.0.0.0       U         0 0          0 eth1
127.0.0.0       0.0.0.0         255.0.0.0       U         0 0          0 lo
224.0.0.0       0.0.0.0         240.0.0.0       U         0 0          0 eth0
0.0.0.0         192.168.1.1     0.0.0.0         UG        0 0          0 eth0
fs1:~ #
```

Be aware that this route is not persistent. If you restart your server, the route information will be lost. To make this persistent, add an entry to the `/etc/sysconfig/network/routes` file that reads as follows (assuming you are using eth0 as your network device):

224.0.0.0 0.0.0.0 240.0.0.0 eth0

After it is configured, your slpd daemon will use the ports shown in Figure 12.9 to communicate between UAs, SAs, and DAs:

FIGURE 12.9
SLP ports.

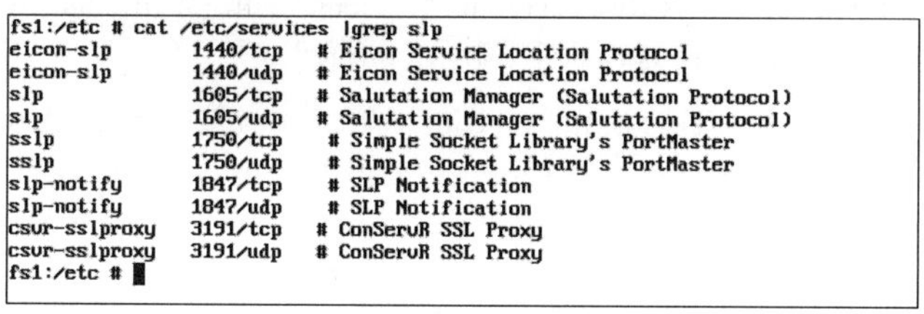

```
fs1:/etc # cat /etc/services |grep slp
eicon-slp       1440/tcp    # Eicon Service Location Protocol
eicon-slp       1440/udp    # Eicon Service Location Protocol
slp             1605/tcp    # Salutation Manager (Salutation Protocol)
slp             1605/udp    # Salutation Manager (Salutation Protocol)
sslp            1750/tcp    # Simple Socket Library's PortMaster
sslp            1750/udp    # Simple Socket Library's PortMaster
slp-notify      1847/tcp    # SLP Notification
slp-notify      1847/udp    # SLP Notification
csvr-sslproxy   3191/tcp    # ConServR SSL Proxy
csvr-sslproxy   3191/udp    # ConServR SSL Proxy
fs1:/etc #
```

With this background in mind, you're ready to start configuring an SLP daemon on your server.

CONFIGURING THE SLP.CONF FILE

When the installation is complete and the multicast route has been added, the slpd daemon is copied to `/usr/sbin` and its configuration file, `slp.conf`, is copied to `/etc`.

After the initial installation, the slpd daemon is configured to run in SA-Only mode. To create a DA, you must edit the `slp.conf` file, shown in Figure 12.10.

FIGURE 12.10
A portion of the `slp.conf` file.

```
# and a DA.  The SLP UA functionality is encapsulated by SLPLIB.
#
##############################################################################


#----------------------------------------------------------------------------
# Static Scope and Static DA Configuration
#----------------------------------------------------------------------------

# This option is a comma delimited list of strings indicating the only scopes
# a UA or SA is allowed when making requests or registering or the scopes a
# DA must support. (default value is "DEFAULT")
;net.slp.useScopes = myScope1, myScope2, myScope3

# Allows administrator to force UA and SA agents to use specific DAs.  If
# this setting is not used dynamic DA discovery will be used to determine
# which DAs to use.  (Default is to use dynamic DA discovery)
;net.slp.DAAddresses = myDa1,myDa2,myDa3


#----------------------------------------------------------------------------
# DA Specific Configuration
#----------------------------------------------------------------------------
./slp.conf lines 7-29/202 14%
```

The following is a list of parameters you can configure in the **`slp.conf`** file:

- net.slp.useScopes—This parameter has two functions. If the slpd daemon is running in SA-Only mode, this parameter specifies which scopes the local SA is allowed to register its services with. If the slpd daemon is running in DA mode, this parameter specifies the name of the scope associated with the local DA. The default value is DEFAULT.
- net.slp.DAAddresses—This parameter forces the local SA to not multicast at startup for DAs. Instead, it forces the SA to register its services, using a unicast, with the specific DAs listed here. This feature is disabled by default.
- net.slp.isBroadcastOnly—This parameter forces the local UA and SA to use broadcasts instead of multicasts when locating services. This feature is disabled by default. Under normal circumstances, you probably will never need to enable this parameter. Doing so would greatly increase the traffic on your network.
- net.slp.passiveDADetection—This parameter configures the local SA to discover Directory Agents passively. The default value is set to TRUE.
- net.slp.activeDADetection—This parameter specifies that the local SA actively discover DAs. This is usually implemented if you have your SAs statically configured to contact a specific DA.
- net.slp.DAActiveDiscoveryInterval—If net.slp.activeDADetection is enabled, this parameter specifies the number of seconds between active DA discovery transmissions. If you set it to 0, it will be disabled.

- net.slp.interfaces—If you have multiple network interfaces in your Linux server, this parameter can be used to specify the network interfaces the local DA and SA should listen on. By default, they listen on all interfaces.
- net.slp.isDA—This is the parameter you need to use if you want to enable a local DA. Remember that the UA and SA always run when the daemon is running. To run a DA, you must set this parameter to TRUE. The default value is FALSE.
- net.slp.DAHeartBeat—This parameter configures the number of seconds between Directory Agent heartbeat packets. The default value is 10800 seconds (3 hours).

To configure your slpd daemon, edit the `/etc/slp.conf file`, making the changes you need for your network. When that is done, you're ready to start the service.

TIP

In the lab for this chapter, you will create a DA and configure it with a scope.

The slpd daemon places an init script file in the `/etc/init.d` directory named slpd. As with the other services we covered in this course, you can manage the SLP daemon using the `rcslpd start¦stop¦restart` commands. If your server provides mission-critical services, you need to configure the slpd daemon to automatically start on runlevels 3 and 5 using chkconfig or the YaST Runlevel Editor module.

When the daemon is running, you can use the slptool utility, which is installed as part of the OpenSLP package, to verify that your configuration is working properly.

The syntax for using slptool is as follows:

`slptool` *`options commands`*

You can use the following options with slptool:

- -v—Displays version information.
- -s scope_name—Specifies a list of scopes to limit queries to.

You can use the following commands with slptool:

- findsrvs service-type—Displays registered services of the type specified.
- findattrs URL—Displays registered services with the specified URL.
- findsrvtypes URL—Lists the services that are available, but not their URLs.
- findscopes—Displays all scopes known to the DAs your local UA and SA have discovered.

TIP

You can use many other commands with slptool. Enter slptool with no options to see a list of what you can use.

Let's get OpenSLP up and running on your SLES 9 system in Lab Exercise 12.1.

Lab Exercise 12.1: Installing and Configuring SLP

In this exercise, you will modify the `/etc/slp.conf` file to create a DA. Complete the following:

1. Boot your SLES 9 server and authenticate as your **`tux`** user with a password of **`SuSE789`**.
2. Open a terminal session and enter **`sux -`** to change to root with a password of **`tuX123`**.
3. Configure your `slp.conf` file by completing the following:
    a. At your shell prompt, enter **`vi /etc/slp.conf`**.
    b. Press **Ins**.
    c. Scroll down to and locate the `net.slp.useScopes` line.
    d. Remove the comment character (;) from the beginning of the line.
    e. Set the value of net.slp.useScopes to **CLE9Scope**. This configures your DA to service a scope named CLEScope.
    f. Scroll down to and locate the `net.slp.isDA` parameter.
    g. Remove the comment character (;) from the beginning of the line. The line should now read as follows:

       ```
       net.slp.isDA = true
       ```

       This enables the local DA on your server. Remember that the SA and UA are run automatically when the service is started.
    h. Scroll up to the `net.slp.DAAddresses` parameter.
    i. Remove the comment character (;) from the beginning of the line; then set the value of this parameter to your server's *IP address*.
    j. The remaining parameters' functions can remain at their default values for your implementation. Press **Esc**; then enter **`:exit`**.
    k. Start the slpd daemon by entering **`rcslpd start`** at the shell prompt.
4. Verify that SLP has been configured correctly by entering **`slptool findscopes`** at the shell prompt. The slptool utility should find the CLE9Scope you configured your DA to service, as shown in Figure 12.11.

FIGURE 12.11
Checking your SLP configuration with slptool.

5. Browse the SLP-registered services on your network with YaST by completing the following:
   a. Start YaST.
   b. When prompted, enter a root password of **tuX123**.
   c. Select **Network Services, SLP Browser**. The screen in Figure 12.12 is displayed:

FIGURE 12.12
The YaST SLP browser module.

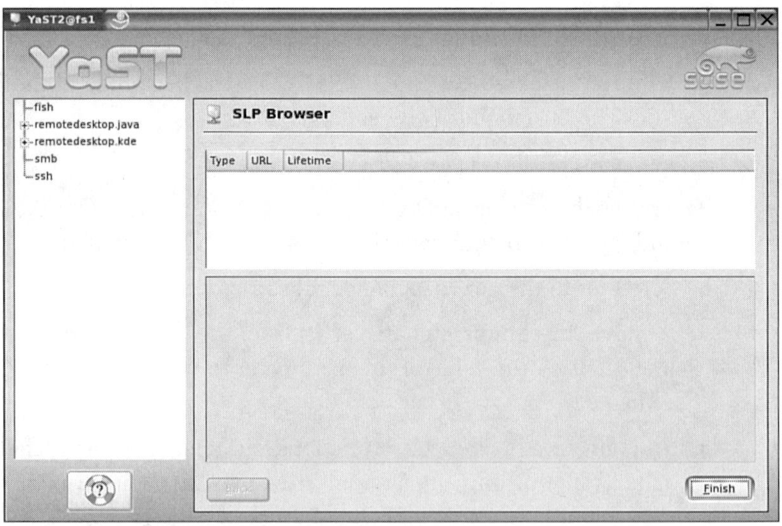

NOTE

You many not see the remotedesktop.kde service. This is displayed only if you have VNC running.

d. If no services are displayed, enter **rcslpd restart** and then try step c again.

e. Browse the services registered with your SLP agents by selecting items on the left side of the screen. When you do, the service type and URL for the registered service is displayed, as shown in Figure 12.13.

FIGURE 12.13
Browsing an SLP-registered service in YaST.

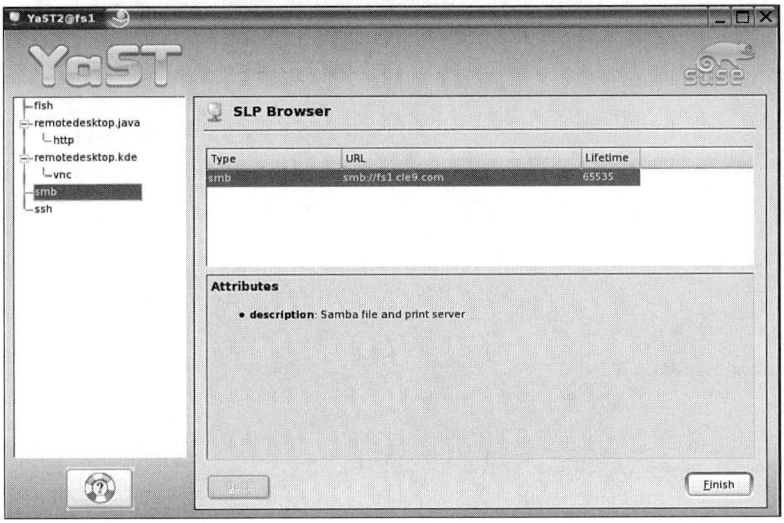

f. Select **Finish**.

6. View registered SLP services with Konqueror by completing the following:

   a. At your shell prompt, enter **kfmclient openProfile webbrowsing**.

   b. In the Location field, enter **slp:/**. The screen in Figure 12.14 is displayed.

   c. Using the icons displayed, browse the services registered by your slpd daemon.

Pretty easy, huh? Using SLP, you can create a dynamic service location service for your IP network. This will save you tons of time over manually configuring DNS records or DHCP options.

FIGURE 12.14
Browsing SLP-registered services in Konqueror.

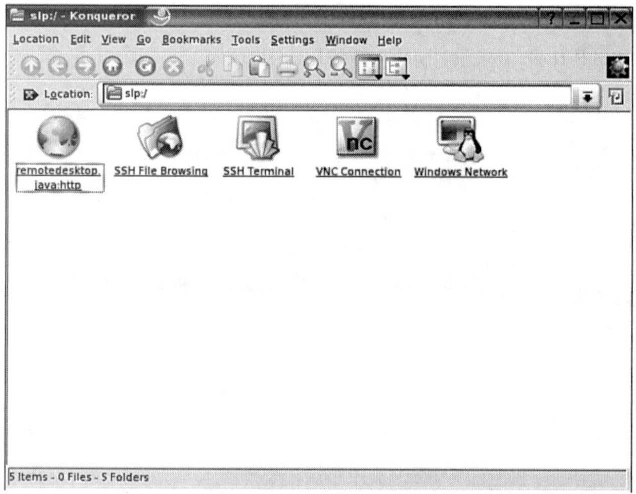

In the preceding exercise, you were able to browse SLP-enabled services running on your server. But what do you do about services that aren't SLP aware? Let's talk about static SLP registration next.

Statically Registering Services with slpd

Many Linux services are already SLP aware, as you saw in Lab Exercise 12.1. When an SLP-aware service is installed on your server, it creates a registration file in `/etc/slpd.reg.d`, as shown in Figure 12.15.

FIGURE 12.15
SLP registration files.

```
fs1:/etc/slp.reg.d # ls
.  ..  inn.reg  ksysguardd.reg  samba.reg  ssh.reg  vnc.reg  xntp.reg
fs1:/etc/slp.reg.d #
```

These registration files are pretty simple. For example, consider the registration file for the VNC service running on my SLES 9 system in Figure 12.16.

FIGURE 12.16
The VNC SLP registration file.

```
#############################################################################
#
# OpenSLP registration file
#
# register VNC remote logins via kdm
# You need also to allow remote logins
#
#############################################################################

# Register VNC service for krdc (KDE VNC client in kdenetwork)
service:remotedesktop.kde:vnc://$HOSTNAME:5901,en,65535
tcp-port=5901
description=VNC remote login [1024x768]

# Register VNC service for krdc (KDE VNC client in kdenetwork)
service:remotedesktop.kde:vnc://$HOSTNAME:5902,en,65535
tcp-port=5902
description=VNC remote login [1280x1024]

# Register VNC service for krdc (KDE VNC client in kdenetwork)
service:remotedesktop.kde:vnc://$HOSTNAME:5903,en,65535
tcp-port=5903
description=VNC remote login [1600x1200]
./vnc.reg lines 1-23/42 55%
```

Notice that each port the VNC service uses has its own registration line using the syntax

service:*service_name*:*protocol*://*host_name*:*port*,*language*,*registration_timeout*

In Figure 12.16, the remotedesktop.kde service is defined. The protocol used is vnc. The `$HOSTNAME` variable pulls the system's hostname from the environment variables. The service is provided on port 5901. The language for the registration is English. The value of 65535 is used to disable the registration timeout (a value of 0 would disable registration). The tcp-port parameter is used to specify that the service runs on TCP port 5901. The description parameter is a text string that provides a description of the service.

As you can see in Figure 12.16, multiple, related service registrations can be defined in the same file. When the slpd daemon is loaded, each file in `/etc/slp.reg.d` is read and the associated services are registered. To register your own services, create a file in this directory (ending with a `.reg` extension) that defines the service using the syntax described previously.

You can also use the `/etc/slp.reg` file to register services. This file functions in much the same manner as the individual registration files in `/etc/slp.reg.d` directory. However, this file contains all the service registrations in a single file. A portion of the `/etc/slp.reg` file is shown in Figure 12.17.

Let's practice statically registering a service in Lab Exercise 12.2.

FIGURE 12.17
The VNC SLP registration file.

```
##############################################################################
#
# OpenSLP registration file
#
# May be used to register services for legacy applications that do not use
# the SLPAPIs to register for themselves
#
# Format and contents conform to specification in IETF RFC 2614 so the
# comments use the language of the RFC.  In OpenSLP, SLPD operates as an SA
# and a DA.  The SLP UA functionality is encapsulated by the libslp library.
#
##############################################################################

#comment
;comment
#service-url,language-tag,lifetime,[service-type]<newline>
#["scopes="scope-list<newline>]
#[attrid"="val1<newline>]
#[attrid"="val1,val2,val3<newline>]
#<newline>

#
# The following are examples entries for this file
./slp.reg lines 1-23/46 55%
```

Lab Exercise 12.2: Creating a Static SLP Registration for CUPS

In this exercise, you will create an SLP registration file for the CUPS service you configured previously in this book. To complete this exercise, you will need DNS, CUPS, and SLP daemons configured and running on your server. Complete the following:

1. Boot your SLES 9 server and authenticate as your **tux** user with a password of **SuSE789**.
2. Open a terminal session and enter **sux -** to change to root with a password of **tuX123**.
3. At the shell prompt, enter **vi /etc/slp.reg.d/cups.reg**.
4. Press **Ins** and then enter the following text in the new file:

```
service:cups:http://$HOSTNAME:631,en,65535
tcp-port=631
description=Cups Server
```

5. Press **Esc**; then enter **:exit**.
6. At the shell prompt, enter **rcslpd restart**.
7. At your shell prompt, enter **kfmclient openProfile webbrowsing**.
8. In the Location field, enter **service:/**.
9. Select **cups:http** > **your_server:631**. Your CUPS page should appear as shown in Figure 12.18.

That's all there is to it. You're now an SLP master!

We're almost done. Before we end this book, there's one more topic you need to be familiar with for your CLE 9 certification: Tomcat. Let's look at this service next.

FIGURE 12.18
The CUPS page.

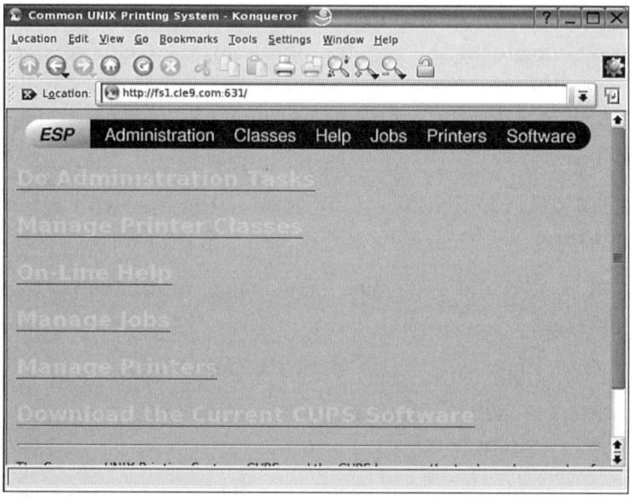

Working with Tomcat on SLES 9

TEST OBJECTIVE COVERED:

2. Configure Tomcat on SLES 9.

I want you to think about some of your favorite websites—those that you visit daily. What kind of pages do you pull down when you visit those sites? One of my favorite pages is http://finance.yahoo.com. On this site, I can pull down quotes for the mutual funds that are in my IRA account to see if I'm going to be a prince or pauper when I retire. This page is shown in Figure 12.19.

On this site, you can enter the stock, bond, or mutual fund symbol in the Enter Symbol field and retrieve extensive information about the particular security that you want to research.

Think about what it would take for the folks at Yahoo to manually create a page for each publicly traded stock, bond, and mutual fund. There are literally thousands of each type. That's a lot of web pages to create. It would require a fairly significant staff to accomplish this task.

FIGURE 12.19
The Yahoo! Finance website.

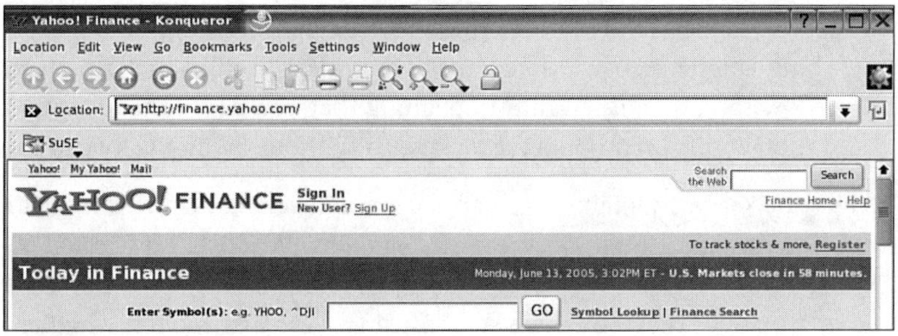

Now that we've established that it would take a tremendous amount of work to create pages for each publicly traded security, consider the fact that this website instantly provides 15-minute delayed quotes for the particular security you're researching. If you thought it would be an overwhelming task to initially create pages for each symbol, imagine how much work it would be to manually update each one every few minutes all day long! Unless you had employees numbering in the tens of thousands, it would be an impossible task. So how do they do it?

The answer is *dynamic* web content. When I visit this site and enter the symbols in my IRA account, a web application server (or servers, in this case) is used on the web server end of the communication to dynamically generate the appropriate web page. The web application server is configured to grab the latest data for the symbol I'm checking and then, using templates, generate a web page on-the-fly and send it down to my web server. Without this technology, most of the websites we visit and take for granted on the Internet wouldn't be possible. The amount of effort required to statically write pages would make them completely infeasible.

In this last topic of this book, we're going to discuss how you can use your SLES 9 system to implement this kind of functionality. Specifically, we're going to discuss how you can use the Tomcat service to dynamically create web pages using the Java programming language.

Before we get going, please understand that this, like most of the topics we've covered in this text, is a huge topic and we can cover only the basics . If you go on to Amazon's or Barnes & Noble's websites, you see that there are many huge, thick books written on Tomcat. What I'm going to give you here is just an overview. If you want to become a Tomcat expert (and many folks do when they learn what Tomcat can do), I encourage you to get one of these mammoth books and start studying. You'll see that the possibilities of what you can do with Tomcat are almost endless.

With that in mind, let's spend some time discussing how Tomcat works.

How Tomcat Works

The Tomcat service is a web server with Java built in. Using Tomcat, web pages can be compiled as they are requested, allowing you to create exceptionally dynamic and relevant content.

Java is a programming language that has become very widely used in the last decade. Java is designed specifically with *portability* in mind, meaning that you can write an application or applet in Java and then run it on any operating system without having to tweak the code.

Tomcat is based on the servlet/container web application server model. This model is based on two components. Yes, you guessed it: *servlets* and *containers*. When I first learned about servlets and containers, I did some serious head scratching. Hopefully, this chapter can impart these concepts to you in a manner that isn't quite so confusing. Let's first look at what a servlet is.

A servlet is a small, standalone Java application that can be run by Tomcat. Tomcat itself is a servlet engine or "container" that is used to run servlets. When a web request is received by Tomcat, it loads the appropriate servlet into memory to process the request and generate the web page that will be returned to the client.

You may be asking, "What about Apache? Do you still need it if you're implementing Tomcat?" The answer is *yes*. Although Apache and Tomcat are both web servers, they are each designed to fulfill a specific role. The Apache web server is designed to serve up static web pages. It does this job very well and is one of the fastest web servers around. Apache can't generate dynamic web pages, however. If you want to do this with Apache, you have to integrate it with some kind of dynamic content engine. That's where Tomcat comes into the picture.

Although Tomcat can serve up static web content, it doesn't do it nearly as robustly as Apache does. It just isn't what it was designed to do. To get the best of both worlds, Tomcat is usually implemented in conjunction with Apache; each service does what it does best.

Apache is configured to run, by default, on port 80 and 443. Tomcat on the other hand, listens on port 8080 for requests. Before you can use Tomcat on your server, you must install the appropriate packages on your server, as shown in Figure 12.20.

These packages are the following:

- jakarta-tomcat—This package contains the Tomcat servlet container designed to support Java servlets and Java Server Pages (JSP).
- apache-jakarta-tomcat-connectors—This package contains modules that allow you to integrate Tomcat with an Apache 1.3 web server. If your server is running Apache 2, you don't need this package.
- apache2-jakarta-tomcat-connectors—This package contains modules that allow you to integrate Tomcat with an Apache 2.0 web server.

FIGURE 12.20
Installing Tomcat.

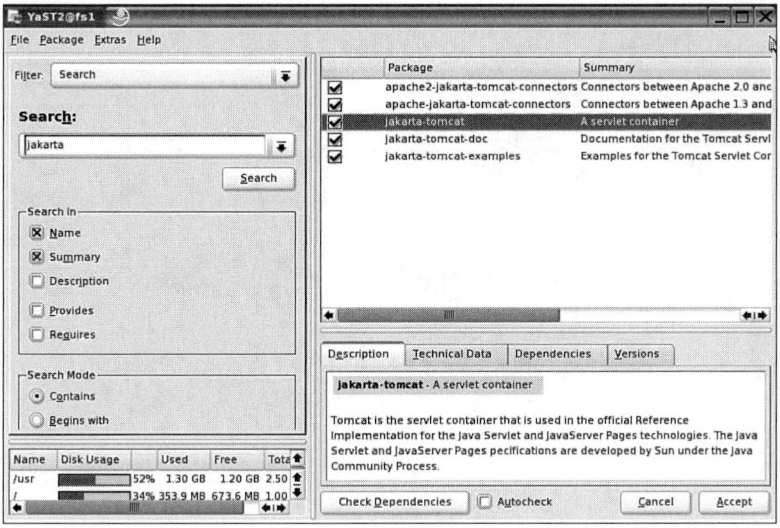

- jakarta-tomcat-doc—This package contains the Tomcat documentation (and there is a lot of it!).
- jakarta-tomcat-examples—This package contains samples that you can use to learn how to implement Tomcat.

To install these packages, start YaST and navigate to the Install and Remove Software module. In the Search field, enter **`tomcat`** and select **Search**. After marking your packages, you'll be presented with a dialog box indicating that YaST doesn't know which Java runtime environment to use. Select **Install java2**, as shown in Figure 12.21.

With the necessary packages installed, it's time to learn some basic Tomcat configuration concepts. Let's do that next.

Configuring Tomcat on SLES 9

Configuring Tomcat is bit different from configuring the other products we've been working with in this book. After installation, the Tomcat files are located in `/usr/share/tomcat`, as shown in Figure 12.22.

FIGURE 12.21
Installing a Java Runtime Environment.

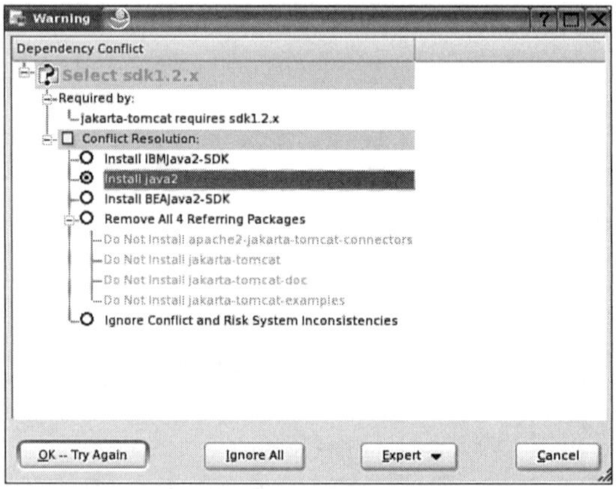

FIGURE 12.22
The Tomcat files in /usr/share/tomcat.

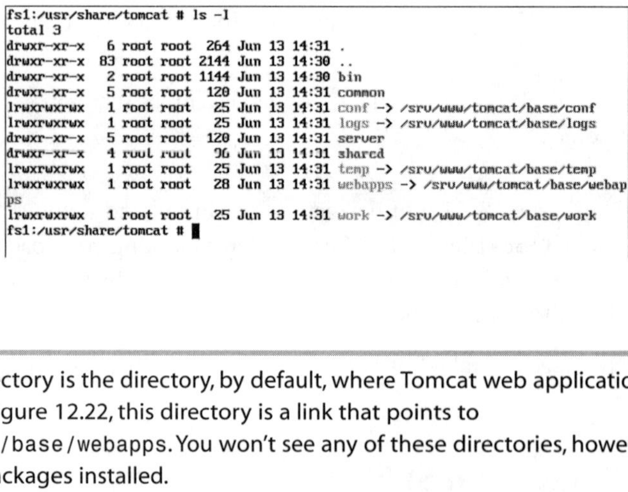

```
fs1:/usr/share/tomcat # ls -l
total 3
drwxr-xr-x   6 root root  264 Jun 13 14:31 .
drwxr-xr-x  83 root root 2144 Jun 13 14:30 ..
drwxr-xr-x   2 root root 1144 Jun 13 14:30 bin
drwxr-xr-x   5 root root  120 Jun 13 14:31 common
lrwxrwxrwx   1 root root   25 Jun 13 14:31 conf -> /srv/www/tomcat/base/conf
lrwxrwxrwx   1 root root   25 Jun 13 14:31 logs -> /srv/www/tomcat/base/logs
drwxr-xr-x   5 root root  120 Jun 13 14:31 server
drwxr-xr-x   4 root root   96 Jun 13 14:31 shared
lrwxrwxrwx   1 root root   25 Jun 13 14:31 temp -> /srv/www/tomcat/base/temp
lrwxrwxrwx   1 root root   28 Jun 13 14:31 webapps -> /srv/www/tomcat/base/webap
ps
lrwxrwxrwx   1 root root   25 Jun 13 14:31 work -> /srv/www/tomcat/base/work
fs1:/usr/share/tomcat #
```

NOTE

The ./webapps directory is the directory, by default, where Tomcat web applications are stored. As you can see in Figure 12.22, this directory is a link that points to /srv/www/tomcat/base/webapps. You won't see any of these directories, however, if you don't have the Tomcat packages installed.

The files used to configure the Tomcat service are located in the **./conf** directory, which, as you can see in Figure 12.22, is a symbolic link to the **/srv/www/tomcat/conf** directory on your server. Within this directory are a number of configuration files, as shown in Figure 12.23:

FIGURE 12.23
Tomcat configuration files.

```
fs1:/usr/share/tomcat/conf # ls -l
total 92
drwxr-xr-x  3 tomcat tomcat   344 Jun 13 14:30 .
drwxr-xr-x  4 root   root     104 Jun 13 14:31 ..
drwxr-xr-x  3 tomcat tomcat    80 Jun 13 14:30 Catalina
-rw-r--r--  1 tomcat tomcat  6804 Feb 14  2004 catalina.policy
-rw-r--r--  1 tomcat tomcat  2715 Feb 14  2004 catalina.properties
-rw-r--r--  1 tomcat tomcat   778 Feb 14  2004 jk2.properties
-rw-r--r--  1 tomcat tomcat  1128 Feb 14  2004 server-minimal.xml
-rw-r--r--  1 tomcat tomcat 18190 Jul  1  2004 server.xml
-rw-r--r--  1 tomcat tomcat   440 Feb 14  2004 tomcat-users.xml
-rw-r--r--  1 tomcat tomcat 37477 Feb 14  2004 web.xml
-rw-r--r--  1 tomcat tomcat  5658 Jul  1  2004 workers.properties
fs1:/usr/share/tomcat/conf #
```

You'll notice in Figure 12.23 that these aren't the typical `.conf` files you're used to. Instead, these files are written using Extensible Markup Language (XML). If you're not familiar with XML, this can be a little confusing at first. With a `.conf` file, you usually use a syntax of *parameter=value*. XML, on the other hand, uses a structure of nested *nodes*, also called *elements*, as shown:

```
<node1>
        <node2>
        <node3>
        </node3>
    </node2>
</node1>
```

An element that resides inside another element is said to be *nested*. The superordinate element is called the *parent* element. The subordinate element is called the *child* element. For example, in the preceding example, `node3` is a child of `node2`. Likewise, `node2` is a child of `node1`.

If you're familiar with HTML, you'll notice some similarities. For example, you enclose elements within `< >` tags. Also, you must close what ever tag you open with a `</element>` tag. A good example of this structure is shown in Figure 12.24.

Each element can have its own attributes defined within the node. For example, in Figure 12.24, the `<Connector>` element has the following attributes:

- className
- port
- minProcessors
- maxProcessors
- enableLookups
- appBase
- acceptCount

FIGURE 12.24
An XML structure example in `server.xml`.

```
<Service name="Tomcat-Apache">

  <Connector className="org.apache.catalina.connector.warp.WarpConnector"
   port="8008" minProcessors="5" maxProcessors="75"
   enableLookups="true" appBase="webapps"
   acceptCount="10" debug="0"/>

  <Engine className="org.apache.catalina.connector.warp.WarpEngine"
   name="Apache" debug="0">

    <Logger className="org.apache.catalina.logger.FileLogger"
            prefix="apache_log." suffix=".txt"
            timestamp="true"/>

    <Realm className="org.apache.catalina.realm.MemoryRealm" />

  </Engine>

</Service>
-->

        <!-- Normally, users must authenticate themselves to each web app
             individually.  Uncomment the following entry if you would like
./server.xml lines 324-346/384 90%
```

Don't be concerned at this point about what each of the attributes specifically does. For now, just understand that each XML element can have its own set of attributes. These attributes are declared within the element tag and have values associated with them. For example, in Figure 12.24, the attribute `enableLookups` is set to a value of `true`.

Each element must be closed with a closing `</...>` tag. If you look at Figure 12.24, you'll see that the `<Service>` and `<Engine>` tags each have a corresponding `</Service>` and `</Engine>` closing tags. However, you probably also noticed that the `<Connector>`, `<Realm>` and `<Logger>` elements don't appear to have a closing tag. Actually they do, it's just hard to see them. In XML, you can close an element with traditional closing tags, such as we've just discussed.

However, you can also close XML elements by including a / character at the end of the tag. For example, find the ending > in the Connector and Logger elements in Figure 12.24. Notice that each of these tags has a / inserted at the very end of the tag. This is a shorthand way of closing the tag. It's used when a particular element doesn't have any child elements. If an element has children, you have to use the separate `<.... />` closing tag.

The file we'll be most concerned with in this chapter is the `server.xml` file. Let's look at it next.

WORKING WITH `server.xml`

Within this file, the elements that can be used in the XML structure are predefined. The following elements are used:

```
<Server>
    <Service>
        <Connector>
        </Connector>
```

```
        <Engine>
            <Host>
                <Context>
                </Context>
            </Host>
        </Engine>
    </Service>
</Server>
```

The `<Server>` element resides at the root of the XML structure in **server.xml**. This element represents the entire Tomcat service. There can be only one `<Server>` element in the **server.xml** file. The default `<Server>` element with its accompanying **port**, **shutdown**, and **debug** attributes are shown in Figure 12.25.

FIGURE 12.25
The <Server> element in server.xml.

```
<Server port="8005" shutdown="SHUTDOWN" debug="0">
```

The port attribute configures the IP port that Tomcat will listen on for the SHUTDOWN command. The default is port 8005, as shown in Figure 12.25. The shutdown attribute configures the text string that must be sent to Tomcat to shut it down. The default value is, surprise, SHUTDOWN.

Within the `<Server>` element in **server.xml** are multiple `<Service>` elements. By default, two `<Service>` elements are defined in **server.xml**: Catalina and Tomcat-Apache. The Catalina `<Service>` element is shown in Figure 12.26.

FIGURE 12.26
The Catalina <Service> element in server.xml.

```
  <!-- Define the Tomcat Stand-Alone Service -->
  <Service name="Catalina">
```

The Tomcat-Apache `<Service>` tag is shown in Figure 12.27.

FIGURE 12.27
The Tomcat-Apache <Service> element in server.xml.

```
  <!-- Define an Apache-Connector Service -->
<!--
  <Service name="Tomcat-Apache">
```

The `<Service>` elements define a collection of `<Connector>` and `<Engine>` elements, which, in turn, define how requests are received by Tomcat. The Catalina service definition defines the standalone Tomcat service, which can directly receive HTTP requests from web clients. The Tomcat-Apache service definition defines how requests from the Apache web server are received by Tomcat.

Within the Catalina service are several `<Connector>` elements that define ports 8080, 8443, 8009, and 8082 for use by the standalone Tomcat service. Some of these `<Connector>` elements are shown in Figure 12.28.

FIGURE 12.28
Catalina <Connector> elements in `server.xml`.

```
    <!-- Define a non-SSL Coyote HTTP/1.1 Connector on port 8080 -->
    <Connector port="8080"
               maxThreads="150" minSpareThreads="25" maxSpareThreads="75"
               enableLookups="false" redirectPort="8443" acceptCount="100"
               debug="0" connectionTimeout="20000"
               disableUploadTimeout="true" />
    <!-- Note : To disable connection timeouts, set connectionTimeout value
     to 0 -->

        <!-- Note : To use gzip compression you could set the following properti
es :

                           compression="on"
                           compressionMinSize="2048"
                           noCompressionUserAgents="gozilla, traviata"
                           compressableMimeType="text/html,text/xml"
        -->

    <!-- Define a SSL Coyote HTTP/1.1 Connector on port 8443 -->
    <!--
    <Connector port="8443"
               maxThreads="150" minSpareThreads="25" maxSpareThreads="75"
               enableLookups="false" disableUploadTimeout="true"
./server.xml lines 91-112/384 26%
```

The Tomcat-Apache service also contains a `<Connector>` element. This configures Tomcat to use port 8008 to communicate with the Apache web server, as shown in Figure 12.29.

FIGURE 12.29
Tomcat-Apache <Connector> element in `server.xml`.

```
<!--
  <Service name="Tomcat-Apache">

    <Connector className="org.apache.catalina.connector.warp.WarpConnector"
     port="8008" minProcessors="5" maxProcessors="75"
     enableLookups="true" appBase="webapps"
     acceptCount="10" debug="0"/>
```

Also within each `<Service>` element is an `<Engine>` element. This element defines how requests will be processed. The Catalina service contains the `<Engine>` element shown in Figure 12.30.

FIGURE 12.30
The <Engine> element within the Catalina service.

```
<!-- Define the top level container in our container hierarchy -->
<Engine name="Catalina" defaultHost="localhost" debug="0">
```

The element in Figure 12.30 contains the **name**, **defaultHost**, and **debug** attributes. These set the name of the engine and define which server will receive HTTP requests received by the standalone Tomcat service.

The Tomcat-Apache service also contains an <Engine> element, shown in Figure 12.31.

FIGURE 12.31
The <Engine> element within the Tomcat-Apache service.

```
<Engine className="org.apache.catalina.connector.warp.WarpEngine"
 name="Apache" debug="0">
```

This element contains the **className** and **name** attributes. These specify the Java class that will process requests received from the Apache web server. They also configure the name of the engine.

Within the <Engine> element for the Catalina service is a <Host> element, shown in Figure 12.32.

FIGURE 12.32
The <Host> element within the <Engine> element.

```
<!-- Define the default virtual host
     Note: XML Schema validation will not work with Xerces 2.2.
 -->
<Host name="localhost" debug="0" appBase="webapps"
 unpackWARs="true" autoDeploy="true"
 xmlValidation="false" xmlNamespaceAware="false">
```

This element defines a virtual host for Tomcat, much like the virtual hosts you should be familiar with in the Apache web server. In Figure 12.32, the <Host> element is defined with the name, debug, appBase, unpackWARs, autoDeploy, xmlValidation, and xmlNamespaceAware attributes defined. The **name** attribute specifies a name for the virtual host. The **appBase** attribute specifies the directory (relative to the Tomcat base directory) where web-based applications are stored. We'll discuss the meaning of the remaining attributes later in this chapter.

Finally, within each <Engine> element is a <Context> element. This is used to map a particular URL to a specific application provided by Tomcat. If you review your server.xml file, you'll notice that there aren't any <Context> elements defined by default. We'll take care of that later in this chapter as we configure a simple web app to deploy with Tomcat.

I hope the preceding description of the `server.xml` file made sense to you. I know the first time I looked at it, my head was swimming. The good news is that the defaults provided in `server.xml` work great as they are, especially if you're new to Tomcat. After you spend some time working with Tomcat, you'll probably want to tweak the `server.xml` to customize it.

To do this, I encourage you to open up `server.xml` in a text editor on your SLES 9 system and study it thoroughly. The comments provided for each element are very useful. In addition, there are a ton of docs available for you to study in `/usr/share/doc/packages/jakarta-tomcat/tomcat-docs`.

In addition to your `server.xml` file, you also need to be concerned with the `/usr/share/tomcat/conf/tomcat-users.xml` file. Let's look at it next.

WORKING WITH tomcat-users.xml

You'll be glad to know that the `tomcat-users.xml` file is much less complex than the `server.xml` file we just looked at. This file is used to define users, passwords, and roles for the Tomcat service.

FIGURE 12.33
The tomcat-users.xml file.

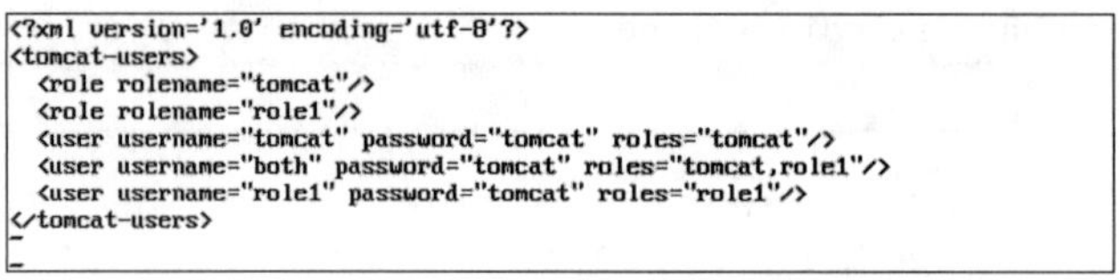

```
<?xml version='1.0' encoding='utf-8'?>
<tomcat-users>
  <role rolename="tomcat"/>
  <role rolename="role1"/>
  <user username="tomcat" password="tomcat" roles="tomcat"/>
  <user username="both" password="tomcat" roles="tomcat,role1"/>
  <user username="role1" password="tomcat" roles="role1"/>
</tomcat-users>
```

As you can see in Figure 12.33, this file uses the following XML structure:

```
<tomcat-users>
    <role />
    <user />
</tomcat-users>
```

The <role> element is used to define specific roles for the Tomcat service. The `rolename` attribute is used to define a name for the role. Tomcat provides two predefined roles that you can declare in `tomcat-users.xml` to create administrative users:

- admin—This role is used to control access to the web-based Tomcat Administration utility.
- manager—This role is used to control access to the Tomcat Application Manager web-based utility.

The role1 and tomcat roles shown in Figure 12.33 are sample roles that aren't actually required for anything. The `<user>` element is used to define usernames, assign passwords, and declare which role they belong to using the username, password, and roles attributes.

TIP

Notice that these usernames and passwords are stored clear-text. You should definitely configure your permissions so that lurking eyes can't get at this file! In addition, there's a way to configure Digest authentication for your Tomcat users. Have a gander at the Tomcat docs installed on your server to learn how to do this.

If you want use to the Application Manager and Administration web-based utilities (I highly recommend them), you need to create the admin and manager roles and then create users to fill these roles. You do this by completing the following:

1. Open /user/share/tomcat/conf/tomcat-users.xml in a text editor.
2. (Optional) Remove the tomcat and role1 roles along with the role1, both, and tomcat users.
3. Add the following child elements to the `<tomcat-users>` element to define the admin and manager roles and assign them to users:

```
<role rolename="manager" />
<role rolename="admin" />
<user username="user_name" password="password" roles="manager" />
<user username="user_name" password="password" roles="admin" />
```

TIP

You can use the same user for both roles by setting the roles attribute to `"admin,manager"`.

4. Save your changes and close the file.
5. Restart Tomcat by entering **`rctomcat restart`** from a shell prompt with root privileges.

After doing this, you can access the web-based Tomcat Administration utility by opening a browser and navigating to **http://localhost:8080/admin**. You will be prompted to authenticate using the *username* and *password* you configured in `tomcat-users.xml` for the admin role. When you do, the Tomcat Web Server Administration Tool page is displayed, as shown in Figure 12.34.

FIGURE 12.34
The Tomcat Web Server Administration Tool page.

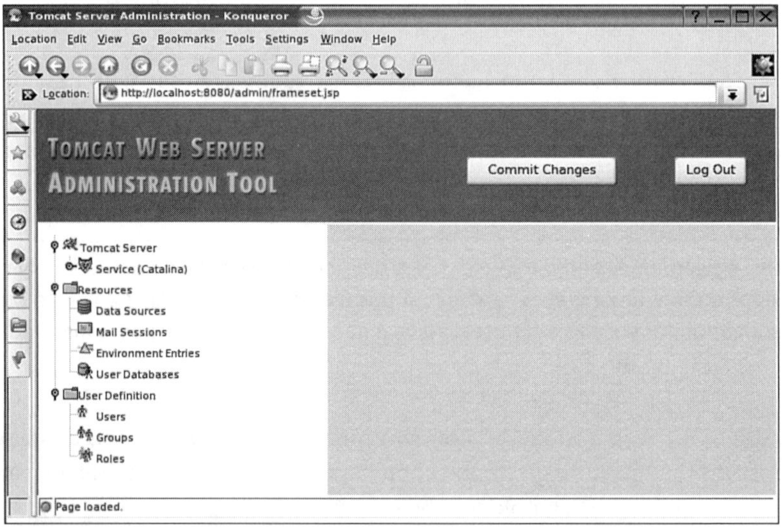

You can use this tool to configure your `server.xml` file as well as other Tomcat service parameters. If you're struggling with the XML code in `server.xml`, using this tool is a great way to get going with Tomcat.

You can also use the roles and users you configured in `tomcat-users.xml` to access the web-based Tomcat Application Manager utility. To do this, complete the following:

1. Open `/usr/share/tomcat/server/webapps/manager/WEB-INF/web.xml` in a text editor.
2. Scroll down to the `<servlet-class>org.apache.catalina.servlets.ManagerServlet</servlet-class>` element and change it to the following: `<servlet-class>org.apache.catalina.servlets.HTMLManagerServlet</servlet-class>`

TIP

Changing this line changes the behavior of the Application Manager to an extensive HTML web-based interface.

3. Save the changes to the file and close it.
4. Restart Tomcat by entering **`rctomcat restart`** from a shell prompt with root privileges.

5. Open `http://localhost:8080/manager/html` in a browser window.
6. When prompted to authenticate, enter the username and password you configured for the manager role. The page in Figure 12.35 is displayed.

FIGURE 12.35
The Tomcat Web Application Manager page.

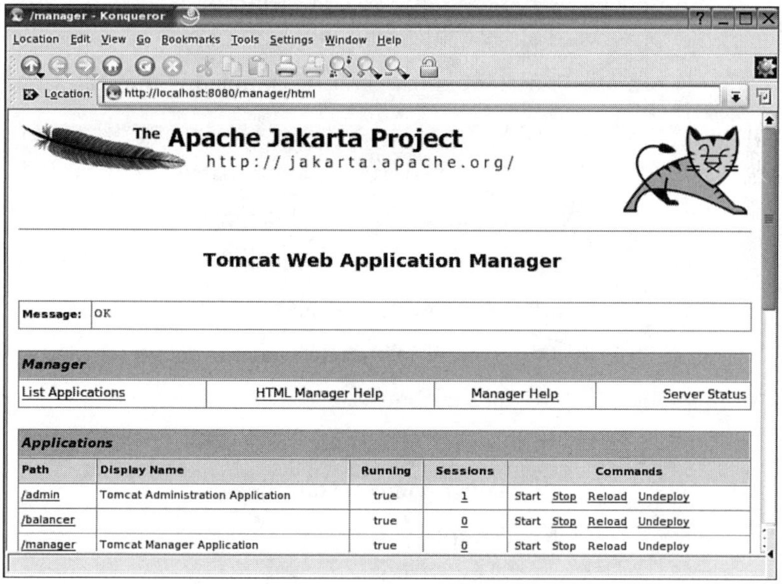

Now that you know how to set up Tomcat, you can practice on your SLES 9 system in Lab Exercise 12.3.

Lab Exercise 12.3: Implementing Tomcat on SLES 9

In this exercise, you will install and configure Tomcat on your SLES 9 system. Then you will configure a sample web app on your server. Complete the following:

1. Boot your SLES 9 server and authenticate as your **`tux`** user with a password of **`SuSE789`**.
2. Install Tomcat on your server by completing the following:
   a. Start YaST.
   b. When prompted, supply a root password of **`tuX123`**.
   c. Select Software, Install and Remove Software.
   d. In the Search field, enter **`tomcat`**; then select **Search**.
   e. Mark the following packages:
      - **apache2-jakarta-tomcat-connectors**
      - **jakarta-tomcat**
      - **jakarta-tomcat-doc**
      - **jakarta-tomcat-examples**

   f. Select **Accept**.
   g. When prompted that there is a dependency conflict, mark **Install java2**; then select **OK-Try Again**.
   h. In the Automatic Changes screen, select **Continue**.
   i. Insert CDs as prompted.
   j. Wait while packages are installed.
   k. When complete, select **Finish**.
3. Configure Tomcat by completing the following:
   a. Open a terminal session.
   b. At the shell prompt, enter **`sux -`** to change to root with a password of **`tuX123`**.
   c. At the shell prompt, enter **`cd /usr/share/tomcat/conf`**.
   d. At the shell prompt, enter **`cp ./server.xml ./server.xml.full`**.

e. At the shell prompt, enter **cp ./server-minimal.xml ./server.xml**.

NOTE

For the purposes of this exercise, we don't need a full-blown Tomcat server integrated with Apache. Instead, the `server-minimal.xml` file can be used to create a simple, standalone Catalina Tomcat server running on port 8080.

f. At the shell prompt, enter **less ./server.xml**.

g. Notice that the minimal server.xml file contains only the Catalina service element with a connector element that runs on port 8080.

h. Press **q**.

4. Configure the Administrator and Application Manager utilities by completing the following:

a. At the shell prompt, enter **vi ./tomcat-users.xml**.

b. Press **Ins**.

c. Add the following elements to the `<tomcat-users element>`:

```
<role rolename=manager />
<role rolename=admin />
<user username=bosspassword=testroles=manager,admin/>
```

d. Press **Esc**; then enter **:exit**.

e. Open `/usr/share/tomcat/server/webapps/manager/WEB-INF/web.xml` in vi.

f. Scroll down to the `<servlet-class>org.apache.catalina.manager.ManagerServlet </servlet-class>` element.

g. Change this element to the following:

```
<servlet-class>org.apache.catalina.servlets.
HTMLManagerServlet
</servlet-class>
```

h. Press **Esc**; then enter **:exit**.

i. Test the configuration by entering **rctomcat start** at the shell prompt.

   j. At the shell prompt, enter **tail /var/log/messages** and verify that Tomcat started without any errors.
   k. At the shell prompt, enter **rctomcat stop**.
5. Install a web-based application.
   a. At the shell prompt, enter **kfmclient openProfile filemanagement**.
   b. Browse to `/usr/share/doc/packages/jakarta-tomcat`.
   c. Right-click the **webdav** directory and select **Copy**.
   d. Browse to `/usr/share/tomcat/webapps`.
   e. Select **Edit**, **Paste**.
   f. Right-click the **webdav** directory and select **Properties**.
   g. Select **Permissions**.
   h. In the User field, enter **tomcat**.
   i. In the Group field, enter **tomcat**.
   j. Mark Apply Changes to All Subfolders and Their Contents; then select **OK**.
   k. Select the **webdav** directory.

TIP

Notice the structure of the application. Tomcat requires that all applications use a standardized file structure. The `index.html` file is located at the top of the application's directory structure along with its associated image files.

Also notice that there is a directory called `WEB-INF`. This directory contains the deployment descriptor file named `web.xml`. This file is used to configure the web app. Some applications use their own Java class files. These are located in `./WEB-INF/classes`. If the application used its own `.jar` files, they would be located in `./WEB-INF/lib`.

Some Tomcat applications come prepackaged in a web archive file (`.war`). To use these, copy them into the webapps directory. If Tomcat is running, it will automatically deploy them for you. If not, they will be deployed when Tomcat is started.

   l. Select the **WEB-INF** directory. You should see the `web.xml` file.
   m. Select **web.xml**; then select **View**, **View Document Source**.

NOTE

Notice that KWrite provides a very nice XML editing interface. You can expand or close the elements in the XML file, making it much easier to get around. Also notice that comments are grayed out, allowing you to easily see the elements in the file.

- **n.** Scroll down to the commented out `<init-param>` element.
- **o.** Remove the `<!--` line immediately preceding the `<init-param>` element.
- **p.** Remove the `-->` line right after the `</init-param>` closing tag.
- **q.** Save the file and close KWrite.
- **r.** At the shell prompt, enter **`rctomcat start`**.

TIP

When Tomcat starts, it looks in its webapps directory and automatically deploys any applications it finds there.

- **s.** Access the Application Management utility by opening a Konqueror window and browsing to **http://localhost:8080/manager/html**.
- **t.** When prompted, authenticate as **`boss`** with a password of **`test`**.
- **u.** Scroll down to the list of applications. You should see an entry for WebDAV Content Manager, as shown in Figure 12.36.
- **v.** Open a new browser window in Konqueror and browse to **http://localhost:8080/webdav/index.html**. The screen in Figure 12.37 should be displayed.

That's all there is to it! You just configured a really cool Tomcat web application: WebDAV. If time permits, you may want to visit http://www.webdav.org to learn more about the application you just deployed. You also may want to edit the web.xml file again and play with the commented-out Security Constraints for Testing section.

Also, if time permits, you may want to try deploying other web-based applications in your Tomcat server. There's a host of applications on the Internet that you can download and try. A good place to check is http://freshmeat.net. You'll find all kinds of Tomcat applications here, including `.war` files that make deployment really easy.

FIGURE 12.36
The WebDAV application deployed in Tomcat.

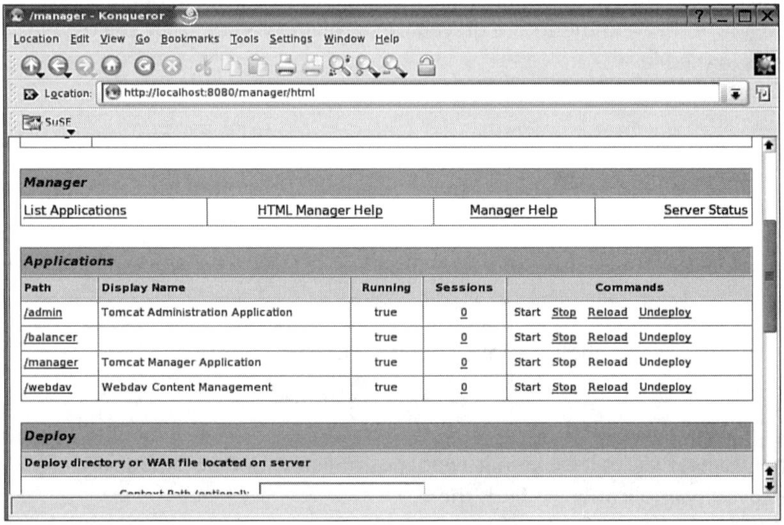

FIGURE 12.37
Accessing WebDAV in a browser.

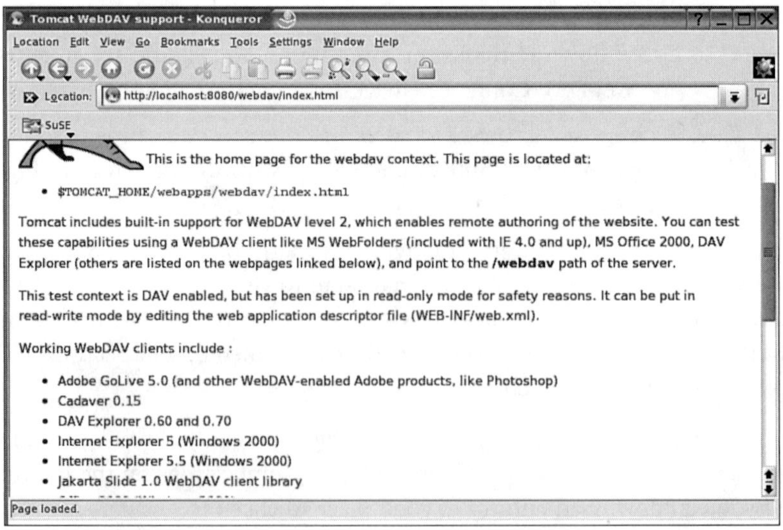

Congratulations! You made it all the way through a very harrowing array of Linux services and concepts. Your head should feel like it's going to explode. Before ending, I want to take a few pages and give you some last-minute strategies for completing your CLE 9 practical exam.

Closing Thoughts: Preparing for the CLE 9 Practicum

Remember from Chapter 1 that the CLE 9 Practicum is a scenario-based, live exam. Instead of a list of questions that test your conceptual knowledge, you will be presented with a deployment scenario in the form of a Business Requirements Document (BRD). The BRD is a list of requirements and expectations you must fulfill to complete the scenario.

You'll notice that the BRD is based on the CLE 9 objectives. However, be aware that the Practicum scenarios may not include all the CLE 9 objectives. Which will and which won't make the cut? I have no idea. The fellows at Novell who develop the CLE 9 practical exams are friends of mine and they are very tight-lipped about what's in the exam scenarios. They are very good at keeping secrets.

NOTE

This brings up one of my pet peeves. As I peruse CLE-related websites on the Internet, I frequently run into folks who beg and plead for CLEs who have taken the exam to divulge what's on it. Don't do this. It's not fair to those who study honestly and, frankly, you're doing yourself a disservice as well. Study hard and gain the knowledge for yourself. It builds character!

If you've ever worked as a consultant, you know that working from a BRD is "real life." Consultants generally sit down with their clients when they start a project and come up with some form of BRD (many companies call it a "Statement of Work"). The BRD is usually included in the contract between the consultant and the client.

The BRD serves as protection for both the consultant and the client. It ensures that the work the client wants done is clearly specified. The consultant knows exactly what it is that the client expects. If the consultant fails to complete any item specified in the BRD, he or she has breached the contract and may not get paid.

The BRD also serves as protection for the consultant. After the BRD is established and a bid issued, the client can't make radical changes to the BRD or add items to it. If you've ever hired a contractor to build a house, you know how this works. If you try to make changes to the building specs after construction starts ("Honey, can't we move the bathroom to the other side of the house?"), they will charge you a horrendous change-order fee (or just tell you "no way!"). That's because you're changing the requirements of the contract.

When you sit down to take your CLE 9 practical exam, you will take the role of a consultant who has been hired to deploy a SLES 9 network. You will be given a scenario in the form of a BRD that you must deploy on a virtual network.

As discussed in Chapter 1, the CLE Practicum is delivered on a series of virtual servers. You need to be absolutely sure you have met each and every requirement specified in the scenario. Remember that the CLE Practicum is a pass/fail exam. If you fail to fulfill a single requirement in the scenario, you will fail the entire exam. I strongly suggest that you review the test-taking strategies presented in Chapter 1 and commit them to memory. Doing so will help you to be in the minority that actually pass the CLE 9 exam!

In addition to memorizing these strategies, you should also practice extensively before going in to take your exam. It's relatively easy to deploy individual services one at a time as we have done in this book. However, it's *much* harder to deploy them all at once in a unified system without the help of a book and under a time constraint.

TIP

If you get stuck while taking your CLE 9 exam, remember that most screens in YaST offer help options and tips that can help you with specific steps for completing a particular task. In addition, all the man pages are at your disposal as well as the product documentation in `/user/share/doc`. Many CLE candidates forget that these are available!

The best way to prepare is to try to deploy each service we've covered without opening this book. If you can do that, you'll be in good shape. Again, the key to passing your CLE exam is *extensive* practice. (Have I said that enough?)

It's much like a football game. If you show up for the big game having only read about the sport, it's very unlikely your team will win. Yes, you may *know* all the rules and the best plays, but you won't be able to *execute* them. However, if your team has practiced itself to the brink of exhaustion well before the game, your chances of winning are much better.

Succeeding in the CLE 9 Practicum works the same way. Conceptual knowledge alone won't cut it. You must know the system intimately, and the only way you can do that is to practice, practice, practice.

With that said, let's review what you learned in this chapter.

Summary

In this chapter, you were first introduced to the Service Location Protocol (SLP). You learned that SLP is used to create a level of service location automation that we used to have with the IPX and NetBIOS protocols. We then reviewed the three types of SLP agents:

- User Agents (UAs)
- Service Agents (SAs)
- Directory Agents (DAs)

We then discussed the various ways in which SLP can be deployed, including SA-Only mode and DA mode. With this in mind, we then discussed how to configure the slpd daemon using the `slp.conf` file. You then learned how to statically register services that aren't SLP-aware with the slpd daemon.

With SLP behind us, we spent the last half of this chapter discussing Tomcat. We talked about how Tomcat creates web pages on-the–fly, eliminating the need to manually write and continuously update static web pages.

Then we turned to a high-level discussion of how to configure Tomcat on your SLES 9 system. We reviewed general XML concepts; then we looked specifically at the `server.xml` file that is used to configure Tomcat. We also discussed how to configure the `tomcat-users.xml` file to support the web-based Application Manager and Administrator utilities. Finally, in Lab Exercise 12.3, we configured Tomcat and learned how to deploy a web-based application.

Before ending, we spent some time reviewing the knowledge and skills you need to have prior to taking your CLE 9 exam. You learned that the CLE 9 Practicum will provide you with a Business Requirements Document (BRD) whose requirements you must satisfy to pass the exam. Missing a single requirement will result in failure.

We then discussed the fact that the best way to prepare for the CLE Practicum is to extensively practice deploying SLES 9 using the services covered in this book.

That's it for this book. Thank you for giving me the opportunity to share what I have learned with you. I hope you found this book to be useful, easy to read, and intuitive. I wish you the best of luck on your CLE 9 exam and in your subsequent Linux pursuits!

Index

NUMBERS

A

D

E

H

I

J - K - L

O

Q - R

S

T

U

X - Y

Z